The Fifties in America

The Fifties in America

Volume I
Abstract expressionism—Golf

Editor
John C. Super
West Virginia University

Managing Editor
R. Kent Rasmussen

SALEM PRESS, INC.
Pasadena, California
Hackensack, New Jersey

Editorial Director: Christina J. Moose

Managing Editor: R. Kent Rasmussen   *Photograph Editor:* Philip Bader
Copy Editor: Sarah M. Hilbert   *Production Editor:* Joyce I. Buchea
Assistant Editors: Andrea E. Miller   *Acquisitions Editor:* Mark Rehn
Elizabeth Ferry Slocum   *Graphics and Design:* James Hutson
Indexer: R. Kent Rasmussen   *Layout:* Eddie Murillo

Title page photo: *Atomic bomb test at Yucca Flats, Nevada.*
(Hulton Archive / by Getty Images)

Library of Congress Cataloging-in-Publication Data

The fifties in America / edited by John C. Super.
    p. cm.
  Includes bibliographical references and index.
  ISBN 1-58765-202-1 (set : alk. paper) — ISBN 1-58765-203-X (v. 1 : alk. paper) — ISBN 1-58765-204-8 (v. 2 : alk. paper) — ISBN 1-58765-205-6 (v. 3 : alk. paper)
 1. United States—Civilization—1945—Encyclopedias. 2. United States—History—1945-1953—Encyclopedias. 3. United States—History—1953-1961—Encyclopedias. 4. Nineteen fifties—Encyclopedias. I. Super, John C., 1944-
  E169.12.F498 2005
  973.92'03—dc22

2004024559

First Printing

■ Table of Contents

■ Publisher's Note

The Fifties in America surveys the events and people of the United States and Canada from 1950 through 1959. Salem Press's second reference set on a twentieth century decade, this three-volume publication is modeled on Salem's popular *The Sixties in America* (1999). However, with its 640 alphabetically arranged essays, *The Fifties in America* is 20 percent larger than the 1960's set and goes beyond the latter's geographical scope by covering Canada in depth.

The 1950's The 1950's are often portrayed as a quiet and comparatively uneventful era in North American history—a period of political and cultural conservatism and conformity when little of consequence happened. However, the decade was in fact a period of domestic political turbulence, mounting world tensions, and significant cultural change. Indeed, it may be fairly argued that the 1950's set in motion most of the changes for which the tumultuous 1960's were later to become famous.

While the decade of the 1940's had experienced the horrors, privations, and dislocations of world war, the 1950's experienced the more subtle horrors of the Cold War, with its concomitant nuclear arms race and rising fears of thermonuclear war, particularly after the Soviet Union was known to possess working nuclear weapons. Within the United States, the strains of the Cold War generated a kind of mass paranoia about communist subversion that gave rise to a second "Red Scare," making possible McCarthyism and a trend toward the suppression of civil liberties. The impact of Cold War fears on North America was both broad and deep. It influenced not only politics but also culture and can be seen in the films, television programs, and literature of the period.

Although the 1950's was an era of civil defense paranoia, bomb shelters, and loyalty oaths, it was also a time of positive changes in American social and economic history. Under the leadership of Chief Justice Earl Warren, the U.S. Supreme Court assumed a more activist role in correcting past social wrongs. When the Court outlawed racial segregation in public schools in *Brown v. Board of Education* in 1954, it helped launch a social revolution that drew focus and force from the Civil Rights movement and leaders such as Martin Luther King, Jr. In 1957, when President Dwight D. Eisenhower sent federal troops into Little Rock, Arkansas, to enforce the Supreme Court's ruling on school desegregation, the lines were drawn for a new civil war that would be fought out during the 1960's.

Meanwhile, the United States and Canada were emerging from the hard times of the Great Depression and World War II into a period of economic growth that brought unprecedented prosperity to both nations. This prosperity was accompanied by the introduction of a vast array of new consumer goods and services, making North America the home of what Harvard economist John Kenneth Galbraith would call the "affluent society." Canada and the United States enjoyed enormous agricultural surpluses. Construction industries boomed, and unprecedented numbers of North Americans were able to buy their own homes and enjoy previously undreamt luxuries. Among the most striking changes of the decade was a huge increase in the production of automobiles. After the stagnation in design and production that the automobile industry had endured during the war years, the industry responded with cars offering revolutionary changes in design, variety, and performance. Among the most memorable new models of the 1950's were the Chevrolet Corvette, the Ford Thunderbird, and the ill-fated Edsel—a car that helped to define the decade. New highways had to be built to accommodate increased motor travel, which also fostered new motel and fast-food restaurant industries.

Among the new consumer products that flooded North American markets were televisions, transistor radios, and long-playing records—all of which prompted revolutions in the entertainment industries and everyday lifestyles. Indeed, the 1950's might justly be described as the decade of television. Television's origins go back to the 1920's, but it was not until the 1950's that television broadcasting began to affect the ways that average people lived. In 1950, fewer than four million American households had television sets, and television had not even begun broadcasting in Canada. By the end of the decade, television was established as the dominant form of entertainment and a powerful force in the communication of culture and news in both countries. Television programming reflected postwar social values, while changing the way that North Americans lived. Television brought the immediacy of national and world events into homes, helped introduce new trends in music and culture, and gave the film industry its biggest scare in history. Competition from television prompted the film industry to make sweeping changes that led to greater use of color and special effects, experiments in 3-D projection, and new wide-screen formats.

One revolution for which the 1950's has always received full recognition is the emergence of rock and roll, an outgrowth of African American rhythm and blues music. Personified by the towering presence of Elvis Presley, rock and roll changed the face of popular music and became the musical voice of the youth movement that would take on more coherent forms during the 1960's.

The 1950's was also an era of new forms of fun that were expressed in such fads as hula hoops, poodle skirts, ducktail hairstyles, two-tone cars, outlandish automobile tail fins, and stunts such as telephone-booth stuffing. The first "flying saucer" sightings of the late 1940's occurred as the world was entering the nuclear bomb and space ages, making the 1950's an era obsessed with the possibilities of thermonuclear war and alien invasions. These concerns were expressed in such films as *The Thing from Another World*, *The War of the Worlds*, *The Day the Earth Stood Still*, and *Invasion of the Body Snatchers*.

Content of This Reference Work *The Fifties in America* covers all these and many other topics in its 640 essays, which range from 300-word articles on individual personages, books, events, films, court cases, inventions, and other subjects, to 3,000-5,000-word overviews on such broad subjects as literature, economics, education, politics, medicine, science, and television. While many essays provide pre-1950's background material and discuss post-1950's developments, the focus of each essay is on the events of the 1950's.

Written with the needs of students and general readers in mind, the articles in this set present clear discussions of the topics, explaining terms and references that may be unfamiliar to readers. The essays are arranged in alphabetical order, with clear, concise titles followed by brief descriptors and italicized summaries of their subjects' significance. The essays

are divided into a variety of easy-to-use formats: 175 overviews; 185 biographical pieces; 78 articles on events; 40 articles on books, plays, and magazines; 22 articles on individual films; 27 articles on television programs; 9 articles on individual court cases; 56 articles on government agencies and organizations of various types; 18 articles on laws and treaties; and 25 articles on individual products and inventions. A fuller list of subject categories can be found at the end of volume 3.

Ready-Reference Tools Important dates and selected facts are highlighted in ready-reference top matter at the beginnings of articles on people, organizations, events, and artistic works. Within the texts of articles, boldfaced subheads such as "Impact" or "Subsequent Events" make finding information quick and easy. Cross-references at the end of each article will guide readers to additional entries on related subjects. Every article, regardless of length, also offers annotated bibliographical notes under the heading of "Further Readings," and readers will find an annotated general bibliography among the appendices at the end of the third volume.

No reference work on the 1950's would be complete without extensive visual elements, and this set contains more than 300 photographs of the decade's events and numerous maps, graphs, charts, and sidebars highlighting the decade's most interesting facts and trends. As an additional aid to readers, volume 3 contains a detailed index to photo subjects.

Other Search Tools *The Fifties in America* also contains a number of useful tools to help readers find the subjects of interest. A complete list of all 640 essays appears at the beginning of each volume. A list of essays sorted under more than fifty categories appears at the end of volume 3, and the third volume contains a comprehensive index and personages index, as well as the photo index. On average, each essay topic is listed three times in the category list, under headings ranging from "African Americans" and "Art and architecture" to "Women's issues" and "Youth culture." The comprehensive index also has aspects of the category list, as it contains collective entries on such subjects as individual films, television programs, plays, novels, awards, and people.

Appendices The third volume contains fifteen appendices that provide additional information about selected aspects of the decade in quickly accessible formats. The five drama appendices list the major films, Broadway plays, television shows, and major awards of the 1950's. The two literature appendices list the best-selling U.S. books and major literary award winners, and the music appendix lists the decade's most popular musicians and their hits. A sports appendix provides a quick look at the winners of the major sporting events of the 1950's. The two legislative appendices look at the U.S. Supreme Court and its major decisions and major legislation passed by Congress during the decade. Other appendices include a glossary of new words and slang from the 1950's, a detailed time line of the decade, an extensive annotated bibliography, and an annotated list of Web sources on 1950's subjects.

Acknowledgments Publications such as *The Fifties in America* would not be possible without the generous contributions of a large team of scholars. The editors of Salem Press would therefore like to thank the 248 scholars who contributed articles and appendices to this set. The editors would also like to thank Professor John C. Super of West Virginia University for serving as the project's Editor and for bringing to the project his expertise on North American history.

■ Contributors

Michael Adams
City University of New York Graduate Center

Bland Addison
Worcester Polytechnic Institute

Richard Adler
University of Michigan, Dearborn

Paul Alkebulan
Virginia State University

Majid Amini
Virginia State University

Carolyn Anderson
University of Massachusetts, Amherst

Bethany Andreasen
Minot State University

Gayle R. Avant
Baylor University

Charles Avinger
Washtenaw Community College

Sylvia P. Baeza
Independent Scholar

Charles F. Bahmueller
Center for Civic Education

Sue Bailey
Tennessee Technological University

Carl L. Bankston III
Tulane University

Garlena A. Bauer
Otterbein College

Frances R. Belmonte
Loyola University Chicago

Alvin K. Benson
Utah Valley State College

Chuck Berg
University of Kansas

Milton Berman
University of Rochester

Anthony J. Bernardo, Jr.
Cecil Community College

Margaret Boe Birns
New York University

George P. Blum
University of the Pacific

Pegge Bochynski
Salem State College

Bernadette Lynn Bosky
Independent Scholar

Gordon L. Bowen
Mary Baldwin College

J. Quinn Brisben
Chicago Public Schools

Dana D. Brooks
West Virginia University

Thomas W. Buchanan
Ancilla College

Michael H. Burchett
Limestone College

Susan Butterworth
Salem State College

José A. Carmona
Daytona Beach Community College

Russell N. Carney
Southwest Missouri State University

Jack Carter
University of New Orleans

Gilbert T. Cave
Lakeland Community College

Ranes C. Chakravorty
University of Virginia

Cheris Shun-ching Chan
Northwestern University

Paul J. Chara, Jr.
Northwestern College

Justin P. Coffey
University of Illinois, Chicago

Susan Coleman
West Texas A&M University

David A. Crain
South Dakota State University

Sarah E. Crest
Towson University

Richard A. Crooker
Kutztown University

LouAnn Faris Culley
Kansas State University

Eddith A. Dashiell
Ohio University

Mary Virginia Davis
University of California, Davis

Nathaniel Davis
Harvey Mudd College

Jennifer Davis-Kay
Education Development Center, Inc.

Andy DeRoche
Front Range Community College

Thomas E. DeWolfe
Hampden-Sydney College

Gordon Neal Diem
ADVANCE Education and Development Institute

Margaret A. Dodson
Independent Scholar

Paula C. Doe
Virginia Museum of Fine Arts

J. R. Donath
California State University, Sacramento

Thomas Du Bose
Louisiana State University, Shreveport

Mark R. Ellis
University of Nebraska at Kearney

Thomas L. Erskine
Salisbury University

David G. Fisher
Lycoming College

Dale L. Flesher
University of Mississippi

Bonnie L. Ford
Sacramento City College

John K. Franklin
Graceland University

John C. Fredriksen
Independent Scholar

Raymond Frey
Centenary College

Leslie Joan Friedman
The Lively Foundation, Inc.

C. George Fry
Winebrenner Theological Seminary

Daniel J. Fuller
Kent State University

Jean C. Fulton
Landmark College

Joy M. Gambill
Appalachian State University

Michael J. Garcia
Arapahoe Community College

Janet E. Gardner
University of Massachusetts, Dartmouth

Paul D. Gelpi, Jr.
Grambling State University

Phyllis B. Gerstenfeld
California State University, Stanislaus

Jan Giel
Independent Scholar

Sheldon Goldfarb
University of British Columbia

Nancy M. Gordon
Independent Scholar

Sidney Gottlieb
Sacred Heart University

Richard W. Grefrath
University of Nevada, Reno

Scot M. Guenter
San Jose State University

Robert E. Haag
Naugatuck Valley Community College

Lawrence W. Haapanen
Lewis-Clark State College

Michael Haas
Political Film Society

John C. Hajduk
University of Montana—Western

Timothy L. Hall
University of Mississippi

Susan E. Hamilton
Independent Scholar

Maurice Hamington
Lane Community College

Randall Hannum
New York City College of Technology

Roger D. Hardaway
Northwestern Oklahoma State University

Dennis A. Harp
Texas Tech University

P. Graham Hatcher
Anderson College

Jim Heaney
AC Flora High School

Bernadette Zbicki Heiney
Lock Haven University of Pennsylvania

John A. Heitmann
University of Dayton

Thomas E. Hemmerly
Middle Tennessee State University

Mark C. Herman
Edison Community College

Steve Hewitt
University of Birmingham

Sarah M. Hilbert
Independent Scholar

Randy Hines
Susquehanna University

Arthur D. Hlavaty
Independent Scholar

Virginia Hodges
Northeast State Community College

Samuel B. Hoff
Delaware State University

Kimberley M. Holloway
King College
East Tennessee State University

Charles C. Howard
Tarleton State University

Mary Hurd
East Tennessee State University

Raymond Pierre Hylton
Virginia Union University

Robert Jacobs
Central Washington University

Ron Jacobs
University of Vermont

Jeffry Jensen
Independent Scholar

Bruce E. Johansen
University of Nebraska at Omaha

Barbara E. Johnson
University of South Carolina, Aiken

Lloyd Johnson
Campbell University

Sheila Golburgh Johnson
Independent Scholar

Yvonne Johnson
Central Missouri State University

David Kasserman
Rowan University

Jarod Kearney
Hallockville Museum & Folklife Center

Joseph C. Kiger
Croft Institute of International Studies

Leigh Husband Kimmel
Independent Scholar

Bill Knight
Western Illinois University

Gayla Koerting
University of South Dakota

Grove Koger
Boise Public Library, Idaho

Obiagele Lake
Independent Scholar

J. Wesley Leckrone
Temple University

Douglas A. Lee
Vanderbilt University

Ann M. Legreid
Central Missouri State University

Denyse Lemaire
Rowan University

Jose C. de Leon
San Jose State University

Leon Lewis
Appalachian State University

Thomas Tandy Lewis
Anoka Ramsey Community College

Peter D. Lindquist
Independent Scholar

Victor Lindsey
Independent Scholar

Alar Lipping
Northern Kentucky University

Janet Alice Long
Independent Scholar

Pietro Lorenzini
St. Xavier University

Denise Low
Haskell Indian Nations University

M. Philip Lucas
Cornell College

R. C. Lutz
cii

Joanne McCarthy
Independent Scholar

Mary McElroy
Kansas State University

John L. McLean
Missouri Valley College

David W. Madden
California State University, Sacramento

Edward W. Maine
California State University, Fullerton

Joseph T. Malloy
Hamilton College

Nancy Farm Mannikko
National Park Service

Martin J. Manning
U.S. Department of State

Henry W. Mannle
Tennessee Technological University

John F. Marszalek III
Xavier University of Louisiana

Sherri Ward Massey
University of Central Oklahoma

Robert R. Mathisen
Western Baptist College

James I. Matray
California State University, Chico

Steve J. Mazurana
University of Northern Colorado

Laurence W. Mazzeno
Alvernia College

Michael E. Meagher
University of Missouri, Rolla

Joseph A. Melusky
Saint Francis University

Scott A. Merriman
University of Kentucky

Beth A. Messner
Ball State University

Andrea E. Miller
Independent Scholar

Tracy E. Miller
Towson University

William V. Moore
College of Charleston

Anthony Moretti
Texas Tech University

Todd Moye
Independent Scholar

Otto H. Muller
Alfred University

Betsy A. Murphy
William Woods University

Alice Myers
Simon's Rock of Bard College

John Myers
Simon's Rock of Bard College

Michael V. Namorato
University of Mississippi

Byron Nelson
West Virginia University

Holly L. Norton
University of Northwestern Ohio

Austin Ogunsuyi
Shorter College

Paul Orkiszewski
Appalachian State University

Robert J. Paradowski
Rochester Institute of Technology

Martha E. Pemberton
Independent Scholar

William E. Pemberton
University of Wisconsin, La Crosse

Andy Perry
Independent Scholar

Alan P. Peterson
Gordon College

Gene D. Phillips
Loyola University Chicago

Michael Phillips
Independent Scholar

Erika E. Pilver
Westfield State College

Betty L. Plummer
Independent Scholar

David L. Porter
William Penn University

Victoria Price
Lamar University

Maureen J. Puffer-Rothenberg
Valdosta State University

Steven J. Ramold
Virginia State University

P. S. Ramsey
Independent Scholar

R. Kent Rasmussen
Independent Scholar

John David Rausch, Jr.
West Texas A&M University

Rosemary M. Canfield Reisman
Charleston Southern University

H. William Rice
Shorter College

Betty Richardson
*Southern Illinois University,
    Edwardsville*

James Riddlesperger
Texas Christian University

Edward A. Riedinger
Ohio State University Libraries

Edward J. Rielly
Saint Joseph's College of Maine

Jeffrey W. Roberts
Independent Scholar

Charles W. Rogers
Southwestern Oklahoma State University

Deborah D. Rogers
University of Maine

JoAnne M. Rogers
Southwestern Oklahoma State University

Jennifer E. Rosenberg
*About.com Guide to 20th Century
    History*

Joseph R. Rudolph, Jr.
Towson University

Lisa M. Sardinia
Pacific University

Sean J. Savage
Saint Mary's College

Elizabeth D. Schafer
Independent Scholar

William J. Scheick
University of Texas at Austin

H. J. Schmeller
Fort Hays State University

Lacy Schutz
Independent Scholar

Rebecca Lovell Scott
Mashpee Family Practice

R. Baird Shuman
*University of Illinois at Urbana-
    Champaign*

Charles L. P. Silet
Iowa State University

William M. Simons
State University of New York, Oneonta

Sanford S. Singer
University of Dayton

Carl Singleton
Fort Hays State University

Rhonda Smith
Eastern Kentucky University

Ira Smolensky
Monmouth College

Larry Smolucha
Benedictine University

Alan L. Sorkin
University of Maryland

Leigh Southward
Tennessee Technological University

Joseph L. Spradley
Wheaton College

James Stanlaw
Illinois State University

August W. Staub
University of Georgia

Barry M. Stentiford
Grambling State University

Glenn Ellen Starr Stilling
Appalachian State University

Roger J. Stilling
Appalachian State University

Lloyd K. Stires
Indiana University of Pennsylvania

Megali Stuart
University of the Pacific

Taylor Stults
Muskingum College

Donald Sullivan
University of New Mexico

Charlie Sweet
Eastern Kentucky University

Glenn L. Swygart
Tennessee Temple University

James Tackach
Roger Williams University

Robert D. Talbott
University of Northern Iowa

Sue Tarjan
Independent Scholar

G. Thomas Taylor
University of Maine

Cassandra Lee Tellier
Capital University

J. W. Thacker
Western Kentucky University

John M. Theilmann
Converse College

Gale M. Thompson
Delta College

Evelyn Toft
Fort Hays State University

Paul B. Trescott
Southern Illinois University

David Treviño
Donna Klein Jewish Academy

Marcella Bush Trevino
Barry University

William T. Walker
Chestnut Hill College

Spencer Weber Waller
Loyola University Chicago

Donald A. Watt
Dakota Wesleyan University

Amy K. Weiss
Appalachian State University

Marcia J. Weiss
Point Park University

Christine A. Wernet
University of South Carolina, Aiken

Winifred Whelan
St. Bonaventure University

George M. Whitson III
University of Texas at Tyler

Richard L. Wilson
University of Tennessee at Chattanooga

Sheri P. Woodburn
Independent Scholar

Susan J. Wurtzburg
University of Canterbury

William A. Young
University of North Dakota

Kristen L. Zacharias
Albright College

■ Complete List of Contents

Volume I

Volume II

Volume III

The Fifties in America

A

■ Abstract expressionism

Definition Art form characterized by individuality and spontaneous improvisation

The devastation and confusion of the war years of the 1940's helped give rise to abstract expressionism—an art form wholly unique to American artists that gained international attention and acclaim.

The end of World War II in 1945 coincided with what American painter Barnett Newman later called the moral crisis of a world in shambles due to a Great Depression followed by a world war. The artists' moral crisis was mainly in relation to subject matter: They felt they could no longer continue to paint the flower still-lifes, reclining nudes, and pleasant domestic interiors that they had been painting before the war, when the dominant styles had been social realism and regionalism. Thus, during the late 1940's and early 1950's, the visual arts took a new course. The changes that came about were due in large part to the events of the war, not the least of which was the extensive emigration of so many of Europe's artists to the United States. As most of these artists settled in New York City and were assimilated into the American art world, New York took the position of leadership left vacant by the devastation of Europe's cultural centers.

Influences and Supporters As many historians have noted, the first major original direction in American painting, abstract expressionism (also called the New York School), came about because of attitudes conditioned by the war—a loss of belief in old systems and forms of expression, as well as a growing sense of alienation from society. Artists began to investigate new forms of intellectual thought, ranging from the psychoanalytic theories of Sigmund Freud and Carl Jung to existentialism, which was the most popular philosophy in the postwar period. The most prevalent influence of existentialism on artistic expression was the conviction that each person is alone in the world, separated from all systems of belief and left to find salvation in art alone, thus requiring the need to reinvent art from the very beginning. This stance arguably led many artists to overemphasize the importance of originality in art.

The abstract expressionists were a diverse group but did have a number ideas and attitudes in common. For example, they were all opposed to any form of social realism and to anything in the visual arts that related to nationalism. They also considered the pure geometric abstraction of artist Piet Mondrian and the members of the American Abstract Artists as trivial, despite the fact that they generally admired Mondrian himself. They were, however, influenced by European Surrealism, especially the abstract, automatist Surrealism of André Masson, Joan Miró, and Roberto Matta. Matta, a New York artist from 1939 to 1948, introduced the abstract expressionists to psychic automatism, a kind of free association in which the pen or brush was allowed to wander on a surface, undirected by the conscious mind. The artists considered this technique more of a way to explore new forms than a means of entering into the subconscious.

Some of the early supporters of the new abstract expressionism included Peggy Guggenheim, who, in her gallery, had exhibited the work of the European Surrealists. She also began to feature work by the Americans Clyfford Still, Robert Motherwell, and Jackson Pollock. Moreover, some influential critics began to champion the new movement: Clement Greenberg, Thomas Hess, and Harold Rosenberg. Greenberg's definition of modernism was particularly important in promoting the new movement. In 1954, in a lecture later published as *Art and Culture* (1961), he declared that art's ability to reveal human experience does not depend upon its representational qualities. Gradually, other critics and dealers, as well as the major museums, began to support the work of the abstract expressionists, resulting in an international recognition of the movement when the Museum of Modern Art mounted an exhibition titled "The New Ameri-

Jackson Pollock moving paintings in his East Hampton, New York, studio in 1953. Pollock's style of painting later earned him the sarcastic nickname "Jack the Dripper." (Hulton Archive | by Getty Images)

can Painting," which toured eight European countries.

Approaches to Art Within abstract expressionism, there were two main tendencies during the 1950's. The first consisted of the Color Field painters, who strove to make an abstract statement through the creation of large, unified color shapes or areas. They believed that this was the way by which abstract art could express universal, timeless ideas. In a letter of manifesto to *The New York Times*, they declared that there is no such thing as a good painting about nothing, therefore subject is crucial and only subject matter that is tragic and timeless is valid. As abstract expressionist Mark Rothko insisted, art, even at its most abstract, could still convey a sense of tragedy, ecstasy, and doom. Besides Rothko, this group included Barnett Newman, Clyfford Still, Adolph Gottlieb, Robert Motherwell, and Ad Reinhardt.

The second tendency of abstract expressionism was gestural painting. These artists were concerned in various ways with brushstroke and texture—that which made each artist's touch or "handwriting"

individual and spontaneous. This group included Jackson Pollock, Willem de Kooning, and Franz Kline, among others. In 1952, the critic Harold Rosenberg used the phrase "action painting" to describe gestural painting, stating that American painters had begun to consider the canvas as an arena in which to act, rather than as a space in which to reproduce, redesign, or analyze an object, actual or imagined. What appeared on the canvas was now an event, rather than a picture. What the term "action painting" failed to acknowledge, however, was the balance between planning and spontaneity that these gestural painters achieved.

Notable Artists One of the most influential artists of the 1950's was Hans Hofmann. Born in Europe, he came to the United States in 1932 and taught successively at the University of California at Berkeley, the Art Students League in New York, and finally, at his own School of Fine Arts in New York and in Provincetown, Massachusetts. Although his principal artistic concern lay in his own concept of pictorial structure based on architectonic principles integral to cubism, he did create a variety of abstractions, ranging from the painterly geometric to lyrical expressionism.

Another foreign-born artist whose work formed a critical link between European Surrealism and American abstract expressionism was Arshile Gorky. After achieving early success with a distinctive figural style, he developed a mature style that combined eccentric hybrid forms with rich, flowing color. His biomorphic imagery, influenced by the Surrealist automatism of Matta and Masson, in turn influenced Willem de Kooning and others of the abstract expressionist movement. A central figure of the movement, de Kooning had the ability to alternate between representational and abstract themes, which he did not consider to be contradictory or exclusive of one another. In 1950, he began his most famous and controversial painting, *Woman I*, which interprets woman as both sex symbol and fertility goddess. During the mid-1950's, de Kooning left the theme of women to concentrate on what he called "abstract urban landscapes," paintings that were intended to call forth the exciting, often coarse atmosphere of New York City streets.

Jackson Pollock is typically considered the quintessential abstract expressionist. His famous "drip" paintings date from the late 1940's and continue into the 1950's, by which time he had become internationally symbolic of the new American style. Early influences on his work included the figural paintings of his teacher, Thomas Hart Benton, as well as the landscapes of Albert Ryder and the work of the Mexican muralists. He was also drawn to the automatism of Masson and Miró.

Pollock's most beautiful drip painting, *Lavender Mist: Number 1, 1950*, is an excellent example of the fact that his painting was not a totally uncontrolled, intuitive act, but rather it combined the elements of intuition and accident with skills developed by his years of experience as a painter. Before Pollock's death in a car accident in 1956, he returned to a figurative art, declaring that when painting out of the subconscious, figures are bound to emerge. While most critics compared these paintings unfavorably to his earlier drip paintings, they were the beginnings of what could have been an important new direction in the art of the 1950's.

Other important abstract expressionists included Lee Krasner, whose work was based on spontaneous gesture and large overall compositions; Franz Kline, who was noted for his large-scale black-and-white abstractions; Mark Tobey, who, like Pollock and de Kooning, utilized both figurative and abstract styles; and Bradley Walker Tomlin, who worked in an abstract cubist style, creating a group of pictographic compositions in which he superimposed forms reminiscent of ancient Egyptian hieroglyphs over colored backgrounds. Philip Guston created his first abstract gestural paintings in 1951, utilizing a Mondrian-inspired motif of short vertical and horizontal lines densely interwoven. Elaine de Kooning created figurative paintings with definite gestural, expressive tendencies throughout the 1950's, including portraits of such notable figures as politician John F. Kennedy. Grace Hartigan, a second-generation abstract expressionist, was influenced by Pollock and Willem de Kooning. Like de Kooning, she was inspired by the commonplace aspects of life in the city.

American sculpture also saw the development of a major new direction with the creation of constructed sculpture—as opposed to sculpture carved from stone or cast in bronze. One of the leaders of this movement during the 1950's was David Smith, who worked primarily in welded steel. As he pointed out, the metal itself has little history in art—what associations it does have are those of the twentieth century: power, structure, movement, progress, suspension, brutality. Throughout his career, Smith worked mainly on themes in series, creating sculpture which was monumental in both scale and conception.

Impact During the 1950's, abstract expressionism affected the visual arts of the last half of the twentieth century in many ways. The movement's concept of the overall painting in which no part of the composition takes formal precedence over any other part—as seen in the works of Pollock, Rothko, and Newman for example—resulted in subsequent compositions that are nonhierarchical, with areas of pictorial importance evenly distributed over the entire surface. This compositional approach, when combined with the large scale of the works, brought about the concept of wall painting, as opposed to traditional easel painting, and led eventually to the painting becoming an environment that encloses the viewer. Moreover, the often-exaggerated emphasis on the artist's individuality prompted that emphasis to become the subject itself in later artworks.

Many artists also practiced a form of self-effacement by immersing themselves and their work in technology, endeavoring to imitate scientific procedure. In the latter half of the century, abstract expressionism was succeeded by many "isms" and movements: pop art, op art, assemblage, kinetic art, minimalism, conceptualism, super realism, and neo-expressionism. In truth, all these movements resulted from a reinterpretation of ideas that were known earlier: For example, abstract expressionism had its roots in Surrealism and, as Marcel Duchamp declared, new realism, pop art, and assemblage are all related to Dada. Where Dada challenged the existing aesthetic and social order, however, later twentieth century art movements turned that challenge into an order.

Further Reading

Crane, Diane. *The Transformation of the Avant-Garde: The New York Art World, 1940-1985.* Chicago: University of Chicago Press, 1987. Essential guide to understanding the importance of New York City as an international cultural center.

Herskovic, Marika. *American Abstract Expressionism of the 1950's: An Illustrated Survey.* New York: New York School Press, 2003. Excellent survey of eighty-eight important abstract expressionists of the 1950's. Each entry includes a statement from the artist, two color reproductions, and individual biographies.

Shapiro, David, and Cecile Shapiro, eds. *Abstract Expressionism: A Critical Record.* Cambridge, England: Cambridge University Press, 1994. Chronicles the history of the movement using a collection of articles, reviews, and essays.

LouAnn Faris Culley

See also Art movements; de Kooning, Willem; Guggenheim Museum; Johns, Jasper; Kline, Franz; Motherwell, Robert; Pollock, Jackson; Rauschenberg, Robert.

■ Academy Awards

Definition American film industry awards given annually by the Academy of Motion Picture Arts and Sciences

The Academy Awards grew in importance and popularity during the 1950's because of the introduction of both televised ceremonies and increasing attention to political and aesthetic issues by the awards' recipients and presenters.

The Academy Awards began in 1929 as a modest celebration of the previous calendar year's achievements in the American film industry and was initially held in a banquet room of Hollywood's Roosevelt Hotel. Fifteen awards were presented for outstanding individual or collective efforts in several categories, including acting, best picture, and direction. Through the ensuing years, award recipients were chosen by secret ballots cast by Academy members. By the early twenty-first century, the number of categories had grown to more than twenty-five.

Public interest in the Academy Awards grew quickly after the first year in which they were given. As early as 1930, the event was broadcast on radio. In 1941 the famous sealed-envelope system was introduced at the awards ceremony, and the recipients were not announced until the moment each award was presented. Prior to that year, winners were announced to newspapers before the ceremonies.

Crisis at Midcentury After two relatively uneventful decades, the Academy Awards faced a major crisis on the eve of the 1950's. In 1948, the five major studios of the American motion picture industry—MGM (Metro-Goldwyn-Mayer), Fox, Warner Bros., Paramount, and RKO—were adversely affected financially when the U.S. Supreme Court ruled that their ownership of both production and distribution of films violated antitrust provisions. To cut costs, the studios withdrew their sponsorship of the Academy Awards, leading to a transfer of the presentation from the 6,700-seat Shrine Auditorium to the Academy's own 950-seat screening theater. The following year, three other studios, Columbia, Universal-International, and Republic, also withdrew their support, and a controversy about national bias for or against British films resulted in a pessimistic forecast from Columbia that the Academy Awards were "going to fold."

A Dow Jones study published in *Fortune* magazine provided statistical evidence that the Academy Awards were the most effective publicity method that the industry possessed, as witnessed by the box-office receipts earned by such Oscar-winning films as *Gentleman's Agreement* (1947) and *The Best Years of Our Lives* (1946). Consequently, the studios agreed to subsidize the awards again, albeit on a year-by-year basis. The awards ceremony was then moved to the Pantages Theater in the center of Hollywood. To enhance the value of each award, the Academy's board of governors declared that the statuettes—which were popularly known as Oscars—would be individually numbered.

As the studios reassessed their commitment to the Academy Awards, a new challenge faced the film industry. The increasing popularity of home television viewing was cutting into motion-picture theater patronage. The film industry became alarmed that it was losing its audiences to free television and sought ways to draw people back to the theaters by offering them things that television could not provide: innovations such as 3-D movies and wide-screen formats, more color films, and an increased emphasis on the industry's glamour. The industry seemed to be suggesting that television was a more plebeian medium, while motion pictures were the true purveyors of style and artistic accomplishment. This claim held some credence while television was still broadcasting only black-and-white programs and most of its stars were considered less stellar actors. Most theatrical film releases were photographed in color and used recognized stars. Eventually, the studios understood that its Academy Awards ceremonies could be used to advertise the industry's strengths.

Studio Influence in 1950 and 1952 The Academy of Motion Picture Arts and Sciences has frequently drawn criticism for overlooking worthy films, giving its awards to undeserving films, and making decisions on criteria other than the merits of the films. The studios have also earned their share of criticism for shamelessly promoting selected films for purely commercial reasons. The early 1950's was a period during which the Academy Awards were subjected to an exceptional amount of criticism.

The apparent power of major studios to influence the awards was evident in the fact that several of the best and most original films of the late 1940's and early 1950's received unexpectedly few awards. For example, Billy Wilder's film *Sunset Boulevard* (1950) received only one award. Wilder's film was a brilliantly corrosive view of Hollywood that won only for best screenplay. Throughout the decade, similar oversights occurred, most conspicuously in the critically acclaimed work of Alfred Hitchcock. In 1952, Humphrey Bogart won an award for best actor for his performance in *The African Queen* (1951), but the film itself was not nominated for best picture.

Moreover, while Vivien Leigh, Karl Malden, and Kim Hunter all won acting awards for their performances in *A Streetcar Named Desire* (1951), its direc-

tor, Elia Kazan, lost in the directing category to George Stevens, who directed *A Place in the Sun* (1951). Vincente Minnelli was not nominated for his direction of *An American in Paris* (1951), which won the best picture award. Marlon Brando's legendary performance in *A Streetcar Named Desire* was not sufficient to overcome the sentimental regard for Bogart, who cooperated in an advertising campaign for the first time. Hitchcock's powerful *Strangers on a Train* was overlooked except for a single nomination for its cinematography.

Cold War Fears In 1951, *All About Eve* (1950) established a record, receiving fourteen Academy Award nominations. That film had the unusual distinction of having two of its actors—Bette Davis and Anne Baxter—nominated for the same best-actress award. Thelma Ritter and Celeste Holm, from the same film, were both nominated for best supporting actress. None of them won, however, as the only acting award for the film went to George Sanders as best supporting actor. Nevertheless, the film won the best-picture award, and its director, Joseph L. Mankiewicz, was named best director and given a second award for best screenplay. That year, José Ferrer was named best actor for his re-creation of the title character of *Cyrano de Bergerac* (1950).

The Cold War and its resulting communist hysteria in the United States began to affect the film industry seriously when Ferrer was subpoenaed by the congressional House Committee on Un-American Activities (HUAC) shortly after his nomination, and Mankiewicz, the president of the Director's Guild, was challenged by director Cecil B. DeMille about not supporting anticommunist loyalty oaths. DeMille tried to have Mankiewicz impeached, but he failed and resigned himself, a move some blamed on the failure of DeMille's biblical epic *Samson and Delilah* (1949) to garner important Academy Awards nominations in the face of the numerous nominations that went to Mankiewicz's *All About Eve* the same year.

By 1952, the furor over communist influence in the film industry was directly affecting the Academy Awards. Kazan's unpopular cooperation with HUAC might arguably have contributed to his loss in the best directing category for *A Streetcar Named Desire*. Carl Foreman, who wrote the screenplay for *High Noon* (1952), was summoned to testify before HUAC while the film was in production. He consciously wrote several scenes in which the sheriff is left stand-

Notable Film Talents Snubbed by the Academy

Year	Film	Nominated but did not win	Not nominated
1950	All About Eve	Actors Bette Davis, Anne Baxter, Celeste Holm, Thelma Ritter	
	Asphalt Jungle	Director John Huston; screenwriters John Huston and Ben Maddow	Actor Sam Jaffe
	Father of the Bride	Actor Spencer Tracy	
	Rio Grande		Actors John Wayne, Maureen O'Hara
	Sunset Boulevard	Director Billy Wilder; actors William Holden, Gloria Swanson	
	The Third Man	Director Carol Reed	Actor Orson Welles
1951	The African Queen	Director John Huston; actor Katharine Hepburn	
	A Christmas Carol		Actor Alastair Sim
	Strangers on a Train		Director Alfred Hitchcock
	A Streetcar Named Desire	Actor Marlon Brando; screenplay writer Tennessee Williams	
1952	The Bad and the Beautiful	Actor Kirk Douglas	
	High Noon	Director Fred Zinnemann	
	The Lavender Hill Mob	Actor Alec Guinness	
	Limelight	Score by Charles Chaplin	Actor Charles Chaplin
	The Quiet Man		Actors John Wayne, Maureen O'Hara
	Singin' in the Rain		Actors Gene Kelly, Donald O'Connor, Debbie Reynolds
1953	The Big Heat		Actor Gloria Grahame
	Calamity Jane		Actor Doris Day
	Gentlemen Prefer Blondes		Actors Marilyn Monroe, Jane Russell
	Shane	Director George Stevens; actor Alan Ladd	
1954	The Country Girl	Director George Seaton; actor Bing Crosby	
	Rear Window	Director Alfred Hitchcock	Actors James Stewart, Thelma Ritter, Grace Kelly

Year	Film	Nominated but did not win	Not nominated
1955	*Bad Day at Black Rock*	Director John Sturges; actor Spencer Tracy; screenwriter Millard Kaufman	
	Blackboard Jungle		Director Richard Brooks
	East of Eden	Actor James Dean	Director Elia Kazan
	Mister Roberts		Actor Henry Fonda
	Picnic		Actors Kim Novak, William Holden, Rosalind Russell
	The Virgin Queen		Actor Bette Davis
1956	*The Man Who Knew Too Much*		Actors Doris Day, James Stewart
1957	*Funny Face*		Director Stanley Donen
	Twelve Angry Men	Director Sidney Lumet	
1958	*Cat on a Hot Tin Roof*	Director Richard Brooks; actor Paul Newman	
	The Last Hurrah		Actor Spencer Tracy
	Vertigo		Director Alfred Hitchcock
1959	*Anatomy of a Murder*	Actor James Stewart	Actor Lee Remick
	The 400 Blows	Screenwriters François Truffault and Marcel Moussy	
	North by Northwest		Director Alfred Hitchcock
	Some Like It Hot	Director Billy Wilder	
	Wild Strawberries	Screenwriter Ingmar Bergman	

ing alone against approaching outlaws, as frightened townspeople cower in dark recesses. Such scenes symbolized the plight of film writers who were blacklisted by the Hollywood establishment. Actor Gary Cooper, who played the sheriff, was the only influential figure who spoke out for Foreman when the writer was attacked by a group of actors, gossip columnists, and publicity agents. Cooper's principled position was not universally popular, but he won the award for best actor, and *High Noon*'s director, Fred Zinnemann, was nominated for best director. However, that year's best picture award went to DeMille's *The Greatest Show on Earth* (1952), an uncontroversial commercial success. John Ford won an unprecedented fourth directing award for *The Quiet Man* (1952), which had seven nominations, but John Wayne's sensitive portrait of the film's title character was overlooked. Wayne's somewhat strident support of the studio's cooperation with HUAC arguably affected voters on both sides of the political spectrum.

Widening the Audience in 1953 The Academy Awards presentation ceremonies were televised for the first time in 1953, when RCA offered $100,000 for the rights to broadcast it on NBC after several studios withdrew their financial support a week before the awards.

Meanwhile, political concerns continued to worry the major studios. However, in 1953, the range of nominated films and performances shifted the focus toward more purely cinematic issues. In a particularly strong year for acting, William Holden won the best actor award for his performance in Billy Wilder's *Stalag 17* (1953). He won over the performances of Marlon Brando in *Julius Caesar*, Montgomery Clift and Burt Lancaster in *From Here to Eternity*, and British actor Richard Burton in *The Robe*. *From Here to Eternity* was also chosen as best picture and its director, Zinnemann, won in his category.

The recognition in 1953 of Belgian actor Audrey Hepburn for her performance in *Roman Holiday* initiated a series of awards for young female actors. That same year, Donna Reed—another ingenue with comparatively little acting experience—was chosen as best supporting actress for her role in *From Here to Eternity*. The film *Shane*, a classic Western noted for being a family film, garnered nominations for director George Stevens, young actor Brandon DeWilde, and veteran actor Jack Palance. However, the film was not supported by the Academy. The lack of recognition for Alan Ladd's title role in *Shane* may have resulted from his decision to work as an independent actor with no studio connections.

Bob Hope (right), a perennial host of the Academy Awards ceremony during the 1950's, tries to wrench away the Oscar won by Marlon Brando (left) for his performance in On the Waterfront *during the 1955 Academy Awards ceremony.* (Hulton Archive | by Getty Images)

Gritty Realism in 1954 In 1954, Marlon Brando was nominated for a best acting award for the fourth consecutive year, this time for his role in *On the Waterfront*. Lee J. Cobb, Karl Malden, and Rod Steiger received supporting actor nominations for their performances in the same film. Brando temporarily relinquished his trademark rebel image, a move that apparently made him more acceptable to the Academy and helped him earn the best actor award. Columbia nominated Eva Marie Saint, Brando's costar in *On the Waterfront*, for the supporting actress award, which she won, and Grace Kelly continued a pattern of young women winning the best actress award for *The Country Girl*. *On the Waterfront* was chosen as best picture, and its director, Elia Kazan, also won an award. Another best director nominee that year was Alfred Hitchcock, for *Rear Window*; it was a rare nomination for the director whose impressive films of the 1950's were generally ignored.

Dorothy Dandridge's best actress nomination for *Carmen Jones* was the first that went to an African American in a best-acting category. There was some grumbling in the industry with Kazan's award because he had been a friendly witness at HUAC hearings. Brando remarked that Kazan was a "songbird," but he respected the director's ability and the powerful role enough to want to take the part.

Mixed Awards in 1955 The gritty realism of *On the Waterfront* reflected the somber mood of the mid-1950's as the war in Korea, the witch-hunt hearings in the Senate by Joseph McCarthy, and the development of devastatingly powerful nuclear bombs inspired the production of many films that either confronted social issues or offered fantasies to avoid them. The 1955 best picture award went to the downbeat *Marty*, with Ernest Borgnine winning the best actor award for the title role, as well as the nomination of James Dean in *East of Eden* and Frank Sinatra in *The Man with the Golden Arm*, and Anna Magnani's win for best actress in the adaptation of the Broadway play *The Rose Tattoo*, contrasted with nominations for romantic films such as *Love Is a Many-Splendored Thing* and *Picnic* and up-beat performances such as Jack Lemmon's Oscar-winning performance as supporting actor in *Mr. Roberts*. However, Dean was not nominated for *Rebel Without a Cause*, and the picture itself was not acknowledged. However, Natalie Wood and Sal Mineo, both new to Hollywood, were given supporting-acting nominations for their performances in the film. Hitchcock's *To Catch a Thief* won an award for Robert Burks's color cinematography.

Spectaculars and Foreign Films in 1956 By 1956, the possibility of films such as Hitchcock's *The Man Who Knew Too Much* or John Ford's *The Searchers* being nominated for Academy Awards was negated by the honors heaped on such lavish productions as DeMille's *The Ten Commandments* and *The King and I*. That year, the winner for best picture was the extravagant but lightweight *Around the World in Eighty Days*.

The relatively puritanical public posture of the Academy led to some controversy over the best actress award to Swedish actress Ingrid Bergman in *Anastasia*. The Academy introduced a best foreign-language film award in 1956. The first such award went to Italian director Federico Fellini's *La Strada*.

In 1956, an Academy loyalty oath made Michael Wilson, the writer of *Friendly Persuasion* who was blacklisted and unable to work in the United States, ineligible, so the writing-award nomination that the film received did not include the writer's name. The winner for best motion-picture story, however, was listed as "Robert Rich," a nom de plume for Dalton Trumbo, one of the original blacklisted Hollywood Ten compelled to work under false names but still employed by the industry because of their talent and the opposition of many people in the industry to such things as the Academy's loyalty oath. After Kirk Douglas used Trumbo's real name on *Spartacus* (1960) and Otto Preminger used it on *Exodus* in 1960, Trumbo returned to favor, and it was later re-

vealed that he had also written *Roman Holiday* (1953), although the script was attributed to the English writer Ian McLellan Hunter, who gave Trumbo the forty thousand dollars he was paid for the story.

Recognition of British Films in 1957 Subterfuge continued in 1957, when the Academy Award for Best Adapted Screenplay for *The Bridge on the River Kwai* was officially awarded to Pierre Boulle, the author of the novel on which the film was based, although Carl Foreman had actually written the script with Michael Wilson. Likewise, in 1959, the screenplay for *The Defiant Ones* was credited to Harold Smith and "Nathan E. Douglas," a pseudonym for Ned Young, another blacklisted writer.

British films received so many Academy Awards during the awards' first decades that there was a negative backlash against British films in the American film industry. Consequently, few British films received awards during the 1950's. However, that trend was reversed in 1957 by *The Bridge on the River Kwai*. That film, set primarily in a Japanese prisoner-of-war camp in Burma during World War II, won Academy Awards for best picture, best direction for David Lean, and best actor for Alec Guinness.

An important change in the Academy during 1957 was the dismissal from the award-voting process of the 15,000 members of the various Hollywood guilds. Academy Awards voting was then returned solely to the Academy's own 1,800 members. That year, for the first time, the films nominated for best picture and best director awards matched exactly. Fellini's *Nights of Cabiria* (*Le notti di Cabiria*) won for best foreign-language film, but a more somber depiction of war than *The Bridge on the River Kwai*, Stanley Kubrick's *Paths of Glory*, was not nominated.

New Directions in 1958 Although *The Defiant Ones*, Stanley Kramer's sensitive examination of racism with Sidney Poitier and Tony Curtis, was widely praised, the best picture award for 1958 went to Vincente Minelli's musical *Gigi*, for which he was also named best director. Poitier and Curtis were both nominated for the best actor award. Poitier's nomination was the first such nomination for a male African American actor, but British actor David Niven won for *Separate Tables*. French actor/director Jacques Tati's *Mon Oncle* won the foreign-language award. Meanwhile, Alfred Hitchcock's *Vertigo* and Orson Welles's *Touch of Evil*—both critically acclaimed films—were overlooked.

Notable Films That Did Not Win "Best Picture"

Year	Film	Academy's snub	Year	Film	Academy's snub
1950	Asphalt Jungle	Not nominated	1955 (cont.)	Mister Roberts	Nominated but did not win
	Father of the Bride	Nominated but did not win		The Night of the Hunter	Not nominated
	King Solomon's Mines	Nominated but did not win		Picnic	Nominated but did not win
	Rio Grande	Not nominated		East of Eden	Not nominated
	Sunset Boulevard	Nominated but did not win		The Virgin Queen	Not nominated
	The Third Man	Not nominated	1956	Bigger than Life	Not nominated
1951	The African Queen	Not nominated		Invasion of the Body Snatchers	Not nominated
	A Christmas Carol	Not nominated		The Killing	Not nominated
	Strangers on a Train	Not nominated		The Man Who Knew Too Much	Not nominated
	A Streetcar Named Desire	Nominated but did not win		The Searchers	Not nominated
1952	The Bad and the Beautiful	Not nominated		The Seven Samurai	Not nominated
	High Noon	Nominated but did not win		The Ten Commandments	Nominated but did not win
	The Lavender Hill Mob	Not nominated		The Wrong Man	Not nominated
	Limelight	Not nominated	1957	A Face in the Crowd	Not nominated
	The Quiet Man	Nominated but did not win		Funny Face	Not nominated
				Paths of Glory	Not nominated
	Singin' in the Rain	Not nominated		Sweet Smell of Success	Not nominated
1953	The Big Heat	Not nominated		Twelve Angry Men	Nominated but did not win
	Calamity Jane	Not nominated	1958	Cat on a Hot Tin Roof	Nominated but did not win
	Gentlemen Prefer Blondes	Not nominated		Indiscreet	Not nominated
	Shane	Nominated but did not win		The Last Hurrah	Not nominated
				Touch of Evil	Not nominated
1954	The Country Girl	Nominated but did not win		Vertigo	Not nominated
	Johnny Guitar	Not nominated	1959	Anatomy of a Murder	Nominated but did not win
	Rear Window	Not nominated		The 400 Blows	Not nominated
	A Star Is Born	Not nominated		North by Northwest	Not nominated
1955	Bad Day at Black Rock	Not nominated		Rio Bravo	Not nominated
	Blackboard Jungle	Not nominated		Some Like It Hot	Not nominated
	Lady and the Tramp	Not nominated		Wild Strawberries	Not nominated

Ben-Hur **in 1959** The decade's awards concluded with the blockbuster film *Ben-Hur*, which won for best picture, William Wyler winning as its director and Charlton Heston winning as best actor in the title role. *Ben-Hur* set a record with eleven awards out of twelve nominations.

Once again, two acclaimed—and now classic—films, Hitchcock's *North by Northwest* and Wilder's *Some Like It Hot*, were not nominated for best picture. The French-Brazilian film *Black Orpheus* (*Orphée Nègre*) was chosen as best foreign-language film, while François Truffaut's *The 400 Blows* (*Les Quatre-Cent Coups*) and Ingmar Bergman's *Wild Strawberries* (*Smultronstället*) were not even nominated. Silent-film star Buster Keaton received an honorary award for his contributions to film comedy.

Impact The Academy Awards survived various threats during the 1950's, became an ABC television staple by the end of the decade, and began a rise to prominence in American cultural life that has made them unique among entertainment award ceremonies.

Further Reading

Biskin, Peter. *Seeing Is Believing: How Hollywood Taught Us to Stop Worrying and Love the Fifties*. New York: Pantheon Books, 1983. This witty examination of the film industry during the 1950's explores ways in which films such as *On the Waterfront* and *Rebel Without a Cause* reflected the social and political tensions of their times.

Holden, Anthony. *Behind the Oscar: The Secret History of the Academy Awards*. New York: Plume/Simon and Schuster, 1995. A candid, revealing, and biting account of the machinations and power struggles behind the polished facade of the Academy Awards Presentations.

Pickard, Roy. *The Oscar Movies*. 4th ed. New York: Facts On File, 1994. Encyclopedic reference work organized by film titles, covering all the films that won Academy Awards through the early 1990's. Includes a variety of appendix lists and more than one hundred illustrations.

Wiley, Mason, and Damien Bona. *Inside Oscar: The Unofficial History of the Academy Awards*. New York: Ballantine Books/Random House, 1987. Entertaining and occasionally gossipy account of the awards, with an extensive index of the results of all the award presentations.

Leon Lewis

See also Actors Studio; *Ben-Hur*; Brando, Marlon; Emmy Awards; Film in the United States; Hitchcock films; House Committee on Un-American Activities; Kazan, Elia; *On the Waterfront*; *Streetcar Named Desire, A*; Trumbo, Dalton.

■ Acheson, Dean

Identification U.S. secretary of state from 1949 to 1953

Born April 11, 1893; Middletown, Connecticut

Died October 12, 1971; Sandy Spring, Maryland

As U.S. secretary of state, Dean Acheson was a primary aide to President Harry S. Truman in the development of American foreign policy during the post-World War II period. He is considered a major architect of the American Cold War policy of containment, which was designed to prevent Soviet expansion and to curtail the influence of communism throughout the world.

After graduating from Yale University in 1915 and Harvard Law School in 1918, Acheson began his career of public service as a secretary to Supreme Court Justice Louis B. Brandeis. During the 1920's, he pursued a successful career as a lawyer. President Franklin D. Roosevelt appointed Acheson as under secretary of the treasury in 1933, but Acheson left that post after several months because of a dispute over fiscal policies. After America's entrance into World War II, Acheson returned to the Roosevelt administration as assistant secretary of state from 1941 to 1945 and continued his service at the Department of State under President Harry S. Truman as under secretary of state from 1945 to 1947. During those years, Acheson became clearly identified as an anticommunist; he played an essential role in the formulation of the Truman Doctrine, which was initiated to support Greece and Turkey in resisting Soviet expansion. Acheson also contributed significantly to the development of the European Economic Recovery Program, commonly known as the Marshall Plan.

In January, 1949, Acheson was appointed secretary of state by President Truman. During his tenure in that position, Acheson continued to advance policies and programs that were focused on containing the Soviet Union. In his autobiography, *Present at the Creation: My Years at the State Department* (1969), Acheson argued his case for containment and provided significant details on the development of the

Dean Acheson. (Library of Congress)

North Atlantic Treaty Organization, American problems with China in the late 1940's, and U.S. involvement in the Korean War.

Impact Acheson was a key proponent of Soviet containment and played an important role in the formation of the North Atlantic Treaty Organization (NATO) in 1949. He developed the American policy of nonrecognition of communist China and established principles of American policy that resulted in American military intervention in Korea and, later, Vietnam, Cambodia, and Laos. While Acheson was anticommunist, he came under attack by the American political right wing for not going far enough in his opposition to communist ideology. In particular, Acheson was attacked by Senator Joseph McCarthy as being soft on communism and for harboring communist employees in the State Department. These accusations were rendered more complex by Acheson's failure to quickly denounce Alger Hiss; Hiss had been identified as a Soviet agent by Whittaker Chambers. In the hysteria of McCarthyism,

Acheson held his ground and was supported by Truman. However, the American right wing continued to view him as a key figure responsible for the loss of China. In 1953, Acheson returned to his legal practice; during the presidency of John F. Kennedy (and to a lesser extent that of Lyndon B. Johnson), Acheson provided substantive advice on American foreign policy.

Further Reading

Chace, James. *Acheson: The Secretary of State Who Created the American World.* New York: Simon & Schuster, 1998. A scholarly, balanced, and highly readable biography of Acheson based on a wide range of sources.

McNay, John T. *Acheson and Empire: The British Accent in American Foreign Policy.* Columbia: University of Missouri Press, 2001. A valuable interpretation of the impact of British history and thought on Acheson's policies during the 1940's and 1950's.

William T. Walker

See also China; Foreign policy of the United States; Germany's postwar occupation; Kennan, George F.; Korean War; Lebanon occupation; McCarthy, Joseph; North Atlantic Treaty Organization; Truman, Harry S.; Truman Doctrine; Vietnam.

■ Actors Studio

Identification Theater company that emphasized a training technique based on actors' psychological and emotional awareness of their characters' motivations

Date Formed in 1947

Place New York, New York

The Actors Studio rose to fame as one of the best acting schools during the 1950's by expanding and promoting famed Russian stage director Konstantin Stanislavsky's "Method" acting and became a major influence on postwar theater.

Founded by Elia Kazan, Cheryl Crawford, and Robert Lewis in 1947, the Actors Studio adapted the techniques of Konstantin Stanislavsky's "system" of acting (later known as the Method) and trained American actors to act from within. Most important, it emphasized that acting was a technique rather than solely an art form.

Stanislavsky challenged the actors he directed to find the character within themselves and used the

Method to prepare them to act in plays of the era that were using a new genre, realism. Stanislavsky felt that the actors' art alone enabled them to perform in classical drama or farce, genres popular in the nineteenth century, but not necessarily in realist performances. During Stanislavsky's tour of the United States and Europe in 1922 with his Moscow Art Theater, two members defected and began teaching at the American Laboratory Theater. A businessman, Lee Strasberg, was impressed by the acting.

Strasberg joined Cheryl Crawford, a successful stage producer, to found the Group Theatre in 1931. This company was the first in the United States that worked as an ensemble. Actors were invited to join, Elia Kazan and Robert Lewis among them. Financial problems and artistic differences split the company in 1941, but some of the original members—Kazan, Lewis, and Crawford—decided to start another group, the Actors Studio, in 1947.

Strasberg Years Initially, Robert Lewis and Elia Kazan taught acting to the original fifty members; in 1949, after several changes of personnel—such as Lewis's resignation—Strasberg was invited to join. He soon became the only person to teach acting, and in 1951, he was named artistic director.

Strasberg taught actors to reach inside themselves for the play's required emotions. This meant that actors had to prepare themselves before each scene, frequently dwelling on events in their own pasts that would evoke emotions similar to those felt by their characters. Actors taught this way were called "method actors." Strasberg initiated the process by which an actor attains inspiration and subsequently created workshops for actors to work on facets of their art apart from the concerns of production.

While the Actors Studio was not the only school teaching method acting (Marlon Brando, studying with Stella Adler, used the technique to bring Stanley Kowalski to life in Tennessee Williams's 1951 screenplay *A Streetcar Named Desire*), most major theater and film actors studied at least for a time at the Actors Studio.

Actors went through a rigorous audition process, and talent, rather than celebrity, was the primary factor in their acceptance. If not accepted, they often re-auditioned several times. Once an actor was a member, the membership was lifelong. Classes were conducted in workshops where actors performed scenes that were critiqued by experienced professionals as well as by other students.

Impact The 1950's was the Actors Studio's heyday, and its approach revolutionized theater and film acting. Strasberg turned the studio into a breeding ground for a generation of theatrical stars, including Brando, James Dean, Montgomery Clift, Joanne Woodward, and Geraldine Page. Audiences were enthralled by method acting and watched as performers seemed to become the character in front of their eyes. Method acting became standard in the world of theater and film, and the list of actors trained by the studio eventually came to include notable performers such as Paul Newman, Ellen Burstyn, Al Pacino, Dustin Hoffman, Jack Lemmon, Meryl Streep, Shirley MacLaine, and Rip Torn.

Subsequent Events The Actors Studio continued its prominence in the world of theater throughout the twentieth century. After Strasberg died in 1982, the company went through some difficult financial times, but its board managed to keep it afloat. Cable television's Bravo network created the program *Inside the Actors Studio*, which provided a regular source of revenue in the early twenty-first century. In 2004 it still had a theater in New York City at which actors, playwrights, and directors displayed their craft.

Further Reading

Frome, Shelly. *The Actors Studio: A History.* New York: McFarland, 2001. The founders of the studio are thoroughly discussed, as are the lives and careers of its early icons.

Hethmon, Robert, ed. *Strasberg at the Actors Studio: Tape-Recorded Sessions.* 1965. Reprint. New York: Theater Communications Group, 1991. The interviews with Strasberg contained in this book give the reader Strasberg's thoughts on acting technique and theater in general.

Hirsch, Foster. *A Method to Their Madness: The History of the Actors Studio.* Cambridge, Mass.: Da Capo Press, 2001. Examines the techniques of the studio and how its alumni shaped theatrical history.

Tracy E. Miller

See also Brando, Marlon; Dean, James; Film in the United States; Kazan, Elia; *On the Waterfront*; *Streetcar Named Desire, A*; Theater in the United States.

■ Adams, Sherman

Identification White House chief of staff from 1953 to 1958
Born January 8, 1889; East Dover, Vermont
Died October 27, 1986; Hanover, New Hampshire

During his service in the Dwight D. Eisenhower presidential administration, Sherman Adams established a powerful model for future White House chiefs of staff.

Perhaps because of his military background, Dwight D. Eisenhower wanted a well-run White House staff. He selected Sherman Adams, former governor of New Hampshire, to oversee White House operations. During his tenure in the Eisenhower White House, Adams acquired substantial influence. Critics of Eisenhower labeled Adams as the nation's co-president. Adams controlled access to the president and determined what information reached the president's desk. Although he was a dutiful member of the Eisenhower administration, he was forced to resign from the White House in 1958 over allegations that he improperly used his influence on behalf of a friend.

Impact Adams envisioned his role as protecting Eisenhower's time. Reasoning that the federal government was too large to micromanage, Eisenhower typically did not study the details of government operations. Critics saw this as evidence that Adams had too much influence. Adams became a lightning rod for pundits to attack the work ethic of President Eisenhower. In reality, Adams was performing a new role in American politics that many people were unable to understand. While reflecting the personal preferences of Eisenhower, Adams established the guidelines for the newly emerging chief of staff office, thus serving as an important role model for his successors.

Further Reading

Adams, Sherman. *Firsthand Report: The Story of the Eisenhower Administration.* New York: Harper, 1961. Provides the personal memoirs of Adams.

Pacho, Chester J., and Elmo Richardson. *The Presidency of Dwight D. Eisenhower.* Lawrence: University Press of Kansas, 1991. This is a balanced account of the Eisenhower years. It provides excellent coverage of the conditions that shaped the career of Adams in the Eisenhower administration.

Michael E. Meagher

See also Eisenhower, Dwight D.; Eisenhower's heart attack; Elections in the United States, midterm.

■ The Adventures of Ozzie and Harriet

Identification Family television comedy series centering on the real-life Nelson family
Producer Ozzie Nelson (1906-1975)
Date Aired from 1952 to 1966

The show depicted an idealized all-American family and became one of the longest-running family television programs in history.

The Adventures of Ozzie and Harriet originated as a radio program in 1944, starring Ozzie Nelson, a bandleader in real life; the band's singer, Harriet Hilliard, a minor actor and Ozzie's wife; and their two sons, David and Eric (Ricky). In 1952, the family moved to television in roles that closely followed their real-life situations. Ozzie, whose actual job was never really clear on the television show, was the jovial head of family and often the foil for Harriet. David and Ricky were "perfect" children—good students, respectful, and with nice friends. While all members of the Nelson family appeared in each early episode, the show gradually incorporated the sons' friends and girlfriends. David eventually left for college and then a career, though he continued to make frequent appearances. As the show continued through the 1960's, Ricky married Kris Harmon, daughter of football star Tom Harmon, and Kris Harmon and David's wife, June, became part of the show. Most episodes finished with a performance by Ricky and his band.

Impact The program depicted American middle-class family life during the 1950's and reflected postwar mores and aspirations. As Ricky grew older on the show, he developed a strong teen following as an entertainer and would eventually become one of the most famous rock-and-roll artists of the day. A talented entertainer, "Rick" Nelson continued with a singing career until his death in a plane crash in 1985.

Further Reading

Brooks, Tim, and Earle Marsh. *The Complete Directory to Prime Time Network TV Shows: 1946-Present.* 8th ed. New York: Random House, 2003. An alphabetical listing of programs with complete details

The real-life Nelson family in 1951: Ozzie, Harriet, Dave, and Ricky. (Hulton Archive | by Getty Images)

about broadcast histories, casts, and plot summaries, as well as behind-the-scenes stories about the shows and the stars.

McNeil, Alex. *Total Television: A Comprehensive Guide to Programming from 1948 to the Present.* New York: Penguin Group, 1996. Provides complete details for all major television programs.

Richard Adler

See also Baby boomers; Conformity, culture of; *Father Knows Best*; *Goldbergs, The*; *Honeymooners, The*; *I Love Lucy*; *Leave It to Beaver*; Rock and roll.

■ *The Adventures of Superman*

Identification Syndicated television series based on a comic book superhero
Date Aired from 1953 to 1957

One of the most popular syndicated series of the early 1950's, The Adventures of Superman *inspired other television shows about superheroes and has itself endured into the twenty-first century.*

The fictional Superman is an alien from the distant planet Krypton whose parents sent him to Earth as a baby when their planet was breaking up. When his rocket ship crash-landed in the American Midwest, he was found and adopted by a childless farming couple, the Kents, who gave him the name Clark Kent. Although young Clark was indistinguishable from a human in appearance, his extraterrestrial origins left him with a dense molecular structure that endowed him with extraordinary powers and near-invulnerability on Earth. When he grew up, he chose to use his powers in the service of humankind and went to the great city of Metropolis, where he became a newspaper reporter for the *Daily Planet*—a job that enabled him to learn of crises as they were unfolding so that he could respond to them. (Although Metropolis is clearly modeled on New York City, the *Daily Planet* exteriors shown in the television series were of Los Angeles City Hall.)

Apart from a single episode explaining Superman's origins, *The Adventures of Superman* revolves around the adult Superman, with most of the action occurring in or near the *Daily Planet* building. George Reeves (1914-1959), a beefy actor of stage and screen experience, played the dual role of Superman/Clark Kent. The cast was limited, and sets were simple. For example, reporters Clark Kent and Lois Lane (Phyllis Coates the first season and Noel Neill the last three seasons) both have private offices—an unlikely luxury for any newspaper reporter, but one that made it unnecessary to put additional actors in office scenes. Indeed, one might draw the impression from the series that the entire *Daily Planet* staff consisted of only a half-dozen or so employees.

Stories were generally simple, and guest casts were mostly limited to character actors, many of whom made multiple appearances on the show. The first season's episodes were more violent than episodes in later seasons; however, Superman himself is rarely seen doing anything that might be construed as responsible for a villain's death.

Although the show was played comparatively straight, it had an underlying feeling of silliness that may have been unavoidable, given the show's preposterous premises. In addition to wondering about Superman's great powers, viewers had good reason to question the intelligence of the people who were nearest to him. Although Superman and Clark Kent are physically identical—except for the fact that Kent wears glasses—no one figures out that they are one and the same person, even though the fact that they are never seen together is frequently mentioned.

Origins and Background The character of Superman first appeared in a comic book in 1938, and he remained a comic-books staple into the twenty-first

Actor George Reeves as the Man of Steel. (Arkent Archive)

century. A popular radio series was built on the success of the comic books during the 1940's, and in 1948 and 1950, Superman made it to big screens in two film serials. The popularity of the radio program and film serials made a series in the new medium of television the natural next step. Production on a syndicated television series began in 1951, but the first regular broadcasts did not begin until May, 1953. Twenty-six episodes were made the first year, and their popularity led to three more twenty-six-episode seasons, through 1957. There was some talk of reviving the series several years later, but the untimely death of lead actor George Reeves in 1959 ended that possibility. However, over the next four decades, the program was frequently rebroadcast in syndication and could still be seen during the early years of the twenty-first century.

Impact The popularity of *The Adventures of Superman* was not fully appreciated until the conclusion of the first season's broadcasts, when the decision was made to produce another season of episodes, and the show then became one of the first dramatic series broadcast in color. Merchandising of Superman toys and other products began in earnest, and the show became a hit among younger viewers. The show's popularity among children probably contributed in later seasons to increasingly whimsical plots that involved invisibility, robots, teleportation, and other science-fiction themes. In 1978, Superman won a new generation of fans when Christopher Reeve (no relation to George Reeves) played him in the first of four big-budget motion pictures. In 1993, Superman returned to television in a new series, *Lois and Clark: The New Adventures of Superman*. In an homage to the original series, Phyllis Coates—the original television Lois Lane—played Lois's mother in a 1994 episode of the new series. Another Superman-related television series, *Smallville*, was introduced on the Warner network in 2001. In that series, Tom Welling plays a teenage Clark Kent; Kent has superpowers, but the show never hints at the existence of "Superman" (or "Superboy"), and the character did not even begin to fly until the 2004-2005 season.

Further Reading

Bianculli, David. *Dictionary of Teleliteracy: Television's Five Hundred Biggest Hits, Misses, and Events*. New York: Continuum, 1996. Contains an appreciative description of the series that places it in the broader perspective of other films and television series about Superman.

Bifulco, Michael J. *Superman on Television: A Comprehensive Viewer's Guide to the Daring Exploits of Superman as Presented in the TV Series*. 1988. Anniversary ed. Grand Rapids, Mich.: Author, 1998. Hard-to-find self-published book, but the most complete guide to the television series in print.

Daniels, Les. *Superman, the Complete History: The Life and Times of the Man of Steel*. San Francisco: Chronicle Books, 1998. Lavishly illustrated and detailed history of the Superman saga. The six-decade evolution of the comic-book hero gets most of the attention, but the book also contains valuable information on the television series.

Grossman, Gary H. *Superman: Serial to Cereal*. New York: Warner Books, 1977. Episode-by-episode history of the 1940's film serials and 1950's television show of the Superman saga. Well illustrated and filled with anecdotes.

Henderson, Jan Alan. *Speeding Bullet: The Life and Bizarre Death of George Reeves*. Grand Rapids, Mich.: Michael J. Bifulco, 1999. Fan biography of actor George Reeves that examines the mysteries surrounding Reeves's death. Discusses his work on *The Adventures of Superman* at length.

R. Kent Rasmussen

See also *Captain Video*; *Cisco Kid, The*; Comic books; *Sky King*; Television for children; Television in the United States.

■ Advertising

Definition Purchased use of the mass media to promote goods and services

During the 1950's, the rapid rise of the baby-boom generation, growing economic prosperity, and television's unprecedented command over the North American public created an unprecedented expansion of advertising.

By the year 1950, the manufacturing facilities of North America had been converted from wartime production to consumer items. A bustling economy resulted in dozens of competitive buying options for the typical growing household income. In the United States, the average weekly wage in 1950 hit a new high of $60.53, which was double that of the pre-Depression era. To help make purchasing decisions easier, the revitalized advertising industry jumped at the opportunity to showcase the proliferation of new products and services for citizens in Canada and the United States. Advertising's role continued to be the preparation and promotion of messages about products, services, and ideas, paid for by an identified sponsor. Because the promotion was paid for, the advertiser (or its agency) had total control over its message, including content, timing, and placement.

Although many differences existed between the United States and Canada, democracy in both countries ensured that mass media were relatively free of governmental control. Thus, advertising served as the principal source of revenue for the media in both Canada and the United States. Equaling only about 10 percent of the U.S. population in size, Canada had fewer media options. However, the vast majority of Canadians lived within one hundred miles of the U.S. border, which meant that much of the U.S. media affected Canadians as well. Television, magazines, and films were imported from the United States, even when they were not welcomed by nationalist Canadian authorities.

The boom economy in the United States and Canada meant that purchases put off during the war years, such as cars and appliances, could now be made at a record pace. Advertisers jumped at this boom and promoted a product's "unique selling proposition"—a term coined during the decade by noted advertising copywriter Rosser Reeves to differentiate the era's many consumer offerings—to give customers ample reason to select one brand over another.

Advertising Agencies Advertising agencies took advantage of the decade's tremendous growth in advertising, and they themselves underwent great expansions. Their bottom line was enhanced thanks to the decades-old commission system. Official agencies were allowed a 15 percent commission for all advertising that they placed in the media. Thus, a $100,000 advertising campaign would result in a $15,000 commission for the agency that prepared the advertisements. The discount was the client company's way of thanking the agency for handling much of the paperwork, artwork, and delivery. The agency also billed the client for such activities as research, development time for the creative staff, and preparation of final advertising proofs. As advertising budgets grew, so did the agencies.

Advertisements were primarily done by hand for print media before approval was given for final pro-

duction. Television commercials were usually shot by following a rough sketch of the major scenes using a storyboard. Common supplies found in the pre-computer 1950's advertising agencies or in publications' advertising departments were drawing tables, rubber cement, erasers, drawing pencils, pens, rulers, T-squares, triangles, large sketch pads, and dry-transfer lettering. Typesetting slowly produced the final advertisement, following the hand-sketched concepts.

With the arrival of television, advertising agencies developed into early versions of later full-service operations. They expanded their staffs so they could handle both print and broadcast media, along with the necessary research to determine the best supposed placements for a client's message. Account executives represented agencies to clients and the clients to the agencies. The account executives—almost all were male during the 1950's—would also try to solicit new business for the agency. Copywriters were responsible for developing a creative advertisement. An art director, with experience in photography and typography, coordinated the finished print advertisement or television commercial. At larger firms other employees (now called creatives) were enlisted to do the artwork, photography, or layout. Agencies also took on social responsibility, developing public service announcements and contributing pro bono work for a variety of local and national clients.

Leaders in the industry emerged during this decade. Leading advertising agencies developed by such powers as Leo Burnett, David Ogilvy, and Bill Bernbach were expanding. Olgilvy's "Hathaway man" and "Commander Whitehead" became common models for brand promotion during the 1950's. Burnett, who had opened his agency in Chicago in 1935, once said that a successful advertisement was one that made a consumer reply not with "That is a great ad!" but with "That is a great product!"

New Medium of Television The growing U.S. and Canadian populations were fascinated by the new medium of television, which allowed advertisers to showcase exciting new products to a long-denied public. RCA had delivered its first black-and-white television sets to market in 1946, but color broadcasts were slower to catch on during the 1950's, even though they existed. Televisions went from being an innovation in a few homes in 1950 to being a staple in almost all homes by the conclusion of 1959. In 1950, 108 commercial and noncommercial stations broadcast to 9 percent of U.S. homes. By decade's end, the number was 583 stations to more than 87 percent of the homes; of that number 13 percent of the homes owned multiple television sets. While it took more than one hundred years for newspapers to reach penetration into 50 percent of U.S. homes, black-and-white television needed only eight years to accomplish the same feat. The growth in Canada, while not quite as dramatic, was also notable. The Canadian Broadcasting Corporation (CBC), founded in 1932, brought television to that country in 1952.

Many of the early programs were produced specifically for advertisers, who directed the content toward their intended audiences. Among the ten top shows by sponsors during the 1950-1951 season were *Texaco Star Theater, Philco TV Playhouse, The Colgate*

Comedy Hour, and *Gillette Cavalcade of Sports.* The popular show *I Love Lucy,* for example, was owned by Philip Morris cigarettes, which is why characters smoked on the air and even promoted the brand during commercial breaks. NBC was the first network to begin selling commercials to several different advertisers to share sponsorship of a single program, a move likely prompted by the quiz-show scandals during the late 1950's. Popular because of their get-rich-quick techniques, quiz shows such as Revlon's *The $64,000 Question* and *Twenty-One* were found to be rigged in 1957. During the investigations, it was discovered that program sponsors provided certain contestants with advance answers in order to create an atmosphere of success and maintain high viewer ratings.

With the advent of television advertising, North American consumers were subjected to advertisements emanating from a variety of companies and us-

Many television programs of the early 1950's were closely linked to their sponsors, whose names were omnipresent during the broadcasts. (Hulton Archive | by Getty Images)

ing sound, motion, and, by decade's end, full color in the United States. Unlike later decades' fast-paced, multiple-commercial breaks from programming, most commercials during the 1950's were one or two minutes in length. Only one sponsor typically was featured during a commercial break early in the decade.

Advertising rates were primarily determined by audience size. The A. C. Nielsen Company, initiated during the decade, determined television audience sizes using its unique rating system and served as the primary yardstick for putting prices on minutes of commercial air time.

Print Media By the beginning of the 1950's, newspapers were approaching their highest production numbers in history. In 1950, the United States had 1,772 morning and afternoon dailies, a number that slowly and steadily dropped in later decades. The newspapers of the era were almost always black and white, with wide pages, narrow columns, and small photographs. More than 75 percent of U.S. adults read a daily newspaper during the 1950's. In the United States, eighty-three cities had two or more competing newspapers by 1954, a total that declined consistently after the decade. Moreover, the number of nondailies was at an all-time high during that time, although their circulation figures continued to increase in later decades.

Because printing prices were low, and circulation was high, newspapers and magazines served as ideal advertising vehicles for reaching households by the millions, especially for local retailers. The amount of space devoted to advertising in the typical daily newspaper averaged about 60 percent during the decade. Despite this kind of success, however, most publishers were becoming anxious about the growth of television advertising. In fact, many papers refused to run television listings or even mention programs within their pages.

Unlike the daily paper, color advertisements did appear frequently in many magazines. Even without extensive research to back their assumptions, magazine advertisers were correct in their thinking that color advertisements attracted higher consumer attention than black-and-white ones.

However, the advent of television soon caused a major loss in national advertising revenue for magazines. Many mass-circulation national publications saw declines by the mid-1950's that would eventually send them into retirement. Such notable titles as *Col-*

lier's, Coronet, American, Look, The Saturday Evening Post, and *Life* closed because national advertising dollars were redirected to television. In fact, both *Life* and *Look* still had circulations of more than six million when they folded. However, television's siphoning of advertising revenue was too much for such publications to overcome.

Most successful magazine starts during this time were specialized publications. Among the launches in 1950 were *Golf Digest* and *Prevention. TV Guide,* capitalizing on the popularity of the new broadcast medium, had 1.5 million subscribers during 1953 in only its first year of national distribution. That same year, Hugh Hefner started *Playboy,* featuring enough high-quality editorial content by top literary writers in addition to the nude female photographs to avoid pornography charges. *Sports Illustrated,* started in 1954, overcame early years of revenue loss to become a leader in its field. *Young Miss* (later *YM*) was launched in 1955. In 1958, *Guns & Ammo* and *Modern Maturity* entered the market. With a renewed emphasis on demographics, advertisers could target magazines and their unique readerships to sell goods and services.

Radio and Outdoor Marketing Radio advertising grew during the decade, largely as a result of the placement of radios inside the new automobiles and the creation of smaller, portable radios. Advertisers recognized the immediate benefit of having their messages broadcast to potential customers as they were mobile and could stop at retail locations. In 1950, there were 2,867 radio stations in the United States. By the end of the 1950's, that number had grown to 4,296. Advertising revenue jumped during that period from $445 million to $560 million. Radio adapted to the growth of television by revamping its format. Soap operas, dramas, and comedies from the 1940's gave way to an emphasis on music, especially with the introduction of rock and roll. Portable radios were produced at lower costs and in smaller-sized transistor versions with batteries. Their portability increased the chances that the commercials would be heard outside the house.

Radio sales staffs during the 1950's, similar to their television counterparts, were responsible for earning a majority of the revenue for the stations. The local retail community was visited frequently by sales representatives to garner support for the local station. Television did take over radio's previous dominance of national advertising, but radio survived through its reliance on local retailers and its relatively low rates.

Outdoor advertising, the oldest form of advertising, became a valuable tool in the decade as more automobiles traveled more miles across North America. Free from the legal restrictions that would arise later, the billboard grew as a popular—if not intrusive—advertising medium. Billboards were placed strategically to alert cross-country motorists or mere suburban commuters about goods and services, which often could be found in close proximity to the signs. Furthermore, in 1956, the popularity of painted barns was evident by the more than nine hundred "See Rock City" signs painted on structures from Canada throughout the eastern United States, encouraging tourists to see the towering rock formation near Chattanooga, Tennessee. An additional barn painting popularized during this time was for Mail Pouch Tobacco.

Another popular advertising form during the decade was skywriting, when airplanes would produce stylized plumes of white against a blue background for all on the ground to see. A related method was the use of blimps. Goodyear started the trend in 1925. Following wartime surveillance use, their promotion practice multiplied during the 1950's when Goodyear tires were being hawked to motorists and others.

In 1958, the U.S. Congress passed the first federal law to control billboards along interstate highways. This legislation was called the Bonus Act because states were provided bonus incentives to control such forms of advertising. Other types of outdoor signs appeared on or inside mass transit vehicles and buildings, especially in metropolitan areas.

Promoting Brands Brand promotion was one of the biggest factors in the increase in advertising during this decade. Because of the influx of consumer goods on the market, products needed to be differentiated from their competitors; advertising the unique qualities of a brand allowed a company to position its products or services as better, faster, cleaner, or less expensive than the competition. With so many brands to choose from, consumers often sought advice from advertising to help them discern a product's special characteristics. Advertising mogul Ogilvy promoted this concept of "brand personality" to sell products and argued that a personality would prove more important to draw customers to products and services than "any trivial product difference" would.

Once a brand was established, brand loyalty followed as customers sought the assurance of an expected level of quality for their favorite products from one purchase to the next.

One early example of brand success after the introduction of television was Hazel Bishop lipstick. Sales zoomed from $50,000 a year in 1950 to $4.5 million following two years of television commercials. A North American advertising campaign reintroduced the chubby-cheeked Campbell Kids, first introduced in 1905 to sell Campbell's soup and brought back during the early 1950's to celebrate the company's fiftieth anniversary. Other cultural icons from the decade that were popular or were introduced included Aunt Jemima for the Quaker Oats Company, Mr. Clean, and Tony the Tiger, developed in 1951 for Kellogg's Sugar Frosted Flakes. Speedy Alka-Seltzer, with his smiling "plop, plop, fizz, fizz" routine, became an early 1950's fixture in print and broadcast promotions and helped introduce inexpensive puppetry into advertising. Automobiles at this time replaced cigarettes and packaged goods as the most frequently promoted product.

In 1955, Leo Burnett attempted to find an effective way to advertise Marlboro cigarettes, a filter-tip brand that for decades had been much more popular among women. When he saw a pictorial on cowboys, Burnett knew that if he could connect Marlboro to the idea in the photographs, American smokers would respond. The successful national "Marlboro Man" advertising campaign began that year. *Advertising Age* magazine ranks the Marlboro man as the number-one brand image of the twentieth century.

By the late 1950's, agencies began to encourage the collaboration between art directors and advertising copywriters to further brand personality and loyalty. This team approach typically had not been used prior to that time. Bill Bernbach, founder of the firm Doyle Dane Bernbach, brought together his creative staff so that advertising headlines and photos or illustrations could work as a unit. He said the key to a successful advertisement was that it had "stopping power" that emanated from text and image. One classic example of this collaboration was the long-running "Think Small" campaign that started in

1959 for the Volkswagen Beetle. It was ranked among the best advertisements of the twentieth century by *Advertising Age*. Unlike large colorful photos for most automobile offerings coming out of Detroit, the Volkswagen advertisements were simple, with black-and-white understated photos. Honesty was a major by-product of the campaign, which benefited the German import as well as the advertising profession.

Not all brand campaigns resulted in successful sales. For example, the 1957 Ford Edsel was called by many the biggest flop of the twentieth century. Despite $30 million in consumer advertising, the most extensive campaign for any new model during the decade, the Edsel fared poorly at its Ford dealerships. It became a classic case of good advertising that failed to sell a product.

Regulation Both Canada and the United States impose certain restrictions on advertising to children as well as the number of minutes per hour commercials are allowed to be broadcast on television. However, the countries' courts have different interpretations of what constitutes commercial speech, which typically is given much less protection than an individual's right to free speech in a democratic society. The main governing body for U.S. advertising regulation is the Federal Trade Commission, established in 1914. In 1942, the U.S. Supreme Court ruled in *Valentine v. Chrestensen* that purely commercial advertising was beyond First Amendment protection.

Bait-and-switch advertising was declared illegal by the American courts. In this scenario, popularized by a few shady retailers during the 1950's, customers would come to a store after seeing an advertised low sales price only to be told that the item was sold out but a much better item was available at a higher price. The sales staff might also try to convince the consumer that the low-priced item was so inferior that the smart thing to do was to buy an alternative higher-priced product.

The Fur Products Labeling Act in 1951 and the Textile Fiber Products Identification Act of 1958 gave the Federal Trade Commission (FTC) authority on the advertising and labeling of such products. One of many differences in U.S. and Canadian regulations concerns puffery, which refers to subjective claims about such qualities as taste, appearance, or smell. Puffery is legally protected in the United States but greatly restricted in Canada.

The FTC addressed the use of puffery during the late 1950's, accepting its inevitable place in advertising, but it cautioned against misstatements of material facts.

The Canadian Code of Advertising Standards, developed by and for its advertising industry, was not officially published until 1963. However, Canadian standards were even more complex than those in the United States during the 1950's. This was attributed to the national and provincial jurisdictions, self-regulatory rules by the advertising industry, and the difficulties of having to deal with both French and English languages and cultures.

Ethical Issues New York City's Madison Avenue—an important locale for advertising agencies and commercial retail—became a household name during the decade but not necessarily in a positive light. Criticisms quickly surfaced about advertising and how it was becoming a powerful force in society. Novels from the decade depicted account executives and advertising copywriters as shady characters. It was no secret that many of the leading advertising executives had proven their effective persuasiveness while serving under George Creel for the U.S. War Advertising Council during World War II, which raised $35 billion in war bonds and encouraged two million women to enter the workforce. Fears of advertising manipulation soon were being voiced as advertising flooded North America during the 1950's. Advertisements were going to make people buy lots of things they did not need, opponents argued.

One controversy that surfaced during this time was subliminal advertising. The premise was that hidden messages, often sexual in nature, would not be seen in print advertisements or commercials except by the subconscious mind, encouraging consumers to make purchases that they might not have considered otherwise. In 1957, James Vicary added to the controversy with research later deemed unethical. His experiment occurred in a motion-picture theater where he flashed the words "Eat Popcorn" and "Drink Coke" on the screen for one three-thousandth of a second. Rumors about the project alleged that sales had increased following the experiment. Subsequent replications showed no such increase. Critics contend that the entire experiment was a futile attempt by Vicary to obtain large consulting fees from advertisers. Before leaving the profession, Vicary finally admitted that the whole project was a hoax. However, the damage to the advertising profession's credibility was permanent.

Vance Packard's *The Hidden Persuaders* (1957) attacked the advertising industry for exploiting consumer vulnerabilities to sell products. With more than one million copies sold, it remained on the best-seller list for eighteen weeks. He claimed that motivation research was used to control consumer thinking and buying decisions. Despite the lack of research confirming Packard's sensational thesis, the National Association of Broadcasters banned subliminal advertising. Martin Mayer added more fuel to the advertising manipulation theory with his 1958 book, *Madison Avenue, U.S.A.*

Historically, the advertising profession sought to present itself in a better light. For example, the American Association of Advertising Agencies adopted an ethics code in 1924, and similar standards were adopted or revised by other advertising organizations. Some observers charged that such actions were too little and too late to reverse the negative attitudes regarding the onslaught of media advertising bombarding the North American public.

Critics also started calling attention to how advertising increased the costs of goods and services, since a company had to pay for the advertising to reach its customers. The advertising industry, in response, pointed out how mass promotion led to mass production, which actually lowered the price. Advertising gave businesses the opportunity to communicate directly with consumers. It also provided potential consumers the opportunity to compare products and services, which could create competition and promote improved customer service and lower costs. That debate was far from settled during the decade.

Targeting Housewives Most women did not work outside the home during the decade. In fact, according to research from the 1950's, women spent more time on household chores than their mothers had, averaging nearly a one-hundred-hour workweek. Advertisements targeted specific products as means to lessen the drudgery of housework. Moreover, they specifically targeted women, for good reason. They were the ones in the family who went shopping. Food preparation and housework topped the categories of advertisements directed at the typical stay-at-home mother of the 1950's. A 1954 advertisement for a Kelvinator automatic clothes dryer proclaimed to its female audience that it was a "new way to end washday drudgery." Similar advertisements decreed that women needed a respite from dishwashing: In order to have more leisure time to spend with husband and children, women were encouraged to buy a new dishwasher. Products were promoted as fashionable, to fit the decor of one's kitchen, for example. Thus, many housewives regularly wanted new and better appliances and colorful products featured in advertisements to keep up with the neighbors. The original Mr. Clean television and radio jingle became a popular tune during the 1950's as the Procter & Gamble Company attempted to prove that it wanted to befriend North American women. Its advertisements promised high-quality assistance with household cleaning in the form of an animated, muscular, bald spokesman.

Frozen dinners were heavily promoted in print and broadcast media so women would not have to prepare meals over a hot stove. They were quickly renamed "TV dinners" during the early 1950's as family members would gather in the living room to watch their favorite television programs while eating their evening meal.

Women would later revolt over their sexist depictions in many of the 1950's advertisements in which they appeared to be overly concerned with a spotless toilet bowl or the whiteness of their husband's shirt collars. There was also concern about the way women were used as sexual objects to pander products to consumers. This was nothing new, but as overall advertising increased, so did such sexist depictions. New-car advertisements, for example, both on television and in print, often had scantily attired, attractive young women adorning the fenders.

Advertising Associations The Association of Canadian Advertisers (ACA), founded in 1914 and acting as an important organization during the 1950's, is a national, nonprofit organization dedicated solely to serving the interests of all companies that advertise and market their goods and services throughout Canada. The ACA functions to promote the common interests of all advertisers. Serving as the voice of the Canadian advertiser, ACA safeguards advertisers' rights to commercial free speech and strives toward an advertising marketplace that is accountable for the value provided to the advertiser. ACA represents the views and concerns of advertisers before government and industry bodies and negotiates with union contracts on behalf of Canadian advertisers. The Canadian Advertising Research Foundation is a not-for-profit entity whose major focus is advertising, communications, and related research. It was chartered under a federal grant in 1949, when it was established in cooperation with the ACA and the Institute of Canadian Advertising.

In the United States, local and state advertising clubs, the American Association of Advertising Agencies (founded in 1917), and the Advertising Council were formed to help regulate the industry, enhance the profession, assist charitable organizations, and provide educational materials. In 1950, the Outdoor Advertising Association of America, founded in 1891, was revamped as that industry expanded. The television division of the National Association of Broadcasters was established in 1952.

The Advertising Council was an outgrowth of the War Advertising Council, established in 1942 to promote patriotism during the U.S. war effort. Its new mission was to conduct significant campaigns on issues that would improve overall society. Members donated their time and talents, while the media typically donated the use of their space or air time. The Ad Council spent considerable resources during the 1950's promoting causes for local and national nonprofit organizations, such as the Red Cross. Moreover, a 1957 public service advertisement in *The New York Times* listing the complete schedule for the upcoming New York Philharmonic season reversed a serious attendance slide.

Impact The tremendous growth of advertising during the 1950's was aided by a 25 percent increase in the population in need of goods and services. Family size increased as did incomes and the need for additional housing units with furnishings. Products proliferated along with the means to promote them over the expanding mass media.

Further Reading

Berger, Arthur Asa. *Ads, Fads, and Consumer Culture: Advertising's Impact on American Character and Society.* Lanham, Md.: Rowman & Littlefield, 2004. Examines advertising in American society and visits topics such as advertising and the communication process, sexuality and advertising, political advertising, and the marketing society.

Key, Wilson Bryan. *Subliminal Seduction: Ad Media's Manipulation of a Not So Innocent America.* New York: Signet, 1973. Explores the psychological aspects of advertising on the American public.

McCallister, Matthew P. *The Commercialization of American Culture: New Advertising, Control, and Democracy.* Thousand Oaks, Calif.: Sage, 1996. Examines advertising from a late-twentieth-century perspective and explores advertising tactics such as place-based media, cross-promotion, and product placement in films.

McDonough, John, and Karen Egolf, eds. *The "Advertising Age" Encyclopedia of Advertising.* Chicago: Fitzroy Dearborn, 2002. A colorfully illustrated book that traces numerous ad campaigns across several decades.

Sivulka, Juliann. *Soap, Sex, and Cigarettes: A Cultural History of American Advertising.* Belmont, Calif.: Wadsworth, 1998. Examines how advertising both shapes and reflects society.

Tellis, Gerald J. *Effective Advertising: Understanding When, How, and Why Advertising Works.* Thousand Oaks, Calif.: Sage, 2004. Summarizes an extensive body of research on advertising effectiveness and focuses especially on the instantaneous and carry-over effects of advertising on consumer choice, sales, and market share.

Randy Hines

See also Affluence and the new consumerism; Communications in Canada; Communications in the United States; Home appliances; Home furnishings; McLuhan, Marshall; *Man in the Gray Flannel Suit, The*; Newspapers in Canada; Newspapers in the United States; Nielsen ratings; Packard, Vance; Television in Canada; Television in the United States.

■ Affluence and the new consumerism

Definition Postwar economic prosperity that ushered in a way of life centered on consumption of material goods

The growing affluence of the 1950's led to a new consumer-driven society that had both rewards and costs. The rewards included luxurious lifestyles, abundant with material goods, for many Americans, while the costs included indebtedness and pollution.

During the 1950's there was more economic growth in the United States than had ever been experienced in any nation in human history. This growth resulted in an affluent American society. There are a number of factors that aided economic growth during the 1950's, including a backlog of construction projects and demand for durable consumer goods as a result of World War II; the Korean War effort; and the baby boom, which occurred primarily in the middle and upper classes.

After the rationing of the early 1940's, when all efforts were directed toward the war effort, soldiers returned home to jobs and new material goods. Building demand for consumer goods resulted from the restrictions placed on purchasing during World War II. These restrictions allowed Americans to save at a rate more than three times higher than that in the decades before or after World War II. Real wages also increased significantly; as a result, Americans had plenty of money to spend during the 1950's.

After World War II, per capita income grew by 35 percent, and many working-class families were able to move into the middle class. By the mid-1950's, 60 percent of the population in the United States had middle-class incomes—between $3,000 and $10,000 a year. This movement of individuals into the middle class was unprecedented; for example, during the "prosperous 1920's," only 31 percent of Americans had a middle-class lifestyle.

Disposable income increased significantly during this time, as did spending. Americans bought homes, automobiles, appliances, and other consumer goods in record numbers. Private affluence on a mass scale emerged as the dominant force in the marketplace, and as a result, consumerism—bolstered by increased production, use of credit cards, and advertising—emerged as a way of life on an unprecedented scale.

A Shift in Values Some argue that there was a shift in American values during the 1950's from hard work, self-restraint, and deferred gratification to instant gratification and flagrant spending. The earlier values encouraged individuals to save, which in turn aided the national growth of industrialism and capitalism; immediate spending fueled late capitalism. The 1950's introduced new levels of materialism into American culture. Consumerism became a natural way of life; it was seen as normal, acceptable, and even good for the economy.

During the 1950's affluence in the United States led to conspicuous consumption among not only the upper classes but commoners as well. Sociologist Thorstein Veblen first identified conspicuous consumption as a practice among the wealthy upper classes of Americans during the late nineteenth century. He believed that in a society dominated by con-

spicuous consumption, the norms of consumption shape one's sense of what is beautiful; for example, an object that serves an honorary purpose of conspicuous waste is therefore considered an object of beauty. Veblen felt that beauty and cost inevitably become linked in this kind of culture. The more costly or rare something is, the more it is valued, and in turn, if something is not costly, it tends to be devalued. Veblen also pointed out that the markers of conspicuous consumption are used to indicate a person's place in the social class hierarchy.

A consumer culture developed during the 1950's and mass consumption infiltrated every aspect of individuals' lives. For the first time, large numbers of people were consuming goods solely for the sake of expressing themselves. When a society moves into consumerism, material possessions are prized less for their durability and more for their roles in fashion. Therefore, people consume in order to express themselves; the products they buy allow them to engage in self-definition. Clothing becomes more than merely a means to cover one's body or to protect oneself from the elements: It becomes a way for one to emphasize values and social position.

The norms of fashion played an important role in fueling the consumer era of the 1950's. Fashions were constantly shaping and reshaping the norms of consumption by dictating what was "in" and what was "out." Those who paid attention to fashions felt compelled to update wardrobes on a yearly basis.

Role of Mass Production American industry manufactured an unprecedented volume of products during the 1950's. Automobile sales rose to record highs, the number of cars produced soared from 2 million in 1945 to 51 million in 1955, and purchases of appliances and household furnishings increased by 240 percent during the decade.

The invention of the assembly line in 1913 by Henry Ford helped lead to the mass production of goods. Ford developed the assembly line to produce cars. The principle, referred to as Fordism, spread to other industries, and as a result of this kind of standardization of goods at low cost, a surplus of material goods were available. Consumer goods that were once considered to be luxurious gradually became everyday items.

Housing starts exploded after World War II: There were more single-family homes purchased between 1946 and 1956 than in the first half of the preceding century. By the year 1960, 62 percent of American families owned their own homes in contrast to 43 percent in 1940. Most of these homes were built in the suburbs. Nearly the entire increase in the gross national product during the mid-1950's was a result of increased spending on consumer durables and residential construction.

Credit Cards and Advertising The credit card was introduced during the 1950's, and it led to increased spending and consumerism. People could buy what they wanted even if they did not have the means to do so. Consumer credit in the United States increased dramatically during this era, rising from $8.4 billion in 1945 to nearly $45 billion in 1958. During the 1950's, consumer debt expanded considerably as the cost of household comforts came at an enormous increase in total indebtedness.

Advertising was another major force that encouraged consumerism during the 1950's. Advertising increased by nearly 400 percent between 1945 and 1960. The new medium of television gave advertisers a fresh venue to reach out to consumers. For the first time, the youth market was directly targeted by advertisers through programs such as *Disneyland* and the *Howdy Doody Show*, which advertised directly to children and bypassed parents. Advertising was ubiquitous; everywhere people turned they were being convinced that their wants were really needs.

As values shifted from deferred gratification to instant gratification, advertisers needed to help individuals justify their desire to engage in conspicuous consumption. Consuming more goods and products than one needed was previously seen as immoral and wasteful. Advertisers had to convey to the public that it was acceptable—even moral and good for the country—to buy that second car or that expensive suit. Not only did advertisers provide consumers with a rationale to shop and consume, but they also linked consumerism with issues surrounding patriotism, freedom, and family. Consumer freedom came to be equated with democracy and political freedom. Consumerism was even seen as patriotic, a way of supporting the country and government. Consumerism and the desire to have more were also sold as a way to make one's family happy and stable.

Impact The affluence of the 1950's led to a culture enthralled with materialism. In order to obtain the level of material comfort desired, many Americans became overworked and overspent. Many Americans began to place the pursuit of material gain above all else, even family, social, and personal obligations. The norms of consumption introduced new standards of expensiveness and wastefulness. For many, this unending quest for material goods left them feeling empty and discontented, a sentiment echoed in many literary works of the era, including J. D. Salinger's *The Catcher in the Rye* (1951) and the works of the Beat poets.

There were those in the United States who did not celebrate the general affluence of the nation as much as some did. John Kenneth Galbraith, in his 1958 book *The Affluent Society*, argued that increased production rates and overall affluence had created important problems in society—namely, a widening gap between the wealthy and the poor. He argued that rather than create false needs through advertising, the United States should focus on improving public spending for schools, infrastructure, and housing. His book was widely read and influenced public policy during the 1960's and President Lyndon B. Johnson's Great Society programs.

With affluence and consumerism came many changes in American life. Increasing suburbanization created urban sprawl and exacerbated problems for the underprivileged and unfortunate left behind in the cities. The affluent who lived in the suburbs bought cars in record numbers for their commutes into cities to work. Shopping malls emerged, creating a venue for the consumer to buy nearly everything one could possibly imagine under one roof.

The affluence and consumerism of Americans also came at great cost to both the environment and people of other nations. High levels of production created problems such as pollution of the air, land, and water. Furthermore, once goods such as televisions, refrigerators, radios, and washing machines are produced and distributed to the consumer, there is a direct increase in the amount of energy consumed, placing even greater demands on Earth's natural resources. Moreover, as corporations in the United States became richer because of increased consumption, their power and reach increased as well. Many American companies began operating overseas as multinational corporations during this era. These corporations did business overseas—often paying much lower wages to the international worker than to American workers—and brought the profits back to the United States, creating an even larger gap between the rich and the poor countries of the world.

Further Reading

Cohen, Elizabeth. *A Consumer's Republic: The Politics of Mass Consumption in Postwar America.* New York: Knopf, 2003. Examines the way in which affluence and consumerism were linked to issues of citizenship (the encouragement to buy for "the good of the nation") in postwar America.

Coontz, Stephanie. *The Way We Never Were: American Families and the Nostalgia Trap.* New York: Basic Books, 1992. This work is an intriguing chronicle of American family life during the mid- to late twentieth century.

Hession, Charles, and Hyman Sardy. *Ascent to Affluence: A History of American Economic Development.* Boston: Allyn and Bacon, 1969. Provides a complete historical account of economic development and its implications in the United States and abroad.

Miles, Steven. *Consumerism as a Way of Life.* Thousand Oaks, Calif.: Sage, 1998. Applies social theory to the history of consumerism and explores topics such as "Consumerism Then and Now," "Consuming Fashion," and "The Consuming Paradox."

Parr, Joy. *Domestic Goods: The Material, the Moral, and the Economic in the Postwar Years.* Toronto: University of Toronto Press, 1999. Examines the differences in the ways American and Canadian housewives used consumer goods and takes a broader look at the production, promotion, and consumption of furniture and appliances in Canada.

Ritzer, George. *The McDonaldization of Society: Revised New Century Edition.* Thousand Oaks, Calif.: Pine Forge Press, 2004. This unique examination of American life looks at many ways in which the changes during the 1950's, including the growth of fast-food restaurants, are still influencing social life today.

Christine A. Wernet

See also Advertising; *Affluent Society, The*; American Dream; Automobiles and auto manufacturing; Conformity, culture of; Fast-food restaurants; Home appliances; Home furnishings; Income and wages in the United States; Levittown; McDonald's restaurants; Mills, C. Wright; Packard, Vance.

■ *The Affluent Society*

Identification Social commentary on the central economic problem facing the United States during the 1950's
Author John Kenneth Galbraith (1908-   )
Date Published in 1958

The arguments and analyses of the American economy included in Galbraith's book influenced popular thinking and executive policymaking with regard to poverty and social spending.

The title of *The Affluent Society* gave a new name to the post-World War II era in the United States. By the 1950's, the United States possessed the world's largest economy, in terms of both total output and output per person. Despite this prosperity, about 20 percent of the population lived in poverty. To John Kenneth Galbraith, a professor of economics at Harvard University, the central economic problem was no longer how to increase production to satisfy basic human needs, which for many had long since been met, but rather how to deal with the growing abundance or affluence in society. He argued that continued focus on increasing output by creating needs through such means as advertising would only widen the gap between the wealthy and the poor. He argued that the real need—and the way to combat poverty—was to improve public services such as schools, infrastructure, and housing through increased government spending.

Impact Galbraith's book, which was widely read in the last years of the 1950's, had a profound impact on American public policy during the 1960's. It provided a foundation for President Lyndon B. Johnson's War on Poverty and Great Society programs, enacted during the decade following its publication.

Further Reading

Collins, Robert. *More: The Politics of Economic Growth in Postwar America.* New York: Oxford University Press, 2000. An exploration of how political attitudes regarding postwar economic growth have evolved.

Sobel, Robert. *The Great Boom, 1950-2000: How a Generation of Americans Created the World's Most Prosperous Society.* New York: St. Martin's Press, 2000. A thought-provoking look at the sources of increased affluence following World War II and its social implications.

Randall Hannum

See also Advertising; Affluence and the new consumerism; Business and the economy in the United States; Conformity, culture of; Gross national product of the United States; Income and wages in the United States; *Lonely Crowd, The*; Mills, C. Wright; *Organization Man, The*; Packard, Vance.

■ AFL-CIO merger

The Event Joining together of the largest craft and industrial unions in the United States
Date December 5, 1955

The largest federations of labor unions, American Federation of Labor (AFL) and Congress of Industrial Organizations (CIO), ended two decades of rivalry, determined to work together to protect their collective interests.

As the economic boom after World War II increased the strength of the American economy, organized labor began to assert its power. Early in 1950, union strikes in the auto and coal industries brought widespread benefits for workers, including company financing of pension plans and health insurance as well as automatic cost-of-living increases in wages. Growing union memberships created a shift in the balance of power between labor and management. As the power of unions increased, strikes occurred against railroads, airlines, and the steel industry.

In the final months of 1952, major events involving the transfer of power to three new leaders directly affected the future of labor unions. The election of Republican president Dwight D. Eisenhower ended two decades of governmental support for labor under Democratic presidents Franklin D. Roosevelt and Harry S. Truman. United Auto Workers president Walter Reuther took over as head of the CIO, and former secretary-treasurer George Meany became leader of the AFL.

Within a short time, Reuther and Meany began planning a merger of the two organizations, estab-

CIO president Philip Murray (left) and United Auto Workers president Walter Reuther at the CIO national convention in Chicago in November, 1950. (AP/Wide World Photos)

lishing a unity committee of leaders from the AFL and CIO to facilitate their plan. The committee spent two years dealing with issues to draw up the agreement. The long-standing rivalry between the AFL and CIO had involved arguments between local chapters over jurisdiction and ongoing "raiding"—the stealing of memberships from the other organization.

Unions faced serious challenges as alleged communist and criminal activities and corruption within their ranks motivated their leaders to take defensive action against the threat of government investigations. In 1953, the AFL forced out the International Longshoremen's Association after a major scandal disclosed evidence of corruption.

When publicity regarding several cases of fraud and graft undermined public trust in AFL leadership, Meany created an ethics committee to investigate associations with mobsters and clear out racketeers from the organization. Other unions conducted their own purges after the CIO ousted eleven member unions with nearly sixty thousand workers because of suspected communist sympathizers.

In 1957, after considering findings of the U.S. Senate committee's investigations on racketeering, the executive board of the AFL-CIO drove out the Brotherhood of Teamsters with almost two million members, along with the Bakery Workers and the Laundry Workers. Early in the decade, Congress had passed laws to prevent unions from becoming too powerful, and when steelworkers threatened to strike in 1952, President Truman called in troops to keep the mills running. President Eisenhower was faced with a similar situation in 1959, when a strike by steelworkers was still unsettled as the decade ended.

Impact Providing a basis for collaboration, the AFL-CIO merger brought nearly sixteen million workers together, strengthening and stabilizing the unions, protecting gains already made, alleviating jurisdictional problems, and creating a single voice of agreement on legislative and political issues.

Further Reading

Dubofsky, Melvyn, and Warren Van Tine. *John L. Lewis: A Biography.* New York: Quadrangle/New York Times, 1977. Details myths and realities about Lewis, president of the United Mine Workers, founder of the CIO, and a man of secrecy, aggression, and egotism.

Robinson, Archie. *George Meany and His Times: A Biography.* New York: Simon & Schuster, 1981. Compiled from taped interviews of family and associates of Meany.

Zeiger, Robert H. *The CIO, 1935-1955.* Chapel Hill: University of North Carolina Press, 1995. In-depth chronology including extensive quotations from key figures in the CIO and AFL.

Zeller, F. C. Duke. *Devil's Pact: Inside the World of the Teamsters Union.* Secaucus, N.J.: Birch Lane Press, 1996. Personal adviser to four Teamsters presidents, Zeller reveals the union's underground history using previously unpublished material from confidential sources.

Gale M. Thompson

See also Canadian Labour Congress; Celler-Kefauver Act of 1950; Chrysler autoworkers' strike; General Motors; Hoffa, Jimmy; Kefauver Committee; Landrum-Griffin Act of 1959; Lewis, John L.; McClellan Committee; Meany, George; Teamsters Union; Unionism in Canada; Unionism in the United States.

■ African Americans

Identification Americans of full or partial African descent

New postwar economic opportunities and the rise of the Civil Rights movement made the 1950's an important turning point in the history of African Americans.

For the African American community at the dawn of the 1950's, there was far greater cause for optimism than had existed in decades prior. The postwar boom in the economy was felt even within the more disadvantaged segments of American society, and African Americans had achieved significant breakthroughs in sports, the military, political and government offices, and the judiciary. However, progress was still slow, and the Harry S. Truman presidential administration's stated commitment to implement a far-reaching civil rights program under Truman's Fair Deal was blocked by Republicans and southern Democrats in Congress.

In 1950, the African American population in the United States was officially stated as standing at barely more than 15 million people, 10 percent of a total national population of 150,697,361. By the year 1960, the totals had risen to 18,871,831, 10.5 percent of a national population of 179,323,175. In 1950, the majority—68 percent—of African Americans lived in the South, while 28.2 percent lived in northern states and 3.8 percent lived in western states. However, the southern proportion of this population had been shrinking since the 1910's "Great Migration," when large numbers of black Americans began leaving the South both because of the violent discrimination to which they were subjected and because of the better employment opportunities in urban areas outside this region.

The 1950's saw the tendency continue—African Americans left at the rate of 146,000 each year—and by the end of the 1950's, only 60 percent of African Americans resided in the South; 34.4 percent lived in the North and 5.6 percent in the West. Regional loss was heavy among those in the agricultural sector, where sharecroppers were squeezed by farm mechanization. Black-owned farms declined from 559,980 in 1950 to 272,541 by 1960; most of the loss was felt in the South. Among those who lived in the North and the West, the overwhelming majority were located in cities. In the northern states, 93.5 percent of African Americans were urban dwellers in 1950; this figure increased to 95.3 percent in 1960. In the West, the parallel totals were 70.1 percent in 1950 and 73.7 percent in 1960.

Socioeconomic Trends Despite certain socioeconomic advances, illiteracy, mortality rates, and unemployment among African Americans remained at levels far higher than those of nearly every other group in American society. Black households without male heads increased during the decade: from 17.6 percent in 1950 to 22.4 percent by 1960. In comparison, white families without male heads were only 8.5 percent in 1950 and 8.7 percent in 1960. Illegitimacy rates for black citizens as measured against the total population maintained at a high level: generally five times greater than the national average.

Unemployment for blacks would remain at consistently higher levels than for the white population and widened by the end of the decade. In 1950, 12 percent of African Americans were out of work compared to only 8 percent of white Americans. By 1960, 10 percent of African Americans were unemployed, a figure that had improved during the decade but remained much higher than the comparable figure of 4 percent of white Americans. Toward the end of the decade, the employment of African Americans in service sectors—for example, as teachers, clerical

workers, health service workers, and sales clerks—as well as in construction and blue-collar labor had increased, although more remained in unskilled and domestic positions than among their white counterparts.

Gains were realized in personal health as a result of scientific breakthroughs. Life expectancy among African Americans increased from 60.8 years in 1950 to 63.6 in 1960. However, this figure stood below the national average of 68.2 years in 1950 and 69.7 in 1960. Poverty, subpar nutrition, and discrimination in health care in some rural and poorer areas contributed to this figure. Although the birthrate among African Americans remained higher than that of white Americans, it did decrease slightly by the end of the decade—from 33.3 live births per thousand in 1950 to 32.1 in 1960 versus 24.1 per thousand for whites in 1950 to 23.7 by 1960.

In terms of housing, outside of gains made by the black middle class, the trend toward "ghettoization" of urban neighborhoods and substandard, inner-city accommodations continued to plague African American communities as "white flight" took white Americans out of the cities and into newly created suburbs.

Though gains in education for African Americans through the 1950's were tangible, progress was still slow and attainment levels remained below those for the white population both in the South and elsewhere. In many cases, the achievement gap stayed the same or even widened during the decade. In 1950, the average years of education for men between the ages of twenty-five and sixty-four stood at less than six for African Americans compared to slightly more than nine for white Americans; in 1960, the discrepancy was virtually the same at seven years to ten years. A modest proportional advance was made in higher education: In 1950, 2.2 percent of the black population attended college, and by 1960, this figure had increased to 3.5 percent. However, college attendance rates for African Americans still fell short of the white percentages of 6.2 percent in 1950 and 7.7 percent in 1960.

Racial Violence Certain events during the early years of the decade also revealed all too clearly that the southern Jim Crow system, and both legalized and ingrained racism in the North, remained powerful forces capable of jeopardizing even the modest gains that organizations such as the Congress of Racial

Future Supreme Court justice Thurgood Marshall (center) was one of the driving forces behind the NAACP's legal battles against segregation throughout the 1950's. Here he is seen being interviewed on the steps of the Supreme Court building in Washington, D.C., after the Court ordered resumption of the integration of Central High School in Little Rock, Arkansas, in September, 1958. (AP/Wide World Photos)

Equality (CORE) and the National Association for the Advancement of Colored People (NAACP) had achieved. On July 12, 1951, for example, a mob took over the streets of all-white Cicero, Illinois, a suburb of Chicago, in anger over a black family moving into town, and National Guard units were dispatched to restore order. On Christmas Day in 1951, Harry T. Moore, the activist state director for the NAACP in Florida, and his wife Harriette, were brutally murdered when a bomb blast tore through their home in the town of Mims. In 1953, riots against blacks who moved into previously all-white neighborhoods broke out in Cleveland and Chicago and were only controlled with difficulty.

Legal Battles Early in the decade, the NAACP's legal attack on segregation, which had begun in 1934 under the direction of Charles Hamilton Houston and Thurgood Marshall, gained added momentum. On June 5, 1950, the Supreme Court, in its decisions

for the cases of *Sweatt v. Painter, McLaurin v. the Oklahoma State University Regents*, and *Henderson v. the United States*, effectively struck down "separate-but-equal" segregation in higher education and on railroad diners. These rulings helped open the way for lawsuits being filed assailing the Jim Crow system in primary and secondary education. In Prince Edward County, Virginia, woefully inadequate facilities at the all-black R. R. Moton High School ignited a student boycott of classes on April 23, 1951, which led to a desegregation lawsuit filed under the brief *Dorothy Davis v. Prince Edward County*. Officials' refusal to allocate money for even a single school bus for black children in Clarendon County, South Carolina, led to the filing of *Briggs v. Elliott*. These cases, combined with other cases, such as *Bolling v. Sharpe* in the District of Columbia and *Gebhart v. Belton* and *Gebhart v. Bulah* in Delaware, were argued by Marshall's team under the rubric of *Brown v. Board of Education*. On May 17, 1954, a unanimous Supreme

Court decision in the *Brown* case declared that the mandating of "separate-but-equal" educational facilities was unconstitutional.

The decision in *Brown*, while ground-breaking in nature, did not usher in immediate progress. Instead, it was the start of a grudging and often violent journey. It was not until more than a year later, on May 31, 1955, that the Court devised a mechanism for enforcement, which became known as *Brown II*. It contained the phraseology that integration should proceed by "all deliberate speed," which was readily interpreted by Southern judges, law enforcement officials, legislators, local officials, and education policy makers as a license to drag their feet or even evade the Court's ruling. Virtually nothing substantial was done to advance desegregation in the first two years after *Brown*. As late as 1959, the Prince Edward County, Virginia, board of supervisors voted to close down the entire public school system rather than implement desegregation.

Murder, Protest, and Government Intervention In 1955, the news media began to focus national attention on the race issue through its national coverage of the horrific kidnapping and murder of fourteen-year-old Emmett Till in Money, Mississippi, on August 28, and the Montgomery bus boycott, which began on December 1 after Rosa Parks refused to relinquish her bus seat to a white passenger. The boycott finally realized its goals on November 13, 1956, when the Supreme Court ruled that segregation on local bus lines was unconstitutional. Moreover, the Till murder case made clear to a national audience that equal justice under the law was denied to minorities in many parts of the United States in general but in the Deep South in particular. The boycott demonstrated the potential effectiveness of nonviolent protest to achieve social justice and brought into national prominence a new leader, the charismatic pastor of Montgomery's Dexter Street Baptist Church, the Reverend Martin Luther King, Jr.

The Civil Rights Act of 1957 seemed to be indicative of a renewed sensitivity to racial injustice on the part of the federal government. Serving as the first Civil Rights Act since 1875, it sought to establish a standing Civil Rights Commission to monitor and report voting rights violations and extend the authority of the Department of Justice regarding legal action against discrimination by state and local governing bodies. However, its scope and effects were quite limited, the enforcement provisions were considered inadequate, and its passage was soon overshadowed by the Little Rock Crisis in September, 1957. In Little Rock, Arkansas, as part of the desegregation order under *Brown*, nine black students were to be admitted to the city's Central High School. The first student to arrive, Elizabeth Eckford, was stopped by National Guard units directed by Governor Orval Faubus and menaced by a white mob. On September 25, 1957, President Dwight D. Eisenhower nationalized the Guard and deployed regular army troops to ensure the admission and protection of the "Little Rock Nine."

Little was accomplished as far as advances in civil rights during the last two years of the 1950's. Civil Rights issues were kept alive by the Southern Christian Leadership Conference (SCLC), an organization rising out of the Montgomery boycott, and student groups. In 1958 and 1959, the SCLC sponsored marches for desegregation in Washington, D.C., which drew an estimated total of 36,000 protesters. Paralleling the advent of nonviolent activist movements such as the SCLC were more radical groups. The most notable was the Nation of Islam, which espoused a militant religious self-help agenda and attracted an increasing percentage of black urban citizens.

Sports Milestones In the fields of drama, entertainment, music, literature, and sports, African Americans began to enjoy a higher level of visibility. Within the National Football League, African American athletes became star performers. The Cleveland Browns' Marion Motley, Jim Brown, and Bobby Mitchell; the Chicago Cardinals' Ollie Matson; and the Baltimore Colts' Lenny Moore are but a few of the decade's prominent football figures. In Major League Baseball, the ground broken by Jackie Robinson and Larry Doby during the late 1940's continued to be harvested through the appearance of players such as Willie Mays with the New York Giants, Henry Aaron with the Milwaukee Braves, Elston Howard with the New York Yankees, Jim Gilliam and Roy Campanella of the Brooklyn Dodgers, and Ernie Banks of the Chicago Cubs.

In the National Basketball Association, the color line was broken when Chuck Cooper was signed to play for the Boston Celtics in 1950. Before the end of the decade, a bevy of talented athletes began their distinguished careers: Bill Russell and K. C. Jones of the Boston Celtics; Elgin Baylor of the Minneapolis Lakers; and Wilt Chamberlain of the Philadelphia Warriors. In 1952, the Harlem Globetrotters basketball team was organized. Some of professional boxing's most outstanding feats were accomplished by African Americans: Ezzard Charles, Jersey Joe Walcott, and Floyd Patterson held the world heavyweight championship titles while Archie Moore was light heavyweight champion from 1952 to 1962, and Sugar Ray Robinson held the middleweight crown on five occasions: 1951, 1951-1952, 1955-1957, 1957, and 1958-1960.

Tennis superstar Althea Gibson became the world's first famous African American female athlete. Gibson's victories included the French Open title in 1956; the Wimbledon women's singles championship in 1957, when she became the first African American to earn a Wimbledon title; and the U.S. women's singles championship in 1957. A breakthrough occurred in professional golf when Charles Sifford became the first African American to win a major tournament, the Long Beach Open.

Entertainment and Literature The first Hollywood film of the 1950's to focus on African Americans and feature black actors playing important roles was *The Jackie Robinson Story* (1950), in which the baseball star portrayed himself. Dorothy Dandridge's sultry performance in *Carmen Jones* (1954) opposite Harry Belafonte earned for her a nomination for an Academy Award, the first black woman to achieve this distinction. Dandridge was at the height of her artistic career during the 1950's, starring in *Bright Road* (1953), *Island in the Sun* (1957), and *Porgy and Bess* (1959) opposite Sidney Poitier and Sammy Davis, Jr. Other notable film performances by African American actors included Eartha Kitt in *New Faces* (1954) and *The Mask of the Hawk* (1958); Ruby Dee and Nat King Cole in *St. Louis Blues* (1958); Ossie Davis in *No Time for Sergeants* (1958); Louis Gossett, Jr., in *Take a Giant Step* (1959); and Sammy Davis, Jr., in *Anna Lucasta* (1959). Sidney Poitier's performance in *The Defiant Ones* (1958) earned him the honor of being the first black man to receive an Academy Award nomination.

Lena Horne continued and highlighted her distinguished career into the 1950's with her role in the Broadway musical *Jamaica*. In 1950, Ethel Waters's singing career was augmented by her role in the Broadway musical *The Member of the Wedding*. The greatest Broadway masterpiece for African Americans arguably was the 1959 production of *A Raisin in the Sun* by Lorraine Hansberry, which starred an all-black cast headed by Poitier and Claudia McNeil and was one of the most critically acclaimed plays of the twentieth century. Other highly visible dramatic performers who continued or began their careers in the 1950's included Mahalia Jackson, Diahann Carroll, Pearl Bailey, Diana Sands, and Ivan Dixon.

Nat King Cole became a well-known musical and television presence. His recording of "Mona Lisa" in 1950 earned for him international renown, and as host of the *Nat King Cole Show*, a fifteen-minute weekly television show that ran from 1956 to 1957, he was the only African American to have his own program during the decade. In 1959, Count Basie became the first African American male to win the music industry's Grammy Award, and Ella Fitzgerald became the first female African American recipient of the award.

Noteworthy literary works by African Americans included Gwendolyn Brooks's *Annie Allen* (1949), which earned the 1950 Pulitzer Prize in poetry, and *Maude Martha* (1953); *Invisible Man* (1952) by Ralph Ellison, which won the National Book Award in 1953; *Go Tell It on the Mountain* (1953) and *Notes of a Native Son* (1955) by James Baldwin; and Billie Holiday's tragic autobiography *Lady Sings the Blues* (1956).

Impact Progress for African Americans could not be discerned readily on every front during the decade of the 1950's; social inequities remained firmly ingrained. The decade served as a bridge between the war years of the 1940's, when most of the racial barriers in American society were intact, and the 1960's, when the Civil Rights movement was at its peak and swept aside a great many racial inequities. While the progress accomplished during the 1950's might appear to be slow and inconsistent, the gains achieved through the Supreme Court, nonviolent action, and individual accomplishments in varied fields of endeavor were crucial ones, and without them, the reform and transformation of living conditions for African Americans would have been even more painfully delayed.

Further Reading
Branch, Taylor. *Parting the Waters: America in the King Years, 1954-1963*. New York: Simon & Schuster, 1988. A detailed account of the background and history of the Civil Rights movement. Though

much of the focus revolves around the activities of Martin Luther King, Jr., and his circle, there is considerable coverage of other personalities and related events.

Brown, Claude. *Manchild in the Promised Land.* New York: Signet/Penguin, 1965. At the time of its publication, it was the definitive autobiographical narrative about life in the Harlem ghetto during the 1950's. It still acts as an indispensable volume for understanding the ground-level history of the times.

Davis, Ossie, and Ruby Dee. *In This Life Together: Ossie Davis and Ruby Dee.* New York: William Morrow, 1998. An autobiographical work by the most prominent of the couples who pioneered the African American presence in drama, television, and film during the 1950's. Offers a personal account of the nature and extent of discrimination in the entertainment industry during the period.

Hine, Darlene Clark, William C. Hine, and Stanley Harrold. *The African American Odyssey.* Upper Saddle River, N.J.: Prentice-Hall, 2000. One of the most definitive surveys of African American history. The 1950's are given their due as pivotal years that foreshadowed the major 1960's movements toward civil rights.

Irons, Peter. *Jim Crow's Children: The Broken Promises of the Brown Decision.* New York: Penguin, 2004. A somewhat pessimistic study that depicts the 1950's as an era of disappointingly slow, misdirected, and ultimately flawed progress for African Americans in education.

Killian, Lewis, and Charles Grigg. *Racial Crisis in America: Leadership in Conflict.* Englewood Cliffs, N.J.: Prentice-Hall, 1964. Though dated in some respects, this study attempts to statistically measure the progress made up to that time and to account for the shortfalls in expectations.

Newman, Dorothy K., et al. *Protest, Politics, and Prosperity: Black Americans and White Institutions, 1940-1975.* New York: Pantheon, 1978. A highly useful amalgam of analysis and statistics that sheds light on the progress (or lack of such) of African Americans during a pivotal period.

Whitman, Mark, ed. *Removing a Badge of Slavery: The Record of "Brown v. the Board of Education."* Princeton, N.J.: Markus Wiener, 1993. Gives a very readable analysis of the background to the *Brown* case and to the myriad arguments of the case.

Raymond Pierre Hylton

See also *Bolling v. Sharpe*; *Brown v. Board of Education*; Civil Rights Act of 1957; Civil Rights movement; Commission on Civil Rights; Congress of Racial Equality; Interracial marriage laws; *Invisible Man*; Little Rock school desegregation crisis; National Association for the Advancement of Colored People; Racial discrimination; School desegregation; Southern Christian Leadership Conference; White Citizens' Councils.

■ Agriculture in Canada

The 1950's witnessed several innovations and changes in Canadian agricultural output and federal policy that helped maintain agriculture as one of the country's most important economic sectors.

The largest country, in terms of land size, in the Western Hemisphere, Canada stretches 3,426 miles from east to west. It consequently encompasses many climate regimes that have strong impacts on agriculture. Agriculture is extensive in nearly every province of Canada.

From an agricultural perspective, there are four major regions of Canada: the Atlantic provinces, those first settled by Europeans, comprising Newfoundland, Prince Edward Island, Nova Scotia, and New Brunswick; the central, most populous provinces, Quebec and Ontario; the plains provinces, Manitoba, Alberta, and Saskatchewan; and, finally, British Columbia, with its mild and rainy Pacific coast climate. Rainfall, a critical ingredient of agriculture, ranges from an ample 40 inches per year in the humid, eastern provinces of Atlantic Canada, to a slightly less generous amount in the central section, through a semi-arid zone in the prairie provinces, all the way to an extremely well-watered Pacific coast, where rainfall can amount ot 100 inches per year in a few locations.

There are some 600,000 units of agricultural production in Canada. These vary in size from small subsistence farms in much of Atlantic Canada to large spreads in the prairie provinces, where the average-sized farm in 1951 was 500 acres. By the 1950's, almost all the agriculturally useful land of Canada had been settled; three-fourths of it was in the prairie provinces.

Innovations and Transitions There were some startling changes in Canadian agriculture during the

1950's. Perhaps the most consequential was the mechanization of farming—the adoption of tractors and other labor-saving devices that enabled far fewer workers to produce far more crops. The result was a drastic reduction in the number of farmworkers, which, combined with the abandonment of marginal land, led to much more productive agriculture. Other measures introduced during the decade helped increase output per farm and per worker: electrification (making possible such things as milking machines), fertilization (used heavily in, for example, the tobacco fields of southern Ontario), and irrigation, enabling farmers to decrease their dependence on uncertain rainfall.

Canada, along with the United States, Australia, and Argentina, is one of the major wheat-producing nations of the world, with its efforts centered in the prairie provinces. Since 1920, Canada has, on average, supplied about 30 percent of the world market;

at least 20 percent of its wheat crop is exported. In 1951, Canada exported a record one billion bushels of wheat. Normally it exports slightly less wheat than the United States, but in 1953, Canadian exports of wheat exceeded those of the United States.

As the 1950's progressed, some wheat acreage was diverted to "coarse grains," that is, to crops such as oats and barley, as farmers turned increasingly to livestock raising and as worldwide wheat production exceeded demand. A special transportation subsidy for coarse grains enabled prairie farmers to ship their production to central and eastern Canada, where much of the livestock was fattened. At the same time, many eastern farmers began producing hay, the best-suited crop for the acidic soils of the Northeast; this hay also made livestock production more profitable, as the livestock grazed pastures during the summer and were fed some hay in the winter. In Quebec, dairying became a major agricultural activity.

Canadian farmer plowing a field at the foot of a mountain range during the early 1950's. (Hulton Archive | by Getty Images)

In the Atlantic provinces, potatoes were a major cash crop. Additionally, farmers with small acreages took to raising poultry, both for its meat and for its eggs. In Quebec and parts of the Atlantic provinces, maple syrup was an important cash producer. In southern Ontario, wine grapes and tobacco became major products of agricultural land.

Apple orchards were prominent in Nova Scotia, but as the years wore on, they tended to be scrapped as the apple-producing potential of British Columbia became recognized. Nova Scotia's humid climate easily enabled the cultivation of a wide variety of fruits and vegetables, which were becoming more important staples in the diets of Canadians during the decade's growing affluence.

Subsidies The Canadian government provides substantial help for Canada's farmers. Wheat marketing bears some resemblance to the U.S. system, in which farmers receive payment for their crop when it is harvested. The Canadian Wheat Board, created in 1930, pays the farmers when their grain is delivered either to a grain elevator or to a railroad car. If, over the course of the next months, the market is sufficiently favorable that the crop sells for more than the "base price," the farmers receive a supplementary payment. The initial payment is guaranteed by the federal government.

The government also subsidizes continuing scientific research into better agricultural methods, through the Dominion Department of Agriculture and the Experimental Farms Service. In addition, agricultural extension workers exist in each province in order to teach farmers better cultivation methods.

In addition, because agriculture is generally carried on with credit, which is then repaid when the crop is harvested, loans are critical. Lending is mostly done by the Canadian Farm Loan Board, created in 1929 by the government, or by the Veterans' Land Act Administration, authorized to help returning veterans get established in business. By the 1950's, the government was guaranteeing such loans. Short-term loans (up to one year) were financed by Canadian banks, with the potential crop or the livestock herd constituting security.

Impact The decade was one of innovation and growth for Canadian farmers. Canada's vast size ensured that agriculture remained a force during the 1950's despite the fact that the country was rapidly facilitating more technological and urban sectors and thus becoming one of the world's most developed nations.

Further Reading

Gleave, Alfred P. *United We Stand: Prairie Farmers, 1901-1975*. Toronto: Lugus, 1991. Gleave, a prairie farmer in Saskatchewan and an official of the United Farmers of Canada, Saskatchewan Section, details his own experiences both as a farmer and as an official of the farmers' union.

Skogstad, Grace Darlene. *Politics of Agricultural Policy-Making in Canada*. Toronto: University of Toronto Press, 1987. Traces federal intervention in Canada's agricultural sectors.

Nancy M. Gordon

See also Agriculture in the United States; Business and the economy in Canada; Farm subsidies; Gross national product of Canada; Income and wages in Canada; International trade of Canada; Urbanization in Canada.

■ Agriculture in the United States

During the 1950's, many scientific, economic, and social forces combined to change the course of North American agriculture and transform it into a modern enterprise.

As the 1950's began, agriculture was one of the most traditional sectors of U.S. society. Farms and ranches—5.7 million of them, each with an average size of 220 acres—were operated by fifteen million people. While some modernization trends were already under way (the twentieth century peak in the number of operating farms had been reached in 1930 with 6.5 million farms), many more technical changes took place in American agriculture during the 1950's than during any previous decade of the twentieth century.

By the year 1950, tractors and combines were no longer unusual sights in the Corn Belt (the lower midwestern states from Indiana through central Kansas) even though twenty years earlier there had been four times as many farms as tractors in this area. In 1950, there were as many tractors as farms in the Corn Belt, yet it was not until 1954 that tractors overtook horses and mules in North American agriculture. Nevertheless, during the 1950's, many of these tractors pulled plows and cultivators that had been converted only recently from horse-powered implements to tractor-powered implements.

The early 1950's was the last time American agriculture would be driven by tradition instead of technology. By the end of the 1950's, irrigation, hybrid crops, and improved animal breeding techniques would start American farmers on a "technology treadmill." A sector that supported 16 percent of the U.S. population would yield to a system in which the quest for lower-priced food to feed the world increased farm productivity but decimated its numbers. In 1950, farmers received 40 percent of every food dollar spent by consumers. By the 1960's, this percentage decreased as consumer demand for processed foods grew. Moreover, farm prices did not keep pace with inflation. Small farmers would soon find the technology treadmill a recipe for financial disaster.

Consolidation in the Countryside Ranches and farms had been consolidating before the 1950's as increased used of farm tractors expanded the acreage a single farmer could cultivate. In 1940, the average farm consisted of 170 acres. By 1950, the average farm had grown to 220 acres and would grow to 300 acres by 1960. Most of this increase in farm size came not from cultivating virgin land but from the dissolution of existing farms and the sale of previously cultivated land to existing farmers. During the 1950's, the value of the average farm doubled from around $10,000 to about $20,000 even though the size of the average farm had only grown by 36 percent during this time. The increase in value was attributed to increases in land prices and an increase in the amount of farm machinery used on the average farm during the decade.

Further consolidation was an indirect result of reduced transportation costs during the 1950's. High transportation costs involved in getting agricultural products to consumers had always plagued American agriculture. During the early eighteenth century, it was cheaper in New England to import grain from Europe than to transport it ten or fifteen miles overland. Moreover, the advent of the railroad made large-scale animal husbandry profitable during the late nineteenth century, but even by the 1940's, local markets were the destination of most of the food grown in North America. The advent of the Eisenhower-administration interstate highway system during the early 1950's and individual states' improvement of their systems of farm-to-

market roads removed most of the barriers to large-scale agriculture.

Increased access to more distant markets made regionalization of many food commodities possible for the first time. The poultry industry, for example, rapidly abandoned colder climates for the more hospitable growing conditions of the southern United States. The ability to ship eggs and meat safely over long distances meant growers could take advantage of warmer weather (and lower wages), eventually resulting in much less expensive poultry for consumers. Producers of most food commodities responded to these pressures to produce lower-priced output by specializing in the particular crops or animals for which they had a comparative advantage in producing. Those who did not find a niche soon failed or were bought out by larger producers.

The "Technology Treadmill" American farmers have been no strangers to innovation. The challenges of farming unfamiliar soil have long required them to abandon tradition and develop new methods of farming in order to survive. The grain elevator, the sod-busting plow, and the McCormick reaper were all invented in North America, and each invention had a significant effect on agricultural productivity in its time.

The term "technology treadmill" was first used during the late 1950's to refer to a pattern in which farmers had to adopt the latest technologies not necessarily to increase their profits but merely to survive the more competitive marketplace for their products. Since the goal of these technologies was to increase production on the same amount of land (or with livestock), in agricultural markets the adoption of new technologies typically has led to lower prices for farm products. The first farmers to adopt a new technology reap the benefits of increased production for themselves without drastically affecting the total market production and, by extension, the market price of the commodity. Eventually, however, enough farmers adopt the new technology that the market price for the commodity falls, and those farmers who do not adopt the technology fail. Hence, the adoption of new technology puts one on a treadmill from which escape is impossible. Just as a runner on a treadmill never makes forward progress, farmers felt that they too were running not to make forward progress but to keep from being trampled by lower-cost competitors.

U.S. secretary of agriculture Ezra Taft Benson demonstrating his ability to milk a cow during a visit to Pennsylvania State University's farm in 1954. (AP/Wide World Photos)

For all the frustration and expense the technology treadmill inflicted upon farmers, U.S. consumers and those abroad reaped significant benefits in terms of lower-cost food and fiber products. During the 1950's, the resources required to harvest 100 bushels of wheat fell from an average of eighteen hours of labor and 5 acres of land to ten hours of labor and 4 acres of land. This productivity increase was eclipsed by the increases during the 1960's and 1970's, but at the time, it was a far greater increase in productivity than was found in most manufacturing sectors in postwar America. The average American family spent 20.5 percent of its income on food in 1950—a percentage that had been falling from 30 percent at the beginning of the twentieth century—and only 17.5 percent by 1960. By comparison, consumers in 2002 spent only 10.1 percent of their incomes on food.

Beef Production Prior to the 1950's, beef production was limited to areas of the arid plains that were too dry, hilly, or otherwise had inferior soil for other crops yet were sufficiently close to railheads. During World War II, price controls were in effect for beef, and when they were lifted, producer prices rose from $15.00 per one hundred pounds in 1947 to $30.60 in 1951. By 1956, production had risen and prices had fallen to an average of $14.10, only to rise to $25.80 in 1959—a price that would not vary much for the subsequent ten years. Cattle ranching has always required a longer-term commitment than row crops. The extreme swings in cattle prices are such that only those ranchers willing to stay in the business indefinitely survive.

Red meat consumption followed general economic conditions, rising during prosperous times and falling during economic recessions. During the 1950's, beef consumers' tastes were changing as well, away from grass-fed beef to grain-fed beef. This change made the establishment of feedlots, on which cattle are fattened before slaughter, economically feasible. Since cattle were no longer shipped to the great stockyards of Chicago, proximity to railheads was no longer a limiting factor in cattle ranching. Furthermore, the advent of large-scale irrigation projects during the 1950's, aided by the federal government's Rural Electrification Administration projects, resulted in locally grown grains (principally milo and sorghum) for the regional feedlot industry in the Texas panhandle.

The federal and state governments in the American Southwest invested many agricultural research and development dollars in the transformation of the beef production industry. Research in forage crops (grains and grasses used to feed livestock) included new varieties of milo and sorghum as well as new technologies for extracting oil from cottonseeds, rendering the waste cottonseed hulls available for feed.

The introduction of Brahman bulls and other new breeds of cattle into Texas during the 1950's was made possible by the elimination of fever ticks during the 1940's and hastened by the development of frozen bull semen for artificial insemination during the early 1950's. Crossbreeding became possible without buying an exotic bull. Scientific research into animal nutrition as well as the introduction of new grasses, such as Coastal Bermuda grass, further strengthened the regional cattle ranching industry in the American Southwest. In Texas alone, the number of beef cattle raised rose from 7.7 million in 1950 to 9.5 million—the largest growth of any decade of the twentieth century.

The Problem of Growing Surpluses Growth in agricultural productivity during the 1950's was (and remained later) both a blessing and a curse. On one hand, lower food prices freed up more consumer income for other purchases. On the other hand, larger farms and a declining agricultural population were in danger of impoverishing rural areas. Concerned with the possibility of precipitous farm price drops after World War II, the U.S. Congress passed the Agricultural Act of 1949. This act, amended later in 2002, imposed no time limits on its price support provisions and formed the basis for all farm bills into the twenty-first century. The act originally specified that farm prices should be supported at 90 percent of parity price. Parity price was defined in the legislation as that price that would give farm commodities the same purchasing power with respect to articles

farmers buy that they had during the 1910-1914 period. The percentage of parity price at which corn, wheat, and the like were supported fell to 60-90 percent (depending upon the crop and contemporary production levels) during the 1950's and generally remained at that level for the rest of the twentieth century. The "market basket" of products a farmer would have purchased in 1910-1914 differed from those products farmers purchased during the 1950's. As time went on, more adjustments had to be made to this "market basket" approach as tractors were added and horses and mules were removed.

The supported prices of the 1949 legislation, coupled with improvements in irrigation and new fertilizers and pesticides, led to rapid increases in the food supply. As consumer incomes rose during the 1950's, food purchases initially increased. Limited in their consumption of beef, dairy products, and eggs during the war years, consumers used their increased income to purchase the increased supply of these products during the decade. However, this growth quickly reached satiation, and consumers diverted much of their increased incomes to other purchases such as cars, new houses, and growing families. Food, while necessary for human life, does not enjoy the unlimited demand of other products.

The federal government was soon faced with the need to dispose of mountains of surplus food. The Agricultural Trade Development and Assistance Act of 1954, also known as PL 480 or Food for Peace, was passed, and in its first year, it exported 69 million dollars' worth of surplus food to needy nations. The bill authorized the U.S. Department of Agriculture (USDA) to ship surplus food in response to disasters in other nations, for sale in exchange for foreign currency, or for barter exchanges for other commodities. Other sources for disposing of surplus food grew during this period, including the school lunch program and the donation of surplus commodities to low-income households in the United States.

Conservation and the Environment Although environmental concerns during the 1950's were far more muted than they would become in the decades to follow, memories of the Dust Bowl conditions of the 1930's continued to haunt policy makers. The U.S. Congress passed the Soil Bank Act of 1956, which paid farmers to take land out of active agricultural production for ten years. The original program converted 28.7 million acres on 306,000 farms in the United States to conservation uses, defined in the bill as planting trees or planting permanent land covers (that is, nonpasture plantings).

The twin goals of the Soil Bank Act of 1956 were to take marginal land out of production and to bolster farm prices by reducing the acreage under production. Marginal farmland was defined as that land that is especially prone to erosion, namely hilly land, or farmland in which a dry year can lead to the type of dust storms experienced during the Dust Bowl era. Farmers, given a choice of which acres to take out of production in order to participate in the Soil Bank Program, most often chose their least productive acres, which tended to be the acres most prone to soil erosion.

The second goal of the Soil Bank Act was to bolster farm prices by reducing the amount of land being farmed. In this respect, the act was less successful because most of the land being taken out of production was not highly productive in the first place. The high (and increasing) rate of agricultural productivity would make this second goal increasingly elusive in the coming decades.

Impact The 1950's witnessed a major turning point in North American agriculture. The farm tractor went from a luxury found on a minority of farms to an essential implement for modern agricultural production. Increased interest and support from federal and state governments uncovered new knowledge in crop and animal nutrition and improved highways made large-scale agriculture possible. During this period, farm size grew by 36 percent, while farm populations shrank by 40 percent and the number of farms fell by 32 percent. However, the value of the average farm doubled during this time period, and a trend toward rapidly increasing productivity (in terms of labor and land) was firmly established. This growth in farm productivity spurred governments to find a use for the surplus food produced and led to programs such as Food for Peace and an expansion of domestic food distribution programs. Environmental concerns led to legislation designed for the first time to reduce the amount of land being farmed.

Further Reading

Cochrane, Willard W. *The Development of American Agriculture: A Historical Analysis.* 2d ed. Minneapolis: University of Minnesota Press, 1993. Although the book covers the vast history of agriculture from 1607 onward, Cochrane devotes a great amount of discussion to the period between 1950 and 1990.

Jones, Lu Ann. *Mama Learned Us to Work—Farm Women in the New South.* Chapel Hill: University of North Carolina Press, 2002. Historical work on the lives of twentieth century farm women in the American southeast, this book tells the story of the impact farm innovations and changes had on families and family farms in the twentieth century.

Levins, Richard A. *Willard Cochrane and the American Family Farm.* Lincoln: University of Nebraska Press, 2000. Story of President John F. Kennedy's primary agriculture adviser and early opponent of the technology treadmill. Although not an unbiased account, this book presents a cogent argument for the preservation of family farms.

Pillsbury, Richard, and John Florin. *Atlas of American Agriculture: The American Cornucopia.* New York: Macmillan Library Reference, 1996. A comprehensive book on the state of agriculture in North America today with an in-depth examination of the historical and technological factors responsible.

Betsy A. Murphy

See also Agriculture in Canada; Bracero program; Business and the economy in the United States; Farm subsidies; Food for Peace; Income and wages in the United States; International trade of the United States; Mexico; Natural resources; Operation Wetback; Soil Bank Act of 1956; United Fruit Company.

■ Ailey, Alvin, Jr.

Identification African American dancer and choreographer
Born January 5, 1931; Rogers, Texas
Died December 1, 1989; New York, New York

Alvin Ailey, Jr., gained acclaim during the 1950's for his unique dance style and his creation of the Alvin Ailey American Dance Theater, which expressed the experience and culture of African Americans.

As a child, Ailey moved through several poor rural Texas towns as his mother looked for work. In 1942, they moved to Los Angeles, which exposed young

Ailey to new worlds of music, theater, and dance. He saw the Ballet Russe, heard Duke Ellington, and watched Katherine Dunham and her all-black dance company in performances inspired by African and Caribbean cultures, jazz, and Broadway musicals. Ailey soon joined noted choreographer Lester Horton's integrated dance studio; at the time, African Americans were seldom seen in major ballet or modern dance companies. Horton required of his dancers an interest in American Indian, Spanish, and other cultures; history; and social justice issues. Ailey's continued involvement with Horton's productions was a creative laboratory for him, and Horton's movement style, approach to the theater, and multiracial company were the greatest influences on Ailey's artistry.

In 1958, Ailey and several dancers presented Ailey's choreography at the Ninety-second Street Young Men's Hebrew Association, a focal point for new dance in New York. This performance and his newly formed all-black American Dance Theater were a huge success. The program included an homage to Lester Horton, danced by Ailey. A piece for the full company, "Blues Suite," presaged many aspects of his future work. It was drawn from characters and images of his southern childhood, used music popular with black Americans and society as a whole, and contained new movements and daring use of subject and dancers.

The acclaim Ailey received led to invitations to choreograph for other dance and theater productions. In 1959, his company was invited to perform at the Jacob's Pillow Dance Festival. At this time he began the masterpiece of his many choreographies. Ailey set this work, *Revelations*, to spirituals and used drama and humor to depict the social and religious lives of African Americans. His company first performed the complete work in 1960.

Impact Alvin Ailey created a company of African American artists who made modern dance exciting and accessible to audiences beyond the narrow dance world. While the Civil Rights movement drew attention to the lives of black Americans, Ailey put his personal experiences into an art form that expressed African American culture to others. By the end of the decade, the Ailey company was thrilling audiences in Europe and Africa and was ready to solidify its presence as a major cultural force in the United States.

Alvin Ailey, Jr. (Library of Congress)

Further Reading

Ailey, Alvin, with A. Peter Bailey. *Revelations: The Autobiography of Alvin Ailey*. Secaucus, N.J.: Carol Publishing Group, 1995. Ailey's own insights on his life, work, and the social context of the arts.

Dunning, Jennifer. *Alvin Ailey: A Life in Dance*. Reading, Mass.: Addison-Wesley, 1996. A thorough biography based on interviews, reviews of Ailey's works, and historical records. It includes photographs and useful lists of choreography and company members.

Leslie Joan Friedman

See also African Americans; Civil Rights movement; Dance, popular.

■ Air pollution

Definition Degradation of physical and chemical air quality

Although air pollution was not perceived as a problem during the 1950's, environmental damage was being done that would require attention at a later date.

During the first half of the twentieth century, several urban areas in the eastern United States experienced problems with coal smoke. Although not all the dangers of coal smoke were recognized (for example, the potential for acid deposition), several cities were beginning to experience difficulties. Air inversions, combined with extensive use of coal by industry and for home heating, produced lingering fogs that had negative health impacts. The most notable of these "killer fogs" occurred in Donora, Pennsylvania, in 1948, but the problem persisted into the 1950's. Beyond its direct health impact, coal smoke also produced a greasy residue that remained on laundry hung outside to dry or any other exposed surface. However, industrial smoke tended to be welcomed by officials and American citizens as a sign of prosperity.

Early Regulation In response to the potential for harming human health, some municipalities began to try to regulate smoke during the early twentieth century. In addition, some would also issue health warnings when air conditions were conducive to killer fogs. Oregon became the first state to enact meaningful air pollution standards in 1952. The federal government enacted the Air Pollution Control Act in 1955, but it did little more than provide funds for states to engage in air pollution research. Moreover, as industry turned to other fuel sources, the problem of coal smoke was alleviated partially. By the end of the decade, the problem of coal smoke appeared to be under control in many areas.

As the use of automobiles increased in the United States and Canada, people became aware that various gases emitted by cars, such as carbon monoxide, degraded air quality, particularly when an air inversion caused the gases to collect near ground level. In the Los Angeles basin, the issue of automobile emissions began to become a public health issue during the 1950's. In 1956, California enacted the first law to deal with automobile pollution, but it had small impact. Although there was public concern regarding automobile-induced smog, little was done to reduce emissions.

Chemical Pollution While Americans were readily aware of the negative impact of smoke during the 1950's because of the media focus on killer fogs, there was less awareness of the impact of the long-term harm produced by the various chemical components of coal smoke. There had long been an awareness that smokestack emissions could contain harmful chemicals. Copper refining, for example, produced a great deal of sulfur dioxide that, when turned to precipitated sulfuric acid, settled on the surrounding landscape and killed all vegetation. The state of Georgia challenged the negative impact of the Copper Hill Refining Company in north Georgia on several occasions, but the smelter continued to produce large amounts of sulfur dioxide throughout the 1950's. Furthermore, in other areas, metal smelting had come under attack, but because these operations generally occurred in isolated areas, they were generally not perceived as a danger.

Long-term exposure to acid deposition was beginning to have an impact on vegetation and water quality during the 1950's. Coal smoke contained both sulfur dioxide and nitrogen oxides that produced sulfuric and nitric acids when combined with water vapor. Little was known of the long-term effects of acid deposition during the 1950's, but the sulfur dioxide and nitrogen oxides being emitted into the air would prove dangerous to the forests and lakes on the Cumberland Plateau, in the northeastern United States, and in southern Canada, especially in the Ontario province.

Several forms of atmospheric pollution existed during the 1950's, although they were unrecognized as being harmful at the time. A notable example was the use of chlorofluorocarbons (CFCs) as refrigerants, cleaning solvents, and aerosol sprays. When released into the atmosphere, these gases cause the ozone layer to break down, contributing to global warming. Additionally, carbon dioxide, a gas component of both coal smoke and automobile emissions, saw its levels increase during the period. In later decades, officials would point to the increase of U.S. industry and America's car culture as key components to the gradual rise of the levels of this gas and the consequent phenomenon of global warming.

Another form of air pollution not recognized during the 1950's was the impact of tobacco smoke.

Cigarette smoking was commonplace in the United States and Canada and widely advertised and accepted. Later research would demonstrate that prolonged exposure to cigarette smoke could cause various respiratory problems such as lung cancer.

Impact For the most part, air pollution was not perceived as a problem in American society during the 1950's. Some efforts were made to ameliorate health problems caused by air inversions, but people generally regarded smoke as a sign of industrial growth. A few cities tried to curb the worst impact of coal smoke, and the federal government addressed the problem superficially, but most of these efforts at control were directed at the visible aspects of air pollution. The more serious and far-ranging chemical impact of air pollution went largely unnoticed and ignored during the decade.

Subsequent Events Starting during the 1960's, the United States and Canada began to cope more diligently with the long-term aspects of air pollution. Research and public outcry would lead to substantial legislation directed toward dealing with all aspects of pollution.

Further Reading

Markham, Adam. *A Brief History of Pollution.* New York: St. Martin's Press, 1994. A good overview of the history of causes and the government's responses.

Portney, Paul R., ed. *Public Policies for Environmental Protection.* Washington, D.C.: Resources for the Future, 1990. Essay by Portney describes the development of air pollution policy

Scheffer, Victor B. *The Shaping of Environmentalism in America.* Seattle: University of Washington Press, 1991. Environmentalists' responses to air pollution.

Somerville, Richard C. J. *The Forgiving Air.* Berkeley: University of California Press, 1996. Details technological changes and their impacts on air pollution.

John M. Theilmann

See also Automobiles and auto manufacturing; Natural resources; *Sea Around Us, The*; Water pollution.

■ Aircraft design and development

During the 1950's, advances in aircraft design changed the way Americans thought of warfare and travel. The advent of jet airliners revolutionized commercial aviation and the American aircraft industry.

Few decades have witnessed such sweeping changes in the aviation industry as the 1950's. Early in the decade the majority of commercial and military aircraft in the United States was propeller driven. By the decade's end, turbojets had replaced piston engines as the power plant of choice in most commercial and military aircraft. Aircraft performance increased as well. Where once a rocket engine was required to break the sound barrier, turbojets were capable of propelling planes at speeds of over twice that of sound by 1960. The 1950's also witnessed a revolution in the commercial aviation business, as the airplane became the preferred means of travel for business people and vacationers alike. Once the province of the elite, air travel became the domain of Middle America.

Commercial Aviation In 1950, the Boeing Stratocruiser, Douglas DC-6, and Lockheed Constellation were the premier four-engine propeller-driven commercial airliners. The Douglas and Lockheed aircraft could each carry more than eighty passengers, but a more comfortable cabin layout restricted the DC-6 to around fifty passengers and the Constellation to around sixty. The high-end Stratocruisers, as commercial airliners, accommodated slightly more than one hundred passengers or had twenty-eight sleeper berths in their most extravagant arrangements. Unlike the other aircraft, the Stratocruiser, which was based on the B-29 bomber airframe, made use of a unique double (over-under) fuselage, a design feature that increased its carrying capacity. Nevertheless, the relatively low passenger volume of the late-propeller-driven airliners restricted the influence of air travel on American life.

In 1952, the Boeing Company drew on its experience with the Stratocruiser, as well as the B-52 bomber, to begin work on a plane that would revolutionize the commercial aviation industry: the jet 707 airliner. Boeing astutely designed its new airliner around an aircraft that could serve as a transport and in-flight refueling platform for the U.S. Air Force. The plane first flew in July, 1954. The 707 began its service with U.S. airlines in the summer of 1958. That fall Pan American Airlines began nonstop jet service between New York City and London. In addition, the 707 proved an excellent airliner for service within the United States because of its ability to carry almost 150 passengers and more than 200 using special configurations. Thus, it had an imme-

A DC-8 taking off on its inaugural flight from California's Long Beach Municipal Airport, which was adjacent to the Douglas Aircraft Company plant in which it was built, in 1958. (AP/Wide World Photos)

diate influence on the commercial aviation business and would stay in production for almost thirty years.

The Douglas Company also entered into the commercial jet airliner field with the DC-8. Douglas began work on its turbojet transport in 1955, and the DC-8 first flew in the summer of 1958. The following summer Delta Airlines and United Airlines received the first DC-8's. Although the DC-8 carried slightly fewer passengers than the 707, the aircraft had a similar influence on commercial aviation.

Convair and Lockheed initially developed turboprop aircraft instead of jets. Like jets, turboprops were faster and had greater lift power than standard piston engines but were more fuel-efficient. In 1955, Convair retrofitted turboprops to its twin-engine Model 340 to produce the Model 540. Lockheed designed a four-engine turboprop that could carry almost one hundred passengers, the L-188 Electra. The Electra first flew in 1957 and began service with U.S. airlines over the next few years. Despite their limited passenger capacity, in comparison to the 707 and DC-8, turboprops would find their niche in short- and medium-range commercial passenger flights because of lower operating costs than the available jet aircraft. By the end of the 1950's, it was possible to transport passengers farther, faster, and more cheaply because of turboprop and jet power.

Military Aviation When the Korean War began in June of 1950, the frontline aircraft of the U.S. Air Force were all World War II vintage planes or improved models of them. Although more advanced jet bombers and fighters were in various stages of design and production, none had entered service. The lessons learned in the war hastened the development of more advanced jet aircraft.

In 1949, Pratt and Whitney revolutionized the aviation industry with its J-57 turbojet engine. The J-57 made possible the United States' first all-jet intercontinental bomber, the Boeing B-52. When used in conjunction with military 707's for in-flight refueling, B-52's could strike targets deep inside the Soviet Union from bases within the United States. During the Cold War, the ability to accomplish such a feat comforted Americans until the Soviet Union launched the satellite *Sputnik* in 1957.

Impact The 1950's was a time of transition for American military aircraft. Convinced that the nation would not fight another Korean War, senior commanders in the U.S. Air Force pushed for faster fighters and increased capacity bombers. Military aircraft went from subsonic flight early in the decade to sustained supersonic flight at its end. Bombers, as well as fighters, were affected by the quest for speed. Convair developed the nation's first supersonic bomber, the B-58 Hustler. A controversial plane within the upper echelons of the U.S. Air Force command, the B-58, which first flew in 1956, would not become operational until 1960 and would be withdrawn from service a decade later. The lengthy development and testing period for military aircraft meant that most of the planes designed during the 1950's would not see service until the 1960's.

Further Reading

Donald, David, ed. *The Complete Encyclopedia of World Aircraft.* New York: Barnes and Noble Books, 1997. Donald's comprehensive volume provides a detailed analysis of the commercial and military aircraft of the twentieth century.

Futrell, Robert F. *Ideas, Concepts, Doctrine: Basic Thinking in the United States Air Force, 1907-1984.* 2 vols. Maxwell Air Force Base, Ala.: Air University Press, 1989. Futrell's history of the U.S. Air Force includes the development of aircraft and air power strategy, as well as an analysis of the service's doctrine.

Irons-Georges, Tracy, ed. *Encyclopedia of Flight.* Pasadena, Calif.: Salem Press, 2002. Details air carriers, airplane types, and issues pertinent to the American airlines industry, among many other related topics.

Knaack, Marcelle Size. *Encyclopedia of U.S. Air Force Aircraft and Missile Systems.* Washington, D.C.: Office of Air Force History, 1978. Knaack's compendium of the aircraft and missile systems used by the U.S. Air Force until the late 1970's gives detailed history and technical information for each weapon system.

Nalty, Bernard C., ed. *Winged Shield, Winged Sword: A History of the United States Air Force.* 2 vols. Washing-

ton, D.C.: Air Force History and Museums Program, 1997. Examines the U.S. Air Force from its earliest beginnings to the end of the twentieth century.

Paul D. Gelpi, Jr.

See also Avro Arrow; B-52 bomber; Boeing 707; Federal Aviation Administration; National Aeronautics and Space Administration; United States Air Force Academy.

■ Alaska statehood

The Event Alaska became the forty-ninth state in the Union
Date January 3, 1959

The decades-long struggle for Alaska statehood ended in 1959 with the admission of the region, allowing Alaskans to participate fully in national political processes.

On March 30, 1867, United States secretary of state William H. Seward signed an agreement with the Russian minister to the United States to purchase Alaska for $7.2 million. Congress enacted legislation in 1868 to make Alaska, nicknamed "Seward's Folly," a customs district of the United States. From 1879 until 1884, the U.S. Navy governed Alaska. The passage of the First Organic Act in 1884 made Alaska a civil and judicial district of the United States and provided the territory with judges, clerks, and marshals. At that time, Alaska was considered a colony of the United States.

The Klondike gold rush of 1897-1898 and smaller gold rushes during the last decade of the nineteenth century brought tens of thousands of new inhabitants to Alaska and the Yukon Territory in Canada. In 1900, President William McKinley called for legislative action to provide for more government in the territory. His efforts resulted in legislation that provided for an official code of civil and criminal procedure and appointed more judges in the territory. In 1912, Congress passed the Second Organic Act, making Alaska an official territory and establishing a territorial legislature. The first statehood bill was introduced in Congress by Alaska delegate James Wickersham in 1916. During World War II, the population of Alaska grew as a result of military activity.

Postwar Alaska In 1945, Edward Lewis "Bob" Bartlett was elected territorial delegate to Congress,

Alaska's only representative in Washington, D.C. Between 1943 and 1953, Alaska's territorial governor, Ernest Gruening, and Delegate Bartlett, working with business and professional men and women in the territory, labored on numerous legislative efforts to achieve statehood for Alaska. A successful referendum in 1946 led to the formation of the Alaska Statehood Association. President Harry S. Truman called on Congress to grant statehood to Alaska in his first state of the union message in 1946. Bartlett introduced a statehood bill in 1948, but it never came to the Senate floor.

In 1949, the Alaska Statehood Committee was formed to intensify statehood efforts. The committee was able to draw national attention to the goals of those Alaskans who desired statehood. A statehood bill passed the House of Representatives in early 1950, but it was killed in the U.S. Senate by a coalition of conservative Republicans and southern Democrats. Republicans feared that Democrats would make up Alaska's first congressional delegation. The Korean War, begun in 1950, overshadowed the statehood drive.

In 1953, the Senate Interior and Insular Affairs Committee traveled to Alaska to hold hearings on statehood. Meeting in Anchorage, Fairbanks, Juneau, and Ketchikan, the committee heard from hundreds of Alaskans. The committee hearings resulted in the organization of the Operation Statehood movement. Alaskan women sent bouquets of artificial forget-me-nots, Alaska's official flower, to members of Congress. Ordinary Alaskans wrote letters to members of Congress and letters to the editors of big-city newspapers. They sent Christmas cards to their friends in the contiguous United States that read:

> Make our future bright
> Ask your Senator for statehood
> And start the New Year right.

President Dwight D. Eisenhower (left) and Secretary of the Interior Fred Seaton (right) with Alaska governor Mike Stepovich on July 1, 1958—the day after the U.S. Senate completed Congress's approval of Alaska's admission to the Union. Stepovich is holding a copy of the Anchorage Daily Times. (AP/Wide World Photos)

President Dwight D. Eisenhower called on Congress to grant statehood to Hawaii in his 1954 state of the union address, but he failed to mention Alaska. Congress developed legislation calling for Hawaii's admission first followed by that of Alaska. However, a new plan called for not admitting the territories but making Hawaii and Alaska commonwealths of the United States instead, giving them the power to elect their own governors. Alaskans opposed this proposal because it would require them to pay federal income taxes without receiving any of the benefits of statehood.

The "Alaska-Tennessee Plan" Meeting in Juneau in January of 1955, Alaska's territorial legislature called for a constitutional convention to meet in November, 1955, on the campus of the University of Alaska in Fairbanks. On the second day of the convention, territorial governor Ernest Gruening delivered the keynote address, "Let Us End American Colonialism." The convention wrote a constitution that Alaskans overwhelmingly approved in a 1956 referendum vote.

A New Orleans businessman and navy veteran presented the convention with a proposal he called the "Alaska-Tennessee Plan." The plan involved electing a congressional delegation without waiting for Congress to act on statehood. This plan had been used in Tennessee, Michigan, California, Oregon, Kansas, and Iowa. In the territory's 1956 general election, Alaskan voters elected William Egan and Ernest Gruening to the U.S. Senate, and Ralph Rivers was elected as a representative. The delegates went to Washington, D.C., for the first day of the 1957 session of Congress but were not seated in their respective chambers.

With their improved access, the men intensified their lobbying for statehood. Territorial delegate Bob Bartlett was able to persuade Speaker of the House Sam Rayburn to change his position on Alaska statehood. The speaker's new position brought an end to southern Democrats' objections to statehood. In 1958, President Eisenhower endorsed Alaska statehood in his state of the union address. Despite the president's support and the support of Texas senator Lyndon B. Johnson, the House Rules Committee blocked the statehood bill for a short time. Energized by a wave of public support spurred by the 1958 publication of Edna Ferber's novel, *Ice Palace*, the bill was discharged from the rules committee and approved by the House in May, 1958. The Senate approved the bill on June 30, 1958. After a referendum vote in which Alaskan voters overwhelmingly approved becoming a state, President Eisenhower signed the proclamation declaring Alaska a state on January 3, 1959.

Impact The efforts by Alaskans to become a state overcame partisan political differences. Joining the Union did not end all of the new state's problems, and it actually caused a few more as the federal and state governments labored to deal with ownership of Native American lands and the tax consequences of large expanses of federal lands. While the state received revenue windfalls from its deposits of natural resources, several decades after statehood, some Alaskans wondered if federal government regulation was becoming so burdensome that the state should secede.

Further Reading

McBeath, Gerald A., and Thomas A. Morehouse. *Alaska Government and Politics*. Lincoln: University of Nebraska Press, 1994. Examines Alaska's state government, paying close attention to the relationship between the state and federal governments and Alaska's political culture.

Naske, Claus-M. *Ernest Gruening: Alaska's Greatest Governor*. Fairbanks: University of Alaska Press, 2004. A chronicle of Gruening's career as territorial governor and his work to bring Alaska into the Union.

_____. *A History of Alaska Statehood*. Lanham, Md.: University Press of America, 1985. A detailed examination of the statehood effort.

John David Rausch, Jr.

See also Eisenhower, Dwight D.; Hawaii statehood; Puerto Rico as a commonwealth; Rayburn, Sam; Truman, Harry S.

■ *American Bandstand*

Identification Long-running television show hosted by Dick Clark that showcased current rock-and-roll artists in a dance hall setting

Date Aired from 1957 to 1987

American Bandstand *was the first and longest-running rock-and-roll show on television.*

American Bandstand began as a local program on WFIL-TV in Philadelphia. From 1952 to 1956 it was

Singer Bobby Rydell and host Dick Clark (with microphone) during a late 1950's broadcast of American Bandstand. *(Hulton Archive | by Getty Images)*

hosted by Bob Horn and called *Bob Horn's Bandstand.* In July of 1956, the show got another host—a clean-cut, twenty-six-year-old Dick Clark. The American Broadcasting Corporation (ABC) picked up the show one month later and christened it *American Bandstand.* Every weekday afternoon, hundreds of thousands of teenagers would rush home after school to tune in and hear the opening strains of the theme song, "Bandstand Boogie." The dancers on the floor included a core of regulars from Philadelphia. The rest of the dancers were young people who lined up every day hoping for the chance to be on television. While popular artists lip-synched their own hit songs, the dancers tried out current dance steps. The audience watched to see their favorite artists, learn the latest moves, and follow the lives of the regulars.

In 1959 the federal government began to investigate entertainment figures such as Dick Clark for possible conflicts between broadcasting interests and financial ones. Payola, or pay-for-play, was a common practice in which radio and television broadcasters were paid, usually by producers or record companies, to promote records by certain artists. Payment could come in the form of cash, a percentage of the publishing royalties, or various gifts. Clark was a canny businessman with many holdings in both the broadcast and music worlds, and he often showcased artists on *American Bandstand* who recorded for labels in which he had a financial stake. When the government began to put pressure on him, Clark drafted a letter stating he would divest himself of his recording and publishing companies, opting to stick with his broadcasting career. He was still required to testify before a congressional committee in 1960. He was given a slap on the wrist for accepting jewelry and a fur stole from a record company executive but was otherwise cleared of any wrongdoing.

Impact *American Bandstand* introduced rock-and-roll music into American living rooms across the nation. It presented a new form of music, often viewed suspiciously by parents, in a benign, nonthreatening way, making it palatable to the mainstream public. Exposure on *American Bandstand* helped build the popularity and careers of many rock-and-roll performers, including Chubby Checker, Buddy Holly, and Chuck Berry, among many others. A single appearance on the show led to the sale of thousands of records. The social and cultural impact of the show was vast. One of the most important things Clark did was insist on a racially integrated program. Many of the performers were African American and for many viewers, *American Bandstand* was the first vision of racial diversity.

For some, the payola scandal signaled the end of an era. *American Bandstand*, however, rapidly recovered. It became a weekly show in 1963 and continued in that format until 1987. It not only influenced generations of teenagers, helping form their musical tastes, but it also was the forerunner of every other musical show on television, including MTV.

Further Reading

Jackson, John A. *American Bandstand: Dick Clark and the Making of a Rock 'n' Roll Empire.* New York: Oxford University Press, 1997. This is a fair and well-researched book that chronicles both music and television history, as well as the cultural portrait that emerged from the rise and long life of *American Bandstand.*

Shore, Michael, and Dick Clark. *History of American Bandstand: It's Got a Great Beat and You Can Dance to It.* New York: Ballantine Books, 1987. An in-depth compendium of the show's history, divided by decade. Includes interviews with the show's regulars and photos of people, fashions, and memorabilia.

Weingarten, Marc. *Station to Station: The Secret History of Rock and Roll on Television.* New York: Simon & Schuster, 2000. Examines the performances, personalities, and television shows that were instrumental in the world of music and entertainment.

Lacy Schutz

See also Berry, Chuck; Dance, popular; Holly, Buddy; Music; Radio; Rock and roll; Television in the United States; *Your Hit Parade;* Youth culture and the generation gap.

■ American Dream

Definition Long-held popular belief that prosperity is within the reach of all Americans

The American Dream reached its fullest expression during the 1950's—an era that saw unprecedented consumer spending and confidence, as well as private accumulation of material, giving rise to widespread hopes of gaining even greater wealth.

Following a decade of poverty for Americans who suffered during the Great Depression of the 1930's and a decade of sacrifice and strife brought on by World War II, a weary people began to experience hope and optimism. Despite the perceived threat of world communism and the possibility of another great war and the social inequalities fostered by racial segregation laws, millions of Americans believed that the 1950's was a good time to be alive and that their efforts to attain the good life would be rewarded if they worked hard enough.

That dream was not precisely defined but generally understood to encompass such goals as greater social equality, personal security and freedom from oppression, better jobs, steadily rising income, home ownership, and eventual comfortable retirement. Almost every aspect of American life contributed to sustaining this dream. For example, unprecedented numbers of Americans were entering the stock market, and American Telephone and Telegraph (AT&T) became the first corporation in the world to have more than a million individual stockholders. The growing prosperity could also be measured in increased spending on recreation and dining outside the home.

Many new products came onto the market: photocopy machines, UNIVAC computers, automobiles with such features as power steering, color televisions, Diner's Club and American Express credit cards, transistor radios, sports cars, prepared frozen meals, disposable diapers, and more. The decade was also a period in which Americans expressed their exuberance in harmless fads, such as the hula hoop. The 1950's saw the beginning of the fast-food industry and a rapid expansion in domestic airline transportation.

Positive Trends The decade was not without strife, but a number of positive developments helped to buoy public optimism and reinforce faith in the

American Dream. For example, Hawaii and Alaska joined the Union and brought the number of states to an even fifty. Racial discrimination was challenged by the Civil Rights movement, Supreme Court rulings, and the first federal civil rights legislation since the nineteenth century. In medicine, the first kidney transplant was done; fluoridation of water greatly reduced tooth decay; mass inoculation against polio, using the Salk vaccine, began. Still feeling the glow of victory in World War II, the nation expressed its technological and military might by developing the hydrogen bomb and competing with the Soviet Union in the exploration of space.

In the cultural field, Leonard Bernstein became the first American-born director of the New York Philharmonic and Van Cliburn became the first American to win the prestigious International Tchaikovsky Piano Competition in Moscow. The Solomon R. Guggenheim Museum, designed by Frank Lloyd Wright, opened in New York City. Book publishing was varied and prolific, and new magazines such as *MAD*, *Playboy*, *TV Guide*, and *Sports Illustrated* began circulating.

The decade saw a virtual revolution in labor-saving appliances for the home, family recreation, and entertainment. Television finally emerged from being an obscure experiment to find its way into almost every American home by the end of the decade, and color television made the medium even more popular. The film industry met the challenge of television by experimenting with 3-D and wide-screen movies and offering increasingly colorful and spectacular films. The music industry benefited from the spread of transistor radios and the introduction of long-playing records that made it possible for rock and roll to become the dominant popular music form.

Impact While not realized by every American, millions of Americans experienced unprecedented prosperity in a new consumer culture that encouraged them to spend freely to fulfill their dreams. Credit cards enabled families to buy now, pay later, and ignore the values of saving and living frugally that had been the norm for their parents and grandparents. Economic prosperity led to a peak in the baby boom that had begun during the early 1940's. Older couples who had delayed beginning families now felt they could afford children, and the average marriage age of women dropped to 20.1 years in

1956, resulting in the largest ten-year increase in population in American history.

Further Reading

Calder, Lendol. *Financing the American Dream: A Cultural History of Consumer Credit*. Princeton, N.J.: Princeton University Press, 2001. Study of the problems arising from consumer overuse of credit to make purchases, with a historical survey of the problem.

Cullen, Jim. *The American Dream: A Short History of an Idea That Shaped a Nation*. New York: Oxford University Press, 2002. Historical study that traces the origins of the "American Dream" back to the seventeenth century.

Hudnut-Beumler. *Looking for God in the Suburbs*. New Brunswick, N.J.: Rutgers University Press, 1994. This book explains the religion of Americans during the 1950's in order to understand what happened to American religion and society in later years.

Luttwak, Edward N. *The Endangered American Dream*. New York: Simon & Schuster, 1993. While acknowledging continued affluence, Luttwak predicts a downward spiral and identifies areas to be affected.

Victoria Price

See also Affluence and the new consumerism; Baby boomers; Business and the economy in the United States; Civil Rights movement; Conformity, culture of; Home furnishings; Housing in the United States; Income and wages in the United States; Levittown; *Lonely Crowd, The*; Packard, Vance; Urbanization in the United States.

■ *Amos and Andy*

Identification Television sitcom with an all-black cast
Date Aired from 1951 to 1953

An amiable comedy about a black New York City cab driver and his unemployed friend, Amos and Andy *aired for only two years during its original run but nevertheless acquired nearly legendary notoriety for its supposedly negative depictions of African Americans.*

Amos and Andy occupies a special place in television history for more than one reason. Not only was it the first network program to feature a predominantly African American cast, but after it and *Beulah*, another series that featured stereotyped African Americans, stopped production in 1953, more than a decade would go by until another network program featured even a single black actor in a lead role. Moreover, even though *Amos and Andy* was for many years the only television show with a black cast, it was reviled by many African Americans and was eventually forced off the air altogether because of its reputation for presenting negative stereotypes of African Americans.

Compared to sitcoms of later decades that featured predominantly black casts, *Amos and Andy* was a relatively inoffensive comedy. It centered on cabdriver Amos Jones (played by Alvin Childress), his friend Andrew H. Brown (Spencer Williams), and the ever-scheming George "Kingfish" Stevens (Tim Moore). Individual episodes dealt with such standard sitcom themes as marital problems, unrealistic money-making schemes, and misunderstandings among friends. What offended many viewers, particularly African Americans, was the impression that the show seemed to convey to audiences that African Americans were stupid, lazy, and irresponsible. It might be argued that the same criticism could have been made about the ways in which white Americans were depicted in shows such as Jackie Gleason's *The Honeymooners*, and Phil Silvers's *You'll Never Get Rich*. However, the difference was that while some shows did, in fact, depict white Americans as stupid, lazy, and irresponsible, such shows represented only a minority of the programs in which ordinary white people were depicted. The dominant image of white Americans on television was that presented in such family sitcoms as *Father Knows Best*, *The Donna Reed Show*, and *Leave It to Beaver*. It would not be until *The Cosby Show* of the 1980's that African Americans had their equivalent. However, there was more to criticisms of *Amos and Andy* than the mere fact that its characters were often buffoonish.

The reputation of the *Amos and Andy* television series is inextricably mixed with that of the much longer-lived radio program of the same name that preceded it. *Amos and Andy* originated in 1928 as a radio program created by Freeman Gosden and Charles Correll, white performers who wrote, di-

Beulah

When *Amos and Andy* began airing on CBS in June, 1951, the only other network television series starring African American characters was ABC's *Beulah*. First broadcast in October, 1950, *Beulah* was a family situation comedy built around a black maid working in a white household. Like *Amos and Andy*, it had begun as a popular radio program created by white actors performing in the black roles. However, *Beulah* differed markedly from *Amos and Andy* in being not about the black community but about the role of African Americans in the white world. The show was essentially a sitcom about a white family, whose comic problems happened to be regularly solved by the family's meddling but well-meaning maid. Like *Amos and Andy*, *Beulah* came under heavy attack from the National Association for the Advancement of Colored People for its negative stereotypes of African Americans, and both shows went off the air in 1953. It would be fifteen years until another television series starred an African American woman—*Julia*, with Diahann Carroll.

Singer Ethel Waters was the first actor to play Beulah on television. The show was popular, but relentless public criticism of the show's depiction of black characters contributed to her leaving it after two seasons. Hattie McDaniel—best known for her Academy Award-winning performance as a maid in *Gone with the Wind* (1939)—then took over the role. McDaniel was already enjoying success as Beulah on the separately produced radio version of the program. In 1952, she made six TV episodes and twelve radio episodes, but her health failed, and she quit both shows. Louise Beavers then took over the TV role, and McDaniel's episodes were never broadcast. Like her predecessors, Beavers was troubled by public criticism of the show. After she completed a full seasons's episodes, she, too, left the show, and the network decided to cancel the series.

Other regular black characters on television's *Beulah* included Oriole, played by Butterfly McQueen, as the maid in a neighboring white home, and Beulah's shiftless boyfriend, Bill Jackson. Jackson was played by Bud Harris during the first season and by Dooley Wilson of *Casablanca* fame through the final two seasons.

rected, and performed in the show, affecting exaggerated imitations of black dialect in their portrayals of their African American characters. The radio program lasted until 1955 and for many years was one of the most popular programs on the air. During the 1930's, some motion-picture theaters drew fans of

Amos and Andy from their homes by providing intermissions during which they broadcast the radio program in their theaters.

Gosden and Correll created the characters of *Amos and Andy* and gave them stereotyped characteristics that many white people associated with African Americans. If the same characteristics had been given to the characters by black creators, African American audiences might have found them less objectionable. However, the fact that *Amos and Andy* was a white creation was in itself objectionable, particularly when photographs of Gosden and Correll in blackface were published. The National Association for the Advancement of Colored People began objecting to *Amos and Andy* during the 1930's and renewed its objections when the television series was broadcast during the 1950's. In June, 1953, after a run of only two years, the television show went off the air.

Impact *Amos and Andy* was immensely popular during both its radio and television runs, but the rise of the Civil Rights movement during the 1950's made Americans more sensitive to the need for the entertainment media to offer positive depictions of members of minorities. Although the humor in *Amos and Andy* was largely harmless, and the show was virtually the only television program to provide work for African American actors, it was driven off television and regarded as something best forgotten.

Subsequent Events After production of new episodes ended in 1953, reruns of *Amos and Andy* were broadcast on national television until 1966, when the program was withdrawn from syndication because of protests by civil rights organizations. Apart from a brief revival on an Atlanta, Georgia, station in 1983, *Amos and Andy* was never again broadcast on American television. By the early twenty-first century, few Americans under the age of fifty had seen even a single episode of *Amos and Andy*. However, by then, many episodes of the show were available in a variety of video formats.

Further Reading

Andrews, Bart, and Ahrgus Julliard. *Holy Mackerel: The Amos 'n' Andy Story*. New York: Penguin, 1986. History of the television series that places it within the broader history of African American depictions on television.

Bianculli, David. *Dictionary of Teleliteracy: Television's Five Hundred Biggest Hits, Misses, and Events*. New York: Continuum Publishing, 1996. Collection of brief articles on individual television programs, including *Amos and Andy*, which Bianculli argues deserves to be reconsidered.

Bogle, Donald. *Primetime Blues: African Americans on Network Television*. New York: Farrar, Straus and Giroux, 2001. Study of African American images on television by an authority on African Americans in the entertainment industries.

Ely, Melvin Patrick. *The Adventures of Amos and Andy: A Social History of an American Phenomenon*. Charlottesville: University of Virginia Press, 2001. Scholarly study of the complete history of the *Amos and Andy* radio and television programs with extensive discussion of the programs' social impact and critical response.

R. Kent Rasmussen

See also African Americans; *Honeymooners, The*; Mutual Broadcasting System scandal; National Association for the Advancement of Colored People; Radio; Silvers, Phil; Television in the United States.

■ *Andrea Doria* sinking

The Event Sinking of famed Italian ocean liner *Andrea Doria*

Date July 26, 1956

Place Atlantic Ocean, southwest of Nantucket, Massachusetts

The sinking of the Andrea Doria *involved the greatest sea rescue ever covered by American print media and television broadcasters.*

The end of World War II soon brought unparalleled affluence to the United States and Western Europe. By the mid-1950's, this prosperity included significant growth in transatlantic passenger liner voyages. Among the most famous of these liners was the *Andrea Doria*, an Italian ship noted for opulent luxury and the safety of its modern design. No one expected that this grand ship's marriage of style and safety would end in a fatal collision.

During the late fog-covered evening of July 25, 1956, the bow of the *Stockholm* ripped into the starboard hull of the *Andrea Doria*. The Italian liner began to list rapidly to starboard. Realizing the *Andrea Doria* was doomed, its captain ordered an evacuation. A flotilla of boats, which included the *Île de*

The Andrea Doria *listed so badly to starboard that none of the lifeboats on its port side could be used.* (AP/Wide World Photos)

France and the damaged *Stockholm*, helped rescue all but 46 of the *Andrea Doria*'s 1,706 passengers and crew. The sea tragedy was so dramatic that Americans sat riveted to their television sets until finally, at 10:09 A.M., July 26, the once-graceful liner sank to a depth of 225 feet.

Impact The sinking of the *Andrea Doria* contributed to a decline of the great age of transatlantic passenger ships and inaugurated American television's leading role in covering the decade's most sensational events.

Further Reading

Goldstein, Richard. *Desperate Hours: The Epic Rescue of the Andrea Doria.* New York: Wiley, 2001. Along with a technical explanation of the sinking of the *Andrea Doria*, the author presents an account of the human drama behind the sea rescue.

Moscow, Alvin. *Collision Course: The Andrea Doria and the Stockholm.* Reprint. New York: Putnam, 1988.

This work offers an objective and thorough analysis of the sinking of the *Andrea Doria*.

Pietro Lorenzini

See also *Bennington* explosion; Grand Canyon airliner collision.

■ Antarctic Treaty of 1959

Identification International treaty that demilitarized Antarctica and ensured international cooperation in its study

Date Signed on December 1, 1959

During the 1950's, Cold War tensions and the quest for new resources made Antarctica a potential battleground for industrialized nations. The treaty forestalled international competition to claim and exploit Antarctica, preserving its pristine environment and promoting international cooperation.

Since its discovery at the beginning of the nineteenth century, Antarctica has been coveted by many world powers that dreamed of mining its huge reserves of coal and harvesting its abundant fish, krill, seal, and whale populations. Before the International Geophysical Year (IGY) of 1957-1958, about one dozen countries led expeditions into Antarctica and began to claim portions of the region. Some claims, like those of Great Britain, Argentina, and Chile, overlapped, setting the stage for international disputes.

When it was decided that the IGY's exploration focus would be Antarctica, twelve countries installed forty-eight scientific bases along the continent's coast, and four countries created bases in the Antarctic interior. The eighteen months of intense scientific cooperation during the IGY were instrumental in convincing the twelve nations with territorial claims that Antarctica had to be protected to ensure continued scientific progress. As a result, the United States organized a conference, held in Washington, D.C., in 1959, at which the governments of twelve nations—Argentina, Australia, Belgium, Chile, France, Japan, Norway, New Zealand, the United Kingdom of Great Britain and Northern Ireland, South Africa, the Soviet Union, and the United States—signed a treaty regulating their actions in Antarctica.

Demilitarization and Scientific Cooperation The first article of the Antarctic Treaty prohibited the use of Antarctica for any military operations, the testing of weapons, or the establishment of military bases. However, it authorized "the use of military personnel or equipment for scientific research or for any other peaceful purpose." For example, the United States' Cold Regions Research and Engineering Laboratory (CRREL) is located on the continent and managed by the Department of the Army. The second article established "freedom of scientific investigation in Antarctica and cooperation toward that end," following the impetus of the IGY that promoted scientific inquiry in a climate of international cooperation. Because scientific cooperation was the ultimate goal in Antarctica, the third article stated that "information concerning plans for scientific programs shall be exchanged to permit maximum economy of and efficiency of operations." This included "exchanging scientists between expeditions and stations" and making scientific observations readily and freely available to the international community.

Article 4 stated that the cooperation required by the treaty should not infringe on the territorial sovereignty of the twelve contracting members. Article 5 prohibited the use of Antarctica for the disposal of radioactive waste or nuclear explosion. Article 6 defined the geographic area in which the treaty was to apply.

Article 7 authorized each contracting party to send observers to any base and to carry out aerial observations "at any time over any or all areas of Antarctica." Article 8 asserted that observers, scientific personnel, and staff should operate under the jurisdiction of their own nations.

Administration and Growth Representatives of all parties, noted article 9, would meet in Canberra, Australia, at regular intervals to discuss "the use of Antarctica for peaceful purposes only," facilitation of scientific research, cooperation, inspection, and "preservation and conservation of living resources in Antarctica." Article 10 required that no contracting party would "engage in activity contrary to the principle of the treaty." Article 11 required contracting members to resolve disputes over Antarctica through peaceful means, such as negotiation, mediation, conciliation, or judicial settlement by the International Court of Justice. Article 12 provided a mechanism by which the treaty could be modified or amended. Article 13 allowed other states, besides the twelve signatory nations, to ratify or access the Antarctic Treaty "if the contracting parties agree." The last article required the treaty to be written in English, French, Russian, and Spanish and that originals of the treaty would be deposited in the United States, with certified copies circulated among the signatory members.

Impact The Antarctic Treaty of 1959 limited the southward expansion of the Cold War and reaffirmed that international cooperation was both useful and attainable. At the same time, it ensured the preservation of Antarctica's pristine environment, ending any significant attempt to exploit its resources.

Further Reading

Trewby, Mary. *Antarctica: An Encyclopedia from Abbot Ice Shelf to Zooplankton.* Toronto: Firefly Books, 2002. A general encyclopedia of Antarctica, which includes information related to the treaty.

Watts, Arthur. *International Law and the Antarctic Treaty System.* Cambridge, England: Cambridge University Press, 1992. Studies the Antarctic Treaty of 1959 and the changes made to the treaty in later years.

Denyse Lemaire and David Kasserman

See also Cold War; Disarmament movement; International Geophysical Year; Natural resources; Science and technology.

■ Archaeology

Definition Study of human habitation through the excavation of buildings and other physical remnants of past occupation

The intensity of archaeological activity in the 1950's greatly enhanced understanding of humankind's occupation of North America, its settlements and migrations, and its antiquity, origins, and relationships.

During the 1950's, archaeology underwent a technological revolution worldwide, with the introduction of carbon-14 dating methods and aerial photography. In North America, these breakthroughs were especially timely. A boom in public engineering projects, such as highways and dams, forced the hurried excavation of hundreds of sites from Alaska to Yucatán, Mexico.

Until the development by Willard G. Libby of carbon-14 dating methods, archaeologists derived the dates for their discoveries from a method called seriation. Statistically based, seriation used the preponderance of types of artifacts, such as tools, ceramics, and jewelry, to sequence the presence of certain human groups. In conjunction with striation, a method that assumed that deeper layers of earth yielded progressively older artifacts, seriation provided a rough chronological framework for North American archaeology. The earliest date for human presence in North America was considered to be about 5,000 B.C.E.; carbon-14 dating reset the earliest known human sites in North America to about 9,000 B.C.E., therefore moving the first migrations to 12,000 B.C.E. at the latest. Libby was himself wary of depending too much on carbon-14 dating, particularly in the American Southwest, warning that radioactive contamination from weapons testing might affect the accuracy of dates based on carbon-14 in the sample. Nevertheless, it proved to be an essentially reliable tool.

Dendrochronology also began to come into its own in the 1950's. Tree rings served to confirm carbon-14 dating and also gave archaeologists information about conditions of climate and aridity during periods of settlement. Some archaeologists began using palynology, the study of pollen preserved in ancient sites, to determine the level of agricultural development, types of crops, and environmental conditions in which a people lived. Paul Martin's influential work analyzed pollen from numerous sites in the Southwest, tracing the domestication of plants and documenting climate change.

Aerial photography enabled archaeologists to see clearly for the first time such large features as the Great Serpent Mound in Ohio, which was known to archaeologists as early as the mid-nineteenth century. Ancient irrigation channels and well-trod routes, invisible from the ground, could be discerned easily from the air. The difference in subsurface soils, either compacted from traffic or lighter and more fertile fill from deposition, produces a difference in plant growth that may be quite vivid from overhead. Harvard archaeologist Gordon R. Willey first used aerial photography to reconstruct settlement over time of the Virú Valley in Peru. This nonintrusive method, called regional archaeology, was then widely used all over North America during the 1950's.

Threats from Development The unprecedented number of civic projects undertaken in the 1950's caused concern to the archaeological community. The interstate highway system and hundreds of dam projects threatened to bulldoze or inundate many unexamined archaeological sites, including cave shelters, villages, and burial grounds. Coordinating with the National Park Service and the Smithsonian Institution, universities provided volunteer archaeology students to excavate and document threatened sites throughout the United States and parts of Canada and Mexico. Budget cuts during the middle of the decade resulted in the loss of hundreds of archaeological sites.

Though hurried, these digs produced vast amounts of information about Native American settlements of North America and early colonization by Europeans. Sites were described and documented and artifacts collected for more thorough study. The earlier understandings of Archaic, Woodland, and Mississippian cultures was greatly expanded, and clearer relationships were drawn between native groups and their ancestors. A number of significant sites were later acquired for historical parks and saved from further degradation.

Excavations Excavations of the 1950's included the Cahokia Mound Group in the Mississippi Valley. The University of Michigan project, under the direction of James B. Griffin, dated materials found at Mound 34 to about 1,100 B.P. (before the present). Gregory Perino followed up Griffin's work in 1956, obtaining engraved shell and ceramics and other ornamental objects that helped develop an outline of cultural development at this important site.

Earlier mounds of the Archaic period also were excavated in Louisiana at Poverty Point. The most important known Archaic trading center in North America, Poverty Point consists of six concentric bisected circles, three small mounds, and the spectacular central Bird Effigy Mound. State highway projects in the 1950's did significant damage to the site, using gravel from the Bird and other mounds for road base, but at the same time unearthing a wealth of flints and other artifacts. The enormous ridges had been considered some kind of naturally formed levee until aerial photographs revealed them to be engineered earthworks with some astronomical function. The complex strongly challenged the traditional notion that such large projects required an agriculturally based society. No evidence of large-scale agriculture exists for Poverty Point, though its influence in the region was felt as far as the Great Lakes.

In the West, a number of sites were worked, including Lava Beds, with its rich trove of petroglyphs, and Fort Ross, a Russian trading settlement, both in northern California. In a remote Nevada site called Tule Springs, Libby used his carbon-14 dating method on charcoal from a site known to have been inhabited by humans in the distant past. A small number of tools and disarticulated bones indicated encampment. In 1954, Libby announced his determination that human hunters had been in the area more than 23,000 years ago. This extraordinary date does not fall within the accepted range, and it is generally believed that the charcoal was not associated with a campfire. The site was problematic for a number of reasons, but the announcement generated excitement, and anthropological outliers continued to hold out hope for a much earlier berengian or even transoceanic migration based on such claims.

In 1953, the first physical remains of a Pleistocene-age human in North America were discovered weathering out of an ancient lake bed by a pipeline welder name Keith Glasscock. The site, located near Midlands, Texas, was later excavated by a team of archaeologists, who successfully associated the skull with Pleistocene-age animals found in the same stratum.

During the 1950's, arctic sites were of particular interest to archaeologists seeking to understand the first migrations. Early cultures were discovered, but contrary to what might be expected, these finds were significantly more recent than Folsom and other paleolithic cultures found south of the arctic. Nevertheless, such finds drew intriguing relationships between the metholithic cultures of the Old and New Worlds. In 1956, a site near the Firth River in the Yukon Territory yielded nine cultural layers, the three deepest holding artifacts from a number of very early hunting groups. The most ancient coastal houses in the American arctic, dating from one thousand to two thousand years old, were found in Alaska in 1957. Additional dwellings on the Choris Peninsula that were somewhat older were discovered in 1959. Traces of the earliest North American pioneers remained elusive.

Historical Archaeology Colonial Williamsburg, Virginia, opened one of the first departments of historical archaeology during the middle of the decade. Prior to the 1950's, the term "archaeology" was not applied to more recent diggings without some resistance. Jean Carl "Pinky" Harrington was probably the greatest advocate for applying archaeological methods to investigating historical colonial sites in North America. The written historical record, he argued, could be supplemented valuably and sites such as Jamestown, Virginia, Plymouth, Massachusetts, and St. Augustine, Florida, could be understood more fully if excavated and interpreted by trained archaeologists. From this new subdiscipline, information about early explorers, Spanish and English colonists, and postcontact Native American societies was gleaned. Most notable is the work of John L. Cotter, who, as head archaeologist at Colonial National Historical Park from 1950 to 1953, directed the excavation of Jamestown.

Impact Before the 1950's, archaeologists had drawn only a very rough chronology of precontact North America. Cultural dates were based on relative dating methods, such as striation, seriation (or typology), and early dendrochronology. Absolute dating methods, such as carbon-14 dating and a more sophisticated implementation of dendrochronology, pinpointed periods of settlement and overthrew assumptions of simultaneous cultural practices and tool development. The acceptance of the regional approach to archaeology, as first introduced by Willey, led to a more complex classification of Paleo-Indian cultures as well as techniques less destructive than surface removal for some archaeological projects. Countless sites, however, were destroyed or degraded during the mid-century public works frenzy.

While a greater understanding of the settlement of North America by North Asian peoples and their descendants was achieved, Native Americans continued to suffer what they perceived as the plundering and desecration of sacred burial sites. Another thirty years would pass before American Indians acquired rights to protect ancestral burial grounds and demand repatriation of anthropological remains.

Further Reading

Deetz, James. *In Small Things Forgotten: An Archaeology of Early American Life*. New York: Anchor, 1996. Expanded edition of a classic work first published in 1977 on the archaeology of colonial America—one of the fields developed during the 1950's. Focusing on colonial New England, Deetz provides examples of how everyday objects such as chairs, musical instruments, and gravestones can help to reconstruct early American life.

Dorrell, Peter G., et al., eds. *Photography in Archaeology and Conservation*. New York: Cambridge University Press, 1994. Clearly written and amply illustrated survey of the equipment, techniques, and principles of photography used in archaeological work.

Gamble, Clive. *Archaeology: The Basics*. New York: Routledge, 1995. Introduction to the most basic principles of archaeological research and interpretation of evidence.

Gibson, Jon L. *The Ancient Mounds of Poverty Point: Place of Rings*. Gainsville: University of Florida Press, 2001. Examination of the information learned since the 1950's about the most important Archaic trading center in North America—Louisiana's Poverty Point.

Stokes, Marvin A., and Terah L. Smiley. *An Introduction to Tree-Ring Dating*. Tucson: University of Arizona Press, 2000. Reprint of a brief 1968 study of the science of dendrochronology, which was developed during the 1950's. Well illustrated.

Young, Biloine Whiting, and Melvin L. Fowler. *Cahokia: The Great Native American Metropolis*. Urbana: University of Illinois Press, 1999. Detailed survey of the work done on the Mississippi Valley's Cahokia Mound Group since the 1950's.

Janet Alice Long

See also Astronomy; *Kon-Tiki*; Native Americans; Science and technology.

■ Architecture

American architecture of the 1950's embodied the social, economic, and technological changes in postwar America that completely remade the national landscape.

As World War II ended, America was able to turn its war machine into a consumer economy almost overnight. By the 1950's, this economic expansion resulted in an extraordinary program of building, in both the commercial and domestic sectors. The years after the war were characterized by a sense of confidence, optimism, and a desire to focus on a twentieth century version of the American ideal of progress, which had been emblematic of so much of the nineteenth century. The ideals of the International Style, which reached the United States during the 1920's and 1930's, were still significant and had a powerful influence on 1950's American architecture. Postwar architects expected that the ideas of a modern architecture that were part of the early twentieth century would continue and even expand in the recovery in the postwar era. In general, they were right, and by the beginning of the 1950's, what had been an avant-garde architectural movement became something of a normative style. The result was a celebration of international functionalism in commercial architecture and the development of an American brand of contemporary design in domestic building, furniture, and consumer products.

The International Style Much of the design of American architecture during the 1950's was derived from the International Style, which flourished in Europe during the 1920's and early 1930's and was imported to the United States when prominent architects who had been members of the German Bauhaus emigrated during the late 1930's. Among the most influential of the expatriate Bauhaus members was Walter Gropius, who, as a professor at Harvard, trained a number of the most important architects of the period. Two other expatriate architects, Richard Neutra and Rudolph Schindler, were also important proponents of an internationally flavored modernistic style. They arrived in the United States before 1920, and their ideas and designs focused on houses and were powerfully affected by their participation in noted architect Frank Lloyd Wright's Taliesin fellowship.

The basic principles of international modernism included an emphasis on simplicity, an interest in texture, a willingness to permit the interpenetration of interior and exterior space, and an intense interest in technological improvements in planning, materials, and design. These certainly were not new ideas to American architects—both Wright and Bernard Maybeck championed much the same program during the early twentieth century. What set International Style apart from these early American prophets of modernism was an almost pathological aversion to ornament and an obsessive desire to systematize, universalize, and industrialize all the components of the design and construction process.

Postwar Corporate Architecture The promises of functionality and pragmatism that were the foundations of the machine aesthetic of modernism held a particular fascination for corporate America during the 1950's, and corporations sought architects who designed buildings that appeared abstractly universal and technically pure.

The first of these types of structures built in New York City was Lever House, constructed between 1951 and 1952 and designed by Skidmore, Owings & Merrill, a firm that would quickly become a leader in postwar commercial architecture. The design by su-

Frank Lloyd Wright, one of the most influential American architects of the twentieth century, revisiting Chicago's Prairie-style Robie House, which he designed decades earlier, in 1957. (AP/Wide World Photos)

pervising architect Gordon Bunshaft was able to make use of a recent change in the city's zoning laws, which permitted the construction of an unbroken rectangular tower, provided that a percentage of the ground area was either left open or used by a low unit. Bunshaft exploited both scenarios and set the building's green glass tower on one end of a one-story base set on raised columns, which defined an enclosed courtyard.

Lever House was among the first of many urban corporate headquarters that displayed the strong influence of the pioneering designs of Ludwig Mies van der Rohe and other members of the European modernist movement of the 1920's. Mies van der Rohe came to the United States in 1937, sponsored by Philip Johnson, and together they developed the "glass box" style of building that came to symbolize American business and modern American living during the era.

The Seagram Building, a Park Avenue tower built between 1954 and 1958 by Mies van der Rohe and Johnson for the liquor manufacturer, was arguably the most significant icon of postwar architecture. A golden-glass, thirty-eight-story tower—which, like the Lever House, made efficient use of its plot—was a sleek column of panes of glass set in an oiled bronze grid. The Seagram Building, like Mies van der Rohe's designs for the Illinois Institute of Technology (1950-1956) and Chicago's Lakeshore Drive Apartments (1948-1951), reflected the architect's belief that modern buildings should be universally functional, simple forms that could be adapted to the complex and multiple demands of modern society while making the best use of modern building methods and technologies.

Other significant International Style buildings were built around the nation and included such masterworks as I. M. Pei's Mile High Center in Denver, Colorado (1955); Eero Saarinen's General Motors Technical Center in Warren, Michigan (1950); William Brown and Gordon Bunshaft's Connecticut Life Insurance Company building in Bloomfield, Connecticut (1957); and the international committee design for the United Nations complex (1953-1957).

During the 1950's, architecture increasingly became a form of public relations and a tool of social organization. The complex nature of modern life and institutions was wrapped in the sleek, blank, uniform, and monotonous International Style struc-

tures. In some ways, the International Style that became the hallmark of modern public buildings during the 1950's presented a vision of an ideal world, one that, perhaps as an understandable response to the horrors of World War II, emphasized rationality, tidiness, and conformity.

Organic Design A less powerful and somewhat contradictory impulse to international modernism was epitomized by Wright's conceptualization for the Guggenheim Museum in New York, in which he sought to create a "natural" but modern postwar design. His designs generally were motivated less by technology than by an interest in creating buildings that reflected American values and the exceptional qualities of the American landscape. Wright's first spiral designs for the Guggenheim Museum emerged during the early 1940's and reflected his fascination with the form of the helix. As was often the case with Wright's preliminary plans, his design for the Guggenheim Museum was an object of public ridicule, and a number of experts were concerned that the building would be subject to fire hazards. As usual, Wright defended his "organic" ideas against those of the design's opponents, and his original design was completed, after his death, in 1959. While the museum does not fit in with the towers of commerce built during the decade to command the skyline of New York, the Guggenheim Museum is a brilliant expression of the symbolic power of natural form.

Eero Saarinen's David S. Ingalls Skating Rink at Yale University in New Haven, Connecticut (1958), is another organic design, which used an elliptical plan with cast concrete walls on the long edges of the ellipse. A central arch spans the major axis of the ellipse, and from the spine of the arch, cabled roofs form convex and concave curves. Saarinen refined his vision of an organic, sculptural building in his 1956 design for the soaring concrete shells that form the Trans World Airlines (TWA) Terminal at New York's Kennedy Airport.

Bruce Goff was an advocate of organic design in domestic architecture, and his work directly contradicts the idealized, abstract program of international modernism. For example, his Eugene Bavinger House in Bartlesville, Oklahoma (1950), is a spiral of stone turning out on a fifty-foot mast from which the roof is suspended. The Bavinger House was a unique combination of primitive cave dwelling and futuristic geometries. It was an iconic example of the organic tradition that provided postwar architects with an alternative vocabulary to modernism, in both public and domestic building design.

The House Goes Modern Throughout the decades, the house form has been a special strength of American architectural design, so it is not surprising that corporate headquarters and commercial structures were not the only buildings influenced by the ideas of international modernism. Philip Johnson domesticated the glass box in several of the houses he designed during the 1950's. The most famous is the Glass House in New Canaan, Connecticut (1945-1949), which he built for himself. Although his house was clearly influenced by Mies van der Rohe's design for the Farnsworth House in Plano, Illinois (1945-1951), Johnson's design interrupted the glassy, rectangular purity of Mies van der Rohe's design by inserting a large brick cylinder into the floor plan of the house, which held the bathroom and a fireplace, and by surrounding the house with large, leafy trees. Johnson produced similar designs for the Rockefeller Guest House in New York (1950) and the Robert Leonhardt House on Long Island (1956).

Other significant experiments in self-conscious modern housing included Gregory Ain's low-cost, mass-produced projects in Southern California for Park Planned Homes in Altadena and Avenel Corporation in Silverlake and Joseph Eichler's modern home developments in the San Francisco Bay Area. The Museum of Modern Art in New York City prepared a temporary display of modern domestic architecture in its 1949 and 1950 installations of designs by Marcel Breuer and Ain as part of the Museum of Modern Art's House in the Garden program.

The promise of manufactured components to provide sanitary, affordable, and modern living spaces was a core component of European modernism during the early decades of the twentieth century and a significant ideological and design concept in the international modernism movement. Wartime technological advances held the promise of the mass production of prefabricated and cheap homes to solve America's severe postwar housing shortage. Arguably, the most innovative concept for factory-built housing was R. Buckminster Fuller's Wichita House, an aluminum home resembling a spacecraft, which could be easily transported and set up by six workers in one day. Although Fuller's design generated significant public interest and industrial support, it never went into production.

The Case Study House Program Certainly, a number of American architects were interested in developing modern house designs, even if most Americans were not really interested in purchasing a house with a modern facade. The Case Study House Program, organized by John Entenza, editor and publisher of *Arts and Architecture* magazine, was one of the most significant efforts to define modern American domestic architecture. Beginning in 1945, *Arts and Architecture* presented Southern California as the center of modern domesticity.

Thirty-six experimental, prototype modern houses were designed (and the majority were built) between 1945 and 1966. The program's main aim was to point the postwar building boom in a modern direction by offering technologically advanced and ultimately affordable housing. The program showcased the talents of some of Southern California's most important architects in its effort to demonstrate the role of modern architecture in the creation of a better society. The best-known works of the program—houses designed by Charles and Ray Eames, Craig Ellwood, Pierre Koenig, and Raphael Soriano—were experiments that attempted to apply industrial methods and materials to residential architecture.

Early houses of the program were intended for typical post-World War II families, and the designs were generally two-bedroom, two-bathroom houses for couples with no servants and one or two children. The Eames House in Pacific Palisades, California (1945-1949), is typical of the Case Study houses of the era and the most internationally known of the Case Study houses. The Eames design was Case Study House Number Eight and presented a functional but family-friendly structure constructed from standard steel H-columns, steel decking, and factory sliding- or fixed-sash window panels.

Although the Case Study House Program was architecturally significant, particularly in the West, Case Study houses seemed to appeal only to American intellectuals. As the Case Study House Program evolved, the houses that were designed and produced emphasized technological innovation in materials and construction. The program's early, progressive vision of democratic, modern, and domestic architecture was never embraced by the majority of American home buyers. The postwar period actually saw only a few, isolated attempts to design and produce domestic architecture that reflected modern ideals. Instead, with rare exceptions, American postwar homes took much more conventional and traditional forms, although they were produced using wartime techniques.

Suburban Housing Developments Although suburbs existed during the late nineteenth and early twentieth centuries and an infrastructure to support suburban development was in place by the end of the Great Depression, a mass exodus to the suburbs did not truly begin until the 1950's. During World War II, there were many books and articles that offered a vision of the postwar home. The house that was envisioned by the popular press was one that had been specially built for modern living, not a remodeled older home. It was also understood that a new postwar home would be suburban and that there would be new homes for a large portion of the population.

In postwar America, the majority of new housing reflected specific and construction-industry agendas more than illustrating any particular architectural aesthetic. As a result of the government's support of new, single-family home construction, developers all over the country began to develop new communities of identical houses. Most of 1950's American residential architecture was of no discernible historical or artistic style but was built as part of the explosion of suburban communities around the country. Developments such as Henry Kaiser's Panorama City in Los Angeles, American Community Builders' Park Forest outside Chicago, and Levitt and Sons' Levittown outside New York City experimented with alternative methods, such as assembly-line, onsite fabrication and alternative materials, such as metal members for framing, to meet the American public's appetite for new houses as components of the American Dream.

Levitt was the most successful at cheaply producing large numbers of single-family houses and marketing them effectively. Individual Levittown houses were small—only about 800 square feet—"Cape Cod" homes with clapboard siding, shutters, unfinished attics, and kitchens equipped with all appliances, including a washing machine, an unheard of luxury in tract housing of the time. Levitt included

modern features and technologies in a house whose form resembled traditional American vernacular architecture. The early Levitt version of classic Cape Cod houses gradually evolved into a bland version of modern-style designs by the end of the 1950's.

Consumerism and the Mall No discussion of postwar American architecture is complete without some attention to the larger changes in the society of which it was a part. After World War II, the Federal Housing Administration (FHA) ensured that prospective home buyers had plenty of funds on which to draw for mortgages, but the agency did not insert itself into the private real estate market, except to favor the development of sites on the outskirts of urban areas. The explosion of postwar automobile production and the creation of the interstate highway system that led to the expansion of suburban housing during the 1950's also facilitated the development of shopping centers outside the city's core.

Curiously, shopping strips and malls of the 1950's owed a great deal to the architectural movements of Europe that spawned international modernism. Like the avant-garde work of German architect Eric Mendelssohn during the 1920's, commercial strip buildings in 1950's America tended to be almost transparent, so that at night, lit from inside, the building acted as a kind of beacon to passing automobile traffic. Indoor shopping malls also became part of the commercial environment, with the first enclosed suburban shopping center, Southdale, built outside Minneapolis, Minnesota, in 1956. Increasingly, by the end of the 1950's, cities were corporate enclaves of international modernism skyscrapers, early modern industrial sites, and home to factory workers and racial minorities. Middle- and upper-middle-class workers and their families had moved to the suburbs, places that were marked by conformity, driven by consumption, promised convenience, and reflected an idealized and isolating vision of postwar domesticity.

Leisure Destinations The idealization of the American landscape that resulted from both international modernism and assembly-line construction of suburbs extended into presentations of America's past, present, and future in leisure and entertainment environments. In many ways, Disneyland, which opened in Anaheim, California, in 1955, represented the contradictory impulses in American architecture of the 1950's—at once nostalgic, traditional, modern, and futuristic. Walt Disney's vision of America's past included a sanitized vision of nineteenth century America in Main Street USA and Frontierland. Tomorrowland and attractions such as "It's a Small World" presented visitors with a reassuring look at the shape of the present and the future. Other entertainment sites of architectural note included Las Vegas, whose "strip" expanded dramatically during the 1950's, and resorts such as Morris Lapidus's "Versaille-modern" Fountainbleu (1954) and Eden Roc (1955) hotels in Miami, Florida. In much of mainstream society during the 1950's, the line between the "real real" world of authentic, individual experience and the constructed world of the built environment began to blur as buildings both reflected and controlled social behavior and attitudes.

Impact American architectural designs of the 1950's embodied the social, economic, and technological changes of postwar America, many of which persisted into the twenty-first century. Though no one style predominated, postwar American architectural designs revealed the beginnings of a global commercial structure, the expansion of a consumer-driven economy, and the rise of an educated middle class. In addition to an interest in organic architecture among elite architects and their clients, an almost overwhelming nostalgia informed the designs of many suburban tract houses and resorts and entertainment sites such as Disneyland. Both public and domestic architecture of the 1950's provided a rich picture of the often contradictory attitudes, hopes, and dreams of American society of the era.

Further Reading

Colquhoun, Alan. *Modern Architecture.* New York: Oxford University Press, 2002. Traces the development of architecture in the modernist style.

F. W. Dodge Corporation. *Eighty-two Distinctive Houses from Architectural Record.* New York: McGraw-Hill, 1952. A glossy look at work by distinguished architects of the postwar period.

Ford, Edward R. *The Details of Modern Architecture: 1928 to 1988.* Vol 2. Cambridge, Mass.: MIT Press, 2003. Analyzes the technical and aesthetic importance of modernist architecture and examines the contributions of architects such as Eero Saarinen and Richard Neutra, and the Case Study House Program, among other discussions.

Hines, Thomas. *Richard Neutra and the Search for Modern Architecture: A Biography and History.* New York: Oxford University Press, 1982. Hines does an excellent job of discussing the influence of the international modernism movement on American housing.

Hitchcock, Henry-Russell, and Arthur Drexler, eds. *Built in the USA: Postwar Architecture.* New York: The Museum of Modern Art, 1952. A museum catalog illustrating the designs of preeminent American postwar architects.

Upton, Dell. *Architecture in the United States.* New York: Oxford University Press, 1998. A concise and thematically organized history of American architecture.

Von Eckhart, Wolf. *Mid-Century Architecture in America: 1949-1961.* Washington, D.C.: American Institute of Architects, 1961. A well-documented review of significant buildings of the 1950's.

J. R. Donath

See also American Dream; Business and the economy in the United States; Disneyland; Geodesic dome; Guggenheim Museum; Home furnishings; Housing in the United States; Levittown; Mackinac Bridge; Motels; Urbanization in the United States.

■ Armour, Richard

Identification American humorist and poet
Born July 15, 1906; San Pedro, California
Died February 28, 1989; Claremont, California

Richard Armour brought his light verse and whimsical style to the study of history and introduced a novel form of literary humor to the American public.

The only child of pharmacist Henry Willard Armour and Sue Wheelock Armour, Richard Armour earned degrees in English philology. In 1945, he became a professor of English at Southern California's Scripps College, where he remained until retirement in 1966, although he also taught at nearby Claremont Graduate School.

Armour published several books of humor and light verse during the 1940's, but he found his niche in 1953 with *It All Started with Columbus.* Like the earlier humorous take on British history, *1066 and All That* (1931) by Walter Carruthers Sellar and Robert Julian Yeatman, to whom Armour dedicated his own book, *It All Started with Columbus* features funny names, puns (for example, early American politician DeWitt Clinton is referred to as "a man of action known as 'Do-It' Clinton"), and running gags. Further books claimed that "it all started with" Europa (1955), Eve (1956), Marx (1958), and Hippocrates (1966), and a similar approach was applied to literature with *Twisted Tales from Shakespeare* (1957), *The Classics Reclassified* (1960), and *American Lit Relit* (1964). The popularity of Armour's prose works inspired his publisher, McGraw-Hill, to bring out several books of his light verses, including *Light Armour* (1954), *Nights with Armour* (1958), and *The Medical Muse* (1963).

After his academic retirement, Armour wrote children's books, with an occasional adult book, usually sharper in its wit than his early work, such as *A Diabolical Dictionary of Education* (1969) and *It All Started with Stones and Clubs* (1967), a mordant antiwar satire.

Impact Armour was a popular writer during the 1950's, appreciated for his wit and irreverence. One can see his influence in later humorists such as Dave Barry.

Further Reading

Allen, Everett S. *Famous American Humorous Poets.* New York: Dodd, Mead, 1968. By examining the body of humorous work, gives context to Armour's contributions.

Armour, Richard. *Drug Store Days: My Youth Among the Pills and Potions.* New York: McGraw-Hill, 1974. Contains some autobiographical information.

Arthur D. Hlavaty

See also Golden, Harry; Lehrer, Tom; *MAD*; Poetry; Shulman, Max.

■ Army-McCarthy hearings

The Event Hearings of a Senate Government Operations Subcommittee involving charges and countercharges between the U.S. Army and Senator Joseph R. McCarthy

Date April-June, 1954

Place Washington, D.C.

The hearings marked a decline in McCarthy's influence and an increase in the effect of television on American politics.

When the Army-McCarthy hearings began on April 22, 1954, recent polls had shown that Senator Joseph R. McCarthy, a Republican from Wisconsin, had the support of 50 percent of the American public while another 23 percent were undecided. McCarthy had been denounced by liberal critics as he was becoming a national figure in 1950, but with little visible effect. He also had been denounced by members of his own party, notably Senator Margaret Chase Smith from Maine and Senator Ralph Flanders from Vermont, who would introduce a resolution of censure against McCarthy after the hearings. President Dwight D. Eisenhower, who sought McCarthy's support during the 1952 elections, found McCarthy distasteful and belatedly was beginning to respond to McCarthy's criticism of his administration. Even Vice President Richard M. Nixon, who also made his national reputation by exposing alleged subversives, was beginning to distance himself from McCarthy.

The Cold War was at its height. The Soviet Union had exploded a hydrogen bomb in 1953, only months after the United States had done so. The French-held Vietnamese city of Dien Bien Phu was about to fall to Ho Chi Minh's nationalist troops. The Communist Party of the U.S.A. was minuscule, infiltrated by informers, and unlikely to grow, but they were feared nonetheless: For officials, attacking it was the easiest route to political popularity.

Television was a new force in American politics. The 1951 Kefauver hearings had attracted much attention where they were held, but the coaxial cable did not link most parts of the country until the political conventions of 1952, and the quality of delayed broadcasts was poor. By April of 1954, all the television networks had competing news divisions. Edward R. Murrow's *See It Now* television program on CBS had exposed McCarthy's high-handed methods on March 29, and McCarthy replied in his typical fashion on April 6: not by answering the criticisms but by making personal attacks against Murrow. Both CBS and NBC opted out of hearings coverage early on, but ABC vacated its daytime schedule in favor of complete live coverage, thereby gaining an enormous new audience.

Background McCarthy's chief counsel, Roy M. Cohn, a lawyer who was part of the team that convicted accused atomic spies Julius and Ethel Rosenberg, brought to his staff G. David Schine, heir to a hotel chain. Schine received a draft notice in July, 1953, and was drafted in November. Cohn tried to get special privileges for Private Schine, putting pressure

Boston trial lawyer Joseph Welch (left) and Senator Joseph R. McCarthy (right) during one of the last sessions of the Army-McCarthy hearings. (AP/Wide World Photos)

on officials such as Secretary of the Army Robert Stevens. The McCarthy committee had begun an investigation of the Army Signal Corps at Fort Monmouth, New Jersey, a search which soon spread to other military facilities. Secretary Stevens denied Cohn access to a facility for which he did not have a proper security badge, which Cohn took as a personal insult.

McCarthy demanded access to confidential Army personnel files, which Stevens, with the backing of the president, refused, although Stevens partially backed down on February 24, 1954. On March 9, the Army released a chronology, prepared by Stevens's counsel John G. Adams, of Cohn's attempts to gain privileges for Schine. The Army and McCarthy agreed to a joint airing of charges and counter-charges before McCarthy's committee, with McCarthy stepping down as chairman in place of Senator Karl Mundt. Cohn served as McCarthy's special counsel, and Ray Jenkins served as chief counsel for the committee's Republicans. Robert F. Kennedy,

who, like his father Joseph Kennedy, had earlier been an enthusiastic supporter of McCarthy, served as counsel for the committee's Democrats. Joseph Welch, a well-known Boston trial lawyer, assisted Counsel John G. Adams for the Army.

Millions Watch McCarthy in Action Despite long stretches of dullness and confused legal wrangling, the thirty-six days of hearings, totaling 187 hours of television airtime, drew a daily audience of approximately twenty million viewers. Thirty-two witnesses gave countless pages of testimony. The scowling McCarthy—with his repeated interjections of "point of order, point of order"—the cool and dapper Welch, the extremely mild-mannered Stevens, and the craggy chain-smoking Jenkins became daily companions for many viewers. The attempts of McCarthy and Cohn to manipulate evidence, and McCarthy's bullying tactics did not play well on television, especially when McCarthy fell into what may have been a carefully laid trap by Welch.

McCarthy and Welch agreed before the hearings that several areas would be off limits, including Cohn's avoidance of the draft during World War II and the one-time membership of one of Welch's staff, Fred Fischer, in the National Lawyers Guild—an organization that later successfully sued to get its name removed from the attorney general's list of subversives. They also may have agreed that Welch would never mention the widely suspected homosexual relationship between Cohn and Schine. Welch became angry when a photograph was introduced to show that Stevens had been especially friendly with Private Schine without outside pressure. It showed Stevens and Schine alone, but Welch determined that it had been cropped from a larger view that showed other people, which completely changed its purported meaning. Welch tried to find out from McCarthy's staff who had cropped the picture. When no explanation was forthcoming, Welch playfully asked if the alteration had been done by a pixie. When McCarthy asked the counsel to define the meaning of "pixie," Welch responded that "a pixie is a close relative of a fairy. Shall I proceed, sir? Have I enlightened you?" The room rocked with laughter. The homosexual allusion was lost on most television viewers but not on Washington insiders, including McCarthy.

On June 9, McCarthy decided to bring up the matter of Fred Fischer's former membership in the National Lawyer's Guild. Welch replied angrily, explaining his associate's essential innocence. Cohn tried to drop the subject, but McCarthy insisted on pursuing the matter. Welch appealed to him to stop maligning Fischer and asked, "Have you left no sense of decency?" The hearing room exploded with applause. After a sharp exchange with McCarthy near the end of the hearings, Senator Stuart Symington, a Democrat from Missouri, said, "The American people have had a look at you for six weeks. You are not fooling anyone." Many supporters of McCarthy were still loyal, but he was now powerless to ruin people merely with accusations.

Impact Public exposure to the methods of Senator McCarthy led to his December, 1954, censure by the Senate. The hearings also gave an indication of the increasingly important role of television in politics, signaling that politicians would have to look convincing as well as sound convincing to the American public from that time forward.

Further Reading

Cook, Fred J. *The Army-McCarthy Hearings, April-June, 1954.* New York: Franklin, Watts, 1971. A good brief summary of the hearings from an anti-McCarthy critic.

Doherty, Thomas. *Cold War, Cool Medium: Television, McCarthyism, and American Culture.* New York: Columbia University Press, 2003. Fascinating examination of television's role in perpetuating but also resisting McCarthy's scare tactics.

Herman, Arthur. *Joseph R. McCarthy: Reexamining the Life and Legacy of America's Most Hated Senator.* New York: Free Press, 2000. A book sympathetic to McCarthy but accurate in details.

J. Quinn Brisben

See also Cold War; Communist Party of the U.S.A.; Congress, U.S.; Eisenhower, Dwight D.; Elections in the United States, 1952; Faulk, John Henry; Kefauver Committee; Loyalty oaths; McCarthy, Joseph; Murrow, Edward R.; Nixon, Richard M.; Smith, Margaret Chase.

■ *Around the World in Eighty Days*

Identification Film about an imaginary round-the-world journey during the late nineteenth century

Director Michael Anderson (1920-   )

Producer Michael Todd (1907-1958)

Date Released in 1956

Exotic vistas and opulent sets conveyed in wide-screen cinematography won for this big-budget epic five Academy Awards, including the year's best picture award.

An adaptation of Jules Verne's 1873 novel of the same title, *Around the World in Eighty Days* is the story of an Englishman named Phileas Fogg who bets he can circle the world and return to London within eighty days. David Niven portrays Fogg in the film, Mexican comedian Cantinflas took on the lively role of Passepartout the butler, and Robert Newton offered some dramatic tension as private investigator Mr. Fix. The film ran for almost three hours and took audiences on a wide array of different transports through Europe, down the Suez Canal, through India, and into Thailand, China, and Japan before crossing the United States back to London. Shirley MacLaine portrayed an Indian princess (complete with dyed skin), and forty-four celebrities revered by 1950's audiences—including John Carradine, Marlene Dietrich, José Greco, Peter Lorre, Buster Keaton, George Raft, and Frank Sinatra—made cameo appearances throughout the film.

Impact *Around the World in Eighty Days* captivated theater audiences and Academy voters when it debuted. It was noted for its use of the lush, wide-screen process created by Mike Todd, called Todd-AO, which provided the movie a sense of grandeur and made audiences feel more a part of the film's action. In 2004, Walt Disney Productions released a remake of the film starring martial-arts performer Jackie Chan as Passepartout.

Further Reading

Osborne, Robert A. *Seventy-five Years of the Oscar: The Official History of the Academy Awards.* 4th ed. New York: Abbeville Press, 2003. This classic overview of American film includes a chapter devoted to cinematic achievements, events, and trends of the 1950's.

Verne, Jules. *Around the World in Eighty Days: The Extraordinary Journeys.* Translated by William Batcher. New York: Oxford Press, 1999. This paperback critical edition includes a select bibliography, a chronology of Verne's life, and additional appendices.

Scot M. Guenter

See also Academy Awards; Film in the United States; Greco, José; Sinatra, Frank; Wide-screen movies.

■ Art movements

Definition Trends and innovations in painting and other visual arts

By the 1950's, American artists responded to postwar uncertainty and rapidly established themselves as the driving force of artistic expression in the world.

After World War II, the United States not only emerged as the leading economic and military power but also took giant strides as a cultural leader. Both Europe and Asia found themselves recovering from the devastation of war, while the United States primarily had been left unscathed. During the late 1940's, several American artists were driven to express themselves with rebellious fervor and emotional abandon. New York City became a hotbed of artistic activity, and young American artists gravitated to the city in order to challenge the status quo

and push American art beyond traditional styles such as realism. New York also became the home of several exiled European artists. The interaction between American and European artists led to a revolutionary turn in American art. Despite their differences, the artists as a whole believed that it was paramount to express a sense of inner self in the visual arts they created.

Abstract Expressionism In 1946, art critic Robert Coates attached the term "abstract expressionism" to the works of Jackson Pollock, Willem de Kooning, and Arshile Gorky. Other terms such as "action painting," "New York School," and "color-field painting" also were used to refer to abstract expressionist artists. Most of the artists who became associated with this movement came of age during the American Depression and World War II, and the disruptions of these events unsettled their own views on the world around them. Because of the uncertainty of the postwar period, the artists felt that they could find sanctuary and could reach the "essence" of who they were as individuals only through the process of art.

In addition to Pollock, de Kooning, and Gorky, Robert Motherwell, Mark Rothko, Adolph Gottlieb, Franz Kline, and Clyfford Still left their mark on the art world with their vibrant, exciting creations. Pollock, however, was the artist who became synonymous with the invigorating and chaotic spirit in contemporary art. He served as the face of this new direction in American art, which attracted dismay from some critics and from a large percentage of the public. With such paintings as *Lavender Mist* (1950) and *Autumn Rhythm* (1950), Pollock established himself as a force of almost mythic proportions. Despite his death in 1956, Pollock continued to hold a larger-than-life presence in American art. By the 1960's though, the abstract expressionist movement relinquished its place of prominence to such movements as pop art and minimalism.

Beat Art, Assemblage, and Combine Painting The term "Beat generation" was introduced by American novelist Jack Kerouac during the late 1940's. While Beat writers such as Kerouac, Allen Ginsberg, and William S. Burroughs garnered the most attention, there also were important visual artists in the movement. The Beats felt alienated from American society, and they were put off by the consumer culture and the racism that festered in postwar America.

Like the Beat writers, Beat artists shared a sense that conforming to such a consumer society would constitute an abomination. Although the visual artists associated with the Beats—Wallace Berman, Jay DeFeo, Robert Frank, Claes Oldenburg, and Larry Rivers, for example—shared a certain mind-set, some of these artists also have been linked to other artistic movements such as assemblage, funk art, and neo-Dada. As a whole, however, they should be considered Beats because of their contempt for the moral hypocrisy that they perceived to be prevalent in 1950's America.

While the first assemblage work of art was created in 1912 by Pablo Picasso and Georges Braque, it was not until the 1950's that the assemblage movement gained international recognition. By the 1950's, a typical piece of assemblage art tended to be a three-dimensional artwork principally constructed of nonart materials. The materials used in some cases were nothing more than junk. Assemblage artists took inspiration from objects found in the "real world." They rejected the abstract expressionists' inward-looking approach to art. One of the most extraordinary examples of assemblage art is Simon Rodia's *Watts Towers*, which was completed in 1954. An Italian immigrant, Rodia began his amazing assemblage during the 1920's. Located in the southern Los Angeles neighborhood of Watts, the completed *Watts Towers* received significant news coverage and inspired many assemblage artists of the 1950's. The towers are nine major sculptural forms made of steel and covered with mortar embedded with pieces of ceramic tile, pottery shards, sea shells, and broken glass.

The term "combine painting" was introduced in 1954 by Robert Rauschenberg to describe the works he did that incorporated sculpture and painting. His works that were created to be mounted on a wall were called "combine paintings," while the works that did not have to be mounted were called "combines." In 1955, Rauschenberg completed *Bed*, one of his most famous combine paintings. For this painting, the artist painted both on canvas and on a quilt and then added a pillow in order to give the composition better balance. In 1958, a *Newsweek* magazine article titled "Trend in 'Anti-Art'" included a photograph of *Bed*. The art community debated whether the mounting of a bed on a wall could be considered innovative. While Rauschenberg was considered no more than a "prankster" by many art critics, his pop-

ularity grew during the late 1950's and early 1960's. By the mid-1960's, there were art experts who considered him as one of the most important American artists since Jackson Pollock.

Pop Art During the late 1950's, Jasper Johns and Robert Rauschenberg directed American art away from abstract expressionism. These artists were inspired by images that could be found in American popular culture. Johns painted such mundane subjects as the American flag, targets, maps, and Arabic numerals, while Rauschenberg created collages that employed newspaper headlines, comic strips, and images from advertising campaigns. Pop art re-created things from everyday life—items that were not considered proper subject matter for art in prior decades. For the pop artist during the 1950's, the consumer culture was king. While abstract expressionism emphasized the psychological, pop art celebrated the concrete. Through the efforts of such artists as Johns, Rauschenberg, Andy Warhol, and Roy Lichtenstein, pop art became influential during the 1960's.

Impact For the United States, the 1950's was a complex period. The complexity of the time can readily be seen in the art movements that gained prominence during the decade. American artists were bold, vital, and had an overwhelming belief in the freedom to take creative chances. This new breed of American artist did not take a backseat to traditional European cultural styles and understood the necessity to wrestle with social issues that lingered from previous eras. Whether through the existential energy that gave rise to the abstract expressionist movement, the purposeful joining together of common objects to form sculptures in the assemblage movement, or the playful, ironic qualities found by reproducing such American icons as the flag in the pop art movement, American artists during the 1950's took a leadership role in the art world. During this American decade, U.S. artists surpassed all expectations and produced a superior body of work.

Further Reading

Ashton, Dove. *American Art Since 1945*. New York: Oxford University Press, 1982. A close examination of how postwar American art grew out of the social and political forces at work in American society.

Dempsey, Amy. *Art in the Modern Era: Styles, Schools, Movements.* New York: Harry N. Abrams, 2002. A detailed study of modern art.

Doss, Erika. *Twentieth-Century American Art.* New York: Oxford University Press, 2002. A thoughtful exploration of the various American art movements that emerged during the tumultuous twentieth century, including abstract expressionism and pop art.

Phillips, Lisa. *The American Century: Art and Culture, 1950-2000.* New York: Whitney Museum of American Art, 1999. A fascinating look at the incredible flourishing of American art during the second half of the twentieth century.

Stich, Sidra. *Made in U.S.A.: An Americanization in Modern Art, the '50s and '60s.* Berkeley: University of California Press, 1987. A striking study of how American art during this period took its inspiration from the United States itself.

Jeffry Jensen

See also Abstract expressionism; de Kooning, Willem; Guggenheim Museum; Johns, Jasper; Kline, Franz; Motherwell, Robert; Painters Eleven; Pollock, Jackson; Rauschenberg, Robert.

■ Asian Americans

Identification Americans of full or partial Asian descent

Relaxation of discriminatory race-based immigration restrictions caused a substantial growth of the Asian American population in the United States in the 1950's, a time when Asian Americans were considered a "model minority" because they placed few demands on American society and generally agreed to strive for success under the rules set by the majority population.

The 1950 census revealed that there were 321,000 people of Asian descent living in the United States. This number represented 0.2 percent of the overall population, which stood at just over 152 million people. About 200,000 more people of Asian descent lived in the U.S. territory of Hawaii, which became a U.S. state in 1959. "Asian" was defined as originating from the Far East, Southeast Asia, or the Indian subcontinent. The vast majority of Asian Americans had come from China, Japan, India, the Philippines, and Korea.

In coming to the United States, Asian Americans faced xenophobia—a fear of foreigners among the majority population—and with it, racial prejudice as well as legal and social discrimination. Therefore, they remained a small minority. Even as legal discrimination diminished during the 1950's, Asian Americans who had been in the United States for some time were often treated as if they were foreigners. By the year 1950, large Asian American communities existed only in the states of California and New York and the territory of Hawaii.

Legal Discrimination The California gold rush of the mid-nineteenth century prompted numerous Chinese immigrants to enter the United States. However, anti-Chinese sentiment among European Americans who disliked labor competition from Chinese workers led Congress to pass the Chinese Exclusion Act of 1882. This act barred Chinese immigrants from entering the country for ten years (later extended indefinitely) and disallowed their attempts for naturalization as citizens. It became the first major restriction on immigration in the United States. This law represented the first in a series of racially based immigration restrictions targeted against Asians that would stay in place until the 1940's and 1950's.

The 1950's saw important changes in America's racially discriminatory immigration policy, which followed the softening of an anti-Asian legal bias begun during the 1940's, largely as a result of the influence of World War II. The modified immigration rules greatly benefited the growth of the Asian American community during the 1950's.

When Japan attacked the United States on December 7, 1941, the vast majority of Asian Americans immediately showed their loyalty to the country where they lived as residents or citizens. This made it harder to maintain the predominant racist attitude that Asian Americans were not "real" Americans. The vast majority of Japanese Americans were loyal to the United States, although those living on the West Coast were nevertheless summarily interned in remote camps that were not abolished until 1944.

Despite the fact that Japanese Americans suffered discriminatory treatment during World War II, the American government was forced to rethink its universal anti-Asian bias during this time. In 1942, Filipinos were allowed to join the U.S. armed forces, which made them eligible for citizenship. In 1943, Congress finally repealed the Chinese Exclusion

Act, and Chinese American residents became eligible for U.S. citizenship.

The next milestone came when the War Brides Act of 1945 was officially extended in 1946 to cover Asian wives of U.S. soldiers. Since Asian Americans had joined the U.S. forces in substantial numbers relative to their overall community, they were now eligible to bring home the wives they married abroad. Until December 31, 1953, when the War Brides Act expired, about seven thousand Chinese women, two thousand Japanese women, and thousands of Filipinas entered America under its provisions. Finally, the 1952 repeal of the Naturalization Law of 1790 represented a legal milestone for Asian Americans. Under the old law, Asians could not become American citizens.

War Brides Overall, for historical reasons, there were many more Chinese and Filipino men than women in the United States before World War II, although the Japanese American community tended to be more gender balanced. During the late 1940's and 1950's, Chinese and Filipina women entered America in record numbers. Asian women initially were able to come to the United States as wives of Chinese and Filipino American soldiers; later, they could enter the country as a result of relaxed immigration policies.

From 1945 to 1953, women made up 90 percent of the twelve thousand Chinese immigrants entering the United States. This trend continued throughout the 1950's, helping to reduce the 3-1 ratio of Chinese American men; the dream of starting a family had become a reality for many Chinese immigrants. The same was true for Filipinos, where men previously had outnumbered women 15-1.

The young Asian brides coming to the United States suddenly found themselves in an alien land. They felt surrounded by a foreign culture which still viewed them with some suspicion. The language barrier added to their feeling of being strangers. The same was true for wives or daughters who had not seen their husbands or fathers for a long time. In

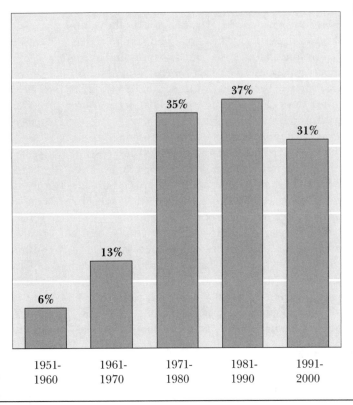

Arrivals from Asia as Percent of Total Immigrants to the United States

Source: 2002 Yearbook of Immigration Studies, U.S. Citizenship and Immigration Services.

turn, they often turned to the support of the existing Chinese, Filipino, Indian, or Japanese communities in the United States. As many of them became mothers, they relied on their families and Asian American neighbors to provide a social environment that lessened the shock of a new country where their facial features alone made them stand out within the mainstream population.

Overall during the 1950's, the Asian American communities matured into more family-based societies. The old stereotypes of lonely Asian bachelors or husbands separated from their families began to fade as new Asian American families grew and infused vibrancy into their neighborhoods.

Communist Refugees By the year 1950, most Chinese Americans viewed with alarm the victory of Mao Zedong's communist forces in China's civil war in October, 1949. However, anticommunist Chinese refugees became eligible to enter America under the Displaced Persons Act of 1948 until it expired on June 30, 1952. Thereafter, the new Refugee Relief Act of 1953 provided a legal framework for the immigration to the United States of Asian refugees fleeing communism. In 1953 alone, two thousand immigration visas were given to Chinese refugees, and more than five thousand Chinese students who had entered America before the communist victory were also given permanent residency.

The Chinese American community gained some highly educated members that helped increase its participation in the professional class. However, racial barriers still caused Asian American job entrance figures and average incomes to lag substantially behind those of European Americans.

Anti-Chinese bias returned to the United States when Mao Zedong intervened against America in the Korean War. Some Chinese Americans feared mistreatment akin to the internment of the Japanese Americans in World War II; this did not happen. Most Chinese Americans supported the Republic of China on the issue of Taiwan, the last noncommunist Chinese foothold.

When North Korea invaded South Korea on June 25, 1950, President Harry S. Truman committed U.S. troops to support its struggle. By the time an armistice was signed in 1953, American public opinion had become decisively more worried about global communist aggression than Asian immigration. Because the two communist superpowers during the 1950's—the Soviet Union and the People's Republic of China—contained both European and Asian populations, it became harder for the United States to continue race-based exclusions of Asians from immigration and naturalization. Instead, refugees from communist-ruled countries, whether in Europe or Asia, began to be welcomed by Americans.

Consequently, the immigration laws designed to exclude Asians were replaced. America's support of South Korea also led to new ties that resulted in stronger Korean immigration. From 1951 to 1959, about ten thousand Koreans immigrated to the United States, most as wives and dependents of U.S. soldiers. Beginning in 1955, the Holt Adoption Agency, founded by Harry Holt of Oregon, brought more than six thousand Korean orphans to America. There, the children were generally adopted by European American parents, even though only 60 percent of them were of biracial heritage. In addition, about eighteen thousand Korean students and nonimmigrants entered America during the 1950's, with some subsequently deciding to stay. Despite these factors, however, the Korean American community was still relatively small.

By the mid-1950's, refugees' worries of further persecution seemed to be justified. American public fear of Chinese communist spies entering America meant that in 1953, the two thousand Chinese refugees entering America had to be cleared by Chiang Kai-shek's government in Taiwan, which was entrusted to weed out spies. In 1955, a new scare was raised. The American consul in Hong Kong pointed out that many Chinese immigrants had illegally circumvented the rules of the old Exclusion Act and were technically ineligible to remain in the United States. The allegations stemmed from fears of communist spies among these immigrants. As the scope of Chinese circumvention became obvious, the administration decided to enact a "confession program." Those Chinese Americans who confessed to past fraud but were not part of criminal or subversive activities were allowed to stay in the United States. In effect, 99 percent of the tens of thousands of Chinese Americans who confessed were permitted to stay.

McCarran-Walter Act America's new superpower interests found their legislative expression in the McCarran-Walter Act of 1952. For Asian Americans, the new law presented a double-edged sword. On one hand, it finally abolished the laws that prohibited naturalization. It also provided an official quota for immigrants from Asia, establishing a crucial pre-

---

"Asian Americans"

The term "Asian American" was not used during the 1950's. During that era, Americans of Asian descent were typically referred to by their ancestral nationalities, such as "Chinese" and "Korean." They were also frequently called "Orientals," a term that later became regarded as pejorative and is now no longer used. Similarly, mainstream American culture had difficulties in distinguishing between Asian Americans who were U.S. citizens and Asians who were permanent residents of the United States.

cedent. For these advantages, the act was actively supported by Asian groups such as the Japanese American Citizens League.

On the other hand, the new law continued to base quotas on the immigrant's country of origin and maintained an anti-Asian bias. Countries in South and East Asia were permitted an annual quota of about one hundred immigrants, compared with quotas for European countries that ranged in the thousands. However, the law also officially removed all direct racial references and allowed Asian Americans of both genders to bring foreign spouses into the United States. Asian Americans immediately focussed on these exemptions. For example, while the quota for Japanese immigrants was set at 185 persons per year after 1952, in reality more than 5,000 Japanese immigrated to the United States each year during the 1950's. This was possible because Japanese immigrants came as wives, children, or husbands of U.S. citizens and residents.

Political Participation One of the biggest political issues that united Asian Americans during the 1950's was the need to change immigration laws. Another major political triumph for Asian Americans was the repeal of California's Alien Land Law by a 2-1 majority in 1956. In 1948, the Supreme Court ruled that the law—which for decades had prohibited the ownership or transfer of land to immigrants, primarily Asians—was unconstitutional, but it was not formally made law until 1956. The official repeal was considered a political watershed.

Throughout the 1950's, Asian Americans did participate as citizens in America's representative democracy. However, their numbers were generally too small to achieve sufficient critical mass for active representation on a state or a federal level. One noticeable exception was Indian American Dalip Singh Saund, who was elected to the U.S. Congress from California in 1956 and served three consecutive terms. When Hawaii became the fiftieth state of the United States, one of its first senators was Chinese American Hiram Fong, and two congressmen were Asian Americans, Representatives Daniel Inouye and Spark Matsunaga.

The experience of racial discrimination led to a certain reserve in the public arena among Asian Americans that proved a bit hard to overcome. Even though Asian Americans were generally still unwilling to draw too much public attention to themselves during the 1950's, they tended to be more active in their communities. Especially in states such as Hawaii, California, and New York, they were elected and appointed to civic boards and judicial posts. An interesting example was Samuel Ichiye Hayakawa. A Canadian by birth, he joined San Francisco State College in 1955 and would become one of the first Asian American college presidents and a Republican senator from California in 1973.

Japanese Americans Rebuild Their Communities
The 1950's was still a traumatic decade for Japanese Americans. The memories of their deportation from their West Coast homes and subsequent internment as "enemy aliens" had caused deep emotional wounds. Racial discrimination against Japanese Americans continued so strongly for some Japanese American families during the 1950's that some told their children to say "Chinese" when asked about their ethnicity by outsiders.

Approximately 25,000 Japanese Americans had fought as U.S. soldiers. However, there were also those individuals who had been offended by the American treatment of their families and who had refused the draft. The Japanese American community was torn by tensions between Japanese American war veterans and the so-called No-No Boys, who said "no" to American demands to foreswear any allegiance to Japan and to submit to the draft.

Immigration of Japanese women during the 1950's also saw the emergence of biracial marriages and children of Japanese and European or African American offspring. Since a large number of U.S. soldiers had been stationed in Japan since 1945, marriages also took place, and the dependents of U.S. soldiers could immigrate to America. In general, Japanese American wives were expected to assimilate to mainstream American culture, and their children were raised accordingly. However, when marriages failed, young Japanese American women often retreated to Japanese American communities. There, they found both comfort and resentment, the latter for having crossed an ethnic line.

Filipino American Community Expands Filipinos had enjoyed better access to the United States than other Asian immigrants before stricter racist barriers were implemented in 1934. They had also suffered widespread hostility and mistreatment at the hands of European Americans. With independence for the Philippines in 1946, the official immigration quota from that country was fixed at one hundred individuals per year. However, utilizing the far more generous rules for nonquota immigration, approximately 32,000 Filipinos came to the United States between 1953 and 1965.

In addition to Filipina war bride immigrants, students and businesspeople also began to immigrate to the United States during the 1950's. Because of the close military, cultural, and social ties between the two countries, and a lowering of race-based immigration barriers, the Filipino American community expanded significantly in the decade, and racist violence against Filipino Americans tended to decrease.

Impact Substantially increased immigration, a small baby boom, and the fact that Hawaii, with its large Asian American population, became the fiftieth American state on August 21, 1959, brought the Asian American population to 980,000 in the 1960 census. This number included Pacific Islanders and Hawaiians and gave Asian Americans a 0.5 percent share of the U.S. population.

By 1959, Asian American communities had changed significantly. The impact of so many Asian-born women, and the addition of Asian students and professionals, gave the Asian American societies more of a family orientation and further intellectual power. Racial bias by the majority population and the English language barrier meant that many Asian Americans often either stayed within their own communities during the 1950's or sought to assimilate to mainstream culture at all costs.

However, the Asian American communities continued to thrive economically in the face of much hardship, adversity, and remaining cultural barriers. With a general emphasis on conservative family values, a strong work ethic, and an immense appreciation of education, Asian Americans succeeded in American society. Important international recognition of the scientific contributions of Asian Americans came in 1957, when Chinese Americans Chen Ning Yang and Tsung Dao Lee shared the Nobel Prize in Physics.

Subsequent Events In 1965, the massive overhaul of immigration policies decisively abolished national quotas in favor of a more equitable system. Once the quota system fell, Asian immigration to the United States surged again. During the 1960's and 1970's, a growing political assertiveness arose. After 1975, communist victories in Southeast Asia brought new waves of refugees, which altered the demographics of the Asian American community. Vietnamese, Cambodians, Laotians, and Hmong would flee communist regimes in their home countries and settle in the United States, where there had been few Southeast Asian immigrants before. The 1980's and 1990's saw integration of these refugees together with an increasing visibility of Asian Americans in mainstream American politics, society, and culture. By 2000, more than ten million Asian Americans lived in the United States, accounting for about 3.6 percent of the U.S. population.

Further Reading

Chang, Iris. *The Chinese in America*. New York: Viking Press, 2003. Well-written overview, includes material on the 1950's.

Chin, Soo-Young. *Doing What Had to Be Done: The Life Story of Yum Kim*. Philadelphia: Temple University Press, 1999. Story of a Korean American community activist who witnessed the growth of the Korean American community in San Francisco during the 1950's and beyond.

Kitano, Harry, ed. *Asian Americans: Emerging Minorities*. 2d ed. Englewood Cliffs, N.J.: Prentice Hall, 1995. Concise historical and sociological study of all Asian American groups. Has important data on the 1950's.

Liu, Eric. *The Accidental Asian*. New York: Random House, 1998. Collection of essays by a second-generation Chinese American. Liu's memories of his parents' daily struggle to cope in mainstream America during the 1950's reveals the price of being seen as a "model minority" while still facing discrimination.

Ng, Francis, ed. *Asians in America*. New York: Garland, 1998. Collection of essays that focus on American immigration policies and Asian American self-awareness.

Segal, Uma. *A Framework for Immigration: Asians in the United States*. New York: Columbia University Press, 2002. Comprehensive study with an excellent chapter on pre-1965 Asian immigration to the United States and discussion of the Asian American experience during the 1950's.

Takaki, Ronald. *Strangers from a Different Shore: A History of Asian Americans*. Rev. ed. Boston: Back Bay Books, 1998. Very readable text, places the Asian American experience of the 1950's in the full context.

Tan, Amy. *The Joy Luck Club.* New York: Putnam, 1989. Even though it is a novel, Tan's vivid account of Chinese American mothers and their daughters in San Francisco's Chinatown during the 1950's demonstrates what it felt like to be Chinese American in that era.

Zia, Helen. *Asian American Dreams: The Emergence of an American People.* New York: Farrar, Straus and Giroux, 2000. Excellent firsthand account of growing up Chinese American in New Jersey during the 1950's, combined with general historical information.

R. C. Lutz

See also California's Alien Land Laws; China; Demographics of the United States; Hawaii statehood; Immigration and Nationality Act of 1952; Immigration to the United States; Interracial marriage laws; Japan; Korean War; Racial discrimination; War brides.

■ Asian flu epidemic

The Event Global pandemic of a new strain of type-A influenza virus

Date Peaked between September and November, 1957, followed by a second wave in 1958

The 1957 flu was a global pandemic of explosive proportions, the worst since 1918, with elevated death rates among the elderly and very young.

The Asian flu of 1957 sickened millions of people globally and was the most dramatic epidemiological event since the influenza pandemics of 1918 and 1889-1890. The 1957 flu variety was the most serious of three influenza epidemics affecting North America during the 1950's. A strain of influenza, which evolved by genetic drift, appeared in China in early 1957, and by late May, it had spread along transportation routes to Hong Kong, Japan, the Philippines, Malaysia, and Indonesia.

The virus entered the United States in June at the Naval Training Station in San Diego, California, as well as aboard a naval vessel deployed along the East Coast out of Newport, Rhode Island. It appeared in additional epicenters in Montana, Arizona, and Florida and by mid-summer was diffusing rapidly inland from the West, East, and Gulf coasts. The disease was geographically localized rather than frontal in its spread. Scientists believe that a small number of infected carriers known as "super-spreaders" may have unwittingly created multiple epicenters of disease throughout North America, especially in heavily populated urban areas.

The full pandemic exploded in both Canada and the United States from September through November; only isolated areas such as parts of Appalachia, interior Texas, the northern Plains, and lightly populated expanses of Canada escaped the worst of the disease. The Maritime Provinces were hardest hit in Canada, while Ontario and British Columbia faired much better, and the other provinces fell in between. The flu dissipated in North America by late autumn, but in the United States, the deadly siege in the fall was followed by another wave in early 1958. Except for the Ontario city of Montreal, Canada escaped the second onslaught. Overall, the flu epidemic in Canada was similar to the epidemic in the United States, with localized outbreaks, mostly from influxes of infected persons into population centers.

The 1957 influenza exhibited a normal age-mortality curve, with mortality the highest among the elderly. Death was normally a result of bacterial pulmonary complications and, in many cases, influenza may have hastened death to those with chronic cardiorespiratory ailments. Morbidity and mortality statistics were a reflection of the intertwining forces of viral strength and human vulnerability. The disease killed about eighty thousand persons in the United States, while Canada experienced a somewhat lower mortality rate.

Impact The epidemic led to controversy over the feasibility and logistics of national inoculation programs. The federal governments did not mobilize to mass vaccinate the American and Canadian populations. A vaccine was developed, but there were diagnostic and distribution problems. This epidemiological event drew greater attention to disease surveillance and diagnosis, vaccine development, and research into the mechanisms of the type-A virus. Research showed its link to the Spanish flu of 1918, the most deadly epidemic in American history, and researchers continue their search for the genetic reservoirs and carriers of these strains. Birds, pigs, and human beings in South China intermingle in a viral breeding ground and have a suspected link to the 1957 flu.

Further Reading

McDonald, J. C. "Influenza in Canada." *Canadian Medical Association Journal* 97 (1967): 522-527. A summary of morbidity and mortality in Canada, primarily 1946 through 1965.

Pyle, Gerald F. *The Diffusion of Influenza: Patterns and Paradigms.* Totowa, N.J.: Rowman & Littlefield, 1986. Covers U.S. patterns of morbidity and mortality, with emphasis on origins and diffusion mechanisms.

Ann M. Legreid

See also Health care systems in Canada; Health care systems in the United States; Health, Education, and Welfare, Department of; Medicine.

■ Astronomy

During the 1950's, new astronomical theories, observations, and technologies, including radio astronomy and the first artificial Earth-orbiting satellites, provided the basis for a revolution in the understanding of the universe.

After World War II, North American astronomers returned from war-related work to their studies of the solar system and beyond. Several technologies developed during the war were adapted and applied to research in astronomy. This was especially true during the 1950's, with the growth of radio astronomy from wartime advances in radar technology and the emergence of space probes and artificial Earth-orbiting satellites from wartime rocket developments. Scientists used these technologies to test new theories and to make new observations and discoveries.

Discoveries in the Solar System Some of the first theories to be developed during the 1950's were related to the origin and structure of comets. In 1950, Harvard University scientist Fred Whipple developed his "dirty snowball" theory of comet structure, suggesting that comets were conglomerates of frozen hydrocarbons cemented together with dust and rocks. As these frozen gases approach the Sun in their elongated orbits, they would vaporize and produce the characteristic comet tail. Whipple was able to account for observed accelerations of comets by the forces produced from the evaporating jets that produce their tails. He based his theory on work done in the Netherlands by Jan Oort, who formulated his comet-cloud theory, in which billions of frozen bodies surround the solar system. In 1950, Oort was able to account for the rate and random orientations of long-period comets (comets requiring more than two hundred years to revolve around the Sun) by

suggesting that they were deflected from this "Oort Cloud" into elongated orbits around the Sun.

In 1951, the Dutch American astronomer Gerard Kuiper developed a theory to explain short-period comets. After graduate work under Oort, he came to the United States and worked at the University of Chicago's Yerkes Observatory, where he discovered satellites of Uranus and Neptune and the atmosphere of Saturn's moon Titan. His 1951 theory postulated that the outer planets and their moons condensed from "protoplanets" in the gaseous disk that formed the solar system, and that the outer rim of the disk condensed into numerous icy objects beyond Neptune. Some of these objects would be deflected from this "Kuiper Belt" to form short-period comets, thus accounting for the fact that such comets orbit in nearly the same plane as that of Earth's orbit.

The Sun was another object of fruitful study during the 1950's. Sydney Chapman suggested the influence of the Sun on Earth's upper atmosphere in 1950. He showed how particles emitted by sunspots produced geomagnetic storms when they were deflected by Earth's magnetic field, thereby producing the northern lights. In 1956, Eugene Parker of the University of Chicago worked out the structure of the solar wind in a detailed mathematical analysis of particles emitted from the Sun and provided the first explanation for the production of comet tails by these particles. In 1952, Horace and Harold Babcock invented the solar magnetograph for measuring the Sun's magnetism, while in 1958, Harold Babcock discovered the periodic reversals of the Sun's magnetic field.

Optical Astronomy The 200-inch Hale telescope at Mount Palomar near San Diego was completed in 1948, and it soon allowed astronomers to make significant contributions to astronomy. During the 1950's, discoveries made with the telescope began to resolve a debate in cosmology over the expansion of the universe, a process discovered in 1929 with the 100-inch Hooker telescope at Mount Wilson near Los Angeles. The big bang theory was the first attempt to explain the expanding universe, but it became suspect when it estimated the age of the universe at about two billion years, compared to an age of more than four billion years for Earth. In 1948, the steady-state theory attempted to solve this discrepancy by suggesting that the universe was eternally expanding through a process of continuous creation, which produced new matter between the galaxies as they moved apart. The Hale telescope helped to resolve this debate in favor of the big bang theory by revealing a much larger and older universe.

Walter Baade did the pioneering work on the Hale telescope. As a German immigrant who was exempt from the armed services, he was one of the only astronomers who continued to work at Mount Wilson during World War II. Taking advantage of dark skies during wartime blackouts, he discovered two distinct populations of stars: younger and brighter blue stars forming from dust in the spiral arms of galaxies, and older and dimmer red stars near the galactic nuclei. In 1952, at Mount Palomar, he found that galactic distances based on younger stars were greater than earlier estimates, which had assumed that they were the dimmer, older stars. This finding greatly increased estimates of the size and age of the universe and thus supported the big bang theory.

In 1954, Baade and Rudolph Minkowski used the Hale telescope to obtain optical spectra from a very powerful radio source, Cygnus A. The men found that its great distance meant that it must radiate more energy than an entire galaxy. Their conclusion that this source of energy was a pair of colliding galaxies was later corrected, leading to its identification a decade later as a quasar. Quasars are newly forming galaxies early in the expansion of the universe, a finding that proved consistent with the big bang theory. The most conclusive confirmation of the big bang theory came a decade later from advances in radio astronomy and the discovery of microwave background radiation.

Radio Astronomy The first work in radio astronomy was done during the 1930's, but the development of radar technology during World War II led to rapid advances during the 1950's. The Naval Research Laboratory (NRL) in Washington, D.C., constructed a radio-telescope reflector with a 50-foot diameter in 1950 for receiving radio wavelengths of a few centimeters. In 1956, the University of Michigan built an

Very-large-array radio telescopes at Socorro, New Mexico, in 1955. (National Radio Astronomy Observatories/Associated Universities, Inc.)

85-foot reflector, and in 1959, Caltech built a similar sized radio telescope in Owens Valley, California. The National Radio Astronomy Observatory (NRAO) was established at Greenbank, West Virginia, in 1959, with an 85-foot reflector, and plans were made for two larger radio telescopes of 140-foot and 300-foot diameters.

In 1951, Harold Ewen, a graduate student of Nobel physics laureate Edward Purcell at Harvard University, reported his discovery of the emission of radio waves from neutral hydrogen in interstellar space. Six years earlier, a Dutch graduate student of Oort, Hendrik van de Hulst, had predicted that such radiation occurred from the changing spin orientation of the electrons in hydrogen atoms, producing 21-centimeter radio waves. Using a small horn antenna and a novel switched-frequency receiver, Ewen was able to detect this predicted radiation. Since 21-centimeter radio waves can penetrate interstellar dust clouds, they became very important in probing the Milky Way galaxy. In the next few years, Oort's group was able to map out hydrogen in interstellar space, estimating the rotation rate of the galaxy and its spiral-arm structure.

Radio waves were also detected from several objects in the solar system. In 1955 at the Carnegie Institute, Bernard Burke and Kenneth Franklin made the unexpected discovery of radio waves from Jupiter. While studying 15-meter radio waves from the Crab Nebula radio source, they noticed bursts of "interference," which were eventually identified with the location of Jupiter. In 1959, Frank Drake and his colleagues used the 85-foot telescope at Greenbank to discover 70-centimeter waves from Jupiter and suggested that the waves were produced by Jupiter's magnetism deflecting electrons surrounding the planet. Using the 50-foot telescope at NRL in 1959, a group led by Cornell Mayer measured thermal radiation at a 145-Kelvin temperature from the atmosphere of Jupiter with 3-centimeter microwaves. A year earlier, this group penetrated the clouds of Venus, measured a 600-Kelvin surface temperature, and probed the atmosphere of Mars, revealing a 210-Kelvin temperature.

Space Astronomy After World War II, the United States expanded its rocket program with several new facilities, including one at Cape Canaveral, Florida, in 1950. The program was boosted with the help of more than one hundred German rocket scientists under the direction of Wernher von Braun. They were moved in 1950 to the Redstone Arsenal in Huntsville, Alabama, to work with the army's Guided Missile Development Group. The scientists launched the Redstone rocket in 1953, and the three-stage Jupiter-C rocket in 1956 from Cape Canaveral. The National Aeronautics and Space Administration (NASA) was established in 1958.

Planning began in 1950 for an international campaign to gather data about the Earth. Scientists established the International Geophysical Year (IGY) for July of 1957 through 1958. On July 29, 1955, the United States announced its plan to place a satellite into Earth's orbit during the IGY to study the Earth and its space environment. Two proposals were considered, one from the Navy and one from the Army, headed by von Braun. The Navy's Project Vanguard was approved, but their work was not yet completed when the Soviet Union launched their *Sputnik I* satellite on October 4, 1957, followed by *Sputnik II* on November 3. On December 3, 1957, *Vanguard I* was launched with a Viking rocket from Cape Canaveral, rising only three feet before crashing back to Earth with its three-pound payload.

On January 31, 1958, von Braun's group used a Juno rocket to place into orbit the thirty-one-pound *Explorer I* satellite built by the Jet Propulsion Laboratory. Using instruments developed by James Van Allen of Iowa State University to detect charged particles, it made the first major discovery of the space age when it detected intense radiation circling the earth above 1,000 kilometers. Ten months later, the Army's *Pioneer III* space probe confirmed the existence of two doughnut-shaped regions of electrons trapped by the Earth's magnetic field lines, one centered at a height of about one earth radius and the other at about 2.5 Earth radii. In addition to confirming the Van Allen radiation belts, the data were used to map the size, shape, and strength of the Earth's magnetic field for the first time. *Pioneer IV* was launched on March 3, 1959, passing within 60,000 kilometers of the Moon before going into a solar orbit. Meanwhile, *Vanguard I* was launched on March 17, 1958, and discovered a slightly pear-shaped surface for the Earth (the North Pole is about 19 meters farther away from the center while the South Pole is about 26 meters closer).

Impact American astronomy during the 1950's provided the basis for a revolution in modern understanding of the universe. New theories for the structure and source of comets were eventually confirmed by space probes to Halley's comet in 1986 and the discovery of several hundred objects in the Kuiper Belt during the 1990's. New knowledge emerged about the effects of the Sun's magnetism and solar winds. The new 200-inch Hale telescope clarified the age of the universe and the big bang theory, which was later confirmed by the microwave background radiation. Radio astronomy began to map the spiral structure of the galaxy and to provide a better understanding of the planet system. The first Earth satellites and space probes began to reveal the nature of the planet's own space environment, leading to a better knowledge of the Earth and its surroundings.

Further Reading

Hey, J. S. *The Evolution of Radio Astronomy.* New York: Neale Watson Academic, 1973. A short history of radio astronomy by one of its pioneers.

Jones, A. W. *Innovations in Astronomy.* Santa Barbara, Calif.: Helicon, 1999. A brief overview and chronology of twentieth century astronomy plus biographical sketches, bibliographic and Internet resources, and a dictionary of terms and concepts.

Lang, Kenneth R., and Owen Gingerich. *A Source Book in Astronomy and Astrophysics, 1900-1975.* Cambridge, Mass.: Harvard University Press, 1979. Contains the most important astronomical articles of the 1950's with helpful introductions and explanations.

McNamara, Bernard. *Into the Final Frontier: The Human Exploration of Space.* New York: Harcourt College, 2001. A history of space exploration.

Joseph L. Spradley

See also *Explorer I*; International Geophysical Year; Mercury Space Program; National Aeronautics and Space Administration; Science and technology; Space race; *Sputnik I*; Van Allen radiation belts.

■ *Atlas Shrugged*

Identification Novel in which one man, vowing to "stop the motor of the world," persuades America's industrialists to shut down their companies and disappear, one by one

Author Ayn Rand (1905-1982)

Date Published in 1957

This epic, best-selling novel, which was reviled by critics, championed capitalism and individualism and featured a strong heroine.

Born in St. Petersburg, Russia, Ayn Rand lived through the Russian Revolution and emigrated to the United States shortly after finishing college. *Atlas Shrugged*, her second best-selling novel, included lengthy monologues, notably Francisco d'Anconia's "money is the root of all good" speech, and John Galt's sixty-page radio address to the world. Rand vividly depicts the inexorable decline of the United States as its infrastructure collapses, the government's stranglehold tightens, and the public sinks into hopelessness, repeating the refrain, "Who is John Galt?" Many reviews of the book were hostile, as Rand expected. Critics found its tone shrill, even hateful; the characters excessively positive or negative; the novel's literary merits limited; and Rand's rejection of the Christian value, altruism, discomfiting.

Impact Despite critics' negative reviews, the novel became a best-seller in 1957, and interest grew in the philosophy it touted, objectivism. In subsequent years, the novel gave impetus to the libertarian movement, influenced future Federal Reserve Board chairman Alan Greenspan, was appreciated by policy advisers during Ronald Reagan's presidency, was read and reread by business executives following the corporate scandals of 2002-2003, and was reexamined by feminists.

Further Reading

Gladstein, Mimi Reisel. *"Atlas Shrugged": Manifesto of the Mind.* New York: Twayne, 2000. This lucid, well-researched, compact companion discusses Rand's life and the book's critical reception, plot, characters, and themes.

Olster, Stacey. "Something Old, Something New, Something Borrowed, Something (Red, White, and) Blue: Ayn Rand's *Atlas Shrugged* and Objectivist Ideology." In *The Other Fifties: Interrogating Midcentury American Icons*, edited by Joel Foreman. Urbana: University of Illinois Press, 1997. Pages 288-306 relate *Atlas Shrugged* to what Rand viewed as the United States' lack of ideology in the postwar era.

Glenn Ellen Starr Stilling

See also *Affluent Society, The*; Conformity, culture of; Literature in the United States.

■ Atomic bomb

Definition Nuclear weapon that generates its energy by nuclear fission

Dates First tested on July 16, 1945; used on Hiroshima, Japan, on August 6, 1945; used on Nagasaki, Japan, August 9, 1945

The atomic bomb was used by the United States as a potent threat to curtail aggression from the Soviets, Chinese, and other countries during the Cold War era and contributed to the concept of "massive retaliation" in the arms race.

The atomic bomb was developed in the United States during the closing months of World War II and was used on Japan in the summer of 1945. Shortly thereafter, the war in the Pacific theater ended. It is unclear how many people died in the Hiroshima and Nagasaki bombings, and estimates vary widely. Most died of burns, many died from flying and falling debris, and some died of radiation exposure. Perhaps as many as 125,000 people died immediately, and an equal number died of injuries over the next five years. During the 1950's, the American public remained sharply aware of the atomic bombing of Japan because of the swiftness and apparent ease with which the bombs destroyed the Japanese landscape and because of the weapons' invisible, deathly radiation. Although U.S. foreign policy makers understood that the atomic bomb was a weapon of unequaled destructive capabilities, they nonetheless held that it was a weapon that the United States would use again if a given situation merited such a response.

When the Soviets tested their first atomic bomb on September 3, 1949, there was strong pressure on U.S. leadership to bomb Soviet targets before the country could amass a threatening arsenal. The Soviets could not directly threaten the United States until 1955, when they first deployed nuclear-armed, long-range bombers. The United States threatened to respond with massive retaliation if the Soviets bombed any American targets. By the year 1960, the United States had amassed 1,515 bombers and 3,083 nuclear bombs with which to carry out this threat.

Updated Weapons for the 1950's The basic bomb designs were improved during the 1950's by making them much lighter, more powerful, and more task specific. Like the Hiroshima bomb, the Mark-8 was a gun-assembly uranium-235 bomb. It began production in 1951, had a yield of 25 to 30 kilotons, and was

an earth-penetration weapon for use against hardened targets. The Mark-12 began production in 1954, had a yield of 12-14 kilotons, and was light enough to be carried to the battlefield by fighter and fighter-bomber aircraft. The Mark-18 began production in 1953 and had a 500-kiloton yield, the highest of any atomic, or fission, bomb ever deployed.

The Honest John was a surface-to-surface missile with a range of 12 miles and a 20-kiloton warhead. It first was deployed in 1954 in Europe, where it was intended to allow the United States to use fewer military personnel to fight larger armies. The Nike Hercules surface-to-air missile was deployed in 1958. It had a range of 88 miles and an adjustable yield of either 2 or 40 kilotons. However, during the mid-1950's, the hydrogen (fusion) bomb began to take

U.S. Marines watch an atomic bomb test at Yucca Flats, Nevada, around 1950. Many troops would later suffer from the effects of their exposure to the radiation released in these tests. (Hulton Archive I by Getty Images)

Hiroshima and Nagasaki

Under the right conditions, atomic nuclei can be ripped asunder in a chain reaction and made to release a million times more energy than an equal weight of chemical explosives. The cantaloupe-sized, uranium-235 core of the bomb dropped on Hiroshima on August 6, 1945, exploded with the energy of 15,000 tons (15 kilotons) of trinitrotoluene (TNT). Its target was an important railhead and a base housing 43,000 soldiers. Despite the terrible destruction and loss of life—largely civilian—caused by the explosion, Japan did not immediately surrender.

At the time the bomb was dropped, the war party that controlled Japan's government was intending to hold out for at least an additional seven months and force an Allied invasion of their homeland. The Japanese government hoped that an invasion would prove so costly to the Allies that it could win favorable surrender terms. An estimated 200,000 Americans and as many as 2,000,000 Japanese were expected to die in such an invasion. Not to be forgotten were the 250,000 people, mostly Asians, who were dying each month of the Japanese occupation because of forced labor and starvation.

Believing that it might be necessary to convince the Japanese that the bomb dropped on Hiroshima was not a fluke, the United States planned a second bombing for August 11, 1945, but the event was moved up to August 9 because of bad weather. Clouds obscured the intended target, Kokura arsenal, so the bomb was diverted to Nagasaki's Mitsubishi Steel and Arms Works. This bomb's softball-sized plutonium core exploded with the energy of 21 kilotons of TNT. Japan surrendered soon afterward.

---

over the role of the high-yield strategic bomb, leaving the atomic bomb to specialized roles, such as acting as a trigger for the hydrogen bomb.

Impact During the 1950's, neither the United States nor its European allies wanted to use the resources necessary to maintain standing armies large enough to defeat the Soviets or the Chinese in a full-scale war. Government strategists determined it was cheaper to build a sufficient number of nuclear weapons to defeat U.S. enemies. The United States extended the protection of its nuclear umbrella to its allies because, among other reasons, it hoped that those countries would then forgo obtaining their own nuclear weapons.

Presidents Harry S. Truman and Dwight D. Eisenhower were pressured to use atomic bombs in the Ko-

rean War (1950-1953). When mainland China bombarded National Chinese troops on Quemoy Island in 1954 and again in 1958, Eisenhower threatened to bomb mainland China. During the 1956 Suez Crisis, both the United States and the Soviet Union threatened to use nuclear weapons. Eisenhower again threatened to use nuclear weapons during the 1959 Berlin crisis. In subsequent decades, countries were able to find means to end international crises short of nuclear war, fulfilling to some degree the hope of many of the scientists who first built the atomic bomb.

Further Reading

Maddox, Robert James. *Weapons for Victory: The Hiroshima Decision Fifty Years Later.* Columbia: University of Missouri Press, 1995. A careful discussion of the necessity of using atomic bombs.

Newman, Robert P. *Truman and the Hiroshima Cult.* East Lansing: Michigan State University Press, 1995. An excellent discussion of the "Japan-as-victim" myth and why the Japan bombings were necessary.

Rhodes, Richard. *The Making of the Atomic Bomb.* New York: Simon & Schuster, 1986. One of the best available popular treatments of the subject.

Tsipis, Kosta. *Arsenal: Understanding Weapons in the Nuclear Age.* New York: Simon & Schuster, 1983. An excellent introduction to the science and politics of nuclear weapons.

Charles W. Rogers

See also B-52 bomber; Bomb shelters; Brinkmanship; Civil defense programs; Cold War; Disarmament movement; Einstein, Albert; Hydrogen bomb; North American Aerospace Defense Command; Oppenheimer, J. Robert; Rosenberg, Julius and Ethel; Seaborg, Glenn; Teller, Edward.

■ Atomic Energy Act of 1954

Identification Federal legislation governing the development of atomic energy in the United States

Date Became law on August 30, 1954

The Atomic Energy Act of 1954 established the fundamental conditions for the private development of nuclear power in the United States.

The Atomic Energy Act of 1946 created the Atomic Energy Commission (AEC) to direct the development and use of atomic energy in the United States. After the submarine *Nautilus* was successfully propelled with nuclear power in 1952, interest in the practical uses of atomic power increased dramatically. On December 8, 1953, President Dwight D. Eisenhower presented his "Atoms for Peace" speech to the United Nations General Assembly. President Eisenhower requested the establishment of the International Atomic Energy Agency (IAEA) to redirect the emphasis of nuclear technology from military to peaceful applications.

After exhaustive congressional hearings were conducted during the spring of 1954 to consider the future development of atomic energy in the United States, the Atomic Energy Act of 1954 was proposed. President Eisenhower signed it into law on August 30, 1954. This amendment to the Atomic Energy Act of 1946 authorized the United States to proceed with the peaceful use of atomic energy wherever practical, as long as constraints for defense and security were maintained. By providing new licensing regulations, greater access to technical data, and the right for private industry to own nuclear reactors, the act opened the door for the private sector to work with the government in the research and development of atomic energy applications that would help promote world peace and provide an increased standard of living throughout the free world. Additionally, the act enabled the AEC to share technical and scientific information with other nations.

Under the Atomic Energy Act of 1954, American industry and government were given the mandate to keep the United States at the forefront of atomic energy development. Using fissionable materials leased from the United States government, private industry could design, build, and test its own nuclear power plants. By the end of 1957, seven experimental reactor designs were in operation. On October 1, 1957, the IAEA was established in Vienna, Austria, to promote peaceful uses of atomic energy worldwide.

Impact The Atomic Energy Act of 1954 provided the necessary link between industry and government for the peaceful development of nuclear energy technology. The right for the industrial sector to own nuclear reactors led to the design and implementation of several reactor designs for the generation of nuclear energy, with applications for the space program, the production of electrical power, and the development of several practical devices powered by atomic energy taking precedence.

Although various modifications and amendments were made to the Atomic Energy Act after 1954, it continued to provide the basic guidelines for both the military and civilian uses of radioactive materials in the United States. The Energy Reorganization Act of 1974 transferred the responsibilities of the AEC to the Energy Research and Development Administration and the Nuclear Regulatory Commission (NRC). The NRC continues to implement the provisions of the Atomic Energy Act of 1954 in the regulation of all companies that use radioactive materials.

Further Reading

Atkins, Stephen. *Historical Encyclopedia of Atomic Energy.* Westport, Conn.: Greenwood, 2000. More than 450 alphabetically arranged entries detail the history of atomic energy use.

Ford, Daniel F. *Meltdown.* New York: Simon & Schuster, 1986. Explains the impact of the Atomic Energy Act of 1954.

Sylves, Richard Terry. *The Nuclear Oracles: A Political History of the General Advisory Committee of the Atomic Energy Commission, 1947-1977.* Ames: Iowa State University Press, 1987. Details the history of the Atomic Energy Commission and the role of the Atomic Energy Act of 1954 in the development of nuclear power in the United States.

Alvin K. Benson

See also Atomic Energy of Canada, Ltd.; Einstein, Albert; *Nautilus*, USS; Oppenheimer, J. Robert; *Savannah*; Science and technology; Seaborg, Glenn; Space race; Teller, Edward.

■ Atomic Energy of Canada, Ltd.

Identification State company in charge of Canada's national nuclear program
Date Founded in 1952

The Atomic Energy of Canada, Ltd. (AECL) represented an effort by the Canadian government during the early years of the Cold War to ensure government control of the nuclear industry.

With the arrival of the Cold War and the acquisition of an atomic bomb by the Soviet Union in 1949, the nuclear arms race between the United States and the

Soviet Union accelerated during the 1950's. Canada found itself in a significant position with its own nuclear program, which had begun during the 1940's in cooperation with Great Britain.

Wishing to ensure a monopoly over the nuclear industry and to centralize existing operations, the Canadian government of Prime Minister Louis St. Laurent created a new crown (government) corporation, the AECL, in 1952. Explicit in its creation was that its mandate would be for the development of the peaceful uses of nuclear energy.

In 1951, Canada already had developed a unique radiation cancer therapy, still in use in the twenty-first century. That research also included the development of nuclear reactors for peaceful purposes. Beginning in 1954, the AECL took a leading role in developing a nuclear reactor to help generate electricity. In 1962, power from this source went online in the province of Ontario for the first time. It also developed a research reactor in 1957.

Impact The AECL symbolized, especially in an era of heightened Cold War tensions, the possibility of the peaceful uses of nuclear power.

Further Reading

Bothwell, Robert. *Eldorado: Canada's National Uranium Company.* Toronto: University of Toronto Press, 1984. Provides a history of Canada's nuclear program.

Whitaker, Reg, and Steve Hewitt. *Canada and the Cold War.* Toronto: James Lorimer, 2003. Canada's nuclear program is discussed in a Cold War context.

Steve Hewitt

See also Atomic bomb; Atomic Energy Act of 1954; Canada and Great Britain; Cold War; Continentalism; St. Laurent, Louis.

■ Automobiles and auto manufacturing

In several important respects the automobile and automobile manufacturing proved to be at the heart of North American life during the 1950's. The decade was one characterized as the age of tail fins and chrome, and the automobile was recognized as something far more than ordinary transportation.

In the consumer-oriented society of the 1950's, the automobile became the ultimate status symbol, an object that was worshiped by some with a religious intensity. The decade marked an age of excess expressed by style. As the 1950's unfolded, cars became longer, lower, heavier, more powerful, and as a result of these developments, more gasoline reliant. Moreover, unlike the late twentieth century, when cars, because of aerodynamic design considerations, appeared alike, every major car brand had its own look or profile during the 1950's. Children growing up during this decade became car spotters, distinguishing from considerable distances the differences between DeSotos and Chryslers and between Pontiacs and Chevrolets, playing close attention to the cars' distinctive grills, hood ornaments, or taillights. Indeed, for many Americans, inspired by car races and off-road excursions in, for example, the dry lakes of California, the automobile became a hobby, as reflected in such popular magazines as *Hot Rod, Motor Trend,* and *Road and Track.*

During the first half of the decade, in addition to the big three companies of General Motors (GM), Ford, and Chrysler, there were several independents, each with a distinctive style. Studebaker had broken away from conventionality in 1948 with Raymond Loewy's "coming and going" design. Packard was attempting to break into the middle-class market with a car that had a bulbous shape. J. Powell Crosley of Cincinnati manufactured a series of economy models despite the fact that the market was geared toward affluence. The Hudson Company pioneered the step-down, lowered-floor design that was coupled with a powerful Hornet engine, making its car a serious contender on southern NASCAR tracks. Nash produced a sporty hybrid Nash-Healy along with a passenger car that had the appearance of an inverted bathtub. Finally, Kaiser-Frazer came out with the economical Henry J, one version of which was sold at Sears Roebuck department stores but was considered ugly by many consumers.

Style The auto industry of the 1950's was dominated by its stylists. Prominent among them was Loewy at Studebaker, whose 1953 Starliner was a style *tour de force.* At General Motors, Harley Earl, inspired by the P-38 aircraft, added fins to the Cadillac during the late 1940's and adopted chrome as his design hallmark. Earl had an uncommon appreciation for the aesthetic value of glitter and chrome and developed a theory of "light value" of chrome trim. By angling beveling and then angling trim at 45 degrees, he was able to reflect light directly to the

Harley Earl, standing next to a full-scale model of a Buick sports car in 1951. General Motors' vice president in charge of styling, Earl was a major contributor to the revolutionary design changes of American automobiles during the 1950's. (Hulton Archive | by Getty Images)

viewer, and a maximum stylistic impact resulted. Along with Bill Mitchell, Earl headed a GM design studio that shaped two automotive icons of the 1950's, the 1955 and 1957 Chevrolets. Perhaps the most innovative of the stylists was Virgil Exner at Chrysler, who, in 1955, introduced the "forward look," a design concept that was perhaps best represented by the 1957 Plymouth. At Ford, Frank Hershey led the team that was responsible for the clean-lined 1955 Ford Thunderbird and the Fairlane Crown Victoria, as well as the four-passenger 1958 Thunderbird.

During the 1950's, automobiles changed not only in shape but also in color, as two- and even three-tone paint schemes became popular. Moreover, thanks to innovations in paint technology, colors became more vibrant and varied. For example, in 1955, Ford offered such unique colors as Regency Purple Iridescent and Tropical Rose, and Oldsmobile enticed customers with Turquoise Iridescent and Bimini Blue Iridescent.

Technology Just as the appearance of automobiles was dramatically altered, so too were the foundational technologies. For much of the 1950's, Detroit manufacturers engaged in a horsepower race, a competition that began with the introduction of the Oldsmobile Rocket V-8 engine in 1949. Gradually six and straight eight engines were displaced with overhead V-8 designs. At Chrysler, hemispherical chambered V-8's, known as "hemis," gained in popularity. In 1955, Chevrolet introduced its small block V-8, quickly a favorite among the hot-rod crowd. By the year 1956, some 80 percent of buyers purchased cars with V-8's, perhaps appropriate given that during the same year the interstate highway system became a reality. Although the Automobile Manufacturers Association banned factory-sponsored racing and discouraged the preoccupation with speed in auto advertising in 1957, horsepower and engine size continued to escalate through the early 1960's.

Concurrently, automatic transmissions became increasingly popular with consumers, including push-button, on-the-dash versions in Chrysler products. In fact, the interiors of automobiles began to be filled with homelike conveniences. Power windows and plush seats, outside mirrors, automatic dimming headlights, transistorized radios, and air conditioning were now options in higher-priced models by mid-decade.

The Consumer Market Within the car industry, 1953 marked an important turning point. Between 1946 and the end of the Korean War in 1953, there were far more buyers than cars, and thus dealers could charge full prices for autos with already inflated price tags as a result of the addition of costly accessories. In 1953, an average American had to work thirty weeks to buy a new car, as compared to thirty-seven weeks in 1925. Consequently, 59 percent of consumers bought their automobiles on credit. Beginning in 1954, however, the tables were turned as it became a buyers' market. Dealers were now squeezed by manufacturers, who unloaded excess inventories with the threat of taking away the franchise from those dealers who did not comply. As a result, unscrupulous sales methods were practiced on a public already wary of dealers' honesty. Suspect practices included high-pressure sales tactics, inflated charges for dealer preparation, high interest rates, bait-and-switch tactics, and "unhorsing" the customer, whereby the prospective buyer found it difficult to get his or her old car back after appraisal.

These abuses and others led to widespread hostility on the part of the public, ultimately leading Congress to pass the Automotive Information Disclosure Act in 1958, which required the attachment to each new car of a sticker that informed customers of the price for each option and total retail price for the vehicle. Not surprisingly, by the late 1950's, critics of the automobile and Detroit manufacturers surfaced, including John Keats, who, in 1958, published *Insolent Chariots.* According to Keats, industry leaders had lost touch with American consumers.

The decade so simplistically characterized as one of "happy days" ended on a turbulent note. In 1957 and 1958, America experienced a short but painful recession, during which unemployment reached approximately 7 percent. It was during this downturn that Ford introduced the ill-fated Edsel, Packard ceased production, and car sales dropped more than 30 percent for the model year. However, Detroit manufacturers continued to build large, heavy,

and expensive-to-operate cars, ignoring the fact that import model sales were up tenfold from 1951. Volkswagen, Volvo, Renault, Fiat, MG, Triumph, and Austin were all making inroads into the American market. In response, in 1959, Detroit automakers released models with features such as upward-soaring tail fins (like those found on the Cadillac), outward extensions on the Chevrolet, and a delta wing design on the Buick. After only one year of record import sales did the big three manufacturers counter with economy cars—the Corvair, Falcon, and Valiant.

Safety Issues Until the 1950's, little attention was paid to the problem of automobile safety in the United States. The typical American automobile featured dashboards with numerous hard protrusions, the absence of seatbelts, poor brakes and tires, noncollapsible steering columns, doors that opened on impact, seats and suspension systems that were too soft, and windshield glass that shattered easily. This neglect was the consequence of manufacturers' hubris, consumer preferences, the psychology of driving, and the failure of government to further public interest in this matter.

Perhaps not surprisingly, more than 30,000 Americans died as a result of traffic accidents in 1950, and that number increased to more than 50,000 two decades later. However, despite obvious evidence to the contrary, the auto industry maintained that it was not automobile design features but drivers and their behaviors that caused accidents and injuries. Nevertheless, several forces for change began to converge during the late 1950's and early 1960's. Indeed, by the end of the 1960's, a once-thought unassailable industry was forced to change by the rising tide of public opinion, regulatory legislation, and a newly created federal government bureaucracy.

A major reason for the emerging emphasis on auto safety during the 1950's came as a result of enhanced technical knowledge about the "second crash"—the collision of the automobile's passengers with the interior after initial exterior impact. Wartime studies done at Wright-Patterson Air Force Base and the Cornell University Medical College in New York on aircraft cockpit injuries were subsequently extended to an examination of similar phenomena inside automobiles at the Cornell Aeronautical Laboratory. Evidence from these studies, coupled with the work of Detroit plastic surgeon Claire Straith on passenger injuries, clearly suggested that relatively simple design modifications could save lives and prevent serious injuries. However, in 1955 and 1956, when the industry was confronted with these facts, it largely failed to respond.

Similarly, change was in process regarding the environmental impact of automobiles. In 1959, the Automobile Manufacturers Association announced that in 1961, cars sold in California would have a crankcase ventilation device. It was hoped that manufacturers could head off government intervention, but the election of 1960 and the presidency of John F. Kennedy signaled increased government intervention, and the auto industry's complacency was soon forced to change.

Impact The 1950's witnessed the emergence of automobility in the United States, as the car moved to the center of culture and society. Economically, approximately one out of every seven Americans owed his or her job directly or indirectly to the automobile, as the glass, rubber, petroleum, and steel industries were all fueled by the manufacture of automobiles. Furthermore, the automobile figured prominently in the advertising, literature, music, and film of the decade. In 1957, Jack Kerouac published his life-as-journey account, *On the Road*, while noteworthy cinema of the decade featured automobiles in the backdrop, including James Dean's *Rebel Without a Cause* (1955) and James Mitchum's *Thunder Road* (1958). Indeed, the automobile was the quintessential technology of mid-century America, and it touched virtually every area of everyday life.

Further Reading

Encyclopedia of America Cars. Lincolnwood, Ill.: Publications International, 2002. Details inventions, makers, designers, and the big-three manufacturers, among other features of America's car culture.

Flammang, James M. *Cars of the Fabulous Fifties: A Decade of High Style and Good Times*. Lincolnwood, Ill.: Publications International, 2002. A colorful and well-illustrated work.

Flink, James J. *The Automobile Age*. Cambridge, Mass.: MIT Press, 1988. An excellent book on the history of the automobile and its cultural influences.

Sedgwick, Michael. *Cars of the Fifties and Sixties*. New York: Beekman House, 1983. Includes European automobiles; this work is outstanding in terms of descriptions of technology.

John A. Heitmann

See also Affluence and the new consumerism; Chevrolet Corvette; Chrysler autoworkers strike; Drive-in theaters; Edsel; Fast-food restaurants; Ford Thunderbird; General Motors; Interstate highway system; Motels; Trans-Canada Highway; Volkswagen.

■ Avro Arrow

Identification Canadian-designed jet interceptor
Dates Test-flown on March 25, 1958

The Canadian-made Avro Arrow had the potential to become the greatest jet fighter-interceptor of its day, but the government of Prime Minister John G. Diefenbaker canceled the project.

In April, 1953, the Royal Canadian Air Force (RCAF) established requirements for a new and highly sophisticated jet interceptor to replace its aging, subsonic CF-100 fighters. Such an aircraft would have to fly at twice the speed of sound, have an operational ceiling of 58,000 feet, and employ state-of-the-art missiles and fire-control systems to facilitate its role as a bomber destroyer. An estimated six hundred machines were considered necessary to protect North America from attack by Soviet aircraft flying over the North Pole.

The RCAF established rigid specifications for the project, and by 1957, the firm of Avro Canada had finalized design of the CF-105, unofficially known as the Arrow. The Arrow was a large delta-winged fighter, powered by twin turbojet engines. The first Arrow was test-flown on March 25, 1958, and it stunned the aviation world with its many sterling qualities. In fact, this aircraft placed Canada at the forefront of military aircraft design and was considered a source of national pride. However, the plane also experienced problems and was viewed by the Conservative government of Prime Minister John G. Diefenbaker as prohibitively expensive. On February 20, 1959, Diefenbaker summarily canceled the entire project and ordered the five prototypes destroyed.

Impact Beyond depriving Canada of one of the world's great aircraft, the Arrow's demise solidified perceptions that Diefenbaker was soft on defense matters and contributed to his eventual defeat at the polls. Moreover, despite the Diefenbaker administration's attempts to distance Canada from the foreign policies of the United States, the cancellation of the Avro Arrow meant that Canada was left to rely on American-built Bomarc surface-to-air missiles, a path which ultimately tied Canada more closely to its neighbor.

Further Reading

Campagna, Palmiro. *Requiem for a Giant: A. V. Roe and the Avro Arrow.* Toronto: Dundurn Group, 2003. An excellent discussion of political factors leading to the aircraft's cancellation.

Peden, Murray. *Fall of an Arrow.* Toronto: Stoddert, 2001. Well-illustrated with a wealth of technical and aeronautical descriptions.

John C. Fredriksen

See also Aircraft design and development; B-52 bomber; Canada as a middle power; Diefenbaker, John G.; Elections in Canada; Foreign policy of Canada; International trade of Canada; North American Aerospace Defense Command; St. Laurent, Louis.

B

■ B-52 bomber

Definition Strategic bomber designed and built by Boeing Company

Date Prototype first flown on April 15, 1952

The development of the B-52 provided the United States with a credible intercontinental nuclear deterrent, increased the U.S.-Soviet arms race, and raised Cold War tensions.

When the B-52 entered U.S. Air Force (USAF) service in 1955, it began a career that continued into the twenty-first century. At a time when the Soviet Union lacked an intercontinental bomber, the B-52 gave the United States an advantage in strategic nuclear strike capacity. The bomber enabled the USAF to strike targets in the Soviet Union from bases within the continental United States. Because of its ability to do so, the B-52 also became a psychological weapon and helped allay some of the Cold War fears of the American public.

The B-52 bomber's true intercontinental range decreased the need for overseas air bases without minimizing the nation's nuclear deterrent. No longer was any part of the Soviet Union beyond the limits of American military power. Only with the launch of the Soviet satellite *Sputnik* in 1957, as well as the development of ballistic missiles, did a challenge emerge to the preeminence of the B-52 as the nuclear weapons' delivery system. Over time, this bomber would come to symbolize the USAF, its Strategic Air Command, and the American nuclear deterrent, and it would serve longer than any other aircraft in USAF inventory.

Design and Development The design of the eight-engine turbojet plane that would become the B-52, the Boeing Model 464, began in 1946. That year, the Boeing Company secured approval for its design and initiated work on its long-range turboprop bomber. Boeing initially designed the aircraft to fly nonstop from bases in the United States and strike targets deep inside the Soviet Union. At the direc-

Profile of the B-52

Length: 152 feet
Wingspan: 185 feet
Gross weight: 390,000 pounds
Power source: eight 8,700-pound jet engines that generate a maximum speed of 556 miles per hour at 40,000 feet
Range: 5,200 miles
Service: A prototype of the B-52 first flew on October 2, 1952. This heavy strategic bomber would form an essential component of the U.S. nuclear arsenal during the Cold War and would see service in the Vietnam, Korean, and Gulf Wars and in the 2002 Afghanistan campaign.

(AP/Wide World Photos)

tion of USAF headquarters in early 1948, Boeing incorporated aerial refueling into the design not only to decrease its size and cost but also to preserve its intercontinental range. The next year, Boeing incorporated the Pratt and Whitney J-57 turbojet engine into the B-52 to give the USAF an all-jet intercontinental bomber. In early 1952, the first B-52 prototype took flight and initial production models were designated the B-52A, but they became test platforms at Boeing. The B-52B entered USAF service in mid-1955.

Impact Throughout the 1950's, the B-52 chalked up numerous distance and speed records; in 1957, it carried out the first globe-circling nonstop flight by a jet aircraft. In service, the B-52 realized the nuclear deterrent goal of President Eisenhower's "New Look," in which the threat of massive retaliation from the Strategic Air Command's bombers would deter communist aggression. Until the introduction of intercontinental ballistic missiles, the B-52 remained the United States' primary nuclear strike platform. Production of the B-52 ceased in 1962, but it remained a mainstay of the Strategic Air Command for the next three decades. Later versions became conventional bomb carriers and continued in USAF service into the twenty-first century.

Further Reading

Futrell, Robert F. *Ideas, Concepts, Doctrine: Basic Thinking in the United States Air Force, 1907-1984.* 2 vols. Maxwell Air Force Base, Ala.: Air University Press, 1989. Futrell's history of the U.S. Air Force includes the development of aircraft and air-power strategy, as well as an analysis of the service's doctrine.

Knaack, Marcelle Size. *Encyclopedia of U.S. Air Force Aircraft and Missile Systems.* Washington, D.C.: Office of Air Force History, 1978. Knaack's compendium of the aircraft and missile systems used by the U.S. Air Force until the late 1970's provides a detailed history of and the technical information for each weapon system.

Nalty, Bernard C., ed. *Winged Shield, Winged Sword: A History of the United States Air Force.* 2 vols. Washington, D.C.: Air Force History and Museums Program, 1997. Nalty's two-volume history examines the U.S. Air Force from its earliest beginnings to the end of the twentieth century.

Paul D. Gelpi, Jr.

See also Aircraft design and development; Atomic bomb; Avro Arrow; Brinkmanship; Eisenhower Doctrine; Hydrogen bomb; Military-industrial complex; *Sputnik I*; United States Air Force Academy.

■ Baby boomers

Definition Nickname for the generation of Americans born between 1946 and 1964

The years between 1946 and 1964 saw the highest birth-rates in U.S. history and dramatic changes in American culture.

Following World War II, sixteen million American soldiers returned home and were eager to start families. During the first year of the boom, 3.4 million babies were born in the United States—at the time, a record number of births for one year. From 1954 onward, more than 4 million boomers were being born each year, peaking at 4.3 million in 1957.

Parents of the baby-boom generation faced housing shortages and overcrowded schools. During this period, thousands of single-family houses and new schools were built, giving rise to suburban tracts bordering most large American cities.

Many "boomers," as they were called, remember their childhood years as a peaceful and optimistic time. After World War II, the United States experienced an unprecedented period of growth and prosperity. Children often grew up in new and safe housing developments, with mothers tending to stay at home while fathers earned the family income. Moreover, the decade witnessed an unprecedented focus on childhood, and middle-class boys and girls enjoyed a remarkable flood in toys marketed to children: comic books, Play-Doh, Tinkertoys, Barbie dolls, hula hoops, Mr. Potato Head, and Easy Bake Ovens, among others.

Until the 1960's, the boomer years were largely an age of conformity in dress, manners, and social relationships. Religion played a major role in most families. Organizations such as Little League baseball, Boy Scouts, and Girl Scouts helped teach cooperation and discipline.

Major Influences Television had a major impact on the lives of baby boomers. They were the first generation of American children to be affected by the new medium. Thirty-minute "situation comedies" or "sitcoms" such as *Leave It to Beaver* and *The Adventures* *of Ozzie and Harriet* portrayed idealized versions of American family life, which for many were quite unlike their everyday experiences while growing up. Although the stereotypes of the families of 1950's and 1960's sitcoms did contain a grain of truth, in fact there were serious cultural undercurrents in American society. Many women who had worked in wartime industries and returned to more traditional roles as housewives and mothers became discontented. Some young people began to challenge the traditional manners of dress and behavior. The most obvious sign of rebellion was the emergence of rock-and-roll music. Borrowing rhythms from African American jazz and blues music, white suburban youths found a new means to express their desire to be different from their parents' generation.

Impact During the 1960's, more baby boomers attended college than any generation before them, giving rise to hundreds of new state colleges, community colleges, and universities. As they grew into adulthood, the large numbers of children born between 1946 and 1964 would profoundly change the culture, economy, and politics of the last decades of the twentieth century.

Although their parents had hoped to create a world that was free from the poverty and war they had endured, the boomer generation would be the first to live under the cloud of nuclear war. By the 1970's, the assassinations of John F. Kennedy, Martin Luther King, Jr., and Robert F. Kennedy, combined with the Vietnam War, the Watergate scandal, and a stale economy, would dash the optimism of their earlier years as baby boomers began to take their place in society.

Further Reading

Halberstam, David. *The Fifties*. New York: Villard Books, 1993. An excellent narrative history that covers a wide range of cultural currents of the decade.

Marling, Karal Ann. *As Seen on TV: The Visual Culture of Everyday Life in the 1950's*. Cambridge, Mass.: Harvard University Press, 1996. Explores the social impact of television on the boomer generation.

Yenne, Bill. *Going Home to the Fifties*. San Francisco: Last Gasp of San Francisco, 2002. Photos and advertising illustrations that depict idealized, middle-class suburban life and culture of the decade.

Raymond Frey

See also American Dream; Conformity, culture of; Demographics of the United States; Education in the United States; Levittown; Rock and roll; Urbanization in the United States; Youth culture and the generation gap.

■ Banks, Ernie

Identification American baseball player
Born January 31, 1931; Dallas, Texas

Ernie Banks was the first African American player for the Chicago Cubs and became known as a power-hitting shortstop.

Ernie Banks was first signed to play professional baseball by the Kansas City Monarchs, a premier team of the Negro League, after a short career on an all-black, traveling "barnstorming" team. He was then signed by the Chicago Cubs as the team's first African American player in 1953, six years after Jackie Robinson broke baseball's color barrier with the Brooklyn Dodgers. Banks joined the Cubs without ever playing minor league baseball.

Banks was the first shortstop with great home run power, hitting the most total home runs in Major League Baseball from 1955 through 1960. He was selected as the National League's most valuable player in 1958 and 1959, despite playing for Cubs teams that finished near the bottom of their league both seasons. He finished with 512 career home runs and ranks among the greatest home run hitters of all time.

Banks steadily improved as a defensive shortstop, eventually setting records for the least errors in a season in 1959 and winning the Golden Glove Award in 1959 and 1960. Injuries led him to shift to first base, where he played from 1962 until his retirement in 1971. He was elected to the Baseball Hall of Fame in 1977.

Impact Awards and statistics do not fully capture the importance of Banks, who became known as "Mr. Cub." His cheery optimism and slogan "Let's play two" symbolized the Cubs and gave hope to fans during an era when the team was unsuccessful nearly every season. He played his entire career for the Cubs and remained closely affiliated with the team after retirement. Banks is generally acknowledged as the greatest player who never had the chance to play in the World Series.

Further Reading

Gentile, Derek. *The Complete Chicago Cubs: The Total Encyclopedia of the Team.* New York: Black Dog & Leventhal, 2002. A thorough sourcebook of games, players and their statistics, and more.

Jacob, Marc. *Wrigley Field.* New York: McGraw-Hill, 2002. A book of photographs that pays homage to Wrigley Field's nine decades of "service" to baseball, accompanied by essays that discuss notable players, games, fans, and much more.

May, Julian. *Ernie Banks: Home Run Slugger.* New York: Crestwood House, 1973. A biography of Banks.

Spencer Weber Waller

See also Baseball; Baseball's exemption from antitrust laws; Campanella, Roy; DiMaggio, Joe; Robinson, Jackie.

Ernie Banks is considered by many to have been one of the greatest baseball players never to have played in a World Series. He spent his entire career with the Chicago Cubs, whose last appearance in the World Series (through 2004) was in 1945—eight seasons before he joined the team. (National Baseball Library, Cooperstown, New York)

■ Barbie dolls

Identification Doll in the form of an adult woman
Manufacturer Mattel
Date Debuted in February, 1959, at the International American Toy Fair in New York City

Barbie was the new American teenage doll. Unlike the traditional baby dolls of the time, she had an adult face and body and an enormous and fashionable wardrobe. An immediate commercial success in 1959, the Barbie doll evolved through later years and remained popular into the twenty-first century.

During the 1950's, Ruth and Elliot Handler operated a successful toy company called Mattel, which had been founded in 1945. Watching her daughter Barbara and her friends play make-believe with paper dolls inspired Ruth to push for the creation of an adult-bodied fashion doll. However, others at Mattel felt that such a doll would be too expensive to manufacture. On a trip to Europe, Handler discovered the German Bild Lilli doll, based on a cartoon character created by Reinhard Beuthien in 1952. Manufactured by the O. M. Hausser Company, Bild Lilli was either blonde or brunette, with an adult female body, high-heeled shoes molded on her feet, painted fingernails, and black earrings. Most of the Lilli dolls were twelve inches in height, but they also came in a seven-inch size. Handler presented the Lilli dolls to the Mattel design department, which began work on designing the Barbie doll, named after Ruth's daughter, Barbara. In 1957, Mattel set up the manufacture of the doll in Japan, where production costs were lower. Charlotte Johnson was hired to design the doll's costumes, which would resemble those worn by teenage and adult women.

In February, 1959, the first Barbie doll, in a black-and-white swimsuit, was presented at the American International Toy Fair in New York. About half the trade people there were skeptical about selling a small, eleven-and-a-half-inch fashion doll, which was so different from the popular baby dolls. However, when Barbie dolls became available in stores at a price of three dollars each in May, 1959, they were an immediate success with children and their parents.

This first Barbie was made of sturdy vinyl plastic, with a definite bust, narrow waist and hips, and joints at the neck, arms, and legs. Her slim legs could move but not bend. She wore curly bangs and a ponytail, and her skin was a pale, ivory tone. The first Barbie had high-arched eyebrows, painted eyes set in a sideways glance, and red pursed lips.

Impact As Ruth Handler had envisioned, her Barbie doll was a three-dimensional representation of paper dolls that encouraged young girls' imagination and fantasies. Like the paper dolls, Barbie had interchangeable clothing and realistic accessories that could be purchased separately. Barbie also symbolized the classic American teenager. From her debut in 1959 to the present, Barbie has been a top-selling toy. Each year brought improvements and innovations, such as ethnic and foreign Barbies, several series of dolls who were relatives and friends, clothing by world-famous designers, and Barbies in various occupations. The Barbie doll became an American icon, an integral part of popular culture, and a collector's item.

Daddy Dolls?

Before introducing Barbie—America's most celebrated plastic doll—to the public, Mattel public relations employees interviewed mothers and their young daughters to get their reactions to the new doll. Many women were horrified, some even disgusted, by the doll's sexy looks and clothing. Author M. G. Lord recounts the following exchange:

> MOTHER NO. 1: I object to that sexy costume. I wouldn't walk around the house like that. I don't like that influence on my little girl. . . . It's hard enough to raise a lady these days without undue moral pressures.
>
> MOTHER NO. 2: [My daughter] loves dolls with figures. I don't think I would buy this for that reason. It has too much of a figure. . . . I think that would be all she would observe.
>
> MOTHER NO. 1: I'd call them "daddy dolls"—they are so sexy. They could be a cute decoration for a man's bar.

Source: M. G. Lord, *Forever Barbie,* 1994.

Further Reading

Greenwood, Marie, et al. *Barbie: A Visual Guide to the Ultimate Fashion Doll.* London: Dorling Kindersley, 2000. A visual guide that tells the Barbie story with beautiful photographs of the dolls and outfits from 1959 until 2000.

Tosa, Marco. *Barbie: Four Decades of Fashion, Fantasy, and Fun.* New York: H. N. Abrams, 1998. A lavishly illustrated, comprehensive biography of Barbie. It is an informative history of Barbie's evolution through four decades and her transformation from doll to icon.

Westenhouser, Kitturah B. *The Story of Barbie Doll.* Paducah, Ky.: Collector Books, 1999. The chapter "Humble Beginnings" is an excellent, detailed account of the creation of the Barbie doll. Includes a bibliography and more than three hundred photographs and illustrations.

Alice Myers

See also Baby boomers; Fads.

■ Bardot, Brigitte

Identification French film actor
Born September 28, 1934; Paris, France

Brigitte Bardot personified sensuality and sexual freedom to repressed, straight-laced American movie audiences.

Encouraged by her mother to study dance as a child, Brigitte Bardot used her precocious beauty soon to build a modeling career, and at the age of fifteen, she posed for the cover of *Elle* magazine. The picture attracted the attention of director and producer Roger Vadim, who eventually married her and cast her in *And God Created Woman* in 1956, a film that created an international sensation. Although she had appeared in fifteen films previously, Bardot's semi-nude scenes and implied wild sexual episodes in this film made her an international sexual icon. Although the film was actually banned in France and lost money, it forever made the actor synonymous with sex, and she became known to the world simply as "Bardot," or "BB." Her combination of innocence and kittenish sexuality fascinated repressed American filmgoers of the 1950's.

Bardot continued making films throughout the 1960's, including Jean-Luc Goddard's *Con-*

Dubbed a "sex kitten" by the media, Brigitte Bardot projected a mixture of innocence and sensuality to 1950's films that helped prepare the way for the more frank treatments of sexuality in American films of the 1960's. (Hulton Archive | by Getty Images)

tempt (1963)—considered one of her best performances—*Dear Brigitte* (1965) starring Jimmy Stewart, in which she played herself, and *Viva María!* (1965), directed by Louis Malle. She also had a singing career, recording five albums during the 1960's. Never an accomplished actor, she did bring attention to the French cinema during the 1950's and 1960's. She retired from films in 1973 and subsequently devoted herself to the cause of animal rights.

Impact Bardot paved the way for a new sexual freedom and candor in American cinema, encouraged a growing acceptance of female sexuality, and was an early precursor of the sexual revolution of the 1960's and 1970's.

Further Reading

Beauvoir, Simone de. *Brigitte Bardot and the Lolita Syndrome.* New York: Reynal, 1960. A treatise on Bardot's sexuality.

Robinson, Jeffrey. *Bardot: An Intimate Portrait.* New York: D. I. Fine, 1994. This biography chronicles both her careers: film star and animal activist.

Mary Virginia Davis

See also Censorship; Film in the United States; *Playboy*; Sex and sex education; Women and the roots of the feminist movement.

■ Barkley, Alben W.

Identification U.S. senator from Kentucky and vice president of the United States from 1949 to 1953

Born November 24, 1877; Lowes, Kentucky

Died April 30, 1956; Lexington, Virginia

Alben W. Barkley was a veteran Democratic senator who served as Senate majority and minority leader during the Roosevelt and Truman administrations and vice president under Harry S. Truman; he was also a candidate for the Democratic presidential nomination in 1952.

Active in local Democratic politics in Kentucky, Alben W. Barkley was elected to the U.S. House of Representatives in 1912 and to the Senate in 1926. During the presidency of Franklin D. Roosevelt, Barkley was a supporter of the New Deal and Roosevelt's foreign and defense policies. Roosevelt regarded Barkley as an ideal liaison between the White House and the Senate and between the northern and southern wings of the Democratic Party within the Senate. Consequently, Roosevelt helped Barkley become Senate majority leader in 1937. Barkley continued to serve as Senate majority leader until the Republicans gained control of Congress in 1946, at which point he became Senate minority leader.

President Harry S. Truman chose Barkley as his running mate during the 1948 election. After his election as vice president and Truman's decision not to run for reelection in 1952, Barkley announced his presidential candidacy. He soon withdrew after he learned that labor leaders opposed his candidacy because of his age. Deciding to return to politics, Barkley was elected to the Senate from Kentucky in 1954. He died of a heart attack in 1956 while speaking to college students in Virginia.

Impact As a liberal senator and vice president from a border state, Barkley was a key figure in trying to resolve the growing party conflicts between northern and southern Democrats during the 1950's.

Alben W. Barkley (standing) with President Harry S. Truman. (AP/Wide World Photos)

Further Reading

Barkley, Alben W. *That Reminds Me*. New York: Doubleday, 1954. Barkley's own memoir.

Davis, Polly A. *Alben W. Barkley*. New York: Garland, 1979. Chronicles key events in Barkley's career.

Sean J. Savage

See also Elections in the United States, 1952; Nixon, Richard M.; Truman, Harry S.

■ Baseball

During the 1950's, Major League Baseball experienced several changes that would expand the popularity of the game, including the introduction of new team markets, the racial integration of teams, and television broadcasts of games.

The major leagues experienced several team relocations during the 1950's. In 1953, National League (NL) owners approved the relocation of the Braves from Boston to Milwaukee—the first NL franchise shift since 1900. As attendance records were set for the Milwaukee Braves as a result of their move from Boston, other owners began to entertain the idea of moving their own teams to more lucrative markets. On September 29, 1953, Bill Veeck sold his controlling interest in the St. Louis Browns for more than two million dollars. The new owners received approval to move the franchise to Baltimore for the 1954 season and changed the team's name to the Orioles. It was the first franchise shift in the American League (AL) since 1903, when the Baltimore Orioles moved to New York to become the Highlanders and later the Yankees. On November 4, 1954, the Philadelphia Athletics were sold for $604,000 and moved to Kansas City. The Dodgers and Giants were lured to the West Coast by economic incentives that included new stadium developments. In 1957, the Dodgers played their last game at Ebbets Field, which had been their home since 1913. A few days later, on September 29, 1957, the Giants played their last game at the Polo Grounds, which had been their home since 1889.

On July 27, 1959, William A. Shea, a New York attorney, announced the formation of the Continental League, which would consist of eight teams and would include a team in New York to fill the void left by the Giants and Dodgers. A year later, on August 2, 1960, Major League Baseball negotiated with Shea to disband the Continental League. As part of the agreement, four teams from the Continental League were added to the NL and AL during the early 1960's: the New York Mets, the Houston Colt 45s (later changed to the Astros), the Los Angeles Angels (later the California Angels and then the Anaheim Angels), and a new Washington Senators (replacing the Washington Senators team that moved to St. Paul-Minneapolis and became the Twins).

Racial Integration The integration of baseball commenced on April 15, 1947, when Jackie Robinson became the first black player in modern Major League Baseball. However, it took another twelve years before all major league teams broke the color line. The Boston Red Sox became the last team to integrate, when, on July 21, 1959, Elijah "Pumpsie" Green entered the game for the Red Sox as a pinch runner.

The 1950's saw the decline of the Negro Leagues as their young players were lured to the major leagues. Players such as Willie Mays, Henry Aaron, Ernie Banks, Sam Jethroe, Jim "Junior" Gilliam, and Joe Black, all of whom starred in the Negro Leagues, would make important playing contributions in the major leagues. They joined Negro League stars such as Jackie Robinson, Satchel Paige, Larry Doby, Monte Irvin, Roy Campanella, Minnie Minoso, Luke Easter, and Don Newcombe, all of whom had ventured into the majors during the late 1940's.

The Negro Leagues experienced a decline during the 1950's, largely as a result of the loss of players to the major leagues. In 1953, the Negro American League was reduced to four teams. In 1963, Kansas City hosted the thirtieth and last Negro League East-West All Star game, and the following year, the famed Kansas City Monarchs stopped touring the nation; the Monarchs had produced more than a dozen major league players. The impact of integration during the 1950's was notable as eight of the ten most-valuable-player (MVP) awards and six rookie of-the-year awards in the National League were won by players who began their careers with Negro League clubs.

However, the decline of segregation on the playing field did not end racial discrimination. Incidents in which African American ball players were not allowed to use facilities during spring training in the South still occurred. Several black ball players such as Jackie Robinson, Frank Robinson, and Luke Easter were frequently the league leaders in being hit by pitches. In cities such as St. Louis and Washington, D.C., black ballplayers could not stay in the same hotels as their white teammates. In addition, little progress was made during the 1950's in integration of administrative positions in baseball. It would be another two decades before baseball integrated management positions, when Frank Robinson, who began his playing career in 1956 with the Cincinnati Reds, would make his debut as the manager of the Cleveland Indians on April 8, 1975.

The Role of Television Television revenues rose significantly during the 1950's, from more than two million dollars in 1950 to twelve million dollars by 1960. Baseball's second commissioner, Happy Chandler, secured six million dollars for broadcast rights

to the next six World Series before stepping down in 1951. Individual teams gained additional revenue by signing television rights to local television companies. In early 1958, the New York Yankees sold the television rights to 140 games to WXIX-TV for more than one million dollars. As a result of television, minor league teams started a decline during the 1950's, going from fifty-nine leagues in 1951 to only nineteen leagues by 1964. Telecommunication technology improvements in subsequent decades played a significant role in elevating the value of many franchises.

Labor Disputes Throughout the history of baseball, there has been widespread player discontent over salaries and the reserve clause. The reserve clause was created on September 29, 1879; it permitted owners to limit competitive pay for players and to reserve the rights of five players on each team to be traded. As early as 1900, and again in 1912, players attempted to organize for reforms, only to be met with resistance from the team owners. Attempts to sue the leagues for monopoly practices eventually led to a Supreme Court ruling in 1922, in which baseball was considered to be a sport and not subject to the laws of interstate commerce.

In 1953, player discontent over salary negotiations came to a head when players organized the Major League Players Association. In summer, 1953, players hired an attorney to represent them in negotiations with owners. Commissioner Ford Frick informed the attorney that he was not welcome at any of the meetings of the owners. In late 1953, team representatives attended the first meeting of the Major League Baseball Players Association in Atlanta. The association was able to make modest concessions, which included a pension plan, a minimum salary, and pay for spring training. The ability of players to make any gains against the monopoly practices of baseball owners was stymied by a November 9, 1953, Supreme Court ruling, *Toolson v. New York Yankees*, which declared that baseball was a sport, not a business, and was not subject to the nation's antitrust laws. By a 7-2 vote, the Court found no cause to overturn the 1922 ruling that permitted baseball to utilize the reserve clause. It was not until the end of the 1960's when players finally achieved negotiation clout with the owners.

New York Dominance Teams from New York dominated baseball performances during the 1950's.

During the decade, fourteen of the twenty pennants and eight of the ten World Series were won by New York teams: The Yankees won eight pennants and six World Series, the Dodgers won four pennants and one World Series (an additional win in 1959 was as the Los Angeles Dodgers), and the Giants won two pennants and one World Series.

In 1951, three New York teams finished in first place. The Giants and Dodgers ended the regular season with identical records of 96 wins and 58 losses. A three-game playoff series was contested for the NL pennant. The first game was played on October 1 at Ebbets Field, which the Giants won; game two was won by the Dodgers. In game three, the Dodgers had a 4-1 lead going into the ninth inning. In the bottom of the ninth, the Giants scored one run and had two runners on base when Bobby Thomson came to bat. On a one-strike pitch, Thomson hit a home run, which became known as the "shot heard 'round the world." Many fans agree that the third playoff game in 1951 was the most memorable game of the 1950's, as well as in baseball history.

During the 1954 World Series, the New York Giants overshadowed the regular-season achievements of the Indians by defeating the Indians, four games to none. The Giants, managed by Leo Durocher—who, in 1947, was released by the Dodgers midseason and was immediately hired by the Giants—succeeded in winning two pennants and one World Series championship during the 1950's. In 1951, Durocher called up Willie Mays at the age of twenty from the minor leagues in mid-season. Mays joined a lineup that included Bobby Thomson and Monte Irvin and a pitching staff that had two twenty-game winners, Sal Maglie and Larry Jansen. The Giants lost to the Yankees four games to two during the 1951 World Series. Mays won the National League's most-valuable-player award in 1954 with a league-leading batting average of .345, 41 home runs, and 110 runs batted in. In 1955, Mays hit 51 home runs, the most of any hitter during the decade. Mays played for twenty-two years, retiring in 1973. His lifetime record included 660 home runs, 3,283 hits, 1,903 runs batted in, 2,062 runs, and a career batting average of .302. In 1979, Mays was inducted into the Hall of Fame.

In 1955, the Brooklyn Dodgers entered the World Series for the eighth time, having lost seven times. The Dodgers roster included four previous Negro League players: catcher Roy Campanella, who had won the league's MVP award in 1951, 1953, and 1955; infielders Jim "Junior" Gilliam, who had won the 1955 rookie-of-the-year award, and Jackie Robinson; and pitcher Don Newcombe, who won the NL MVP award in 1956. The Dodgers included hitters Duke Snider, who hit 42 home runs and a league-leading 136 runs batted in; Gil Hodges, who had 27 home runs; and Carl Furillo, who had a batting average of .314 with 26 home runs. The 1955 World Series was played in the full seven games, and the Dodgers prevailed four games to three. The following year, the Dodgers faced the Yankees again in the World Series. During game five, Yankee pitcher Don Larsen pitched a perfect game. The feat of pitching a perfect game in the World Series was not duplicated in subsequent decades. The Yankees won the championship in seven games.

On December 13, 1954, the Dodgers signed nineteen-year-old Sandy Koufax. On August 31, 1959, Koufax tied Bob Feller's 1938 major league single-game strikeout record of eighteen against the Giants in the Los Angeles Coliseum, the temporary home for the Dodgers until the construction of their new stadium was completed. In 1956, Don Drysdale became a member of the Dodger pitching staff. In 1959, Drysdale led the league in strikeouts with 242, the highest of any pitcher during the 1950's.

New York Star Players On October 12, 1948, the Yankees announced the hiring of Casey Stengel to replace Bucky Harris as manager. During his twelve-year tenure as manager of the Yankees, Stengel won ten pennants and seven world championships. On December 11, 1951, Joe DiMaggio announced his retirement after playing for the Yankees for thirteen years. To fill the void left by DiMaggio's retirement, Stengel cultivated a team of new Yankees stars. He turned to his young players, such as infielder Jerry Coleman, second-string catcher Yogi Berra, and Mickey Mantle. On April 17, 1951, Mantle made his major league debut playing right field against the Red Sox. Eventually Mantle would be moved to center field to replace DiMaggio. During the 1950's Berra and Mantle became the nucleus for Yankee hitting, while pitchers Vic Raschi, Allie Reynolds, Eddie Lopat, and Whitey Ford secured the pitching game for the Yankees.

During the 1950's, Yogi Berra was voted the most valuable player three times (1951, 1954, and 1955), while Mantle won the honor twice (1956 and 1957).

During a 1951 game, Bill Veeck, the owner of the St. Louis Browns, pulled off one of the most famous stunts in Major League Baseball history by having a three-foot-seven stunt man, Eddie Gaedel, sent to the plate as pinch hitter. After Gaedel walked on four straight pitches, he was replaced by a pinch runner, and his baseball career was over. (AP/Wide World Photos)

Mantle also won the home-run race three times, and in 1956, he became a "triple crown" winner with a batting average of .353, 52 home runs and 130 runs batted in. The World Series performances of Berra and Mantle remain in the record books: Berra appeared in seventy-five World Series games, the most of any player in history; he had 71 hits, 10 doubles, 12 home runs, and 39 runs batted in. Mantle appeared in sixty-five World Series games, second only to Berra; he was first in series home runs with 18 and first with runs batted in with 40.

Cleveland Indians Although New York teams dominated the 1950's, the Cleveland Indians achieved the best record of any team during the 1950's in 1954. The Indians finished the season with a record of 111 wins and 43 losses with a percentage of 721, setting a record for that time. The pitching staff consisted of three pitchers, each later elected to the Baseball Hall of Fame: Bob Feller, Bob Lemon, and

Early Wynn. Feller started his career with the Indians in 1936 and announced his retirement in early 1957. During his eighteen years with the Indians (he did not play between 1941 and 1944), he won 266 games and had 162 losses. He had 2,581 strikeouts, a statistic that led the league seven times; he was inducted into the Hall of Fame in 1962.

Bob Lemon started with the Indians in 1946 and retired after the 1958 season. He had 207 wins and 128 losses, with 1,277 strikeouts. During the 1950's, Lemon led or was tied for the league lead in wins three times. He was inducted into the Hall of Fame in 1976. Early Wynn played for the Indians from 1949 to 1957. In 1954, Wynn tied with Lemon for the league lead in wins with twenty-three; he was inducted into the Hall of Fame in 1972. In addition to pitching, the Indians had formidable hitters: Al Rosen, Larry Doby, and Rocky Colavito. In 1953, Rosen was the league's most valuable player, leading with 145 runs batted in and 43 home runs, and having a slugging average of .613. His batting average in 1953 was .336, barely missing the league's leading status by one point; James Vernon of the Senators led the league with an average of .337. Rosen missed winning the triple crown by two points in his batting average. Many baseball historians regard his 1953 hitting achievements as the best ever by a third baseman. Larry Doby, who was the first black ballplayer to integrate the American League, would lead the league in home runs in 1952 and 1954.

Milwaukee Braves In 1953, the Braves began the season in Milwaukee after playing in Boston for seventy-seven years. In 1954, the Braves set an attendance record with more than two million in their audience. The Braves had one of the most dominating pitchers of the decade: Warren Spahn began his career with the Braves in 1942. During the 1950's, he won twenty or more games eight times, led or tied the league's record five times and led or tied the league's record in strikeouts three times.

In addition to Spahn, the pitching staff included Lew Burdette, who was a two-time, twenty-game winner during the 1950's, and Bob Buhl. Henry Aaron and Eddie Matthews provided the hitting power for the Braves. Aaron joined the Braves in 1954. In 1957, Aaron was the league's MVP; he led the league in batting average in 1956 and 1959 and in home runs in 1957. Matthews led the league in home runs in 1953 and 1959. Aaron played with the Braves until 1976, retiring as the team's all-time home-run leader with a career 755 home runs. In 1957, the Braves beat the Yankees in the World Series, four games to three. In 1958, the Yankees beat the Braves in the World Series, four games to three.

Other Notable Players A number of players during the 1950's demonstrated their playing ability despite not playing on teams that participated in the World Series. Veteran players such as Stan Musial of the St. Louis Cardinals led the NL league in hitting in 1950, 1951, 1952, and 1957, and Ted Williams of the Red Sox led the American League in hitting in 1957 and 1958. In early 1958, Musial signed a $100,000 contract with the Cardinals, setting a league record for a one-year contract. On February 6, 1958, Williams became the highest-paid player in baseball when he signed a contract for $135,000 with the Red Sox.

The year 1954 saw a number of rookies who would later become Hall of Fame members: Ernie Banks, Roberto Clemente, Harmon Killebrew, Brooks Rob-

inson, and Sandy Koufax. In 1959, Willie McCovey joined the Giants, Bob Gibson recorded his first win with the Cardinals, and Billy Williams made his debut with the Cubs. On May 7, 1959, 93,103 fans assembled at the Los Angeles Coliseum to honor Roy Campanella, who had been paralyzed in an automobile accident prior to the Dodgers' moving to the West Coast. It was among the largest baseball crowds ever to have gathered.

Women's Baseball Women's prefessional baseball, which had begun during World War II to compensate for the loss of major league players to military service, continued into the 1950's for a few years and was marked by performances of many notable players. The All-American Girls Professional Baseball League was launched by Dodger president Branch Rickey and Cubs owner Phil Wrigley in 1943, but it folded after the 1954 season. In 1953, the Indianapolis Clowns of the Negro Leagues signed a woman, Toni Stone, to play second base for $12,000. On July 21, 1954, a Negro Leagues contest between the Kansas City Monarchs and the Indianapolis Clowns included three women players: Toni Stone (now playing for the Kansas City Monarchs), Mamie Johnson, and Connie Morgan of the Clowns.

Impact The events that occurred in baseball during the 1950's contributed significantly to shaping the game in subsequent decades. The relocation of baseball teams to new markets prompted baseball to consider further expansion during the 1960's. The complete integration of baseball teams demonstrated the quality of players from the Negro Leagues and would finally lead to integration of managerial positions during the 1970's. Finally, the creation of the Major League Baseball Players Association would eventually lead to the breakdown of the dreaded reserve clause.

Further Reading

Koppett, Larry. *Koppett's Concise History of Major League Baseball.* Rev. ed. New York: Caroll and Graf, 2004. Chronicles the long history of the game, from its beginnings in the nineteenth century to modern-day events and players.

Moffi, Larry, et al. *Crossing the Line: Black Major Leaguers, 1947-1959.* Iowa City: University of Iowa Press, 1996. Details the importance of the Negro Leagues for fueling the success of Major League Baseball.

Solomon, Burt. *The Baseball Timeline.* New York: DK Publishing, 2001. Gives a narrative of significant events that occurred in baseball during the 1950's.

Ward, Geoffrey C., and Ken Burns. *Baseball: An Illustrated History.* New York: Alfred A. Knopf, 1994. One chapter, titled "The Capital of Baseball," details the 1950's.

Alar Lipping

See also Banks, Ernie; Baseball's exemption from antitrust laws; Berra, Yogi; Campanella, Roy; DiMaggio, Joe; Dodgers and Giants relocation; Larsen's perfect game; Mantle, Mickey; Mays, Willie; New York Yankees; Robinson, Jackie; Snider, Duke; Stengel, Casey; Thomson, Bobby.

■ Baseball's exemption from antitrust laws

The Event Reaffirmation of U.S. Supreme Court decision that baseball was not interstate commerce

Date Exemption granted in 1922; reassessed between 1951 and 1953

As television and radio rights increased revenues for Major League Baseball teams, the game became subject to claims that it was indeed an interstate business and should be held accountable to laws governing such enterprises.

In *Federal Baseball Club of Baltimore, Inc. v. National League of Professional Baseball Clubs, et al.* (1922), the U.S. Supreme Court declared that baseball was merely a game rather than a business engaged in interstate commerce. Team owners and the commissioner used this advantage to prevent teams from relocating and to enforce the "reserve clause," which bound a player to one team until that team released or traded him. When minor league pitcher George Toolson rejected a demotion to a lower minor league team in 1951, the New York Yankees banned him from playing for any team. Toolson challenged Major League Baseball's reserve clause and its antitrust exemption. Baseball during the 1950's, Toolson's lawyers argued, was far different from what it was in 1922. The revenues from radio and television made baseball a business that fell within the conventional definition of interstate commerce.

Congress also threatened the owners. Representative Emanuel Celler of the House Judiciary Committee opened hearings in 1951 investigating monopolies in sports, specifically in baseball. The investigation focused on Major League Baseball's geographical limitations and why it had not expanded into prosperous West Coast markets.

In 1952, the Celler Committee report expressed concerns about the reserve clause and the lack of baseball expansion but recommended no antitrust legislation unless the Court reversed its 1922 decision. In *Toolson v. New York Yankees* (1953), the Supreme Court declined to overthrow the *Federal Baseball* decision. Instead the Court declared that if the antitrust exemption was unjust, federal legislation should address it.

Impact Major League Baseball was a prosperous business during the 1950's and a bedrock of American culture. Neither Congress nor the Supreme Court wished to subject this national institution to antitrust legislation. Between 1953 and 1957, owners allowed five franchises to relocate. Toolson, however, never pitched for the Yankees or any other major league team again.

Further Reading

Abrams, Roger I. *Legal Bases: Baseball and the Law.* Philadelphia: Temple University Press, 1998. Baseball's special place in law presented in layperson's terms.

White, G. Edward. *Creating the National Pastime: Baseball Transforms Itself, 1903-1953.* Princeton, N.J.: Princeton University Press, 1996. The rise of baseball as both big business and symbolic national pastime.

M. Philip Lucas

See also Baseball; Congress, U.S.; Dodgers and Giants relocation; Sports.

■ Basketball

During the 1950's, popularity of both college and professional basketball grew, thanks to changes in the game's rules, the rise of attention-getting dynasties, the introduction of athletic big men, and the end of racial segregation.

During the 1950's, the game of basketball centered on teams in the National Collegiate Athletic Association (NCAA) and the professional National Basketball Association (NBA). The latter began in 1946 as the Basketball Association of America and became the NBA later. Salaries in the NBA were modest during the 1940's and rose slowly during the 1950's. Average players earned about four thousand dollars per season. More experienced players earned between five and seven thousand dollars a year. Only a handful of players earned more than ten thousand dollars a season. Although professional salaries were slowly increasing, the numbers of spectators and revenue did not rise greatly. Most fans got information about basketball games from radio and newspapers. Television was still in its infancy, and NBA games were rarely televised. Some owners of NBA teams feared that television broadcasts would hurt attendance at games.

In 1953, the NBA negotiated its first television contract, but the college game remained more popular than the pro game. The only NBA game that could match attendance with top college games was the annual all-star game, which was first played on March 2, 1950, at Boston Garden.

Problems Within the NBA The NBA had problems with low attendance figures, slow games, limited publicity, and the integration of black and white players. The league was also plagued by a scandal when it had to ban referee Sol Levy from the league in 1953, after he was charged with taking bribes to change the outcomes of games several years earlier. In early 1954, rookie Jack Molinas admitted that he had bet on NBA games while playing for the Fort Wayne Zollner Pistons. He said that he bet small amounts on the Pistons to win games. The owner of the Pistons, Fred Zollner, suspended Molinas, and the league banned him for life.

Some people saw problems within the game itself. The professional game was a slow, bruising, body-contact affair. Before the shot-clock rule (see below) was introduced, the game was slow and saw frequent free throws as the result of fouls. Referees could also be physically threatened by fans, which could quickly become mobs. In fact, coaches and home-team players frequently incited the fans against the referees. Team owners often sat on the benches, alongside their teams, and joined in fracases.

Many owners wanted to develop a higher-speed game more like that of college basketball, with fewer trips to the foul line. Without a shot clock, there was no limit on how long a team could hold the ball. When a team got a lead, it would typically go into a stall, leaving the other team no choice but to foul to get the ball back. In one 1953 game, for example, between the Syracuse Nationals and Boston Celtics, the two teams combined for 128 free throws. In 1950, the Fort Wayne Pistons beat the Minneapolis Lakers by the score of 19 to 18, with both teams scoring a combined eight field goals and the rest of the points coming from free throws. By the 1953-1954 season, the owners were forced to make changes.

Bill Russell (with ball) was one of the new big men who helped to revolutionize basketball during the 1950's. (AP/Wide World Photos)

The Shot-Clock Rule Danny Biasone, the owner of the Syracuse Nationals, suggested that teams should be required to shoot the ball within a time limit. He calculated that each team had to make at least sixty shots in forty-eight minutes for a game to be exciting. That figure resulted in an average of one shot every twenty-four seconds. Other NBA owners and league commissioner Maurice Podoloff initially ignored Biasone's idea, but in 1954 they finally approved the twenty-four-second clock, which remained in use into the twenty-first century. During the 1980's, Podoloff maintained that Biasone's invention was the most important rule change in NBA history.

Another early 1950's change in the professional game was widening of the six-foot foul lane to twelve feet. This change helped open up the area under the basket after free throws, because players had to stand farther from the basket while free throws were being attempted.

Dynasties, Big Men, and Integration The 1950's was still an age of two-handed set shooters. However, jump shooters such as Paul Arizin, Jim Pollard, and Bob Pettit were paving the way toward a more vertical game in the future. Although players frequently dunked the ball during pregame warmups, they rarely did so in actual games. The introduction of the shot clock and widening of the foul lane encouraged a faster pace that began to attract more fans.

The 1950's also saw the emergence of dominant big men in the middle—the centers. The first significant big man of the era was six-foot-ten George Mikan of the Minneapolis Lakers. Mikan led the Lakers to league titles in 1949, 1950, 1952, 1953, and 1954. The Lakers were the first NBA dynasty, and when Mikan retired in 1954 at the age of thirty, that dynasty came to an end. He did return for a partial season in 1955-1956, but the spark that ignited him before was no longer there.

African American players began appearing on NBA rosters in 1950, following the lead of Major League Baseball, which had integrated three years earlier. Basketball was slower to integrate for several reasons. Most NBA franchises were not financially stable, and their owners feared that if they were to integrate their teams, they would lose white patronage. The Boston Celtics were the first team to draft an African American player, Chuck Cooper, a six-foot-five forward from Duquesne University. He was not the first African American player to appear in an NBA game, however. That honor belongs to Earl Lloyd of the Washington Capitols, who played on October 31, 1950. Cooper played in his first NBA game the following night. Once the doors of segregation were broken down, increasing numbers of African American players entered the league.

Another dominant team during the 1950's was the Boston Celtics, led by their coach and general manager Red Auerbach. Auerbach traded to get draft rights to a player who would become the heir to Mikan—the University of San Francisco's Bill Russell. Throughout the 1950's, most of basketball's greatest players were either prolific scorers or flashy ball-handlers, but Russell was unique because he was neither. In addition to leading the University of San Francisco to two NCAA titles during the mid-1950's and helping the United States win a gold medal in the 1956 Olympic Games, he revolutionized shot-blocking and rebounding. He was the first truly athletic big man in basketball and joined a well-established team that had such future Hall of Fame players as guards Bob Cousy and Bill Sharman. Russell led the Celtics to their first NBA championship during his first year in the league. He could defend, block, and rebound like no other player. The Celtics won eleven NBA titles over the next thirteen years and were arguably the greatest dynasty of any sport.

The Harlem Globetrotters Despite the improvements in the NBA, the most entertaining basketball was not being played by NBA teams but by Abe Saperstein's Harlem Globetrotters. For a long time, the Globetrotters had the best African American players in the world. Whenever they played NBA teams, attendance skyrocketed, and NBA owners did not want to challenge Saperstein's rights to the best black players. The Globetrotters began in Chicago in 1926 and during the 1950's remained as popular as ever. They toured Alaska in 1949 and traveled to Western Europe and North Africa in 1950. In 1951, they toured South and Central America. They were also asked by the U.S. government to tour Berlin to help improve relations with Germany after World War II. In 1952, the team performed in front of Pope Pius XII. In 1958, they added Wilt Chamberlain to their roster. A seven-foot-one center, Chamberlain left the University of Kansas a year early and was waiting to join the NBA, where he became the dominant big man of the 1960's and early 1970's. Even after entering the NBA, Chamberlain still toured with the Globetrotters during the summer months.

The College Game and Future Stars College basketball was widely popular during the 1950's. During the 1950-1951 college basketball season, the NCAA tournament expanded its field to sixteen teams. In that season, the University of Kentucky became the first school to capture a third NCAA title, under coach Adolph Rupp. However, during the spring of 1951, newspaper headlines told of an expanding gambling investigation involving a handful of college basketball squads. These were not merely any basketball teams; they were powerhouses of NCAA basketball, including City College of New York (the winner of both the National Invitational and NCAA tournaments in 1950), Long Island University, Manhattan College, Bradley University, University of Toledo, and University of Kentucky. Players on those teams were charged either with having connections with gamblers or with being asked to fix games by reducing their teams' margins of victory. By 1953, NCAA investigators had implicated six teams and thirty-three players. Several players then in the NBA were accused of fixing games when they played in college and were banned from the game. Other college players were barred from playing in the NBA.

As in the NBA, college basketball became racially integrated during the 1950's. However, this process developed more unevenly than in the professional league because of the different attitudes in various regions and schools. By the late 1950's, college basketball was producing many future NBA stars, such as Oscar Robertson, Elgin Baylor, Jerry West, and Wilt Chamberlain. However, none of these players' schools could stop Rupp's Kentucky Wildcats from capturing a fourth NCAA title in 1958.

Impact The 1950's witnessed an increase in the professional game's popularity because of dynamic dynasties, athletic big men, and new rules. Despite scandal, the college game increased in popularity and sent many future stars into the NBA. The Harlem Globetrotters became the ultimate ambassadors of the game, undertaking tours to South and Central America and Europe. Both professional and college basketball continued to develop a strong fan base in the decades to come.

Further Reading

Peterson, Peter. *Cages to Jumpshots: Pro Basketball's Early Years.* New York: Oxford University Press, 1990. This work provides information on the greatest players and coaches of the NBA, including team-by-team profiles.

Rosen, Charles. *Scandals of '51: How the Gamblers Almost Killed College Basketball.* New York: Holt, Rinehart and Winston, 1978. Examination of the college point-shaving scandal.

Shouler, Ken, et al., eds. *Total Basketball: The Ultimate Basketball Encyclopedia.* Toronto: SPORT Media Publishing, 2003. Excellent book that covers all aspects of NBA history. It includes essays from sports writers on teams, players, and coaches, and has statistics on every player and significant game in NBA history.

Strauss, Steven D. *The Complete Idiot's Guide to the NBA.* New York: Alpha Books, 2003. This book analyzes the history of basketball in the United States from 1891—when James Naismith invented the game—to the middle of the twentieth century.

David Treviño

See also Basketball point-shaving scandal; Chamberlain, Wilt; Cousy, Bob; Harlem Globetrotters.

■ Basketball point-shaving scandal

The Event Criminal activity involving point fixing by college basketball players
Date 1951

The point-shaving scandal of 1951 exposed an illegal component to the game of college basketball and resulted in the arrest and jail sentencing of several players.

By the 1950's, college basketball was emerging as a major sport attraction. College basketball games were drawing more than ten thousand fans per game, and more than sixteen thousand fans regularly filled New York City's Madison Square Garden, which had become the arena for college basketball programming. However, the game's appeal prompted a heightened interest in gambling on game results, and the number of illegal bookies increased steadily during this era.

During the early 1940's, gamblers began to use the point spread as a means to attract gambling on games. To achieve an advantage, gamblers tried to influence college basketball players to "fix" games to the advantage of gamblers. The point spread allowed basketball players not to lose a game necessarily but to make the game close enough in order to meet the point spread.

In January, 1951, Junius Kellogg, a Manhattan College basketball player, was offered $1,000 to fix a game with DePaul University. Hank Poppe, who was a co-captain of Manhattan College during the 1949-1950 season, made the offer. Kellogg reported the bribe offer to the authorities, and Poppe was arrested.

Arrests Increase Following the arrest of Poppe, District Attorney Frank Hogan of New York began further investigations into point shaving. On February 18, 1951, he announced the arrests of Ed Roman, Alvin Roth, and Ed Warner, players on the basketball team of City College of New York (CCNY). These players had been instrumental in helping CCNY win both major national basketball tournaments in 1950. Connie Schaff of New York University (NYU) and Eddie Gard, a former Long Island University (LIU) player, were also arrested. Gard was accused of being the middleman between players and Salvatorre Sallazzo, a New York jeweler and gambler. The CCNY players admitted to losing three games deliberately during the 1950-1951 season. Each player received $1,000 or more for each of the three games. Further arrests were made involving CCNY players. Floyd Layne admitted to accepting $3,000 to fix three games, while teammates Irwin Dambrot, Norm Mager, and Herb Cohen were also charged with fixing games during the 1949-1950 season.

After the arrests of the CCNY players, three players from LIU were arrested: Sherman White, Adolf Bigos, and Leroy Smith, all of whom confessed to receiving $18,500 to shave points in seven games during the 1949-1950 and 1950-1951 seasons.

The scandal was not isolated to teams located in the New York City area. It extended to players at the University of Toledo, where three players admitted to shaving points during the 1950 game against Niagara. At Bradley University in Peoria, Illinois, three players were found guilty of point shaving in 1949 during a National Invitational Tournament (NIT) game against Bowling Green at Madison Square Garden. At the University of Kentucky, Ralph Beard, Alex Groza, and Dale Barnstable were discovered to have thrown Kentucky's first-round NIT game against Loyola at Madison Square Garden in 1949. Evidence indicated that eleven of Kentucky's games were fixed during the 1948-1949 season.

In November of 1951, Judge Saul Streit began sentencing the first indicted players and gamblers, including the CCNY, NYU, and LIU players, along with Sallazzo and Gard. Players Warner, Roth, White, and Schaff received jail sentences. Gard re-

Manhattan College basketball player Junius Kellogg (center) being congratulated by Bronx district attorney George B. DeLuca for reporting the bribe that was offered to him. At Kellogg's side is his coach, Kenny Norton. (AP/Wide World Photos)

ceived a jail term of up to three years, and Sallazzo received a sentence of eight to sixteen years.

Impact The 1951 point-shaving scandal clearly identified the exploitation of college athletics. Many of the athletes who were arrested lost their opportunities to pursue a professional career in basketball: The National Basketball Association refused to draft any of the players who were arrested. In light of the scandal, it would seem that strict guidelines would have been implemented to avoid future gambling activities. However, this would not be the case, as a new scandal in college basketball surfaced in 1961.

Further Reading

Figone, Albert J. "Gambling and College Basketball: The Scandal of 1951." *Journal of Sport History* 16, no. 1 (1989): 44-61. Chronicles the events of the scandal as well as its impact.

Rosen, Charles. *Scandals of '51: How the Gamblers Almost Killed College Basketball.* New York: Holt, Rinehart and Winston, 1978. Details how the point-shaving scandal was accomplished and by whom.

Alar Lipping

See also Basketball; Sports; *Sports Illustrated*; West Point honor code scandal.

■ Beat generation

Definition Avant-garde literary community that rebelled against the social and political mores of the Cold War era

Forging the way for the counterculture of the 1960's, the Beat writers rejected middle-class values, advocated a bohemian lifestyle, and flouted literary convention to create a new age in American letters.

The term "Beat generation" was originally coined by Jack Kerouac during a conversation in 1948 with fellow writer John Clellon Holmes. The term encapsulated the feelings of disillusionment and alienation many young people were experiencing during the postwar years. During the early 1950's, "Beat" took on a different meaning as the members of the new literary movement fused their feelings of despair with a mythic quest for transcendence. The word "beat" became associated with the "beatific" quality of blessedness, whereby an individual experiences illumination after being "beaten" down to the point where he or she is psychologically desolate.

After the history-making flight of the Russian satellite *Sputnik* in 1957, the suffix "nik" was added to "beat" by *San Francisco Chronicle* columnist Herb Caen to describe a cultural phenomenon whose "far out" adherents wore black berets, sported goatees, smoked marijuana, banged on bongo drums, and used words such as "cool" and "crazy." The popular image of a beatnik was epitomized by Maynard G. Krebs, a character in the television program *The Many Loves of Dobie Gillis* (1959-1963). Although the beatnik fad faded during the early 1960's, Beat prose and poetry continued to have a significant impact on popular culture and eventually became recognized as a major development in modern American literature.

Beat Beginnings Jack Kerouac, Allen Ginsberg, and William Burroughs formed the nucleus of the Beat generation. Former Columbia University students, Ginsberg and Kerouac crossed paths in 1944 in New York City. Later the same year, they met Burroughs. For several months, Ginsberg, Kerouac, and Burroughs lived communally in the apartment of Joan Vollmer, who would become Burroughs's common-law wife and the mother of his son. The men formed a lifelong emotional and professional bond despite their very different backgrounds: Kerouac was raised in blue-collar Lowell, Massachusetts; Ginsberg, whose mother was schizophrenic, grew up in a leftist household in Paterson, New Jersey; and Harvard-educated Burroughs lived a privileged early life in St. Louis, Missouri.

Central to the relationship among Beat writers was a shared "New Vision." The term implied a dynamic, avant-garde worldview that ran counter to the conformist outlook of the 1950's. Although sometimes portrayed as anti-intellectual, these writers were well read in modern Western literature, including works by William Butler Yeats, W. H. Auden, Franz Kafka, James Joyce, and German philosopher Oswald Spengler. Spengler's dark view of the end of culture in *Decline of the West* (1918-1920) particularly fueled the New Vision and reinforced the idea that because the dominant culture was moribund, only art could deliver it from social and political corruption. The Beat writers continued to refine their New Vision until four characteristics emerged that would drive the movement's future: unfettered self-expression, sensory derangement as a means of perceiving truth, sexual experimentation, and the idea that art transcends conventional morality.

The alternative lifestyle of the Beat writers mirrored these characteristics of the New Vision. They believed that the use of drugs and alcohol would free them spiritually, psychologically, and artistically. By exploring homosexuality and bisexuality, they defied prevailing sexual norms of the day. In their writings, they experimented with open-verse forms, spontaneous composition, and vernacular language. Geographical boundaries were no more inhibiting to them than social conventions or literary traditions. After leaving Vollmer's apartment, the three men went their own ways. However, even when they were living in different parts of the country or the world, they remained close friends, acting as agents, editors, typists, readers, and promoters of one another's work.

Beat Literature Three men influenced the work and lives of Kerouac, Ginsberg, and Burroughs. Raised in flophouses and reform schools, Neal Cassady was the son of an alcoholic and an accomplished thief. A child prodigy, Carl Solomon was a communist, schizophrenic, and mental patient. Herbert Huncke ran away from home at the age of twelve and became a drifter, drug dealer, addict, and convict. Each man embodied the archetypal antihero, whom the Beat writers transformed into beatific literary icons.

Kerouac's semiautobiographical novel, *On the Road* (1957), is based on a 1948 cross-country trip he undertook with Cassady, who was the model for the story's main character, free-spirited Dean Moriarty. The picaresque novel chronicles the experiences of a group of aimless wanderers who drive and hitchhike across the United States, seeking spiritual enlightenment through fast living, sex, and drugs. At first, Kerouac was unsure how to structure the story. He repeatedly shelved the manuscript but went back to it whenever he corresponded with Cassady. Finally, in the spring of 1951, fueled by Benzedrine, he taped together sheets of paper, forming a scroll, and began a marathon writing session that lasted three weeks. This new method of composition—Kerouac called it "bop prosody" or "spontaneous prose"—was related to the automatic-writing practices of the Surrealists and was rooted in the rhythms of jazz.

Ginsberg's celebrated poem, "Howl," also reflected jazz influences and the works of poets Walt Whitman and William Carlos Williams, as well as Kerouac and the Old Testament. Prophetic in tone,

the poem consists of three parts. The first, which is reminiscent of Kerouac's *On the Road*, describes the community of artists, addicts, hustlers, psychotics, and sexual deviants of which Ginsberg was a part. He included references to Cassady, Huncke, and Burroughs, "the best minds of my generation," who were wounded by drugs, despair, and alienation.

The second part of Ginsberg's poem launches into a diatribe against Moloch, an Old Testament Canaanite god to whom children were sacrificed. Moloch represents the false values, spiritual and social bankruptcy, and technological menace of the 1950's that threatened to swallow America's youth whole. Carl Solomon, to whom the poem is dedicated, was named as one of the victims of Moloch. The third section addressed Solomon directly and included the refrain, "I am with you in Rockland," the mental hospital to which Solomon had been committed. The poet's identification with Solomon reflected his preoccupation with his mother's insanity, as well as his own bout with mental illness. Because of his use of vulgar images and words, Ginsberg believed the poem would never be published.

Huncke introduced Burroughs to the underworld of drug pushers and petty thieves, and Burroughs became a drug addict himself. His book, *Naked Lunch* (published in France in 1959 and the United States in 1962), reflected his experience with drugs and crime. The main character is addicted to opiates and is subsequently cured through apomorphine treatments. The novel consists of disjointed images and hallucinations, contains objectionable language, and portrays frankly the amoral existence of addicts, criminal, and sexual deviants. The somewhat incoherent structure of the book was due in part to the way it was composed. Burroughs worked on the manuscript while living in an apartment in Tangier, Morocco. When he finished typing a page, he would throw it on the floor and begin another. In 1957, he finally asked for help from his friends, and Ginsberg, his partner Peter Orlovsky, and Kerouac arrived in Tangier to help Burroughs organize his chaotic work. Like Ginsberg's "Howl," *Naked Lunch* was deemed pornographic and would not be published in the United States for another five years.

"Howl" In October, 1955, an event occurred that would bring the Beat generation international fame. Ginsberg performed "Howl" at a poetry reading organized by Kenneth Rexroth at the Six Gallery in San Francisco, which marked the beginning of the San Francisco Renaissance. Fellow poet and publisher of City Lights Books Lawrence Ferlinghetti was so impressed that he asked Ginsberg for the manuscript. Ferlinghetti published *Howl and Other Poems* in August, 1956, and he was arrested subsequently on obscenity charges in May, 1957, after selling the book to plainsclothes police officers. Amid the glare of the media, the case went to trial during the summer of 1957. Lawyers hired by the American Civil Liberties Union defended Ferlinghetti on the grounds that his freedom of speech had been violated. The judge agreed and, in a precedent-setting verdict, acquitted him.

Burroughs's *Naked Lunch* underwent a similar trial. In 1959, a nine-page excerpt was printed in *The Chicago Review*, the publishing arm of Chicago University. The piece was immediately denounced as "filth" and subsequent publication of excerpts was prohibited. Subsequently, the book was published in Europe by Olympia Press, a publisher of pornography. Finally in 1962, the novel appeared in the United States and was banned in Boston. The presiding judge ruled it obscene. The case was appealed to the Massachusetts Supreme Court in 1966, and the previous judgment was overturned. This landmark ruling ended literary censorship in the United States.

Fellow Travelers on the Road Although Kerouac, Ginsberg, and Burroughs are considered the pioneers of the Beat generation, other writers made significant contributions to Beat literature. During the early 1950's, while drinking in a bar in New York, ex-convict Gregory Corso shared some of his poems with Ginsberg, who became his mentor. Self-educated, Corso was well read in classic poetry, especially the works of Percy Bysshe Shelley. Corso's poetry was unpretentious, humorous, and anarchic. "Bomb," one of his best-known pieces, was written in the shape of a mushroom cloud and satirized the government's love of atomic weaponry.

Gary Snyder met Kerouac in San Francisco in the fall of 1955. Snyder was a student of Zen Buddhism, Asian languages, and Native American culture. At the time he and Kerouac met, he lived a simple, self-sufficient lifestyle based on his Buddhist beliefs. The main character in Kerouac's novel *The Dharma Bums* (1958) was modeled on Snyder. Snyder's poetry reflected his interest in Zen, pacifism, and environmental concerns and encouraged some Beat writers in their Buddhist faith, notably Kerouac and Ginsberg.

Philip Whalen was also a Zen Buddhist and was Snyder's roommate at Reed College in Portland, Oregon. He attended the Six Gallery reading at Snyder's invitation and was inspired to follow a career as a poet after hearing Ginsberg read "Howl." His work was characterized by humor, by a focus on the commonplace, and unlike Snyder's work, by its lack of political content. Whalen also appeared in Kerouac's *The Dharma Bums* as Warren Coughlin.

Michael McClure's literary career was launched at the October, 1955, Six Gallery event. When he was young, he wanted to become a naturalist, and his interest in the natural world, animal consciousness, and Zen Buddhism was reflected in his work. He appears as Pat McLear in Kerouac's *Big Sur* (1962) and went on to become a leader during the 1960's hippie movement.

Impact Because of the notoriety surrounding the Beats' work and lifestyles, their cultural and literary influence did not begin to be fully appreciated until the late 1960's and 1970's. The Beat generation revived the power of the spoken word through readings in coffeehouses and bookstores, which set the stage for the emergence of contemporary performance poetry. The Beats' unconventional writing style, infused with jazz rhythms, not only influenced the postwar youth culture but also shaped the work of subsequent generations of counterculture artists and musicians, from psychedelic hippies to punk rockers and hip-hop performers. For example, legendary blues singer Janis Joplin, Grateful Dead leader Jerry Garcia, and folksinger Bob Dylan were heirs of the Beat generation. One of Joplin's hits, "Lord, Won't You Buy Me a Mercedes Benz," was written by McClure. As members of author Ken Kesey's antiestablishment group the Merry Pranksters, Garcia and Cassady traveled across the country together. Dylan, regarded as a poet as well as a composer and performer, was a close friend of Ginsberg.

The philosophy of the Beats significantly influenced the social and political climate of the 1960's. Following their Buddhist beliefs, Ginsberg, Snyder, and McClure all protested against the Vietnam War. McClure and Snyder were also leaders in the ecology movement, which in turn spawned the formation of other socially conscious groups such as the Green parties of the 1970's and the antiglobalization movement of the 1990's. Ginsberg in particular became a major force within the Love Generation of the 1960's and championed a variety of causes. In addition to protesting against the Vietnam War, he spoke in favor of gay liberation, religious freedom, civil rights, legalization of marijuana, and the right to free expression. Many of these issues remain controversial and continue to spark public debate.

Further Reading

Campbell, James. *This Is the Beat Generation: New York, San Francisco, Paris.* Berkeley: University of California Press, 1999. An accessible introduction to the Beat generation, this book draws extensively on Beat literature, personal letters, and contemporary newspaper articles.

Warren, Holly George. *Rolling Stone Book of the Beats: The Beat Generation and American Culture.* New York: Hyperion, 2000. Essays, book reviews, memoirs, interviews, and photographs reveal the impact of the Beat generation on American culture.

Watson, Steven. *The Birth of the Beat Generation: Visionaries, Rebels, and Hipsters, 1944-1960.* New York: Pantheon Books, 1995. A well-organized over-

view that chronicles the rise to fame of Kerouac, Ginsberg, and Burroughs. Includes information on the San Francisco Renaissance and the Black Mountain poets.

Pegge Bochynski

See also Burroughs, William; Censorship; Conformity, culture of; Corso, Gregory; Ferlinghetti, Lawrence; Ginsberg, Allen; Kerouac, Jack; Literature in the United States; Poetry; Rexroth, Kenneth; San Francisco Renaissance; Youth culture and the generation gap.

■ Belafonte, Harry

Identification American singer of West Indian heritage
Born March 1, 1927; New York, New York

Harry Belafonte's distinctive voice and appealing style brought him wide recognition in the performing arts during the 1950's, and he balanced that successful career with social activism, winning numerous arts and humanitarian awards.

Singer Harry Belafonte (right), with bodybuilder Mickey Hargitay (left), actor Jayne Mansfield, and columnist Mike Connolly at Los Angeles's Cocoanut Grove night club, where Belafonte was performing in January, 1957. (AP/Wide World Photos)

Born in the Harlem neighborhood of New York City, Harry Belafonte moved with his Jamaican parents back to Jamaica when he was eight years old. He joined the U.S. Navy during World War II and later returned to New York and worked in the garment district. A production at the American Negro Theatre inspired him to turn his attention to acting. Subsidized by the G.I. Bill, Belafonte enrolled in Erwin Piscatory's famed Dramatic Workshop, where Marlon Brando and Walter Matthau also studied. Belafonte spent evenings at jazz clubs listening to Dizzy Gillespie and Miles Davis. While researching folk music in the early 1950's, he began to build a repertoire with songs from many cultures and genres, including West Indian music and jazz.

Belafonte starred in and produced several films during the 1950's. He also won Broadway's Tony Award in 1954 for *John Murray Anderson's Almanac*, completed numerous concert tours, enjoyed several television appearances, and was both the first performer with a million-seller album and the first black performer to win the Emmy Award.

A respected human rights activist, Belafonte was deeply involved in the Civil Rights movement. A financial supporter of close friend Martin Luther King, Jr., as early as 1956, Belafonte helped lead a youth march for integrated schools in 1958, supported voter-registration drives, and financed the 1961 Freedom Rides, which challenged segregation on interstate buses.

Impact In his concerts, Belafonte encouraged the audience to participate, and a whole generation learned to appreciate folksinging. More than fifty years after he introduced the phrase "Day-O" from his "Banana Boat Song," that familiar call still rings out at baseball games and the crowd responds, emblematic of the ongoing influence of Harry Belafonte. In 1985, Belafonte's song, "We Are the World," generated seventy million dollars to fight famine in Ethiopia. As goodwill ambassador for UNICEF, Belafonte also received the Distinguished American Award in 2002.

Further Reading

Belafonte, Harry. *Belafonte Sings*. New York: Duell, Sloan and Pearce, 1962. Music, lyrics, and commentary about Belafonte's famed songs, including "Banana Boat Song," "Jamaica Farewell," and "Mathilda."

Fogelson, Gina. *Harry Belafonte: Singer and Actor*. Los Angeles: Melrose Square, 1999. A succinct biography.

Gale M. Thompson

See also African Americans; Civil Rights movement; Film in the United States; King, Martin Luther, Jr.; Music.

■ Bellow, Saul

Identification Canadian American author
Born June 10, 1915; Lachine, Quebec, Canada

Saul Bellow created new narrative styles and moved the American Jewish novel to the forefront of mainstream American literature.

Saul Bellow was born in Quebec to Russian Jewish parents. When he was nine years old, his family moved to Chicago, where he absorbed the sights and sounds of his immigrant community, peopled by memorable characters who would later serve as raw material for his autobiographical novels. In 1944, Bellow published his first novel, *Dangling Man*, followed in 1947 by *The Victim*, and the literary establishment recognized him as a rising star.

Bellow's breakthrough came in 1953 with *The Adventures of Augie March*, which won the National Book Award. The first sentence announced the arrival of a new voice in American fiction, as the narrator proclaimed that he intended to tell his story wide-open and in his own freewheeling style. Augie depicts Chicago during the 1920's and 1930's and exuberantly relates his own struggle to find himself and to achieve success in an America that had been closed to people like him. Bellow's characters often are destined to lose in life's struggles but, like Augie, valiantly engage in an "underneath battle."

Bellow's 1956 novella *Seize the Day* follows Tommy Wilhelm through a few hours on the day that his life falls to pieces. His poor decisions leave his family shattered and his career wrecked, but, like many Bellow characters, he carries on even as his mistakes overwhelm him. He ends his day battered and humiliated but not quite crushed.

If Bellow's lead characters typically struggle against endless, often self-inflicted wounds, Eugene Henderson in *Henderson the Rain King* (1959) has a unique solution: He takes his blundering quest for spiritual fulfillment to Africa. Henderson is a self-destructive man who, when he makes a decision

Nobel laureate Saul Bellow. (©The Nobel Foundation)

about his life, knows that it inevitably will wreak havoc on him and everyone around him. During his stumbling, destructive path through Africa, the wise and self-possessed King Dahfu calms Henderson and helps him gain insight into his tormenting needs and insatiable wants. Henderson returns to the United States to prepare for his new mission in life, that of a physician-healer. *Henderson the Rain King* became a best-seller and brought Bellow new readers.

Impact Bellow became an outspoken critic of the cultural and political currents of his time, but he rejected despair and disappointment with one's present circumstances. His self-destructive characters always seem to pull something positive from the ruins they have made of their lives. To be disappointed by life is extremely shallow, Bellow seems to say. One may not be strong enough to live in the present, but

one should never be disappointed by it. In evaluating Bellow's sixty-year writing career, distinguished British author and literary critic Martin Amis ranked him as the supreme American novelist, surpassing Nathaniel Hawthorne, Herman Melville, Henry James, and William Faulkner.

Subsequent Events After the 1950's, Bellow went from success to success. In 1964, *Herzog* stayed on the best-seller list for forty-two weeks and won a National Book Award. In 1971, *Mr. Sammler's Planet* (1970) won him a third National Book Award. In 1976, *Humboldt's Gift* (1975) won a Pulitzer Prize, while Bellow's 1976 Nobel Prize in Literature secured his position in world literature.

Further Reading

Atlas, James. *Bellow: A Biography.* New York: Random House, 2000. A biography based on Bellow's letters and other important biographical material.

Miller, Ruth. *Saul Bellow: A Biography of the Imagination.* New York: St. Martin's Press, 1991. Written by a friend of Bellow, it has special insight into aspects of his thinking.

William E. Pemberton

See also Jewish Americans; Literature in the United States.

■ Bell's swim across Lake Ontario

The Event First person to swim across the width of Lake Ontario
Date September 8-9, 1954

An event that captured great public attention in Canada, Marilyn Bell's swimming achievement inspired women athletes and helped reduce public resistance to women competing in long-distance sports.

Prior to swimming across Lake Ontario, sixteen-year-old Marilyn Bell's prior swimming accomplishments included completing the 1954 Atlantic City Marathon as the first female finisher. She decided to swim Lake Ontario when the Canadian National Exhibition and *Toronto Telegram*, seeking publicity, promised Florence Chadwick, an accomplished American swimmer, ten thousand dollars to become the first person to swim thirty-two miles across that lake. The *Toronto Daily Star* sponsored Bell during an intense rivalry with the *Toronto Telegram*.

An hour before midnight on September 8, Bell and her competitors began their swims at Youngstown, New York. Conditions were miserable, but Bell persevered. Waves and currents pulled her off course, adding about eight miles to her swim. Chadwick swam fifteen miles before quitting. Although her legs were numb, Bell determinedly pulled herself through the cool water. Bell came ashore in Toronto approximately twenty-one hours later. The news media praised Bell's accomplishment in special editions, transforming her into a Canadian national hero.

Impact Bell's swim publicly proved that female athletes were capable of participating in sustained activities that require strength and endurance. At the time Bell conquered Lake Ontario, most women were denied the right to compete in sporting competitions involving distances. Many people thought such sports were harmful to women. Despite Bell's athletic accomplishments, women could not run in Olympic marathons until thirty years after her Lake Ontario swim. Canada's Sports and Swimming Halls of Fame inducted Bell, acknowledging her superb athleticism.

Further Reading

McAllister, Ron. *Swim to Glory: The Story of Marilyn Bell and the Lakeshore Swimming Club.* Toronto: McClelland & Stewart, 1954. This contemporary account discusses Bell's athleticism and her work with handicapped swimmers.

Morrow, Don, et al. *A Concise History of Sport in Canada.* Toronto: Oxford University Press, 1989. A comprehensive survey that comments on Bell's contribution to advancing women's sports.

Elizabeth D. Schafer

See also Newspapers in Canada; Sports; Women and the roots of the feminist movement.

◾ *Ben-Hur*

Identification Epic film set in biblical times
Director William Wyler (1902-1981)
Date Premiered on November 18, 1959

Based on Lew Wallace's 1880 novel of the same title, Ben-Hur *is the story of a Palestinian Jew defying the Roman Empire. It is remembered as one of the grandest historical films of the 1950's, featuring an epic-scale sea battle and a chariot race.*

The plot of *Ben-Hur,* which was directed by William Wyler, concerns the relationship of a Jewish man, Judah Ben-Hur (played by Charlton Heston), and a Roman man, Messala (Stephen Boyd). The pair grew up together as friends but went their separate ways in adult life. As adults, Messala, a Roman officer, has a bitter quarrel with Ben-Hur, who opposes the Roman occupation of Judea. Ben-Hur and Messala subsequently part and swear mutual enmity. The vindictive Messala later allows Ben-Hur to be unjustly convicted of treason.

As the story proceeds, Ben-Hur serves a term as a galley slave aboard a Roman ship and displays great valor by saving the admiral (Jack Hawkins) when the ship is attacked by the enemy. As a result, he is released from his servitude, is adopted by

The famous chariot race scene in Ben-Hur. *Judah Ben-Hur (Charlton Heston) is driving the team of white horses at the right.* (AP/Wide World Photos)

the admiral, and becomes a champion charioteer. After he returns to Palestine, he competes in a chariot race in which Messala is his principal adversary. As the race progresses, Messala's recklessness causes his chariot to crash, and he is mortally injured. Later Ben-Hur happens upon Christ carrying his cross to Calvary to be crucified; Ben-Hur maintains a vigil at the foot of the cross as Christ dies.

Ben-Hur realizes that Christ prayed for his persecutors before he died; Christ's example in forgiving his enemies inspires Ben-Hur to relinquish his hatred of Messala for the wrongs that Messala had done him. In the end, Ben-Hur emerges as a heroic figure who has risen above his sufferings and learned to forgive the injustices done to him.

Impact Known as an intimate epic (a film that does not lose sight of its characters amid its large-scale production) and noteworthy for its wide-screen cinematography and 217-minute length, *Ben-Hur* won an unprecedented eleven Academy Awards in 1959, making it one of the most honored films of all time. *Ben-Hur* was also one of the biggest critical and popular film triumphs of the 1950's.

Further Reading

Herman, Jan. *A Talent for Trouble: The Life of Hollywood's Most Acclaimed Director, William Wyler.* New York: Da Capo, 1997. A solid, well-researched survey of Wyler's entire career, containing interesting production information on *Ben-Hur.*

Heston, Charlton. *In the Arena: An Autobiography.* New York: Simon & Schuster, 1997. Includes a personal, lively account of the arduous demands that Wyler made on his actors, with special reference to Heston's work with Wyler on *Ben-Hur.*

Gene D. Phillips

See also Academy Awards; Film in the United States; Wide-screen movies.

■ *Bennington* explosion

The Event Deadly explosion on the U.S. fleet carrier USS *Bennington* during a cruise

Date May 26, 1954

Place Seventy-five miles off Rhode Island's Narragansett Bay

The explosion on the U.S. naval vessel was a peacetime tragedy that garnered media attention for the deaths of crew members and for the heroism that ensued in rescue efforts.

Named after a Revolutionary War battle that took place in Vermont in 1777, the USS *Bennington* was an Essex class aircraft placed into service in 1944. After serving in the Pacific campaign during World War II, the carrier was recommissioned during the early 1950's and commanded by Captain William F. Raborn, Jr. From May, 1953, to May, 1954, the ship operated along the eastern seaboard and also made cruises to Halifax, Nova Scotia, and the Mediterranean region.

On May 26, 1954, a series of explosions rocked the ship between 6:15 and 6:30 A.M.; 103 crewmen were killed and 201 were injured. Rescue operations began with four helicopters evacuating seriously injured men, but the ship managed to reach shore under its own power at Quonset Point, Rhode Island. The *Bennington* then moved to the New York Naval Shipyard for repairs, and the carrier was completely rebuilt by March, 1955. On April 22, Secretary of the Navy Charles S. Thomas boarded the ship to award letters of commendation and medals to 178 members of the crew for heroism. The carrier continued to serve with the Atlantic Fleet until the fall of that year, when it began making cruises in the Far East.

Impact Newspaper reporters described the tragedy as one of the worst peacetime disasters in U.S. naval history. A court of inquiry was later convened to investigate the cause of the explosions. It was determined that the fluid in one of its port catapults, a device for launching airplanes from the deck, ruptured, setting off fires and secondary explosions.

Further Reading

Callahan, M. Catherine. "*Bennington* Crew Remembers Mates Lost in Explosion." *Newport Daily News,* January 5, 2004. Article that commemorates the fiftieth anniversary of the naval disaster.

Fenton, John H. "Catapult Linked to Carrier Blast." *New York Times,* May 30, 1954. Two officers from the *Bennington* testified in a naval court of inquiry that they smelled hydraulic oil coming from the port catapult shortly before the explosions.

Muschett, James O., et al., eds. *U.S. Navy: A Complete History.* Westport, Conn.: Levin, Hugh Lauter Associates, 2003. Chronicles key events in the U.S. Navy's history.

Gayla Koerting

See also *Andrea Doria* sinking; Cold War; Grand Canyon airliner collision; Korean War; *Nautilus,* USS.

■ Berle, Milton

Identification American comedian and songwriter
Born July 12, 1908; New York City
Died March 27, 2002; Beverly Hills, California

Known as "Mr. Television," Milton Berle was the first entertainer to become a television star, drawing millions of viewers to the new medium.

Born Mendel Berlinger, Milton Berle was a child actor in silent films and vaudeville. During the 1930's and 1940's, he performed music and comedy in nightclubs and on radio. In 1948, he began hosting radio's *Texaco Star Theater*; the program became a weekly television series on NBC later the same year. *Texaco Star Theater* was reminiscent of vaudeville, featuring variety acts but also showcasing Berle's slapstick humor and outrageous costumes. The program proved so popular, businesses closed on Tuesday nights so people could watch "Uncle Miltie." Berle became known as "Mr. Television" and in 1950, won an Emmy Award for "most outstanding kinescoped personality."

In 1953, *Texaco Star Theater* became the *Buick-Berle Show*. Faced with slipping ratings, the program traded its fast-paced zaniness for a more structured format, featuring Berle as a recurring character. Buick ended its sponsorship in 1955; the program continued as *The Milton Berle Show*.

Impact *Texaco Star Theater* was television's first hit show, and Berle was the medium's first big star. His popularity drove television sales until the number of American families owning television sets had nearly quadrupled. Berle's success proved that television entertainment (and advertising) could attract millions.

Further Reading

Berle, Milton, with Haskel Frankel. *Milton Berle: An Autobiography.* New York: Applause Theatre Books, 2002. Berle's no-holds-barred account of his professional progress from vaudeville to television and his tumultuous personal life.

Wilde, Larry. *Great Comedians Talk About Comedy.* Mechanicsburg, Pa.: Executive Books, 2000. Includes an interview with Berle covering different types of comedians and the mechanics of comedy performance.

Maureen J. Puffer-Rothenberg

See also Gobel, George; *Honeymooners, The*; Martin and Lewis; Marx, Groucho; Nielsen ratings; Radio; Television in the United States.

Jack Benny (left), Laurence Harvey, Milton Berle (as Cleopatra), Kirk Douglas, and Charlton Heston in a skit set in ancient Rome on the Milton Berle Show. *The show aired during the late 1950's, after Douglas had starred in the film* Spartacus *and Heston had starred in* Ben-Hur—*both of which were set in ancient Rome. (Hulton Archive | by Getty Images)*

■ Bernstein, Leonard

Identification American composer and conductor
Born August 25, 1918; Lawrence, Massachusetts
Died October 14, 1990; New York, New York

The first American-born and American-educated conductor of a major symphony orchestra, Leonard Bernstein also wrote both serious and theater music, combining traditional techniques with popular elements in a highly individualized style.

After graduating from Harvard and the Curtis Institute, Leonard Bernstein studied with Russian conductor Serge Koussevitzky. In 1943, he earned acclaim and prominence by substituting on short notice for an ailing conductor at Carnegie Hall, a performance that was broadcast on national radio. Since Bernstein had also written music for Broadway productions and the concert stage, he was torn between conducting and composing.

In 1953, Bernstein's musical *Wonderful Town* opened on Broadway, and he was the first American to conduct at the famed La Scala opera house in Milan, Italy. In 1954, Bernstein composed the highly regarded score for the film *On the Waterfront.* That same year, when he presented the first of several lectures for the television program *Omnibus,* his work brought music appreciation into millions of homes. In 1956, his operetta *Candide* debuted, which, after several revisions, continued for several decades to be produced. Its overture is one of Bernstein's most popular concert pieces. In 1957, the groundbreaking musical *West Side Story* opened. Although the play was considered his masterpiece and brought him fame for his compositions, Bernstein regretted being recognized as a composer for Broadway rather than for opera. When Bernstein became music director of the New York Philharmonic in 1958, his televised "Young People's Concerts" created an opportunity for millions of people to experience symphonic music.

Impact One of the most important musical figures of his century, Bernstein influenced musical life worldwide for almost five decades. He conducted more than one thousand concerts and made some four hundred recordings. His stage music ranks with the best, and he saw the advantages of television and used it effectively as an educational medium.

Further Reading

Burton, Humphrey. *Leonard Bernstein.* New York: Doubleday, 1994. Provides a chronology and lists of Bernstein's compositions and publications.

Secrest, Meryle. *Leonard Bernstein: A Life.* New York: Alfred A. Knopf, 1994. A biography based on anecdotes from associates.

JoAnne M. Rogers

See also Broadway musicals; *On the Waterfront; Peter Pan;* Theater in the United States; *West Side Story.*

■ Berra, Yogi

Identification American baseball player
Born May 12, 1925; St. Louis, Missouri

An all-star catcher, Yogi Berra anchored the New York Yankees, the team that dominated baseball during the 1950's.

Lawrence Peter "Yogi" Berra joined the New York Yankees in 1946, and by 1950 he was a star player on the greatest dynasty in baseball history. Berra was a

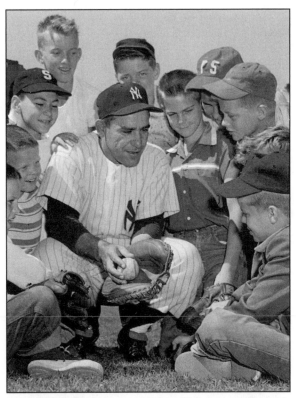

Yogi Berra gives pointers on catching to Little League players during the Yankees' 1957 spring training period in Florida. (AP/ Wide World Photos)

hard-hitting, good fielding catcher, who was considered by manager Casey Stengel as the most valuable member of a team loaded with star players. Berra's American League hitting accomplishments during the 1950's were extraordinary: seven times in the top ten in slugging percentage, total bases, and extra base hits; eight times in the top ten in home runs and runs batted in. In that decade, Berra was selected as an all star every year, and he finished in the top four in most-valuable-player voting seven times, winning in 1951, 1954, and 1955. He also played in eight World Series during the 1950's, compiling a .271 batting average, with nine home runs and twenty-five runs batted in.

Impact Berra holds important World Series records for most games, at bats, hits, and doubles, and his lifetime 358 home runs was a record for catchers at that time. He was elected to the Baseball Hall of Fame in 1972. He also gained tremendous popularity because of his likable personality and humorous malapropisms such as "Ninety percent of this game is half mental." Berra's advertisements for the drink "Yoo-hoo" skyrocketed its sales and boosted Berra's celebrity status. That status reached legendary proportions in 1958 when a new cartoon character, Yogi Bear, was named after the Yankee icon.

Further Reading

Berra, Yogi. *Ten Rings: My Championship Seasons.* New York: William Morrow, 2003. Berra details his life and accomplishments.

_____. *When You Come to a Fork in the Road, Take It! Inspiration and Wisdom from One of Baseball's Greatest Heroes.* New York: Hyperion Press, 2001. Witticisms, inspiring anecdotes, and simple yet profound advice about living abound in this delightful book.

Paul J. Chara, Jr.

See also Banks, Ernie; Baseball; DiMaggio, Joe; Larsen's perfect game; Mantle, Mickey; New York Yankees; Stengel, Casey.

■ Berry, Chuck

Identification African American guitarist and singer
Born October 18, 1926; St. Louis, Missouri

The African American performer Chuck Berry was one of the earliest breakthrough rock-and-roll artists and played an incalculable role in shaping the genre and influencing subsequent acts.

Charles Edward Anderson Berry took up guitar playing at the age of fourteen. He moved to Chicago in late 1954, where he introduced himself to blues legend Muddy Waters. Waters helped Berry persuade Leonard Chess of Chess Records to record a single. Although he was a fan of the blues, Berry's first single, "Maybellene" (1955), was an interpretation of a hillbilly song titled "Ida Red." The song was arguably the first rock-and-roll hit single. Berry's guitar playing technique was reminiscent of the blues stylist Lightnin' Hopkins, and like Elvis Presley, Berry's live performances were legendary, if only because he exhibited a sexuality that appealed to young people and shocked their elders. He toured endlessly,

Chuck Berry performing during the mid-1950's. (Hulton Archive | by Getty Images)

spending months at a time on the road. He released a string of hits beginning in 1955, including "Sweet Little Sixteen," "Roll Over Beethoven," "Brown Eyed Handsome Man," and the rock classic "Johnny B. Goode." In addition to touring and recording, Berry appeared in four films during the decade.

Impact Berry's musical influence is immeasurable, and he is credited with inventing rock and roll. His musical style inspired musicians in bands such as the Beatles, the Jimi Hendrix Experience, the Rolling Stones, and the Grateful Dead. His songs have been performed by dozens of other performers and are part of the standard rock repertoire.

Further Reading

Berry, Chuck. *The Autobiography*. New York: Harmony Books, 1987. Berry's account of his life and contributions to music.

Peg, Bruce. *Brown-Eyed Handsome Man—The Life and Hard Times of Chuck Berry: An Unauthorized Biography*. New York: Routledge, 2002. Uses public records and numerous interviews to chronicle Berry's life.

Ron Jacobs

See also *American Bandstand*; Diddley, Bo; Freed, Alan; Lewis, Jerry Lee; Little Richard; Music; Presley, Elvis; Rock and roll; Youth culture and the generation gap.

■ **Betty Crocker cookbooks**

Identification Series of popular cookbooks published by a food company
Publisher General Mills
Date First published in 1950

Betty Crocker's Picture Cookbook *provided many housewives of the 1950's with advice and instruction for cooking and housekeeping and reinforced domestic ideals of the era.*

In 1921, the Lashburn Crosby Company, a flour producer, began using the pen name Betty Crocker to sign replies to mailed requests for cooking advice. "Betty" was chosen as a common woman's name, and "Crocker" was chosen in memory of the late secretary and director of the company, William G. Crocker. In 1928, the Lashburn Crosby Company merged with numerous other flour producers to form the General Mills corporation. In 1936, artist Neysa McMein created the first portrait of Betty Crocker.

In 1950, General Mills published the first edition of *Betty Crocker's Picture Cookbook* in both hardbound and three-ring binder formats (to allow readers, assumed to be women, to add recipes from magazine advertisements). *Betty Crocker's Picture Cookbook* became a best-seller and was designed to make the preparation and serving of food easy, creative, and fun, while encouraging the use of General Mills products wherever possible. It was designed to be a comprehensive source of information on all aspects of food and cooking, from the most basic of cooking information to advice on how a homemaker should plan her daily routine.

Impact Since the 1950's, more than two hundred Betty Crocker cookbooks have been published. The 1950's found many housewives having the responsibility of cooking and caring for a nuclear family but without the ready advice and instruction available within an extended family. Betty Crocker became the resource to which housewives could turn from, and when they did, the recipes, cooking techniques, and ingredients were often different than those handed down by previous generations. Betty Crocker's advice was extended when she became a television personality during this era. During the early 1950's, Adelaide Hawley began portraying Betty Crocker in advertising and on programs titled *The Betty Crocker Show* and *The Betty Crocker Star Matinee.*

Further Reading

Lovegren, Sylvia. *Fashionable Food*. New York: John Wiley, 1995. Traces the changes and trends in foods, including those emerging during the 1950's.

Manchester, Alden C. *The Food Marketing Revolution, 1950-1990*. Washington, D.C.: USDA Economic Research Service, 1991. Chronicles the rise of convenience foods marketing.

Robert E. Haag

See also Advertising; Fast-food restaurants; Home appliances; McDonald's restaurants; Tupperware; TV dinners; Women and the roots of the feminist movement.

■ **Birth control**

Definition Ability of parents to choose, in an effective manner, the number and timing of their children's births

Combined with the discovery of "the pill," medical advancements, and changes in social mores, the 1950's witnessed growing awareness and usage of birth control and concomitant changes in policies regarding its use in the United States and Canada.

Birth control was available and used in some forms prior to the 1950's; from ancient times, people were aware of herbs, shields, and pessaries. By the late 1830's, a cervical cap and rubber condoms became available. By the 1950's in the United States and Canada, rhythm and barrier methods had been available for some time. Society in general, however, was neither familiar with nor disposed to use these methods. Since the passage of the federal Comstock Law in 1873, labeling birth control information as an "obscenity" and forbidding its dissemination through interstate commerce or the U.S. mail, citizens tended to feel it was wrong and generally were lacking in education about it. Some states had laws against contraception, churches were far from countenancing birth control, and medical personnel evinced little ease in recommending it.

By the Anglican Lambeth Conference in 1930, which allowed limited use of birth control at the discretion of couples, the United States was warming to the idea of birth control for medical or therapeutic purposes. During the 1930's, the American Medical Association recognized birth control as a legitimate aspect of medical practice. Subsequently, a combination of events elicited a change of mind in the American public: birth control advocate Margaret Sanger's scrapes with the government, the isolation of estrogen and progesterone, the discovery of the rhythm method, the Crane decision, the passage of the Nineteenth Amendment to the U.S. Constitution, and concerns about world population. Although thirty states still had laws against contraception on their books by 1950, the following decade witnessed major breakthroughs in preventing and planning pregnancies.

In fact, the 1950's capped a century of negative attitudes toward birth control and witnessed a social upheaval, emblematic in the development of the pill, or Enovid. From the mid-nineteenth century through the mid-twentieth century, the growing push toward women's rights, slowly changing attitudes toward sexuality, and medical technology eventuated in a politics of reproduction and an eventual movement of churches and government out of the bedrooms of the citizenry. In the words of President Dwight D. Eisenhower, with respect to regulating birth control, it was "not a proper political or government activity or function or responsibility"; in short, it was "not our business."

The rise of television expanded media outreach as a herald of scientific discoveries and afforded the social body greater access to political discussion. In the postwar climate, as women symbolized by "Rosie the Riveter" were sent home from the experience of doing "men's work" during World War II, they forged a new sense of control over their lives. Slowly, discussions about sexuality began to be carried on above a whisper, aided by the relatively new discipline of psychology, which found itself attached to medicine rather than philosophy.

The Pill By 1951, when Planned Parenthood of America—an outgrowth of Margaret Sanger's first birth control clinic—operated two hundred birth control clinics, and the American public had become more comfortable with the thought of contraception, the use of educational pamphlets and lectures began to increase, and work on using hormones as a birth control method was under way after a small grant was given to researcher Gregory Pincus by Planned Parenthood. By mid-decade, Pincus and John Rock of Massachusetts had found a way to create an oral birth control pill. In a paper delivered at the Laurentian Conference on Endocrinology in Canada, Rock put forth his work that showed how progesterone inhibits ovulation.

Eventually, the drug company G. D. Searle's formulation of the birth control pill, called Enovid, was submitted for the approval of the Food and Drug Administration (FDA). Given state laws against birth control, Rock and Pincus could not conduct the large-scale studies necessary for FDA approval in the United States. Rather, they arranged for the first large-scale clinical trails to be held in Puerto Rico.

By October 29, 1959, G. D. Searle had filed an application to the FDA to license Enovid, with its stated purpose being for alleviation of menstrual problems, and on May 9, 1960, the FDA approved it to be used only under a doctor's prescription. By August 18, 1960, the first commercialized oral contraceptive was available in Skokie, Illinois.

Impact By late 1959, more than 500,000 women in the United States were taking Enovid, presumably for its "off-label" purpose of preventing conception. After the decade's discoveries concerning the hor-

Birth Control Time Line

1950	From the late 1940's into the early 1950's, an estimated 200,000-1,300,000 illegal abortions are performed annually in the United States, where public information on family planning is virtually nonexistent.
1951	Dr. Gregory Pincus shows that injections of progesterone suppress ovulation in laboratory animals, and the G. D. Searle Company undertakes research to develop a contraceptive pill or injection.
1952	The International Planned Parenthood Federation is launched at a conference in India.
1953	For the twentieth successive year, Connecticut's state senate debates retention of a law against contraceptive use by women, both married and unmarried.
	Publication of Alfred Kinsey's report *Sexual Behavior in the Human Female*, based on interviews with 8,000 women, reveals that 22 percent of married women have had abortions and that 90 percent of pregnancies outside marriage end in abortion.
1954	Volunteers participate in the first human experimental trials of oral contraceptives at the Worcester Foundation for Experimental Biology in Massachusetts.
1955	Lucille Ball's character on her TV show *I Love Lucy* gives birth to Little Ricky. In an unprecedented move in television history, Ball continued to make the show throughout her own, real-life pregnancy and let her pregnancy show on the screen, proving that mothers could remain career women.
1956	Margaret Sanger, as the first woman to address the Japanese Diet, urges that nation's citizens to practice birth control.
1957	An award-winning series of articles in the *New York Post* documents the existence of an unwritten ban on contraceptive counseling in New York City's public hospitals, sustained by the influence of the Roman Catholic Church.
1958	The city commissioner of hospitals in New York orders an obstetrician at King's County General Hospital not to fit a diaphragm for a Protestant, diabetic mother of three. The hospital policy banning birth control counseling, based on the influence of one religious group, is widely and publicly condemned. A new policy is instituted recognizing contraceptive measures as proper medical practice, though this was condemned by the local Catholic archdiocese as immoral. In the years following, women's right to use contraception had to be tried and won in other cities throughout the United States.
1959	The G. D. Searle Company files its application with the U.S. Food and Drug Administration for a license to sell "the pill" as a contraceptive.
	The American Medical Association sanctions birth control, which had by then been available for years.
	A presidential commission on foreign aid recommends giving family planning assistance to foreign governments that request it. President Dwight D. Eisenhower dismisses the suggestion after Catholic bishops denounce it.
	The American Law Institute recommends that states allow licensed physicians to carry out abortions under limited circumstances. Opposition to reform of abortion laws begins to gather momentum under the leadership of the Catholic Church.

monal implications of pregnancy avoidance, the development of Enovid, and the changed mindsets in the United States and Canada, the question of birth control became entirely reframed.

Further Reading

Kaledin, Eugenia. *Daily Life in the United States, 1940-1959: Shifting Worlds*. Westport, Conn.: Greenwood Press, 2000.

McFarlane, Deborah, and Kenneth Meier. *The Politics of Fertility Control: Family Planning and Abortion Policies in the United States*. New York: Seven Bridges Press, 2001.

McLaren, Angus, and Arlene T. McLaren. *The Bedroom and the State*. Toronto: McLelland and Stewart, 1986.

Watkins, Elizabeth S. *On the Pill: A Social History of Contraceptives, 1950-1970*. Baltimore: Johns Hopkins University Press, 1998.

Frances R. Belmonte

See also Demographics of Canada; Demographics of the United States; Medicine; *Second Sex, The*; Sex and sex education; Women and the roots of the feminist movement.

tions offered by a lonely and seductive fellow teacher. The students fight every effort he makes to connect with them until he screens a cartoon to win over hearts and minds. A violent, last-ditch effort by an unredeemable, racist thug (Vic Morrow) to take back control of his peers forces a confrontation, which Dadier wins with the help of a charismatic, African American student (Sidney Poitier). The upbeat ending does not completely relieve the mood of youthful alienation and rebellion that pervades the film.

Impact With its "Rock Around the Clock" opening song, a strong cast of veteran and upcoming actors, and gritty script and direction, *Blackboard Jungle* shook complacent suburbanites with its harsh look at the lives of students and teachers in an embattled urban vocational school.

Further Reading

Considine, David M. *The Cinema of Adolescence*. Jefferson, N.C.: McFarland, 1985. Thematically arranged study with extensive discussion of the film.

Doherty, Thomas. *Teenagers and Teenpics: The Juvenilization of American Movies During the 1950's*. Rev.

■ *Blackboard Jungle*

Identification Film about the threat of gang disorder in inner-city American high schools

Director Richard Brooks (1912-1992)

Date Released in 1955

Blackboard Jungle *was a controversial movie that capitalized on the fascination of the public with juvenile delinquency, troubled schools, and the rise of rock-and-roll music.*

The plot of *Blackboard Jungle* follows the struggles of idealistic, first-year English teacher, Richard Dadier (played by Glenn Ford), in a rough, underfunded vocational high school. Among the obstacles Dadier faces are unmotivated and disruptive students; a run-down, noisy school building; bitter, cynical colleagues; and the tempta-

Glenn Ford (left) as the harassed inner-city high school teacher confronts one of his students, played by Sidney Poitier. In 1967, Poitier reversed his role by playing a conscientious teacher in a rough East London school in To Sir, with Love. *(Museum of Modern Art, Film Stills Archive)*

ed. Philadelphia: Temple University Press, 2002. Accessible and thorough look at teenagers and films during the 1950's.

Roger J. Stilling

See also Dance, popular; Education in the United States; Film in the United States; Haley, Bill; Poitier, Sidney; *Rebel Without a Cause*; Rock and roll; *Rock Around the Clock*; Youth culture and the generation gap.

■ Boeing 707

Identification First American jet-propelled transport and passenger plane to go into commercial service
Date Entered service in 1954

The Boeing 707 set new standards for aviation travel, efficiency, and safety while carrying record numbers of passengers.

The age of commercial jet transportation officially began in May, 1952, with the deployment of Great Britain's De Havilland Comet airliner. Two years later, the Americans followed up with Boeing's revolutionary model 367-80, more commonly known as the 707, which performed its maiden flight on July 15, 1954. The 707 was an ultra-modern, swept-wing aircraft with features adapted from the famous Boeing B-47 Stratojet bomber. Foremost among these features was the positioning of four jet engines in pods below the wings to minimize metal fatigue. Sleek and powerful, the new 707 prototype set several aerial speed and range records for jet aircraft while the British Comet was beset by inexplicable crashes. Within months, Boeing received large orders from Pan American and American Airlines as the United States pioneered the jet transportation revolution. The 707 helped establish America's dominance of commercial jet manufacture.

Impact The Boeing 707 established new aviation standards for passenger travel in terms of range, safety, reliability, and ease of maintenance. The com-

pany received orders from airlines around the world and ultimately more than one thousand of the planes were built and sold. The commercial fleet of 707s was gradually phased out by newer designs commencing in 1970, but it remains the backbone of cargo air fleets around the world.

Further Reading

Francillon, René J. *Boeing 707: Pioneer Jetliner.* Osceola, Wis.: MBI, 1999. Fully illustrated history by an aviation authority.

Winchester, Jim. *Boeing 707/720.* Shrewsbury, England: Airlife, 2002. A unique British perspective on the American aircraft.

John C. Fredriksen

See also Aircraft design and development; Avro Arrow; B-52 bomber; Federal Aviation Administration; Grand Canyon airliner collision; Military-industrial complex; United States Air Force Academy.

Profile of the Boeing 707

Length: 144.5 feet
Wingspan: 130.83 feet
Gross weight: 257,000 pounds
Power source: four 12,500-pound turbojet engines that provided a cruising speed of 571 miles per hour
Payload: 124 to 179 passengers
Range: 3,075 miles
Service: The prototype of the 707 made its inaugural flight on December 20, 1957.

(AP/Wide World Photos)

■ *Bolling v. Sharpe*

Identification U.S. Supreme Court decision on school segregation in Washington, D.C.
Date May 17, 1954

Together with its companion case, Brown v. Board of Education, *this Supreme Court decision overturned the doctrine of "separate but equal" that allowed school segregation by race.*

In 1950, a group of parents attempted to enroll eleven African American students in a new high school in the District of Columbia. The school's refusal to admit them led to the 1954 ruling that the Court's decision in *Brown v. Board of Education* (1954), which prohibited school segregation by state and local governments, applied to the District of Columbia as well. In *Brown,* the Court relied on the Fourteenth Amendment's equal protection clause to prohibit school segregation by state and local governments. It then stated in *Bolling v. Sharpe* that the same prohibition applied to the federal government through the Fifth Amendment's due process clause. Although the Court stated that the two clauses were not interchangeable, it did hold that "discrimination may be so unjustifiable as to be violative of" the Fifth Amendment due process clause, and therefore, there is also an equal protection component of the due process clause.

Impact This decision made clear that equal protection of the laws applies not only to local and state governments but also to the federal government. Thus, the fifty-year-old "separate but equal" doctrine emanating from *Plessy v. Ferguson* (1896) and used as a basis for segregation was eliminated.

Further Reading

Berman, Daniel M. *It Is So Ordered: The Supreme Court Rules on School Segregation.* New York: Norton, 1966. Short but complete analysis of the three major cases leading to public school desegregation. It includes actual text of the decisions as appendices.
Henig, Jeffrey R. "Patterns of School-Level Racial Change in D.C. in the Wake of *Brown*: Perceptual Legacies of Desegregation." *PS: Political Science and Politics* 30, no. 3 (1997): 448-453. Scholarly but readable discussion of changes in school enrollment in the District of Columbia, including interesting graphs and tables.
Klarman, Michael J. *From Jim Crow to Civil Rights: The Supreme Court and the Struggle for Racial Equality.* New York: Oxford University Press, 2003. Traces the key legal developments in the struggle for civil rights.

Lisa M. Sardinia

See also African Americans; *Brown v. Board of Education*; Civil Rights movement; Education in the United States; Little Rock school desegregation crisis; National Association for the Advancement of Colored People; Racial discrimination; School desegregation; Supreme Court decisions, U.S.; Warren, Earl.

■ Bomb shelters

Definition Structures built to protect people during atomic attacks

The discussion about and construction of bomb shelters directly represented the American public's constant fear of a nuclear holocaust during the Cold War.

Before the invention of atomic bombs, military targets consisted primarily of military bases, factories, and bridges; after atomic bombs, military targets became civilians. When the Soviet Union built its first atomic bomb in 1949 and its first hydrogen bomb in 1953, Americans (who in 1945 had been first to build and use the bomb) became potential targets for nuclear war.

Civilians, accustomed to military protection during war, looked to the government for answers. In order to protect Americans, a massive, government-sponsored sheltering program was recommended. However, the numerous large shelters required to hold all Americans were expected to cost between twenty and thirty billion dollars. During the early 1950's, the Eisenhower administration considered these costs too high and advocated for a much cheaper policy—evacuation. Though a few people built bomb shelters themselves during the early 1950's, they received little advice on proper construction and tended to focus their efforts on shelters that would offer protection from bombs such as those that devastated Hiroshima and Nagasaki, Japan, at the end of World War II.

A Shift in Government Policy In 1955, the U.S. government released the surprising results of the 1954 hydrogen bomb test, dropped on Bikini Atoll. The explosion was more than one thousand times larger than the Hiroshima bomb, and the radioactive fallout spread much farther than expected. The government began to realize that evacuation would not work.

Because government-sponsored shelter programs were too expensive, officials realized it was going to be each family's responsibility to protect itself. Many families, however, seriously contemplated whether or not they wanted to survive a nuclear attack only to live in the hostile and dreadful world depicted in the apocalyptic books and films that were ubiquitous during this decade.

Those who wanted bomb shelters had to decide what types of shelters to build. A family could fortify a basement, construct something new, or buy a prefabricated shelter. They also had to decide what size shelter would accommodate their family and what they would do if an unprepared neighbor demanded refuge during an atomic attack. Shelters needed to be prestocked with food and supplies, but they also needed to have bathroom facilities, radiation detectors, and enough uncontaminated air for several weeks. Tight seals along doors and thick walls were essential. With all of these requirements, shelters could quickly become expensive.

Picture on the face of an early 1950's educational toy designed to teach children about taking shelter in the event of an atomic bomb attack. (Library of Congress)

Impact Bomb shelters offered civilians a proactive response to the fear of an atomic attack and inspired numerous debates about the ethics of atomic warfare. Though the threat of a nuclear holocaust remained constant, few families had built a shelter by the end of the decade. Most families still expected the government to establish a plan to save them during a nuclear war.

Subsequent Events On July 25, 1961, President John F. Kennedy made a speech concerning the Soviet threat to the German city of Berlin in which he advocated that every family should prepare itself for an imminent Soviet nuclear attack. This speech sparked a popular demand for bomb shelter information along with copious questions regarding the effectiveness of bomb shelters.

Further Reading

Dowling, John, and Evans M. Harrell, eds. *Civil Defense: A Choice of Disasters.* New York: American Institute of Physics, 1987. A scientific view of the effects of nuclear weapons and the physical attributes bomb shelters needed in order to withstand an attack.

Kerr, Thomas J. *Civil Defense in the U.S.: Bandaid for a Holocaust?* Boulder, Colo.: Westview Press, 1983. A chronological analysis of the civil defense policies within the United States, especially regarding shelters.

Rose, Kenneth. *One Nation Underground: The Fallout Shelter in American Culture.* New York: New York University Press, 2001. Examination of the concept of bomb shelters during the Cold War period.

Jennifer E. Rosenberg

See also Atomic bomb; Civil defense programs; Cold War; Disarmament movement; Fads; Hersey, John; Hydrogen bomb; *On the Beach*; Pauling, Linus.

■ Book publishing

The return of soldiers after World War II produced a new generation of readers in the United States, while new technologies and marketing strategies gave publishers opportunities to produce books for a wider audience than had ever existed. Through the selection and distribution of both popular titles and textbooks, book publishers shaped Americans' attitudes on topics ranging from appreciation of the arts to understanding complex political, social, and religious issues.

In the years following World War II, publishers found themselves doubly blessed. First, many soldiers had become avid readers, having devoured paperbacks issued by the armed forces to help them while away idle hours. Millions had entered college under the G.I. Bill and became eager book purchasers. Second, the paper shortage created by government rationing that had hampered book production during the war ended. Cheap paper allowed publishers to take greater risks on larger "lists"—their annual collections of new titles. As a result, annual production of trade books, which had averaged 7,800 during the war years, increased by 1950 to 11,000.

Even in these favorable times for the industry, however, leadership frequently made the difference between strong growth and lackluster performance. The record for Macmillan Company, the largest publisher before World War II, proves this point. Though the firm issued a number of distinguished titles, a trend toward stagnation was reversed only by Bruce Brett's appointment as chief executive officer in 1958. Moreover, Bennett Cerf, who built Random House into a flourishing firm before the war, became a national celebrity during the 1950's. He may be the only publisher in American history whose charm and wit have been witnessed by millions of Americans, as he was a regular panelist on one of America's earliest hit quiz shows, *What's My Line?*

Sales Strategies For a brief period at the beginning of the decade, some publishers, especially those publishing Left-leaning authors, came under the scrutiny of communist hunter Senator Joseph McCarthy. These investigations took a toll: Sloan & Company, unable to sustain the attacks, went out of business, while Little, Brown suffered for a time as well. The industry as a whole, however, rebounded quickly from this temporary setback. Publishers actually had more to do with limiting the range of titles than did McCarthy. Advertising and marketing expenses drove overhead to twice its prewar level. Producing a best-seller became imperative to justify costs and provide a return to the business. Hence, there was a growing tendency for firms to issue fewer books and focus on promoting them heavily. Booksellers, too, became caught up in the phenomenon. Heavy federal taxes on inventory made it increasingly difficult for small, independent bookshops to stock anything but best-sellers and reference works, which were certain to attract buyers and keep inventories modest. During the 1950's, the number of retail outlets specifically devoted to selling books decreased.

Publishers found other venues to replace retail outlets. One important accommodation used increasingly by major publishers was an alliance with the book club industry. Once seen as a threat, the various clubs became a lucrative marketing outlet. Publishers and editors at major houses frequently worked hand in hand with their counterparts at the clubs to coordinate introduction of new titles. Publishers also found a new source of revenue in the Reader's Digest Condensed Book series; executives at Reader's Digest bought rights to both new and previously published works. Finally, the prediction that the glut of new novels and plays would lead to a reduction in the modest amounts paid for movie rights did not materialize. Instead, those sums increased markedly; for example, the rights to *Peyton*

Place, Grace Metalious's 1956 account of New England sexual liaisons, brought $265,000. During the 1950's, money could be made in many ways from a best-seller.

Whereas publishers during the first half of the twentieth century had often operated on a business model analogous to the specialty boutique, during the 1950's, the major houses became more like department stores, producing trade, text, and specialty books to diversify revenue streams and hedge against bad decisions by individual acquisitions editors. The role of diversification in producing healthy bottom lines can be seen in the activities of McGraw-Hill. That firm, always a leader in trade books, established a line of scientific and technical publications that captured a large market share.

The textbook departments of major publishing houses proved to be sound fiscal investments as well. At Harcourt Brace Jovanovich, for example, the elementary and high school division accounted for more than 60 percent of net sales in 1959 and the college department for another 20 percent. Houghton Mifflin, for years a leader in trade book sales, also increased its textbook sales during the decade. Firms that specialized in textbook publishing, such as Ginn & Company and Scott Foresman, saw sales increase consistently. E. P. Dutton remained strong by making a wise decision to overhaul and reissue its Everyman's Library texts. Works in this series were a staple for both libraries and college classrooms.

Paperback Revolution The 1950's can justifiably be called the decade of the paperback revolution. Established publishing houses found themselves competing with dozens of start-up companies, who developed a lucrative formula for mass market publishing. While paperbacks had been in existence since the eighteenth century, the birth of the modern paperback industry can be traced to 1939, when Robert de Graff established Pocket Books. Intended for sale in drug and department stores and other places where people purchased sundries, paperbacks soon began selling by the millions. New players such as Avon and Ballantine Books entered the publishing arena during the 1950's, as executives from established houses branched out to take advantage of new marketing opportunities. Deals began to be negotiated for simultaneous publication of new titles in hardcover and paper.

Early mass-market paperbacks tended to focus on genres such as mystery, science fiction, and Westerns. Millions purchased works by writers such as Erle Stanley Gardner, Mickey Spillane, Louis L'Amour, and Arthur C. Clarke. However, the increased reliance on mass marketing as a means of diversifying a publisher's income stream led in many instances to a homogenization of both fiction and nonfiction. Quite a number of new titles in fiction actually followed a formula that could be counted on to generate sales: strong story lines and simplistic characterization. Many mass-market paperbacks had heavy sexual content inside titillating covers. Publishers helped readers select books by dyeing the edges in specific colors coded to subject matter. These books were produced inexpensively and distributed through wholesalers, further reducing costs. The long-established policy that allowed bookstore owners to return unsold hardbacks was modified for the paperback trade. Frequently retailers were instructed to tear off and return covers to receive credit for unsold merchandise—and toss out the books.

The paperback revolution was not limited to mass-market offerings. A number of publishers initiated new lines known as trade paperbacks: high-quality, paperbound versions of works previously issued in hardcover or new titles initially printed as a paperback. Doubleday's Anchor Press and Knopf's Vintage Books made the work of scholars and established authors available to a wider-than-ever readership. Some mass-market publishers found a successful formula in combining high literary quality with contemporary marketing and distribution techniques. The New American Library, Mentor Books, Signet, and others issued classics of British, American, and world literature and history, while firms such as Basic Books were established to promote the social sciences. Rinehart was one of several firms that specialized in paperback texts for classroom use.

Start-ups, Mergers, and Acquisitions Not only did established publishing houses flourish during the decade; the climate was also good for start-ups in the industry. In 1950, immigrant Frederick Praeger established Praeger Press, a successful trade and reference firm that survived for nearly three decades before being assimilated into a larger house. Another key publishing enterprise, begun in 1952, was St. Martin's Press, which became known quickly for its high-quality reference books. The firm would branch out in succeeding decades to rival some of the new, larger houses formed by mergers and acquisitions. Another start-up that would have significant influence on the industry in later years was Time-Life Books. Originally a by-product of Time, Inc.'s magazine business, the firm grew gradually to become a giant in the picture-book and "how-to" fields.

Book publishing during the 1950's was transformed into a corporate industry. Smaller firms joined forces to maximize efficiencies in editorial work and production. The 1960 merger of three successful firms into Holt, Reinhart, Winston created a company whose previous years' individual company sales totaled more than forty million dollars. Somewhat ironically, however, the most newsworthy "merger" occurred in 1957, when key executives from Harper & Bros., Random House, and Knopf joined forces to establish Atheneum Press, a firm expressly established to rival the trade giants. The success of Atheneum was assured in 1961 when Theodore H. White's *The Making of the President* appeared under its imprint. This account of the rise of John F. Kennedy sold 150,000 copies in hardcover and more than one million copies in paper.

A second trend commonplace during the 1950's was the acquisition of family-owned firms by business conglomerates, many of which had never been involved in book production. In fact, many bought publishing houses principally as a means of diversifying the assets of the parent company, and quality often was sacrificed to high-volume sales. Editors and publishers began to select works for publication solely on a book's potential to attract wide readership, giving further impetus to the trend toward homogenization of content. Writers of truly experimental poetry and prose and those with highly controversial theories of history, science, or psychology found it increasingly difficult to have their works accepted by the industry giants. The result was a proliferation of small presses and the growth of academic presses, which were less dependent on large sales. Companies such as Grove Press, established in 1949 and bought in 1952 by iconoclast Barney Rosset, published reprints and new works that were considered too controversial for mainstream publishers.

Impact The introduction of mass marketing techniques, coupled with the trends toward merging publishing houses into fewer and fewer firms with ever greater resources, shaped both editorial policy and reading habits for decades to come. The acquisition of publishing houses by conglomerates whose principal business was not book production further shaped the industry, as fewer publishers were willing to take risks that might jeopardize profit margins not only for the publishing house but for the parent company as well. The establishment of paperback books as a staple of the trade houses and college textbook suppliers had a major influence in widening reading audiences for all forms of published work. Not until the introduction of print-on-demand books during the 1990's would the publishing industry see major changes that rivaled those that took place during the 1950's.

The economic impact of these developments was significant as well. From 1950 through 1959, increases of 8-20 percent annually in hardcover sales were the norm. During this time, the average price of a novel rose by approximately 25 percent, while high-quality nonfiction such as biographies and histories rose in excess of 20 percent. A Gallup poll conducted in 1959 revealed that more than 20 percent of Americans had read at least one book within a month of the survey date. In that year, the mainstream publishing industry reported annual sales of $1.2 billion. Clearly, people were willing to pay the price for a commodity they believed added value to their lives.

Further Reading

Bonn, Thomas L. *Heavy Traffic and High Culture.* Carbondale: Southern Illinois University Press, 1989. Examines the influence of New American Library, a mass-market publisher.

_____. *Under Cover: An Illustrated History of American Mass Market Paperbacks.* New York: Penguin, 1982. Analyzes the success factors of paperbacks, which dominated publishing beginning during the 1950's.

Davis, Kenneth C. *Two-Bit Culture: The Paperbacking of America.* Boston: Houghton Mifflin, 1984. Examines the impact of paperback books on shaping American ideas and culture.

Madison, Charles A. *Book Publishing in America.* New York: McGraw-Hill, 1966. A detailed, contemporary examination of individual publishing houses and summaries of major trends in the industry.

Tebbel, John. *The Great Change, 1940-1980.* Vol. 4 in *A History of Book Publishing in the United States.* New York: Bowker, 1981. Explores general trends after

World War II, highlighting changes at major publishing houses.

Laurence W. Mazzeno

See also Advertising; Censorship; Comic books; Great Books movement; Literature in Canada; Literature in the United States; Poetry; Pulp magazines.

■ Boone, Pat

Identification American pop singer
Born June 1, 1934; Jacksonville, Florida

With his signature white buck shoes, Pat Boone personified the clean-cut, all-American teenager, becoming the "anti-Elvis" to Americans apprehensive about rebellious adolescents.

Charles Eugene "Pat" Boone grew up in Tennessee and began performing at the age of ten, appearing on popular shows such as *Arthur Godfrey's Talent Scouts* and the *Ted Mack Amateur Hour* during the early 1950's. Boone signed with Dot Records and began recording smooth, bland versions of rhythm-and-blues hits. This formula of making "race music" more palatable for white audiences worked well for him: He had hits with Fats Domino's "Ain't That a Shame," Little Richard's "Tutti Frutti" and "Long Tall Sally," and Ivory Joe Hunter's "I Almost Lost My Mind."

Boone's career reached its peak in 1957, when he recorded the hit ballads "Love Letters in the Sand" and "April Love," hosted his own television variety show, and starred in the hit films *Bernadine* and *April Love*. Boone also authored several advice books for teenagers, including the popular *'Twixt Twelve and Twenty* (1958). Boone's career began to slip during the 1960's, and his contract with Dot Records ended in 1966. His later career was in Christian and country music; he recorded several albums with his wife and daughters as the Boone Family Singers.

Impact Boone's wholesome image allowed him to introduce African American rhythm-and-blues music to white, middle-class America. Although his versions of these songs were bland and watered-down, many Americans got their first taste of rhythm and blues from his early hits.

Further Reading

Davis, Paul, Cliff Richard, and George Hamilton IV. *Pat Boone: The Authorized Biography*. Grand Rapids, Mich.: Zondervan, 2002. Authorized biography by Christian music journalists.

Rock and Roll Generation: Teen Life in the 1950's. Alexandria, Va.: Time-Life Books, 1998. Lavishly illustrated survey of popular music that focuses primarily on white youth.

Mary Virginia Davis

See also Domino, Fats; Little Richard; Music; Presley, Elvis; Rock and roll.

Actors Shirley Jones and Pat Boone relaxing at a Lexington, Kentucky, amusement park, where they made the film April Love *in 1957. (AP/Wide World Photos)*

■ Bowden, Don

Identification American track and field athlete
Born August 8, 1936; San Jose, California

Dan Bowden was the first American to run a mile in less than four minutes.

Don Bowden was a high school track star in California when British runner Roger Bannister ran the world's first mile in under four minutes in 1954. Only three years later, on June 1, 1957, Bowden clocked a 3:57:8 mile to become the first American to break the four-minute barrier.

Bowden reached his maturity as a runner during the golden age of the mile. As a prep star at Lincoln High School in San Jose, California, he specialized in the 880-yard run. He won the state championship in that event in 1953 and 1954 and held the national high school record until 1957. At the University of California at Berkeley, he set college records while training under Brutus Hamilton, the coach of the 1952 U.S. Olympic team. During his freshman year, he set a National College Athletic Association (NCAA) record for the freshman mile. In 1957, he won the NCAA title in the 880, and in 1958, he anchored the university's world-record-setting 4x800 relay team. Bowden also ran the 1,500 meters at the 1956 Olympic Games in Melbourne, Australia.

Unlike Bannister's sub-four-minute-mile race, which was well promoted and paced by two runners, Bowden broke the four-minute barrier while running at a small track meet at the College of the Pacific with few spectators and no pacers. Bowden finished the third lap at close to three minutes flat, and using his half-mile speed, he clocked a sub-one-minute final lap. Bowden's time was the third-fastest mile up to that point. A severed Achilles tendon ended Bowden's track career in 1960.

Impact Once a nationally recognized figure in track and field, Bowden and his record-setting performance set the stage for later American runners such as Jim Ryun and Bill Rodgers, who set world records during the 1960's and 1970's.

Further Reading

Denison, Jim. *Bannister and Beyond: The Mystique of the Four-Minute Mile.* Halcottsville, N.Y.: Breakaway Books, 2003. Interviews with record-breaking track and field stars.

Mark R. Ellis

See also Mathias, Bob; Oerter, Al; Olympic Games of 1956; Sports.

■ Bowles, Chester

Identification American advertising executive, liberal politician, public official, and diplomat
Born April 5, 1901; Springfield, Massachusetts
Died May 25, 1986; Essex, Connecticut

Chester Bowles worked for economic rather than military support for underdeveloped nations in an effort to achieve peace and stability during the Cold War.

At the onset of World War II, Chester Bowles left his advertising career to enter public service. He held various positions in state and federal government, including governor of Connecticut and special adviser to the secretary-general of the United Nations. In 1951, Bowles was appointed U.S. ambassador to India and Nepal. The Indian government of Jawaharlal Nehru practiced a policy of nonalignment, or neutrality, in the growing Cold War. Pakistan, however, aligned itself with the United States and allowed American military bases on Pakistani soil. Bowles pushed for economic support for India, as opposed to military support for Pakistan, as a means of fostering stability in Asia.

After the election of President Dwight D. Eisenhower in 1952, Bowles resigned his ambassadorship and wrote several books, including *The New Dimensions of Peace* (1955) and *Africa's Challenge to America* (1956). He later served as a United States representative, undersecretary of state, and again as U.S. ambassador to India.

Impact Bowles used his position as ambassador to one of the largest and poorest countries to champion the liberal idea that peace and stability would come from economic rather than military support to other nations. His perspective was novel for the time and to some degree influenced foreign policy making during the conservative Cold War era.

Further Reading

Hlavacek, Pegge, and Janet B. Tilden. *Diapers on a Dateline: The Adventures of a United Press Family in India During the 1950's.* Campbell, Calif.: Writers Club Press, 2002. A look at Bowles-era India through the eyes of an American journalist family stationed there during the 1950's.

Schaffer, Howard B. *Chester Bowles: New Dealer in the Cold War.* Cambridge, Mass.: Harvard University Press, 1993. The seminal work on Chester Bowles written by a fellow diplomat.

Robert E. Haag

See also Cold War; Economic Stabilization Agency; Food for Peace; Foreign policy of the United States; Liberalism in U.S. politics.

■ Bowling

Definition Individual participant sport that involves knocking over wooden pins with a heavy ball

Bowling was one of the top participant sports in the United States and Canada during the 1950's. Postwar prosperity, increased leisure time, and the introduction of automatic pinsetters resulted in a spectacular rise in bowling's popularity in communities across the continent.

Versions of bowling most likely have been in existence for five thousand years, but the American version probably is descended from the German and Dutch nine-pins, brought to New Amsterdam in the seventeenth century and played in New York City's Battery Park. In medieval Germany, bowling, or "kegling," was a religious ritual whereby parishioners tried to knock down war clubs or heathens in the aisles of cathedrals. Theologian Martin Luther decided that the game would have nine pins.

In the New World, bowling became associated with gambling and heavy drinking in alleys alongside taverns. New York and Connecticut outlawed the sport in the nineteenth century, but enthusiasts sidestepped the law by setting up ten pins rather than nine. The American Bowling Congress (ABC) was established in 1895 to clean up the sport, standardize the rules, and act as chief governing body. The Women's National Bowling Association was established in 1916 and was renamed the Women's International Bowling Congress (WIBC) in 1971.

Rising Popularity Bowling was an important morale booster during the years of the Great Depression and World War II. It also suited the frugality of the times when gasoline was in short supply. Bowling experienced a spectacular rise after World War II, especially among the working classes. Service people bowled in military camps during the war and brought enthusiasm for the sport back to their home communities. Moreover, bowling appealed to the masses because it was easy to learn, required simple equipment, brought the family together, and could be enjoyed by all ages the year round. The bowling alley was an important community meeting place. Beginning during the 1950's, television embraced bowling and greatly accelerated its growth through series and tournament broadcasts. *Championship Bowling* on NBC was the first network broadcast of the sport; *Make That Spare, Celebrity Bowling,* and *Bowling for Dollars* gave bowling even greater popularity.

Proprietors of bowling alleys fueled the growth of the sport when they established leagues, recruited people from schools and workplaces, and built modern, inviting bowling allies. Automatic pinsetters were the game's major technological development of the decade, introduced first by American Machine and Foundry in 1951 and later by Brunswick in 1954, the two largest bowling equipment suppliers of the decade. No longer dependent on human setters, who were usually in short supply, automatic setters did much to stabilize the sport and invite investment. In 1952, the ABC approved plastic sheathing of balls to improve durability.

Impact In 1940, bowling was the third-most popular sport in the United States, behind skiing and fishing. By the 1960's, it was the fastest growing and number-one participation sport in the United States. The men's Professional Bowlers Association, established 1958, and the Professional Women Bowlers Association (1960) promoted and supported tournament competition. American-style bowling replaced candlepins and duckpins as the preferred form in Canada, where bowling also experienced exponential growth during the 1950's.

In subsequent decades, the centers of bowling's popularity across the North American continent corresponded closely to areas of heavy Germanic settlement, especially in Ohio, Illinois, and Wisconsin. The International Bowling Museum and Hall of Fame is located in St. Louis, Missouri.

Further Reading

Baker, William J. *Sports in the Western World.* Totowa, N.J.: Rowman & Littlefield, 1982. A chronological history of the sport set in a broad social context.

Herbst, Dan, and Parker Bohn. *Bowling: How to Master the Game.* New York: Universe Books, 2000. Gives secrets and strategies for successful bowling along with an illustrated history of the sport.

Sullivan, George. *The Complete Book of Family Bowling.* New York: Coward-McCann, 1968. Includes rules and techniques as well as a history of league and professional bowling, organizations, and other bowling-related games.

Ann M. Legreid

See also Fads; Sports.

■ Bracero program

Identification Federal program created through agreements with the Mexican government to employ temporary "guest" workers in the United States, chiefly in agriculture

Date 1942-1964

The bracero program prevented projected labor shortages during World War II and the Korean conflict but depressed wages and prevented farmworkers from effectively organizing into unions throughout the 1950's.

The first formal guest worker arrangement between the United States and Mexico began in 1917, when severe American labor shortages occurred as a result of massive enlistments in the armed forces and a wartime manufacturing boom. The program ended in 1920, but many workers stayed on illegally until employment prospects waned during the 1930's, when large numbers of laborers were forcibly deported.

Similar conditions prevailed after the bombing of Pearl Harbor in 1941 and America's entry into World War II. The war itself resulted in the usual labor shortages, but the military evacuation from the west coast of Japanese, mostly agrarian families exacerbated the crisis, leaving growers worried that crops would be left rotting in the fields. The Bracero Act of 1942 was passed, named after the Spanish word for "strong armed ones." The agreement, under a proviso to the Immigration Act of 1917, remained in effect—amid a war in Korea—until 1951, when the

Mexican farmworkers participating in the bracero program register at an Hidalgo, Texas, labor center in 1959. Most of the workers went no farther than Texas, but some ventured as far north as Michigan. (AP/Wide World Photos)

Agriculture Act of 1949 was amended to become Public Law 78, which regulated the bracero program until its demise in 1964.

The bracero program benefited both U.S. agribusiness and the Mexican government. U.S. farmers gained a reliable, nonunion labor supply while Mexico gained a substantial stream of U.S. dollars from the money sent back to laborers' families. Nevertheless, mindful of the exploitation and expulsions its citizens had suffered in the past, the Mexican government insisted on safeguards to protect workers' welfare, including the provision of transportation to and from the recruitment centers in Mexico, living expenses while traveling, a minimum wage, and employment or subsistence payments for at least 75 percent of the contracted work period. By the time Public Law 78 was enacted, however, domestic unemployment had increased, resulting in further provisions to protect domestic workers. "Braceros" were to be employed only when sufficient domestic workers were unavailable and when employment of braceros would not adversely affect wages and working conditions of similarly employed domestic workers. In addition, employers were to make serious efforts to hire domestic workers before resorting to braceros.

Impact Real damage was felt within rural American economies over the twenty-two years the program remained in effect. Farmers contributed to the rise in rural unemployment by ignoring regulations to hire domestic workers, preferring the uncomplaining braceros, who could be fired and deported without recourse. Moreover, appalling working conditions resulted in local taxpayers footing the bills for health care while rural wages remained artificially depressed, contributing to an overall increase in rural poverty even as profit margins for farmers increased.

Further Reading

Calavita, Kitty. *Inside the State: The Bracero Program, Immigration, and the INS.* New York: Routledge, 1992. Overview of U.S. policies regarding illegal aliens from Mexico, legal agricultural migrants, and the Immigration and Naturalization Service.

Galarza, Ernesto. *Merchants of Labor: The Mexican Bracero Story.* Santa Barbara, Calif.: McNally and Loftin, 1964. History of the bracero program and farmworkers in California from 1942 to 1960 from the first Mexican American to be nominated for the Nobel Prize in Literature.

McWilliams, Carey. *Factories in the Field: The Story of Migratory Farm Labor in California.* Berkeley: University of California Press, 2000. This classic piece of journalism was originally published in 1939.

Mitchell, Don. *The Lie of the Land: Migrant Workers and the California Landscape.* Minneapolis: University of Minnesota Press, 1996. Details the role of the migrant worker in the labor history of the state and the material and ideological struggles over living and working conditions for the workers.

Sue Tarjan

See also Agriculture in the United States; Immigration to the United States; Income and wages in the United States; Latinos; Mexico; Operation Wetback; *Pocho*; Unionism in the United States.

■ Bradley, Omar

Identification Chairman of the U.S. Joint Chiefs of Staff during the Korean War
Born February 12, 1893; Clark, Missouri
Died April 8, 1981; New York, New York

As the highest-ranking officer in the U.S. armed forces and one of President Harry S. Truman's leading advisers during the Korean War, Omar Bradley played a critical role in formulating American strategy in the conflict and helped shape the North Atlantic Treaty Organization (NATO).

Omar Bradley grew up in rural Missouri and graduated from the Military Academy at West Point in 1915, a classmate of Dwight D. Eisenhower. He missed service overseas during World War I and spent most of his early career training troops. In 1941, he was named head of the Infantry School by General George C. Marshall.

Bradley was placed in command of the newly formed 82d Infantry Division and promoted to major general in December, 1941. During World War II he played important roles, both domestically and internationally, for the war effort, commanding troops, evaluating military training, and participating in preparatory stages for the Normandy invasion in 1944.

Bradley became the first chief of the Joint Chiefs of Staff in 1949, serving until his retirement in 1953. In this position, he played an important role in the ongoing disputes over nuclear deterrence and service roles and missions. Once NATO was formed, he became the first chairman of the organization's military committee. During the Korean War, Bradley was part of the contingency that advised Truman to limit the war to the Korean Peninsula, and he supported Truman's decision to dismiss General Douglas MacArthur from his military duties in April, 1951. After the Truman administration was criticized for its decisions on MacArthur and a limited war, Bradley appeared before Congress to defend the administration's actions. He was promoted to general of the army on September 22, 1950, the last man to hold that rank.

Impact Bradley was known as the "G.I.'s general" during his career because of the care and concern he showed the soldiers under his command. He became one of the primary architects of the defense buildup during the Korean War. His memoirs, *A Soldier's Story*, were published in 1951.

Further Reading

Bradley, Omar. *A Soldier's Story*. New York: Henry Holt, 1951. Bradley's memoirs of World War II.

Bradley, Omar, and Blair, Clay. *A General's Life*. New York: Simon & Schuster, 1983. Bradley's autobiography finished posthumously by Clay Blair.

Weigley, Russell. *Eisenhower's Lieutenants*. Bloomington: University of Indiana Press, 1981. Provides a balanced account of Bradley's command of the 12th Army Group.

J. W. Thacker

See also Cold War; Eisenhower, Dwight D.; Korean War; MacArthur, Douglas; Marshall, George C.; Truman, Harry S.

■ Brando, Marlon

Identification American film actor
Born April 3, 1924; Omaha, Nebraska
Died July 1, 2004; Los Angeles, California

Marlon Brando became recognized as one of the most influential American actors during the 1950's for his smoldering and tortured film portrayals.

The third child and the only son of Dorothy Pennebaker Brando and Marlon Brando, Sr., young Marlon Brando grew up in a turbulent family environment. While his mother struggled with alcoholism, his father was a salesman who dominated his children. Through his mother's involvement in local theater, Brando became intrigued with acting. He was a rebellious youth; he eventually was expelled from the military academy to which his father sent

him. He moved to New York City's Greenwich Village at the age of eighteen in order to study acting. He lived with his sister Frances and enrolled in a course taught by Stella Adler at the Dramatic Workshop of the New School for Social Research. Adler had studied at the Moscow Art Theater with the legendary Konstantin Stanislavsky during the early 1930's. It was Stanislavsky who had introduced the "method" approach to acting. By employing the "method," an actor would delve into his or her "emotional memory" in order to bring a role to life.

In 1944, Brando made his Broadway debut in the play *I Remember Mama*. He was named the most promising new actor on Broadway in 1946 after his performance in *Truckline Café*. However, even with all his early promise as an actor, the theater world was turned upside down by his 1947 performance as Stanley Kowalski in Tennessee Williams's *A Streetcar Named Desire*. The intensity and sexual energy that Brando brought to the role stunned the acting world and made him a star.

Film Star In 1950, Brando played a paraplegic veteran in the film *The Men*. Although the film was not a huge success, Brando was praised for his sensitive portrayal of the soldier. In 1951, director Elia Kazan and Brando teamed up again in order to do the film version of *A Streetcar Named Desire*. As he had done on the stage in the role of the earthy and barbaric Kowalski, Brando was a force of nature in the film and became popular with the youth of America. He garnered his first Academy Award nomination for best actor and created one of the seminal characters in screen history. He also would receive best actor nominations for *Viva Zapata!* (1952) and *Julius Caesar* (1953). In 1953, Brando played the leader of a motorcycle gang in the low-budget film *The Wild One*. His image as a rebel was enhanced by this role, and the growing numbers of disenfranchised young Americans saw him as their hero.

Brando again worked with Kazan on the powerful film *On the Waterfront* (1954). He played the down-and-out fighter Terry Malloy and mesmerized audiences with his ability to bring dignity to a common man struggling against all odds. For his performance, Brando finally won an Academy Award. By 1955, he had become one of the most popular actors in the world. However, always mistrustful of his celebrity status, Brando found it difficult to play the role of a Hollywood star. During the second half of

Marlon Brando as Stanley Kowalski in the film adaptation of Tennessee Williams's play A Streetcar Named Desire. *(AP/ Wide World Photos)*

the 1950's, he made a number of eclectic films, including *Guys and Dolls* (1955), *Sayonara* (1957), and *The Young Lions* (1958).

Impact Brando was a groundbreaking actor who shattered all preconceived notions of acting with his naturalistic approach to performances. There was a fresh spontaneity in his performances that rang true with audiences. Along with actors such as James Dean and Montgomery Clift, Brando ushered in a new definition of what a screen hero could be. He reflected the changes that were transforming post-World War II America. Brando inspired many of the serious American actors who came after him, including Paul Newman, Warren Beatty, Jack Nicholson, Robert De Niro, Al Pacino, and Sean Penn.

Although Brando's career was uneven at best after his remarkable achievements of the 1950's, he garnered acclaim for his performances in such landmark films as *The Godfather* (1972), *Last Tango in Paris* (1972), and *Apocalypse Now* (1979). In 2004, Brando died of pulmonary fibrosis at the age of eighty.

Further Reading

Bosworth, Patricia. *Marlon Brando.* New York: Viking, 2001. Gives an incisive look at the troubled life of a screen legend.

Schickel, Richard. *Brando: A Life in Our Times.* New York: Atheneum, 1991. An insightful portrait of Brando's acting career and tumultuous life.

Jeffry Jensen

See also Academy Awards; Actors Studio; Clift, Montgomery; Dean, James; Kazan, Elia; *On the Waterfront*; *Streetcar Named Desire, A*; Theater in the United States; *Wild One, The*; Williams, Tennessee.

■ Brinkmanship

Definition Uncompromising approach to Cold War foreign policy

Brinkmanship reflected the Dwight D. Eisenhower administration's hard-nosed approach to foreign policy, wherein the United States would rather risk war than give in to communist demands.

An article praising Secretary of State John Foster Dulles appeared in the January 16, 1956, issue of *Life* magazine. The piece claimed that Dulles had saved the United States from the "brink" of a major war on three separate occasions. Dulles noted that the key to his successes was his refusal to back down from tough diplomatic decisions even if war might be the result. Reporters quickly picked up on the term "brinkmanship" (also known as "brinksmanship"), which came to describe the unflinching foreign policy of the United States during the Cold War.

Impact Brinkmanship came to hold a negative connotation for many Americans during the 1950's. Provided that U.S. enemies backed down when faced with the prospect of war, the policy worked well, but critics often wondered what would happen if the Soviets stood their ground and inflexibility pushed the superpowers into nuclear war. In combination with the theory of massive retaliation, the development of the hydrogen bomb, and the launch of the Soviet satellite *Sputnik*, brinkmanship helped fuel the paranoia of nuclear war that was pervasive during the 1950's.

Further Reading

Marks, Frederick W. *Power and Peace: The Diplomacy of John Foster Dulles.* Westport, Conn.: Praeger, 1995.

A study of Dulles's foreign policy that seeks to show that he was more flexible than terms such as "brinkmanship" would suggest.

Paterson, Thomas G., and J. Garry Clifford. *America Ascendant: U.S. Foreign Relations Since 1939.* Lexington, Mass.: Heath, 1995. A survey of foreign policy in the Cold War era that shows the lasting impact of brinkmanship while providing a suitable contrast to other diplomatic styles.

John K. Franklin

See also Atomic bomb; B-52 bomber; China; Cold War; Dulles, John Foster; Eisenhower, Dwight D.; Espionage and Sabotage Act of 1954; Foreign policy of the United States; Hydrogen bomb; Korean War; Teller, Edward; United Nations.

■ Brink's robbery

The Event Robbery of a well-known armored car company
Date January 17, 1950
Place Boston, Massachusetts

Often called "the crime of the century," the Brink's robbery was the largest armed theft of money at that time in U.S. history, and the thieves would elude capture for six years.

At 7:00 P.M. on January 17, 1950, seven men entered the Brink's building in Boston, Massachusetts, wearing identical coats, caps, and Halloween masks. The men tied and gagged five Brink's employees at gunpoint, and less than thirty minutes later had disappeared with nearly three million dollars in cash, checks, and other securities.

It took the Federal Bureau of Investigation (FBI) six years to identify and prosecute the eleven men who had planned and executed the robbery. The FBI quickly identified the gang as career criminals in the Boston area but could not prove a case against them until, in 1956, Joseph "Specs" O'Keefe confessed. O'Keefe had fallen out with the other gang members, and three attempts had been made on his life.

Based on O'Keefe's information, eight men were arrested and tried. In October, 1956, all were found guilty and sentenced to life in prison.

Impact A nearly "perfect" crime, the Brink's robbery captured the public's imagination; many hoped the thieves would never be captured. The FBI's investi-

gation cost an estimated $29 million, but authorities recovered only $57,000 of the stolen money.

Further Reading

Behn, Noel. *Big Stick-Up at Brink's!* New York: Putman, 1977. Popular account of the robbery, illustrated with photographs.

O'Keefe, Specs, and Bob Considine. *The Men Who Robbed Brink's.* New York: Random House, 1961. O'Keefe's inside story of the elaborately planned robbery, with a detailed account of the FBI investigation.

Maureen J. Puffer-Rothenberg

See also Federal Bureau of Investigation; Organized crime.

■ British Empire Games

The Event Quadrennial sports competition similar to the Olympic Games that brought together athletes from around the British Empire and Commonwealth
Dates 1950, 1954, and 1958

The 1950's witnessed changes in the British Empire Games that reflected the changing political climate of the immediate post-World War II decade and set precedents for future events.

The British Empire Games were the product of discussions and ideas that emanated from Reverend John Astley Cooper's proposal, during the late nineteenth century, for a sports- and cultural-oriented gathering for English-speaking nations. The idea continued to evolve over a thirty-year period, and the first British Empire Games were held in 1930 in Hamilton, Ontario. After a hiatus during World War II, the games resumed in 1950 in Auckland, New Zealand.

During the 1950 games, fencing made its debut as a competitive sport for both men and women. It was added to the only two sports—athletics and swimming—in which women were allowed to compete; the three competitions continued to be the only ones open to female competitors throughout the 1950's. For men, fencing and weight lifting were part of the traditional rivalries, which also included athletics, boxing. cycling, lawn bowling, rowing, swimming, and wrestling. Ceylon, Fiji, and Malaysia were first-time participants during the 1950 games.

With the 1954 games, held in Vancouver, Canada, the event became known as the British Empire and Commonwealth Games. The name change reflected the evolving nature of the British Empire into one in which several former colonies became emerging and independent nations. It also highlighted a new Elizabethan age, of sorts, with the 1952 accession of Elizabeth II to the British throne. As newly independent nations participated, others withdrew for political reasons or because they achieved independence. Pakistan and Uganda were first-time participants. However, the 1954 games might be best known for the "Miracle Mile" match between Roger Bannister of Britain and John Landy of Australia that resulted in the first mile race in which two runners finished under four minutes.

Cardiff, Wales, was the site of the 1958 games. It was the last competition for twenty-eight years in which athletes from South Africa participated; there were demonstrations against the all-white South African team both in London and in Cardiff. The Isle of Man, Kenya, Singapore, and Trinidad and Tobago became first-year participants during the 1958 games. Moreover, the tradition of the Queen's Baton and Message started in Cardiff. The first Queen's Message Relay began, in 1958, at Buckingham Palace, led by champions from the 1954 games; the baton was taken north through Britain into Wales, down the country's west coast, and back to Cardiff.

Impact The games of the 1950's were modernized by geopolitical factors that affected the event's team rosters. Dissolution of Britain's colonial ties and the subsequent emergence of newly independent nations gave the event a more multinational flare and brought a revitalized competitive event to Canada's doorstep in 1954. From 1966 to 1974, the name "British Commonwealth Games" was used, but in 1978, they became known as the "Commonwealth Games."

Further Reading

Bell, Daniel. *Encyclopedia of International Games.* Jefferson, N.C.: McFarland, 2003. Contains an excellent essay on the Commonwealth Games; it has facts and statistics for each game and serves as a good overview.

Dheenshaw, Clive. *The Commonwealth Games: The First Sixty Years, 1930-1990.* Sydney: ABC Books for the Australian Broadcasting Corporation, 1994. Good background on the games; focuses on the spectrum of the games' events and competitors rather than narrowly focusing on participation by specific countries.

Phillips, Bob. *The Commonwealth Games: The History of All the Sports.* Manchester, England: Parrs Wood Press, 2002. Excellent history of the games from its earliest days.

Martin J. Manning

See also Olympic Games of 1952; Olympic Games of 1956; Sports.

Roger Bannister crosses the finish line of the British Empire Games' "Miracle Mile" in 3:58.8, followed closely by John Landy who finished in 3:59.6. (AP/ Wide World Photos)

■ Broadway musicals

Definition Musical plays staged in New York City's Broadway district

Broadway musicals achieved new sophistication and popularity by skillfully integrating dialogue with songs and dances, usually in optimistic and romanticized depictions of American life.

The 1950's was the golden age of the American musical comedy. A dazzling succession of musicals featured tuneful scores, witty song lyrics, and "books" (the spoken portions of the show) by fine composers, lyricists, and playwrights. Many were performed eight times a week by some of the most revered performers in American musical theater. Inspired by the example of *Oklahoma!* (1943), which integrated songs, dance, and dialogue within a more tightly unified format than the genre had attempted previously, the creators of the 1950's Broadway musicals produced a succession of critical and popular hits.

The decade was framed by two of the greatest hits of Richard Rodgers and Oscar Hammerstein II, who enjoyed one of the most fruitful collaborations in the history of the American musical theater. *South Pacific* (1949) was an evocation of the romantic side of World War II in the Pacific. Ten years later, the final collaboration of the composer and lyricist, *The Sound of Music* (1959), won the Tony Award for best musical—just as *South Pacific* had a decade earlier—and it featured the same female star, Mary Martin. In 1965, *The Sound of Music* found a huge international audience in the Hollywood film version starring Julie Andrews. Despite the non-American settings for both shows (*The Sound of Music* was set in Nazi-occupied Austria), Hammerstein's lyrics celebrated characteristically American values—openness, naïveté, optimism, and ingenuity in confronting danger—while Rodgers's music was relentlessly tuneful. *The King and I* (1951) showed the forthright behavior of a Victorian governess at the Thai royal court, while *Flower Drum Song* (1958) slyly commented on Chinese immigrants in San Francisco and their acculturation to life in the United States.

To their detractors, the sunny optimism of Rodgers and Hammerstein seemed an endorsement of the negative aspects of American life during the 1950's: mindless conformity, inflexible gender roles, and a complacent optimism that ignored the more troubling aspects of Dwight D. Eisenhower's Amer-

ica. Other Broadway creators offered a darker view of American culture. Frank Loesser's *Guys and Dolls* (1950) was arguably the embodiment of American musical theater and the perfect example of the genre. However, its characters—gamblers, racetrack touts, and showgirls—cheerfully refute the optimism of Rodgers and Hammerstein. For many viewers, the most endearing musical of the decade was Meredith Willson's *The Music Man* (1957), which comically subverted wholesome midwestern values and celebrated an apparent con man, Professor Harold Hill, memorably portrayed on both stage and screen by Robert Preston.

While "Some Enchanted Evening" from *South Pacific* was probably the favorite romantic song of the era's musical, "Seventy-Six Trombones" from *The Music Man* was its marching song. The most widely admired musical comedy of the 1950's, *My Fair Lady* (1956), by Alan Jay Lerner and Frederick Loewe, had a sardonic British tinge. It featured the wittiest lyrics and most tuneful score of the decade, and it offered the two most famous performances of the Broadway musical theater, with Rex Harrison as Henry Higgins and Julie Andrews as Eliza Doolittle.

Leonard Bernstein composed the scores for three hits during the 1950's. *Wonderful Town* (1953) won the Tony Award for best musical. *Candide* (1956) likely offered the richest musical score of any show of the decade, but its book failed to match the witty lyrics of Richard Wilbur and John Latouche or the sparkle of Bernstein's mock-operetta score. *West Side Story* (1957) combined the talents of Bernstein, Stephen Sondheim, Jerome Robbins, and Arthur Laurents in a modern retelling of William Shakespeare's *Romeo and Juliet* in a gritty urban setting. *Gypsy* (1959), the ultimate backstage musical, provided Ethel Merman with her greatest star turn. It offered, in its portrait of the mother of Gypsy Rose Lee, one of the few three-dimensional characters in the Broadway musical. Jule Styne's score and Stephen Sondheim's lyrics were remarkably incisive, and the show fully achieved the integration of plot, music, and character in the pattern laid out by *Oklahoma!*

Broadway musicals have always been known for the excellence of their dancing, but the 1950's saw a succession of remarkable choreographers who understood the psychological implications of dance. Bob Fosse won Tony Awards in 1955 and 1956 for his distinctive choreography for *The Pajama Game* (1954) and *Damn Yankees*, featuring rakishly tipped hats and an aggressive style. Gwen Verdon was the embodiment of the Fosse style in a succession of shows during the 1950's: *The Pajama Game, Damn Yankees, New Girl in Town* (1957), and *Redhead* (1959). Jerome Robbins moved to Broadway from classical dance and provided the ultimate example of the integration of dance and characterization in *West Side Story*.

Impact The Broadway musical of the 1950's was widely understood and enjoyed as affirming the most positive values of American culture, and Mary Martin's line from *South Pacific* seemed to set the tone for the decade: "I'm just a cock-eyed optimist." For critics, the majority of the shows failed to challenge the complacent conformity of the Eisenhower years. At their best, however, as in *Guys and Dolls, West Side Story*, and *Gypsy*, the musical productions offered a distinctively American theatrical experience, combining good music, singing, and dancing with compelling narratives. During this period, subject matter became more intricate and plots more human and complex. The best musicals showed awareness of troubling, even controversial aspects of American life while simultaneously giving immense pleasure to the Broadway audience and, through their long stage runs and Hollywood movie versions, to a far wider international audience.

Further Reading

Bernstein, Leonard. *The Joy of Music*. New York: Simon & Schuster, 1959. A chapter on the "American Musical Theater" by a great Broadway composer and serious classical musician, then at the peak of his influence, gives a good overview of the Broadway musical at the moment of its greatest artistic success.

Mordden, Ethan. *Coming Up Roses: The Broadway Musical During the 1950's*. New York: Oxford University Press, 1998. Details the golden age of Broadway theater and analyzes why the 1950's was a period when "no one knew what the rules were any more."

Steyn, Marc. *Broadway Babies Say Goodnight: Musicals Then and Now*. New York: Routledge, 2000. Chronicles seven decades of American theater on Broadway, giving strong attention to the 1950's productions.

Byron Nelson

See also Belafonte, Harry; Bernstein, Leonard; *Damn Yankees*; Film in the United States; Long-playing records; Music; *My Fair Lady*; *Peter Pan*; Rodgers and Hammerstein musicals; Sumac, Yma; Theater in the United States; *West Side Story*.

■ Brown, Jim

Identification African American football player
Born February 17, 1936; St. Simons Island, Georgia

Jim Brown excelled as an all-around college athlete and professional football running back, setting records that lasted many years.

During his high school years in Manhasset, New York, in the early 1950's, Jim Brown earned thirteen varsity letters in football, basketball, lacrosse, and track and field. As a senior, he averaged 14.9 yards per carry in football and thirty-eight points a game in basketball. He then entered Syracuse University, where he earned a bachelor's degree in physical education in 1957. During his three-year college playing career, he gained more than two thousand yards rushing and scored twenty-five touchdowns and 187 points as a halfback. Among the records he broke were the major-college record of 43 points, scored against Colgate University in 1956, and 21 points against Texas Christian University in the 1957 Cotton Bowl. In 1956, he made all-America teams in both football and lacrosse and also played basketball. These achievements later earned him memberships in the Lacrosse Hall of Fame (1985) and the College Football Hall of Fame (1995).

Brown's real fame, however, came during his spectacular professional football career. The Cleveland Browns selected him first in the 1957 National Football League (NFL) draft. Brown's size, toughness, and quickness made him a powerful fullback for the Browns. During his first season, he won the league's rookie of the year award and set a single-game rushing record of 237 yards against the Los Angeles Rams. He also led the league in scoring. During his second season, he established a season rushing record with 1,527 yards.

During a professional career lasting from 1957 through 1965, Brown gained totals of 12,312 rushing yards and 15,459 all-purpose yards. He also set NFL records for average yards per carry (5.2), seasons leading the league in rushing (8), and seasons leading the league in touchdowns (5). He made the pro bowl nine times and was named all-pro eight times. Meanwhile, he appeared in three NFL championship games and was selected the league's most valuable player in 1958 and 1965. In 1971, he was inducted into the Pro Football Hall of Fame. By that time, he had started new careers as a film actor and social activist.

Impact Brown's electrifying play helped attract new fans to professional football during the 1950's, and he set a standard for running backs that many people believe has never been equaled, even though most of his records were eventually broken.

Further Reading

Brown, Jim. *Off My Chest.* Garden City, N.Y.: Doubleday, 1964. Brown's first attempt at autobiography focuses on his athletic achievements.

Brown, Jim, with Steve Delsohn. *Out of Bounds.* New York: Kensingston, 1989. Candid autobiography that does not gloss over the darker sides of Brown's life on and off playing fields.

Marvis, B. *Jim Brown: Football Great.* New York: Chelsea House, 1996. Details the life and times of Brown.

David L. Porter

See also African Americans; Fitzgerald, Ella; Football; Sports; Unitas, Johnny.

■ Brown v. Board of Education

Identification U.S. Supreme Court decision holding school segregation unconstitutional

Date Decided on May 17, 1954

The Supreme Court's unanimous ruling that legally mandated segregation of American public schools was unconstitutional launched a social and political upheaval during the 1950's that helped give rise to the modern Civil Rights movement.

In 1896, in the case *Plessy v. Ferguson*, the U.S. Supreme Court held that state governments could mandate racial segregation by law in public facilities so long as "equal but separate accommodations" were provided. The result of this decision was the passage of a broad range of "Jim Crow" laws, particularly in the South. These laws established racial segregation in nearly all public facilities, including the public schools.

Legal attacks on the segregation laws began in earnest during the 1930's under the leadership of

the National Association for the Advancement of Colored People (NAACP). Because state universities had made no provision for black students, the NAACP's campaign focused at first on segregation in graduate and professional schools. By 1950, several cases forcing the admission of minority students to graduate and law schools had been won. In 1947 and 1948, cases challenging elementary and secondary school segregation were filed in Delaware, Kansas, South Carolina, and Virginia. In each case, black children had been denied admission because of their race to schools attended by white children. In all but the Delaware case, the state courts upheld the segregation statutes under the *Plessy v. Ferguson* separate-but-equal rule.

Supreme Court Action Because the myriad cases all involved the same fundamental issue, they were consolidated into one case presented before the U.S. Supreme Court under the title *Brown v. Board of Education, Topeka, Kansas.* The Legal Defense Fund of the NAACP, led by Thurgood Marshall and Jack Greenberg, briefed and argued the cases for the plaintiffs. They argued that separate schools for blacks and whites were not equal and could not be made equal, and therefore, state statutes that require racial segregation violate the equal protection clause of the Fourteenth Amendment to the Constitution. The NAACP's position was reinforced by a brief filed by Attorney General Herbert Brownell on behalf of the Department of Justice. The states were represented by John W. Davis, a prominent appellate attorney. Davis argued that *Plessy* had settled the issue and that its precedent ought to be binding, especially since it reflected the way of life to which people had become accustomed, especially in the South.

After hearing arguments in the case in 1952, the Supreme Court asked the parties for additional arguments in its 1953 term. Re-argument dealt primarily with the historical circumstances under which the Fourteenth Amendment had been written and passed. Meanwhile, changes were coming to the Court. Early in 1953, President Dwight D. Eisenhower had appointed Earl Warren, the former governor of California, to be chief justice. It fell to Warren rather than his less imaginative predecessor, Fred Vinson, to organize the Court in the case. A majority of justices were in favor of overruling *Plessy* and doing away with segregation. Warren felt strongly that in a decision of such magnitude, the Court

Linda Brown Smith, the third-grade Topeka, Kansas, child whose exclusion from an all-white neighborhood school helped prompt the Brown v. Board of Education *case that was named after her father.* (AP/Wide World Photos)

should speak with a single unanimous voice. He spent much time persuading justices Tom Clark and Stanley Reed—who were from Texas and Kentucky—to join the majority.

In its unanimous decision, the Court held that "in the field of public education the doctrine of 'separate but equal' has no place." Separate facilities were held to be inherently unequal, regardless of the physical facilities of the schools in question. The Court asked for further argument on how the decision was to be enforced, and a year later it held that federal courts would have the power to issue injunctions requiring the desegregation of public schools.

Impact The moral and political impacts of *Brown* were enormous. On the legal side, it quickly became clear that courts would no longer tolerate racial segregation, and during the remainder of the 1950's and beyond, school systems were desegregated in

spite of massive southern resistance. Federal troops had to be deployed on several occasions to enforce court orders, most notably in Little Rock, Arkansas, in 1957. Moreover, the same legal analysis of segregation that characterized *Brown* subsequently was applied to racial segregation in all public facilities, and one after another, the manifestations of Jim Crow began to disappear. In northern states, school segregation existed also, brought about primarily by discriminatory school zone boundaries. This segregation too was ended by federal courts. The legal and moral basis for these kinds of later developments can be traced back to *Brown*.

On the political side, *Brown* was the genesis of the massive Civil Rights movement of the 1960's. Demonstrations and political action for equality eventually resulted in the end of most private racial segregation and, in 1964, in the passage of a powerful civil rights act by Congress. The new law prohibited racial discrimination in places of public accommodation; it was subsequently strengthened to prevent discrimination in employment, housing, and education.

Further Reading

Branch, Taylor. *Parting the Waters: America in the King Years, 1954-1963.* New York: Simon & Schuster, 1988. Pulitzer Prize-winning history of the Civil Rights movement, from *Brown v. Board of Education* to the death of President John F. Kennedy. Very strong on the moral and psychological impact of the *Brown* case.

Kluger, Richard. *Simple Justice: The History of "Brown v. Board of Education" and Black America's Struggle for Equality.* New York: Alfred A. Knopf, 1975. Fascinating discussion of NAACP activities and the legal strategy for overturning the separate-but-equal rule.

Raffel, Jeffrey. *Historical Dictionary of School Segregation and Desegregation: The American Experience.* Westport, Conn.: Greenwood, 1998. A comprehensive compilation of entries for important court decisions, persons, concepts, and organizations that proved central to the history of school segregation and desegregation in the United States.

Williams, Juan. *Thurgood Marshall: American Revolutionary.* New York: Times Books, 1998. Biographical study of Marshall's legal philosophy as desegregation advocate and his twenty-four-year career as justice of the Supreme Court.

Robert Jacobs

See also *Bolling v. Sharpe*; Civil Rights Act of 1957; Civil Rights movement; Education in the United States; Eisenhower, Dwight D.; Little Rock school desegregation crisis; National Association for the Advancement of Colored People; Racial discrimination; School desegregation; Southern Manifesto; Supreme Court decisions, U.S.; *Sweatt v. Painter*; Vinson, Fred M.; Warren, Earl.

■ Brubeck, Dave

Identification American jazz pianist, group leader, and composer
Born December 6, 1920; Concord, California

Dave Brubeck's unique improvisational and compositional techniques helped solidify his reputation as one of the best-respected jazz musicians in the United States.

In 1950, the Dave Brubeck Trio, based in San Francisco, began to attract national attention. Brubeck had developed his own version of modern jazz, heavily influenced by his studies with French composer Darius Milhaud, and he soon formed a new group, the Dave Brubeck Quartet, with alto saxophonist Paul Desmond. The trio's first long-playing (LP) record, *Jazz at Oberlin*, recorded in 1953, along with *Jazz at the College of the Pacific* (1953) and *Jazz Goes to College* (1954), were successful. As the album titles suggest, Brubeck was very popular with college audiences.

What was to become one of the most popular albums in jazz, *Time Out*, was recorded in 1959 by Brubeck's quartet. Each of the album's pieces was in a different meter. One of the pieces, Desmond's "Take Five," became the first jazz instrumental recording to sell one million copies.

Jazz pianist Dave Brubeck, drummer Cal Tjader, and bassist Ron Crotty rehearsing in a studio around 1950. (Hulton Archive | by Getty Images)

Impact Brubeck's complex time signatures and his ability to play in two keys at once, known as polytonality, proved to critics and audiences alike that a creative and innovative approach to the genre could attain popular success. In subsequent decades, Brubeck continued to perform and compose, inspiring generations of musicians and listeners.

Further Reading

Hall, Fred. *It's About Time: The Dave Brubeck Story.* Fayetteville: University of Arkansas Press, 1996. Biography with descriptions and recollections.

Lees, Gene. "The Man on the Buffalo Nickel." In *Cats of Any Color.* Oxford, England: Oxford University Press, 1994. Long, far-ranging interview with a great deal of biographical material and many anecdotes.

Storb, Ilse, and Klaus-Gottthard Fischer. *Dave Brubeck Improvisations and Compositions: The Idea of Cultural Exchange.* New York: Peter Lang, 1994. Combines a detailed analysis of Brubeck's music with an extensive narrative describing the highly diverse sources of inspiration for the material.

John Myers

See also Jazz; Long-playing records; Music; Newport Jazz Festival; Peterson, Oscar; Sahl, Mort; San Francisco Renaissance.

■ Bunche, Ralph

Identification African American scholar and diplomat

Born August 7, 1904; Detroit, Michigan

Died December 9, 1971; New York, New York

Ralph Bunche negotiated an armistice between Israel and the Arab states, and in 1950, he was the first African American to win the Nobel Peace Prize for his efforts.

Ralph Bunche was the only son of Olive and Fred Bunche. In 1916, both of his parents died, and Ralph was taken to Los Angeles by his grandmother. He excelled in school, graduating as valedictorian of his classes in high school and the University of California at Los Angeles (UCLA). He earned a doctorate in international relations from Harvard and taught political science at Howard University. During World War II, he served as an intelligence officer and later helped in the planning of the United Nations (U.N.). In 1949, he became the U.N. mediator for the first Arab-Israeli war, and his success in attain-

Nobel laureate Ralph Bunche in October, 1950, shortly after he became the first black professor in the history of Harvard College. (AP/Wide World Photos)

ing a cease-fire earned for him the Nobel Peace Prize in 1950.

During the early 1950's, Bunche refused an offer to serve in the State Department because of the prevalence of racial segregation in Washington, D.C., and instead accepted the post of under secretary-general at the United Nations in 1954. In 1956, he organized the peacekeeping mission in the Suez Canal Zone following the Suez Crisis. He focused on similar efforts for the rest of the decade. Bunche remained active as a scholar and supporter of the Civil Rights movement but spent most of his time at the United Nations until his death in 1971.

Impact By winning the Nobel Peace Prize in 1950, Bunche inspired African Americans to become involved in diplomacy and served as an example to all Americans regarding the possibilities of the United Nations.

Further Reading

Henry, Charles. *Ralph Bunche: Model Negro or Amer-*

ican Other? New York: New York University Press, 1999. Thoroughly researched yet concise discussion on the contradictions of Bunche's career.

Urquhart, Brian. *Ralph Bunche: An American Life.* New York: Norton, 1993. A solid biography written by a colleague.

Andy DeRoche

See also African Americans; Foreign policy of the United States; Israel; Nobel Prizes; Suez Crisis; United Nations.

■ Burroughs, William

Identification American novelist associated with the Beat generation
Born February 5, 1914; St. Louis, Missouri
Died August 2, 1997; Lawrence, Kansas

William Burroughs's friendships with other writers and the publication of his own outspoken works led to a literary revolution.

After studying English literature and traveling in Europe, William Burroughs befriended writers Jack Kerouac and Allen Ginsberg in 1944, forming the nucleus of what would later be known as the Beat generation. Burroughs moved to Mexico City in 1949 to escape trial for possession of illegal drugs and firearms and there began writing *Junkie* (1953).

In 1951, Burroughs accidentally shot and killed his common-law wife, an incident that forced him to leave Mexico. After further travels, he settled in the Moroccan city of Tangier in 1953. With Ginsberg's help, *Junkie* was published the same year in the United States under the pseudonym William Lee. A short, relatively realistic novel growing out of Burroughs's addiction to morphine, it expressed its narrator's need to escape the confines of his privileged, middle-class existence.

By the time *Junkie* appeared, Burroughs had begun writing *Naked Lunch.* Published in France in 1959 and the United States in 1962, the novel was greeted with critical acclaim but legal condemnation. Its sexually explicit and violent subject matter and disjointed narrative techniques would reappear in *The Soft Machine* (1961), *The Ticket That Exploded* (1962), and *Nova Express* (1964), all of which Burroughs had begun writing during the late 1950's. Although he published many other books, Burroughs would remain best known for *Naked Lunch.*

Impact During the 1950's, William Burroughs's work, combined with that of other Beat authors, helped create a literary atmosphere of greater openness and experimentation in the United States. Critics point to Burroughs's black humor, his use of taboo subject matter, and his daring narrative techniques as his contributions to the literary scene during this time. His book *Naked Lunch* spoke to the disaffected generation of the era and achieved cult status.

Further Reading

Caveney, Graham. *Gentleman Junkie: The Life and Legacy of William S. Burroughs.* Boston: Little, Brown, 1998. Inventive and profusely illustrated biography reflecting Burroughs's compositional techniques.

Miles, Barry. *William Burroughs: El Hombre Invisible.* New York: Hyperion, 1993. Biography devoting considerable attention to *Naked Lunch.*

Grove Koger

See also Beat generation; Book publishing; Censorship; Ferlinghetti, Lawrence; Ginsberg, Allen; Kerouac, Jack; Literature in the United States; *Lolita*; *Naked Lunch*; Rexroth, Kenneth; San Francisco Renaissance.

■ Business and the economy in Canada

As Canada changed from a frontier colonial society to a full member of the developed world, business sectors and the economy became the engines of this transformation.

During the 1950's, Canada experienced a marked sectoral change that signaled the shifting of national economic priorities. This change was mirrored in the decline of the primary sector, defined as agriculture, forestry, mining, quarrying, fishing, and hunting, from 15.6 percent of the economy to 9.6 percent. The major reason for this change was the drop in the portion of the economy dedicated to agriculture, from 9.5 percent to 4.8 percent.

Agriculture became heavily mechanized during the 1950's. Farms increased in size and, more important, they employed machinery to a much greater extent, notably in the use of tractors and combines. The use of mechanical methods enabled employment in agriculture to drop to nearly half of what it had been before World War II. Mechanization also empowered manufacturers of agricultural equipment, notably Massey-Harris-Ferguson, a Canadian company, though U.S. manufacturers of agricultural machinery, such as John Deere and International Harvester, also benefited.

In the secondary sector, manufacturing dropped slightly, from 26.2 percent in 1950 to 23.2 percent in 1960, but only because the entire Canadian economy was very much larger by the end of the decade. Construction, the other part of the secondary sector, declined a minuscule amount, from 4.9 percent to 4.8 percent, but again, this change obscured an actual growth in construction since it was part of a much larger economy.

In the tertiary sector, as well as in the category "other," both of which encapsulated service-related employment, there was measurable growth. The tertiary sector grew from 44.6 percent to 51 percent, and the "other" sector rose from 8.7 percent to 11.4 percent. Both of these figures indicated a marked shift during the decade to what is known as a service economy.

The growth in the manufacturing-, construction-, and tertiary-sector businesses was powered by a great increase in urbanization of the Canadian population. Along with the substantial increase in the population itself, the shift from agriculture to other kinds of businesses was a consequence of the decision of many people to move off the farm and into the city, and to seek wage employment. Further, the many immigrants who came to Canada during the 1950's, mostly from Great Britain and northwestern Europe, were typically already urbanized in their old home countries, and they brought with them skills that could best be employed in an urban setting.

Natural Resources Canada's geographical location, notably its central location on the Laurentian shield, made it a major source of the minerals required for much of the world's manufacturing capabilities. During the 1950's, Canada became a major exporter of iron ore, partly as a result of the discovery of deposits in Labrador. New finds in northern Ontario and in Newfoundland added to the available resources. As the U.S. supply of iron-rich ore in the Mesabi range of northern Minnesota declined, a good deal of Canadian iron ore went to the United States as a replacement. Moreover, because of the heavy cost of shipping unrefined ore, Canada quickly developed a processing capability. At the time, the country was the largest global producer of nickel, which was mined and processed by the giant International Nickel Company in Sudbury, Ontario. Some of the world's largest deposits of asbestos are located in Quebec and were heavily mined at that time. During the 1950's, Canada was the second largest producer in the world of gold, zinc, cadmium, and selenium, and the third largest producer of silver, molybdenum, and barite. It was also a major producer of copper and lead, mostly from mines stretching across the relatively unpopulated northern fringe of the provinces.

Canada also became increasingly important as a source of petroleum and natural gas during the 1950's. Pipelines from the Alberta oil and gas fields were completed during the early 1950's and joined with terminals on the Great Lakes as well as British Columbia, where the oil could be loaded on tankers. The completion of a gas pipeline from the Alberta fields freed the heavily populated cities of central Canada, notably Toronto and Montreal, as well as the port cities on the Pacific, from dependence on imported gas and oil. Canada's oil and gas resources remained a major national asset in subsequent decades.

Along with mineral resources, forest products were a major factor in the Canadian economy during the decade. A large portion of the forest output was in the form of pulpwood, and it was converted in Canada into paper, which became a major export item, mostly in the form of newsprint. British Columbia produced a large quantity of lumber, which made possible the rapid growth of the home construction industry in both Canada and the United States.

Investment Canada's conversion from a frontier, colonial society to a developed nation was possible only with a vast amount of investment. Besides empowering the mechanization of agriculture, investment was essential for transportation purposes. In a country a little larger than the United States, products of agriculture and industry relied on efficient transportation to reach the world market. Although transcontinental railroads had been built in the nineteenth century, they needed expansion and modernization to be the primary means by which agricultural products and other items could reach the markets. The Canadian railroads, notably the Canadian Pacific and the Canadian National, converted from coal-

The trading floor of the Toronto Stock Exchange during the mid-1950's. (Hulton Archive | by Getty Images)

fired engines to diesel locomotives during the 1950's and thereby retained their ability to move Canada's agricultural surpluses to Great Lakes, Atlantic, and Pacific ports.

Although most mineral resources were developed by private companies, there were situations in which either the amount of capital needed or the uncertain prospects of a suitable return made private enterprise unwilling to undertake development. Those were situations in which the Canadian provinces retained ownership (as they did of most of the land in Canada), and they often resorted to a special device, the crown corporation, to organize exploitation of the resource. One of Canada's two transcontinental railroads, the Canadian National, was a crown corporation, and it was used for the development of other resources. The large deposit of potash in Saskatchewan was developed by a crown corporation,

as was the production of uranium. Hydroelectric power was the property of the provinces, and each province had its own operating system. The Canadian Broadcasting Corporation (CBC) is a public entity, as is Trans-Canada Airlines. In 1956, the Canadian Overseas Telecommunications Corporation, another crown corporation, was responsible for laying a new undersea cable between Newfoundland and Europe.

Much of the investment during the 1950's was, however, wholly in the public sector. By agreement within the dominion government, a greater portion of the income tax revenue collected was transferred to the provinces, whose expenditures rose dramatically. In turn, the provinces funded much municipal investment under agreements in which the municipalities recorded the investment as a loan, to be paid back to the province over an extended period.

Through this system, many Canadian municipalities acquired municipal water and sewer systems. In Ontario, for example, the Ontario Water Resources Commission was specifically authorized in 1956 to build and finance water and sewer facilities in the small and medium-sized towns that had previously lacked such infrastructure.

Another major area of public sector investment was the health care system. Hospital employment doubled during the 1950's, as part of the gradual introduction of a government-financed health care system. Saskatchewan and British Columbia pioneered the development of the system. Government-financed old age pensions were first introduced in 1952.

Financing The banking system of Canada consisted of the Bank of Canada at its head and nine "chartered" or privately owned banks. Historically, the Bank of Canada can affect the reserves of the chartered banks through its purchases or sales of government securities. It can also change the rediscount rate, the rate at which banks borrow from the Bank of Canada, but during the 1950's, this seldom happened. Technically, the Bank of Canada was responsible for fighting inflation, but it tended during the 1950's to follow an anti-inflationary policy. Only when the economy slowed down, as it did during the late 1950's, did the Bank of Canada adopt a slightly inflationary stance.

Large private banks operate through numerous branches located throughout the country. However, they did little to provide long-term corporate financing during the 1950's, concentrating instead on providing short-term commercial loans, of the sort required in the agricultural sector to cover the costs of a single production season. During the 1950's, the commercial banks provided much of the money required by grain dealers to purchase crops. During the 1950's, the large commercial banks did not finance mortgages, which were supplied instead by "building societies" modeled on those in Great Britain.

A major source of debt financing was Canada's life insurance industry. This industry was a primary means by which savings were made available through debt instruments to expand the economy. Although some foreign life insurance companies also operated in Canada, the domestic industry dominated the field; the assets of domestic life insurance companies exceeded those of foreign companies by four to one.

Foreign Control A major concern of all Canadians, especially during the economic expansion of the 1950's, was the risk of foreign control. Having been, a settlement colony of Great Britain during the nineteenth century, many Canadians feared the domination that was implied by a colonial relationship. Moreover, Canada's location on the border of the American colossus, the United States, whose economy exceeded that of Canada by a factor of at least ten, posed the risk that the United States would dominate Canada's economy.

Some of the major corporations playing large roles in Canadian business were, in fact, controlled by U.S. interests. This control most often took the form of ownership of the largest blocks of stock in the company. Three of Canada's top corporations during the 1950's—Alcan, Massey-Ferguson and Canada Packers—were dominated by U.S. financial interests. Foreign interests controlled 70 percent of International Nickel; 50 percent of that figure was located in the United States. Foreign control of Canada's manufacturing sector grew during the 1950's from 50 percent to 56 percent. An important element consisted of the plants of the major U.S. auto manufacturers located in Windsor and Oshawa, Ontario.

Impact Canada's economy grew substantially during the 1950's, powered by an increasing population, by urbanization, by a shift to manufacturing and resource processing, and by heavy investment, both public and private. Despite Canadian concerns, the dominant influence of the colossus to the south, the United States, remained a potent factor in the economic expansion of the decade.

Subsequent Events Canada continued to grow economically in the subsequent decades but always in the shadow of the United States. Nevertheless, its role as a major market for U.S. goods and as a source of many of the materials used by U.S. manufacturers helped to make Americans aware that Canada was a separate country. Because it did not participate in the Vietnam War, Canada served as a haven for many Americans who wanted to protest against the war. Even later, its public health system served as a model, both negative and positive, for the fractured health care system in the United States.

Further Reading

Aitken, Hugh G. J. *American Capital and Canadian Resources.* Cambridge, Mass.: Harvard University Press, 1961. Long a specialist on Canada, Aitken provides insight into the question of foreign control.

Bothwell, Robert, Ian Drummond, and John English. *Canada Since 1945: Power, Politics, and Provincialism.* Rev. ed. Toronto: University of Toronto Press, 1989. Comprehensive survey of Canadian development since World War II, a number of chapters are dedicated to the economy.

Dominion Bureau of Statistics. *Canada 1957.* Ottawa: Author, 1957. This volume, part of an annual survey published by the Canadian government, is full of statistical information.

Marr, William L., and Donald G. Paterson. *Canada: An Economic History.* Toronto: Macmillan, 1980. A good descriptive account of the Canadian economy.

Nancy M. Gordon

See also Agriculture in Canada; Canada and U.S. investments; Canadian Labour Congress; Elections in Canada; Gross national product of Canada; Immigration to Canada; Income and wages in Canada; Inflation in Canada; International trade of Canada; Trans-Canada Highway; Unemployment in Canada; Unionism in Canada; Urbanization in Canada.

■ Business and the economy in the United States

The 1950's was a period of growth and stability. Conditions were a welcome contrast to the instability and hardships of the Depression of the 1930's and World War II.

The 1950's was an era of unprecedented economic growth in the United States. The gross national product (GNP) measured at current prices increased from $285 billion in 1950 to $484 billion in 1959. Removing the effect of price increases, the GNP in 1958 increased by about one-third. This was not a notably high rate of growth for the period—it was far behind the rates of West Germany, Japan, France, and Italy. However, most adult Americans were more aware that their incomes and purchasing power enabled them to live far better than they had a decade or two earlier.

Business Cycles Fear that the economy would lapse into another major depression gradually gave way to confidence that the government had developed knowledge and policy instruments that would prevent such a disaster. During the Korean War boom years 1951-1953, unemployment fell to around 3 percent of the total labor force. The step-up in the military draft took many young men with few skills or little experience—people who would have been prime candidates for unemployment. Thereafter unemployment showed an upward trend, partly due to reduction in military personnel. Cyclical increases accompanied mild recessions in 1954 and 1958, going as high as 6.5 percent in 1958. Unemployment compensation, which had been introduced during the 1930's, reduced the pain of unemployment. Benefits were sensitive to the business cycle and helped insulate consumer spending against recessions. For example, between 1957 and 1958, benefits rose from $1.7 billion to $3.5 billion, the latter going to 7.9 million individual workers.

The outbreak of the Korean War in 1950 set off a wave of consumer scare buying and drove prices up by about 10 percent between 1949 and 1952. Price controls were reimposed, and tax increases and monetary restraint helped prevent further excess growth of demand. The subsequent rise in prices was probably no greater than the improvements in product quality. Even so, a 3.4 percent rise in consumer prices in 1957 caused alarm among economists.

Many economists believed that the national economy was operating below its potential during the late 1950's. Such views came out in a massive inquiry by the Joint Economic Committee of Congress into employment, growth, and price levels, concluded in 1959, and carried over into John F. Kennedy's presidential campaign in 1960. Some economists attributed the sluggish growth to inadequate increase in aggregate demand for goods and services. Others blamed the continuing high rates of taxes on personal incomes and corporate profits.

Demographics The national population increased from 152 million people in 1950 to 178 million in 1959. The "baby boom" was in full swing. The number of births surged upward from 3.6 million in 1950 to a peak of 4.3 million in 1957, then receded slightly. About 250,000 immigrants entered the country each year, far below the levels of the early twentieth century. The foreign-born population actually declined slightly over the decade. The proportion of immigrants from Europe fell below half, while the proportion from the Western Hemisphere, particularly Mexico, showed a pronounced increase.

The growing population needed more houses. Because of the economic hardships of the 1930's and 1940's, the country faced a severe housing shortage at the end of World War II. Consequently, the 1950's witnessed a sustained high level of home building. Housing starts actually peaked at around 2 million in 1950, then fluctuated around 1.5 million starts through the remainder of the decade. The number of occupied housing units rose from 43 million in 1950 to 53 million in 1960. Over the same period, the proportion of homes that were owner-occupied rose from 55 percent to 62 percent. These homes became an important component of the total wealth of most households. The new homes also contributed to upgrading national air quality, as many employed natural gas rather than coal for heating and cooking.

The development of a nation of home owners was encouraged by federal government policies. Interest payments on home mortgage loans were deductible in calculating federal income tax. The government provided home-loan guarantees or insurance through the Federal Housing Administration (FHA) and the Veterans Administration (VA). These programs covered about one third of the new housing started during the decade. Housing purchases were very sensitive to the costs and terms of credit. Government policies that adjusted these were able to bring about an increase in housing starts during the business-cycle recessions of 1954 and 1958.

New housing was typically financed by mortgage loans. Home-mortgage indebtedness skyrocketed from $43 billion in 1950 to $126 billion in 1959—but the market value of the mortgaged homes rose much more. Mortgage loans were typically amortized—a fixed monthly payment covered interest, taxes, insurance, and a modest repayment of the principal. The repayments constituted an element of forced saving that helped to increase household wealth. The principal institutional source of home mortgage credit was savings and loan associations, which benefited from numerous federal aids: deposit insurance, cheap loans from Federal Home Loan Banks, FHA and VA risk-sharing, and interest-rate ceilings on deposits. The sustained high level of housing-market activity helped increase employ-

ment in finance, insurance, and real estate from 1.9 million in 1950 to 2.6 million in 1959.

Consumer Durables New houses needed to be furnished—not merely with traditional tables and chairs, beds and dressers, couches and lamps, but with an expanding array of electrical appliances. By 1950 most homes, even in rural areas, were wired and connected for electricity.

The spread of television was a major cultural development. That spread was inhibited during the early 1950's by government-imposed restrictions on the number of broadcasting stations. Even after these were eased in 1953, only twelve channels were available for VHF (very high frequency) transmissions, and high-quality transmissions had relatively small viewing areas. However, millions of Americans found ways to enjoy the sitcoms of Milton Berle, Lucille Ball, and others. Attendance at the movies and sporting events fell. Radio stations had to reorganize their programming; they were aided by the introduction of light-weight portable transistor receivers. There were complaints that public morality was being undermined by television sex and violence. More serious concerns were directed at the possible long-run negative impact on young people's reading skills, exercise, and diet.

The mere numbers of electrical devices do not reveal the important upgrades in product specifications. Durable long-playing phonograph records had replaced the easily broken 78-rpm variety; teenagers stocked up on 45-rpm records—with big center holes—to listen to the emerging rock-and-roll music. Color television sets became available in 1954, but the more expensive color sets did not begin to outsell black-and-white sets until the late 1960's. The typical washing machine of 1950 was still a cumbersome wringer device that required tedious (and somewhat dangerous) hand labor. Over the next decade, automatic machines became common. Their spin-dry features greatly facilitated adoption of electric driers, saving the extensive labor entailed in hanging wet wash outdoors. Most washables still needed ironing (the new steam irons helped), but experimental drip-dry garments were on the market by 1959.

Automobiles Much of the housing construction and the appliance installation of the 1950's took place in the suburbs. Cities were crowded, dirty, and crime-ridden; rural areas were too isolated and lacked amenities. Families wanted places to raise their children that had lawns but not fields, houses rather than apartments.

Suburban life revolved around the automobile. Commuters drove to work or to train stations. Mothers drove children to school and drove to shop—often at the new shopping malls that were springing up. Automobile production had been shut down during World War II, but manufacturers expanded production rapidly once peace returned: Output surged to 6.7 million cars in 1950. This was surpassed by the 7.9 million produced in 1955, but through most of the decade, production fluctuated at slightly lower levels. About 40 million cars were on American roads in 1950. By 1959, the total was 59 million—nearly 50 percent higher.

Most of domestic auto production came from the Big Three: General Motors, Ford, and Chrysler. Each produced a wide range of models and placed great emphasis on annual model changes emphasizing style factors such as tail fins. Ford gained a lot of attention with the Thunderbird (introduced in 1954) and the Edsel (which failed in 1957). Most American-made cars were big, used fuel inefficiently, and seldom ran well for 100,000 miles. Automobiles came in for heavy cultural criticism from John Kenneth Galbraith (*The Affluent Society*, 1958), Vance Packard (*The Hidden Persuaders*, 1957), and John Keats (*The Insolent Chariots*, 1958). Dissatisfied consumers responded by purchasing imported cars. The most conspicuous was the Volkswagen Beetle, a durable and economical compact car that had no major annual model changes. By 1959, imported cars were accounting for about one-eighth of the American market.

The automobile industry constituted a tightly knit oligopoly, with profits (and wages) well above competitive levels, protected against entry of new firms by economies of large-scale operation and by their intricate networks of suppliers and distributors. A determined effort to create a serious competitor was launched by Henry Kaiser, whose production feats during World War II had won much praise. He offered the compact Henry J in 1950 but closed operations in 1955. By 1959, only two independent manufacturers remained.

On the Road The automobile boom of the 1950's spread to many related activities. The oil-refining industry provided another example of a highly profitable oligopoly. The major gasoline brands greatly expanded their roadside filling stations, many of them leased from the brand owners. Availability of overnight accommodation was greatly improved after 1954, when Kemmons Wilson opened his first Holiday Inn near Memphis, Tennessee. He developed an important franchising system, with local ownership and management backed by rules, standards, centralized purchasing and nationwide reservations service. Howard Johnson's roadside restaurants were a familiar landmark for hungry Americans. Beginning in 1955, tourists could visit Disneyland, which opened in Anaheim, California. During the mid-1950's, Ray Kroc was beginning his own franchising empire. Impressed by the mass-production techniques of the McDonald brothers' hamburger stand in California, he bought out the company, name and all. His franchisees paid a fee to use the company's name and logos, menu, recipes, and supplies.

Streets and roads were being expanded and upgraded in step with the automobile boom. Gasoline tax revenues were typically earmarked for highway expenditures by state and local government. A major upgrade was added in 1958 with the National Highway Act, which created a nationwide network of interstate highways. Construction standards emphasized gentle grades and curves, divided lanes, and limited access. The toll-free highways were ideally adapted for long-distance travel by cars and trucks.

Government support for road travel (and to a limited extent air travel) greatly reduced the role of railroads in passenger transport. Already by 1950, rail passenger traffic was less than half its wartime peak in 1944. Passenger miles dropped from 32 billion in 1950 to 22 billion in 1959. The coming of commercial jet airliners hastened the trend. In 1955, Pan American placed a massive order for jet planes with Boeing and Douglas and in 1958 launched the first scheduled jet service between New York and Paris.

Agriculture The number of farmers continued to decline, a trend that had become strong during World War II, reflecting the military draft and the great expansion of nonfarm job opportunities. The farm population dropped from 23 million in 1950 to 17 million in 1959, from 15 percent to 9 percent of total population. While the number of farms declined by one-third, actual acreage in farms remained relatively constant. Smaller farms were absorbed into larger units, a process that greatly facilitated mechanization. The number of tractors increased from 3.4 million to 4.7 million, grain combines from 714,000 to 1,045,000, and corn pickers from 456,000 to 775,000. Not only were these items more numerous; they also became larger, more efficient—and more expensive.

Farming became much more efficient. Total farm output increased about 10 percent despite a decrease in labor input of almost one-third. Besides mechanization, productivity was increased by increased use of chemical fertilizers, pesticides, and herbicides.

The number of farm operators fell from 5.4 million to 3.7 million. Much of this decline was concentrated in the South, where cotton farming became highly mechanized. The number of African American farm operators dropped by one-half, from 586,000 to 291,000. The price of cotton dropped from $0.40 to $0.32 per pound as domestic cotton clothing producers suffered competition from synthetics and from imports. Acreage in cotton fell dramatically, from 27 million in 1949 to 15 million in 1959, partly in response to government efforts to curtail production. Because productivity increased so much and because the best acreage remained in production, output declined only slightly, from 15.4 to 13.9 million bales. The introduction of mechanical cotton pickers greatly reduced the demand for field labor. All of these developments produced a huge migration of poorly educated blacks from the cotton South into northern cities. Many of the racial tensions of the 1960's had their origins in this process.

Abundant harvests refuted the traditional bleak forecasts that population growth would outrun food supplies. By 1950, it was estimated that the labor of one American farmworker fed nearly sixteen persons; by 1959, the estimate was nearly twenty-five persons. Much of the benefit of higher agricultural productivity went to consumers, as farm prices declined after 1953. Foreign consumers also benefited, as a substantial portion of American output was exported: farm products made up more than one-fifth of U.S. exports during the 1950's.

Political discourse, however, constantly referred to a "farm problem." Farmers' incomes were chronically lower than those available in nonfarm work (although farm families drew an increasing share of their income from nonfarm occupations). Federal government efforts to improve farm incomes fo-cused on trying to raise farm prices. Restrictions were imposed on acreage to be planted in specific crops or on amounts marketed. Agricultural exports were subsidized. Price-support programs paid farmers above-market prices for "staples" which were easy to store. During the 1950's, about 45 percent of marketed farm products fell under price-support programs. These programs excluded perishable, high-nutrition products such as meats, fruits, and vegetables. Most of the benefits went to large farms with low costs and higher incomes. Despite these apparent unfair features, the programs helped subsidize the increased capital and improved technology that kept the country well fed.

Jobs and Wages During the 1930's and 1940's, there was much concern that the economy could not maintain full employment of its growing labor force. Congress had adopted the Employment Act of 1946 to fix attention on this problem, primarily in management of the government's monetary and fiscal policies. These were relatively well managed, but much of the good performance of the labor market came through the inherent vigor of free competitive markets.

The economic boom attending the Korean War brought increased employment in virtually every listed sector. Draft calls more than doubled the number in military service. After 1951, however, the sectors display greater divergence. Nondurable manufacturing—such as clothing—showed no increase, while mining, transport, and federal government sectors all registered decreases. There were large employment declines in coal mining, textiles, and rail and bus transport. The sectors showing growth were mostly harbingers of an increasingly service-oriented economy—wholesale and retail trade, finance, insurance, real estate, state and local governments, and other services. Local governments hired many new schoolteachers to keep up with the baby boom. This job growth was important to absorb the reduction of three million in the agricultural labor force.

More than half of the job growth during the 1950's reflected the increased employment of women. Their share in the labor force rose from 18 percent in 1950 to 23 percent in 1959.

Income and Wages Money wage rates rose steadily over the decade at an average level that could support middle-class lifestyles. Full-time workers in manufacturing averaged annual incomes of $3,300 in 1950; this figure increased to $5,200 by 1959. About half of this increase reflected inflation; removing the price increases leaves the increase in real wages at about 30 percent for the decade. Cash income was supplemented by "fringe benefits" in many sectors, primarily employer-financed contributions to retirement funds and medical insurance. Fringe benefits enabled employers to evade wage controls and offered reduced tax liability.

While the federal minimum wage was raised from seventy-five cents per hour in 1949 to one dollar in 1955, most workers were paid more than the statutory minimum. The chief forces raising wages were growth of aggregate demand and increase in labor productivity, both making workers more valuable to employers. Productivity per person-hour in non-farm sectors increased by 22 to 24 percent over the decade. A number of forces contributed to rising productivity.

These forces included improvement in labor quality through raised educational levels. The proportion of the population aged twenty-five and over who were at least high school graduates rose from 33 percent in 1950 to 43 percent in 1959. Another force was increased amounts of capital goods per worker. The extremely low interest rates after 1945 encouraged business firms to expand their plants and equipment. Electric power and aluminum and petroleum refining were highly capital intensive sectors. The farm sector also experienced much "capital deepening." A final force was technological innovation. Estimated expenditures on research and development rose from $5.2 billion in 1953 to $12.5 billion in 1959. The transistor (introduced in 1948) was working its way through many electronic products and processes, including the first crude and expensive computers. Industries installed automatic monitoring and control systems, and there was much talk of "automation."

Labor Unions Union membership rose rapidly after the National Labor Relations Act of 1935 gave unions protected status. By 1950, there were about 15 million union members, representing about one-third of the nonfarm labor force. Membership grew in step with the total labor force, and the unionized proportion remained relatively constant. Public concern about abuses of union power had resulted in the Taft-Hartley Act of 1947.

Strikes periodically disrupted the economy, although the publicity usually exaggerated the damage. "Wildcat" strikes (unauthorized by union leadership) in the coal industry in 1950 reduced coal output by one-third. In 1952, the steelworkers union threatened to strike, provoking President Harry S. Truman to seize control of the industry as necessary to support the war. The Supreme Court soon overruled the seizure. The strike occurred but was soon settled. The steel industry was again shut down by strikes in 1956 and 1959. The impact of work stoppages on total labor input was relatively small—seldom more than one-half of one percent.

In 1950, most labor unions were affiliated with either the American Federation of Labor (AFL) or the Congress of Industrial Organizations (CIO), which had parted company during the mid-1930's. In 1955, the two organizations recombined, forming the AFL-CIO under the presidency of George Meany. One motive was to try to improve the image of unions held by the public and the government. Several unions had been expelled from the CIO in 1949-1950 for alleged communist domination. In 1954, the AFL expelled the longshoremen's union for criminal involvements, and the AFL-CIO threw out the Teamsters Union for similar reasons in 1957. After congressional investigations into union corruption, Congress adopted the Landrum-Griffin Act in 1959. Its focus was an effort to increase democratic processes and financial accountability within unions.

The Business World Private business continued to provide the largest share of production and employment. The government share of nonfarm employment rose from 13 percent in 1950 to 15 percent in 1959 (excluding the military), but this was concentrated among the traditional functions of state and local governments. In 1950, there were about 7.5 million business firms, more than 90 percent of them unincorporated proprietorships or partnerships. By 1959, the number had grown to 11.2 million firms, of which slightly over one million were corporations. Most firms, even corporations, were small. However, the small number of corporations with $100 million in assets held about half total corporate assets in 1950 and increased their share to 55 percent in 1951. Corporations generated slightly more than half of the gross national product, a fraction that showed only slight increase over the decade.

There was concern about the powerful role of large corporations. American Telephone and Telegraph, the largest employer, provided nationwide telephone service and still employed vast numbers of operators, although automatic dialing was rapidly spreading. Other large firms were found in petroleum refining, railroads, and chemical and electrical manufacturing.

Concern about the power of large firms led Congress in 1950 to adopt the Celler-Kefauver antimerger law, making it easier for the government to block mergers. In 1957, the government successfully required DuPont to sell its significant holding of General Motors stock, arguing this gave DuPont an unfair advantage in trying to sell its paints and other products to GM. The new antimerger law was used to block combination of Bethlehem Steel and Youngstown Sheet and Tube in 1958. As time passed, it became evident that giant firms were not significantly increasing their role in the economy in any harmful manner.

In general, American business was profitable. In response, stock prices soared. The Standard and Poors stock-price index, which stood at 18.4 in 1950, reached 57.4 in 1959. Thus stocks on average had tripled in market value. One response—and contributing factor—was the increased popularity of mutual-fund investment companies. These grew from a modest $2.5 billion in assets in 1950 to nearly $16 billion in 1959—a harbinger of much greater growth yet to come. These funds accepted investments in small denominations and acquired diversified portfolios that helped reduce risk for investors.

As stock prices were rising, so were interest rates. Rates on government bonds, which averaged less than 2.5 percent during the 1940's, rose steadily to exceed 4 percent in 1959. Keynesian economists blamed the rising rates on restrictive monetary policy. However, rates were responding to a tidal wave of borrowing. Consumer credit indebtedness rose from $23 billion in 1950 to $52 billion in 1959, much of it to buy cars and household appliances. Corporations borrowed heavily to expand their plants and equipment—their debts doubled, from $142 billion in 1950 to $283 billion in 1959. The federal government's debt changed very little, despite the Korean War. However, state and local governments added $40 billion to their debts, mostly to finance construction of highways and other public works. Generally,

the increases in debt were financing increases in assets, wealth, and productivity.

The commercial banking system furnished a large share of the funds for increased borrowing, mostly derived from the inflow of the public's deposits, which rose from $129 billion in 1950 to $193 billion in 1959. The proportion of families with checking accounts rose from about one-third in 1946 to 57 percent in 1960, and banks reported forty-six million personal accounts in early 1961. Commercial banks continued to enjoy protection against competition dating from the Great Depression—entry was restricted, and the Federal Reserve maintained relatively low ceiling rates on deposits.

Income Distribution The 1950's saw a major upshift in the distribution of family incomes. In 1950, three-fourths of families had incomes below $5,000. By 1959, nearly one-third of this number had moved into higher levels. Part of this was a reflection of the inflation of prices. However, after removing the impact of inflation, there was still a major reduction in the under-$5,000 group.

The Congressional Joint Economic Committee estimated that 32 million people were in poverty in 1957. A quarter of the people counted as poor were elderly; another quarter were single women who were heads of their households. About two-thirds of the poor (including many in the previous two categories) were in households whose heads had only eighth-grade educations or less. About one-fifth were nonwhite, and another quarter were members of farm families.

Powerful forces were at work to reduce many of the poverty categories. Social Security benefits to the elderly were expanding rapidly, rising from $651 million in 1950 to $7.6 billion in 1959—more than a tenfold increase. Education levels were improving rapidly, and many low-income farm families were moving to better-paying nonfarm jobs.

International Involvements By 1950, the areas of the world most damaged by World War II were well on their way to recovery. However, the United States government was still providing large sums in foreign economic and military aid—more than $3 billion per year in 1950 and 1951.These payments then receded to an annual average of about $2 billion. American private investment abroad increased substantially, averaging well in excess of $2 billion a year after 1955. These flows, plus a seemingly insatiable foreign demand for American goods and services, gave the U.S. a consistent surplus of exports over imports, ranging from a low of $500 million in 1953 to a high of $5.9 billion in 1957. Leading exports included farm products, capital goods, and other industrial supplies and materials for a world eager to rebuild and develop.

The U.S. government played a leading role in the newly formed institutions to promote international trade and investment. The General Agreement on Tariffs and Trade (GATT), formed in 1947, provided a framework for negotiating multilateral reductions in trade barriers. The World Bank (created in 1944) provided long-term loans, initially for postwar reconstruction, but increasingly for development of low-income countries. The International Monetary Fund (IMF), also created in 1944, attempted to promote stable exchange rates and discourage the use of direct restrictions on trade and payments by making short-term loans available to countries suffering international deficits. The currency of each member nation in IMF generally maintained a fixed exchange rate with the U.S. dollar.

The U.S. Treasury stood ready to buy or sell gold at a fixed price of $35 an ounce in transactions with foreign governments or central banks (but not with ordinary U.S. citizens). Although there was much talk of "dollar shortage" as a chronic problem facing other countries, revival of their economies and downward adjustments of their foreign-exchange rates enabled them to make significant net gold purchases from the U.S. in 1958-1959.

Government and the Economy The Employment Act of 1946 committed the federal government "to promote maximum employment, production, and purchasing power." The law created a three-person Council of Economic Advisers in the executive branch and a Joint (Congressional) Committee on the Economic Report (later the Joint Economic Committee). Although these agencies had no policy-making authority, they produced many useful and influential research studies.

The outbreak of the Korean War in 1950 unleashed a burst of inflation. The government responded by reimposing wage and price controls, but also moved to restrict aggregate demand for goods and services. Tax rates were increased and government spending restrained. In 1951, the Federal Reserve reached an "Accord" with the Treasury that

freed the Federal Reserve to adopt a restrictive monetary policy. As a result, the inflation was relatively mild and short-lived.

Impact The U.S. economy's performance during the 1950's dispelled fears that the hard times of the 1930's would return. At a time when much of the world was experimenting with collectivist policies, the U.S. demonstrated that a system based on private property and free enterprise could deliver comfortable incomes to most families, with steady if unspectacular improvement over time. As a result, there were few major changes in economic policy during the 1950's. Rather, the economy was adapting to policy changes introduced during the 1930's and 1940's.

Subsequent Events Economic conditions of the late 1950's figured prominently in the election campaign of 1960. After his election, President John F. Kennedy fulfilled his promise to "get the country moving again" by sponsoring major reductions in tax rates. In 1960-1965, the economy enjoyed prosperity and economic growth, but inflationary pressures began to build as military involvement in Vietnam intensified. Many structural trends of the 1950's continued—a rise in service industries, increased employment of women, and a decrease in poverty. Large corporations did not take over an increasing share of the economy, but encountered increasing competition from overseas. Government sponsored programs and policies—notably Medicare (medical insurance for the elderly), Lyndon B. Johnson's War on Poverty, and efforts to reduce the influence of discrimination—began in the 1960's and would have a significant impact on the U.S. economy for years to come.

Further Reading

Brozen, Yale. *Concentration, Mergers, and Public Policy.* New York: Macmillan, 1982. Scope is broader than the title suggests, extending to an appraisal of the extent and effectiveness of competition; much data is drawn from the 1950's.

Feldstein, Martin, ed. *The American Economy in Transition.* Chicago: University of Chicago Press, 1980. Essays on financial markets, macroeconomics, international trade, population, labor, industry, and economic well-being.

Galbraith, John Kenneth. *The Affluent Society.* Boston: Houghton Mifflin, 1958. Witty, critical argument that the American economy neglects high-priority social services and public goods.

Hickman, Bert G. *Growth and Stability of the Postwar Economy.* Washington, D.C.: Brookings Institution, 1960. Careful examination of the behavior of the macroeconomy during the 1950's.

Rapp, David. *How the U.S. Got into Agriculture and Why It Can't Get Out.* Washington, D.C.: Congressional Quarterly, 1988. Good review of the "farm problem" and policies.

Rockoff, Hugh. *Drastic Measures: A History of Wage and Price Controls in the United States.* New York: Cambridge University Press, 1984. Excellent survey facilitating comparison of Korean episode (chapter 6) with earlier and subsequent experience.

Stein, Herbert. *The Fiscal Revolution in America.* Chicago: University of Chicago Press, 1969. An insider's readable narrative and analysis; chapters 10-14 deal with the 1950's.

Trescott, Paul B. *Financing American Enterprise: The Story of Commercial Banking.* New York: Harper and Row, 1963. Chapters 10-11 view monetary policy and business-bank interaction from 1945 to 1960.

Vatter, Harold G. *The U.S. Economy in the 1950's.* New York: W. W. Norton, 1963. A compact yet comprehensive and critical overview—best single source on the decade.

Wilcox, Clair. *Toward Social Welfare: An Analysis of Programs and Proposals Attacking Poverty, Insecurity, and Inequality of Opportunity.* Homewood Ill.: Richard D. Irwin, 1969. Historical as well as analytical treatment.

Paul B. Trescott

See also Agriculture in the United States; Celler-Kefauver Act of 1950; Chrysler autoworkers' strike; Gross national product of the United States; Housing in the United States; Income and wages in the United States; Inflation in the United States; International Business Machines Corporation; Recession of 1957-1958; Small Business Administration; Unemployment in the United States; Unionism in the United States.

C

■ Caesar, Sid

Identification American television and film comedian

Born September 8, 1922; Yonkers, New York

Sid Caesar's work on television during the 1950's helped create the comedy-variety genre and made Caesar a fixture on the small screen throughout the decade.

The son of a Yonkers, New York, restaurant owner, Sid Caesar mastered in his youth the dialects and accents he later used in his comedy routines. Although he began as a musician (he studied the saxophone at the Juilliard School), he added comedy to his repertoire while serving in the Coast Guard during World War II. He had a role in a Broadway show after the war, and in 1949, he had a television variety show titled *Admiral Broadway Review*, which was carried on the NBC and DuMont networks. That show, produced and directed by Max Liebman, included Imogene Coca, a talented comedian who was his partner in several shows.

Caesar's next foray into television, *Your Show of Shows*, ran for four years and consisted of monologues, parodies, and skits. Its writers included such future luminaries as Carl Reiner, Mel Brooks, and Neil Simon. The show included a parody of popular films and allowed Caesar and Coca to create comical characters such as the Hickenloopers, the Professor, and the mechanical clock that featured the duo striking each other as well as the hour. In 1954, Caesar split with Coca and began another show, *Caesar's Hour*, with Reiner and Nanette Fabray, but was reunited with Coca for *Sid Caesar Invites You*, which ran for several months in 1958.

Impact Caesar won several awards for his comedic talents, including *Look* magazine's Best Comedian on Television Award in 1951 and 1956 and the Emmy Award for best comedy-variety show in 1958. His best work was captured in Liebman's 1973 feature film *Ten from Your Show of Shows*. Other comedians have testified to Caesar's influence on their careers, and the screenwriting for his shows is said to be the inspiration for Reiner's *The Dick Van Dyke Show*.

Further Reading

Adir, Karen. *The Great Clowns of American Television.* Jefferson City, N.C.: McFarland, 1988. Profiles seventeen comic talents, including Caesar, and includes information about their early years, their personal lives, and their characters, among other facts.

Sid Caesar and his comic costar Imogene Coca. (Hulton Archive | by Getty Images)

Caesar, Sid, and Eddy W. Friedfeld. *Caesar's Hours: My Life in Comedy, with Love and Laughter.* Boulder, Colo.: Perseus, 2003.

Thomas L. Erskine

See also Freberg, Stan; Gobel, George; *Honeymooners, The*; Linkletter, Art; *MAD*; Radio; Silvers, Phil; Television in the United States.

■ California's Alien Land Laws

Definition Laws denying land ownership to foreign-born residents of California

Date Declared unconstitutional by the California Supreme Court on April 17, 1952; officially repealed by popular referendum on November 4, 1956

The end of the laws by judicial and popular decision removed an important obstacle to racial equality in California during the 1950's.

Anti-Japanese sentiment in California led to the state's first Alien Land Law in 1913. The law prohibited land ownership by aliens who were ineligible to become U.S. citizens. Under the amended federal 1790 Naturalization Law—effective until its repeal by the 1952 McCarran-Walter Act—only Europeans or Africans could become United States citizens. California's law targeted Japanese immigrants who often had the money to buy land.

Since American-born children received citizenship regardless of the citizenship of their parents, the Alien Land Law of 1920 prohibited ineligible alien parents to act as guardians for their underage citizen children and forbade land transfer to noncitizens. Land sold in violation became property of the state. While there were only twenty court cases involving this law before 1941, it had a chilling effect on Japanese families.

Legal Challenges In *Sei Fujii v. State of California,* California's supreme court declared California's Alien Land Laws unconstitutional because their racially discriminatory nature violated the equal protection clause of the Fourteenth Amendment to the U.S. Constitution. The verdict, announced on April 17, 1952, built on a series of U.S. Supreme Court decisions handed down during the late 1940's. The most important of those was *Oyama v. California* in 1948, which upheld an alien father's right to act as guardian for his citizen son's real estate. In the 1952 4-3 de-

cision, the California supreme court agreed that the state had no right to exclude any particular racial group from owning land.

For Sei Fujii, this decision in 1952 proved an important victory. A resident alien and law school graduate from the University of Southern California, Fujii had purchased a small plot in East Los Angeles to challenge the law in 1948. When the state began escheat action, a legal process designed to return the land to the state, Fujii challenged the authorities. On appeal, he won his landmark case and gained a crucial victory for Japanese and other Asian American communities.

Even though the alien land laws were ruled unconstitutional, they still were used in some areas. The Japanese American Citizens League (JACL) lobbied strongly to have this racially discriminatory legislation repealed. During the mid-1950's, their efforts gathered steam. Californians saw through the legalistic ruses of the alien land laws and rejected their racist intentions. Working together in a broad popular effort, the JACL and political allies gathered enough signatures to place Proposition 13 on the November, 1956, state ballot. The proposition asked for the repeal of the alien land laws. On November 4, it passed by a wide margin.

Impact The legal challenge and the popular repeal of these laws marked an unusual display of Asian American political passion during the 1950's. Too often, Asian Americans remained a silent minority during this decade and did not openly challenge unjust laws or social practices. The legal and political rejection of California's alien land laws represented a significant landmark in successful Asian American political action during the decade.

Further Reading

McClain, Charles, ed. *Japanese Immigrants and American Law: The Alien Land Laws and Other Issues.* New York: Garland, 1994. Scholarly essays provide in-depth discussion of the laws and the legal challenges to them; places the conflict in the context of overcoming anti-Japanese sentiment during the 1950's.

Takaki, Ronald. *Strangers from a Different Shore: A History of Asian Americans.* Rev. ed. Boston: Back Bay Books, 1998. Widely available, covers the issue from an Asian American point of view.

R. C. Lutz

See also Asian Americans; Demographics of the United States; Immigration and Nationality Act of 1952; Immigration to the United States; Japan; Racial discrimination.

■ Campanella, Roy

Identification African American baseball player
Born November 19, 1921; Philadelphia, Pennsylvania
Died June 26, 1993; Los Angeles, California

Roy Campanella was an exceptional ballplayer and a key figure in the racial integration of Major League Baseball

Roy Campanella's father was of Italian descent, his mother an African American. While racial taunts were not unknown to Roy, he maintained an enthusiastic approach to life and was an avid baseball player. At age fifteen, he joined the Baltimore Elite Giants of the National Negro League and was a powerful catcher for them through 1945. Major League Base-

ball was racially segregated at that time; being of mixed heritage, Roy was considered "colored" and therefore ineligible for the major leagues. In 1946, Branch Rickey, general manager of the Brooklyn Dodgers, took steps to change this segregation. He signed Jackie Robinson to a minor league contract, and Campanella was signed soon afterward. By 1948, Campanella joined Robinson on the Dodgers team. Over the next decade, the pair helped the Dodgers win five National League Pennants and, in 1955, the only World Series championship—against the mighty New York Yankees—in Brooklyn Dodgers history.

Impact Campanella was legendary both as a defensive catcher and as a hitter. During Campanella's career, he was named the National League most valuable player three times (1951, 1953, 1955). During the 1953 season, he set major-league records for a catcher with 41 home runs, 142 runs batted in, and 807 putouts. He was elected to the Baseball Hall of Fame in 1969.

Campanella was also part of an extraordinary team effort that accomplished important social and athletic goals. The Dodgers not only were champions on the field but also showed that racial cooperation was possible and rewarding. Campanella proved an important figure in the team's racial integration, and the 1950's proved an important era for the game's race relations. However, the era came to a sad end when Campanella's career was shortened by a tragic auto crash in 1957 that paralyzed him. The Dodgers moved to the West Coast a year later.

Further Reading

Campanella, Roy, and Jules Tygiel. *It's Good to Be Alive.* Reprint. Lincoln: University of Nebraska, 1995. Campanella's autobiography after his career-ending automobile accident.

Kahn, Roger. *The Boys of Summer.* New York: Perennial Books, 2000. First published in 1972, an account of key figures on the legendary Brooklyn Dodgers of the 1950's, including Campanella.

Ira Smolensky

See also African Americans; Baseball; Robinson, Jackie; Sports.

Roy Campanella in 1952. (AP/Wide World Photos)

■ Canada and Great Britain

During the 1950's, Canada remained an active partici-
pant in British Commonwealth affairs, although its ties
with Great Britain continued to recede as the influence of
the United States increased within its borders.

Established in 1867 as a self-governing dominion of
the British Empire, Canada remained closely tied to
its British colonial heritage and traditions for many
decades. Although the former colony became independent in domestic affairs, and the role of the governor general—the British monarchy's representative
in Canada—was largely symbolic and limited, the dominion still deferred to Britain on foreign policy. A
Canadian Department of External Affairs did not
exist before 1909, and as late as 1920, the dominion
had no treaty-making power, no independent diplomatic representation abroad, and no right to declare
war on its own. At various times, this strong imperial
connection and the obligations it sometimes entailed
led to strains with Canada's large French-speaking
minority, who felt no such attachment to Britain.

World War I and the period following was an era
during which Canada consistently pressed for, and
Britain gradually conceded, autonomy and more input in foreign affairs and imperial matters. In 1926,
under pressure from Canada and South Africa, a
new definition of the dominions' status was affirmed
as that of autonomous communities within the British Empire. Canada and South Africa came to be
referred to as freely associated members of the Commonwealth of Nations. Furthermore, the 1931 Statute of Westminster clearly affirmed the independent and equal status of commonwealth members in
declaring that the British parliament could not pass
legislation affecting them unless requested.

Meanwhile, the British connection in Canada, although still somewhat important to English-speaking conservative nationalists wary of U.S. encroachment, was steadily weakening as American cultural
and economic influence increased. World War II
and its aftermath witnessed the further decline and
unraveling of the British Empire and the rise of the
United States as the world's premier superpower.
During the war, Canada and the United States had
cooperated at many levels. The Cold War period that
followed only accelerated this trend toward an even
closer relationship while the British connection continued to wane.

Era of Growing Autonomy By the 1950's what remained of the imperial tradition and connection
was mostly confined to symbolism and ceremony.
The British monarch's picture appeared on currency. The office of governor general also remained,
but in 1952, the tradition of British aristocrats holding this post gave way to appointment of the first of a
continuing series of Canadian-born officials. The judicial practice whereby constitutional issues were appealed beyond the Canadian Supreme Court to the
Judicial Committee of the Privy Council in London
had ceased in 1949. By this time, Canada also maintained its own embassies and diplomatic staff in
forty-six foreign nations. However, Canada's national
flag still bore the Union Jack, and an unofficial national anthem celebrated the British conquest and
heritage while ignoring the nation's important
French heritage.

Canada's British-style parliamentary system of
government and its ceremonies, procedures, and
constitutional practices differentiated the Canadian
political system from the American presidential system of government and was based in the British
North America Act (BNA), an 1867 legislative measure of the parliament in London.

By the 1950's, Canada participated in new ways
within the commonwealth, whose composition had
changed with the addition of some former underdeveloped colonies which became independent nations after World War II. Within the new and racially
diverse British Commonwealth, Canada was interested in the view of India's prime minister, Jawaharlal
Nehru, who promoted the commonwealth as a force
for reconciliation in world affairs. Among the older
member dominion states, Canada was most noted
for its enthusiastic and friendly attitude toward the
new membership and roles of Third World member
states. This approach led to close ties between Canada and the developing nations. In the case of India
and Canada, the relationship became known as the
Indo-Canadian entente. Through its participation in
the commonwealth's Colombo Plan, created in January of 1950, Canada joined in aid and development
programs that provided starvation relief, technical
assistance, and capital equipment to poorer member nations. In summary, Canada assumed a role in
the commonwealth second only to that of Britain.

Suez Canal Crisis During the Suez Crisis in the summer of 1956, Canadian foreign policy boldly took

British Commonwealth Nations in 1959

Country	Year Joined
Australia	1931
Canada	1931
Ceylon	1948
Ghana	1951
India	1947
Malaya	1957
New Zealand	1931
Pakistan	1947
South Africa	1931
United Kingdom	1931

the initiative in a situation that greatly affected relations between Britain, Canada, and other commonwealth members. When President Gamal Abdel Nasser of Egypt nationalized the Suez Canal on July 26, Britain worried about possible future interruptions of vital oil supplies and acted with force by sending troops, along with France and Israel, into the Suez area. This action met with strong opposition from the United States as well as the Soviet Union and also threatened to explode the commonwealth. Australia and, to a lesser extent, New Zealand backed the British position. India and other Asian commonwealth members were strongly opposed to what appeared to be imperialistic actions against another Third World state and sided with angry nonaligned countries. Britain seemed determined to act on this matter even if it entailed a break with the United States, and it did not regard full commonwealth support as essential. Only Canada seemed concerned about the impact of British actions on commonwealth unity and goodwill.

Both Prime Minister Louis St. Laurent and Minister of External Affairs Lester Pearson felt that Canada's international image would suffer if it became associated with an action likely to fail. Furthermore, this risky power play signaled a possible Anglo-American rift, condemnation of Britain in the United

Nations, and hostility in the Middle East region toward the Western powers. While Pearson, like the Americans, deplored the British decision, he also felt that negative reactions of the U.S. government were overly harsh and rude. Under Pearson's handling of the crisis, Canada sought to occupy a middle-ground position between its two major allies and serve as a bridge between them.

World opinion and diplomatic pressures led Britain, France, and Israel to agree to a cease-fire and withdraw their troops, thereby giving way to a multinational United Nations military force, the solution Pearson advocated. A Canadian general assumed command of this hastily patched together peacekeeping contingent. In the end, a dangerous Cold War confrontation was avoided, and Egypt retained control of the canal. Pearson's diplomacy and the Liberal government's position in the crisis drew heavy criticism from the Progressive Conservative opposition, who saw this event as a betrayal and abandonment of Great Britain. However, others believed that Canada's action had possibly saved the commonwealth from dissolution and had extricated Britain from the unfortunate consequences of a serious miscalculation. Subsequently, Pearson received the Nobel Peace Prize for his diplomacy.

Growing U.S. Influence Another development during this decade that affected Canada's relations with Britain and the commonwealth was the noticeable increase in U.S.-Canadian ties and continuing rapid American penetration of many spheres of Canadian life. Canadian-U.S. trade skyrocketed, American capital made greater inroads into the nation's economic structure, and Canada became enmeshed in common military defense policies with its large neighbor. The statistics for this period in areas such as international trade and the degree of American economic investment speak dramatically. Between 1939 and 1960, American investment amounted to 75 percent of total foreign investment in Canada. During the same period, British investment in Canada had fallen from 36 percent to 15 percent. Likewise, by the late 1950's, Canada's trading patterns underlined its position as a North American country whose significant trade and financial links would be with the United States rather than with Britain and the commonwealth.

Before 1957, Canadians, who were enjoying unprecedented prosperity and reaping some benefits from the inflow of American capital, seemed unconcerned about issues such as foreign ownership in the economy or the vital importance of the British connection: A Gallup poll conducted before the queen's visit in 1957 revealed that nearly half of Canadians were indifferent about her trip and 22 percent expressed negative opinions. On the other hand, nationalistic concerns over the extent of U.S. economic influence finally began to emerge as a public issue. Not all Canadians were pleased by Americanizing trends, which many worried might pose a threat to the nation's sovereignty. This stance would become more evident under the government of John Diefenbaker between 1957 and 1963.

On June 10, 1957, Diefenbaker led the Progressive Conservatives to a stunning upset over the long-reigning Liberals. The Liberal government's demise came about partly as a result of its seemingly arrogant decision to cut off parliamentary debate and force through a bill that aroused the opposition's objections about American economic control. Canada's new prime minister was a traditional conservative nationalist; he was strongly attached to the British connection and averse to the trend of continentalism, the increasing integration of Canada into a single North American economic, cultural, political, and military framework.

During the election campaign, Diefenbaker had promised he would seek to increase Canadian-British trade as a means of reducing dependence on the United States. A month after taking office, the prime minister proposed to divert 15 percent of Canada's import trade from the United States to the United Kingdom. This arrangement never materialized, not only because of policy restrictions accompanying Britain's membership in the General Agreement on Tariffs and Trade (GATT) but also as a result of Britain's growing interest in the European Common Market, which was formed just before Diefenbaker's government took office in 1957.

A few days after his government was installed, and again in the fall of 1958, Diefenbaker undertook long, extended world tours. The Canadian leader attended numerous commonwealth conferences and visited commonwealth capitals with the purpose of strengthening ties through personal diplomacy and finding new trade partners. In addition to being a staunch Canadian nationalist, Diefenbaker was a populist and reformer who sympathized with the poor and oppressed. Being a strong advocate of human rights, Diefenbaker became a determined opponent of South Africa's racist apartheid policies and took an active part in commonwealth actions leading to that state's withdrawal from the organization in 1961.

Impact The Conservative government's efforts during the late 1950's to stem the onslaught of Americanizing trends by strengthening relations and connections with Britain and the commonwealth were not crowned with success, and in 1963, the pro-American Liberals returned to power. Diefenbaker's commonwealth tours may have succeeded in furthering goodwill, but nothing concrete was achieved and his overtures to Britain came to naught. Canada's American connection and ties were destined to be weightier and more important than the past imperial tradition. The realities of geographic proximity, the new power relationships in the world, and a close and familiar American market were difficult to overcome. However, the commonwealth provided Canada with a forum and opportunity to assert itself in world affairs independent of the United States and without straining relations. Canada's humanitarian aid and technical assistance programs boosted its international image. Furthermore, the dominion's lack of imperialist credentials, a nearly unique situation for an industrialized Western state, also enhanced its standing with Third World countries and allowed it occasionally to assume the role of "middle power," honest broker, and peacekeeper.

Further Reading

Creighton, Donald. *The Forked Road: Canada, 1939-1957.* Toronto: McClelland & Stewart, 1976. Monograph by a prominent Canadian historian reflecting a conservative nationalist viewpoint about the weakening of imperial ties and other matters.

English, John. *The Worldly Years: The Life of Lester Pearson, 1949-1957.* New York: Alfred A. Knopf, 1992. Useful biographical study of an important Liberal statesman associated with Canada's "middle power" foreign policy in this era.

Grant, George. *Lament for a Nation: The Defeat of Canadian Nationalism.* Montreal: McGill-Queens University Press, 2003. Study of the Diefenbaker government's failed efforts to distance Canada from the United States.

Miller, J. B. D. *Survey of Commonwealth Affairs: Expansion and Attrition, 1953-1969.* New York: Oxford University Press, 1974. Excellent study by an Australian scholar on the commonwealth during this period.

Robinson, H. Basel. *Diefenbaker's World: A Populist in Foreign Affairs.* Toronto: University of Toronto Press, 1989. The outlook and policies of a Canadian prime minister who sought to strengthen Canada's ties with Britain and the commonwealth.

David A. Crain

See also Canada as a middle power; Continentalism; Diefenbaker, John G.; Elections in Canada; Elizabeth II's visit to North America; Foreign policy of Canada; International trade of Canada; North Atlantic Treaty Organization; Pearson, Lester B.; Suez Crisis.

■ Canada and U.S. investments

A dramatic increase in U.S. capital investment, growth of multinational firms, and American ownership in important sectors of the Canadian economy began to generate some concern in Canada by the late 1950's.

Fear of being absorbed politically and economically into a rising American empire motivated Canada's first prime minister, Sir John A. Macdonald (1867-1888), to retain strong political and economic ties with Canada's former colonial mentor, Great Britain, and to pursue economic nationalist policies in dealing with the United States. Macdonald established his long-standing "National Policy," which included protectionism for Canadian industry under a very restrictive tariff. Ironically, high tariffs helped local industry survive while simultaneously contributing to a significant American economic presence in the national economy.

Denied Canadian markets by a high tariff barrier, U.S. firms eventually decided to vault the wall and establish branch firms in Canada, where they could also enjoy special British trade preferences given to the products of nations associated with the empire and Commonwealth. Canada faced a dilemma in economic policy of being inundated either by American goods or by American branch plants. The National Policy had in fact contributed to the branch plant economy. During the 1950's, however, both trade and the American economic presence were expanding simultaneously at an unprecedented pace.

Post-World War II Boom The 1950's witnessed the continuation of a great postwar economic boom in Canada that unfolded from the late 1940's to the latter part of the next decade. The recent wartime partnership had resulted in close political, economic, and military ties between Canada and the United States. Canada's wartime leader, William L. Mackenzie King, who had fostered this cross-border relationship, began to make vocal his fears about U.S. intentions and the fate of Canadian sovereignty in a relationship between neighbors of such unequal size and strength.

Mackenzie King's successor had no such compunctions. The Liberal government of Prime Minister Louis St. Laurent (1949-1957) attempted to sustain the momentum of economic growth and bolster infrastructure by encouraging foreign investment, especially that of the United States. Minister of Trade C. D. Howe, a naturalized Canadian of American birth, was the most influential person after St. Laurent in this government. Howe was credited with organizing production, and his policies turned Canada into an economic power. Howe promoted great megaprojects such as the St. Lawrence Seaway, the Trans-Canada Highway, and a Trans-Canada Pipeline, which provided industrialized eastern Canada with natural gas from the western provinces. Apparently, Howe was not worried about who actually owned industry as long as the profits rolled in. Since the minister of trade viewed foreign investment as a force driving further economic growth, he urged American businesses to show faith and invest in Canada.

Considering the old tradition of jumping the tariff wall, American businesses required no such encouragement. Moreover, Canada's considerable supply of raw materials and natural resources now beckoned as an increased incentive. The United States, whose status and military responsibilities as a world superpower had expanded as a result of the war, wanted a reliable source for vital products such as uranium and petroleum. In 1952, an American economic report warned of depletion of natural resources at home and spoke of the "El Dorado" to the north. Canada's proximity and the relative ease with which these resources could be bought made them easier to control and protect.

Foreign investment increased rapidly during this period in Canada's history. U.S. State Department figures show that U.S. investment in Canada rose from $3.58 billion (U.S.) in 1950 to $8.3 billion by late 1957, exceeding the growth rate of American investment in Latin America. Manufacturing attracted $3.5 billion while the energy, mining, and smelting sectors accounted for $3.15 billion. According to Canadian figures, by the end of 1960, U.S. investment amounted to 75 percent of all foreign investment, which represented a jump from 60 percent in 1939. In terms of foreign ownership of Canadian industry, by late 1959, 73 percent of petroleum and natural gas production was foreign owned; 69 percent was in U.S. hands. The figures for foreign ownership of smelting, refining, and mining ores were 61 percent and 53 percent respectively. U.S. mining multinationals such as American Smelting and Refining and the American Metal Corporation controlled much of the production of lead and zinc. The manufacturing sector was 51 percent foreign owned, with U.S. capital accounting for 41 percent. The United States owned 90 percent of the auto industry. Foreign ownership of all Canadian industries was 34 percent, with 26 percent of the total belonging to the United States.

The Gordon Commission For most of the decade, Canadians in general were not alarmed over massive foreign investment. When a prominent Canadian businessman complained that Canada's economic role was becoming limited to that of a supplier of raw materials for the U.S. economy, the public turned a deaf ear and remained too busy with their private lives to comprehend a possible negative impact. U.S. investment, after all, did help to bring about a decade of rising prosperity for Canadians, and certainly the American demand for petroleum and minerals sparked a resource boom. Even in 1956, a major Canadian textbook on economics underscored only the positive aspects of foreign investment without mentioning less favorable consequences.

It was not until late in the decade that a warning was sounded and this issue brought to the public's attention by the report of a Royal Commission on Canada's Economic Prospects established under the Liberal government. The commission's chairman was a Liberal Party outsider named Walter Gordon. Gordon viewed C. D. Howe as autocratic and felt that Howe was overly friendly with American business interests. The chairman, four colleagues, and a research staff composed mainly of university-affiliated economists began their work in 1955. The Gordon Commission's written report angered both Howe and St. Laurent, who saw a preliminary 1956 release. The official release was dated November,

1957, but it did not become public until April, 1958, after the Liberal government had left office.

The Gordon Commission's section addressing foreign investment made up only a small part of the study but sounded some warnings. Noting the rapid increase of American capital investment since the war and its high concentration in certain sectors, the report made the following observation: "No other nation as highly industrialized as Canada has such a large percentage of industry controlled by nonresident concerns." The report's tone was generally moderate in discussing the dangers of this situation and noted that most foreign-owned firms were good corporate citizens. Mild recommendations included the employment of high-level Canadian personnel and inclusion of independent Canadians on boards of directors, full disclosure of operations, better access for Canadians to research opportunities, and share holding.

Diefenbaker Administration Interestingly, the issue of foreign capital and ownership was connected to an event known as the Pipeline Debate (May 8-June 6, 1956) in which nationalistic views surfaced over the presence of American capital in this Canadian project. The high-handed tactics of the government used to shut off debate and ram through this measure was one factor in its defeat during the 1957 elections. John Diefenbaker, a Conservative nationalist, consequently became prime minister.

Diefenbaker shared a number of the concerns expressed by the Gordon Commission, although he was hostile to it as a result of its Liberal political composition. The prime minister wished to halt the transfer of Canadian industry and natural resources into the hands of American corporate interests. Noting that foreign investment in Canada amounted to 65 percent of the national income, he posed the question of how long the country could continue on this path and maintain a separate, independent existence. In September, 1957, Diefenbaker told an American audience that their companies should make their stock available to Canadians and not view Canada as simply an extension of the American market.

Impact In spite of his nationalistic leanings and pronouncements, Diefenbaker's government, which lasted until 1963, did not lead to a radical change in the matter of foreign investment and control. Limited measures, included issuing some new regulations for resource development in the Northwest Territories, required that foreign companies in Canada be controlled and the majority of their shares be Canadian owned. However, some critics argued that the tight credit monetary policies pursued by Diefenbaker's governor of the Central Bank actually contributed to an increase in foreign capital inflow at this time. While the issue was raised during the late 1950's, public opinion was still not aroused sufficiently over this issue. However, this situation would change during the late 1960's under the Liberal government of Pierre Trudeau, who embarked on a course of economic nationalism.

Further Reading

Bothwell, Robert, and William Kilbourn. *C. D. Howe: A Biography.* Toronto: McClelland and Stewart, 1979. Study of an influential Liberal cabinet member who was a key figure behind Canada's economic policies and development during the postwar period.

Levitt, Kari. *The Silent Surrender: The Multinational Corporation in Canada.* Toronto: Macmillan, 1989. Critical study of multinationals and their influence in Canada.

Safarian, A. E. *Foreign Ownership of Canadian Industry.* 2d ed. Toronto: McGraw-Hill, 1973. Analyzes the performance of foreign-owned firms in the commodity-producing sectors of Canadian industry. Contains useful statistical tables.

Smith, Denis. *Gentle Patriot: A Political Biography of Walter Gordon.* Edmonton: Hurtig, 1973. Useful study of one of the early advocates of Canadian economic nationalism.

David A. Crain

See also Business and the economy in Canada; Continentalism; Diefenbaker, John G.; Gross national product of the United States; International trade of Canada; International trade of the United States; Niagara Treaty.

■ Canada as a middle power

Definition Canada's emerging diplomatic role in world politics

Following World War II, Canada supported international and regional organizations in a diplomatic manner to achieve its foreign policy goals. Relations with the United States also had a significant impact on Canada's foreign and defense policies.

Canada's participation as a member of the victorious allied coalition during World War II created opportunities for an emerging role in world affairs after 1945. However, Canada's relatively small population of twelve million in 1950 restricted the size and significance of its military forces. Its decision to prohibit nuclear weapons also limited significant military influence. Consequently, Canada's foreign policy adopted a style identified as the "middle power" approach, which relied on diplomacy. Its membership in international and regional organizations provided opportunities for the Canadian government to support policies that promoted peace and stability.

Nonetheless, Canada agreed to take military action if its national interests were affected. It was a founding member of the North Atlantic Treaty Organization (NATO), the western military alliance facing the Soviet Union and its allies during the 1950's. The major conflict involving the Canadian military during the 1950's occurred during the Korean War, when approximately twenty thousand Canadians served under United Nations authority to resist the communist invasion of South Korea. However, Canada's combat role after 1945 was limited, and beginning during the early 1950's, Canadian troops participated as peacekeepers during the decade to oversee truces and other agreements in world trouble spots, especially in Asia and the Middle East. These diplomatic efforts sought to separate adversaries, usually through monitoring truce lines between the antagonists and using negotiations to seek a peaceful outcome.

A notable example of this approach occurred in 1956, when Britain, France, and Israel invaded Egypt. When a cease-fire between the combatants took effect late that year, Canadians participated in creating and staffing the United Nations Emergency Force (UNEF) to supervise the truce and occupation lines between the opposing countries. This undertaking continued until 1967. While not a permanent resolution of the problem, the UNEF effort maintained peace for a decade.

By the later 1950's, such Canadian peacekeeping activities were widely recognized for their contributions. To honor these efforts and achievements, the Norwegian Nobel Peace Prize Committee conferred the 1957 Nobel Peace Prize on Lester Pearson, the Canadian minister of external affairs. Although the award designated Pearson specifically, Canadians

The commandant of Quebec's Civil Defense Technical Training Centre uses a map of the city and a model of an atomic bomb's mushroom cloud to demonstrate what an atomic bomb blast would do to the city, in 1952. (Hulton Archive | by Getty Images)

were justly proud of this honor and believed that it belonged to the Canadian people.

However, Canada's recognition as a peacekeeper also highlighted its comparative military weakness. Canadians generally supported membership in the United Nations, NATO, and the Commonwealth organization composed of former British colonies. Public opinion and the government consistently opposed nuclear weapons as part of Canadian national defense, but few advocated an isolationist approach.

Foreign policy issues and concerns, including the Cold War rivalry of the superpowers and Canada's close but complicated relationship with the United States, periodically affected domestic politics and government policies during the 1950's. These kinds of issues affected the 1957 national election, which shifted political power from the Liberal Party of Prime Minister Louis St. Laurent to the Conserva-

tive Party led by John Diefenbaker. The Diefenbaker administration sought a more assertive national and independent policy, rather than too easily following the powerful United States as its close ally and neighbor. However, the attempt to increase a more independent role in world affairs largely failed by the later 1950's. For example, the ambitious plan to develop a new Canadian supersonic jet fighter (the Avro Arrow) proved so expensive that the government canceled the project in 1959. The demise of the project helped increase unemployment, a topic which became a domestic political issue and increased anti-Diefenbaker sentiment. Moreover, the cancellation of this project forced the Canadian government to become even more dependent on American weapons systems and United States protection. Canadians often were divided over their close ties to the American economy and its foreign policies. By contrast, Americans continued their traditional practice of paying scant attention to their northern neighbor.

Despite occasional differences, the U.S. and Canadian governments cooperated during the 1950's to face a potential Soviet military attack on North America. Construction of extensive radar systems across Canada to track offensive Russian long-range bombers and missiles illustrated this relationship. In addition, in 1958, both governments created an important joint air defense system, the North American Aerospace Defense Command (NORAD). With the potential for Soviet aggression, civil defense also became important during the 1950's, and the Canadian public had to prepare for the possibility of an attack on its territory. However, disagreements over the degree of potential danger and the level of preparation needed to cope with a nuclear conflict divided public opinion during the decade.

Impact Canadians during the 1950's had to cope with the tensions of the Cold War period and the uncertainty of a fragile peace. Their preference was to avoid crises or reduce disputes, and thus the public tended to give their support to government efforts to use its limited resources and influence to achieve success derived by means other than military strength. Overall, Canada's reputation and influence as a middle power in world affairs during this period stayed remarkably steady, confirming the sense among most Canadians that their nation had adopted the appropriate methods to act effectively on the world stage.

Further Reading

Granatstein, J. L., ed. *Canadian Foreign Policy Since 1945: Middle Power or Satellite?* Toronto: Copp Clark, 1973. Informative coverage of Canada's role in world affairs, including relations with the United States.

Hawes, Michael K. *Principal Power, Middle Power, or Satellite? Competing Perspectives in the Study of Canadian Foreign Policy.* Toronto: York University Press, 1984. Includes a useful description of the middle power concept.

Keating, Tom. *Canada and World Order: The Multilateralist Tradition in Canadian Foreign Policy.* New York: Oxford University Press, 2002. Stresses Canada's success as a middle power by working through regional and world organizations to achieve foreign policy objectives.

Morton, Desmond. *A Military History of Canada: From Champlain to Kosovo.* Toronto: McClelland and Stewart, 2000. Readable account of Canada's long military history, including the post-World War II period.

Thompson, John H., and Stephen J. Randall, eds. *Canada and the United States: Ambivalent Allies.* Athens: University of Georgia Press, 1997. The political, economic, and strategic relationship of the two neighbors and allies includes both cooperation and disagreements.

Taylor Stults

See also Avro Arrow; Canada and Great Britain; DEW Line; Diefenbaker, John G.; Elections in Canada; Foreign policy of Canada; Isolationism; North Atlantic Treaty Organization; Pearson, Lester B.; St. Laurent, Louis; St. Lawrence Seaway.

■ Canadian Broadcasting Corporation

Identification Canada's publicly owned broadcasting system for radio and television

Date Began television broadcasting on September 6, 1952

As a result of rising concerns about cultural sovereignty in the post-World War II period, Canada expanded the Canadian Broadcasting Corporation (CBC) to include a nationally owned television network.

Canadian nationalists striving to promote an independent, distinct national culture faced several major obstacles throughout the twentieth century. These difficulties involved regionalism, the lack of a single cultural identity, and a shared three-thousand-mile border with a colossal world superpower containing ten times more inhabitants. The advent of radio broadcasting in the post-World War I period led to the rapid penetration of U.S. popular culture since the great bulk of Canada's population resided within 150 miles of the U.S.-Canadian boundary line. A national network, known as the Canadian Broadcasting Corporation (CBC), took shape during the early to mid-1930's, and CBC programming became closely associated with Canadian nationalism and culture. In its effort to promote Canadian culture, unify the nation, and displace American programming, the CBC waged an uphill battle. Moreover, by 1946, television was beginning to attract some Canadian viewers, who purchased sets and were able to receive broadcasts transmitted from nearby cities in the United States.

Concern over the status of national culture led to the appointment of a Royal Commission on National Development in the Arts, Letters, and Sciences, also known as the Massey Commission. The commission's 1951 report recommended that Parliament develop a Canadian television network through the CBC with transmitters in a number of large cities. CBC television would be supplemented by private CBC affiliates. The project was launched in early September of 1952 as broadcasting started from Montreal and Toronto and reached 30 percent of the nation's inhabitants. Within two years, rapid expansion of the network made national television available in French and English to 66 percent of Canadians.

In 1957, another Royal Commission, the Fowler Commission, charged with doing a follow-up study after the initial trial period, issued its report. This commission found that television had appropriated all the old formats developed for radio and forced its shift over to transmitting news and recorded music, most of which originated in the United States. On CBC television, American productions were as prominent as those from Canada. To counteract this trend and promote more Canadian content, the commission advocated subsidies, protectionism, and a regulatory change. A single system of public and private radio and television networks was to be created and regulated by an agency representing the public interest and responsible to Parliament. Shortly thereafter, the Diefenbaker government carried out these recommendations in the Broadcasting Act of 1958, which created the Board of Broadcast Governors (BBG). In 1959, the BBG introduced content regulations, a type of quota system, to take effect in 1961.

Impact The Massey Commission's recommendations on broadcasting reflected a conservative and elitist view of the Western cultural tradition that favored "high culture" and, particularly, Canadian culture over American "mass" popular culture. Although CBC radio and television produced a number of high-quality, home-grown, English-language programs, stemming the penetration and popularity of programming from the United States proved to be a daunting task in successive decades. Only in French-speaking Quebec province have locally produced programs consistently flourished.

Further Reading

Bothwell, Robert, Ian Drummond, and John English. *Canada Since 1945: Power, Politics, and Provincialism.* Rev. ed. Toronto: University of Toronto Press, 1989. Covers political, economic, and cultural developments during the post-World War II decades. Chapters 12 and 18 deal with popular culture and discuss the CBC.

Peers, Frank W. *The Public Eye: Television and the Politics of Canadian Broadcasting, 1952-1968.* Toronto: University of Toronto Press, 1979. Traces the development of the broadcasting system in Canada from the inception of television in 1952 to passage of the Broadcasting Act of 1968.

David A. Crain

See also Communications in Canada; Education in Canada; Hockey; Literature in Canada; *Maclean's*; Newspapers in Canada; Television in Canada; Television in the United States.

■ Canadian Labour Congress

Identification Canada's largest labor union, formed through the merger of two major unions

Date Formed in April 23, 1956

The creation of the Canadian Labour Congress strengthened the position of Canadian labor and symbolized its growing nationalism.

Historically, American parent unions dominated organized Canadian labor. This domination caused divisions within the Canadian labor movement as the politics of American organized labor spilled over north of the border. In 1939, the American Federation of Labor (AFL) pressured the Trades and Labour Congress (TLC)—a traditional Canadian labor body that dated from the 1870's and contained a number of distinct unions—into expelling the more radical unions of the Congress of Industrial Organizations. The expelled unions, along with the All-Canadian Congress of Labour (ACCL), merged in 1940 to create the Canadian Congress of Labour (CCL), a more fully national labor body.

The expulsion left a major split in the Canadian labor movement. At the same time, ongoing events helped push the two organizations increasingly closer, and each annually passed motions calling for unification. They worked together during World War II on various measures designed to aid workers, and beginning in 1948, they repeatedly pursued partnerships in common causes. Further momentum toward unity came as workers found themselves in an increasingly strong position because of an economic boom that began after World War II and a favorable court ruling, which recognized the ability of unions to collect dues even from nonmembers in organized bargaining units. Despite all of the energy, divisions within the American labor movement blocked reform in Canada.

Merger and the Birth of the CLC During the 1950's, the impetus toward Canadian labor unity became unstoppable. In 1953, the CCL and TLC established a "Unity Committee," which, in turn, created an agreement not to raid each other's members. The ratification of the agreement, coupled with the amalgamation in the United States of the AFL and CIO, created a groundswell for a merger. On April 23, 1956, more than fifteen hundred delegates from both bodies, representing more than one million workers, gathered together to create a newly united organization, the Canadian Labour Congress (CLC). Over the following months, additional unions and labor bodies joined; only Roman Catholic-dominated unions in the province of Quebec remained excluded.

The CLC had to create policies that addressed traditional areas of division within the labor movement, particularly questions surrounding how politically active organized labor should be. As a compromise, the CLC gave its various affiliated members—including not only labor unions but also other bodies at the provincial level—the freedom to decide on their own courses of action. Efforts also were begun to build a broader coalition among those pursuing similar social agendas, including farm organizations and political parties, specifically the social-democratic Cooperative Commonwealth Federation (CCF). These efforts were largely unfruitful before the 1957 election of the Progressive Conservatives under John Diefenbaker, but eventually the hard work of the CLC and CCF led to the creation of the New Democratic Party in 1961.

Impact The creation of the Canadian Labour Congress symbolized the growing power of a distinctive Canadian labor voice during the 1950's.

Further Reading

Abella, Irving. *Nationalism, Communism, and Canadian Labour: The CIO, the Communist Party, and the Canadian Congress of Labour, 1935-1956.* Toronto: University of Toronto Press, 1973. Definitive historical examination of Canadian labor politics prior to the birth of the CLC.

Morton, Desmond, with Terry Copp. *Working People.* Ottawa: Deneau, 1984. Traditional history of Canadian labour.

Palmer, Bryan. *Working-Class Experience: Rethinking the History of Canadian Labour, 1800-1991.* Toronto: McClelland & Stewart, 1992. History of Canadian workers from a Marxist perspective.

Steve Hewitt

See also AFL-CIO merger; Business and the economy in Canada; Cold War; Continentalism; Diefenbaker, John G.; Unionism in Canada.

■ Canadian regionalism

During the 1950's, Canadian regionalism was particularly evident in Quebec's cultural distinctiveness and nationalism, which was expressed in its resistance to federal powers and policies and in its economic disparity among the various provinces.

Regionalism, a reality with which Canada's founders had to struggle in uniting several provinces into a self-governing dominion, was still evident during the 1950's. Throughout history, various factors, including geography, posed problems in forging national unity. Distance and landforms created a variety of regions that are relatively isolated from the other parts of the country. A vast and scenic but harsh wilderness, known as the Precambrian or Canadian Shield, constitutes more than half of the national territory separating east from west and north from south. The United States had no such barrier to transportation and settlement in the center of its territory. Although a transcontinental railroad finally linked Canada from coast to coast in 1885, a paved Trans-Canada Highway project was launched in 1949 but was not complete by the end of the 1950's.

Moreover, demographic, cultural, ethnic, economic, and political factors contributed to regional identities. Canada was not founded on a single cultural and linguistic heritage. Although Great Britain conquered French Canada in the eighteenth century, and English speakers eventually outnumbered francophones, or French speakers, the British failed to assimilate the large French minority concentrated primarily in Quebec. During the 1950's, franco-phones accounted for 30 percent of Canada's population. The persistent and successful historical struggle of Quebec's Roman Catholic, French-speaking population for cultural survival set this province apart as a distinct region within the larger nation.

In addition to the so-called French factor, later waves of immigration and ethnic settlement patterns contributed to creating regional cultures. The mix of cultural heritage is different for each region in terms of the historical timing and ethnic content of settlement. Economic inequality has also played a role in promoting regionalism. Population, resources, industry, employment opportunities, and personal income are unevenly distributed among the various sections of the country. This situation has contributed to regional grievances and stereotypes. Thus, some scholars note that Canada is, in reality, a collection of small countries with boundaries defined by regional consciousness.

Finally, the nation's political system and institutions at times have increased the intensity of regionalism. The electoral system benefits regional parties with narrowly concentrated support. Although Canadian provinces are powerful and exercise considerable jurisdiction within their boundaries, many Canadians feel disadvantaged by lack of clout in the federal parliament. The U.S. Constitution created a Senate with equal representation for all states to counterbalance the lower House, which gives representation based solely on population. Canada's Senate, filled by appointed members, does not serve this purpose. During the 1950's, Ontario and Quebec alone accounted for more than 60 percent of the 265 seats in the House of Commons. The perception that the two central Canadian provinces wield too much power at the federal level exacerbates regional resentments.

Quebec Stands on Its Own While historical factors continued to play important roles in extending Canadian regionalism during the 1950's, it was Quebec's assertion of its distinctiveness and the existence of economic disparity between the Maritime provinces and the rest of the country that attracted public attention.

Quebec, once a relatively backward province in its social and economic development, was progressively becoming more urban and industrial under the impact of modernizing forces. Politically, the province

was under the control of Premier Minister Maurice Duplessis and his Union Nationale Party. Known as *le chef* (the boss), Duplessis ran the province in an authoritarian and paternalistic style. He also cultivated traditional conservative French-Canadian clerical nationalism, which promoted Quebec's distinctiveness and isolation from the rest of Canada. On the national scene, Duplessis was a leading and persistent advocate of provincial rights in opposition to federal powers.

The issue of taxation led to a clash between Quebec and the federal government during the early 1950's. Demands of the wartime period had strengthened the federal government's authority, and the scope of its activities widened. This trend carried over into the postwar period as government-oriented national leaders assumed that economic policy making was its exclusive right.

In 1946, Liberal prime minister William L. Mackenzie King persuaded provinces to agree to a "tax rental" scheme. Under this arrangement, only the federal government could levy income, corporation, and succession (inheritance) taxes. In return for provinces surrendering the right to collect these taxes, the national government would distribute payments to them based on various complicated formulas. The poorest provinces with small tax bases were most receptive; each soon acquiesced except wary Quebec and wealthy Ontario. When Ontario changed its mind and came on board in 1952, only Quebec remained outside the tax rental plan.

In 1954, Quebec, which did not have an income tax yet, decided to impose one of its own. Duplessis boldly inserted a legal argument in the preamble to his legislation that provincial authority took precedence over federal authority in the areas of direct taxation. This challenging assertion rankled the ruling Liberal prime minister, Louis St. Laurent, who was Mackenzie King's successor. Although a Quebec native, St. Laurent was a national-minded Canadian and an advocate of strong federal authority who thought that all provinces should participate in this plan. In September, 1954, he made speeches in Quebec seeking to influence public opinion and criticized those elements in the province that did not support the concept of a strong and united Canada. Duplessis was hard-hitting in his response to the plan in order to exploit sensitive Québécois nationalism, but he also struck a deal and arranged for a meeting with St. Laurent in Montreal. Although both sides compromised and made some concessions that eased the situation, Quebec nevertheless remained outside the tax rental agreement.

The precedent set by Quebec both in refusing to participate and in imposing its own income tax jeopardized the future of the federal government's tax rental plan: Authorities were worried that other provinces might follow Quebec's example in the future. This factor, combined with the realization that the plan was probably not adequate to meet the growing needs and financial burdens of many provinces, led the federal government to implement the new tax scheme of equalization payments in 1957. Since this plan amounted to subsidizing "have-not" provinces to make their revenues more on par with those of prosperous Ontario and British Columbia, even Quebec now agreed to participate.

In defending his successful opposition to the earlier tax plan, Duplessis claimed he was resisting the intrusions of federal authority to defend Quebec's language and institutions. The conservative French-Canadian nationalist viewpoint was also reflected in the 1956 report of a Royal Commission on Constitutional Problems (the Tremblay Commission), established by Quebec. In its critique of the political system, the report asserted that Quebec differed from other Canadian provinces because of religion, culture, and the historical experiences of its majority French-speaking population. To protect Quebec's cultural uniqueness, the commission embraced an old interpretation of Canadian federalism, known as the compact theory, which favors a loose arrangement with weak central authority and strong provincial autonomy.

Regional Disparities During this same period, the important reality of political and economic regional disparities was universally recognized. The postwar economic boom, with its unprecedented economic growth and rising living standards, bypassed Canada's Maritime Provinces. The Atlantic region's heavy dependence on a resource economy subject to changing demands in the world market was a disadvantage. Major economic activities there were logging, fishing, and mining. When Newfoundland finally joined Canada in 1949 to take advantage of federal subsidies and social programs, its underdevelopment greatly affected the overall economic statistics for the Maritime Provinces. Near the end of the decade, federal figures on per-capita in-

come showed Ontario to be the wealthiest province, followed closely by British Columbia. Ontario's per-capita income was more than twice that of Newfoundland and three-fourths more than the figure for the other Maritime Provinces. The region's higher unemployment rates and relatively depressed conditions prompted a noticeable outward migration during the 1950's and 1960's of Atlantic Coast residents seeking better economic opportunities in other regions of Canada. "Newfie" jokes and stereotypical views about Maritimers also became more common.

Regional economic disparity was one of the matters discussed by a Royal Commission on Canada's Economic Future (the Gordon Commission), whose report was publicly released in 1958. In its study, the Gordon Commission did not offer a great deal of hope for the future development and prosperity of Canada's Atlantic provinces and implied that the residents were backward but content with the region's slower, more placid pace of life, which contrasted with the tense and crowded urban scene. The commission's suggestion that the government provide generous assistance to those residents seeking to relocate to other parts of Canada raised some concern in the Maritime Provinces, and one of the local newspapers characterized the report as another "rape of the Acadians," a historical reference to the tragic expulsion and exile of the area's original French-speaking inhabitants by the British in the eighteenth century.

Political Factors Finally, a political aspect of regionalism was one of the important factors that weakened the Progressive Conservative government of Prime Minister John Diefenbaker during the late 1950's and early 1960's. Diefenbaker, a conservative Canadian nationalist who encouraged American influence in Canada, led his party to a stunning but narrow upset victory over the long-reigning Liberal Party in June of 1957. A political blunder on the part of his opponents allowed Diefenbaker to call a snap election in early 1958 and win the largest victory in Canadian political history, gaining 208 of 265 seats. The magnitude of this triumph was a result of the massive defection of Quebec from the Liberal Party. Historically a safe Liberal province in federal elections since the late nineteenth century, Quebec gave Diefenbaker's party fifty of its seventy-five parliamentary seats. Duplessis had no love for the Liberals, whom he accused of trying to erode provincial autonomy with federal bribes.

The unusual political honeymoon between Quebec and the Progressive Conservative government did not endure. Diefenbaker spoke little French and showed no real interest in French-Canadians or Québécois issues. Quebec also felt insulted when he failed to appoint a Quebec lieutenant as a secondary party leader, a standard Canadian political practice, and put only three French-Canadians in his cabinet. Furthermore, his conservative nationalism, which appealed to the country's British heritage as the basis of a common Canadian identity, only further alienated Quebec. During the 1962 and 1963 elections, when the Conservatives clung to power with a minority government, then lost a close election, their representation in Quebec fell to fourteen and eight respectively. The remainder of seats were divided between the Liberals and the Quebec branch of the Social Credit Party, which championed provincial rights.

Impact Regionalism in several of its forms had an impact on Canada during the 1950's, but its divisive effects were not necessarily critical. Regional economic inequality was a matter of concern for both policymakers and those who were disadvantaged, but the perpetually sluggish Maritime economies did not pose a major threat to national unity. However, Quebec was a more serious matter. St. Laurent, in allowing the demands and local interests of a province to dominate his agenda for a national government, failed to use his prestige and political clout to bring Duplessis into conformity with federal policy.

Further Reading

Behiels, Michael, and K. S. Mathew. *Canada: Its Regions and People*. New Delhi: Munshiram Mancharlal, 1998. Useful source on Canadian geography, history, and ethnic relations.

Black, Conrad. *Duplessis*. Toronto: McClelland and Stewart, 1976. Well-researched study on Quebec's influential premier, who championed provincial rights and traditional French-Canadian nationalism.

Bothwell, Robert, Ian Drummond, and John English. *Canada Since 1945: Power, Politics, and Provincialism*. Rev. ed. Toronto: University of Toronto Press, 1989. An informative account of Canadian political, economic, and cultural developments during the post-World War II decades.

McCann, L. D., ed. *Heartland and Hinterland: A Geography of Canada*. Scarborough, Ont.: Prentice Hall, 1987. Discusses economic conditions, regional disparities, and underdevelopment in the post-World War II period.

David A. Crain

See also Health care systems in Canada; Hoof-and-mouth epidemic; Income and wages in Canada; Literature in Canada; Minorities in Canada; Religion in Canada; Theater in Canada; Unemployment in Canada; Urbanization in Canada.

■ Cancer

Definition Often fatal disease characterized by growth and spread of malignant tumors

The 1950's saw meaningful changes in all aspects of cancer management, including government and private organizations aimed at controlling the disease.

During the 1950's, radiological examination was performed mainly with diagnostic X rays, especially for cancers of the lungs and bones, and contrast studies were performed for cancers of the gastrointestinal and urinary tracts. Tomography, a method of producing three-dimensional images of internal body structures, was available at selected centers; however, computer-assisted tomography (CT scans) and magnetic resonance imaging (MRI) were yet to be developed. Mammographic techniques were developed and routine mammographic screenings were advocated and practiced in an attempt to diagnose early cancers of the breast. Mass radiography of the lungs was also organized for the diagnosis of early lung lesions. Except for radioiodine studies for thyroid cancers, most radioisotopic diagnostic tests and radioimmune assay measurements were yet to be developed.

Fiber-optic techniques were not available during the 1950's, so diagnostic endoscopy was done with rigid instruments. Direct laryngo-pharyngoscopy, rigid bronchoscopy, esophagoscopy, proctosigmoidoscopy, and colposcopy (examination of the uterine cervix through a speculum) were the usual tools. As a painful and technically difficult process, rigid gastroscopy was done only in a few centers even though gastric cancer was quite common. Cystoscopy and transurethral ureteric catheterization were well-established procedures. Laparoscopic examination of the intraabdominal viscera was mainly done for the pelvic organs.

Immediate frozen section diagnosis to determine the pathological nature of masses and frozen section examination of the margins of resection for determining freedom from neoplasia became standard practices. The cytodiagnosis of cancer had been developed during the 1930's and came into general and widespread use during the 1950's. The method was used in screening for uterine cervical cancer and lung cancer (and to a lesser extent for cancers at other sites). Diagnostic aspiration biopsy of suspect masses had been initiated during the 1930's and also came into general use for cytologic examination of such things as metastatic neck nodes, lymphomatous nodes, hepatic masses, and soft tissue tumors.

Treatment Methods and Results

In 1955, twelve U.S. hospitals were devoted exclusively to treating cancer patients, and 176 cancer detection clinics and 539 cancer treatment clinics were approved by the American College of Sur-

Cobalt radioscopes, such as this one being installed by workers in University Hospital at the University of Saskatchewan, were used during the 1950's to check the growth of cancer cells in patients by exposing them to concentrations of the radioactive cobalt 60 isotope. (Saskatoon Cancer Centre, Royal University Hospital)

geons. Improvement in anesthesia and postoperative support of patients (especially with improved understanding of electrolyte imbalances) had made radical and super radical surgical procedures practicable. As radiotherapy was still generally dependent on low-voltage X-ray machines, efficacy was low and side effects significant. Supervoltage machines and teletherapy units using radioisotopes such as cobalt and cesium were introduced during the 1950's. Implantation of radioactive isotopes—either temporarily or permanently—was investigated and came into use.

Chemotherapy also was limited to a small number of agents with relatively limited activity. Treatment methods were therefore mainly surgical. In the belief that the wider the excision, the better the chance of "cure," "super" radical procedures were developed for breast cancer and gastric cancer which included wide resection of the involved organ with the associated lymphatics.

Breast Cancer Data from the 1950's show that the breasts were the commonest site for cancer among women and the prostate and lungs in men. Colorectal cancer and gastric cancer were also frequent, as was cancer of the cervix uteri. The incidence of cancer of the lungs was rising and a relationship with external pollutants, especially with tobacco smoke, was strongly suspected.

Breast cancers were routinely treated with radical mastectomy (removal of the entire breast with a large segment of the periareolar skin and complete removal of the lymphatics and fibro-fatty tissues of the axilla). For selected cancers of the breast this was associated with removal of the internal mammary nodes together with a section of the chest wall and on occasion removal of the lymph nodes in the lower neck of the same side.

In patients who had metastatic breast cancer, the ovaries, the adrenal glands, and even the pituitary gland were removed on occasion. Orchiectomy and adrenalectomy were also used for disseminated prostate cancer. "Second look" operations were recommended in apparently cancer-free patients operated upon for stomach, colon, and rectal cancers.

For cancers of the lung, entire lungs were often removed, together with the lymphatics of the mediastinum. For melanomas (a relatively uncommon form of skin cancer at the time) a wide-excision of the primary site was done with a strip of skin with the underlying subcutaneous tissues (supposedly containing the draining lymphatics) excised to the site of the nearest lymphnodal aggregation which was excised in continuity. Among the cure rates reported in 1953, cervix uteri cancer was 25 percent, lung cancer less than 5 percent, breast cancer 35 percent, oral cavity and larynx cancer 35 percent, and skin cancer 85 percent.

New ideas about the biology of cancer included the views that there was a biological predeterminism in each individual cancer, that a bigger operation was not necessarily a better operation, and that some cancers could reappear after a long, apparently disease-free interval.

Organization The American Society for the Control of Cancer was founded in 1913. The name was changed to the American Cancer Society, and its activities increased substantially during the 1950's. In 1950, the journal *CA* was launched by the society. Initially, it had a small subscription base, but it ultimately was freely distributed to physicians and appropriate other professionals and organizations. A program aimed at helping patients with breast cancer in all aspects of their recovery —Reach to Recovery, largely managed by volunteers—was launched in 1954. The International Association of Laryngectomees was started in 1952 under the guidance of the American College of Surgeons. In 1954 the American Cancer Society took it over as a project. The American College of Surgeons mandated tumor registries in all hospitals in 1955.

The 1950's saw the beginnings of multiorganizational cooperation in investigating various aspects of cancer diagnosis and treatment, and a standardized method of reporting end results was jointly established by the American College of Surgeons, the College of American Pathologists, the American College of Radiology, and the American Cancer Society. In 1951 the American Cancer Society published the *Manual of Tumor Nomenclature and Coding*. The TNM system of cancer staging as accepted by the International Union Against Cancer was not accepted in the United States, and the American Joint Committee for Cancer Staging and End-Result Reporting was established in 1958 with representation from the American College of Surgeons, the American College of Radiotherapy, the American College of Radiology, the College of American Pathologists, the American College of Physicians, the American Cancer Society, and the National Cancer Institute.

In 1952, a Teletherapy Evaluation Board was established with twenty medical schools and the Medical Division of the Oak Ridge Institute of Nuclear Studies to "investigate, develop and evaluate radioisotopes" for teletherapy. In 1954 the American Cancer Society set up an ad hoc committee (with representation from various other organizations) to look into the relationship of tobacco consumption to cancer incidence.

Impact The 1950's was an important period in the evolution of all aspects of research, diagnosis, and treatment of cancer. However, virtually every aspect of cancer diagnosis and treatment has changed remarkably since the 1950's. There have been particularly notable improvements in diagnostic radiology, identification of tumor markers, chemotherapy, radiotherapy, and surgery. Multicenter, rigorously statistically controlled investigative methods have become common in deciding optimal methods in the management of cancer.

Further Reading

Lee, H. S. J., ed. *Dates in Oncology: A Chronological Record of Progress in Oncology over the Last Millennium.* New York: Parthenon, 2000. Summary of the study and treatment of cancer throughout recorded history that actually begins in early Greek and Roman times and covers developments through the twentieth century.

Lerner, Barron H. *The Breast Cancer Wars: Hope, Fear, and the Pursuit of a Cure in Twentieth-Century America.* New York: Oxford University Press, 2003. Thoroughly researched and highly readable history of medical research on breast cancer.

Ravitch, Mark M. *A Century of Surgery: The History of the American Surgical Association.* 2 vols. Philadelphia: Lippincott, 1981. This meticulously researched, massive text details mainly the progress of surgery in the United States and Canada by decades; however, changes in radiotherapy and chemotherapy are also touched upon.

Ranes C. Chakravorty

See also Air pollution; Atomic Energy of Canada, Ltd.; Health care systems in Canada; Health care systems in the United States; Medicine; Smoking and tobacco.

■ Capp, Al

Identification American syndicated comic-strip artist

Born Alfred Gerald Caplin; September 28, 1909; New Haven, Connecticut

Died November 5, 1979; Cambridge, Massachusetts

Al Capp's hugely popular, long-running (1934-1977) comic-strip Li'l Abner *drew a large readership during the 1950's and often poked fun at modern society. Many critics consider* L'il Abner *to be the best comic strip of all time.*

Al Capp became a popular culture hero during the 1950's with the parody and satire of his *Li'l Abner* comic strip, delivered daily to the doorsteps of millions of North Americans.

After losing his left leg in a trolley accident at age nine, Capp was encouraged by his artistic father to develop his cartooning skills. He became the youngest syndicated cartoonist in the United States by age nineteen. In 1934, he began his *Li'l Abner* strip through United Features Syndicate. His characters made front-page news in 1952 when the naïve hillbilly Abner finally married pure, innocent beauty queen Daisy Mae. Baby Honest Abe arrived in 1953. The strip's popularity led to a successful Broadway musical with the strip's title in 1956 and a movie in 1959.

Impact Not as shy as his Li'l Abner character, Capp became a media darling during the 1950's. He was often interviewed and appeared numerous times as a guest on the *Tonight Show.* His politics were reflected

in the strip, with its characters combating city slickers, business tycoons, and government officials in subtle parody. He had a newspaper column, a radio show, and speaking engagements on college campuses throughout his career. He talked openly about his disability and encouraged amputees returning from the Korean War.

Further Reading

Berger, Arthur Asa. *Li'l Abner: A Study in American Satire.* Jackson: University Press of Mississippi, 1994. Examines Capp's political and social viewpoints.

Capp, Al. *My Well Balanced Life on a Wooden Leg: Memoirs by Al Capp.* McKinleyville, Calif.: Daniel & Daniel, 1991. A posthumous look at Capp's self-publicized disability contrasted with the physical prowess of *Li'l Abner.*

Theroux, Alexander. *The Enigma of Al Capp.* Seattle, Wash.: Fantagraphics Books, 1999. This small vol-

Al Capp admires the May, 1956, issue of Time *magazine, whose cover uses cartoons that he drew of himself and his most famous comic-strip characters, L'il Abner and Daisy Mae.* (Hulton Archive | by Getty Images)

ume examines changes in the strip over Capp's lifetime, including his shift from liberalism to conservatism during its four decades of popularity.

Randy Hines

See also Comic books; Gaines, William M.; *MAD*; *Peanuts*; *Pogo*.

■ *Captain Kangaroo*

Identification Children's television show
Date Aired from 1955 to 1984

Popular program for preschoolers, combining live action, puppetry, and animation.

In 1955, twenty-eight-year-old Bob Keeshan, previously known as Clarabell the Clown on the *Howdy Doody Show*, launched this gentler, slower-paced CBS weekday morning program, aiming to entertain and educate preschool children. Keeshan's grandfatherly character wore a jacket with large, pouchlike pockets, thus giving rise to his name.

Keeshan's sidekick, Mr. Green Jeans (Hugh Brannum), played guitar, sang, and introduced viewers to gardening and many different animals. Puppeteer Cosmo Allegretti played the other regulars: Bunny Rabbit, who bamboozled the Captain into giving him carrots; Mister Moose, who tricked the Captain into speaking words that triggered a cascade of Ping-Pong balls; Grandfather Clock, who woke up only long enough to recite a poem; and Dancing Bear.

Regular segments included "Reading Stories" and the animated *Tom Terrific and Mighty Manfred the Wonder Dog*. A picture was "magically" drawn on Magic Drawing Board to fit an accompanying song. Skits and musical performances included both regulars and guest stars.

Captain Kangaroo's twenty-nine years on CBS made it the longest-running children's show on television. Keeshan followed it with a Public Broadcasting System (PBS) version combining new footage with clips from the older program. An updated 1997 version with a new Captain Kangaroo failed to find an audience.

Impact *Captain Kangaroo* was a favorite among young baby boomers and their parents, whose letters forestalled a threatened cancellation during the late 1950's. Its slow pace and direct involvement with its viewers stood out amid the trends in children's tele-

vision, and it served as a touchstone in the development of the first "television generation."

Further Reading

Keeshan, Robert. *Good Morning Captain: Fifty Wonderful Years with Bob Keeshan, TV's Captain Kangaroo*. Minneapolis: Fairview Press, 1996. Keeshan's memoir of his career in children's television.

Woolery, George W. *Children's Television: The First Thirty-Five Years, 1946-1981*. Metuchen, N.J.: Scarecrow, 1985. An encyclopedic listing of live-action television programs for children.

Bethany Andreasen

See also *Howdy Doody Show*; *Kukla, Fran and Ollie*; *Mickey Mouse Club*; Silly Putty; Television for children.

■ *Captain Video*

Identification Television show for children
Date Aired from 1949 to 1955

Captain Video *was the first science-fiction show on television and featured television's first space hero.*

Captain Video and His Video Rangers was the first and longest-running science-fiction program on television. Created and produced by a DuMont network vice president, the pioneering program was broadcast live as a continuing serial six nights a week, using developing technology to give the illusion of time and space travel. The title character was a technological wizard living in the year 2254. Captain Video's mission was to maintain world safety by battling a variety of space aliens and enemies using such futuristic wonders as the Opticon Scillometer, an X-ray machine that saw through walls, and a paralyzing Cosmic Ray Vibrator. Operating from secret headquarters and overseeing a network of video rangers, Captain Video also invited children to imagine themselves as rangers, sending special civic-minded messages for would-be rangers between breaks in the drama and offering Captain Video merchandise.

Impact The success of *Captain Video* inspired numerous subsequent science-fiction programs on television and fit in well with the public's fascination with Cold War space exploration, science, and struggles between good and bad forces.

Further Reading

Bianculli, David. *Dictionary of Teleliteracy: Television's*

Five Hundred Biggest Hits, Misses, and Events. New York: Continuum Publishing, 1996. Gives a breezily written article on *Captain Video* that includes fun facts and offbeat information.

Javna, John. *The Best of Science Fiction TV: The Critics' Choice: From "Captain Video" to "Star Trek," from "The Jetsons" to "Robotech."* New York: Harmony Books, 1987. Discusses *Captain Video* as the founder of an important television genre; places it within the context of a golden age of television space shows.

Lucanio, Patrick, and Gary Coville. *American Science Fiction Television Series of the 1950's: Episode Guides and Casts and Credits for Twenty Shows.* Jefferson, N.C.: McFarland, 1998. Article on *Captain Video* details characters, technical innovations, cast, directors, writers, critical commentary, and coverage of individual episodes.

Margaret Boe Birns

See also *Adventures of Superman, The; Cisco Kid, The;* DuMont network; *Lone Ranger, The; Sergeant Preston of the Yukon; Sky King;* Television for children; Television in the United States.

■ Carnegie, Dale

Identification American motivational speaker, author, and educator
Born November 24, 1888; Maryville, Missouri
Died November 1, 1955; Forest Hills, New York

The 1950's saw rapid domestic and worldwide expansion of Dale Carnegie's motivational courses and educational facilities, setting the stage for his wide popularity in subsequent decades. Carnegie is especially well known for his self-help book How to Win Friends and Influence People.

Dale Carnegie was a sought-after lecturer, writer, and teacher who founded a worldwide network of educational facilities designed to motivate people to be the best they could be. As a motivational speaker, he spread his message via personal counseling, small classes, radio programs, newspaper columns, and books.

After receiving his education at Warrensburg State Teachers College in Missouri, Carnegie moved to New York City, where he taught public-speaking classes to adults at the Young Men's Christian Association (YMCA). In 1912, he started his Dale Carnegie Courses. In 1915, he coauthored a book on public

Dale Carnegie reading his own book, How to Win Friends and Influence People, *in 1955.* (AP/Wide World Photos)

speaking. Because his last name was similar to that of Andrew Carnegie, a famous industrialist of the time, Dale Carnagey found that people were confusing his name with that of the industrialist. Rather than trying to correct the world, Carnagey changed the spelling of his surname to Carnegie.

Carnegie retired from the organization that he had founded in 1951, and his wife, Dorothy, became company president. Several of his earlier books were edited and republished during the 1950's. In 1954, the company incorporated under the name Dale Carnegie & Associates, and worldwide expansion of his empire began. By the late 1950's, Dale Carnegie & Associates held courses in places such as Central America and the British Isles.

Impact Dale Carnegie's influence grew tremendously during the 1950's, making him an important precursor to later decades' motivational speakers and the self-help industry. More than fifty million copies of Carnegie's books are in print in thirty-eight languages, and by the early twenty-first century, his organization employed approximately 2,700 motivational instructors.

Further Reading

Carnegie, Dale. *How to Win Friends and Influence People.* New York: Simon & Schuster, 1936. This is Carnegie's best-known book, covering both public speaking and human relations. It was reissued beginning in 1952.

Kemp, Giles, and Edward Claflin. *Dale Carnegie: The Man Who Influenced Millions.* New York: St. Martin's Press, 1989. A biography of Carnegie.

Dale L. Flesher

See also Fads; Peale, Norman Vincent.

■ Castro, Fidel

Identification Cuban president since 1959
Born August 13, 1926, or 1927; near Birán, Cuba

During the 1950's, Castro led a revolution against Cuba's dictatorial regime and went on to become Cuba's president. His transformation of Cuba into the first communist state of the Western Hemisphere made the island nation a major Cold War hot spot.

Fidel Alejandro Castro Ruz was born to Ángel Castro, an affluent landowner, and Lina Ruz González. He later described himself as a child who was violent, devious, given to tantrums, and defiant of all authority. During the 1940's, Castro participated in an aborted invasion of the Dominican Republic and found himself in the center of a bloody uprising in Bogotá, Colombia, where he was helping to organize a student congress against the government.

On July 26, 1953, Castro led an attack on the Moncada army barracks in Santiago, Oriente Province, against the Cuban dictator, President Fulgencio Batista y Zaldívar. Batista had overthrown Carlos Prío Socarrás, a democratically elected president, in a pre-election coup on March 10, 1952. Following the failed Moncada attack, Castro was sentenced to fifteen years in prison. However, he received amnesty in 1955 and was allowed to leave the country.

Preparing for Revolution In 1955, Castro went to the United States to raise funds for his planned revolution. He returned to the United States in 1959, when he met Vice President Richard M. Nixon and entertained guests at the Cuban embassy in Washington, D.C.

In Mexico, he founded the 26th of July Movement and met Argentine revolutionary Che Guevara, with whom he planned the liberation of Cuba. In December of 1956, Castro and eighty-one others landed in Cuba and hid in the Sierra Maestra, where they launched guerrilla warfare against Batista. Success from the Cuban urban underground—people who rebelled within different sections of the country—and the warfare emanating from Castro led to Batista's political fall on New Year's Eve, 1958.

In January of 1959, Castro marched into Havana as the new president of Cuba. Later, he declared Cuba a communist country following Marxist-Leninist ideals. However, in 1959, the Cuban people began to realize his communist tendencies, and

Shortly after making himself president of Cuba, Fidel Castro (left) visited Washington, D.C., where he met U.S. vice president Richard M. Nixon. (Hulton Archive I by Getty Images)

many fled to the United States. Most émigrés were from the upper classes and from the political elite; they tended to seek refuge in Miami, Florida.

Impact Castro's well-known bitterness toward the United States dates back to his student days, when he was involved in anti-imperialist organizations in Havana. It may also stem from the American supply of bombs and ammunition to Batista during the fight from the Sierra Maestra. On June 5, 1956, as U.S. bombs fell upon the area where he hid, he sent a private message to his companion Celia Sánchez, stating "I have sworn that the Americans will pay very dearly for what they are doing. When this war has ended, a much bigger and greater war will start for me, a war I shall launch against them. I realize that this will be my true destiny."

Castro's communist ideals, dictatorship, and anti-American sentiments led to Cuba's alliance with the Soviet Union, which in turn laid the groundwork for the Cuban Missile Crisis of October, 1962. The United States broke its diplomatic relations with Cuba and imposed a trade embargo on the island nation.

Further Reading

Castro, Fidel, and Pedro Alvarez Tabio, eds. *Fidel Castro Reader: Forty Years of the Cuban Revolution.* New York: Ocean Press, 2001. A chronology of Castro and the Cuban Revolution.

Quirk, Robert E. *Fidel Castro.* New York: W. W. Norton, 1993. A good biography of Castro.

Sweig, Julia E. *Inside the Cuban Revolution.* Cambridge, Mass.: Harvard University Press, 2002. A study of Castro and the Cuban urban underground leadership between 1956 and 1958.

José A. Carmona

See also Cold War; Cuban Revolution; Diefenbaker, John G.; Foreign policy of the United States; Guatemala invasion; Immigration to the United States; Latin America; Latinos; Mills, C. Wright; Nixon, Richard M.; Organization of American States; United Fruit Company.

■ *Cat on a Hot Tin Roof*

Identification Psychological drama set in the Mississippi Delta
Author Tennessee Williams (1911-1983)
Date First produced in March, 1955
Place New York, New York

By exploring both marital and homosexual relationships, Cat on a Hot Tin Roof *challenged the social assumptions of the family-oriented 1950's.*

Cat on a Hot Tin Roof is set in a plantation house in the Mississippi Delta, where the Pollitt family is celebrating the birthday of Big Daddy, the wealthy plantation owner. Although Big Daddy believes he is free of cancer, everyone except his devoted wife, Big Mama, knows that he is dying from the disease. Throughout the play, Big Daddy's older son, Gooper, and his wife, Mae, try to keep his attention on their five children, hoping that he will leave the plantation to Gooper rather than to his favorite son, Brick. As Mae keeps pointing out, Brick and his wife, Maggie, have no children. Moreover, Brick is an alcoholic. He tells his father that he has to drink to escape from the world's mendacity, but Big Daddy will not accept that excuse. As he points out to Brick, he himself lives amid lies. He can stand neither his fat, foolish wife nor Gooper, Mae, and their ill-behaved offspring.

Like Big Daddy, Brick has developed an aversion to his wife. However, Maggie is the same young, beautiful woman that Brick once loved. Their marriage foundered after what Brick insists was an innocent relationship with a male friend, which led to Maggie's single act of infidelity and to the male friend's death by overdrinking. Maggie is determined to win back the only man she has ever loved. However, Big Daddy's impending death makes Maggie reconsider her relationship with Brick, who has no job and no source of income; Maggie does not want to be thrust into poverty once Big Daddy dies. The only solution is for her to produce a child, thus making sure that Big Daddy will leave Brick the plantation. In the final act of the play, Maggie stops pleading with Brick and takes decisive action. First she announces to the family that she is pregnant; then she locks up Brick's liquor and tells him what he must do before he can have it back.

Tennessee Williams always insisted that *Cat on a Hot Tin Roof* was about a struggle for an inheritance. However, audiences also were intrigued by its outspoken treatment of sexual issues, including homosexuality. The fact that the playwright changed the ending before the play appeared on Broadway has made interpretation of *Cat on a Hot Tin Roof* even more difficult. A film version of the play appeared in 1958 and starred Elizabeth Taylor and Paul Newman.

Impact Although homosexuality is only one of the themes in a complex play about family ties, marriage, greed, love, life, and death, the fact that *Cat on a Hot Tin Roof* mentioned it and even hinted that such a relationship might be socially acceptable paved the way for more open discussions of the subject in the years to come. In 1955, the play earned for Williams his second Pulitzer Prize.

Further Reading

Crandell, George W. "Cat on a Hot Tin Roof." In *Tennessee Williams: A Guide to Research and Performance,* edited by Philip C. Kolin. Westport, Conn.: Greenwood Press, 1998. Discusses the content of the play and lists stage productions, film versions, and television broadcasts.

Devlin, Albert J. "Writing in 'A Place of Stone': *Cat on a Hot Tin Roof.*" In *The Cambridge Companion to Tennessee Williams,* edited by Matthew C. Roudane. Cambridge, England: Cambridge University Press, 1997. Describes the genesis of the play and explains its later revisions.

Thompson, Judith J. *Tennessee Williams' Plays: Memory, Myth, and Symbol.* Reprint. New York: Peter Lang, 2002. Points out how Williams's dramatic works reflect classical mythology and traditional archetypes.

Rosemary M. Canfield Reisman

See also Film in the United States; Homosexuality and gay rights; Kazan, Elia; Taylor, Elizabeth; Theater in the United States; Wide-screen movies; Williams, Tennessee; Women and the roots of the feminist movement.

■ *The Catcher in the Rye*

Identification Popular novel about adolescent angst
Author J. D. Salinger (1919-   )
Date Published in 1951

The immediate appeal of The Catcher in the Rye *was its appealing description of adolescent rebellion, but thoughtful readers soon recognized how well the book expressed their own uneasiness with the conservative, conformist, and materialistic society of the 1950's.*

Although the protagonist of *The Catcher in the Rye,* Holden Caulfield, attends an expensive prep school and lives in an elegant Manhattan apartment, the fact that he rebels not only against adults, whom he sees as "phonies," but also against all the values of his class and his society, made him one of the heroes of an entire generation of high school and college students during the 1950's. Holden's fictional school, Pencey Prep, must have seemed like a foreign country to American veterans of modest backgrounds who were returning home from World War II and able to attend college only because of the G.I. Bill. However, the crooks and bullies whom Holden meets in the novel likely seemed all too familiar to the veterans. Moreover, Holden's annoyance with people who are not worried about the ducks in Central Park or who are shocked by the obscenities written where innocent young girls might see them spoke broadly to those from all social classes and age groups; in other words, the book resonated with those during the 1950's who believed that life should have a moral and spiritual basis.

Impact In reading of Holden's experiences, Americans found concrete examples of what they had

Author J. D. Salinger in 1951. (AP/Wide World Photos)

sensed was wrong with their society: its essential self-ishness. Holden seems so odd to those around him because he cares so much about other creatures, a comment on the egocentric society of the era. Holden's willingness to defy society, even to become an outsider if he feels a particular cause demands it, was an important influence on those who would become leaders in the social revolution of the 1960's. *The Catcher in the Rye* is also considered a milestone in literary history. Critics agree that in his novel, J. D. Salinger showed the other writers of the 1950's how the contemporary urban landscape could be described so as to reveal the desperate situation of those who were trapped in it.

In the decades that followed the novel's publication, the book became a classic. Today it continues to be widely read by young adults and still frequently appears on high school reading lists. Ironically, however, the book also remains the target of efforts to have it banned from schools and public libraries, usually because of the foul language it contains. Most would-be censors do not seem to see that though he swears, smokes, and rebels against authority, Holden is essentially a highly moral person, an urban knight fighting for right in a society which seems to have rejected chivalric values and the spiritual truths on which they are based.

Further Reading

Kotzen, Kip, and Thomas Beller. *With Love and Squalor: Fourteen Writers Respond to the Work of J. D. Salinger.* New York: Broadway Books, 2001. Lively essays, some of them parodic. Most deal with *The Catcher in the Rye* or focus specifically on the character of Holden Caulfield.

Pinsker, Sanford. *"The Catcher in the Rye": Innocence Under Pressure.* New York: Twayne, 1993. Sees the book primarily as a study of innocence. The initial chapters of Pinsker's work, in which the book's historical background is described and an assessment is made of the ongoing importance of the novel, are especially useful.

Steinle, Pamela Hunt. *In Cold Fear: "The Catcher in the Rye"—Censorship Controversies and Postwar American Character.* Columbus: Ohio State University Press, 2000. With the aid of questionnaires, interviews, and psychological analysis, the author attempts to determine why the novel continues to be banned.

Rosemary M. Canfield Reisman

See also Affluence and the new consumerism; *Affluent Society, The;* Censorship; Conformity, culture of; Education in the United States; Literature in the United States; *Rebel Without a Cause;* Youth culture and the generation gap.

■ Celler-Kefauver Act of 1950

Identification First effective federal law to prevent corporate mergers and acquisitions that lessen competition

Date Enacted on December 29, 1950

The Celler-Kefauver Act closed important loopholes in federal antitrust laws and prohibited certain types of mergers between firms in the same industry.

The Sherman Act, the first federal antitrust law, was passed in 1890 to punish price-fixing agreements (cartels) and monopolies that injured competition, competitors, and consumers through higher prices, restricted production, and restrictions on innovation. Corporations reacted by simply buying up their competitors, suppliers, and customers in ways that the law did not cover. Congress then passed the Clayton Act in 1914, which contained provisions barring certain mergers that tended to lessen competition substantially or create a monopoly. However, corporate lawyers quickly found loopholes around these prohibitions as well. Congressional hearings during the 1930's and 1940's highlighted how the economy was becoming more and more concentrated in the hands of fewer and fewer companies.

In 1950, Congress, led by Emanuel Celler of New York and Senator Estes Kefauver of Tennessee, passed the Celler-Kefauver Act, which prohibited all mergers and acquisitions of any form if they threatened to compromise competition or create a monopoly.

Impact Historians have argued that Celler and Kefauver were successful in their efforts to pass the act because of the manner in which they emphasized the evils of big business. By arguing that big business would require big government and a powerful bureaucracy to regulate the country's monopolies, the congressmen successfully used Cold War rhetoric to heighten fears of anything that might compromise U.S. democratic foundations.

During the early twenty-first century, the act was enforced by both the Antitrust Division of the Justice

Department and the United States Federal Trade Commission. Most significant mergers and acquisitions had to be reported in advance to the two agencies so that the federal government could decide whether to challenge the mergers in court before they actually took place.

Further Reading

Adams, Walter, and James W. Brock. *Antitrust Economics on Trial: A Dialogue on the New Laissez-Faire.* Princeton, N.J.: Princeton University Press, 1991. A dialogue in the form of a mock trial discussing the evolution of antitrust policy from the 1950's through the 1990's with an emphasis on mergers and acquisitions.

Kwoka, John E., Jr., and Lawrence J. White, eds. *The Antitrust Revolution: Economics, Competition, and Policy.* 4th ed. New York: Oxford University Press, 2004. A series of case studies showing evolution of antitrust policy from the 1950's to the end of the twentieth century.

Report of the Federal Trade Commission on the Merger Movement: A Summary Report. Washington, D.C.: United States Government Printing Office, 1948. A landmark study of corporate mergers and acquisitions which helped lead to the passage of the Celler-Kefauver Act.

Spencer Weber Waller

See also AFL-CIO merger; Baseball's exemption from antitrust laws; Business and the economy in the United States; Cold War; Kefauver, Estes.

■ Censorship

Definition Legal and extralegal restrictions placed on freedom of expression

During the 1950's, fears over communist infiltration and national security, combined with a conservative and conformist population, led to legal restrictions and cultural attitudes that supported several forms of censorship in the United States and Canada.

Censorship has had an erratic but long history in North America. Its effects have been felt most within media of all types—print, audio, and visual. Prosecutions of printers and publishers for seditious libel began in the eighteenth century, and the Sedition Act of 1798 imposed severe restraints on free expression. However, President Thomas Jefferson ended these restraints, and overt political censorship fell

dormant until the world wars of the twentieth century.

As a period following the fissures and uncertainties of the Great Depression and World War II, the 1950's saw previously accepted standards, social mores, and religious traditions being challenged more frequently. Although the era was one that tended toward conformity, patriotic values, and conservatism, it was also a time when court cases and news stories took up issues of political and cultural censorship. The Cold War helped set a tone of suspicion and distrust early in the decade, and U.S. senator Joseph R. McCarthy's campaign against alleged communists in government agencies heightened the effects of this climate.

Political Censorship In U.S. history, censorship has periodically been justified by the demands of national security, political expediency, cultural tradition, or religious standards. During the 1950's, material considered harmful to the national interest or to established norms was increasingly feared, and those fears were framed in newly manufactured terms in order to capitalize on issues of Cold War security and defense. For example, journalists found that General Douglas MacArthur held intractable power over press coverage of the Korean War. Over the course of that conflict, MacArthur's policies evolved from a virtual lack of military censorship of war information to such guarded release of information that journalists were subjected to trial for serious violations.

The House Committee on Un-American Activities (HUAC), an investigating committee of the U.S. House of Representatives, was established in 1938 to investigate un-American propaganda during the troubled years leading up to the nation's entry into World War II. However, by the 1950's, HUAC had been accused by many of persecuting people for their personal political beliefs and thus ruining for their lives and careers. At the time, uneasy relations between the United States and the Soviet Union threatened to undermine national security, and any activity associated with the Communist Party of the U.S.A. was suspect in the eyes of HUAC.

A frequent practice of HUAC was to investigate an organization and label it a "communist front" if, in the committee's judgment, the Communist Party or known party members held undo influence over the organization. Individuals from a range of profes-

Comic books were also subjected to censorship during the 1950's. Here, members of the Women's Auxiliary of the American Legion in Norwich, Connecticut, collect comic books from children, whom they rewarded with copies of "clean" books. The organization's plan to burn the collected books was opposed by the American Civil Liberties Union and the American Book Publishing Council. (AP/Wide World Photos)

sions were called to testify before HUAC and were often forced to "name names" of their own associates who might have suspect connections. The Hollywood film and television industry was targeted especially, and this scrutiny resulted in the "blacklisting"and jailing of a handful of screenwriters and directors for contempt of Congress in failing to disclose their political affiliations.

Meanwhile, McCarthy's pursuit of communist subversives in the U.S. government inaugurated a phase in the country's history that came to be known as McCarthyism. While McCarthyism did not hold censorship as one of its overt goals, the ramifications of McCarthy's congressional hearings can easily be identified as political censorship. Many American citizens, especially those in public life, were fearful of expressing political views to the left of mainstream

conservative views. HUAC held no official power to punish, but the people it named as communists or communist sympathizers often lost their jobs or were ostracized. McCarthyism thus became an effective tool of pressure, harassment, or blacklisting in order to instill conformity with the prevailing political order.

Cultural Censorship Until the landmark Supreme Court cases *Roth v. United States* and *Alberts v. California* (both in 1957), federal and state laws commonly criminalized traffic in books, photographs, and films judged to be sexually "indecent," including works by authors D. H. Lawrence, James Joyce, and Gustav Flaubert. In 1956, Samuel Roth, a New York publisher and dealer in erotic literature, was sentenced to five years in prison for violating the federal

Comstock Act. With the assistance of the American Civil Liberties Union (ACLU), Roth appealed his conviction to the Supreme Court. His lawyers argued that the Comstock law was inconsistent with the liberties protected in the First Amendment. The *Roth* and *Alberts* decisions were landmark rulings in which the Court, for the first time, severely limited government's discretion for selecting which erotic materials could be outlawed. By the end of the decade, lower courts also were liberally applying the ruling.

Before laws regarding dissemination of literary publications were liberalized, however, the climate in the mid- to late 1950's had been particularly restrictive. During the 1950's, books became targets of censors. For example, Detroit police banned John Griffin's *The Devil Rides Outside* (1952) and John O'Hara's *Ten North Frederick* (1955); the courts later overturned these bans. Michigan passed a law banning all books it deemed to be harmful to children, and across the United States, several books became controversial. Allen Ginsberg's poem "Howl" set in motion a legal case that was to prove instrumental in setting the stage for challenges to charges of obscenity and pornography.

In 1957, the U.S. Customs Service confiscated poet Lawrence Ferlinghetti's copies of "Howl." Ferlinghetti had published the poem in *Howl, and Other Poems* in August, 1956, and he was arrested on obscenity charges in May, 1957, after selling the book to plainclothes policemen. The case generated substantial media attention as it went to trial that summer. Lawyers hired by the ACLU defended Ferlinghetti on the grounds that his freedom of speech had been violated. The judge agreed and, in a precedent-setting verdict, acquitted him. Other publishers and authors felt the sting of censorship and endured similar legal cases. William Burroughs, like Ginsberg and Ferlinghetti a Beat generation member, had his work *Naked Lunch* (1959) denounced as "filth" after excerpts were published; subsequent publication of the book's excerpts was prohibited. It was not until the 1960's that the issue was resolved legally and the book was allowed to be published in the United States.

Meanwhile, D. H. Lawrence's novel *Lady Chatterley's Lover* had been banned in Europe, the United States, and Canada since its publication in Italy in 1928. In 1959, when Grove Press published a paperback edition of the novel and sold it through the U.S. mail, the postmaster general banned its sale, and the matter immediately came to federal court. In July, 1959, Judge Frederick van Pelt Bryan in the U.S. District Court of New York ruled that the novel was not obscene and was a work of art—a landmark ruling that signaled the end to censorship of sexual content in artistic expression in the United States and made available previously censored literary works at book stands across the country.

Also during the late 1950's, the New American Library published *Lady Chatterley's Lover* in Canada, where it met charges of obscenity and was also banned. In 1960, a judge in Montreal upheld the censorship; his decision was overturned in June, 1962, by the Supreme Court of Canada. In a 5-4 decision, the court ruled that the book could be legally bought and sold throughout Canada.

In 1959, the Supreme Court handed down two other significant judgments that further liberalized obscenity laws. In *Kingsley Pictures Corp. v. Regents*, the Court struck down a New York ban on a film version of *Lady Chatterley's Lover* (1955). The Court affirmed that the First Amendment protected the liberty to advocate all ideas, even those considered immoral. Later that year, in *Smith v. California*, the Court invalidated a statute that punished booksellers for the mere possession of obscene literature. The Court held that to require a bookseller to be familiar with the content of every book in a bookstore unreasonably restricted the public's access to literature.

Canadian authorities also censored print media. James Joyce's *Ulysses* (1922) was allowed into Canada in 1949 after twenty-six years of being on the prohibited importations list and sixteen years after being cleared of obscenity charges in the United States. During the early 1950's, 505 books remained banned in Canada, including short stories by Guy de Maupassant, William Faulkner's *Sanctuary* (1931), and the sixteen-volume *The Book of the Thousand Nights and a Night*, translated by Richard Burton. In 1956, Canada barred *Peyton Place* (1956) from entering the country.

Pressure Groups Along with government agencies, there were other organizations and groups that pressed for increased censorship of literature. Using economic pressure and other forms of persuasion, the groups sought to induce distributors and retailers to comply with their demands. Frequently these citizens' committees had the support of the local police and could brandish the threat of legal action against hesitant retailers or distributors. Religious associations were the most important of the groups in moral influence, and of these, the most powerful was the National Office for Decent Literature (NODL). NODL was established by the American Catholic Bishops in 1938 to mobilize the moral forces of the country against lascivious literature. Armed with NODL lists, local Roman Catholics visited retailers to monitor book offerings, and the lists were used for boycott purposes. NODL's lists also were employed as guides to harmful literature by police officials and commanders at army posts. A similar group, the Protestant Churchmen's Commission for Decent Publications, was set up in 1957.

The American Civil Liberties Union (ACLU) campaigned against such lists and their use by police and military officials, arguing that government officials were imposing their values on the whole society. The ACLU also contested the use of boycotts against recalcitrant retailers. In Canada, similar organizations, such as the National Affairs Committee of PEN (originally the acronym stood for Poets, Playwrights, Essayists and Novelists) Canada, founded in 1926, challenged legislation and private pressure groups who challenged freedom of expression.

Film The National Association of the Motion Picture Industry in the United States faced demands for censorship as early as 1918. Its members voted for self-censorship by adopting a code of standards, including a list of subjects and situations that were unacceptable. To implement the code, an organization called the Motion Picture Producers and Distributors of America was set up; it represented more than 80 percent of producers and was headed by U.S. president Warren G. Harding's postmaster general, Will Hays. It was not until 1930 that the Hays Office embarked on forming a Motion Picture Code (to be revised in 1956), which was drafted by two Roman Catholics. The code prohibited the depiction of illegal drug traffic, use of liquor in American life, white slavery, miscegenation, and pointed profanity.

For the benefit of Catholics, the Legion of Decency was formed in 1934 to evaluate the suitability of movies. Before 1957, the Legion had employed a set of four categories and thereafter another set of five classifications. Ratings of films were decided by the combined efforts of Catholic priests and lay members. The Legion's judgments carried increasing authority because of its powerful and far-flung organizational efforts, as well as the willingness of the Hays Office to have the Legion as an ally. Objections to a film by the Legion often resulted in pre-release alterations to the film. A loose but effective system of cooperation evolved among compliant producers, the fine-wielding Hays Office, and the Legion.

In 1950, this informal system of censorship was destabilized. The issue of whether the ownership or operation of theaters by movie producers violated antitrust laws was brought before the U.S. Supreme Court, which ordered the separation of production and exhibition. This led to the emergence of independent theaters, which could show any motion picture by any producer, with or without the code's seal of approval. The effect of this sea change was evident by 1953, when *The Moon Is Blue*, which was denied the code's blessing and was condemned by the Legion, was shown in seven thousand cinemas. *I Am a Camera* (1955), *The Man with the Golden Arm* (1955), and other films that failed to obtain the code's seal also met with wide box-office success. *The Man with the Golden Arm* was the first film produced in Hollywood to tackle the topic of drug addiction, which had been taboo subject matter for American films up until that time. Its release defied the censorship codes, and its success signaled moviegoers' growing interest in adult themes.

Depicting code-defying social issues was not without its harmful ramifications, however, such as the risk of being labeled sympathetic to communism. In the first half of the 1950's, there were many overtly anticommunist films, such as *My Son John* (1952). The film studios had to maintain a balance: On one hand, they sought to offer greater realism to audiences who had endured the Depression and World War II; on the other, they had to avoid offending other components of the potential film audience, politicians, and censors.

Radio and Television Censorship of radio and television programs was more insidious and intractable, although radio and television codes were less immediate in their effects than the movie codes. The initial federal regulation of radio resulted from the Federal Communications Commission (FCC), which was established in 1934 to assign a particular frequency to each radio station to prevent broadcasting interferences. FCC pronouncements, combined with the restrictions of the 1934 Federal Communications Act and its subsequent revisions, constituted the only governmental restraints upon radio programming.

The overriding concerns of each radio station were to acquire sponsors and to avoid the FCC's scrutiny. Major restraints on radio content, therefore, came from individual stations, sponsors, networks, and producers. In 1939, the National Association of Broadcasters announced a set of self-regulatory "Standards of Practice," outlining its attitude toward problematic radio topics. The standards underwent revision in 1954. During the 1950's, station executives were sensitive about the content of their programs, especially in airing unorthodox opinions. For example, in February, 1957, Eric Sevareid's news broadcast for CBS (Columbia Broadcasting System) Radio was canceled because he was considered too editorial in his treatment of the State Department's ban on American newsmen entering communist China.

The 1950's saw the rising popularity of television: By 1958, there were fifty million television sets and 526 television stations. The accessibility of television, coupled with the passivity of its audience, turned the medium into an unrivaled influence on viewers' opinions and values. Television could count on large audiences and could capture their attention for relatively long periods of time. In 1952, the National Association of Broadcasters promulgated a television code, and controls on television practices paralleled the controls placed on radio; sponsors, agencies, and producers of television shows were more restrictive than the government.

Sponsors were adamant about what they would finance, shunning issues like police brutality and malpractice of justice. For example, Rod Serling faced difficulties in 1958 with his script "A Town Has Turned to Dust" for *Playhouse 90*. It was a dramatization about the true story of Emmett Till, a fourteen-year-old African American who was murdered in Mississippi in 1955 for addressing the wife of a white storekeeper. The show was rejected by all but one sponsor because its treatment of race issues had the potential to adversely affect sales of the advertisers' products. Serling prepared a new script: The locale was transferred to a small southwestern town during the 1870's, and the protagonist became a romantic Mexican in love with the storekeeper's wife but only

"with the eyes." This plot shift left a Mexican as the object of the small town's wrath, yet eschewed any uncomplimentary epithets that might have been incendiary to the viewing audience.

Not all of television's troubles came from sponsors. Powerful action groups were eager to ensure their interests as well. The classic case of such anxiety occurred in Chicago in 1956, when station WGN-TV announced that it would show the film *Martin Luther*. The broadcast was canceled because WGN-TV did not want to cause enmity among Catholics. Protestants in the Chicago area decried the cancellation and accused the station of caving to the pressures of the Roman Catholic Church.

Impact The 1950's was a transitional period in North American censorship. The era was dominated by Cold War fears and—especially in the United States—anticommunist hysteria that generated pressures to impose censorship. However, the era was also a time when the courts were moving to restore civil liberties, paving the way for greater freedom of expression during the 1960's.

Further Reading

Cohen, Mark. *Censorship in Canadian Literature*. Montreal: McGill-Queens University Press, 2001. Scholarly study of literary censorship in Canada.

Foerstal, Herbert N. *Banned in the U.S.A.* Westport, Conn.: Greenwood Press, 2002. Survey of book censorship in American school and public libraries.

Haney, Robert W. *Comstockery in America: Patterns of Censorship and Control*. New York: Da Capo Press, 1974. Detailed and analytically sensitive treatment of censorship in the United States through the 1950's.

Hutchinson, Allan C., and Klaus Petersen, eds. *Interpreting Censorship in Canada*. Toronto: University of Toronto Press, 1999. Broad examination of patterns of censorship in Canada.

Magee, James. *Freedom of Expression*. Westport, Conn.: Greenwood Press, 2002. Well-documented introduction to the vicissitudes of freedom of expression to the end of the twentieth century.

Robbins, Louise S. *Censorship and the American Library*. Westport, Conn.: Greenwood Press, 1996. A review of the American Library Association's response to threats to intellectual freedom from 1939 to 1969.

Majid Amini

See also Book publishing; *Catcher in the Rye, The*; Comic books; Ferlinghetti, Lawrence; Film in the United States; Ginsberg, Allen; Hemingway, Ernest; House Committee on Un-American Activities; *Lady Chatterley's Lover*; *Lolita*; McCarthy, Joseph; *Peyton Place*; *Roth v. United States*; Supreme Court decisions, U.S.

■ Central Intelligence Agency

Identification Foreign intelligence service of the United States
Date Founded in 1947

In the context of the Cold War, the Central Intelligence Agency (CIA) played a crucial role on behalf of the American government during the 1950's. It did so less as a traditional intelligence agency dedicated to collecting and analyzing intelligence than through "covert action" in support of American foreign policy objectives against the Soviet Union in the presidential administrations of Harry S. Truman and Dwight D. Eisenhower.

During the 1950's, the CIA, in what some would later refer to as the agency's golden age, not only collected valuable intelligence about the Soviet Union for American policymakers but also, at the behest of the U.S. presidency, toppled governments in Iran and Guatemala; aided dissent in Eastern Europe, the Middle East, and Southeast Asia; and provided support to governments faced with communist insurgencies.

Created in 1947 as part of the Truman administration's strategy for dealing with the Soviet Union, the original Central Intelligence Agency lacked a clear role in terms of what it was to do abroad and largely was designed, as its name suggests, to coordinate intelligence from a variety of American agencies. By the end of 1947 and into 1948, however, the agency began operations that were not part of its original mandate: covert efforts in Italy and France to influence elections and ensure that communist parties in the respective countries would not achieve power.

Through measures passed by the National Security Council, the CIA gained a permanent role in launching covert operations abroad to further American interests. In 1948, it created the Office of Special Operations (OSO) to deal with foreign intelligence-gathering and covert operations. Later during the same year, covert operations efforts were centralized in the newly created Office of Policy Coordination (OPC) under the leadership of lawyer Frank Wisner. Although funded and staffed by the CIA, the OPC enjoyed autonomy until 1950, when the CIA's newly appointed director, General Walter Bedell Smith, took back control of the OPC. Two years later, that body was merged with the OSO to become the Directorate of Plans with Allen Dulles, soon to be director, as its head. As a Princeton University graduate, Dulles was an apt choice for this role since during the early days of the agency, many of its members were drawn from a social elite educated at Ivy League universities.

Initially, inspired by the American government's determination to launch an all-out effort to "contain" communism, the CIA directed its attentions toward Eastern Europe in an attempt to create problems for the Soviet Union in its own backyard. The CIA placed agents behind the Iron Curtain and offered resources to existing opposition groups.

Under the direction of Wisner, the CIA simultaneously sought to ensure the loyalty of Western Europe through a series of covert operations centered in the cultural field. In June, 1950, a group of intellectuals met in West Berlin and created the Congress for Cultural Freedom, a body that would sponsor academic meetings and journals during the decade. The financial and inspirational force behind this group was in fact the CIA, which viewed the organization as a means of combating Soviet propaganda directed at intellectual and cultural elites. It similarly employed real and front charitable foundations to funnel money into cultural and youth organizations that it believed would aid the anticommunist cause.

Overall, during the Truman period, the fledgling CIA's record was a mixed one. Positive examples of its influence include the case of the Philippines: Through the skill of one CIA operative, Colonel Edward Lansdale, the government of the Philippines managed to defeat a communist insurgency. Lansdale would later move on to Vietnam and work with the government of South Vietnam in its efforts to curtail a North Vietnamese-led communist insurgency. The CIA's negative impact was seen in the case of the Korean War. In 1950, the agency's analysts failed to predict North Korea's invasion of South Korea, and after the attack, the agency continued to provide inadequate intelligence to the Truman government. Problems also arose elsewhere in Asia,

CIA director Allen W. Dulles in his Washington, D.C., office in 1954.(AP/ Wide World Photos)

able faith in the work of the CIA. Part of the new prominence of the CIA also related directly to the exceptional situation whereby Eisenhower's choice to head the agency, Allen Dulles, also happened to be the brother of Eisenhower's secretary of state, John Foster Dulles. These fraternal ties put the CIA in a unique and powerful position to carry out administration policy while helping to shape it.

Early in Eisenhower's first term, the CIA launched its most ambitious covert operation to date. The target was the nationalist government of Prime Minister Mohammed Mossadegh in Iran. Mossadegh angered Great Britain and brought himself and his government to the attention of the Truman administration in 1951, when his government nationalized his country's oil industry. Despite approaches by the British, the Truman administration refused to authorize U.S. involvement in efforts to overthrow the Iranian government. This changed, however, with the Republican victory during the 1952 presidential election. On the campaign trail, Eisenhower had pledged to take an aggressive approach to dealing with what were perceived as efforts by the Soviet Union to spread communism, and Iran, portrayed as a potential Soviet client state, became the first test case of Eisenhower's promised resolve. The CIA was authorized to participate with British intelligence in overthrowing the Iranian government, and—through its man on the scene, Kermit Roosevelt, the grandson of President Teddy Roosevelt—succeeded and helped bring the shah back to power.

Emboldened by this success, the following year the Eisenhower administration targeted the democratically elected government of Guatemala. Its leader, President Jacobo Arbenz, pursued policies of reform and nationalization that threatened American economic interests, particularly those of the United Fruit Company. Once more, however, the rationale for toppling the Guatemalan government was its ties to communism, a tenuous charge at best. The CIA proceeded to train an armed insurgency in Honduras, which, in June of 1954, invaded Guatemala and toppled Arbenz.

where the CIA launched covert operations against the Chinese communist regime of Mao Zedong.

Taiwan was one base for such activities: The agency trained Chinese Nationalists for infiltration efforts against mainland China. These operations had little impact, and in 1952, two CIA agents were captured in the People's Republic of China. Similarly, the agency's efforts to foster unrest in Eastern Europe largely failed, most spectacularly in Poland, where an underground network supplied and financed by the CIA was publicly revealed in late 1950 to have been under the control of Polish intelligence.

The Eisenhower Administration The fortunes of the CIA changed dramatically in 1952 with the presidential election of Dwight D. Eisenhower. Unlike his predecessor, Eisenhower, from his time in the military, valued intelligence and would put consider-

Elsewhere during the 1950's, the CIA continued its efforts against communist China, this time with operations focused on Tibet, which was occupied by China in 1951. The CIA trained Tibetan guerrillas in the United States before transporting them back to Asia and then parachuting them into Tibet.

Domestically, through a program under the leadership of Sidney Gottlieb and code-named MK-Ultra, the agency began the research and covert financing of drug and mind control experiments. The rationale for such work, which involved unwitting human subjects, was that communist nations were conducting similar research. Decades later, revelations of this field of work would cause the CIA considerable damage.

The End of the 1950's Despite the fact that the 1950's are remembered as an era of CIA successes, the agency in fact experienced a series of prominent setbacks. For example, CIA efforts in Syria to replace the government with one friendlier toward the United States failed. Equally ineffective were attempts to bring down the government in Indonesia of President Achmad Sukarno, which was considered to be too friendly toward communists. The CIA attempted to discredit Sukarno by producing and distributing a pornographic film with an actor pretending to be the Indonesian leader. When that failed, the agency funded and supplied Indonesian insurgents, and CIA members flew air support on their behalf. This plot proved embarrassing when an American CIA pilot was captured and put on trial. He was later released in a prisoner swap.

An even more embarrassing episode occurred in May, 1960. Beginning in 1953, the CIA led efforts to develop and manufacture U.S. intelligence-gathering capabilities through spy planes and satellites. This approach proved controversial, as the CIA found itself in a bureaucratic struggle with the U.S. Air Force over which body would control the new technology. In the case of the satellite imagery, this dispute led Eisenhower to create the National Reconnaissance Office in 1960. The results in terms of the Cold War, however, proved immensely beneficial to the Eisenhower administration. A new spy plane, the U-2, began flights over the Soviet Union in 1956 and brought back detailed photos of Soviet military sites. In 1960, the first spy satellite, code-named Corona, was launched and started photographing the Soviet Union as well.

With the U-2 flights, however, there was a danger of Soviet detection. Twenty-three flights followed the first one in 1956 until a CIA pilot, Francis Gary Powers, was shot down over the Soviet Union. Confident that the pilot could not have survived the incident, Eisenhower publicly denied any such missions had taken place. A consistent principle with respect to CIA operations was "plausible deniability," whereby the president could be kept free of any entanglements emerging from covert operations. After the public denial, the Soviet Union, much to the embarrassment of the American government, produced Powers, who had survived. This was a preview of an even worse disaster that would befall the CIA in 1961, with the failure of the Bay of Pigs invasion of Cuba.

Impact Little recognized at the time because of the secretive nature of its work, the Central Intelligence Agency performed a leading role in the covert efforts of the United States government to fight the Cold War against the Soviet Union. The CIA served as a vital arm of U.S. foreign policy, particularly in Europe, Latin America, the Middle East, and Asia.

Further Reading

Grose, Peter. *Gentleman Spy: The Life of Allen Dulles.* Boston: University of Massachusetts Press, 1996. A study of the life of Allen Dulles, director of the CIA between 1953 and 1961 and a key force in the agency.

_____. *Operation Rollback: America's Secret War Behind the Iron Curtain.* New York: Houghton Mifflin, 2000. Discusses the United States' covert Operation Rollback plan, which worked in tandem with CIA efforts and proved to be a bold strategy of espionage, subversion, and sabotage to foment insurrection in the Soviet satellite countries.

Kinzer, Stephen. *All the Shah's Men: An American Coup and the Roots of Middle East Terror.* New York: John Wiley & Sons, 1996. A detailed examination of the CIA's role during the 1953 overthrow of the Iranian government of Mohammed Mossadegh.

Ranelagh, John. *The Agency: The Rise and Decline of the CIA.* New York: Simon & Schuster, 1986. The definitive history of the Central Intelligence Agency by a British journalist. It offers an in-depth analysis of the entire history of the agency, including the period during the 1950's.

Thomas, Evan. *The Very Best Men: Four Who Dared— The Early Years of the CIA.* New York: Simon &

Schuster, 1996. Biographical study of four early members of the CIA. Of particular relevance to the 1950's is Thomas's examination of Frank Wisner, who played a leading role in designing covert operations against the Soviet Union.

Steve Hewitt

See also Cold War; Dulles, John Foster; Eisenhower, Dwight D.; Espionage and Sabotage Act of 1954; Federal Bureau of Investigation; Foreign policy of the United States; Guatemala invasion; Radio Free Europe; Truman, Harry S.; Truman Doctrine; U-2 spy planes; United States Information Agency; Vietnam.

■ Chamberlain, Wilt

Identification African American basketball player
Born August 21, 1936; Philadelphia, Pennsylvania
Died October 12, 1999; Bel-Air, California

Considered by many sports historians to be one of the greatest basketball players ever, Wilt Chamberlain first earned notice during his high school career at Philadelphia's Overbrook High School and his college career at the University of Kansas during the mid-1950's.

The eighth of eleven children, Wilt Chamberlain was born in Philadelphia. During his athletic career at Overbrook High School, Chamberlain demonstrated athletic prowess in basketball and track and field. In his three varsity years at Overbrook, he led his basketball team to a combined record of fifty-six wins and three defeats and helped earn the team a state public school title during his sophomore year.

Chamberlain was highly recruited and decided to attend the University of Kansas. In his first collegiate basketball game, he scored 52 points. One of the saddest days in his two-year college career was when his team lost to North Carolina in triple overtime

during the 1957 National Collegiate Athletic Association (NCAA) title game, although he was named the tournament's most outstanding player.

Chamberlain's style of play led to several NCAA basketball rule changes, which included the rule that offensive players could not throw the ball over the backboard to inbound pass and the rule that free throws had to be shot from behind the free-throw line.

Impact Chamberlain played for the Harlem Globetrotters during the 1958-1959 season. He was then drafted into the National Basketball Association (NBA) and played from 1959 to 1972. During his fourteen-year pro career, he played for three teams (Philadelphia, San Francisco, and Los Angeles). His physical style of play and his scoring and rebounding records became the standards by which other NBA centers were measured. His rookie-season honors included NBA rookie of the year, all-star game most

Wilt Chamberlain grabs a rebound during a 1957 University of Kansas basketball game. (AP/Wide World Photos)

valuable player, and NBA finals most valuable player. Chamberlain was elected to the Naismith Memorial Basketball Hall of Fame in 1978.

Further Reading

Chamberlain, Wilt. *A View from Above.* New York: Villard Books, 1991. Chamberlain's memoir, which details his career and provides his thoughts on the later decades' sports and sports stars.

Greenberger, Robert. *Wilt Chamberlain.* New York: Rosen, 2002. A biography of Chamberlain aimed at young adults.

Dana D. Brooks

See also Basketball; Cousy, Bob; Harlem Globetrotters; Sports.

■ Chevrolet Corvette

Identification American sports car
Manufacturer General Motors
Date First produced in June, 1953

The Corvette was General Motors' answer to postwar America's invasion by European roadsters and quickly established itself as "America's sports car."

Before World War II, two-seater sports cars were essentially the toys of the rich and mostly restricted to European roadways. During the late 1940's, however, imports such as the Jaguar XK-120 and MG-TD became increasingly visible in metropolitan America. The most expensive cars were still purchased largely by the wealthy, but the relatively affordable MGs revealed an appetite for fun-to-drive sports cars in middle-class America.

By the early 1950's, Detroit's automobile designers were trying to meet America's growing demand for sports cars. Chevrolet struck first, premiering its Corvette in 1953 auto shows and pushing the car into production by June of that year. Curvy like the Jaguars but lower priced and constructed out of rustproof fiberglass, the Corvette was an instant success. The Ford Motor Company followed with its own two-seater, the Thunderbird, in 1955. However, like the initial Corvettes, the Thunderbird roadsters had very unsporty, carlike automatic transmissions throughout the three years they were produced before Ford abandoned their design in favor of a four-seater, personal touring car in 1958. By then, Corvette was offering performance pack-

Owners of early Chevrolet Corvette models gather at a rally in New York during the mid-1950's. (Hulton Archive | by Getty Images)

ages that fulfilled the images of quickness and power its design evoked.

Impact By 1960, with synchronized four-speed transmissions, Positraction rear ends, dual four-barrel carburetors, and even fuel injection paired with powerful V-8 engines available to Corvette buyers, the Corvette had established itself as America's only true sports car.

Further Reading

Egan, Peter, and Michael Dregni, eds. *This Old Corvette: The Ultimate Tribute to America's Sports Car.* Stillwater, Minn.: Voyageur Press, 2003. A short anthology of articles, advertisements, and illustrations which capture the Corvette's impact on America's culture.

Schefter, James L. *All Corvettes Are Red: The Rebirth of an American Legend.* New York: Simon & Schuster, 1996. A well-illustrated telling of the Corvette's story and the passion the car inspires.

Joseph R. Rudolph, Jr.

See also Automobiles and auto manufacturing; Edsel; Ford Thunderbird; General Motors; Interstate highway system; Volkswagen.

■ Chiang Kai-shek

Identification President of the Republic of China (Taiwan), 1949-1975
Born October 31, 1887; Zhejiang Province, China
Died April 5, 1975; Taipei, Taiwan

Chiang Kai-shek's anticommunism made him an important U.S. ally in Asia during the Cold War years, and his support was greatly aided by the American public's admiration of his wife.

As a Christian and strong anticommunist, Chiang Kai-shek had the full sympathies of the American public during the 1950's. He had risen to power in postimperial China during the 1920's. Although he was initially impressed by social transformations in the Soviet Union, he subsequently expelled the communists from his Nationalist Party, the Guomindang, in 1927. However, he failed to defeat the communists under Mao Zedong and had to forge an uneasy alliance with them during the late 1930's, when Japan invaded China. After the Japanese surrender in 1945, Chiang Kai-shek and the communists resumed their civil war, which ended with Chiang Kai-shek's defeat in 1949. After fleeing to

Taiwan—then known as Formosa—Chiang Kai-shek set up his exile government that became known as the Republic of China.

America's Chinese Ally Initially, the United States was not committed to ensuring the survival of Chiang Kai-shek in Taiwan. However, when the Korean War broke out on June 25, 1950, the United States changed its policies. It sent the Seventh Fleet into the Taiwan Strait, separating the island from the mainland in order to protect Taiwan from a communist Chinese invasion and to prevent Chiang Kai-shek's launch of an invasion of the mainland that would have widened the war. Beginning in 1950, it was understood that America would protect Taiwan.

Chiang Kai-shek's political standing in the United States was greatly aided by the eloquence, intelligence, and beauty of his second wife, American-educated Soong Mei-ling. Madame Chiang Kai-shek, as she was called in the United States, represented for many Americans the plight of the noncommunist Chinese suffering from Mao Zedong's repression. Conservatives also viewed the couple as a path to regaining a China they considered "lost" to the communists. Madame Chiang Kai-shek, and her husband by extension, became one of the few Asian world leaders familiar to Americans during the 1950's. She became such a popular icon in the United States that one U.S. poll consistently placed her on the annual list of the ten most admired women in the world—a position that she held until 1967.

Utilizing his American popular support, Chiang Kai-shek received much U.S. economic and military aid. In December of 1954, he signed a mutual defense treaty with the United States, which pledged itself to the defense of Taiwan. When the Chinese communists shelled the Taiwanese-held islands of Quemoy (Chin-men Tao) and Matsu in April, 1958, the United States intervened by sending a naval force and by persuading the Soviet Union to end its support for this action. Throughout the 1950's, Chiang Kai-shek had the unqualified support of the United States.

Impact Without the popularity of Madame Chiang Kai-shek and her husband in the United States during the 1950's, Taiwan might have been conquered. Instead, America made Chiang Kai-shek an integral part of its anticommunist strategy. For several years,

Chiang Kai-shek inspecting Nationalist Chinese troops in 1952. (National Archives)

the United States vetoed the attempt within the United Nations to move China's seat, held by Chiang Kai-shek's government, to that of the People's Republic of China in Beijing. However, while his country continued to prosper economically, Chiang Kai-shek was an autocratic ruler who governed under martial law. The American public grew disenchanted with him during the 1960's. Chiang Kai-shek died in 1975 before the United States broke off diplomatic relations with Taiwan in 1979.

Further Reading

Bodenhorn, Terry Dwight. *Defining Modernity: Guomindang Rhetorics of a New China, 1920-1970.* Ann Arbor, Mich.: Center for Chinese Studies, 2003. Studies Chiang Kai-shek's ideological struggle with communists.

Crozier, Brian. *The Man Who Lost China.* London: Angus & Robertson, 1976. Covers Chiang Kai-shek's life, with emphasis on the civil war in China and its aftermath. Illustrated.

Moorwood, William. *Duel for the Middle Kingdom.* New York: Everest House, 1980. Portrays Chiang Kai-shek's U.S.-supported struggle with Mao Zedong.

R. C. Lutz

See also China; Cold War; Foreign policy of the United States; Formosa Resolution; Immigration to the United States; Korean War; Southeast Asia Treaty Organization; *Ugly American, The.*

■ China

Hostilities between China and the United States emerged and deepened as a result of the war in Korea, and the relationship became entrenched in Cold War tensions over feared communist expansion in Asia.

The Cold War was a critical factor in determining the apprehension and hostility between China and North American countries during the 1950's, just as Cold War tensions colored all U.S. foreign policy during the decade.

With the communists' success in driving Chiang Kai-shek and his Nationalist Party forces from the mainland and onto the Chinese island of Taiwan (then called Formosa), U.S. foreign policy received a major blow. Since President Harry S. Truman and Secretary of State Dean Acheson initially were skeptical about the willingness of Chiang Kai-shek to make the necessary reforms to save his government, the United States did not commit itself fully against the new communist government in China and might have shown some flexibility with it had the Korean War not broken out in June of 1950. With the North Korean invasion of South Korea and Truman's determination to resist such open aggression, the situation between China and the United States changed for the worse. The United States felt it had to protect the Nationalists on Taiwan in case Korea was a diversionary pretext to a Taiwan invasion.

After the war between North Korea (which stood as a Russian and Chinese ally) and South Korea (which stood as a U.S. ally) erupted, General Douglas MacArthur, the U.S. commander in Korea, was convinced that America should fight China directly in an attempt to restore Chiang Kai-shek to power, and he made public these views. When he followed up his successful landing at Inchon with a move to push the North Koreans almost to the Chinese border, he also threatened the Chinese, who intervened and pushed the Americans back to the thirty-eighth parallel, the border between the two Koreas. Although Truman fired MacArthur for insubordination and installed the more politically moderate General Matthew B. Ridgway in his place, the hostility in the region intensified.

Fears on the Domestic Fronts American fears of any communist success were fueled in 1949 by the stunning news that the Russians successfully had developed the atomic bomb. Although the United States went on to develop the more powerful hydrogen bomb during the early 1950's, the Soviet Union matched that U.S. achievement as well a short while later. When the Russians launched *Sputnik I*, the first artificial space satellite, in 1957, many thought the Soviet Union was surpassing America in the critical space race. The Cold War fueled fears that had direct political consequences. Republican Senator Joseph McCarthy made a career out of attacks on the U.S. Communist Party and asserted that its members had infiltrated important U.S. government offices.

Anticommunism was evident in organizations such as the John Birch Society and in the decisions of the U.S. Supreme Court. In the "culture of conformity" of the 1950's, it was difficult to contradict the prevailing view of hostility toward China.

Fears of communist success at home and abroad fueled the election of President Dwight D. Eisenhower in 1952 with his pledge to "go to Korea" to end the conflict there. He did successfully negotiate an armistice, but this did not ease tensions with China. Indeed, his selection of the anticommunist John Foster Dulles as his secretary of state arguably exacerbated the tensions. Dulles became identified with "brinkmanship," or bluffing the communists with threats of military action "up to the brink of war." Dulles's foreign policy included encircling communists by defense treaties with nations hostile to communism, as evidenced by his initiation of the Southeast Asia Treaty Organization. Through various provisions, the United States undertook commitments to the defense of the anticommunist regime in South Vietnam, again bringing America into conflict with China and ultimately leading to U.S. involvement in Vietnam.

Since Canada was a member of the British Commonwealth, and Britain maintained diplomatic relations with the People's Republic of China to protect its interests in Hong Kong (then a British colony), Canada's relations with China, although strained by the Cold War, were not as hostile. China also benefited by the fact that Canadian doctor Norman Bethune was a hero to the communists for his medical assistance to the Chinese during the Japanese war.

From the Chinese point of view, the hostility with the United States was equally great. The communists pointed to General MacArthur's speeches and the drive to the Chinese border as evidence of evil U.S. intentions. Chinese fears of a U.S. invasion generated patriotic fervor there and strengthened the communist control by unifying China against America. When China forced America to a stalemate in Korea, the Chinese took it as a sign that they had successfully resisted Western capitalist countries and that communism would prevail eventually over capitalism. Government-sponsored street demonstrations against America were accompanied by hate-filled slogans.

Asian American Communities The strained relations between the United States and the People's Re-

Time Line of China, 1949-1958

1949	Chinese Communist Party (CCP) gains control of mainland China, formally establishing the People's Republic of China (PRC), with Mao Zedong as its chairman.
	Chiang Kai-shek and his followers flee to Formosa (later called Taiwan).
	Soviet Union recognizes the PRC.
1950	China and the Soviet Union sign Treaty of Friendship, Alliance, and Mutual Assistance. The agreement also seeks to counter Japan or any nation that joins Japan for the purpose of aggression.
	China absorbs Tibet.
	Mao, believing in the exportation of communist revolution, involves China in the Korean War. North Korean and Chinese troops halt the United Nations offensive, and U.N. troops soon withdraw southward.
	After entering the Korean War, China begins propagandized drive against the "enemies of the state." At first, foreigners and missionaries are the major targets of this campaign. Soon ideological reform drives such as these demand self-criticisms and public confessions from university faculty members, scientists, writers, and other artists.
	Agrarian Reform Law launches land redistribution, initiating a class struggle between landlords and wealthy peasants.
1951	The Three-Anti, Five-Anti, and Thought Reform campaigns. The *san fan*, or "three anti" movement, is aimed at eliminating incompetent public officials. The *wu fan*, or "five anti" movement, is aimed at eliminating corrupt businessmen and industrialists. Millions of people are affected by the various reform or punitive drives.
	Denouncing China's aggression in Korea, the United Nations calls for a global embargo on arms shipments to China. It becomes clear that the PRC will not soon replace Nationalist China as a member of the United Nations.
1953-1957	Transition to Socialism, or China's first Five-Year Plan, comprises goals of centralizing political operations, collectivizing agriculture, and becoming industrialized. During this time, Chinese industry grows at a rate of 15 percent per year.
1954	United States signs a mutual defense treaty with Chiang Kai-shek's government.
1956-1957	"Hundred Flowers" period arrives. Mid-1956 sees the beginning of an official attempt to liberalize the political climate, as the CCP realizes that intellectuals are needed within its ranks. Intellectuals and artists are encouraged to speak openly on government policies. By mid-1957, criticism of the party, and especially the excesses of its leaders, pours in. Angry and humiliated party cadres launch the Anti-Rightist campaign.
1957	Important Chinese industries are all under government control by this time.
1958	The Great Leap Forward, China's second Five-Year Plan, begins; it is a disastrous attempt at rapid industrialization. Tremendous labor, but little technological ability or capital, is invested in the widely propagandized program. The resulting economic depression lasts through 1961. During this time Mao builds a cult of personality around himself, giving credence to his infallibility.
	PRC bombards Taiwanese-controlled islands of Quemoy and Matsu.

public of China caused conflict within the United States' Asian American communities. The passage of the Immigration and Nationality Act of 1952 and the Refugee Relief Act of 1953 affected immigration to the United States, and immigration from the People's Republic of China and other communist countries virtually ceased. While some immigration from other Asian countries was permitted under tight quotas, only a small number of well-known political refugees had any realistic hope of coming to the United States. Among the Chinese immigrants already in the United States, serious political conflicts between supporters of the Nationalists and the communists occurred; those who resided in the United States but supported the communists were silenced, persecuted, or forced to leave the country.

Impact The strained relations between China and the countries of North America were a product of the larger Cold War struggle between all communist nations and the United States and were themselves an additional source of tension. Each country directed intense negative media attacks against the other. Moreover, the hostile relations between the two countries led the United States to intensify its attempts both to establish a democratic system in Japan to fight perceived communist Chinese infiltration and to conclude a final Japanese peace treaty so that Japan could rebuild industrially and serve as a strong force against China. The United States also strengthened its diplomatic and military commitments to the Nationalist Chinese government on the island of Formosa and to South Korea. These actions were a part of a political doctrine of containment that was also applied to the government of South Vietnam. During the 1960's, the intense mutual hatred would become evident in the war in Vietnam.

Further Reading

Fairbank, John King. *China: A New History.* Cambridge, Mass.: Harvard University Press, 1992. An excellent survey of the country from one of America's greatest Chinese historians.

Faust, John R., and Judith F. Kornberg. *China in World Politics.* Boulder, Colo.: Lynne Rienner, 1995. An excellent overview of China in world affairs.

Lu Ning. *The Dynamics of Foreign-Policy Decisionmaking in China.* Boulder, Colo.: Westview Press, 2000. The most recent analysis of Chinese foreign policy from a Chinese scholar.

Pye, Lucian. *China: An Introduction.* 4th ed. New York: HarperCollins, 1991. A good starting point for a political analysis of China in the twentieth century.

Spence, Jonathan. *The Search for Modern China.* New York: Norton, 1990. A classic history of modern China.

Zhao, Quansheng. *Understanding Chinese Foreign Policy.* New York: Oxford University Press, 1996. A good analysis of Chinese foreign policy.

Richard L. Wilson

See also Acheson, Dean; Asian Americans; Brinkmanship; Chiang Kai-shek; Cold War; Communist Party of the U.S.A.; Dulles, John Foster; Eisenhower, Dwight D.; Formosa Resolution; Korean War; Ridgway, Matthew B.; Southeast Asia Treaty Organization; *Ugly American, The*; Vietnam.

■ Chrysler autoworkers strike

The Event Strike by United Auto Workers (UAW) against Chrysler
Date January 25, 1950, to May 4, 1950

One of the longest strikes in U.S. labor history, the Chrysler autoworkers strike established precedents for employer contributions to medical and other insurance.

The autoworkers strike began on January 25, 1950, after six months of negotiations between the UAW and Chrysler. The major issue involved the form, funding, and administration of a pension fund for retired workers. The union demanded a minimum one-hundred-dollar-per-month contribution to the workers' pension fund for each worker. In addition, the union negotiators asked for a wage increase and an allowance to cover employee hospitalization and medical expenses. The UAW had won similar benefits from Ford Motor Company one year earlier. Chrysler management responded to the demand with an offer to make up the difference between Social Security payments and the one-hundred-dollar-per-month payments. However, Chrysler wished to have complete control over the pension plan, with no union input. It was at this point that UAW president Walter Reuther stepped into the negotiations. After rejecting Chrysler's offer as inadequate, the union set a January 25, 1950, strike date for the 89,000 Chrysler workers. On the morning of that date, the workers began leaving the shop floors of twenty-five Chrysler plants around the United States.

The strike was the first authorized against a major U.S. company since the UAW strike against the Ford Motor Company the previous May. Because the majority of the Chrysler plants were in Detroit, that city was most affected, especially as suppliers that had contracts with Chrysler began to shut down and lay off workers. Negotiations did not resume until early February. After several weeks of give-and-take with minimal results, Chrysler offered to set up a thirty-million-dollar pension fund instead of agreeing to the union's demand for a wage increase that would pay directly into the fund. The union rejected the offer at first because there was no suggestion that the funds would be kept in a separate account. Reuther characterized the offer as an attempt to deceive the workers, the stockholders, and the public. Chrysler reacted to Reuther's charges by stating that the company had no "double-bookkeeping intentions." After another week of talks, the union agreed essentially to the company's offer as long as the fund was separate and guaranteed. Other important aspects of the union counterproposal were the five-year length of the contract and an agreement that the one-hundred-dollar-per-month payments to retirees were to be in addition to any payments from Social Security.

Agreement Is Reached Finally, on April 27, 1950, verbal agreements had been reached on all but one issue in the contract. This issue concerned the contribution from each side to the cost of medical insurance, which to that point was paid by the workers. Both sides were cautiously optimistic and began a round of nonstop negotiations, which lasted two days, broke up for a few hours, and were quickly resumed. On May 4, 1950, both sides made separate announcements about a contract agreement being reached. The final agreement included a pension fund set up and maintained by the company; company contributions to workers' medical, life, and disability insurance; a five-year term for the contract; and no closed shop. UAW leadership was bitter, despite the contract, with President Walter Reuther's attack on Chrysler for its intransigence. Chrysler, for its part, suffered a net loss of $1,782,790.

Impact The UAW strike against Chrysler set a new standard for labor contracts by including agreements that involved pension and medical insurance contributions from the employer.

Further Reading

Amberg, Stephen. *The Union Inspiration in American Politics: The Autoworkers and the Making of a Liberal Industrial Order.* Philadelphia: Temple University Press, 1994. An examination of the history of auto industrial relations and the modern labor movement.

Barnard, John. *Walter Reuther and the Rise of the Auto Workers.* Boston: Little, Brown, 1983. Details Reuter's role during the 1950 strike.

Ron Jacobs

See also AFL-CIO merger; Automobiles and auto manufacturing; Business and the economy in the United States; Unionism in the United States.

■ The Cisco Kid

Identification Television Western series designed for children

Date Produced for syndication from 1950 to 1956

Because The Cisco Kid *was filmed rather than produced live, as were most programs during the 1950's, and was one of the first syndicated television series, it was able to be seen in all television markets and enjoyed enormous popularity.*

Television's Cisco Kid was a Mexican "Robin Hood of the Old West," a fictional Western adventurer created by William Sydney Porter, who wrote under the pen name O. Henry. The Cisco Kid character was introduced in O. Henry's 1907 short story "The Caballero's Way."

Before *The Cisco Kid* became a television program, its character was featured on a radio program from 1942 until the mid-1950's; he also appeared in a comic book and more than twenty motion pictures. Cisco Kid films were released by several studios over many decades and featured four different actors in the title role. The last actor to star as Cisco on the movie screen, Duncan Renaldo, made the transition to television as the program's title character.

Cisco's jovial sidekick, Pancho, added a sense of humor and spirit to each show. The setting for the series was the territory of New Mexico during the 1890's. The duo's primary mission was to ride the countryside fighting injustice and defending the weak and oppressed. However, Cisco and Pancho were often mistaken by law officials as desperados. Renaldo was in his fifties when he portrayed Cisco, and Leo Carrillo was beyond the age of seventy when he played Pancho.

Impact *The Cisco Kid* reflected the era's preoccupation with law and justice, and the character found a niche, along with other television heroes such as the Lone Ranger and Captain Video, with first-generation television audiences. Scriptwriters were urged to avoid controversial material and to include at least three action sequences per episode. A decision to film in color enhanced the value of the show and the market for extended syndication. In the show's six years of syndication, 156 episodes were produced and aired. *The Cisco Kid* television show continued in syndication into the twenty-first century.

Further Reading

Aaker, Everett. *Television Western Players of the Fifties: A Biographical Encyclopedia of All Regular Cast Members in Western Series, 1949-1959.* Jefferson, N.C.: McFarland, 1997. Collection of brief biographies of television actors, including those on *The Cisco Kid.*

Nivens, Francis. *The Films of the Cisco Kid.* Boalsburg, Pa.: World of Yesterday, 1998. A complete account of the Cisco Kid feature-length films.

Rothel, David. *Those Great Cowboy Sidekicks.* Metuchen, N.J.: Scarecrow Press, 1984. A book with considerable information about various "saddle pals" of children's television.

Thummin, Janet. *Small Screens, Big Ideas: Television in the 1950's.* London: I. B. Tauris, 2001. Explores the way in which television reflected and prompted social change in postwar America and Britain. Includes many illustrations and photographs.

Dennis A. Harp

See also *Captain Video; Gunsmoke; Lone Ranger, The; Sergeant Preston of the Yukon; Sky King;* Television for children; Television Westerns.

■ Civil defense programs

Definition U.S. federal programs designed to respond to the threat of nuclear attack

At the height of widespread Cold War paranoia during the 1950's, the U.S. government initiated a variety of civil defense programs that were designed to build public awareness about the consequences of nuclear attack and the means to survive it.

At the end of World War II, the United States was the only country with nuclear weapons. America's status changed in 1949, when the Soviet Union detonated its own atomic bomb. By 1950, the American Central Intelligence Agency (CIA) estimated Soviet atomic stockpiles would reach more than two hundred weapons within the following three years. This growing Soviet nuclear capability threatened the security of the United States and its European allies by creating a potential for a third world war.

In response to Soviet nuclear advances, President Harry S. Truman ordered an assessment of the Soviets' future military capabilities, a move which resulted in the publication of National Security Document 68 (NSC-68) in late 1950. That report, kept secret until 1975, recommended a number of measures the United States needed to take to counter Soviet nuclear and conventional military buildup. Thus, under the auspices of NSC-68, the United States laid its foundation for a Cold War nuclear deterrent policy that would guide the country in the subsequent four decades.

America's new Cold War security policy called for a U.S. nuclear retaliatory capability and a civilian civil defense program, both of which were presumed capable of thwarting a Soviet nuclear attack. Civil defense programs became an emblematic feature of the decade's Cold War fixation. To carry out the civil defense component of NSC-68, President Truman issued an executive order on December 1, 1950, establishing the Federal Civil Defense Administration (FCDA). The next month, Congress passed the Federal Civil Defense Act, beginning a decade of civil defense programs aimed at elevating public awareness about the effects of nuclear war and convincing the American population that survival from nuclear attack was possible if the country were prepared sufficiently. The underlying goal of a sound civil defense program was to demonstrate to the Soviets that the American people had the will to survive any form of Soviet nuclear military aggression.

Easing National Fears One of the first measures taken by the federal government to convince the American public that the nation could weather a nuclear attack was the publication in January, 1951, of a civil defense booklet titled *Survival Under Atomic Attack.* Within a year, twenty million copies of the publication had been distributed nationwide. The booklet attempted to diminish fear of atomic warfare by describing preemptive measures that could lessen the effects of nuclear fallout. For the remainder of the decade, similar publications were produced in tandem with media propaganda, each espousing the benefits of civil defense.

By the mid-1950's, television had become a dominant part of American life. The government took advantage of this new information medium by producing a number of television shows promoting civil defense themes. One such film produced by the FCDA in 1956, titled *Operation Alert*, depicted a realistic portrayal of Americans surviving an atomic attack that hit targets across the country. The following year, the FCDA collaborated with CBS television to produce another civil defense film titled *The Day Called X*. This film depicted the citizens of Portland, Oregon, successfully evacuating the city prior to a nuclear attack. A series of additional films followed for the remainder of the decade, thus marking the marriage of government and television as a force in combating communism.

Public information was not the sole focus of the 1950's national civil defense policy. To ensure public acceptance that civil defense would work, the FCDA and the Office of Civil and Defense Mobilization (OCDM) also engaged themselves in a number of initiatives that would reassure citizens that the country was prepared for war. Schools were required to conduct air-raid practice drills and, with government support, stockpile supplies. Many public buildings both were labeled with a familiar civil defense triangle logo noting the civilian capacity of the structure and were supplied with fifty-gallon filled water cans. The Emergency Broadcast System conducted periodic siren tests on television and outdoors that were meant to warn the public of an incoming attack. The FCDA and OCDM even made readily available information explaining the procedures for building basement and backyard fallout shelters.

Impact America's civil defense efforts during the first half of the 1950's served as a Cold War era response to the threat of Soviet nuclear aggression and

Elementary school children practice taking cover in their classroom during a mid-1950's air-raid drill. (Hulton Archive I by Getty Images)

a potential third world war. America convinced its civilian population that an atomic attack was a survivable experience. However, the government began to change this view by the middle of the decade as it concluded that the survivability of an atomic attack on the United States was unrealistic. In 1956, President Dwight D. Eisenhower came to the conclusion that the country could not cope effectively with the hysteria and subsequent disorganization that would follow a nuclear attack. Despite Eisenhower's thinking and at the risk of deceiving the public, the administration had to continue supporting civil defense in order to convince the Soviets that a preemptive strike against the West was futile. However, because officials recognized the limitations of civil defense, American Cold War deterrence policy shifted and emphasized a nuclear arms buildup, a move that resulted in an escalating global arms race.

Further Reading

McEnaney, Laura. *Civil Defense Begins at Home: Militarization Meets Everyday Life in the Fifties.* Princeton, N.J.: Princeton University Press, 2000. Explores the nexus of military and domestic arenas during the decade and argues that the militarization of the home placed additional demands on already overworked housewives.

Oakes, Guy. *The Imaginary War: Civil Defense and American Cold War Culture.* New York: Oxford University Press, 1994. Argues that civil defense programs were not intended realistically to protect Americans but to ingrain in them the moral resolve needed to face the hazards of the Cold War.

Winkler, Alan M. *Life Under a Cloud: American Anxiety About the Atom.* Urbana: University of Illinois Press, 1999. Examines the impact of the nuclear age on popular culture, scientific thought, military strategy, and political history.

Michael J. Garcia

See also Atomic bomb; Bomb shelters; Cold War; DEW Line; Hydrogen bomb; Truman, Harry S.

■ Civil Rights Act of 1957

Identification U.S. federal law protecting the voting rights of members of minorities
Date Signed on September 9, 1957

The Civil Rights Act of 1957 was was the first federal civil rights legislation since the Civil Rights Act of 1875—an act that had been rescinded in 1883. The 1957 law was also noteworthy because it gave the federal government the right to enforce the Fifteenth Amendment that guaranteed all citizens the right to vote.

The Civil Rights Act of 1957 authorized the U.S. attorney general to take civil action against any person who threatened or violated a citizen's attempt to vote. It also allowed the attorney general to file injunctions against any person who attempted to interfere with someone else's right to vote. The law was written to undo a variety of obstacles that southern states had established over the previous century to prevent former slaves and their descendants from exercising their Fifteenth Amendment rights.

African Americans who tried to vote in southern states typically encountered discriminatory legal obstacles and sometimes even physical violence. In some states, poll taxes required voters to pay fees. Because of the low economic status of most African Americans, the poll taxes alone often prevented them from voting. Other legal gimmicks included literacy tests and "grandfather clauses." Literacy tests might have barred many illiterate white citizens from voting, along with illiterate African Americans; however, the grandfather clauses effectively reinstated whites by permitting them to vote if they could show that they had grandfathers who had voted—something virtually no African American could do.

The federal Civil Rights Act established a framework that would allow the federal government to enforce constitutional law that was put in place during Reconstruction. In spite of the 1957 act, southern city officials and other citizens continued to intimidate African American voters in an effort to keep them from fully participating in the democratic process. Segregation laws also barred African Americans from eating in public restaurants, entering many public establishments, and enrolling in all-white schools.

At the moment the the U.S. Congress was about to pass the Civil Rights Act, Arkansas governor Orval Faubus mobilized his state's National Guard troops to prevent the integration of a high school in Little Rock. President Dwight D. Eisenhower signed the law on September 9; two weeks later, he sent federal troops into Little Rock to enforce the the school's integration. In 1960, Eisenhower signed into law another Civil Rights Act, which further outlined penalties for civil rights violations.

Impact At the time of the law's passage, many civil rights activists opposed it, arguing that the law was too limited because it only addressed voting rights and ignored other areas of discrimination in the United States. Despite the symbolic significance of the 1957 law, African American voting increased only slightly during the late 1950's, as southern whites continued to resist the law's enforcement. Protests against these injustices provided the impetus for the more sweeping Civil Rights Act of 1964, which legislated an end to racial segregation in all public accommodations. The Voting Rights Act of 1965 carried these changes further by eliminating most of the legal obstacles that had long been used to prevent African Americans from voting.

Further Reading

Collier-Thomas, Bettye, and V. P. Franklin. *My Soul Is a Witness: A Chronology of the Civil Rights Era, 1954-1965.* New York: Henry Holt, 2000. Comprehensive study of the Civil Rights movement that explores civil rights legislation beginning during the 1950's.

Riddlesperger, James W., and Donald W. Jackson, eds. *Presidential Leadership and Civil Rights Policy.* Westport, Conn.: Greenwood Press, 1995. Thorough treatment of federal civil rights policies from Reconstruction through the 1990's. Includes a full discussion contrasting the Civil Rights Act of 1957 with the Voting Rights Act of 1965.

Obiagele Lake

See also African Americans; *Brown v. Board of Education*; Civil Rights movement; Commission on Civil Rights; Education in the United States; Eisenhower, Dwight D.; Faubus, Orval; *Hernández v. Texas*; Kefauver, Estes; Racial discrimination; Rayburn, Sam.

■ Civil Rights movement

The Event National movement led by African Americans to extend full rights to all citizens, regardless of race or creed

Date Mid-1950's to the late 1960's

The Civil Rights movement coalesced around several key events during the 1950's to move Congress to pass the first new federal civil rights legislation and launch an era of unparalleled social change.

Although it is difficult to assign a precise time to the beginning of the modern Civil Rights movement,

the 1950's can be identified as the decade when efforts to achieve equal rights for minorities in the United States became a mass movement. At this time, several historical trends promoting such a movement came together. America's largest minority group, African Americans, lived mainly in rural areas at the beginning of the twentieth century. By the 1950's, many were living in cities, where they had sufficient concentration and organization to begin a widespread political struggle.

Groups such as the National Association for the Advancement of Colored People (NAACP) had developed the skills and strategies to challenge legal discrimination. The American fight against Nazi Germany in World War II had heightened awareness of the embarrassing gap between democratic American ideals and racially oppressive American realities. African Americans who served in the military during World War II and the Korean War were frustrated by the failure of the nation they served to recognize their full rights of citizenship. Moreover, during the 1950's, television entered homes throughout the United States, bringing scenes from Little Rock, Arkansas, Montgomery, Alabama, and other civil rights flashpoints to all Americans.

Historical Origins With the end of the U.S. Civil War (1861-1865), Americans were faced with the question of the status of newly freed slaves. In order to protect these former slaves from those who had claimed to own them, the U.S. Congress passed the Civil Rights Act of 1866 over the veto of President Andrew Johnson. This key piece of legislation guaranteed equal protection of the law in contracts, lawsuits, trials, property transactions, and purchases, and it prescribed penalties for interfering with this equal protection.

The U.S. Congress passed two more pieces of Civil Rights legislation during the 1870's: the Civil Rights Act of 1871 (the Enforcement Act), which was intended to overturn laws preventing black Americans from voting, and the Civil Rights Act of 1875, which sought to guarantee freedom of access to public places and to give jurisdiction over cases of violation of this freedom to the federal courts. However, in 1877, the troops who could protect black citizens in the South were withdrawn, and in 1883, the Supreme Court declared the Civil Rights Act of 1875 unconstitutional.

Throughout the late nineteenth century and the

Oklahoma City children stage a peaceful sit-in in a segregated department store lunchroom, where after three days, they still had not been served, in 1958. (AP/Wide World Photos)

first half of the twentieth century, state and local governments acted to limit the freedoms of African Americans and members of other minority groups. Segregation, the forced separation of minority groups from the institutions of the majority population, became the law of the land in many places. By 1950, the following states had laws requiring racial segregation: Alabama, Arkansas, Delaware, Florida, Georgia, Kentucky, Louisiana, Maryland, Mississippi, Missouri, North Carolina, Oklahoma, South Carolina, Tennessee, Texas, Virginia, and West Virginia. Arizona, Kansas, New Mexico, and Wyoming did not require segregation, but these four states allowed local governments to pass ordinances for segregation.

Key Organizations In the absence of governmental assistance, African Americans began to develop in-

stitutions of their own to protect their interests. African American church congregations emerged in the United States during the years immediately following slavery and served as centers of community life. During the 1950's, these organizations would serve as bases for action in events such as the Montgomery bus boycott, which followed Rosa Parks's refusal to give up her bus seat to a white rider. Perhaps the most important explicitly political organization of black Americans has been the National Association for the Advancement of Colored People (NAACP), founded in 1909 as a response to lynchings. Through its Legal Defense Fund, the NAACP would win critical civil rights victories in the courts during the 1950's.

At the same time that the NAACP came into existence, a white philanthropist, Ruth Standish Baldwin, and a black social worker and scholar, George

Edmund Haynes, founded the Committee on Urban Conditions Among Negroes in New York to work to lessen the discrimination and other problems faced by African Americans moving to northern cities. Merging with several other organizations over the following decade, in 1920 the organization became known as the National Urban League (NUL). African Americans also formed labor unions in the years before 1950. One of the most active and effective of the black labor organizations was the Brotherhood of Sleeping Car Porters, organized and led by A. Philip Randolph.

Civil Rights During the 1940's In September of 1940, after the military draft had been established, Walter White of the NAACP and T. Arnold Hill of the NUL met President Franklin D. Roosevelt to discuss racial discrimination in the armed forces and in the defense industries. When Roosevelt took no action, Randolph of the Brotherhood of Sleeping Car Porters began to organize a black protest march on Washington, D.C. Under this pressure, President Roosevelt issued Executive Order 8802, creating the wartime Fair Employment Practices Committee. Although this order had little practical effect, African Americans began to feel that the time for equal citizenship was coming, and membership in the NAACP increased rapidly during and immediately after World War II.

In 1948 President Harry S. Truman signed Executive Order 9981, which ordered the racial integration of America's armed forces. The Korean War, during 1950-1953, saw the first racially integrated combat units since the Civil War, demonstrating that racially integrated institutions were possible for Americans.

During the late 1940's, under the leadership of Legal Defense Fund director Thurgood Marshall, the NAACP began a struggle to end the segregation of American educational institutions. At first, legal efforts concentrated on graduate and professional schools, on the grounds that exclusion from these whites-only institutions usually left aspiring black students without any options and therefore such exclusion could not claim the justification of "separate but equal."

Civil Rights and the Schools In 1950, the new decade saw one of the first major legal victories for school desegregation. In that year, in the case *Sweatt v. Painter*, the U.S. Supreme Court ruled that the state of Texas could not deny a black man entry to the University of Texas law school by quickly setting up a separate law school for African Americans. As NAACP legal efforts turned from graduate and professional schools to elementary and secondary schools, the *Sweatt* decision served as a precedent recognizing that separate schools were often unequal schools.

In several cases around the nation, the NAACP backed African American families who were suing school districts because state laws had forbidden their children to attend schools with whites, even when the white schools were closer and had better resources than black schools. The case *Oliver Brown et al. v. Board of Education of Topeka, Kansas* went to the Supreme Court to test the legality of school segregation in all parts of the United States. The *Brown* case began in 1951 when the daughter of a minister in Kansas had been refused entry to a local white school.

On May 17, 1954, the Supreme Court, under the leadership of Chief Justice Earl Warren, ruled that separate schools were inherently unequal and that separate schools were therefore illegal. This ruling is generally known as *Brown I*. A year later, on May 31, 1955, the court issued a second ruling on the case, known as *Brown II*. This ruling ordered local school boards to desegregate "with all deliberate speed," and it handed over direction of school desegregation to lower federal courts.

Opposition to School Desegregation The *Brown* decision made the segregation of schools illegal, but it also met with opposition. In 1956, one hundred southern senators and congressmen signed what became known as the Southern Manifesto, declaring that the *Brown* decision itself had been illegal. Little Rock, Arkansas, became the site of the most famous struggle to enforce the *Brown* decision.

Initially, it appeared as if Little Rock schools would quietly follow the orders of the Supreme Court. The school superintendent of Little Rock, Virgil Blossom, had devised a plan to first integrate the city's Central High School in 1957 and then gradually integrate lower grades. By concentrating on bringing good students from middle-class African American families into white schools, he hoped to avoid conflict.

At the time, Arkansas governor Orval Faubus was searching for political support to win a third term in office. He decided that he could appeal to whites eager to preserve segregation. Governor Faubus declared that he would not be able to maintain order if Central High School were integrated, and he ordered the National Guard to protect the area around the school. His stand drew public attention to the situation and attracted white segregationist mobs into the streets. The NAACP, under the local leadership of Daisy Bates, organized the African American students slated to enroll in Central High to arrive in a group. They were met by National Guardsmen, who turned the students away with bayonets. One of the students arrived after the others and was confronted by screaming segregationists. Television, which occupied a central place in most American homes by 1957, broadcast the scenes from Little Rock around the nation.

President Dwight D. Eisenhower was forced to send in the 101st Airborne Division to enable the nine African American students to attend Central High. After that, Eisenhower placed the National Guard under federal control and ordered it to see that Little Rock conformed to national law. Eight of the nine students remained at Central High until they graduated.

Other places in the South showed resistance to school desegregation. In New Orleans, Louisiana, where a federal judge had ordered white schools to admit African American pupils in 1956, the school board president conducted an opinion poll of parents. In this poll, 82 percent of white parents said that they would rather shut down the public schools than accept any integration. The Virginia Assembly passed legislation authorizing the closing of any school that allowed blacks and whites to attend together. In 1959, the Prince Edward County school board in Virginia did shut down the entire school system for five years rather than allow black children to sit next to white children in the same classrooms.

Opposition in Mississippi Some of the most determined opposition to the extension of civil rights took place in the state of Mississippi. After the *Brown* decision, white Mississippians formed White Citizens' Councils to oppose school desegregation. These councils organized economic pressure against African Americans known to work for desegregation, refusing credit and taking away jobs from those who asserted their rights.

The struggle involved violence as well as economic pressure. In the spring of 1955, the Reverend George Lee, an NAACP official involved in trying to register African American voters, died from gunshot wounds in Belzoni, Mississippi. A few weeks later, Lamar Smith, an African American who had registered to vote and was encouraging other voters, was shot and killed in the middle of the day in front of the Brookhaven, Mississippi, courthouse.

The most widely reported act of violence in Mississippi was not committed against a potential voter, but against a fourteen-year-old boy. Emmett Till had come from Chicago to visit his mother's family in Tallahatchie County, Mississippi. After he reportedly flirted with a white woman, Till was beaten, shot, and dumped in the Tallahatchie River. The trial of the accused murderers drew attention to the absence of even the most basic civil rights for African Americans in Mississippi.

Resistance in Montgomery While the legal struggle for school desegregation proceeded, a different kind of struggle began in Montgomery, Alabama. Segregation laws required separate public facilities for African Americans and whites. On public transportation, such as buses and streetcars, African Americans frequently had to sit in the rear, with front seats reserved for whites. In Montgomery, according to law there had to be a row of vacant seats on buses between white and African American riders.

On December 1, 1955, Montgomery seamstress Rosa Parks, who had earlier served as secretary for the local chapter of the NAACP, refused to give up her seat so that the vacant row could be maintained after a white man sat down. Parks was arrested. After she was bailed out of jail, black leaders of Montgomery began to organize a boycott to force the bus system to drop its discriminatory practices. E. D. Nixon, head of the Alabama NAACP, contacted two ministers, the Reverend Ralph David Abernathy and the Reverend Martin Luther King, Jr., and a leader of local African American women's groups, Jo Ann Robinson. The leadership created the Montgomery Improvement Association (MIA), which was directed by the young King, then only twenty-six years old. The MIA managed the boycott and arranged carpools to enable African American citizens to avoid riding the buses.

The boycott lasted for a year. Dr. King received national attention for his calls for nonviolent resis-

Time Line of the Civil Rights Movement

1948	President Harry S. Truman signs Executive Order 9981, banning racial discrimination in the armed forces and other federal employment.
1950	In *Sweatt v. Painter* the Supreme Court holds that Texas's effort to establish a separate law school for African Americans violates the Constitution's equal protection clause.
1952	Immigration and Nationality Act eliminates racial and ethnic proscriptions against naturalization, while retaining national origins quotas.
1954	In *Brown v. Board of Education*, the Supreme Court rules that racial segregation in public schools violates the equal protection clause.
1955	Interstate Commerce Commission bans racial segregation on interstate buses and trains.
	Fourteen-year-old Emmett Till is murdered in Mississippi for whistling at a white woman; a jury ultimately acquits the two white men charged with his murder.
	In its second *Brown v. Board of Education* case ("*Brown II*"), the Supreme Court orders desegregation of public schools "with all deliberate speed."
	Rosa Parks's arrest for refusing to surrender her seat to a white man on a segregated bus triggers the Montgomery bus boycott.
1956	Southern congressmen and senators sign the Southern Manifesto to protest the Supreme Court's *Brown v. Board of Education* decision.
1957	Martin Luther King, Jr., and other African American leaders found the Southern Christian Leadership Conference (SCLC).
	Congress passes the first Civil Rights Act since Reconstruction.
	After Arkansas governor Orval Faubus uses National Guard troops to block the integration of Little Rock's Central High School, President Dwight D. Eisenhower federalizes the guard and mobilizes additional troops to oversee the school's integration.
1958	In *Cooper v. Aaron*, the Supreme Court rejects efforts by states to delay desegregation of public schools.
1960	Civil Rights Act of 1960 expands protections of voting rights.

tance, which became the primary strategy of the Civil Rights movement in the years that followed. As the Montgomery bus company lost money, the police and local government began to harass those taking part in the boycott. Police arrested some of the drivers and arrested Dr. King himself, supposedly for speeding. Dozens of members of the MIA faced legal charges of conspiracy. The houses of Dr. King and other leaders were dynamited. Once again, events reached the American public through the mass media.

In February of 1956, five African American women sued to overturn the law requiring separate seating.

By November, the case reached the U.S. Supreme Court. A month later, the Court ordered that Montgomery end segregation on its buses.

The Civil Rights Act of 1957 The growth of civil rights activities throughout the nation pushed the United States government to act. The federal government had not enacted any major civil rights laws since 1875. From 1945 to 1957, however, bills for a new civil rights act came before Congress every year.

In many parts of the United States, particularly in the South, African Americans had been systematically denied the right to vote during the late nineteenth and early twentieth centuries. Their votes were taken away either by outright threats of violence or by maneuvers such as competency tests administered by white voter registrars. As the Little Rock school crisis brought national attention to civil rights, Congress considered a new law intended to protect voting rights.

Opposition to a new act was strong in the South. However, Texas senator Lyndon Baines Johnson, the Senate majority leader, put his support behind the bill. A skillful politician, Johnson managed to move the act through Congress. The Civil Rights Act of 1957 established the Civil Rights Commission, which would investigate complaints of civil rights violations. Interference with the right to vote was made a federal crime, to be acted on by the attorney general. It also gave the Civil Rights Section of the Justice Department the higher status of a division and placed an assistant attorney general at the head of this new division.

Although African Americans in some southern states continued to be denied the right to vote after 1957, the new act was an important legal step. It set the stage for additional Civil Rights Acts in 1960, 1964, 1968, and 1991, as well as for the Voting Rights Acts of 1965 and 1982. By the end of the twentieth century, there were no known locations that still denied African Americans the right to vote, and the federal government gave extensive protections to the legal and political rights of minority group members.

Impact Civil rights activities during the 1950's began a long struggle to achieve equal rights for all groups of people in the United States. These activities met with opposition from many white Americans, but many other white Americans began to recognize the injustice of racial inequality. After the events in Little Rock and in Montgomery, the nation entered a decade of protest, legislation, and debate concerning the obligations of government to protect the rights of minority citizens.

Subsequent Events Throughout the 1960's both the quest for civil rights and the concept of civil rights became wider in scope as activists moved into many arenas of effort. In 1960, protesters, primarily students, participated in widespread sit-in demonstrations against segregated lunch counters and other segregated public facilities. The sit-in movement was quickly taken up in other cities. In a series of cases, beginning with 1961's *Garner v. Louisiana*,

the U.S. Supreme Court upheld the right of protesters to use restaurants and other public facilities.

The freedom rides grew out of the sit-in movement and had the same goal of desegregating facilities. These began in 1961, when the Congress of Racial Equality (CORE) sponsored a bus tour to desegregate terminals. Others began freedom rides on the railroads. These activities pushed the Interstate Commerce Commission, in September of 1961, to prohibit discrimination in interstate buses and bus facilities.

Voter registration became a major part of the Civil Rights movement in 1961 and 1962. The movement reached its highest point in the August, 1963, March on Washington. More than 200,000 marchers from all over the country gathered in the capital to demand immediate equality in political rights, employment, and other areas.

Further Reading

Abernathy, Donzaleigh. *Partners to History: Martin Luther King, Jr., Ralph David Abernathy, and the Civil Rights Movement.* New York: Crown, 2003. An insider's view of the Civil Rights movement, written by the daughter of a prominent activist. Text is supported with more than 350 candid and news photos of notable activists and events.

Branch, Taylor. *Parting the Waters: America in the King Years, 1954-1963.* New York: Simon and Schuster, 1988. One of the best-known histories of the Civil Rights movement, told with a focus on the central figure of Martin Luther King, Jr.

Brinkley, Douglas. *Rosa Parks.* New York: Viking, 2000. A biography of the woman who touched off the Montgomery bus boycott, written by a prominent historian.

Kasher, Steven. *The Civil Rights Movement: A Photographic History, 1954-1968.* New York: Abbeville Press, 2000. Provides photographs, with text, of the main events of the Civil Rights movement during the 1950's and 1960's.

Levy, Peter B. *The Civil Rights Movement.* Westport, Conn.: Greenwood Press, 1998. Six essays examine such topics as the role of women in the movement and the lasting effects of the events during the 1950's and 1960's. Also includes twenty biographies of prominent activists, photographs, and a time line.

Rowan, Carl T. *Dream Makers, Dream Breakers: The World of Justice Thurgood Marshall.* Boston: Little,

Brown, 1993. A well-known African American newspaper columnist tells the story of Thurgood Marshall, main attorney for the NAACP during the *Brown* case and later Supreme Court Justice.

Carl L. Bankston III

See also African Americans; *Bolling v. Sharpe*, *Brown v. Board of Education*; Civil Rights Act of 1957; Commission on Civil Rights; Education in the United States; King, Martin Luther, Jr.; Little Rock school desegregation crisis; Montgomery bus boycott; National Association for the Advancement of Colored People; Racial discrimination; School desegregation; Supreme Court decisions, U.S.; *Sweatt v. Painter*.

■ Cliburn, Van

Identification American concert pianist
Born July 12, 1934; Shreveport, Louisiana

Van Cliburn won the first International Tchaikovsky Competition in Moscow in 1958—a musical achievement that was viewed in both Russia and the United States as a promising break in the international confrontation between the two countries during the Cold War.

Harvey Lavan Cliburn, Jr. showed great promise as a youthful prodigy after winning a number of piano competitions, one of which enabled him to appear as soloist with the Houston Symphony at age twelve. From 1951 to 1954, he studied at the Juilliard School of Music in New York. His student years were capped by his first prize in the Edgar M. Leventritt competition in 1954, which in turn led to a performance with the New York Philharmonic Orchestra at Carnegie Hall.

The American public lionized Cliburn following his triumphant win in Moscow. His return to the United States was marked by a ticker-tape parade in New York City, his picture on the cover of *Time* magazine, and personal congratulations from President Dwight D. Eisenhower. His subsequent recording of Tchaikovsky's First Piano Concerto was the first classical album to sell more than one million copies. In 1960 he returned to Europe and Russia, repeating his earlier success as a pianist and musical statesman. He temporarily interrupted his public concert career in 1978 but resumed limited appearances with a performance before President Ronald Reagan and Soviet general secretary Mikhail Gorbachev at the White House in 1987.

Van Cliburn performing during the final round of the first International Tchaikovsky Competition in April, 1958. (AP/Wide World Photos)

Impact Cliburn was hailed as an American response to the Soviet Union's achievement of placing the first human-made satellite, *Sputnik*, in Earth orbit in 1957. His popularity among the Russians was interpreted as a harbinger of more cordial relations between the two countries. He became a figure of national pride as his achievements renewed America's faith in its own people and institutions at a time of increasing tension in international politics. Above all, Cliburn was a young American who succeeded in a highly competitive field which was, at that time, dominated by performers from abroad.

Further Reading

Chasins, Abram. *The Van Cliburn Legend*. Garden City, N.Y.: Doubleday, 1959. The first extensive study of Cliburn's background and early triumphs.

Reich, Howard. *Van Cliburn*. Nashville: Thomas Nelson Publishers, 1993. A thoroughly documented summary illustrating many of the pitfalls which often follow success in the world of arts and entertainment.

Douglas A. Lee

See also Bernstein, Leonard; Cold War; Music; *Sputnik I.*

■ Clift, Montgomery

Identification American film actor
Born October 17, 1920; Omaha, Nebraska
Died July 23, 1966; New York, New York

Montgomery Clift introduced a new brand of leading man to Hollywood: sensitive, vulnerable, introspective, and sexually ambiguous.

Montgomery Clift began his acting career early, appearing on Broadway by the age of fourteen. Although initially uninterested in a movie career, he was finally persuaded to appear in Howard Hawks's *Red River* (1948), a role he quickly followed with a starring role in *The Search* (1948), which earned him the first of four Academy Award nominations.

Clift was an overnight success in Hollywood, and his relatively short career yielded several unforgettable performances. His portrayal of a troubled young man blinded by love and money in *A Place in the Sun* (1951) brought his second Oscar nomination, and an equally memorable depiction of the sensitive soldier Maggio in *From Here to Eternity* (1953) yielded his third. In 1957, Clift was severely injured in an automobile accident, but he resumed working soon after.

Clift's brilliant career stood in stark contrast to his troubled personal life. He was plagued with health problems and both alcohol and drug abuse and was allegedly consumed with guilt over his homosexuality. Although his personal life deteriorated after the accident, he gave moving performances in *The Young Lions* (1958) and Tennessee Williams's *Suddenly, Last Summer* (1959) and received his fourth Oscar nomination for *Judgment at Nuremberg* (1961). Clift's career tapered off during the early 1960's, and he died in 1966 of heart failure before reaching his forty-sixth birthday.

Impact Clift's sensitive, moody screen presence marked a new era in Hollywood leading men, becoming a symbol of his talented yet rebellious generation of stars and influencing such actors as James Dean, Marlon Brando, and later, Robert De Niro.

Further Reading

Bosworth, Patricia. *Montgomery Clift: A Biography.* New York: Harcourt, Brace, Jovanovich, 1978. Compelling, insightful biography.

Capua, Michelangelo. *Montgomery Clift: A Biography.* Jefferson, N.C.: McFarland, 2002. A detailed biography of Clift.

Hoskyns, Barney. *Montgomery Clift: Beautiful Loser.* London: Bloomsbury, 1991. Biography with film stills, candid photos, and bibliography.

Mary Virginia Davis

See also Academy Awards; Brando, Marlon; Dean, James; Film in the United States; *From Here to Eternity*; Homosexuality and gay rights; Taylor, Elizabeth; War films; Williams, Tennessee.

■ Cold War

Definition Struggle for world power carried on between Eastern and Western nations during the post-World War II years of ostensible peace
Date 1945 to 1991

The Cold War had profound and long-lasting effects on both Canadian and American society; those effects were mostly destructive and could still be felt at the beginning of the twenty-first century.

"Cold war" differs from "hot war" in the matter of violent conflict. In a hot war, actual military hostilities occur. No such hostilities occur in a cold war, but it is the nature of the concept that a cold war can erupt into a hot war at any time. In the historical struggle between the West, led by the United States, and the Soviet Union and its satellites in Eastern Europe, no hot war ever developed. However, a nuclear catastrophe nearly did occur during the Cuban Missile Crisis of 1962. Moreover, tensions over the status of West Berlin through the Cold War threatened to erupt militarily at various times. Nevertheless, the two dominant superpowers managed to avoid open hostilities largely because they came to realize what ruin they faced if they allowed their conflict to develop into nuclear warfare.

Although the Cold War never developed into a violent conflict, it had vast effects on both Canadian and American society. In assessing its effects, it must be remembered that the United States was engaged in a prolonged, titanic struggle for the dominance of democracy and freedom—first, against Soviet communist dictatorship, later against an Asian version of communism that threatened Southeast Asia. The vantage point of the Western victory over Soviet communism in 1991, with the virtual collapse of the worldwide communist movement, places the anxieties and social damage inflicted by the Cold War in a positive light to those who value liberty.

The 1950's in the United States are often characterized as years of placid conformism presided over by a reassuring, fatherly president, Dwight D. Eisenhower, the heroic Allied commander in chief during World War II. This characterization is only partly true, however, since strong undercurrents of fear were generated by Cold War events, often breaking out into public expression.

Pervasive, at times nearly hysterical, fear of atomic weapons and the vast swath of death and destruction such weapons could inflict on North America became a marked feature of 1950's American life. Added to the fears of the influence of domestic communists, their "fellow travelers" (a favorite category of the period), and Soviet spies in their midst, the fear of Soviet nuclear weapons lay over the nation like an invisible blanket throughout the period.

Rise of the "Iron Curtain" Immediately after World War II, U.S. leaders believed that the need for military might had passed, at least for the moment. The government rapidly demobilized most of its military forces, leaving occupation forces to maintain order and supervise transitions to constitutional government in Germany and Japan. Peace, most Americans thought, had come at last. Events in Eastern Europe spoke otherwise, however. Throughout the region, agents under the direction of Soviet dictator Joseph Stalin worked to subvert democratic regimes. Soon, free government had disappeared in Eastern Europe, and a pall of fear spread across Western Europe—fear that communist parties beholden to or controlled by Moscow might take power.

Less than a year after the collapse of German resistance to the Allies, British statesman Winston Churchill gave voice to these fears and provided a name for what was proceeding wherever the Soviet Union's Red Army had been situated at the war's end. In a memorable speech delivered at a small college in Missouri in March, 1946, he said that from the Baltic to the Adriatic, "an iron curtain has descended across Europe." The "iron curtain" analogy at once stuck, and the American public now had a graphic image of what was occurring across the At-

lantic, where, such a short time before, American soldiers had sailed for home secure in the belief that their victory would endure.

After Churchill's call for the West to recognize Soviet policy for what it was—the ruthless extension of communist tyranny wherever opportunity presented itself—events establishing the Cold War as a fact of international life followed in rapid succession. In 1947, President Harry S. Truman called for military aid to Greece and Turkey to save them from communist takeovers. In 1948, the Marshall Plan, named after Secretary of State George C. Marshall, began pouring billions of dollars in economic aid into Western Europe to save its nations from the imminent communist menace.

During the same year, the Soviet Union initiated a blockade of Berlin. The city, divided into Soviet and Western-controlled sectors, was surrounded by the Soviet-controlled Germany, soon to become "East Germany." The blockade was intended to starve it into submission to communism. However, against the advice of his advisers, Truman ordered an air lift in June, 1948, to provision Berlin. Fifteen months of harrowing and heroic flying eventually broke the Soviet will and ended the blockade.

China If 1949 was a year of triumph in the former German capital, it also saw an event that in the context of the Cold War was to have a remarkable—and deeply malignant—effect on American domestic politics during the 1950's and beyond. This event was the victory of the Chinese communists under Mao Zedong over the Nationalist forces of Generalissimo Chiang Kai-shek. On October 1, 1949, Mao proclaimed the People's Republic of China in Beijing.

At once a cry went up in the West: "Who lost China?" This meant, first, that some U.S. officials, perhaps disloyal and perfidious individuals, must have been responsible for the loss of the U.S. alliance and friendship with China. It was, and was perceived to be, a grievous loss to the nation. China, the world's most populous nation and its oldest culture in continuous existence, had been an ally of the United States since the 1930's. Madame Chiang Kai-shek, a graduate of Wellesley College in Massachusetts, had visited Franklin and Eleanor Roosevelt in the White House during the 1940's, drawing much publicity.

Throughout China's ordeal after invasion by Japan during the 1930's, the United States was attuned to China's fate partly through the influence of publisher Henry R. Luce's flagship *Time* magazine, which had carried extensive pronationalist government and anti-Chinese communist reporting from the 1930's and throughout the 1940's. The departure of China from the camp of American allies came as a shock to Americans. Answers to the question of "who lost China" were not long in coming.

A number of American foreign service officers who had served in China and written analyses of its political and military landscape for the State Department during the 1940's, and who were in fact both loyal and highly competent public servants, were singled out for blame. During the 1950's, these individuals, known as "Old China Hands" for their expert knowledge of the country, endured repeated, highly publicized investigations of their loyalty. Though exonerated, talented China professionals such as John

Carter Vincent were nevertheless drummed out of government service, under a cloud of suspicion. Another, Owen Lattimore, a highly respected China scholar, was accused of being a communist. Though there was no truth to the charge, Lattimore left the country for England, where he remained in exile for many years.

Altogether, it would be difficult to exaggerate the toxic effect that the debacle in China created in American politics during the 1950's, especially when Americans and Chinese met, face to face, in a hot Asian war in Korea that began in 1950. This poisonous atmosphere had both open and subtle influences on American public life. Chinese communists became viewed as well-nigh subhuman evil creatures; no criticism of their Nationalist opponents, corrupt and ineffective as well as infested with the influence of organized crime though they were, could

At an August, 1953, session of the United Nations General Assembly, Soviet delegate Andrei Vishinski (right) shakes his fist at the U.S. delegate, Henry Cabot Lodge (left) and Great Britain's Sir Gladwyn Jebb, accusing them of trying to force through an ultimatum relating to the makeup of the Korean War peace conference. Such confrontations among U.N. diplomats were common during the Cold War. (AP/Wide World Photos)

be tolerated. For decades, China, to which no American could legally travel, became a closed subject.

Korea As if the loss of China to communism was not trauma enough, the year 1950 saw further events in Asia that would add materially to the American public's perception of the communist menace. On June 25, the communist government of North Korea made a surprise attack on South Korea. The United States, acting with some fifteen allies under the auspices of the United Nations, took up the task of defending the South against the communist onslaught. In November, China entered the war. By June, 1953, neither side had defeated the other, and a truce was signed. Some 54,000 Americans and more than 300 Canadians lost their lives in the process. Korea illustrated the stark reality that aggression might precipitate a hot war at any time. The shadow of war thus hung like a shroud over American society throughout the 1950's.

Espionage As the 1950's opened, further events were unfolding that would roil the placid surface of American society throughout the decade and after. Public fear of spying, spurred by prolonged public accusations of widespread spying by Soviet agents, was among the principal influences of the Cold War on American society during the 1950's. Soviet spies were found to have taken atomic secrets and handed them to the Soviet Union. The most notorious of these spies was Klaus Fuchs, who had gained access to the U.S. atomic bomb project during World War II and, with his fellow spies, was responsible for the Soviets' explosion of their first atomic weapon in 1949, years before it otherwise would have been possible.

Another accused spy, Alger Hiss, a former high official in the U.S. State Department and a personal friend of U.S. secretary of state Dean Acheson, was accused by onetime communist courier Whittaker Chambers of transmitting secret U.S. government documents to the Soviet Union, was convicted of perjury in January, 1950, and was sentenced to five years in prison. The case generated enormous public controversy throughout the 1950's and for decades afterward. The Federal Bureau of Investigation (FBI) was accused of evidence tampering, and Hiss, along with his many champions, aggressively maintained his innocence until the end of his life. By the mid-1990's, however, evidence had appeared that convinced most scholars of Hiss's guilt.

A further, enormously publicized, case at about the same time was that of Julius and Ethel Rosenberg, who were arrested in January, 1950, and accused of spying for the Soviet Union, passing top-secret data on nuclear weapons in 1944 and 1945. Several others were accused along with them. Convicted in 1951, the Rosenbergs were executed in June, 1953, again to much publicity. However, the damage had been done, for much to the horror of the American public, in 1949 the Soviets had exploded their atomic bomb.

The existence of Soviet spies and the revelation that America's atomic secrets had been compromised during the 1940's increased the pervasive fear of domestic subversion that characterized the Cold War's effect on American society throughout the 1950's.

Canada and the Cold War Canada became embroiled in the Cold War in part through its proximity to its southern neighbor and its huge expanse of northern territory close to the Soviet Union. In 1958 Canada became a target for Soviet missiles on account of its participation in the DEW Line defense system of the North American Air Defense Agreement, which placed a line of powerful radar facilities on Canadian territory. Canada, too, had been shaken by the Soviet takeover of Eastern Europe, by the Soviet atomic bomb, by the blockade of Berlin, and by similar events. By 1950, it had long been familiar with the problem of Soviet spies, since in 1945 a Soviet cipher clerk named Igor Gouzenko had defected from the Soviet embassy in Ottawa and revealed that Canada was host to a large number of spies.

Canada was drawn into the Korean War through its membership in the North Atlantic Treaty Organization (NATO), of which it was a charter member, as well as through its membership in the United Nations. In the autumn of 1950, in an address in Toronto, Canadian prime minister Louis St. Laurent sounded a warning about the Soviet threat, in which he said that the number of those deceived by Soviet propaganda "diminishes week by week." Protecting civilization, he said, requires "building up armed strength" to deter Soviet aggression. During the course of the Cold War, however, Canada tended to reduce its military in favor of welfare state spending. Nevertheless, the nation became caught up in a mentality of fear not unlike the preoccupations of its neighbor.

Rise and Fall of Joseph R. McCarthy The high point of public fear of domestic communist subversion was the phenomenon that became known as McCarthyism, after the red-baiting Wisconsin senator Joseph R. McCarthy. In essence, McCarthyism meant wild accusations of connections to communism, with little or no evidence, that ruined reputations and lives and created a general climate of fear.

When McCarthyism first appeared in early 1950, the soil had been well tilled: The Fuchs, Hiss, and Rosenberg cases had begun during the late 1940's, and China had fallen under a communist regime in 1949—the same year that the Soviet Union exploded its first atomic bomb. By then, communism had taken over most of Eastern Europe and threatened to engulf Berlin, which had to be rescued by the airlift. All of this and more being fresh in the public memory, the stage was set for sensational charges mounted in February, 1950, by the hitherto obscure Senator McCarthy.

In a Lincoln's birthday speech delivered in Wheeling, West Virginia, McCarthy waved to his audience a piece of paper, which, he said, listed some 205 "known communists" in the U.S. Department of State. Soon afterward in another speech, he made a similar claim, though the number of alleged communists had fallen to 57. Amid nationwide headlines, McCarthy soon afterward took the Senate floor for five hours repeating the charges, now charging that 81 communists infested the State Department.

McCarthy kept up his barrage of accusations for several years, embroiling the nation in fear of domestic spying and secret Communist Party influence in government. After Republican gains in the 1952 election, McCarthy gained new powers of investigation as chairman of a Senate subcommittee and set about making further reckless charges of communist infiltration of government. In 1954 he charged that the U.S. Army was suppressing evidence of espionage at an Army installation.

Lack of hard evidence for his charges eventually caught up with McCarthy. A Senate investigation under Millard Tydings exonerated the State Department and branded McCarthy's claims fraudulent. At the end of 1954, the Senate passed a resolution censuring him, and his influence rapidly waned. A few years later he was dead of alcoholism at the age of forty-nine. Meanwhile, the lives of many who had been called before his investigating committee had been ruined through accusation of communist sympathies or actual Communist Party membership.

The passing of McCarthy's power did not, however, mean the end of the influence of McCarthyism, as its effects lingered throughout the decade. Some of this lingering influence accounts for the perverse and shameful refusal of certain prominent New York intellectuals, such as writer Susan Sontag, to oppose communist tyranny. They were refusing, they thought, to succumb to McCarthy's continuing malignant hold on the public imagination.

It must not be thought, however, that McCarthy and his tactics were unopposed by a universally cowering public. Pamphlets in his home state of Wisconsin denounced him; students at such institutions as City College of New York held robust rallies denouncing him. Even a suburban Philadelphia public grade school teacher was not intimidated by the atmosphere of fear and denounced McCarthy to his class each day for weeks. Nevertheless, many Americans were intimidated, and damage was done to the public weal.

House Committee on Un-American Activities Another fixture of American society throughout the 1950's was the House Committee on Un-American Activities (HUAC), a congressional committee that investigated the influence of communism in American society. Those called before it were asked if they were members of the Communist Party, and if they declined to answer on grounds of the Fifth Amendment to the U.S. Constitution, which protects people from coerced self-incrimination, they became known as "Fifth-Amendment communists."

HUAC operated throughout the 1950's and well into the following decade. Its activities were usually given wide publicity, so those who refused to answer its queries often found themselves ostracized in one way or another. The most usual consequence for those who failed to acquit themselves before the committee was the loss of their jobs. One study found that perhaps ten thousand Americans lost their jobs. Major corporations, including General Electric and U.S. Steel, fired employees who invoked the Fifth Amendment before an investigating committee.

In a number of avenues of society individuals came under public scrutiny for their political beliefs and associations. Among the institutions seeking to purge communists or their sympathizers were universities, which set up systems of loyalty oaths. Those refusing to sign these oaths were dismissed.

Another section of society in which suspected subversives lost their jobs or were refused work was the entertainment industry. In 1947 HUAC made its first foray into Hollywood, accusing various writers, actors, and others of communist complicity. Soon a blacklist was created in the industry denying employment to those on it. HUAC returned to Hollywood in 1951 and continued its work. Prominent blacklisted members became known as the "Hollywood Ten." A 213-page book, known as *Red Channels* and published in 1950, listed hundreds of suspects who thereafter found it difficult or impossible to find professional employment. Some were permanently disbarred from the business, though others were eventually rehabilitated.

Democracy thrives on openness—on information being freely available to the electorate to inform its judgments. The Cold War caused a great chill to descend upon the nation. A cult of secrecy gained force within the federal government, lest secrets find their way into the hands of spies or subversives. The Cold War, it is true, made much secrecy in defense and allied matters necessary and legitimate. However, secrecy often went beyond necessity, injuring democratic values and processes. The Cold War spread fear of nuclear war far and wide in American society.

Cries of "witch-hunt" objected to all of this—to secret accusations and lists, to congressional committees that seemed to their opponents more like medieval inquisitions than instruments of democratic rule. To protest the excesses of public efforts to search out and expose communists, famed playwright Arthur Miller wrote *The Crucible* (1953) about the literal "witch-hunting" in seventeenth century Salem, Massachusetts. The charge of "witch-hunt," however, intended as pointed criticism of the search for communists in government and elsewhere in national life, while not without substance, was wide of the mark, for the term "witch-hunt" referred to the search for something that did not exist and was therefore futile to seek. However, there were real spies in the United States, some of whom had done irreparable damage to American security.

Sputnik Besides all else, there was also objective evidence of the challenge Soviet communism posed to America's self-confidence in its place as campion of the free world. This evidence came in the form of a startling announcement in 1957. The Soviet Union had, Americans awoke one morning early in October to discover, launched the world's first artificial satellite, *Sputnik I.* Although the United States launched its own satellite less than four months later, Americans were shocked by the technological achievement of a rival it had considered its inferior.

Sputnik gave rise to far more than redoubled efforts of the American space program. It occasioned a period of national self-examination and soul searching. Was the nation really the light of the world that its famous statue in New York Harbor implied? Americans felt a need to prove that their nation was by launching new efforts in education for science. Suddenly, budgets for science education in schools and colleges became fully funded, as the nation geared up to meet the Soviet challenge. However, the reality of what appeared to be the strength of its Soviet rival, which suppressed every vestige of liberty in its society, had taken its toll in renewed anxiety.

Impact The domestic consequences of the Cold War for the United States included deep and unbridgeable divisions between the Left and the Right over the issue of communism and how deeply it did or did not threaten the nation. Mutual contempt between the two sides became a hallmark of American politics that has never really been transcended. The American approach to Cold War issues did not necessarily coincide with Canada's, and by about the end of the decade the two nations had moved apart on some foreign policy matters. For example, in future years, Canada recognized the communist government of Fidel Castro in Cuba, while the United States refused to do so and maintained an economic embargo against Havana throughout the Cold War period and beyond.

A second consequence was the pervasive fear of nuclear war and communist subversion that lay just beneath the placid surface of American society, home during the 1950's of such comforting symbols of normality and everyday confidence and good humor as the television shows *I Love Lucy, Leave It to Beaver,* and *The Honeymooners.* Children who watched these reassuringly comic entertainments by night might be engaging in rehearsals for atomic attack in their schools by day. At the same time, their parents might be building a backyard bomb shelter for surviving the nuclear holocaust that might suddenly eclipse the Cold War. Canada, for its part, had its "Diefenbunker"—the sarcastic nickname for the bomb shelter that Prime Minister John Diefenbaker had built at the close of the decade for government leaders.

Other consequences were more far-reaching. Upon leaving office in January, 1961, President Dwight D. Eisenhower, military hero of World War II, who had presided reassuringly over most of the decade, gave a farewell address. In that speech he urged the nation in a memorable and endlessly repeated passage to "beware of the military-industrial complex." In so doing, the president alluded to further consequences of the Cold War for American society.

The need for national defense against communism had given rise to a new set of industries that were allied with the armed forces and would seek to further their interests in Washington, not necessarily to the country's benefit. Eisenhower's warning of the rise of such a "military-industrial complex" reflected fears of the corrosive effects on the national budget, political life, and even social life of an economic alliance between military contractors and the government.

The Cold War also played a significant role in fostering a climate that promoted social conformism and political orthodoxy. It also gave rise to extremist political organizations such as the John Birch Society, whose hysterical anticommunism threatened to undermine legitimate concerns about the existence of subversives. President Eisenhower himself, the society proclaimed, was "a knowing and conscious member of the international communist conspiracy."

Conformism reached deep into society, extending, for example, to strict controls on public display of eroticism. While the cultural revolution of the 1960's would change all that, now even the word "pregnant" was banned from the airwaves, along with suspected communists.

In November, 1960, John F. Kennedy, a handsome and dashing U.S. senator from Massachusetts, was elected to the presidency by a slim margin. Even so, the coming to Washington of a new elegance and cultural energy (the White House was soon dubbed "Camelot") in the form of a young chief executive, Kennedy, and his beautiful and cultivated wife, Jacqueline, signaled that one era had passed and another had begun.

Further Reading

Bowie, Robert, and Richard Innerman. *Waging Peace: How Eisenhower Shaped an Enduring Cold War Strategy.* New York: Oxford University Press, 2000. Examines how the Eisenhower administration formulated policies for preventing Soviet expansion and mitigating Soviet hostility.

Brands, H. W. *Cold Warriors: Eisenhower's Generation and American Foreign Policy.* New York: Columbia University Press, 1988. Well-written and organized study of Eisenhower's foreign policy and its impact on later U.S. policy toward the Soviet Union.

Doherty, Thomas. *Cold War, Cool Medium: Television, McCarthyism, and American Culture.* New York: Columbia University Press, 2003. Study of television's role in both perpetuating and resisting McCarthyism

Engelhardt, Tom. *End of Victory Culture: Cold War America and the Disillusioning of a Generation.* 2d ed. Amherst: University of Massachusetts Press, 1998. Explores the Cold War's contributions to American political culture and public disillusionment with U.S. foreign policy.

Halberstam, David. *The 1950's.* New York: Random House, 1996. Expansive survey of American culture of the 1950's that includes numerous Cold War subjects, which are treated in their cultural and historical contexts.

Larson, Deborah Welch. *Anatomy of Mistrust: U.S.-Soviet Relations During the Cold War.* Ithaca, N.Y.: Cornell University Press, 1997. Details key events in the U.S.-Soviet relationship during the early Cold War era.

Parry-Giles, Shawn J. *The Rhetorical Presidency, Propaganda, and the Cold War, 1945-1955.* Westport, Conn.: Praeger, 2002. Analytical examination of Truman's and Eisenhower's foreign policies and their use of propaganda and the news.

Whitaker, Reg, and Gary Marcuse. *Cold War Canada: The Making of a National Insecurity State, 1945-1957.* Toronto: University of Toronto Press, 1994. A detailed examination of Canada, in particular its foreign policy, in the early years of the Cold War.

Whitfield, Stephen J. *The Culture of the Cold War.* 2d ed. Baltimore: Johns Hopkins University Press, 1996. Scholarly work covering a whole range of cultural issues prominent during the Cold War years.

Charles F. Bahmueller

See also Brinkmanship; Central Intelligence Agency; Dulles, John Foster; Eisenhower Doctrine; Foreign policy of the United States; House Committee on Un-American Activities; Hydrogen bomb; Isolationism; Korean War; Military-industrial complex; North American Aerospace Defense Command; North Atlantic Treaty Organization; Southeast Asia Treaty Organization; Tripartite Security Treaty; Truman Doctrine; U-2 spy planes; Warsaw Pact.

■ Cole, Nat King

Identification African American popular singer, composer, jazz pianist, and actor
Born March 17, 1919; Montgomery, Alabama
Died February 15, 1965; Santa Monica, California

During the 1950's, Nat King Cole became a successful crossover musician and the first African American to have his own television show.

Early on, Nathaniel Adams Coles (he later dispensed with the "s" in Coles) learned to play the piano by ear. By the time the family moved to Chicago, he played the church organ and sang in the choir. He took music lessons in the European piano tradition, learning to play a variety of classical compositions ranging from works by Johann Sebastian Bach to those of Sergei Rachmaninoff. The Chicago jazz scene and the rhythmic accents of noted jazz pianist Earl Hines also heavily influenced him. When Nathaniel's devout Baptist parents refused to buy a piano for their home because they did not want him to play secular music, he painted a complete keyboard on a windowsill in order to practice.

Throughout the late 1930's and the 1940's, Cole formed several jazz combos and toured, recorded, and performed successfully in a range of venues in Europe and in North and South America. In particular, his King Cole Trio was wildly successful in live performance and record sales. Its unique rhythmic style influenced other jazz musicians and excited audiences.

Chart and Screen Successes By the early 1950's, Cole had become one of the world's most popular and recognizable songsters. His June, 1950, release of "Mona Lisa" topped the charts for eight weeks, selling one million copies. This success was quickly followed by the hits "Orange Colored Sky" in November and "Frosty the Snowman" in December. His string of chart-topping hits continued throughout the 1950's with, among others, "Too Young," "Unforgettable," "Answer Me, My Love," "Pretend," and "A Blossom Fell." In 1959, Cole's Top 40 hit "Midnight Flyer" won a Grammy Award for best performance by a Top 40 artist.

Cole was able to parlay his vocal success into roles on both big and small screens and on stage. During the early 1950's, he took various bit parts, played himself, and sang the title songs in several films. He also was the first African American to headline a network television program. *The Nat King Cole Show* premiered on NBC in November, 1956, and the music-oriented program ran until December, 1957.

Nat King Cole with Eartha Kitt in the 1958 film St. Louis Blues. *(AP/Wide World Photos)*

Impact Nat King Cole became a noted figure during the era for his accomplishments on stage, in films and on television, and within the recording industry. His silken voice became synonymous with the popular music of the 1950's. Moreover, he succeeded during one of America's most racially charged eras, and he was among the first African American performers to have a sustained presence at the top of the popular music charts. Cole's efforts at integration, which included suing hotels that refused to admit him and moving into the previously all-white Hancock Park neighborhood in Los Angeles, often caused indignation among racist groups in the United States.

Further Reading

Epstein, Daniel Mark. *Nat King Cole.* New York: Farrar, Straus & Giroux, 1999. A good biography of Cole.

Gourse, Leslie. *Unforgettable: The Life and Mystique of Nat King Cole.* Lanham, Md.: Rowman & Littlefield, 2000. Another well-researched biography of Cole.

Sarah E. Crest

See also Domino, Fats; Fitzgerald, Ella; Jazz; Music.

■ Comic books

Comic books were popular among both children and adults during the 1950's, until prominent social critics and the U.S. government began to make connections between juvenile delinquency and the reading of comic books. The comic book industry adopted a code of self-regulation that sanitized the content of comic books, put publishers out of business, and put the continued existence of the industry in doubt.

Comic books rose to popularity during the 1940's, riding on the capes of the superheroes who helped fight World War II in the pages of *Action Comics, Marvel Mystery Comics, Master Comics,* and dozens of other titles. Comic books were commonly considered a cheap and disposable form of entertainment—ten cents typically bought sixty-four pages or more of illustrated stories and features. Their easy accessibility made them popular among adults, including bored and weary servicemen, as well as children. In 1946, 90 percent of all children in the United States were readers of comic books.

By the late 1940's, interest in superheroes had waned, and other genres such as romance, funny animals, crime, and Westerns had emerged to fill a growing demand. Comic-book reading had become so widespread among children that educational organizations, parent groups, social critics, and lawmakers expressed concern about the effects of comics on children. In this atmosphere of widespread popular acceptance and growing official criticism, comic books stepped into the 1950's.

Opening the Crypt: The Birth of EC Comics In 1950, William Gaines, son of EC Comics founder Max Gaines, and editor Al Feldstein initiated what they called a "New Trend" in comics publishing, transforming their moderately successful line of crime, Western, and adventure comics into a publishing powerhouse of horror, crime, science-fiction, and fantasy comics. The crypt door was opened; EC Comics was born, and the company's output would become some of the best-known, most-loved, and most viciously reviled comic books of all time.

EC's horror titles included *Vault of Horror, Haunt of Fear,* and *Crypt of Terror.* The titles contained lavishly illustrated stories with surprise endings, moral lessons, and warnings against misdeeds. Later in 1950, the company added *Weird Science* and *Weird Fantasy* to its lineup. Like their horror predecessors, these two books offered gorgeously illustrated, sophisticated science-fiction and fantasy stories. *Crime Suspenstories* contained horror-tinged mystery and murder stories, and *Two-Fisted Tales,* the last title added in 1950, provided well-researched and historically accurate war stories.

It was EC's horror comics, however, that drove its business and solidified its reputation. EC set the standard in comics publishing, and dozens of imitators arose to offer their own brand of ghoulish horror. Many were good, and some were atrociously bad, but none could compare with the original. EC's position within the industry, and among its fiercely loyal fan base, remained strong.

War and Science-fiction Genres Superheroes were in decline and horror and crime comics on the rise during the early 1950's, but other genres of comic books continued to flourish as well and did so throughout the decade.

The Korean War, which started in 1950, provided fodder for a new generation of war comics. Though not as overtly patriotic as the war comics of the 1940's, books such as *Combat, Battle, Star-Spangled War Stories,* and *War Action* pitted American military might against communist forces in North Korea and elsewhere.

Science-fiction films, UFO sightings, and the space race spurred interest in science-fiction comics. DC Comics' *Strange Adventures*, one of the company's flagship science-fiction titles, debuted in 1950. The first issue of *Strange Adventures* featured an adaptation of the 1950 movie *Destination Moon*, heralding a long run of space stories and interplanetary science fiction. DC also published *Mystery in Space*, which offered science-fiction tales with unexpected themes and terrestrial twists, such as space prisons, Martian cowboys, space-train robberies, and interplanetary kidnappings. Marvel's *Journey into Unknown Worlds*, first published in 1950, contained traditional science-fiction stories before the title converted to the horror genre. American Comic Group (ACG) issued *Adventures into the Unknown*, which premiered in 1948, and *Forbidden Worlds*, first published in 1951, which initially offered horror stories but shifted to adventure tales and science fiction in the latter half of the decade.

Influence of Television and Films Television became more prominent in American households during the early 1950's, and the once-eager readers of comic books found a brighter, louder, more easily accessible form of leisure entertainment on television. Some comic-book publishers reacted to the erosion of their audiences by putting out comics based on popular television programs and entertainment figures. Western-Dell (later simply Dell) inaugurated the decade as a prominent player in media-based comics, beginning with the *Howdy Doody Show* in 1950 and continuing with titles based on the programs *I Love Lucy*, *Gunsmoke*, *Captain Kangaroo*, *Zorro*, and *Leave It to Beaver*. Other publishers gave the ink-and-paper treatment to *The Honeymooners*, *The Adventures of Bob Hope*, and *The Adventures of Dean Martin and Jerry Lewis*. When the fabled Martin and Lewis comedy team broke up in 1956, publisher DC simply continued the book as *The Adventures of Jerry Lewis*. Dell also specialized in adaptations of motion pictures and published comics based on films such as *The Hunchback of Notre Dame* (1939), *Ben-Hur* (1959), *The Searchers* (1956), and *Moby Dick* (1956).

Many of Dell's television and movie comics appeared in *Four Color*, a long-running omnibus comics series of changing characters and features—a character might appear more than once over a run of *Four Color*, but each month brought a new television story, movie adaptation, Western, humor story, or other full-length feature. *Four Color* also served as a tryout book for features such as *Turok, Son of Stone*, a title featuring Native Americans Turok and Andar of the Mandan tribe as they searched for a way home after becoming lost in a dinosaur-infested, caveman-populated sunken valley. Debuting in *Four Color* number 596 in 1954 and appearing again in *Four Color* number 656 in 1955, *Turok, Son of Stone* graduated to his own title beginning with number 3. The series enjoyed a lengthy run into the 1970's, though latter issues consisted mostly of reprints of earlier material.

Westerns, Literary Adaptations, and Humor Comics
Television and films helped generate interest in Western comics. Popular screen cowboys such as Gene Autry, the Lone Ranger, Roy Rogers, Rocky Lane, Lash LaRue, and Gabby Hayes; cowgirls such as Dale Evans; and even animal heroes such as the Lone Ranger's horse, Silver, and Gene Autry's steed, Champion, all appeared in their own comics, most published by Fawcett or Dell. Joining them on the range were a number of original characters, including St. John's Hawk, DC's Johnny Thunder, and Magazine Enterprises' Ghost Rider and Black Phantom. Marvel comics introduced more than fifty Western titles such as *Kid Colt*, *Two-Gun Kid*, *Rawhide Kid*, *Billy Buckskin*, *Ringo Kid*, and a host of other gunslingers.

Classics Illustrated offered adaptations of prose literature in comics form. First published in 1941 as *Classic Comics*, the book changed to its more familiar title in 1947 and ran throughout the 1950's. Many children likely were exposed first to great literature through *Classics Illustrated*, and the title sometimes served as the surreptitious basis for school reports. Among the dozens of works adapted in the series were William Shakespeare's *Hamlet* (1600-1601); Erich Maria Remarque's *All Quiet on the Western Front* (1929), Sir Walter Scott's *Rob Roy* (1817), Lewis Wallace's *Ben Hur: A Tale of the Christ* (1880), James Fenimore Cooper's *Last of the Mohicans* (1826), Mark Twain's *Adventures of Huckleberry Finn* (1884), and Herman Melville's *Moby Dick* (1851).

Humor comics and comics aimed at younger readers became more prevalent as worries increased about the content of horror comics and their effects on children. Funny animal comics, popular since their inception during the 1940's, remained a mainstay for younger readers. Most of the books in this genre contained anthropomorphic talking animals in humorous stories or slapstick adventures. Books such as *Walt Disney's Comics and Stories*, featuring Donald Duck; *Comic Cavalcade*; *Funny Stuff*; and *The Fox and the Crow* were popular during the early 1950's. Other Disney characters such as Mickey Mouse, Pluto, and Uncle Scrooge continued to maintain a presence in comics, as did Warner Bros. characters such as Bugs Bunny, Daffy Duck, and Elmer Fudd; Walter Lantz's Woody Woodpecker and Andy Panda; and Metro-Goldwyn-Mayer's (MGM's) cat-and-mouse duo, Tom and Jerry, all published by Dell. Comics in the funny-animal genre were appealing to children and considered safe by parents.

Other popular humor comics of the 1950's placed children and teenagers in the starring roles. Perpetual teenager Archie Andrews, a mainstay of a stable of Archie comics, continued to cavort around

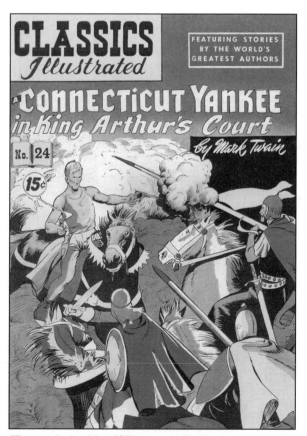

The comic books of the 1950's were not all silliness or violence. The Classics Illustrated *line contained intelligent and faithful adaptations of literature that helped lead many young people to elevate their reading habits as they grew older.* (Arkent Archive)

Riverdale with Betty, Veronica, Reggie, and Jughead. Harvey Comics introduced *Little Dot*, about a young girl obsessed with circles and dots, in 1953, and *Little Lotta*, about an overweight, phenomenally strong girl of prodigious appetites, in 1955. Richie Rich, one of comics' well-known child stars, first appeared in *Little Dot* number 1 in 1953 and went on to headline his own series as well as dozens of other spin-off titles about "the poor little rich boy" and his friends.

Harvey Comics also revived two characters based on animated cartoons and originally published by St. John: *Little Audrey* and *Casper the Friendly Ghost*. Ghost or not, Casper's earthly form appeared to be that of a young boy whose innocence and sincerity carried into the spirit world. Both Little Audrey and Casper enjoyed long publishing runs at Harvey. Casper became particularly successful, serving as the anchor for other characters such as Wendy, the Good Little Witch; Spooky, the Tuff Little Ghost; and Hot Stuff, the Little Devil. *Dennis the Menace*, based on the successful newspaper comic by Hank Ketchum, appeared in 1953. Little Lulu, star of a comic series that ran almost forty years, first appeared in Dell's *Four Color* number 74 in 1945, attained her own title in 1947, and ran strong throughout the 1950's and 1960's. Based on a series of humor cartoons by Marge Henderson Buell in *The Saturday Evening Post*, *Little Lulu* was brought to comics fame by John Stanley, who worked on the feature until his death in 1961. Bright, independent Lulu and her friends could often be seen outsmarting the boys, pondering the actions of adults, or having understated but clever, intelligently written adventures in their neighborhood.

Romance, 3-D, and Superhero Comics Romance comics enjoyed great popularity during the early years of the 1950's. Comics legends Joe Simon and Jack Kirby, who produced the *Captain America* comics of the 1940's, are credited with creating the first romance comic, *Young Romance*, in 1947. Geared toward an adult audience, *Young Romance* quickly achieved phenomenal success and circulation of more than one million copies per issue. A companion title, *Young Love*, introduced in 1948, also did well. In 1949, romance comics were selling better than all of the other genres, and interest in romantic titles carried over solidly into the 1950's. Romance comics, along with horror comics, accounted for nearly half the comic books published in 1952.

The 3-D (three-dimensional) effect, popular in films, also was adapted to comic books. Beginning in 1953 with *Three Dimension Comics*, featuring Mighty Mouse, 3-D comic books enjoyed a short spate of popularity. Popular characters such as Batman and Superman were rendered in 3-D, and most of the genres were represented by 3-D comics. In less than a year, however, the 3-D fad in comic books died out.

Of the hundreds of superhero titles that DC had published during the 1940's, only the Superman, Batman, and Wonder Woman titles remained by the early part of the 1950's. The Timely (Marvel) superheroes were gone from the scene, and Atlas, the company that Timely became, published horror comics instead. Publishers made a number of attempts to revive the superheroes. Marvel brought back Captain America, the Human Torch, and the Sub-Mariner, and Charlton relaunched *Blue Beetle*, but all had short, unsuccessful runs. A handful of new superhero titles were launched, including Simon and Kirby's *Fighting American*, from Prize Group; *Strong Man*, published by Magazine Enterprises; and *Captain Flash*, from Sterling Comics, but most of these efforts also failed after a few issues. Superheroes, once the staple of the industry, had faded almost completely by 1953.

Overall circulation of comic books remained strong at the end of 1953. More than five hundred individual titles were available, accounting for sales of more than sixty-eight million copies per month. Even at a dime each, comics proved to be very profitable for publishers.

Seduction of the Innocent As horror and crime comics increased in popularity during the early 1950's, their content became more gruesome. Scenes of bloody decapitation, torture, shootings, stabbings, and bondage were commonplace. Sexually suggestive scenes and images of exaggerated female anatomy could be found regularly on comic book covers and within stories. EC Comics remained the leader in a field of dozens of competitors. Children loved these types of comics; parents found them reprehensible.

In 1954, psychiatrist Fredric Wertham, a longtime critic of comics, found a wider voice and larger audience with the publication of his book *Seduction of the Innocent*. Wertham devoted *Seduction of the Innocent* to linking comic books and the growing social problem of juvenile delinquency and juvenile crime. Wertham asserted that comics' graphic violence, suggestive sex, and blatant depictions of crime corrupted children and led them to emulate what they saw. He presented incidents in which children had committed a crime, injured themselves or others, or even committed suicide, all influenced, he said, by images and stories in comic books. Wertham placed the blame for juvenile delinquency and, indeed, a host of child behavior problems squarely at the feet of comic books.

In retrospect, *Seduction of the Innocent* has been seen as a classic example of poor scientific investigation and faulty reasoning. Wertham's basic assertion was that since juvenile delinquents read comics, comics therefore cause juvenile delinquency. This overly simplistic conclusion, however, was based on little more than anecdotes and interviews with his own psychiatric patients and known delinquents. Wertham's conclusions ignored other social, economic, and personal factors that would contribute to behavior problems in children. Nevertheless, Wertham's pronouncements were widely accepted, and his indictment of comics galvanized response throughout the country. Comics were suppressed at every opportunity, and parents and concerned children staged burnings of comics, seemingly oblivious to the undertones of censorship and oppression of such behavior.

Government Criticism and New Standards The U.S. Senate Subcommittee to Investigate Juvenile Delinquency in the United States held a series of public hearings on the effects of comic books on children in 1954. Chaired by U.S. senators Thomas Hennings and Estes Kefauver, the committee probed the content of comics and heard testimony from critics, including Wertham, and prominent figures in the comics industry, including William Gaines, embattled publisher of EC Comics. During the hearing, Gaines defended EC, engaged with Kefauver in a debate on what constituted good taste and bad taste in comics, and found himself in the unenviable position of trying to justify to the U.S. government the appropriate way to depict a scene of decapitation on the cover of a comic book. The committee's conclusions were harsh and uncompromising: Comic books, they said, were indeed detrimental to children. New standards were required that would remove not only the existing objectionable content but even potentially harmful and demoralizing material from comics.

In the aftermath of the congressional hearings, the comic book industry formed a self-regulating organization, the Comics Magazine Association of America. This organization created the Comics Code Authority and produced a stringent set of guidelines that prohibited most of the content that made EC Comics famous and drove the phenomenal growth of comics during the early 1950's. Comics approved by the association were allowed to place the Comic Code Authority seal on their covers, signifying that the contents had met the association's standards. Few publishers were willing to resist this trend.

The effects of the Comics Code on the comic book industry were immediate and devastating. Comic book distributors and retail sales outlets refused to carry comics that did not have the Comic Code seal. Publishers scrambled to ensure comics in production conformed to the code. Gaines refused to publish the line of horror comics that had made his company successful; instead, he launched a line of "New Direction" books with titles such as *Valor, Impact, Aces High,* and *Psychoanalysis.* EC's new direction failed, and the company was left with only the stalwart *MAD,* revamped into magazine format and thus exempt from the strictures of the Comics Code.

Of all the publishers of the mid-1950's, only Dell Comics emerged virtually unaffected by the Comics Code Authority and the wide-ranging clampdown on the content of comics. Dell steadfastly retained a dedication to wholesome comic book fare even while competitors rushed to exploit the more lucrative arenas of horror and crime. Its motto, "Dell Comics are good comics," proclaimed to all readers, concerned parents, and skeptical watchdogs that Dell's stories were suitable for even the youngest children. Many issues of Dell's comics contained a "Pledge to Parents" that offered printed reassurance that the comics were clean and safe for children. It was this resolute standpoint that allowed Dell to continue successfully publishing comics—largely the same type it had always produced—even in the midst of the turmoil that enveloped the industry during the middle of the 1950's. Dell's comics were so well trusted that the company was not required to place the Comics Code Authority seal on its books. The company's demonstrated adherence to its own high standards—stricter even than the Comics Code—was considered sufficient evidence of its good intentions.

In other venues, comic stories became bland and predictable, and to stay in business, publishers opted to avoid risks and publish stories safely within the definitions of the Comics Code Authority. Readers began to lose interest in comics that were "safe" but uninteresting. Changes in distribution systems made it more difficult for comic books to gain space and compete on newsstands. Other factors, such as the increasing prevalence of television in American households, drained children's interest in comics. By the end of 1956, the number of comic books available had dropped by half, to little more than three hundred titles. Dozens of publishers had gone out of business. The industry was at a low point, and some speculated whether or not it would even survive.

Superhero Resurrected The 1950's had seen the gradual decline in popularity of superheroes. By 1955, the genre had all but disappeared. However, in the industry's darkest days following *Seduction of the Innocent* and the Comics Code Authority, superheroes characters revitalized a weakened comic book industry.

In 1956, DC Comics published a tryout series called *Showcase,* which featured stories suggested by the book's readers. Under the guidance of legendary editor Julius Schwartz, *Showcase* number 4 would be a landmark issue that ushered in what would come to be known as the Silver Age of comics. The book featured the Flash, the fastest man alive, a superhero with amazing powers of speed and reflexes. Drawn by Carmine Infantino, the new Flash was a revamped version of the 1940's character of the same name. Sales of *Showcase* number 4 were very encouraging, and the Flash appeared three more times there before being given his own title in 1959. Meanwhile, Schwartz continued to resurrect and rework popular characters from the golden age. An updated version of Green Lantern, with art by Gil Kane, appeared in three issues of *Showcase* before the character was granted his own title in 1960. Schwartz reworked the idea of a superhero team in the Justice League of America, which appeared in three issues of another tryout book, *Brave and the Bold* numbers 28 through 30, before graduating to a separate title. Although other genres continued to dominate the comic-book market in 1956 and 1957, superheroes made rapid advances. Schwartz had hit on the right combination of science fiction, adventure, and superheroics; sales of DC's superhero books soared, and readership, including adults who remembered the earlier versions of the characters, multiplied.

In 1958, at the height of the popularity of *The Adventures of Superman* television program, Lois Lane appeared in the first issue of her own title, following two solo stories in *Showcase* numbers 9 and 10. Supergirl, Superman's cousin, appeared in *Action* number 252 in 1959. Archie Comics, long known for the lighthearted adventures of perpetual teen Archie Andrews and his friends, offered a number of significant entries into the superhero market during the late 1950's, including *Adventures of the Fly*. DC's main rival, Marvel Comics, primarily published comics featuring monsters and menaces from space, though a few years later, Marvel would surge to the top of the market, leading yet another renaissance in the comics field with landmark titles such as the *Fantastic Four*, the *Amazing Spider-Man*, and the *Incredible Hulk*.

Impact Comic books during the 1950's became more than a source of entertainment; they became the emblem of a contemporary social problem. They emerged as a scapegoat, a convenient target of opportunity for attacks that ignored the real causes of child crime and juvenile delinquency. *Seduction of the Innocent* clearly demonstrated what happens when bad information, no matter how sincerely meant, is provided to the public under the guise of authority and expertise. Although the saga of comic books during the 1950's demonstrated the benefits of careful attention to the content of material aimed at children, it also clearly pointed out the hazards of accepting conclusions offered by experts without critical thought or demand for genuine scientific proof by audiences.

Further Reading

Benton, Mike. *The Comic Book in America*. Dallas, Tex.: Taylor, 1989. A solid, well-presented history of American comics, from the appearance of the first comic book in 1933 to the landmark anniversaries of Batman and Superman during the late 1980's. Provides detailed coverage of comic book genres and dozens of individual publishers.

Goulart, Ron. *Great American Comic Books*. Lincolnwood, Ill.: Publications International, 2001. A detailed history of American comics by a well-respected comics historian.

Sassienie, Paul. *The Comic Book*. Edison, N.J.: Chartwell Books, 1994. A chronological overview of American and British comic book history. Includes numerous full-color and full-page illustrations of comic book covers and interiors. Provides an index of creators, an index of comic book titles and publishers, and a glossary of terms.

Wertham, Fredric. *Seduction of the Innocent*. Mattituck, N.Y.: Amereon, 1996. Reprint of Wertham's influential 1954 book that encouraged censorship of comics.

Jeffrey W. Roberts

See also *Adventures of Superman, The*; Baby boomers; Capp, Al; Censorship; Gaines, William M.; *MAD*; *Peanuts*; *Pogo*; Pulp magazines; Youth culture and the generation gap.

■ Commission on Civil Rights

Identification Nonpartisan federal agency charged with investigating civil rights violations at the local, state, and federal levels, as well as with advising the president and Congress and recommending legislation

Date Created by the passage of the Civil Rights Act of 1957

Despite its limited powers, the establishment of the Commission on Civil Rights marked a significant first step on the part of the federal government to eradicate civil rights abuses and disestablish the segregated society enshrined in southern state laws.

In 1870 and 1875, Congress enacted civil rights legislation to enforce the Fourteenth and Fifteenth Amendments to the Constitution, but within eight years, the Supreme Court declared the later legislation unconstitutional. Before the nineteenth century ended, the civil rights of African Americans would be further eroded by the Court's ruling in *Plessy v. Ferguson* (1896) and the actions of southern state legislatures in the wake of the decision. Although demand grew for federal civil rights legislation during the New Deal of the 1930's, southern congressmen blocked all attempts to pass such laws.

By the mid-1950's the divisions between the liberal and southern conservative factions of the Democratic Party threatened to split it. Northern Republicans anticipated that civil rights legislation would hasten the split, to the benefit of their party. Concerns, therefore, were less for the civil rights of African Americans than for the Republican Party's political gains. However, President Dwight D. Eisenhower recognized the need to address civil rights violations, which he viewed as one of the foremost domestic problems the nation faced. In his annual state of the union address to Congress in January of 1957, Eisenhower outlined his civil rights agenda. He called for the establishment of a commission to investigate civil rights abuses, the creation of a new assistant attorney general whose office would be devoted to civil rights issues, the passage of federal legislation to protect voting rights and to guarantee existing civil rights, and legislation to allow the federal government to seek redress via the nation's court system.

The president signed into law the first U.S. civil rights legislation since Reconstruction on September 9, 1957, known as the Civil Rights Act of 1957. In so doing, Eisenhower created the Commission on Civil Rights, which was provided for by Title I of the act as an independent, bipartisan federal agency. The commission was established to investigate *de facto* and *de jure* civil rights abuses at the federal, state, and local levels, as well as to evaluate the civil rights practices and policies of the federal government.

Impact Federal lawmakers intended the commission to enforce existing federal voting-rights guarantees, but its powers were limited to advising the president and Congress. Although the commission could recommend legislation, it lacked any real power to compel state officials to comply with existing civil rights legislation because the enforcement procedures proved ineffective in the face of southern resistance. Moreover, measures brought before Congress, on the recommendation of the commission, would be subject to the influence of southern lawmakers on Capitol Hill. These shortcomings prompted Congress to revisit the issue three years later with the Civil Rights Act of 1960, but that law did not result in a more effective commission.

Further Reading

Dulles, Foster Rhea. *The Civil Rights Commission: 1957-1965*. East Lansing: Michigan State University Press, 1968. Details the history leading to the establishment of the commission and explores its lasting contributions and weaknesses.

Levy, Peter B. *The Civil Rights Movement.* Westport, Conn.: Greenwood Press, 1998. Six essays examine such topics as the role of women in the movement and the lasting effects of the events during

the 1950's and 1960's. Provides good context for understanding the benefits and detractions of the Commission on Civil Rights.

Paul D. Gelpi, Jr.

See also Civil Rights Act of 1957; Civil Rights movement; Eisenhower, Dwight D.; Racial discrimination.

■ Communications in Canada

The 1950's witnessed major expansion and restructuring of Canada's communications networks. At the same time, Canada was pulled into the U.S. communications orbit to an unprecedented degree. New technologies were powerful tools that bound the country together and had lasting social, economic, and political consequences.

The inventor Alexander Graham Bell patented the Bell telephone and started a new craze when he demonstrated the gadget at the Philadelphia World's Fair in 1876. By the end of World War II, Canadians used the telephone more than any other population. In 1956, Canada introduced a national microwave relay network for long-distance connections. Bell Telephone introduced direct distance dialing in 1957, thus beginning the phase-out of human operators, who had been integral to the telephone network from its inception. By 1957, Canadians could phone Great Britain for the first time via an underwater cable, a system that was finished and formally opened in 1961, when the prime minister placed a call from Ottawa to Queen Elizabeth II in London's Buckingham Palace. The first telephone hot line was implemented in 1959 for emergency assistance. By the early 1960's, touch-tone dialing and airplane phones were realities even in the remotest northern regions. Telephone services were provided through both public and private companies, although the Bell Company was dominant.

Radio Canada's first nationwide radio transmission occurred on July 1, 1927, when Dominion Day celebrations were broadcast from Parliament Hill. The Canadian Broadcasting Corporation (CBC) was established by the Canadian government as a Crown Corporation during the 1930's. CBC radio was a national service intended to have broad appeal; thus, it served both national languages early in its history: the English-language Trans-Canada network, the French Radio-Canada, and the evening-only Dominion network. Canadian radio reached its golden age

Workers drag the first transatlantic cable onto a Newfoundland shore to provide direct telephone service between Europe and North America, in June, 1956. (Hulton Archive I by Getty Images)

during the 1950's with a high volume and diversity of programs. For example, it broadcast the long-running *Rawhide* (1946-1962), *The Happy Gang* (1937-1959), *Just Mary* (1938-1960), and *Tante Lucille* (1948-1974).

Television and the CBC Television entered Canada from the United States in September, 1952, and the medium quickly outpaced radio in popularity. During the 1950's, television was the fastest-growing industry in Canada, and by 1961, more homes had television sets than cars or flush toilets. Television held mass appeal for its versatility, visual action, and ability to combine radio, stage, and cinema into a single package. Over the years, the CBC added regional radio and television towers and base stations; video recorders made possible delayed broadcasts for audiences in the far North. During this era, radio

and television were powerful agents in building and maintaining national identity and cohesion over a massive land area.

In 1959, more than 96 percent of Canadian homes had radios, about 90 percent had televisions, and television broadcasting ran nine hours daily, usually longer on Sundays. By 1960, the *CBC Times* magazine predicted that the CBC would produce ten thousand television and fifty thousand radio programs in the coming year. The CBC routinely bought out its competition; in fact, efforts to build up private television companies largely were thwarted by the government until the end of the 1950's, and efforts to enact pay television never got off the ground. Alphonse Ouimet, considered the father of Canadian television, was CBC's chief operations officer. CBC documented for Canadian television viewers notable events during the 1950's, including the coronation ceremony of Queen Elizabeth II in 1952 and the opening of the St. Lawrence Seaway in 1959.

Addressing American Influence Fears that American media would dilute Canadian culture prompted the government to order several investigations, beginning in 1949. Independent stations, for example, relied heavily on American programming, both imported and emulated, and posed a growing threat to the CBC with each passing year. The government-sponsored Massey and Fowler reports called for a made-in-Canada approach to the country's media production. To ensure programming of Canadian origin, the government eventually set up the Canadian Radio and Television Commission, which became in subsequent decades the industry's chief governing body.

Other Canadian media faced varying degrees of competition from U.S. media. The commercial film industry in Canada was seminal during the 1950's, easily dwarfed by the giant companies in Hollywood, while the National Film Board of Canada continued to build its reputation as a producer of high-quality, educational programming. *Maclean's* and *Liberty*, the most popular Canadian magazines, faced stiff competition from their American counterparts. Canadian newspapers managed to maintain the greatest degree of independence from American influences through the decade.

Impact Leisure and prosperity after World War II set the stage for a revolution in Canadian communications. New or improved technologies reduced distance barriers across the vast country, gave rise to a host of new entertainment options, and contributed to the absorption of increasing doses of American mass culture. By the 1950's, Canadians had a well-developed, highly integrated communications system.

Further Reading

Collins, Richard. *Culture, Communication, and National Identity: The Case of Canadian Television.* Toronto: University of Toronto Press, 1990. Examines the relationship of television to Canadian identity, with a brief history of television technology, marketing, and programming.

Oslin, George P. *The Story of Telecommunications.* Macon, Ga.: Mercer University Press, 1992. A historical view of the technologies from telegraph to satellite.

Rutherford, Paul. *When Television Was Young: Primetime Canada, 1952-1967.* Toronto: University of Toronto Press, 1990. A study of the structures and genres of television from its first years in Canada.

Ann M. Legreid

See also Canadian Broadcasting Corporation; Communications in the United States; Education in Canada; Film in Canada; Newspapers in Canada; Pay television; Telephones; Television in Canada; Transistors.

■ Communications in the United States

During the 1950's, Americans changed the way they communicated, and advances in communication changed the way they lived. Chatting face to face gave way to telephone calls, letters gave way to long-distance telephone calls, and radio gave way to television. As the world grew smaller, more intimate, and more immediate, American identity began to become associated with a collection of numbers on databases.

At the beginning of 1950, most communication occurred between people who knew one another, either via in-person speech or written correspondence. In many cities, mail was delivered to homes twice a day, "junk mail" had not yet been invented, and the cost of mailing a first-class letter had remained at three cents for nearly two decades. Telegrams generally meant deaths in families, and personal long-distance phone calls were practically unknown.

As the decade began, phone service for many people involved an interaction with a human being—the telephone operator. All telephones were black, and many had no dials. To use one without a dial, the user would lift the earpiece off its hook and then speak to the person who answered, usually with a cheery, "Number, please. . . ." That person, invariably a woman, was the operator, and she could establish connections with any other user in her exchange. She could also connect to other operators in other exchanges to establish long-distance connections. Those operators were people with similar knowledge of their own areas and the folks they served.

It was entirely possible to make phone connections with scant information: "I'm trying to reach the man who married Janice Thornby last year. I think he lives in a town west of Syracuse with a funny name. And I know that he has a good-sized apple orchard." The Syracuse operator might well guess that the town involved was Skaneateles, and the Skaneateles operator might know Janice Thornby and her new spouse. If not, she probably did know a few apple farmers in the area and might ask a couple of them to see if anyone knew who married Janice. Privacy concerns typically did not exist, as almost everyone being called wanted to talk with the caller and appreciated the operator's efforts to establish a connection.

By the end of the 1950's, it was possible for individuals to make their own unique connections to people on the opposite side of the country, as long as they knew the correct area codes and local phone numbers. Such information could be obtained from an information operator, but only if one knew the name under which the phone was listed and, if there were many phones listed under the same name, the address of the party one wished to reach. The connection was made almost instantaneously using electric switching equipment, and the call was transmitted over microwave stations across the continent or through transatlantic telephone cables beneath the sea. Equipment that had been invented and constructed during this decade enabled such advances in phone communications.

Local Phone Service At the end of World War II, phone companies had long lists of people who wanted telephone service but had been unable to obtain it because of the shortages produced by the war. However, by the early 1950's, most homes had telephones. Having a phone and using it were two different things, however, and there was some opposition to this new form of communication. Facial expressions, body language, and gestures help convey a context within which one's words can be understood better, and the telephone eliminated these communication cues. At the time, many articles were written deploring this loss and criticizing the use of the telephone in general. Moreover, phone conversations were seen as being less courteous than a face-to-face conversation and much less courteous than a written letter. It was unacceptable to call someone to express thanks for a gift, for example.

Naturally, the teenagers of the day ignored such formalities and quickly embraced the telephone. Because each family had at most one phone line, tying up the telephone was a common source of fric-

tion within families. In 1950, 75 percent of the residential telephone users shared a party line with several other families. Thus, monopolizing a phone line could produce friction between families as well.

Party lines had multiple users. Each phone would have a different ring pattern, so that families could tell when their phones were being called. When a call was placed, there was no way of knowing if another family sharing a party line was already using it without picking up the handset and listening. If others were using it, and if the conversation was particularly interesting, the temptation not to hang up often proved irresistible.

Phone Numbers As the 1950's progressed, switching systems were developed and deployed that allowed users to establish their own connections within their local area. Phones had dials that were rotated in order to send each number. As the dial rotated back to its original position, the switching system would effectively see how long it took. The longest return was for zero, the shortest for one. Major cities had many exchanges, and initially the first two digits indicated an exchange while the next four gave the number within that exchange. This system provided too few exchanges for the rapidly expanding networks and soon was replaced by a system in which the first three digits determined the exchange. To make the growing length of a telephone number more agreeable to subscribers, the first two digits were referred to by letters, which were printed on the telephone dial along with the numbers. Furthermore, these letters were referred to by a word that started with those letters. A number such as "GR2-8789," for example, was transformed into "472-8789," in which the number "4" served as "G," and "7" served as "R," so that phone books would list the number as "GR2-8789," and anyone giving the number to someone else orally would say, "Granite 2 (pause), 8, 7, 8, 9." To avoid confusion between the numbers "0" and "1" and letters, the alphabet was printed, in groups of three letters, over the numbers "2" through "9."

At the time, no one seriously considered how this system would expand to serve a global community or even a national one, but before the 1950's were over, this issue had to be addressed. Early in the decade, a long-distance call required operator assistance and the cost was substantial: Calls were charged a particular fee for the first three minutes, which paid for getting the connection established, and then at an-

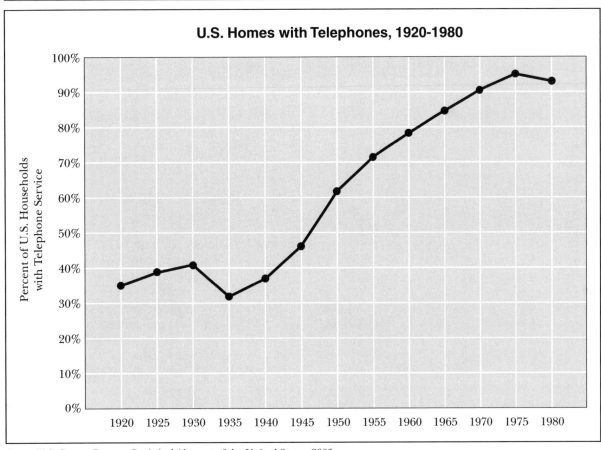

U.S. Homes with Telephones, 1920-1980

Source: U.S. Census Bureau, *Statistical Abstract of the United States*, 2003.

other rate for each additional minute. Many families kept three-minute egg timers near their phones to keep their calls within three minutes.

Operator assistance, though often a tremendous convenience to the user, was an expensive part of running a telephone system, so the American Telephone and Telegraph Company (AT&T) worked diligently to replace it. Two modifications of the telephone number were made. First, a set of "superexchanges," each with its own set of exchanges within it, was established. Next, names and letters for exchanges disappeared and the system moved to All Number Calling for international calls since different languages use alphabets other than that of Western countries. Later in the decade, however, when the Bell systems tried to get people to give up their named and lettered exchanges, resentment developed.

Super exchanges were made easier by a system of three-digit "area codes," which a switching system

would not confuse with a local exchange because the second digit was a "0" or a "1." This provided more than 160 unique area codes, which seemed more than adequate at the time. The first directly dialed telephone call was made on November 5, 1951, but it would take much of the decade before the entire system switched over. Because directly dialed calls were cheaper and connections were made much more quickly, the public rapidly embraced these improvements.

As computers proliferated and databases were developed during this era, assigning a customer number to a customer, a student number to a student, or a social security number to a citizen became a common way to establish a unique record. Because Americans increasingly shared their names with others, additional information—an address and a birth date, for example—needed to be combined with one's name in order to establish a unique identity. Computer memory was expensive, so clients were often each assigned a number. It was not common for different systems to use the same number.

When a ten-digit number could be assigned to each phone on the continent, identity issues became apparent. Removing the letters from phone numbers focused attention and outrage on the telephone system. Many of the names used had local significance, and converting them back to numbers seemed to be an unnecessary surrender to technology and another step away from any personal connection.

Long before a 911 system was envisioned, the telephone operators provided this service for fire departments and police forces. Any child during the 1950's knew that to report a fire you should dial the operator, who could be reached by dialing "0." Clearly printed on the faceplate of every telephone dial was the telephone number of that particular phone, and the operator would ask for that number right away. By using an "inverse phone book," the operator could look up the address for that phone and alert the relevant agency to the emergency. Existence of such resources, even if they were supposed to be restricted to phone company and emergency agencies, worried some people, as they might be used, for example, to determine the identity of someone placing a classified advertisement in the newspaper. Interestingly, privacy issues were not prevalent before the switch to All Number Calling, even though the inverse phone books were certainly in use.

Long Distance Improves As a direct result of war-related research on radar, Bell Labs, a division of AT&T throughout the 1950's, developed the ability to transmit thousands of phone conversations simultaneously over a system of microwave towers spread out across the continent. However, making connections across the oceans was considerably more difficult. The first transatlantic telegraph cable had been successfully placed at the bottom of the sea in 1866. Because information sent by telegraph is a series of dots and dashes, static and audio fidelity mattered little, and this cable was simply a wire. Voice communication, however, required an audio signal to be detected at the far end of the wire. The signal needed to be amplified along its route approximately every twenty miles. The real problem was that the cost of repairing or replacing even one of the amplifiers would be so great that it might jeopardize the entire

fiscal viability of the project. To meet this challenge, Bell Labs developed tube-based amplifiers, which it maintained would last at least twenty years at the bottom of the sea.

The cable was laid in 1956 and carried fifty-one simultaneous phone calls. Over its twenty-two-year lifetime, not a single amplifier failed, despite ten million phone calls being placed and completed. For the general public, the cost was too great for routine use, however. It would be well into the 1960's before there were enough cables going across the ocean to bring the cost down to price levels most Americans could afford.

Federal Regulation Throughout the 1950's, the telephone systems in the United States were regulated monopolies. They were required to make their accounting records available to regulators, and their rates were set by regulators at levels that would provide adequate profits to encourage innovation and improvement of the system, while still ensuring the rate-paying public good value for their money. This approach was also used with respect to other utilities, such as gas and electric companies. However, a somewhat different approach developed for television stations.

The need to regulate the airwaves had been demonstrated convincingly during the early days of radio. Stations intentionally chose frequencies used by other stations in the area and then tried to drown out their competitors by blasting more powerful signals into the air. The resulting cacophony and interference made it difficult for anyone to receive a high-quality signal. The Federal Communications Commission (FCC) was established, and with it, a form of regulated monopoly. It divided up the radio frequency spectrum and allocated various channels to various stations that had applied for a channel.

During the early days of television, a similar procedure had been used. Problems developed, however, when the demand for channels grew rapidly after World War II. Swamped by applications, motivated to include nearby Canadian stations in its planning, and criticized continuously for its methods of allocating stations, the FCC stopped processing applications on September 30, 1948. This freeze was intended to allow for technical input to produce adequate safeguards and rational guidelines, and it was thought that six to nine months would suffice. The freeze subsequently lasted nearly four years.

Color Television Standards As the FCC wrestled with how to allocate VHF (very high frequency) and UHF (ultrahigh frequency) channels, the need for another type of regulation developed. Color television was coming into its own, but there were competing technologies. If the continent was to have one set of standards governing how color signals were to be encoded by the transmitters and decoded by the consumers' receivers, these matters would need to be established by government decree. The airwaves were owned by all, and the government felt it had a responsibility to ensure that the signals propagating through them would be of greatest benefit to the public.

The Columbia Broadcasting System (CBS) had developed a workable system, which produced good pictures and passed several important field tests. However, it required 405 scan lines per frame, instead of the NTSC (National Television Systems Committee) standard of 525 lines per frame. (The European system, PAL, uses 625 lines per frame.) The American Broadcasting Company (ABC) and some smaller companies were working on a very different system, which had some technical difficulties but was compatible with black-and-white television.

In 1950, the FCC decided that the CBS system was superior and made it the national standard, encouraging television manufacturers to develop systems that could use either 405 or 525 scan lines per frame. ABC objected and sued, and television manufacturers balked at raising the cost of their black-and-white units to incorporate the two standards. The Supreme Court ruled against ABC in May, 1951, but by then it was almost a moot point, as the Korean War brought television development to a halt.

By the end of the war, the Radio Corporation of America (RCA) system had been improved, and thousands of additional black-and-white television sets using the 525 line standard had been sold. The FCC reversed its decision in December, 1953. The CBS system, too, was improved and has been used in nonpublic broadcasting applications, for organizations such as the National Aeronautics and Space Administration (NASA) and for medical schools.

Impact During the decade of the 1950's, Americans moved from personal forms of communication, usually face-to-face contacts between people who knew one another, to impersonal forms, whereby knowledge of a telephone number or some other number assigned to a name or an account was more important than any acquaintance with the individual person. Facilitated by developments in technology, these changes persisted and laid important foundations for future technological advances in the years to come.

Further Reading

Brock, Gerald W. *The Telecommunications Industry: The Dynamics of Market Structure.* Cambridge, Mass.: Harvard University Press, 1981. Details government regulation and controlled monopolies and concentrates on barriers to market entry.

Brooks, John. *Telephone.* New York: Harper and Row, 1975. Written to commemorate the first one hundred years of the telephone industry, this book concentrates on AT&T.

Oslin, George. *The Story of Telecommunications.* Macon, Ga.: Mercer University Press, 1992. Written from the perspective of the telegraph industry, this book gives interesting historical insights from someone who lived through much of that about which he writes. Personal anecdotes and black-and-white photographs add interest to the text.

Slotten, Hugh. *Radio and Television Regulation: Broadcast Technology in the United States, 1920-1960.* Baltimore: Johns Hopkins University Press, 2000. Although a little heavy on regulations and legal developments, this book gives an excellent, accessible treatment of the technical details of how color television evolved during the 1950's.

Otto H. Muller

See also Communications in Canada; Computers; *Lonely Crowd, The;* Murrow, Edward R.; Mutual Broadcasting System scandal; Newspapers in the United States; Radio; Science and technology; Telephones; Television in Canada; Television in the United States.

■ Communist Party of the U.S.A.

Identification Political party dedicated to establishing communism in the United States

Date Founded in 1919

Although the power of the Communist Party of the U.S.A. (CPUSA) was at a low point during the 1950's, many Americans saw the party as a symbol of the threat of communism during the Cold War. Laws against the party raised many questions about the democratic rights of individuals thought to be working against democracy.

Inspired by the 1917 Russian Revolution, in which communists under the leadership of Vladimir I. Lenin took power in Russia, radical American socialists met in Chicago in 1919 to form a communist party of their own. Disagreements on policy and strategy led the Chicago radicals to form two parties instead. The parties merged in 1922 on orders from the Communist International (Comintern), the Soviet organization in charge of directing worldwide communist activities. The Communist Party of the U.S.A. reached its maximum membership of about 75,000 followers by 1938 and then began a period of decline.

During the late 1940's, the United States government brought twelve top leaders of the Communist Party, including Party Secretary Eugene Dennis, to trial for violation of the Smith Act, a 1940 law that made it illegal to advocate the overthrow of the U.S. government. In the same period, fears that communists were plotting with foreign governments against the United States grew when former communist Elizabeth Bentley named a number of government officials as Soviet agents and former communist Whittaker Chambers accused Alger Hiss, previously a high-ranking official of the State Department, of espionage for the communists. Throughout the 1950's, the government's House Committee on Un-American Activities would be a center of American anticommunism.

Communism in the Spotlight As the 1950's began, Wisconsin senator Joseph McCarthy drew national attention with his charge that communists had worked their way into the U.S. State Department. In 1950, Congress adopted the Internal Security Act. This act created a Subversive Activities Control Board (SACB) to identify groups promoting communism. Members of these groups had to register

During the U.S. Senate's Army-McCarthy hearings in June, 1954, Senator Joseph R. McCarthy presented a map that he claimed showed the organization of the Communist Party throughout the United States. (AP/Wide World Photos)

with the U.S. attorney general, and membership in communist organizations could bar a person from government employment, labor union participation, and the procurement of a U.S. passport. That year also saw accusations of espionage and treason brought against Julius and Ethel Rosenberg. After the Supreme Court ruled in 1951 that the conviction of the communist leaders was constitutional and even more communists were convicted under the Smith Act, much of the Communist Party moved underground.

Senator McCarthy's accusations against communists made him a political star, and in 1953, he was appointed chairman of the Senate Permanent Subcommittee on Investigations. McCarthy lost much of his influence in 1954 when his investigation of communism in the U.S. Army and his ruthless methods of investigation led to executive and popular anger. McCarthy himself was investigated and censured by the Senate in December, 1954.

Crisis in the Party Already under assault from outsiders, the CPUSA plunged into an internal crisis in 1956 after Soviet Premier Nikita Khrushchev declared that his predecessor, Joseph Stalin, had been a dictator responsible for the unjust imprisonments and deaths of Soviet citizens. Among the American communists, John Gates, editor of the *Daily Worker*, became the leader of those who believed that American communism should distance itself from the Soviet model. In September of 1956, the national committee for the party passed a resolution stating that American communists needed to find their own way to socialism. However, William Z. Foster, a longtime American communist leader, emerged as a spokesman for those who did not believe that the party needed any fundamental reforms. The Soviet Union communicated its support for the Foster position to the American party. Under pressure from the Soviets, Eugene Dennis backed Foster, and the party moved away from efforts at reform.

The crisis in the party grew greater with the Soviet Union's suppression of a revolt in Hungary in 1956. Those leaving the Communist Party included many followers of John Gates, and the party was left in the hands of a relatively small group of pro-Soviet hardliners. When the party reregistered its members in 1957-1958, it found that its rolls had shrunk to only three thousand members.

In 1959, the party selected a new general secretary, Gus Hall. Hall, who had been among those convicted under the Smith Act, served as leader of the CPUSA for the next four decades. He never veered from his support for the Soviet Union, but he did manage to broaden the party's support somewhat by linking it to the New Left, a radical American political movement during the 1960's, taking on African American activist Angela Davis as his running mate in two of his four unsuccessful campaigns for the American presidency.

Impact Documents released from Soviet archives after the fall of the Soviet Union in 1991 made it clear that the Communist Party of the U.S.A. had received substantial Soviet economic support and direction throughout its history. Ironically, however, the American party was at the weakest point in its history during the 1950's, when it was in the spotlight of national concern and arguably had little influence on American life and government. However, fear of internal subversion by communists expressed the insecurities of Americans during this decade.

Further Reading

Klehr, Harvey, John E. Haynes, and Kyrill M. Anderson. *The Soviet World of American Communism.* New Haven, Conn.: Yale University Press, 1998. Uses documents from Russian archives to examine historical ties between the Soviet Union and the American Communist Party.

Powers, Richard G. *Not Without Honor: The History of American Anticommunism.* New York: Free Press, 1995. A history of opposition to communism in the United States that is sympathetic to anticommunism but is critical of the excesses of the McCarthy period.

Scales, Junius Irving, and Richard Nickson. *Cause at Heart: A Former Communist Remembers.* Athens: University of Georgia Press, 1987. Memoir of a former communist activist who was sentenced to six years in a maximum security prison under the Smith Act.

Carl L. Bankston III

See also Army-McCarthy hearings; Cold War; *Dennis v. United States*; Faulk, John Henry; Hoover, J. Edgar; House Committee on Un-American Activities; Immigration and Nationality Act of 1952; John Birch Society; Landrum-Griffin Act of 1959; McCarthy, Joseph; Mills, C. Wright; Rosenberg, Julius and Ethel; *Yates v. United States*.

■ Computers

Stored program computers became commercially available during the early 1950's and were used to solve many problems thought insoluble up to that time. As computers proliferated throughout society and their use became commonplace, people began to expect quick and accurate solutions to problems involving numerous calculations.

In 1945, John von Neumann described a new type of calculator that could store a set of instructions for a series of computations as well as the data used in the calculations. His automated calculator came to be known as the stored program computer. John Mauchly and Presper Eckert developed the first stored program computer, the Electronic Numerical Integrator and Computer (ENIAC), in 1945, and during its ten-year lifetime, it was used to solve a number of problems, such as simulating liquid drop fusion, which were impossible to solve using an ordinary calculator.

Hardware The technology developed for the computers of the 1950's set the stage for the rapid growth of the mainframe computer industry for the rest of the century. Shortly after the deployment of the ENIAC, a number of other stored program computers appeared at universities, businesses, and military research centers. These computers were used to solve a wide variety of problems, which demonstrated the value of the stored program computer. In 1947, William Shockley, John Bardeen, and Walter Brattain developed the transistor, which replaced vacuum tubes and switches as the hardware used for the memory and processing units of computers such as the mid-1950's UNIVAC III.

In 1958, Jack Kilby of Texas Instruments invented the integrated circuit, which laid the foundation for the high-capacity second-generation computers such as the IBM 1620/1790 of International Business Machines Corporation, first marketed in 1959. The second-generation computers not only had larger memory and more powerful processors but also were less expensive. Their affordability supported many small business applications in addition to the applications of the scientific community and the military.

Software At the beginning of the 1950's, all programming was in machine language. In 1952, Grace Hopper described how symbols could be used to make the programming process easier, and over the remainder of the 1950's, a number of assemblers and compilers were developed that allowed scientists and businesspeople to program computers easily and efficiently.

Processors and memory were implemented with vacuum tubes and resistors in 1951, then with transistors by 1957, and finally with integrated circuits in 1964. In 1953, the first high-speed printer was developed by Remington-Rand for the UNIVAC, and the first high-speed magnetic tape device was introduced for the IBM 726 during the same year. In 1957, IBM introduced the first hard disk for its 305 RAMAC system, and the first FORTRAN compiler was also introduced for the IBM 704 during the same year.

Calculating Solutions At the beginning of the 1950's, mechanical calculators were used to do the mathematics required for defense and scientific applications. Generally, much time was spent on developing efficient formulas because of the limitations of the calculating devices. In some cases the problems could not even be solved. The successful simulation in 1950 of the flow of air over the wing of an airplane would have taken hundreds of years before the invention of computerized problem solving. The UNIVAC I computer was used to predict that Dwight D. Eisenhower would win the 1952 presidential election in time for the result to appear in the morning papers, a feat of prediction that impressed the world since it could not be done with the calculators of the day. However, while some scientific problems of the 1950's could be solved in a reasonable amount of time, the solutions often arrived too late to be useful.

Impact As stored program computers became widely available during the 1950's, military, scientific, and business applications increasingly were turned over to the devices. Programmers began to spend less time developing formulas to process the data efficiently and instead concentrated on solving a wider range of problems, such as oil well depletion, census tabulations, and banking. Society started expecting computers to make information available in a more timely fashion so that, for example, weather predictions were more accurate and stock market information or banking transactions were generated more quickly.

In addition to the benefits to society provided by the development of computers during the 1950's, the advances in computer hardware and software during the decade set the stage for the development of computers for the rest of the century and made a significant change in how people lived their lives.

Further Reading

Fritz, W. Barkley. "ENIAC: A Problem Solver." *IEEE Annals of the History of Computing* 16, no. 1 (1994): 25, 45. A very good article documenting the development of the first-generation computers from the ENIAC to the UNIVAC I.

Rojas, Raul. *The First Computers: History and Architectures.* Cambridge, Mass.: MIT Press, 2002. Discusses many of the computers developed in the United States, with special emphasis on their hardware.

Wurster, Christian. *Computer History.* Los Angeles: Taschen America, 2002. Interesting book on the development of the hardware and software of computers with many references to the computers of the 1950's.

George M. Whitson III

See also Communications in the United States; ENIAC computer; FORTRAN; International Business Machines Corporation; McLuhan, Marshall; Photovoltaic cell; Science and technology; Telephones; Transistors; UNIVAC computer.

■ *Confidential*

Identification American scandal magazine
Publisher Robert Harrison
Date Published from 1952 to 1958

Confidential magazine shocked and delighted U.S. readers with its depictions of the misbehavior of Hollywood movie stars.

In 1982, the writer Tom Wolfe called *Confidential* magazine "the most scandalous scandal magazine in the history of the world." During its brief history, the magazine outraged Hollywood movie studios and terrified the actors who worked for them. A press agent once accused it of starting a reign of terror. However, it also became one of the most popular magazines in the United States, with a circulation of more than four million, higher than that of such respected magazines as the *Saturday Evening Post* and *Look.*

Confidential magazine was the brainchild of Robert Harrison, a publisher of naughty glamour maga-

zines with titles such as *Wink, Titter,* and *Flirt.* When the glamour magazines started to lose money in 1952, he turned to something new: a magazine that would go behind the scenes and reveal titillating information about Hollywood movie stars and other entertainment figures.

Confidential ran stories that exposed the supposed source of Frank Sinatra's alleged sexual prowess and detailed how one well-known actor took off all his clothes at a party, while another actor arranged for his own party guests to spy on couples making love. Harrison especially liked stories about adultery and interracial romance—something that was especially scandalous at the time. The magazine also ran stories suggesting that various celebrities, such as pianist Liberace, were homosexual; such allegations could be terribly damaging to the celebrities' careers. One such story that *Confidential* agreed not to run was about Rock Hudson and his homosexuality. To protect Hudson's reputation, his studio offered *Confidential* some scandalous information about a lesser star, and the magazine agreed to print that story instead.

Despite their public outrage at the magazine, the studios sometimes leaked information to *Confidential* for their own purposes, at times to punish one of their stars. Some stars even provided information about themselves, considering the publicity beneficial. *Confidential* also obtained information using private detectives and informants, including one actor who said she would sleep with subjects if necessary to get information from them. The magazine also ran exposés on organized crime and corruption and, especially during the brief editorship of Howard Rushmore, political exposés about supposed communists in Hollywood.

On Trial In 1957, *Confidential*'s reign came to an end as a result of a criminal libel trial. The U.S. Post Office had tried previously to have the magazine banned from the mail, and a California state senator held hearings into the magazine's activities. Actor Ronald Reagan, then the chairman of the Motion Picture Industry Council, called for a campaign against the magazine, and one studio even produced a film, *Slander* (1956), attacking it. The libel trial finally accomplished what these other efforts were unable to do.

The Trial of a Hundred Stars, as some newspapers called it, ended in a mistrial when the jury failed to

Actor Errol Flynn expresses his disapproval of Confidential *magazine in August, 1957, when he was scheduled to testify in a criminal libel trial of the magazine.* (AP/Wide World Photos)

reach a verdict, but to avoid having to go through a new trial, Harrison agreed to a settlement in which he promised to abandon sensationalism. Without sensationalism, however, *Confidential* lost its appeal: Sales slumped, and Harrison sold the magazine the following year.

Impact *Confidential* magazine told tales from the other side of the innocent and conformist 1950's, shocking the innocent and refusing to go along with the sanitized version of reality provided by the Hollywood movie studios. The magazine is sometimes praised for daring to tell the truth, but critics say that its main achievement was to pave the way for the sensationalist tabloid journalism of later decades.

Further Reading

Gabler, Neal. "*Confidential*'s Reign of Terror." *Vanity Fair* 512 (April, 2003): 190-206. A survey of the magazine's history and impact.

Kashnir, Sam, and Jennifer MacNair. "Wink, Titter, and Flirt: *Confidential* Magazine." In *The Bad and*

the Beautiful: Hollywood in the Fifties. New York: Norton, 2002. Focuses largely on the activities of anticommunist editor Howard Rushmore.

Wolfe, Tom. "Purveyor of the Public Life." In *The Purple Decades.* New York: Farrar Straus Giroux, 1982. Surrealistic magazine article based on an interview with Robert Harrison, first published in 1964.

Sheldon Goldfarb

See also Censorship; Homosexuality and gay rights; Hudson, Rock; Reagan, Ronald; Sex and sex education; Sinatra, Frank; Telephones; Turner-Stompanato scandal.

■ Conformity, culture of

Definition Set of beliefs and practices that promote uniformity in the ways that people live and think

Americans began to grow concerned that they were living in a culture of conformity during the 1950's, and there were a number of trends in history, economics, communication technology, and politics that probably did encourage such a culture.

During the 1950's, many Americans began to identify conformity, an unquestioning similarity in belief and behavior among the majority of people, as a characteristic of their society. In the years following the 1950's, people continued to think of the decade as a period of conformity, especially in contrast to the social upheavals of the 1960's.

A number of connected historical influences contributed to the apparent uniformity of American culture during the decade. First, adult Americans during this time had lived through the crises of the Depression and World War II. These experiences made them value stability and material prosperity as goals in their own lives. Also, prosperity was widely available to Americans. The rapid growth of the American economy made possible a standard of living that would have been beyond the dreams of earlier generations. This relatively high standard of living tended to focus on the consumption of consumer goods, which were abundant as a result of mass production and thus were consumed by a large portion of the population.

The construction of standardized housing in the suburbs made home ownership more common than ever before. The suburbs also tended to put people in rows of similar houses. Moreover, the baby boom from the late 1940's to the early 1960's tended to make suburban residents into nuclear families that were primarily concerned with taking care of children. Parenthood often encouraged people to seek lifestyles that were safe and orderly, instead of those that were varied and experimental. The rise of network television tended to create uniformity in entertainment and communication and to promote a standardized consumerism through advertising. Finally, the Cold War competition with the Soviet Union frequently led to fear of unorthodox ideas. The general suspicion of new or unusual ideas, combined with the concentration on material prosperity, made many Americans uncomfortable with broad plans for personal or social change.

Legacy of the Depression and War The Great Depression was the most severe economic crisis among Western industrialized nations in modern history. Historians and economists usually identify the beginning of the Depression as the collapse of stock market prices on the New York Stock Exchange in October, 1929. From 1929 to 1932, prices of stocks dropped by 80 percent. Since banks had invested their customers' money in the market, banks lost money and nearly half of them closed between 1929 and 1933. Bank failures and a loss of confidence in the economy led businesses and consumers to cut back on spending. In turn, companies cut back on production, and employment decreased drastically. By 1932, one-fourth to one-third of those in the U.S. labor force were unemployed.

The Great Depression lasted throughout the 1930's. For adults during the 1950's, hard economic times were a recent experience and often a defining experience of childhood or adolescence. As a result, Americans during the 1950's often saw job security and financial stability as their most important goals. Ownership of a home was an especially central symbol of a stable way of life.

Although the economy improved somewhat over the course of the 1930's, the Depression did not end until the United States entered World War II in 1941. By 1945, more than twelve million Americans were on active service in the military. Those who remained at home as civilians experienced shortages and rationing of goods, as well as anxiety over the safety of friends and family members in uniform.

Conformism in an Affluent Society In 1958, economist John Kenneth Galbraith published his influen-

tial book *The Affluent Society*. Galbraith argued that throughout most of human history, the central economic problem had been the production of enough goods to meet basic human needs. However, by the 1950's, he argued, the modern economy of North America had largely solved this problem. Instead, the problem of the affluent society had become what goods should be produced and how those goods should be distributed. Galbraith maintained that production by profit-seeking companies led to an emphasis on meeting the desires of individual consumers and on stimulating those desires through marketing. In his view, this process led to too little investment in public goods, such as schools, social services, and public transportation.

Some economists and social scientists might disagree with Galbraith that there was too little public spending during the 1950's. Nonetheless, the prosperity that came after so many years of economic hardship and war did encourage Americans to concentrate on consuming goods. The mass production of these goods made them widely available, and it also meant that people in the United States and Canada were purchasing and using the same sorts of products.

Many people were conscious of the conformity of their materialistic society and felt uncomfortable about it. In 1950, sociologist David Riesman published a widely read analysis of the consequences of prosperity, *The Lonely Crowd: A Study of the Changing American Character*. In it, Riesman argued that different types of economies tend to produce different character types: For example, agricultural economies had resulted in "tradition-directed" people, who modeled their lives on ideas of the past. The changes brought about by industrializing societies tended to make people "inner-directed," individualistic, and driven by their own consciences. Riesman described his own time as "other-directed": In a time of abundance, consuming goods and interacting with other people became the most important activities, so that the prevailing character tended to become sensitive to others but also conformist.

Other authors also drew links between the postwar economy and the culture of the 1950's. The 1955 best-selling novel *The Man in the Gray Flannel Suit*, by Sloan Wilson, portrayed what Wilson and many of his readers saw as the emptiness of nuclear-family life in the suburbs. Sociologist William H.

Whyte published a less dramatic expression of a similar view in his book *The Organization Man* (1956), which portrayed corporate conformity as becoming the dominant pattern in American life. Despite these kinds of criticisms, however, the culture of conformity tended to persist.

Growth of the Suburbs During the nineteenth century, North American society was primarily rural. The 1920 U.S. Census was the first to show a majority of Americans living in urban areas. Fifty years later, the 1970 Census was the first to show a suburban majority. The greatest suburban growth occurred during the 1950's as a result of the mass production of housing and the construction of an extensive highway system.

Americans had suffered from a shortage of housing in the war years. After the war, they began to find new homes in the suburbs, made affordable by new approaches to building. The Levittowns, built by William J. Levitt with his brother Alfred, became symbols of suburbia. Levittown architecture dispensed with basements and built rows of nearly identical houses on concrete slabs. Other builders followed the success of the Levitts. By 1955, three quarters of all new housing in the United States consisted of subdivisions based on the Levittown model. Throughout the decade, 83 percent of all population growth in the United States occurred in the suburbs. Canada, with its lower population density, moved to the suburbs at a lower rate, but it followed a similar trend.

The automobile industry made the growth of the suburbs possible. Automobile sales during this decade broke all previous records. New road construction enabled people in the suburbs to travel daily from their homes to their jobs. When the U.S. Congress approved the interstate highway system in 1956, road construction became a national priority that fed the expanding suburbs.

Life in the suburbs contributed to a culture of conformity by placing Americans in similar homes that varied relatively little between regions or within subdivisions. In the suburban tract, it was difficult to find families that strayed from the nuclear model, one that held fairly well-defined roles for each member and emphasized the enjoyment of material goods. The conformity of the suburban lifestyle was encouraged, further, by the patterns of family life and entertainment within suburban homes.

The Baby Boom and Class Change In her books of the later twentieth century, sociologist Arlene Skolnick described the dream of the suburbs during the 1950's as a dream of a happy family life. Men and women began settling into family life in record numbers from the end of World War II until 1965. The three- and four-child family became a widespread ideal, so much so that about 75 million babies were born in the United States during the two decades of the "baby boom." Sociologists notes that people who are caring for children tend to seek security and stability, rather than diversity and new ways of doing things. The baby boom therefore worked together with suburban uniformity to promote a culture of conformity during the 1950's.

Moreover, North Americans largely participated in a society with a rising middle class, the members of which enjoyed prosperity because they had jobs in offices and factories. This class change meant that the ability of American workers to provide for their families depended heavily on workers' conformity to the rules of the workplaces. It also meant that they saw their children's prospects for getting good jobs as dependent on their children's habits of conformity. The prosperity of the times and the experience of most adults with less prosperous times made parents inclined to encourage getting along with others and following the rules as essential traits to cultivate in children.

Mass Media and Conformity Conformity in the home was further encouraged by the kinds of information and entertainment most 1950's homes received. North American manufacturers produced fewer than six thousand television sets in 1946. Seven years later, these manufacturers produced seven million sets. In 1952, Canada's first television station began broadcasting in Montreal. By the end of the 1950's, more than eight out of ten North American households owned televisions. These sets rapidly came to occupy central positions in American homes, and families commonly gathered in front of their small screens every evening.

Three major networks—NBC, ABC, and CBS—broadcast television programming, and there was relatively little variety in the programs watched by families across the American continent. One of the most popular types of shows was the family situation comedy. Set in the suburbs, such programs typically portrayed middle-class nuclear families that were idealized versions of those that actually lived in many places in North America. The programs left out many parts of American life. There were almost no low-income characters, and with the exception of Cuban Desi Arnaz, the television and real-life husband of Lucille Ball on *I Love Lucy*, ethnic and racial minorities virtually did not exist on television after the early 1950's. The fathers were generally not shown at work, and they never discussed their jobs at home. Nevertheless, shows such as *Leave It to Beaver* and *The Adventures of Ozzie and Harriet* offered comfortable portrayals of family life that influenced popular notions of how life ought to be.

The Cold War Political trends also had an impact on the predominant culture of conformity. After World War II, the United States and Canada began a period of competition with the Soviet Union, an ally of the North American countries during the war. During the late 1940's, many Americans began to fear that Soviet communism threatened them from inside their borders. This fear was compounded when former communists Elizabeth Bentley and Whittaker Chambers accused numerous U.S. government officials of being Soviet agents. In 1949, communist forces took over China, and the Soviet Union tested its first atomic bomb. A year later, U.S. citizens Julius and Ethel Rosenberg were accused of spying to help the Soviets acquire U.S. nuclear secrets.

Fear of communist subversion promoted conformity in thought and education. The U.S. government established the "Zeal for Democracy" program in 1947. The purpose of the program was to help local school districts create anticommunist courses. Across the United States, and to a lesser extent in Canada, school officials began to look for ways to eliminate teachers who were suspected of being communist sympathizers. The National Education Association (NEA) made its position clear in 1949, when the association stated that communists should not be allowed to teach in public schools. Perhaps the best-known effort to identify and purge subversion during the decade was led by Senator Joseph R. McCarthy, whose congressional hearings on communist sympathizers and influence led many critics to compare the era to that of the seventeenth century Salem witch-hunts.

Popular entertainment was also affected by the Cold War. In 1947, the House Committee on Un-American Activities (HUAC) began investigating pos-

sible communist infiltration of the motion-picture industry. A number of prominent Hollywood figures were blacklisted, or banned from working in the industry, when they refused to cooperate with HUAC. Films and television programs often avoided controversial topics out of fear that they might be seen as contributing to the threat of communism. Many forms of popular entertainment expressed the fear of the communist threat either openly or symbolically. Mike Hammer, the hard-boiled detective hero of Mickey Spillane's novels, killed communists. A number of films about alien invasions may well have appealed to viewers because the films expressed feelings that society was being taken over by alien forces. The most successful of these films, *The Invasion of the Body Snatchers* (1956), portrayed a small town being taken over by emotionless creatures, grown in pods, who took on the bodily forms of the town dwellers. One of the reasons this film might have had such appeal was that it could be taken equally well as representing fear of communist takeover or fear of the creeping culture of conformity.

Nonconformists of the Era Despite the identification of the 1950's as a time of general conformity, there were a number of notable exceptions. In painting, the dominant school of abstract expressionism pioneered new nonrepresentational artistic forms. During the late 1940's and 1950's, abstract expressionists such as Jackson Pollock and Franz Kline rebelled against earlier artistic conventions.

In literature, the "Beat" writers such as Allen Ginsberg, Jack Kerouac, and William S. Burroughs defied mainstream American practices and expectations both in their works and in their lives. Rejecting the culture of the white middle class, the Beats drew much of their inspiration from African American jazz and bebop musicians.

Although many intellectuals and academics came under pressure for defying convention, especially the scholars who were accused of communist tendencies, a number became widely known for their challenges to established social norms. The sociologist C. Wright Mills, for example, was an outspoken critic of the social and political structure of the United States at mid-century. The critic Dwight Macdonald denounced what he saw as the shallowness of mass culture. At the end of the decade, in 1959, the classics scholar Norman O. Brown turned his attention to modern civilization and questioned that civilization's very basis in his book *Life Against Death: The Psychoanalytical Meaning of History*, a radical fusion of Marxist and psychoanalytic theory.

Impact The identification of a culture of conformity caused many North Americans both then and in later years to question their lives and the nature of their society. Many of the trends that helped to perpetuate this culture, especially the spread of the suburbs, continued. However, a period of reaction against the 1950's American culture through self-conscious nonconformity also emerged, paving the way for countercultural upheavals of the 1960's.

Many of the children who grew up during the 1950's rebelled against the culture of their childhood during the 1960's and 1970's, giving rise to the counterculture. This rebellion probably had several roots during the 1950's culture of conformity. For example, those who had spent their early years in the prosperous 1950's often took material well-being for granted and tended to be less insecure than their parents, who had experienced the Great Depression and World War II. The U.S. generation of the baby boom also faced its own war, the Vietnam War. This was an extremely unpopular war, though, and it caused many young people to turn against their society. Both opposition to the Vietnam War in Canada and the movement of military draft evaders across the border spurred the growth of a Canadian counterculture. Rejection of convention was also a result of the fact that members of the baby-boom generation reached late adolescence and early adulthood during the 1960's and 1970's. This demographic meant that large numbers of people in North America were reaching the most rebellious times in their lives at that time.

Further Reading

Cohen, Elizabeth. *A Consumer's Republic: The Politics of Mass Consumption in Postwar America.* New York: Knopf, 2003. Examines the way in which affluence and consumerism were linked to issues of citizenship (the encouragement to buy for "the good of the nation") in postwar America.

Miller, Douglas T., and Marion Nowak. *The Fifties: The Way We Really Were.* Garden City, N.Y.: Doubleday, 1977. A good general work on the culture of the 1950's.

Mills, C. Wright. *White Collar: The American Middle Classes.* New York: Oxford University Press, 2002. A new edition of an influential book originally published in 1951 that argued that the American middle classes were new social classes who were without extensive property and willingly conformed to the demands of their corporate employers.

Riesman, David. *The Lonely Crowd: A Study of the Changing American Character.* Rev. ed. New Haven, Conn.: Yale University Press, 2001. Revised edition of a book originally published in 1950, which expressed and analyzed the culture of conformity during the 1950's.

Skolnick, Arlene. *Embattled Paradise: The American Family in an Age of Uncertainty.* New York: Harper-Collins, 1991. A good general look at American family life that includes discussion of family trends during the 1950's.

Whyte, William H. *The Organization Man.* Philadelphia: University of Pennsylvania Press, 2002. Reissue of a 1956 classic that argued that safety, security, and conformity had become the primary values of American workers in an increasingly corporate setting.

Carl L. Bankston III

See also Affluence and the new consumerism; American Dream; *Atlas Shrugged*; Baby boomers; Dance, popular; Homosexuality and gay rights; House Committee on Un-American Activities; Loyalty oaths; McCarthy, Joseph; Mills, C. Wright; *Organization Man, The*; Packard, Vance; Youth culture and the generation gap.

■ Congress, U.S.

Identification The two houses constituting the legislative branch of the government of the United States

During the 1950's, the U.S. Congress faced and responded to diverse challenges, including unprecedented issues involving defense and national security, civil and constitutional liberties, labor-management relations, and foreign affairs.

When the decade of the 1950's opened, the U.S. Congress was in the second year of the two-year period known as the Eighty-first Congress. The Democratic Party commanded majorities in both houses: 54 Democrats to 42 Republicans in the Senate, and 263 Democrats to 171 Republicans and 1 independent in the House of Representatives. The major preoccupation of congressional members that year centered on the perceived threat posed by internal subversion by communist elements and the Korean War.

The president pro tem of the Senate was Kenneth McKellam, a Democrat from Tennessee; the majority leader was Scott W. Lucas, a Democrat from Illinois. The Speaker of the House was Sam Rayburn, a Texas Democrat, and the majority leader was Democratic senator John W. McCormack of Massachusetts.

During the early years of the Cold War, a spirit of bipartisanship had characterized the relationship between Congress and the presidency. However, this spirit began to fade during the early 1950's, and later sessions of Congress had greater trouble working with President Harry S. Truman, especially after the moderate conservative senator Arthur Vandenberg, a Michigan Republican, began exerting influence over his party colleagues. However, after Vandenberg relinquished his chairmanship of the powerful Foreign Relations Committee in 1948, the more abrasively conservative elements within the Republican Party, who were led by Senator Robert A. Taft of Ohio, were more openly critical of the Truman administration and less amenable to accepting its foreign policy and domestic security initiatives.

McCarthyism and Television In February, 1950, Wisconsin senator Joseph R. McCarthy delivered a speech in Wheeling, West Virginia, in which he claimed that large numbers of communists were infiltrating the federal government. That claim raised McCarthy to public notoriety but also drew a stinging denunciation from nine of his Senate colleagues, who were led by Maine's Republican senator Margaret Chase Smith. The nine senators issued a public "Declaration of Conscience," denouncing McCarthy's methods of making serious charges based on unfounded accusations and innuendo.

The declaration did little to halt the momentum of McCarthyism, in part because of the outbreak and dangerous progress of the Korean War and the continuing drama of the Rosenberg espionage arrests. McCarthy's well-publicized Senate hearings on communist subversion continued to be a focus of public attention over the next four years. In March, 1950, the Senate Committee on Foreign Relations set up a subcommittee to investigate McCarthy's allegations. Chaired by Senator Millard Tydings, a Democrat from Maryland, the subcommittee concluded that the charges were unfounded. However, even this report did not slow down McCarthy. When Tydings was defeated in his next bid for re-election, McCarthy openly claimed credit for his electoral defeat.

With the advent of television as the dominant media form, televised congressional committee hearings came into being, and for the first time members of the general public could look directly in on congressional activities. Through 1950 and 1951, the Kefauver Committee held televised hearings to investigate organized crime, and the McClellan Committee held hearings on labor racketeering in 1956-1957. Hearings involving McCarthy and the U.S. Army were televised in 1954, and hearings conducted by the House Committee on Un-American Activities were televised throughout the early 1950's.

The Internal Security Act In 1950, both houses of Congress passed the Internal Security Act over President Truman's veto. Sometimes called the McCarran Act, after its chief sponsor in the Senate, Patrick McCarran, a Democrat from Nevada, the law mandated that Communist Party members in the United States register with the Justice Department. The law provided penalties for noncompliance and set up the Subversive Activities Control Board to monitor and document the activities of members of organizations deemed to pose threats to national security. Among the law's more controversial provisions was a prohibition against members of suspect organizations entering the United States.

By contrast, the Foreign Economic Assistance Act of 1950 followed the bipartisan model by authorizing implementation of Truman's technical aid program to developing nations. The Celler-Kefauver Antimerger Act of 1950 was a significant antitrust measure designed to prevent the buying out of a competing firm's assets in order to reduce business competition.

The Eighty-second Congress, 1951-1952 The midterm elections of 1950 brought in the Eighty-second Congress, in which the party balance tightened. The new Congress put 49 Democrats and 47 Republicans in the Senate, and 234 Democrats, 199 Republicans, and 2 independents in the House. Senate leadership remained essentially the same, except that Ernest W. McFarland, a Democrat from Arizona, succeeded Lucas—who lost his bid for re-election—as Senate majority leader. Another notable change was that Texas Democrat Lyndon B. Johnson became the

Senate's majority whip. House leadership remained as it had been.

One of the most important pieces of legislation passed by the Eighty-second Congress was the Immigration and Nationality Act of 1952, also known as the McCarran-Walker Act for its sponsors. This law set a ceiling on immigration to the United States, based on the figures of the 1920 census, and established specific quotas for each nation. The law was criticized for the large disproportion of quota spaces that it awarded to European nations over Asian nations.

The Eighty-third Congress, 1953-1954 With the election of Republican president Dwight D. Eisenhower in 1952, the balance of party power shifted in Congress. In the Eighty-third Congress, which sat from 1953 to 1955, the Republicans had 48 Senate seats to 47 for the Democrats and 1 independent, and 221 seats to 213 for the Democrats and 1 for an independent in the House.

Leadership posts also switched parties. Styles Bridges became president pro tem of the Senate, and Robert A. Taft became Senate majority leader. However, Taft died on July 31, 1953, shortly after the new session of Congress opened. California senator William Knowland then replaced him as majority leader. Lyndon Johnson, majority leader up to that time, assumed the post of Senate minority leader. In the House of Representatives, Joseph W. Martin, Jr., became speaker, and Charles Halleck of Indiana became majority leader.

During the Eighty-third Congress, Joseph McCarthy finally met his match. As chairman of the Senate's Permanent Investigating Subcommittee, he had persisted in waging smear campaigns against government agencies and consequently had created many enemies. From April to June, 1954, he was exposed as an unprincipled demagogue on national television during hearings with representatives of the U.S. Army. Afterward, the Senate voted to censure him by a vote of sixty-seven to twenty-two. That vote effectively end his reign of terror, and he died only three years later.

Eisenhower and the Congress The new Eisenhower administration pursued a policy of consensus-building with Congress, and Eisenhower's own style proved less confrontational than President Truman's had been. More reasoned and moderate dialogue and changes in congressional leadership increased the effectiveness of Congress in the post-McCarthy era.

One of the leading pieces of congressional legislated during the Eighty-third Congress was the Atomic Energy Act of 1954, which amended an act of the same name that had been passed in 1946. The new law allowed for dissemination and exchange of limited nuclear power information and technology with certain allies and for the furtherance of research into the peaceful application of atomic energy. To moderate the negative effects of the Immigration and Nationality Act of 1952, Congress passed the Refugee Relief Act of 1953, which authorized emergency immigration visas to up to 217,000 people who qualified as refugees, over a three-year span.

In 1953, Congress passed Public Law 280, which transferred the federal government's jurisdiction over criminal and civil cases on Native American reservations in most western states and Alaska to the individual state and territorial courts. The Espionage and Sabotage Act of 1954 allowed the death penalty to be imposed in cases of conviction for peacetime spying and sabotage against the United States.

The Eighty-fourth Congress, 1955-1956 In the midterm elections of 1954, the Democrats regained control of the Senate, by a margin of forty-eight to forty-seven, with one independent member. Walter George, a Democrat from Georgia, became president pro tem, and Lyndon Johnson rose to the position of majority leader—a post that he would hold until 1961, when he was elected vice president of the United States.

The Democrats also retook control of the House, with a majority of 232 to 203 over the Republicans. Sam Rayburn returned as speaker, and John McCormack as majority leader, with Carl Albert of Oklahoma assuming the post of majority whip. Joseph W. Martin returned as the Republicans' minority leader. Leslie Arends, who was the Republican whip, was the most enduring of the decade's congressional leaders: He held the post of Republican Party whip from 1943 to 1975.

With the self-destruction of McCarthyism and the growing influence of Lyndon Johnson in the Senate, the 1940's spirit of foreign affairs bipartisanship enjoyed a renaissance. Johnson and fellow Texan Sam Rayburn, the Speaker of the House, were arguably the most skillful political managers in Congress dur-

President Dwight D. Eisenhower delivering his first State of the Union address to a joint session of Congress on February 2, 1953. (AP/ Wide World Photos)

ing the 1950's. They had a talent for cooperating with the Republican Eisenhower administration and forming nonpartisan coalitions, while maintaining at least the necessary degree of solidarity within the Democratic Party. Johnson himself had long been committed to the idea of bipartisanship and would demonstrate increasing interest in international affairs as the decade wore on. The Formosa Resolution of January, 1955, was the earliest significant example of this renewed cooperation. Under its provisions, the president was authorized to take any necessary steps to safeguard Taiwan and the Pescadores Islands from threats by the People's Republic of China.

The Agricultural Act of 1956 (Title I of which became known as the Soil Bank Act, though it was not, strictly speaking, a separate piece of legislation) was designed to reduce the stocks of subsidized farm produce, and it authorized subsidies to farmers to remove land from production.

The Eighty-fifth Congress, 1957-1958 In the Eighty-fifth Congress, the Democratic Party widened its majority over the Republicans in the Senate to a margin of forty-nine to forty-seven. Carl Hayden of Arizona became Senate president pro tem, and William Knowland was again minority leader. Mike Mansfield of Montana replaced Earle C. Clements as majority whip, and Everett Dirksen of Illinois took up the post of minority whip. In the House, the new alignment was 234 Democrats and 201 Republicans. McCormack and Martin retained their posts as majority and minority leaders, as did the party whips, Albert and Arends.

Congress's vote to approve the Eisenhower Doctrine, in March, 1957, marked a further extension of bipartisanship. Through that resolution, Congress empowered the president to commit American troops in the Middle East in the event of threats to U.S. interests in that region.

A notorious highlight of the Eighty-fifth Congress

was South Carolina senator Strom Thurmond's record-setting twenty-four-hour filibuster, which he staged in an effort to block passage of the Civil Rights Act of 1957. That act, the first federal law of its kind since the Civil Rights Act of 1875, grew out of the Supreme Court's desegregation ruling in *Brown v. Board of Education* (1954), which many southern states resisted implementing. Another example of congressional resistance to civil rights was a document dubbed the Southern Manifesto, which denounced the *Brown* decision as unconstitutional. Ninety-six members of Congress signed that document in March, 1956.

Another important piece of legislation passed by the Eighty-fifth Congress was the National Interstate and Defense Highways Act of 1957. One of the most far-reaching measures of the decade, this legislation authorized the establishment of the interstate highway system. Through the National Defense Education Act of 1958, responding to what the bill termed an "educational emergency," the federal government allotted college loan funds on an incremental basis from 1959 to 1962, with provisions for fellowships and stipends and special grants.

As the presidential election of 1960 approached, Democratic leaders in Congress became more critical of the Eisenhower administration, particularly of its foreign policy decisions. Among the Democratic leaders who aspired to the presidency were Lyndon Johnson, Estes Kefauver, Hubert H. Humphrey, Stuart Symington, and John F. Kennedy.

The Eighty-sixth Congress, 1959-1960 The Eighty-sixth Congress witnessed a dramatic electoral upheaval as the Democrats assumed substantial control for the first time since 1951. The 1958 midterm elections put sixty-five Democrats in the Senate and only thirty-five Republicans. Carl Hayden once again became president pro tem of the Senate, but Everett Dirksen replaced William Knowland as Senate minority leader.

The House of Representatives also saw an increased Democratic majority: 282 Democrats to 153 Republicans. However, because conservative southern Democrats in both houses often aligned themselves with Republicans on certain key votes, the numerical disparity was not as significant as it appeared to be.

Among the important decisions made by the new Congress were votes to admit Alaska and Hawaii to the Union. The Landrum-Griffin Act of 1959—a response to the findings of the McClellan Committee—attempted to safeguard the rights of workers from abuses by organized labor. That law required unions to elect officers with secret ballots and generally required more accountability from union leaders.

Impact The Congresses of the 1950's faced unprecedented and diverse challenges, particularly in the fields of national defense and national security, civil rights and liberties, and labor-management relations. While they left a legislative record with significant accomplishments, the Congresses of the 1950's are generally viewed as being too eager to seek publicity—particularly in televised hearings—too quick to react to Cold War hysteria, and too slow to take important legislative initiatives.

Further Reading

Caro, Robert A. *The Years of Lyndon Johnson: Master of the Senate.* New York: Alfred A. Knopf, 2002. Analytical survey of the workings of the Senate leader and future president who may have been the most accomplished congressional politician of the 1950's.

Cheney, Richard, and Lynne B. Cheney. *Kings of the Hill: Power and Personality in the House of Representatives.* New York: Simon & Schuster, 1996. Profiles great leaders of the House of Representatives, including Sam Rayburn.

Diamond, Robert A., ed. *Powers of Congress.* Washington, D.C.: Congressional Quarterly, 1976. Focuses on areas of overlapping jurisdiction and conflicts between the legislative and executive branches.

Eisenhower, Dwight D. *Mandate for Change: The White House Years, 1953-56.* Garden City, N.Y.: Doubleday & Company, 1963. Necessarily biased point of view that sheds certain light on executive-legislative interaction at mid-decade.

Moore, John, ed. *Guide to U.S. Elections.* Washington, D.C.: Congressional Quarterly, 1994. Includes excellent summaries of both presidential and midterm elections, with abundant statistical information and tables.

Pemberton, William E. *Harry S. Truman: Fair Dealer and Cold Warrior.* Boston: Twayne Publishing, 1989. Highlights Truman's difficulties in dealing with the early 1950's Congresses.

Sundquist, James C. *The Decline and Resurgence of Congress.* Washington, D.C.: Brookings Institution,

1981. Critical view of Congress, which Sundquist sees as having been comparatively ineffectual during the 1950's.

Raymond Pierre Hylton

See also Army-McCarthy hearings; Celler-Kefauver Act of 1950; Civil Rights Act of 1957; Eisenhower Doctrine; Formosa Resolution; House Committee on Un-American Activities; Kefauver Committee; McClellan Committee; Rayburn, Sam; Southern Manifesto; Twenty-second Amendment.

■ Congress of Racial Equality

Identification Interracial civil rights organization
Date Founded in 1942

Better known by its acronym, CORE, the Congress of Racial Equality was the first modern civil rights organization to use civil disobedience in the form of sit-ins and freedom rides to destroy segregation.

CORE originated from within the Fellowship of Reconciliation (FOR) as the Committee of Racial Equality. In 1941, James Farmer, a committed pacifist and equal-rights worker, accepted a position with FOR as a race-relations secretary and speechmaker. In early 1942, he produced a plan to destroy segregation by implementing a nonviolent Gandhian philosophy of civil disobedience. He also organized one of the first sit-ins in a Chicago restaurant and co-founded CORE along with George Houser and Bayard Rustin. CORE held its first national conference in 1943, and two years later, it formally separated from FOR, renaming itself the Congress of Racial Equality.

In its first years, CORE depended on local chapters and volunteers, both white and black, to protest segregation. When CORE volunteers were refused entrance or service in restaurants and department stores, they would refuse to leave until served or admitted. In 1947, CORE and FOR joined forces to protest segregated seating on interstate buses. In what was known as the Journey of Reconciliation, volunteers who refused to move to segregated seating traveled on buses to the upper South. The Journey had little immediate impact on segregation, and four of the volunteers, including Bayard Rustin, were arrested.

The 1950's was a seminal decade in the development of CORE. In 1950, Jimmy Robinson became executive secretary of CORE. Although Robinson's fund-raising skills and photo-offset letters kept the organization afloat, it suffered from declining membership and disagreements over strategy in the first years of the decade. Lula Farmer served as the organization's accountant, and Jim Peck edited the *CORElator*, CORE's official publication. Both Farmer and Peck offered their services on a volunteer basis.

By the mid-1950's, Robinson's successful fund-raising techniques had reestablished the organization's viability. The Montgomery, Alabama, bus boycott, led by Martin Luther King, Jr., also breathed new life into the organization. CORE traveled to Montgomery to offer training in nonviolent resistance to bus boycotters. By the end of the 1950's, the organization had established fifty-three chapters throughout the United States and had moved its focus to the South.

Impact CORE was among the first civil rights organizations to use nonviolent protest and to reveal the national scope of segregation. During the 1950's, CORE established new chapters and relocated to the South, allowing it to assume a leadership role in the Civil Rights movement the following decade. CORE volunteers offered support and training to protesters, encouraged southern "sit-ins," and inspired the Freedom Rides across the South in 1961.

Subsequent Events In 1961, Farmer, who left CORE to work as a union organizer, returned to the organization to become the national director. CORE volunteers broadened their activities, participating in sit-ins in North Carolina, picketing grocery chains in Denver and Seattle, and fighting discrimination in trade unions in Philadelphia. CORE leaders also planned another integrated ride on interstate buses. Outside Anniston, Alabama, the first bus was assaulted and destroyed by firebombs. The riders of the second bus were arrested in Jackson, Mississippi, and incarcerated in the county jail and Parchman State Prison.

In 1964, three CORE volunteers, Andy Goodman, Mickey Schwerner, and James Chaney, were murdered during the Freedom Summer voter registration project. By the mid-1960's, many blacks in CORE became convinced that whites should not hold positions of leadership, and in 1966, CORE delegates to the national convention formally joined forces with the Black Power movement. Internal conflicts and debate over CORE's membership caused organizational decline during the late 1960's, and the organization slipped from the forefront of the Civil Rights movement.

Further Reading

Bell, Inge Powell. *CORE and the Strategy of Nonviolence.* New York: Random House, 1968. A contemporary exploration of the group's philosophies and strategies.

Farmer, James. *Lay Bare the Heart: An Autobiography of the Civil Rights Movement.* New York: Arbor House, 1985. Farmer's memoirs of his experiences within CORE.

Yvonne Johnson

See also African Americans; *Brown v. Board of Education*; Civil Rights movement; Liberalism in U.S. politics; *National Association for the Advancement of Colored People v. Alabama*; Southern Christian Leadership Conference.

■ Connolly, Maureen

Identification American tennis player
Born September 17, 1934; San Diego, California
Died June 21, 1969; Dallas, Texas

Maureen Connolly was the world's top female tennis player during the early 1950's, winning nine major tournaments and tennis's grand slam, all before she turned twenty years of age.

Unable to afford horseback riding lessons, Connolly began playing tennis at age nine and demonstrated a natural talent for the game. She caught the eye of the Southern California tennis establishment and quickly advanced to the national scene. In 1949, at the age of fourteen, she became the youngest champion of the U.S. Junior Girls team.

Connolly had already earned a reputation as a determined competitor, and she would commonly put together significant winning streaks. Only five feet, four inches tall, Connolly had strength and accuracy that soon earned her the affectionate nickname "Little Mo." As a sixteen-year-old, she won her first U.S. Championship singles title in 1951, impressing everyone with her strong determination. The following year she conquered Wimbledon, and in 1953 she became the first woman ever to win tennis's grand slam. Her Wightman Cup record was a perfect nine wins and no defeats. Her last major championship was a third consecutive Wimbledon, solidifying her as a popular and inspiring tennis champion.

Sixteen-year-old Maureen Connolly, shortly after winning the Women's National Lawn Tennis Championships at Forest Hills, New York, in September, 1951. (AP/Wide World Photos)

Connolly announced her premature retirement in 1954, following an unusual horseback-riding accident. The next year she married Norman Brinker, with whom she had two daughters. Occasional exhibitions, tennis lessons, and promotions kept her involved in the game she loved.

Impact Connolly was voted the Associated Press woman athlete of the year for three consecutive years, 1951-1953. Though the injury ended her competitive career, her legacy continued with the establishment of the Maureen Connolly Brinker Tennis Foundation, organized shortly before her death in 1969 to promote opportunities for aspiring young players.

Further Reading

Brinker-Simmons, Cindy. *Little Mo's Legacy: A Mother's Lessons, a Daughter's Story.* Irving, Tex.: Tapestry Press, 2001. Connolly's daughter's reflections on growing up as the child of a tennis legend.

King, Billie Jean. *We Have Come a Long Way: The Story of Women's Tennis.* New York: McGraw-Hill, 1988. King explores the history of women's tennis, including the way in which Little Mo helped shape the game.

P. Graham Hatcher

See also Gonzáles, Pancho; Sports; Tennis.

■ Connolly, Olga

Identification Czechoslovakian athlete who married an American athlete she met at the Olympics

Born November 13, 1932; Prague, Czechoslovakia

At a time of hostility between the United States and the Soviet bloc, the love story of Olga and Harold Connolly captured the imagination of Americans.

In 1956, Olga Fikotova represented Czechoslovakia at the Melbourne Olympics, winning the gold medal in the discus throw. While competing there, she met American hammer thrower Harold Connolly, who also won a gold medal in his event. They fell in love, and Connolly proposed marriage to her. However, the tensions between East and West meant that the couple had to return to their homelands.

The two lovers corresponded, and in early 1957, Harold Connolly traveled to Czechoslovakia to ask President Antonin Novotny to allow them to marry and live in the United States. After a bit of encouragement from the U.S. State Department, Novotny agreed. Harold and Olga were married on March 27, 1957, with legendary Czechoslovakian distance runner Emil Zatopek serving as best man. They then returned to the United States to live, and Olga took Connolly as her last name. In 1960, both competed for the United States in the Olympics, though neither won a medal.

Impact The story of love across the Iron Curtain inspired many. Olga Connolly remained a successful athlete, breaking the American women's discus record four times. She competed in later Olympic Games but did not win additional medals. The love

Harold and Olga Connolly during their honeymoon. (AP/Wide World Photos)

story did not last forever, however. The Connollys divorced in 1975, and Harold married another athlete, Patricia Winslow. Olga Connolly remained in the United States and later started the Olympic Truce movement to encourage nations to put aside their conflicts during the Olympics, as symbolized by her own love story.

Further Reading

Connolly, Olga. *The Rings of Destiny*. New York: D. McKay, 1968. Connolly's autobiography.

Schaap, Dick. *An Illustrated History of the Olympics*. 3d ed. New York: Knopf, 1976. A children's book that covers the Connolly romance.

Arthur D. Hlavaty

See also Cold War; Olympic Games of 1956; Sports.

■ Conservatism in U.S. politics

Definition American political ideology that embraced anticommunist efforts and worked against federal intervention in business and individual rights

The Cold War, high inflation, the unpopularity of the Truman administration, the Korean War, and public fear of communism contributed to landslide Republican victories in the national elections of 1952, the development of an influential conservative intellectual movement, and a public rejection of liberal social welfare programs during the 1950's.

The word "conservative" is often used to describe many aspects of the United States during the 1950's: social, economic, cultural, political, and even psychological. Before 1950, conservatism was often identified with an ideology that opposed the New Deal and Fair Deal in domestic policies; that is, liberal Democratic programs and proposals in social welfare, the economy, civil rights, health care, and education that often required greater power and spending by the federal government.

Although conservative intellectuals and activists who emphasized social and cultural issues did not achieve significant national political influence until the 1980's, they were influenced by Russell Kirk's book *The Conservative Mind* (1953). Unlike most conservatives of the 1950's, Kirk perceived American corporate capitalism, automation in industry, and consumerism to be almost as detrimental to traditional Western political, moral, religious, and intellectual values as communism. Consequently, Kirk rejected the probusiness emphasis of many conservatives.

In foreign policy, conservatism was either ambivalent or hostile toward the bipartisan internationalism of the Roosevelt and Truman administrations, which emphasized the United Nations (U.N.), substantial foreign economic aid, and collective security alliances such as the North Atlantic Treaty Organization (NATO). Within the two-party system, conservatism in national politics in general and within Congress in particular was personified by Republican senator Robert A. Taft of Ohio. Taft was widely regarded as the spokesman of the right wing of the Republican Party and for conservative ideas and policies. He was dubbed "Mr. Republican" but was never nominated for president and died in 1953.

Following the Republican nomination of Wendell Willkie, a former Democrat, for president in 1940, the Taft-led conservative wing of the Republican Party resented the domination of its party's presidential nominations and platforms by moderate and liberal Republicans. Immediately after World War II, most conservative intellectuals, such as essayist Frank Meyer and economist Friedrich A. Hayek, saw little hope in achieving conservative domination of the Republican Party in the near future. Instead, they tried to influence public opinion by publishing books and articles on economics, foreign policy, and culture. In foreign policy, though, there was a conflict between the conservatives who wanted more aggressive foreign and defense policies against communism and those who desired a return to isolationism.

Anticommunism In 1949 and 1950, several major events dramatized the dangers of domestic and international communism. Their cumulative political effect energized and united American conservatives, strengthened their influence on the Republican Party, and made conservative criticism of the Truman administration's anticommunist policies more credible and appealing to the American public. During these two years, the Soviet Union, benefiting from secrets obtained from American communist spies, exploded its first atomic bomb; communists led by Mao Zedong gained control of China; the Korean War began; and Alger Hiss, a former State Department official, was convicted of perjury because of his testimony before the House Committee on

Un-American Activities (HUAC). Richard M. Nixon, a Republican congressman from California and HUAC member, was instrumental in finding evidence against Hiss. Nixon was elected to the Senate in 1950 as a harsh critic of Democratic foreign and domestic policies toward communism. Public frustration with the stalemate in the Korean War also contributed to the Republican gains of five Senate seats and twenty-eight House seats during the 1950 congressional elections.

Even more than Nixon or General Douglas MacArthur, who insisted on "total victory" in the Korean War, Republican senator Joseph R. McCarthy of Wisconsin popularized militant anticommunism as the foundation of conservatism during the 1950's. In a February 11, 1950, speech in West Virginia, McCarthy claimed that there were known communists working in the State Department. For the next four years, a political phenomenon known as McCarthyism pervaded American society. McCarthy failed to prove his most specific, extreme charges of communist infiltration and subversion of American foreign policy. Nevertheless, McCarthy's frequent, dramatic, and widely publicized assertions that the Truman administration and liberal Democrats were incompetent and even treasonous in their treatment of communism made McCarthyism the most appealing aspect of conservatism for many American voters during the early 1950's. McCarthyism influenced Dwight D. Eisenhower's presidential campaign rhetoric in 1952, his choice of Nixon as his running mate, and split-ticket voting among Roman Catholic and southern Democrats, which arguably contributed to the Republican capture of the presidency and Congress during the 1952 elections.

The Eisenhower Administration Conservative intellectuals and activists—especially libertarians wanting less federal intervention on economic and social welfare issues and anticommunist militants seeking an aggressive "rollback" of communism in Eastern Europe and elsewhere—were soon disappointed with the Eisenhower administration. In domestic policy, Eisenhower did not threaten the legacy of New Deal and Fair Deal liberalism. Furthermore, he consolidated many of these domestic programs by creating the Department of Health, Education, and Welfare (HEW). Eisenhower also approved the expansion of Social Security coverage and greater federal funding and regulations for education, high-

ways, and urban renewal. Conservatives, who were alarmed at what they regarded as a gradual loss of American sovereignty and independence in foreign policy, perceived Eisenhower's foreign policy to be too similar to that of Roosevelt and Truman, especially because of Eisenhower's emphasis on the United Nations, NATO, and bipartisan cooperation in Congress.

Conservatives soon scorned Eisenhower as another "me too" moderate Republican whose ideas and policies did not provide a distinctly conservative alternative to the liberalism of nonsouthern Democrats. The brief popularity that Eisenhower enjoyed among conservative southern Democrats ended shortly after he appointed Earl Warren, a liberal Republican, as chief justice of the United States in 1953. Warren wrote the court's unanimous 1954 *Brown v. Board of Education* decision, which ordered the racial integration of public schools. Warren continued to lead the Supreme Court in making liberal decisions on civil rights and civil liberties that outraged conservatives throughout the 1950's and 1960's.

After Democrats regained control of Congress during the 1954 elections, President Eisenhower further enhanced his centrist, bipartisan policy behavior, especially in foreign policy. He developed a cooperative, constructive relationship with Democratic congressional leaders, especially Speaker of the House Sam Rayburn and Senate Majority Leader Lyndon B. Johnson. American voters during the mid-1950's seemed to prefer this bipartisan centrism, as Eisenhower was reelected by a landslide and the Democrats gained seats in Congress during the 1956 elections. The most prominent domestic legislative accomplishments reflecting bipartisan moderation and cooperation during Eisenhower's second term were the Civil Rights Act of 1957, the National Defense Education Act of 1958, and the Landrum-Griffin labor reform law of 1959.

Conservative Publications and Organizations Frustrated by their failure significantly to influence the Eisenhower presidency, voters, and public opinion, conservatives resumed their effort to formulate a more persuasive, popular ideology through publications, radio programs, and conservative organizations independent of the Republican Party. By the end of the 1950's, *National Review* and *Human Events* were the most prominent conservative magazines.

In addition to articulating and advocating conservative ideas, they tried to unite the different, sometimes conflicting, factions of conservatives, such as economic libertarians and social conservatives, and move the Republican Party to the right by persuading more Americans to become conservatives. Various conservative student organizations united and became the Young Americans for Freedom (YAF) in 1960. In 1958, Robert Welch established the John Birch Society, an organization that expressed a McCarthyistic, conspiratorial type of militant anticommunism. Welch's most dramatic accusation was that President Eisenhower and Secretary of State John Foster Dulles were communist agents. William F. Buckley, Jr., a founder of the *National Review*, the YAF, and the Conservative Party of New York, along with other conservative activists, later denounced Welch.

Barry Goldwater After Senator Taft's death in 1953 and Senator McCarthy's political decline in 1954, conservatives lacked a prominent, unifying spokesman for their ideology in Congress until the national emergence of Republican senator Barry Goldwater of Arizona during the late 1950's. Goldwater won a narrow, upset victory in the 1952 Senate race and was reelected by a wider margin in 1958, despite a Democratic sweep of that year's congressional elections. Goldwater's conservatism was a combination of economic libertarianism, the protection of states' rights and individual liberty against greater federal intervention, and aggressive anticommunism. Its tone was a straightforward, principled sincerity that appealed to conservative activists and intellectuals, the right wing of the Republican Party, and a growing number of American voters. In particular, Goldwater's clear, consistent opposition to civil rights legislation and court decisions attracted not only white southern Democrats but also other Americans who believed that conservative opposition to federal intervention in civil rights could be nonracist and politically feasible nationally.

Impact The intellectual and political activities and contributions of the conservatives of the 1950's did not develop a broad national appeal by the end of the decade. The Democratic sweep of the 1958 midterm elections and the narrow victory of Democratic senator John F. Kennedy during the 1960 presidential election seemed to indicate that most Americans wanted more liberal domestic policies and the con-

tinuation of a centrist, bipartisan approach in Cold War foreign and defense policies.

Conservatism in American politics during the 1950's is often associated with such individuals, events, and ideas as Eisenhower, Taft, McCarthyism, and hostility to the *Brown* decision and the early Civil Rights movement. Despite the popular perception of the Eisenhower presidency as the exemplification of 1950's conservatism, many conservatives felt alienated from Eisenhower and the Republican Party because of the cautious, bipartisan centrism that characterized many of his policies and those of most mainstream Republican politicians. Nevertheless, the 1950's was a crucial decade for the development, synthesis, and advocacy of conservative ideas on social, economic, and foreign policy issues that eventually dominated the Republican Party and then the nation by the 1980's.

Further Reading

Buckley, William F., Jr. *Up from Liberalism.* New York: McDowell, Obolensky, 1959. Buckley's contemporary explanation of why he rejected the liberalism that dominated American politics and higher education.

Kirk, Russell. *The Conservative Mind.* Chicago: Regnery, 1953. A study of the origins of conservative Western political, religious, social, and cultural values and how modern capitalism and liberalism threaten them.

Muccigrosso, Robert. *Basic History of American Conservatism.* Malabar, Fla.: Krieger, 2001. A two-part book that examines the history of conservatism and then provides key texts, such as Goldwater's speech opposing the Civil Rights Act of 1964, that helped defined the movement.

Nash, George H. *The Conservative Intellectual Movement in America Since 1945.* Wilmington, Del.: Intercollegiate Studies Institute, 1996. A survey and analysis of the major intellectuals, activists, publications, and organizations of post-World War II American conservatism with an especially strong focus on the 1950's and early 1960's.

Sean J. Savage

See also Cold War; Eisenhower, Dwight D.; Elections in the United States, midterm; Elections in the United States, 1952; Elections in the United States, 1956; *God and Man at Yale*; John Birch Society; Korean War; McCarthy, Joseph; Truman Doctrine; Twenty-second Amendment; Veterans organizations.

■ Continentalism

Definition Government policies and factors that promote the political, economic, and cultural integration of the North American countries

Continentalist trends accelerated during the 1950's and became an important political, economic, and cultural issue for Canadians.

The concept of "continentalism" has occasionally arisen as a lively issue in Canadian history. In Canada's early period of nationhood, continentalism was frequently associated with a perceived U.S. threat to absorb Canada in its process of expansion. Although this threat subsided, the more sensitive or potentially negative aspects of continentalism subsequently surfaced at various times, especially in connection with opposition to proposed free trade pacts. A continuing trend of ever closer Canadian-U.S. relations and a gradual weakening of the British connection began with Canada's involvement in World War I. This pattern accelerated in World War II as Liberal prime minister William Lyon Mackenzie King and American president Franklin D. Roosevelt cultivated a warm friendship and cooperated on many levels in the wartime effort. In the meantime, American popular culture was making headway in Canada.

Trade, Military, and Cultural Influences Under Prime Minister Louis St. Laurent, whose tenure spanned 1948 to 1957, government policy encouraged further U.S.-Canadian linkages and integration into a continental system. St. Laurent's government eagerly sought foreign capital as a means of sustaining a period of economic boom and growth. One consequence was a powerful American presence in Canada's economy. This period saw the rise of the large multinational corporation with headquarters in the United States and a branch operation in Canada. By 1959, 34 percent of Canadian industry was foreign owned, with 29 percent in American hands. American capital dominated in oil, gas, mining operations, and manufacturing. Foreign trade also exhibited growing continentalist tendencies. By 1957, Canada was swiftly becoming integrated into the American trading market. It was becoming evident that Canada was a North American country whose trade and financial connections would be with the United States rather than Britain. Can-

ada also set the value of its dollar in terms of the American dollar.

During the Cold War era, concern over a possible Soviet bomber or missile attack brought increasing integration of Canadian forces into a common defense network. By 1957, the Distant Early Warning Line (DEW Line), a radar and communications network constructed by an American firm, stretched across the Arctic. Then, in 1956, discussions began about developing a coordinated air defense program.

Culture was another area area where continentalist trends were evident. During the 1950's, American cinema, magazines, radio, and television influenced a majority of Canadians, many of whom resided near the international border. Maintenance of a distinct Canadian national and cultural identity became a concern among Canadian intellectuals. In 1951, a special royal commission formed to address the current state of culture and the arts and issued the Massey Report, named after its chairman, Vincent Massey. The report inaugurated state support for the arts and Canadian scholarship, which ostensibly was used to offset the effects of American mass culture.

Dissension and Debate Until 1957, objections to policies bringing continental integration were not in evidence. However, some began to raise concerns about the branch-plant economy and the dangers of becoming a cultural colony and military satellite of the United States. A royal commission on Canada's economic prospects observed that no other nation as highly industrialized as Canada had so much of its industry under the control of foreign interests. Nationalistic views surfaced in a 1957 debate over a natural gas pipeline energy project. Opposition forces led by Progressive Conservative leader John Diefenbaker objected to the presence of American capital in the pipeline construction and favored giving the contract to a Canadian firm. When the government used a parliamentary device to shut off debate, it was accused of arrogance and of ignoring legitimate nationalist concerns. In an ensuing election, the Conservatives upset the long-ruling Liberals. Diefenbaker, a conservative nationalist, became prime minister. Diefenbaker's vision for Canada included promises to try and halt the transfer of Canadian industry and natural resources into the control of American capital, to restore Canada's traditional close relations with the British Commonwealth, and to put an end to its subservient acceptance of American policy.

During his tenure as prime minister from 1957 to 1963, Diefenbaker found it hard to reverse powerful trends that had been in motion for more than four decades, including the decline of the British Empire and the growth of a continentally organized North America. Diefenbaker's plan to divert 15 percent of all Canada's imports from the United States to the Commonwealth was thwarted by Britain's interest in the European Common Market and by policy restrictions that accompanied membership in the General Agreement on Tariffs and Trade (GATT) organization. Although he occasionally defied U.S. policy on certain issues, Diefenbaker accepted further military commitments that bound Canada to the United States. In 1957, he apparently decided that the earlier agreements on a joint air defense system had gone too far to be rejected. The new North American Aerospace Defense Command (NORAD) had a American commander in chief and a Canadian second in command. At the end of his tenure, Diefenbaker failed to strengthen or improve Anglo-Canadian relations, and his time in office witnessed Canada's more complete identification in a continental defense system.

Impact Despite determined opposition from some Canadians during the 1950's, continentalism continued as a powerful force and helped lead to developments such as the 1994 North American Free Trade Agreement (NAFTA). In his work *Lament for a Nation: The Defeat of Canadian Nationalism* (1965), the conservative nationalist scholar George Grant concluded that Diefenbaker's efforts to maintain a conservative nationalist tradition had little chance of success against modernizing forces of universalism and homogeneity.

Further Reading

Bothwell, Robert, Ian Drummond, and John English. *Canada Since 1945: Power, Politics, and Provincialism.* Rev. ed. Toronto: University of Toronto Press, 1989. Informative treatment of Canadian political, economic, and cultural developments during the postwar decades.

Creighton, Donald. *The Forked Road: Canada, 1939-1957.* Toronto: McClelland & Stewart, 1976. Monograph by a prominent Canadian historian reflecting a conservative nationalist viewpoint.

Grant, George. *Lament for a Nation: The Defeat of Canadian Nationalism.* Montreal: McGill-Queens University Press, 2003. Another important conservative nationalist treatment of this period but much shorter that Creighton's work.

Thompson, John Herd, and Stephen J. Randall. *Canada and the United States: Ambivalent Allies.* 3d ed. Athens: University of Georgia Press, 2002. Definitive work on Canadian-U.S. relations from the American Revolution to present times.

David A. Crain

See also Atomic Energy of Canada, Ltd.; Canada and Great Britain; Canada and U.S. investments; Canadian Labour Congress; DEW Line; Diefenbaker, John G.; Foreign policy of Canada; Foreign policy of the United States; International trade of Canada; North American Aerospace Defense Command; St. Laurent, Louis; Trans-Canada Highway.

■ Cooke, Sam

Identification: African American singer
Born: January 22, 1931; Clarksdale, Mississippi
Died: December 11, 1964; Los Angeles, California

Cooke was one of the first African American artists to cross over successfully from gospel to popular music. His vocal ability and broad commercial appeal laid the foundation for what came to be known as soul music.

Cooke began singing in his father's church when he was a child. He joined the legendary Soul Stirrers when he was nineteen and soared to the top of the gospel charts as their featured singer. He then made the difficult transition to pop music in 1957 with his number-one single "You Send Me." His gospel fans were deeply shocked and found it difficult to reconcile their love for Cooke's gospel music with his unexpected transition into the world of popular music. Cooke, however, refused to be bound by contemporary music categories and was equally skilled in performing romantic ballads, rhythm-and-blues songs, and pop tunes. During the 1960's, Cooke wrote such hits as "Cupid," "Bring It on Home to Me," and the hauntingly beautiful "A Change Is Gonna Come," which was considered by many young civil rights workers to be an unofficial anthem of the movement.

Impact Cooke succeeded during an era when social, cultural, and legal standards began to be forcefully challenged, and his music was instrumental in breaking down cultural and racial barriers during the decade. The sterling quality of his tenor voice and the deep, rhythmic emotion of his music appealed to a youthful audience of African American and white fans who were ready for new experiences.

Cooke's wide-ranging popularity ushered in the new cultural era of soul music that grew exponentially in the coming years. His career inspired other gospel singers, such as Aretha Franklin, to enter the pop music world. Cooke's controversial shooting death in a Los Angeles motel in 1964 brought a premature and tragic end to a great talent.

Further Reading

Cooke, Sam. *Sam Cooke: Portrait of a Legend, 1951-1964.* New York: Warner Bros., 2004. Posthumously published collection of Cooke's music with arrangements for piano and guitar.

Wolff, Daniel, et al. *You Send Me: The Life and Times of Sam Cooke.* New York: HarperCollins, 1995. Full-length biography of Cooke that examines his untimely death and includes a complete discography of his music.

Paul Alkebulan

See also Baby boomers; Rock and roll; Youth culture and the generation gap.

■ Corso, Gregory

Identification American poet, educator, and philosopher
Born March 26, 1930; Greenwich Village, New York
Died January 17, 2001; Robbinsdale, Minnesota

Corso came to symbolize the nonconformist lifestyles and literary talents of the Beat generation and inspired social activist writers of the 1960's.

Born to an unwed sixteen-year-old mother during the Great Depression, Gregory Corso endured a truly miserable childhood. After being abandoned by his mother, he was reared in a succession of foster homes. He was incarcerated on theft charges, but he put the time to good use by constantly reading poetry and writing some of his own. Upon his release in 1950, Corso met fellow writer Allen Ginsberg, an encounter that would transform both of their lives.

Beat Generation Icon Allen Ginsberg was a monumental influence on Corso, encouraging his writing and introducing him to Jack Kerouac, William Bur-

roughs, and other talented, nontraditional literary figures. Corso's first collection of poetry was published in 1954, but it was the release of another collection, *Gasoline,* in 1958 that cemented his reputation. During the late 1950's, often accompanied by Ginsberg, Corso crossed the nation giving a series of unconventional readings, which made him a nationally known figure. By the mid-1960's, his fame had declined but he continued to publish, teach, and do some acting. In 2001, he had recently finished a volume of poetry when he died in his sleep at his daughter's home in Minnesota.

Impact Corso's voluminous writings and association with Ginsberg and Kerouac contributed to his reputation as a leader of the social movement marked by nonconformist and disenchanted creative artists, broadly called the Beat generation.

Further Reading

Miles, Barry. *The Beat Hotel: Ginsberg, Burroughs, and Corso in Paris, 1958-1963.* New York: Grove Press, 2000. A narrative about the Beat poets' tenure in Paris, based almost entirely on primary data such as diaries, interviews, and letters.

Watson, Steven. *The Birth of the Beat Generation: Visionaries, Rebels, and Hipsters, 1944-1960.* New York: Pantheon Books, 1995. Focuses primarily on Kerouac, Burroughs, and Ginsberg, although Corso features prominently as well. Examines how the poets came to associate with, and influenced, one another.

Thomas W. Buchanan

See also Beat generation; Ginsberg, Allen; Kerouac, Jack; Literature in the United States; Poetry; San Francisco Renaissance.

■ Cousy, Bob

Identification Professional basketball player
Born August 9, 1928; New York, New York

Bob Cousy helped transform the game of professional basketball into a fast-paced sport in the days before the shot clock arrived to force quick turnovers.

Robert Joseph Cousy will long be remembered as one of the all-time great basketball players. A flashy player at a time when the set shot still dominated basketball, he developed a razzle-dazzle style that resulted in part from an accident as a thirteen-year-old. A broken right arm inspired Cousy to learn to dribble and shoot with his left hand. His resulting ambidexterity led to him becoming a star player first in high school and later at Holy Cross College and in the National Basketball Association (NBA). His skill at dribbling behind his back, as well as making other plays that were virtually unknown during the 1940's, turned him into a star. Cousy was a small man for a professional basketball player, standing six-foot-one and weighting only 175 pounds; however, his passion and skills made him a three-time All-American in college. Drafted by the Tri-Cities Blackhawks in 1950, Cousy was traded to the Chicago Stags. That franchise dissolved soon after, and Cousy joined the Boston Celtics.

Impact Beginning with the 1952-1953 season, Cousy, a point guard, garnered eight consecutive assists ti-

The Boston Celtics' Basketball Hall of Fame guard Bob Cousy, in 1953. (AP/Wide World Photos)

tles. Over his career, he averaged 7.5 assists per game. Fellow players still describe him as an absolute offensive master, a player who truly earned his nickname as "the Houdini of the Hardwood." Cousy retired in 1963 at the age of thirty-five, having helped the Celtics win five straight NBA championships. He coached at Boston College for six years, then moved back to professional sports as coach of the Cincinnati Royals.

Subsequent Events In 1974, Cousy left coaching for sports broadcasting as a commentator and announcer for the Celtics and served as commissioner of the American Soccer League. In 1989, he became the first player inducted into the Basketball Hall of Fame to serve as the organization's president.

Further Reading

Berger, Phil. *Heroes of Pro Basketball.* New York: Random House, 1968. Cousy is included in discussions of great basketball players.

Devaney, John. *Bob Cousy.* New York: Putnam House, 1965. Provides a good discussion of Cousy's career during the 1950's.

Grabowski, John F. *The Boston Celtics.* San Diego, Calif.: Lucent Books, 2002. Details the rise of the Boston Celtics dynasty and the people and players who made it happen.

Nancy Farm Mannikko

See also Basketball; Chamberlain, Wilt; Sports.

■ *Creature from the Black Lagoon*

Identification Film about a prehistoric creature discovered in South America
Date Released in 1954
Director Jack Arnold (1916-1992)

One of the most enduring horror films of the 1950's, Creature from the Black Lagoon *has joined the pantheon of all-time classic monster films.*

Universal Pictures made *Creature from the Black Lagoon* in 1954 to take advantage of the 3-D movie craze. However, the craze was dying as the film was being released, so the film was rarely shown in its original 3-D format. Nevertheless, the black-and-white film proved to be one of the most successful horror or science-fiction films of the 1950's, and it contributed one of the classic screen monsters to film lore: the gill man.

The film's story is based on a theme familiar for its time: A team of well-meaning scientists (actors Richard Carlson, Richard Denning, Whit Bissell, and Julia Adams) take a boat up a remote South American river, hoping to find additional evidence of an exciting new fossil discovery. Instead, they find a living specimen of the fossil's species, one previously unknown to science, that traps them in a lagoon and threatens all their lives. Apparently a survivor from a prehistoric age, the creature is an intelligent aquatic animal that closely resembles a human man in size and form. The creature appears only rarely in the film, but H. J. Slater's musical score builds tension by frequently signaling when he is nearby. As is the case in the best-made horror films, *Creature from the Black Lagoon*'s most frightening moments occur when audiences merely anticipate the creature's appearance.

The gill man in *Creature from the Black Lagoon* follows in the tradition of the great Universal monster films of earlier decades, such as *King Kong* (1933), *Frankenstein* (1931) and its sequels, and *The Wolf Man* (1941), in being at once frightening and sympathetic. Although audiences can only surmise that the creature wants to kill the members of the scientific party for having invaded and threatened his domain, he is portrayed as a creature with human feelings, particularly because of his evident infatuation with the party's sole female member, the beautiful Julia Adams. In the film's most lyrical scene, the gill man performs a beautiful underwater ballet (well suited for 3-D) with an unknowing Adams, who is swimming near the surface of the lagoon. The film ends in a scene reminiscent of the beauty-and-the-beast climax of *King Kong*, with the gill man attempting to carry away the woman, only to be overtaken and killed.

Sequels The popularity of *Creature from the Black Lagoon* inspired two quick, and less engaging, sequels. In the first, *Revenge of the Creature* (1955), the gill man proves not to have died in the original film, after all—much as the monster in *Frankenstein* survives his apparent death at that film's climax. The gill man is captured and taken to an aquatic park in the United States, only to escape and endure an ending similar to that of the first film. In *The Creature Walks Among Us* (1956), the gill man is recaptured. After losing his gills in a fire, he is surgically transformed into an air-breathing creature. In this film he appears to die his final death, and so does the series.

Impact The legacy of *Creature from the Black Lagoon* is assured by the familiarity of its title and by the instantly recognizable face of the gill man. However, its impact on film history is both deeper and subtler. The film is a direct ancestor of Stephen Spielberg's 1975 thriller about a human-eating great white shark, *Jaws*. Both films frighten audiences by playing on their fears of the unknown—both figuratively and literally, fears of what lies just below the surface.

Further Reading

Fry, Ron, and Pamela Fourzon. *The Saga of Special Effects.* Englewood Cliffs, N.J.: Prentice-Hall, 1977. Study of the technical aspects of special effects that includes a chapter titled "The Creature-Ridden Fifties."

Skal, David J. *The Monster Show: A Cultural History of Horror.* New York: W. W. Norton, 1993. Survey of the horror film genre and its impact on popular American culture.

Thorne, Ian, and Howard Schroeder. *Creature from the Black Lagoon.* Morristown, N.J.: Silver Burdett Press, 1982. Illustrated novelization of the film, with an essay on the film's production that includes a discussion of its 3-D process.

R. Kent Rasmussen

See also Film in the United States; *Invasion of the Body Snatchers; Thing from Another World, The; War of the Worlds, The;* Wood, Ed.

■ Cuban Revolution

The Event Communist takeover of the Cuban government
Date 1956-1959

After Fidel Castro took over the Cuban government in 1959, President Dwight D. Eisenhower's administration reacted strongly to the new regime's agenda, especially the seizure of U.S. property without fair market compensation.

During the 1950's, Cuba and the United States were closely intertwined. Thousands of Americans, including author Ernest Hemingway and actor Errol Flynn, lived on the island. American gangsters such as Meyer Lansky built impressive casinos for tourists. U.S. investors owned and controlled a significant percentage of the island's economy, which was largely dependent on the fluctuating international market for sugar, and Cubans often resented their more prosperous neighbor. Although the per-capita income of Cubans was only about 20 percent of that of Americans, the island had the third-highest per-capita income of the Latin American countries.

Dictator Fulgencio Batista y Zaldívar, a former army commander, dominated Cuban politics from 1934 to 1959. During his tenure, he presided over mild reforms, which included limited land reform and support for labor unions. His second term as president was enabled by a military *coup d'état* and was characterized by brutal repression: He suspended the liberal constitution of 1940, censored the press, authorized torture, and jailed opponents. The U.S. government nevertheless supported Batista with arms and economic assistance.

The Path to Revolution Until the late 1950's, Fidel Castro appeared to be committed to a left-of-center, noncommunist ideology. He was affiliated with the Cuban People's (or Orthodoxo) Party, which advo-cated clean government and mild programs of social reform. On July 26, 1953, Castro led a small group of rebels in an attempt to take the Moncada army barracks near Santiago de Cuba. This "July 26 Movement" called for a return to the Constitution of 1940, education reform, limited land redistribution, and an end to political corruption. The attack failed, but Castro's defiant speech at his trial, known as his "History Will Absolve Me" speech, made him a national hero. Although he was given a fifteen-year jail sentence, he was released in a general amnesty in 1955.

After his release, Castro moved to Mexico to organize an anti-Batista group and visited the United States several times to raise money. He was not committed completely to the Marxist-Leninist ideology, even though his closest associates included a few communists, most notably his brother Raúl Castro and Ernesto (Che) Guevara. In 1956, Castro and eighty-one other rebels boarded the small boat *Granma* and sailed for Cuba. After their first battles were unsuccessful, Castro and a small band of survivors escaped into the Sierra Maestra of eastern Cuba, from where they carried out guerrilla raids. In February, 1957, Castro was interviewed by Herbert Matthews, a well-known writer for *The New York Times*. Matthews's story romanticized Castro's movement, helping to attract international financial support as well as additional recruits.

As Batista's position weakened, the Eisenhower administration decided to dissociate itself from the despised dictator. In 1957, the administration insisted that the Cuban military could not use American-supplied military equipment in domestic conflicts. In 1958, it suspended all arms shipments to Cuba. Without American assistance, Batista had no hope of defeating the rebels. On January 1, 1959, he and his closest allies fled to Miami. Guevara entered Havana and occupied key military points. A few days later, Castro arrived at the capital to the enthusiastic cheers of most inhabitants. For the

Rebel leader Fidel Castro (with cigar) shortly before his triumphal arrival in Havana in January, 1959. (AP/Wide World Photos)

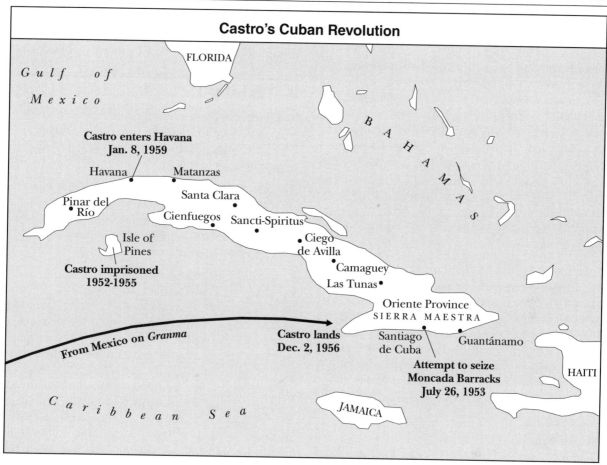

Castro's Cuban Revolution

figurehead leaders, Castro chose anti-Batista liberals, including Manuel Urrutia as president and José Cardona as prime minister.

U.S. Relations with Castro's Government During 1959, relations between the United States and Castro rapidly deteriorated. In April, when Castro visited Washington, Vice President Richard M. Nixon concluded that Castro was procommunist. By this time, Castro's left-leaning policies included redistribution of land ownership, centralized planning, executions of Batista's officers, and a rejection of multiparty elections. These policies alienated Castro's middle-class supporters. In July, President Urrutia was replaced by Osvaldo Dorticós Torrado, and Prime Minister Cardona was replaced by Castro. A few months later, the chief military leader of the revolution, Major Huber Matos, a prominent anticommunist, was imprisoned for treason and for disrupting agrarian reform. In November,

the Eisenhower administration decided to work with Cuban dissidents in Cuba in order to overthrow Castro.

In February of 1960, Castro signed a five-year trading agreement with the Soviet Union. Shortly thereafter, he publicly accused the Central Intelligence Agency (CIA) of responsibility for an explosion of a small arms shipment in a Havana harbor. On March 17, Eisenhower approved "A Program of Covert Action Against the Castro Regime," which authorized the CIA to spend thirteen million dollars to train Cuban exiles for an invasion of the island. In July, the Cuban government passed a law providing for the expropriation of foreign-owned property in Cuba. Eisenhower responded by reducing the purchase of Cuban sugar by 95 percent. Castro, in turn, nationalized numerous American-owned properties. On August 16, the CIA launched an attempt to assassinate Castro with poisoned cigars, and in October, Eisenhower ordered a full trade embargo, an action that set off a new wave of American-property seizures.

Impact The trade embargo and the antagonistic relationship established in 1959-1960 between the two countries continued well into the first decade of the twenty-first century. During his first two decades in power, Castro had limited success in popularizing socialist ideas within many of the less-developed countries of the world. Some historians argue that Eisenhower's anti-Castro policies pushed Castro in a far-left direction to secure his political survival. Other historians think that Castro's actions were determined primarily by the logic of his ideological convictions.

Subsequent Events On January 3, 1961, the outgoing Eisenhower administration suspended diplomatic relations with Cuba. President John F. Kennedy, who continued the policy of supporting an invasion by the refugees, was greatly embarrassed by the Bay of Pigs fiasco of 1961, which was one of the major causes of the dangerous missile crisis of the following year. There would be numerous other American-Cuban confrontations, including the "Mariel boat exodus" of 1980.

Further Reading

Higgins, Trumbull. *Perfect Failure: Kennedy, Eisenhower, and the CIA at the Bay of Pigs.* New York: W. W. Norton, 1987. A fascinating account that includes the planning and training for the covert military operation.

Leonard, Thomas. *Castro and the Cuban Revolution.* Westport, Conn.: Greenwood Press, 1999. A concise narrative history followed by biographical sketches, primary documents, and an annotated bibliography.

Morley, Morris. *Imperial State and Revolution: The United States and Cuba, 1952-1986.* New York: Cambridge University Press, 1988. Interprets Castro as a patriot standing up to an essentially imperialistic and exploitative giant.

Paterson, Thomas. *Contesting Castro: The United States and the Triumph of the Cuban Revolution.* New York: Oxford University Press, 1995. A balanced and compelling diplomatic history of U.S.-Cuban relations during the early period of the revolution.

Thomas Tandy Lewis

See also Castro, Fidel; Cold War; Dulles, John Foster; Eisenhower, Dwight D.; Foreign policy of the United States; Guatemala invasion; Latin America; Latinos; Mexico; Nixon's Latin America tour; Organization of American States; United Fruit Company.

■ Cyclotron

Identification Device that repeatedly uses a single high voltage to accelerate charged particles to high energies as they spiral outward within a magnetic field

The first successful cyclotron began operation in January, 1931. During the 1950's, technological advances made the cyclotron more efficient at producing medical isotopes and also made it a better tool with which to study the nuclear force and the atomic nucleus.

Ernest Lawrence, the cyclotron's inventor, described the device as a merry-go-round for protons. A cyclotron consists of an evacuated chamber equipped with an ion source and radio-frequency, high-voltage electrodes and is placed between the poles of a magnet. Ions leaked into the center of the chamber are forced by the magnetic field to circle the center of the chamber with a frequency (called the cyclotron frequency) that is directly proportional to the magnetic field strength and inversely proportional to the mass of the particle. The genius of the cyclotron is that if the high voltage is switched on and off at the cyclotron frequency, ions can be accelerated by the same voltage each time they circle the chamber.

The 1950's saw the development of better ways to extract the particle beam from the cyclotron and send it to stations where more sophisticated experiments could be done. There was also increasing use of two techniques to produce higher-energy particles. Adding pie-shaped wedges of iron to the magnet pole faces resulted in "sector focusing"; that is, the rapid change in magnetic field experienced by particles passing over the hills and valleys of iron concentrated the particles into the median plane of the chamber instead of allowing them to diffuse away. Proton energies above about 10 million electron volts (MeV) were difficult to achieve because the proton's mass appears to increase with speed— as predicted by physicist Albert Einstein—so that the proton's orbits are no longer synchronized with the accelerating voltage. Synchrocyclotrons are cyclotrons in which the frequency of the accelerating voltage is periodically lowered to stay in step with a flock of increasingly massive particles.

Technetium, an artificial radioactive element widely used in medical procedures, was first produced by bombarding a molybdenum target with deuterons (a proton combined with a neutron) at the Berkeley cyclotron in 1937. In 1940 and 1941, Glenn T. Seaborg and others used the sixty-inch Berkeley cyclotron to bombard a uranium target with deuterons and neutrons to produce the first known transuranic elements, neptunium and plutonium. Working with microscopic amounts of plutonium, Seaborg showed that plutonium-239 was highly fissionable and could be used for a nuclear weapon.

Impact The cyclotron played a major role in the investigation of the characteristics of the strong nuclear force. In 1950, the neutral pion (a subatomic particle) was discovered with the 350-MeV Berkeley cyclotron. When the Chicago 450-MeV cyclotron began operation in 1951, it was the highest-energy accelerator in the world. Enrico Fermi led a team that used it to make two fundamental discoveries: first, that the proton could exist in an excited state (at 180 MeV) and therefore must be composed of more fundamental particles (now called quarks); and second, that the strong nuclear force is charge independent—it treats protons and neutrons in the same fashion. The nature of the spin dependence of the nuclear force (particles can be thought of as spin-ning like toy tops) was explored with the Harvard cyclotron in 1956, and polarization effects (alignment of spins) were explored at the Rochester cyclotron.

Further Reading

Livingston, M. Stanley. *Particle Accelerators: A Brief History.* Cambridge, Mass.: Harvard University Press, 1969. Popular-level discussion by a person who helped build the first cyclotron when he was a student.

Seidel, Robert W., and J. L. Heilbron. *Lawrence and His Laboratory: A History of the Lawrence Berkeley Laboratory.* Berkeley: University of California Press, 1990. Careful and fascinating account of the development of the cyclotron.

Wilson, Richard. *History of the Harvard Cyclotrons.* Cambridge, Mass.: Harvard University Press, 2004. Account of one of the world's longest-running accelerators, which was used from 1949 until 2002.

Wilson, Robert R. "Particle Accelerators." *Scientific American* 198, no. 3 (March, 1958): 64-76. Written by a key player during the 1950's, this article details the evolution from cyclotron to synchrocyclotron to higher-energy machines.

Charles W. Rogers

See also Atomic bomb; Atomic Energy Act of 1954; Atomic Energy of Canada, Ltd.; Einstein, Albert; Science and technology; Seaborg, Glenn; Teller, Edward.

D

■ *Damn Yankees*

Identification Musical comedy about baseball and a deal with the devil
Authors Music by Richard Adler and Jerry Ross; book by George Abbott and Douglass Wallop
Date Opened on May 4, 1955
Place 46th Street Theatre, New York City

The only successful musical comedy about baseball, Damn Yankees *ran for 1,019 performances before leaving Broadway and was made into a feature film.*

Stories of people who sell their souls to the Devil in exchange for worldly goods can be traced back to Johann Wolfgang von Goethe's *Faust: Eine Tragödie* (pb. 1838; *The Tragedy of Faust*, 1823). However, only in the United States could it become the story of a baseball fan who wants to see his beloved Washington Senators win the World Series. Adapted from Douglass Wallop's novel *The Year the Yankees Lost the Pennant* (1954), *Damn Yankees* is the story of Joe Hardy, a middle-aged couch potato given the opportunity by the diabolical Mr. Applegate to become a youthful superstar. There is a catch, however—Hardy must return to his wife, Meg, by 9 P.M. on the night of the last game of the World Series or his soul is forfeit.

When Hardy seems poised to succeed in his game, Applegate summons his seductive assistant, Lola, to lure Hardy away from Meg, in the hope of causing Hardy to forfeit his soul. In spite of Lola's wiles, Hardy resists her attempts, manages to help the Senators win despite being turned back to middle age by Applegate, and returns home to his beloved Meg. The play's title used a touch of humor by referring to some baseball fans' exasperation with the New York Yankees, a team that placed in the World Series nearly every season during the 1950's while the Senators were perennial underachievers.

Impact *Damn Yankees* resonated strongly with the values current during the 1950's—personal responsibility, fidelity, teamwork, and self-sacrifice. It was

such a success on Broadway that it was subsequently produced for the cinema in 1958, with many members of the cast reprising their stage roles.

Further Reading

Jones, John Bush. *Our Musicals, Ourselves: A Social History of the American Musical Theater.* Waltham, Mass.: Brandeis University Press, 2003. A lively look at the role played by the musical comedy in the popular culture of the era.

Judge, Mark Gauvreau. *Damn Senators: My Grandfather and the Story of Washington's Only Win.* San Francisco, Calif: Encounter Books, 2003. A memoir of the star first baseman of the Senators, written by his grandson. Details the friendship that developed between his grandfather and Douglass Wallop, and how Wallop used him as the prototype for Joe Hardy.

Swain, Joseph P. *The Broadway Musical: A Critical and Musical Survey.* 2d ed. Lanham, Md.: Rowman & Littlefield, 2003. A more scholarly look at the topic, but with plenty of familiar examples.

Leigh Husband Kimmel

See also Baseball; Broadway musicals; DiMaggio, Joe; Music; New York Yankees; Theater in the United States.

■ Dance, popular

The 1950's was a transition period in dance. The decade began with people dancing much as they had during the late 1940's, but by the end of the decade, a television-driven national dance form was the norm.

When the 1950's dawned, people danced in pairs, whether they danced in each others' arms to the still-popular Big Band sounds or held onto one of their partner's hands as they jitterbugged in dance halls and school gyms. Moreover, different regions of the country had their own specialized dances: For example, in the Carolinas, people danced "The Shag." Two forms of media, one old and one new, played a large role in changing the dances and the attitudes toward dancing, as did politics.

Influence of Films and Television The early years of the decade produced a series of films depicting teenage rebels. Not only did a new group of stars gain fame, but so also did a new attitude. Marlon Brando's *The Wild One* (1953) showed the effects on a complacent town when a motorcycle gang storms through: While the older generation is upset and terrified, some of the young people are intrigued. The film questioned the values of the townspeople and, by extension, of middle-class America. *Blackboard Jungle* (1955) featured Bill Haley's song "Rock Around the Clock," a song that later served as a backdrop for 1956's *Rock Around the Clock*, a film that depicted teen rebellion in a high school. *Rebel Without a Cause* (1955) secured James Dean's image as a disaffected and alienated rebel.

As teenagers watched these films, their dancing became wilder; even the jitterbug became more sexual as it became a statement of rebellion. Soon, the music and the dancing played off each other as both went increasingly beyond the adults' level of tolerance. When Elvis Presley first appeared on *The Ed Sullivan Show*, a Sunday night variety show that whole families watched together, Presley's gyrations were deemed much too sexual, and the cameras were ordered to film him only from the waist up, leaving any hip movements out of the images broadcast to homes.

Sullivan's show was not the only television program on which teenagers could see current dancing. In 1952, a television show debuted in Philadelphia, *American Bandstand*. In 1957, *The Buddy Deane Show* captured the attention of Baltimore's teenagers. Both shows appeared on television in the afternoons as teenagers were returning home from school. The shows were inexpensive to run, needing only a disc jockey, a crew, records, and dancers, but they soon garnered huge audiences. Teenagers wanted to be able to dance on these shows, even though it meant a large commitment of time. Before long, the teen regulars became celebrities in their own right, and

Teenagers dancing on the nationally televised American Bandstand, *hosted by Dick Clark (upper left), in 1958.* (AP/Wide World Photos)

record companies, anxious to promote a new record or singer, would try to get their talent on the programs in order to provide widespread exposure for performers and songs.

By 1957, *American Bandstand*, now hosted by Dick Clark, aired nationally. The regular dancers on the show were able to demonstrate to teenagers across the United States the steps for the newest dances and even originated some of their own. *American Bandstand* is credited with introducing "The Stroll" to teenagers across the country, and the regulars performed dances such as the "Bunny Hop" and the "Hokey Pokey," both of which became popular even for children's parties.

Baltimore's Buddy Deane was proud to be the first to host Bill Haley and the Comets, the group that had provided a rock-and-roll soundtrack for *Blackboard Jungle*. "The Madison," a line dance, also gained popularity on Deane's show. One important feature distinguished *The Buddy Deane Show* from *American Bandstand*: When *American Bandstand* went national, Dick Clark insisted, over the objections of network bosses, that it be racially integrated. Deane's show was cancelled by its television station in 1964 to keep it from becoming integrated.

As dance programs, particularly *American Bandstand*, gained national popularity, teenagers incorporated more of the moves they witnessed on television and less of those that were regional in origin. "The Shag," for example, became a part of local Carolina dances.

The country's fascination with Cuba, the vacation playground of many, led to an interest in Latin rhythms and movement. Latin dances such as the rhumba were mostly danced by adults, but teenagers made the "cha-cha" their own, swinging their hips in a sexual nature. Teenagers dancing on television had to tone down their movements, or the cameras would focus on other performers whose dancing was less suggestive. As it became acceptable for white teenagers to listen to the mostly African American rhythm-and-blues music, they danced the dances in forms related to this style of music. By the early 1960's, teenagers were dancing without touching one another at all in dance styles such as "The Twist," "The Watusi," and "The Pony."

Impact Popular dance during the 1950's paved the way for the much less structured popular dance of the 1960's. Dance also became a way for teenagers to reflect their growing distance from previously established societal norms, thus reflecting the "generation gap." In the late twentieth and early twenty-first centuries, aging baby boomers looked back to the now-tame dances with nostalgia: Just as swing dancing enjoyed a resurgence during the late twentieth century, so too did the songs and dance styles of the 1950's, proving their enduring quality in American culture.

Further Reading

Cohen, Selma, ed. *International Encyclopedia of Dance.* Rev. ed. New York: Oxford University Press, 2004. An ongoing encyclopedia that documents dance trends and notable figures within the art form and provides historical perspectives.

Jackson, John A. *American Bandstand: Dick Clark and the Making of a Rock 'n' Roll Empire.* New York: Oxford University Press, 1997. Chronicles the rise of the program and explores the influence it had on American popular culture.

Rock and Roll Generation: Teen Life in the 1950's. Alexandria, Va.: Time-Life Books, 1998. A well-illustrated survey of youth culture and its music during the decade.

Tracy E. Miller

See also Ailey, Alvin, Jr.; *American Bandstand*; *Blackboard Jungle*; Conformity, culture of; Haley, Bill; Little Richard; "Louie Louie"; Music; Presley, Elvis; Rock and roll; Top 40 radio; Valens, Ritchie.

■ Davis, Benjamin O., Jr.

Identification African American Air Force general
Born December 18, 1912; Washington, D.C.
Died July 4, 2002; Washington, D.C.

In 1954, Benjamin O. Davis, Jr., became the first African American general in the U.S. Air Force and the second African American general in any U.S. armed force.

Davis led a life of firsts. He was born into a military family, and his father, Benjamin O. Davis, Sr., was the first African American general officer in the U.S. Army. The younger Davis rose through the ranks of the Air Force and became the service's first African American brigadier general in 1954. In 1936, he became the first African American to graduate from the U.S. Military Academy, and he was a member of the first pilot cadet training class for blacks in Tuskegee, Alabama, in the U.S. Army Air Corps, from which he was graduated in 1942. Davis led the graduates of this program—the so-called Tuskegee Airmen—into World War II combat in 1943. The success of the Tuskegee Airmen during the war effort, which many attributed to Davis's leadership, disproved the widespread belief in the military that African Americans could not fly airplanes in combat. The Tuskegee Airmen's accomplishments led in part to President Harry S. Truman's order to desegregate the armed forces in 1948. Davis helped draft the Air Force plan for implementing this order.

Davis left his command of the nearly all-black Lockbourne Air Force Base in Ohio in 1949. He was the first African American to study at the Air War College at Maxwell Air Force Base, Alabama. After graduating from its program in 1950, he worked for a short time at the new Pentagon building in Washington, D.C. Davis received flight training in the Air Force's new class of jets in 1953 and left for Korea just as hostilities there were ending. He commanded the integrated Fifty-first Wing of the Fifth Air Force for a year until he moved to Tokyo, Japan, where he was responsible for maintaining the Air Force troops' combat readiness in that volatile region. Davis became the first African American to earn a star in the U.S. Air Force when President Dwight D. Eisenhower promoted him to the rank of brigadier general in 1954. Davis remained in Asia, focused on the potential threat of communist China and the combat readiness of the Far East Air Force through most of the 1950's.

Impact Davis was instrumental in helping lead the Air Force, and the military in general, into the era of desegregation. He was promoted to lieutenant general in 1965. His military decorations included the Air Force Distinguished Service Medal, Army Distinguished Service Medal, Silver Star, Legion of Merit with two oak leaf clusters, Distinguished Flying Cross, Air Force Commendation Medal with two oak leaf clusters, and the Philippine Legion of Honor. President Bill Clinton awarded Davis his fourth star, making him a full general, in 1998.

Further Reading

Davis, Benjamin O., Jr. *Benjamin O. Davis, Jr., American: An Autobiography.* Washington, D.C.: Smithsonian Institution Press, 1991. Provides details of Davis's life in his own words.

Propman, Alan A. *Air Force Integrates, 1945-1964.* 2d ed. Washington, D.C.: Smithsonian Institution Press, 1998. Argues that the integration of the air force was not for moral or political reasons but to improve military effectiveness.

Todd Moye

See also African Americans; Cold War; Eisenhower, Dwight D.; Korean War; United States Air Force Academy.

■ Davis, Sammy, Jr.

Identification African American entertainer
Born December 8, 1925; Harlem, New York
Died May 16, 1990; Beverly Hills, California

One of the most multitalented entertainers of his generation, Sammy Davis, Jr., was a dancer, a recording star, an actor, and a popular television personality. However, he is best remembered as a performer who bridged the divide between African American and white entertainers.

Born in New York City's predominantly African American Harlem district and raised in a vaudevillian family, Sammy Davis, Jr., grew up as an entertainer and had a wide variety of show business experiences by the time he entered the U.S. Army during World War II. After the war, he returned to performing in a trio with his father and uncle and worked with some of the top jazz performers of the time. By the early 1950's, the trio was leading at nightclubs, and Davis was winning acclaim as a performer in his own right. He was noted especially for the exceptional energy that he projected.

Davis started recording albums for Decca in 1954 and was receiving top bookings in Las Vegas. In 1956, he made his Broadway debut in the musical comedy *Mr. Wonderful*, which Jule Styne and George Gilbert produced especially for him. The show appeared to be autobiographical in that it was about an African American nightclub entertainer who overcomes race prejudice on his road to success. The show played for an entire year, thanks largely to Davis's charismatic performance.

By the time *Mr. Wonderful* closed in 1957, the family trio in which Davis had performed for many years had dissolved. However, by then, Davis was appearing regularly on television, recording hit records, and acting in occasional films. In 1959, he scored another stage success as Sportin' Life in George Gershwin's folk opera, *Porgy and Bess.*

Sammy Davis, Jr., in 1956. (AP/Wide World Photos)

Impact By the end of the 1950's, Davis was one of the most successful African American entertainers in the United States and was generally credited with being the first major black entertainer to be equally popular among both black and white audiences. During the ensuring decades, he went on to even greater successes and gained a new kind of fame for his membership in the so-called Rat Pack of Frank Sinatra and Dean Martin.

Further Reading

Davis, Sammy, Jr. *Sammy: An Autobiography.* Edited by Burt Boyar and Jane Boyar. New York: Farrar, Straus and Giroux, 2000. Posthumously edited version of Davis's two candid autobiographies, *Yes, I Can* (1965) and *Why Me?* (1980).

Haygood, Wil. *In Black and White: The Life of Sammy Davis, Jr.* New York: Alfred A. Knopf, 2003. Penetrating biography of Davis that attempts to explain the forces that drove him.

R. Kent Rasmussen

See also African Americans; Martin and Lewis; Music; Racial discrimination; Sinatra, Frank.

■ *Davy Crockett*

Identification Television program about the life and adventures of the early nineteenth century frontier hero
Producer Bill Walsh
Director Norman Foster
Date Aired from 1954 to 1955

The Disney production represented the first television program that had a tangible commercial impact on the buying interests of children. Commercial "spin-offs" and hype set off a buying mania of Crockett material among the general public and increased interest in U.S. and Texas history. Moreover, the program's emphasis on Crockett's efforts to free Texas from Mexico held resonance for an American public living in the shadow of the Korean War and Cold War.

The real-life Davy Crockett was an authentic frontier hero of early nineteenth century history, considered as such even during his own lifetime. Born in Greene County, Tennessee, Crockett was a strong supporter of farmers and homesteaders all his life. In 1813, he fought with General Andrew Jackson in the Creek War, an event that became the basis for part of the later television series.

In 1821, Crockett was elected to the state legislature. Though he had strong support among his local constituency, he was defeated in a bid for Congress in 1825. However, in 1827 he was elected. His most notable political achievement was his support of a land bill that allowed homesteaders to purchase land at a reasonable price. Breaking with President Andrew Jackson over the issue, he was defeated in 1830. In 1836, Crockett went to Texas, where, on March 6, he was killed while defending the Alamo.

Television Hero Disney created *Davy Crockett* as a "miniseries" within the *Disneyland* television series and designed the series to promote the Frontierland attraction at Disneyland. The program consisted only of three episodes, "Davy Crockett, Indian Fighter," "Davy Crockett Goes to Congress," and "Davy Crockett at the Alamo," which aired over a three-month period. The episodes were later combined into a movie, with the addition of two "prequels," and continued to appear sporadically in syndication. The series starred Fess Parker as

Crockett and Buddy Ebsen as his side-kick, George Russell. It was one of the first programs to be filmed in color, although the show initially was broadcast only in black and white. Each episode was self-contained and presented a fictionalized account of Crockett's life and events related to a certain period or milestone in his life. The final show ended as Crockett was shown swinging his gun at the Mexican soldiers pouring into the fort.

Impact While Davy Crockett was well known among historians, and the story of the Alamo had a life of its own among Texans, younger generations were not as familiar with his story. The widespread popularity of the programs generated a renewed interest in this facet of American history. Children flocked to libraries in droves not only to learn about Crockett but also to read about the Old West and historical figures such as Annie Oakey, Buffalo Bill, and Sitting Bull.

Moreover, although the Crockett series was one of several Western-genre shows included on weekly Disney programming, its commercialization set it apart from the others. The anthem of the series, "The Ballad of Davy Crockett," became one of the most popular hits of the year. Children carried lunch boxes and wore coonskin caps and T-shirts depicting the character. The program became a national phenomenon.

Davy Crockett was the Harry Potter craze of the 1950's, and coonskin caps became the rage among young boys. (Hulton Archive | by Getty Images)

Further Reading

Aaker, Everett. *Television Western Players of the Fifties: A Biographical Encyclopedia of All Regular Cast Members in Western Series, 1949-1959.* Jefferson, N.C.: McFarland, 1997. Collection of brief biographies of television actors, including those on *Davy Crockett.*

D'Angelo, Ruby. *Television's Cowboys, Gunfighters, and Cap Pistols.* Iola, Wis.: Krause, 1999. Details several television Westerns of the 1950's and 1960's that were based on real-life heroes. Also includes biographies of the historical characters and photo-graphs and price guides for promotional toys and outfits that have since become collectibles.

Davis, William. *Three Roads to the Alamo: The Lives and Fortunes of David Crockett, James Bowie, and William Barret Travis.* New York: HarperCollins, 1999. Serves as a biography for three pivotal figures in the Alamo battle.

Richard Adler

See also Baby boomers; Disneyland; Fads; *Gunsmoke, Lone Ranger, The, Mickey Mouse Club, Sergeant Preston of the Yukon*; Television for children; Television Westerns.

■ Day, Doris

Identification American film actress and singer
Born April 3, 1924; Cincinnati, Ohio

Doris Day used her singing and acting talents to become a leading film star during the 1950's.

Born Doris von Kappelhoff, Doris Day was the daughter of Frederick Wilhelm and Alma Sophia (Welz) von Kappelhoff. Originally an aspiring dancer, Day fractured her leg in an automobile accident in 1937, and her hope of becoming a professional dancer ended abruptly. During her recuperation, Day began voice lessons and made her singing debut on a Cincinnati radio station. While singing professionally with Barney Rapp and his band, the singer changed her surname to Day, after the song "Day After Day."

In 1946, Warner Bros. hired Day to star in the film *Romance on the High Seas* (1948). Following that film's success, Day began to move into the role of leading lady in several films and starred in fourteen additional Warner Bros. movies. Romantic musicals such as *My Dream Is Yours* (1949), *I'll See You in My Dreams* (1951), and *Calamity Jane* (1953) solidified Day's nice-girl image. Day also gave powerful dramatic performances in movies such as *Love Me or Leave Me* (1955) and the Alfred Hitchcock film *The Man Who Knew Too Much* (1956). In 1959, she starred in the bedroom farce *Pillow Talk* for which she was nominated for an Academy Award.

Before Day became known as an actress, she was a popular singer and had several hit songs. The 1950's saw her combine her acting and singing talents to become a well-loved actor. In *The Man Who Knew Too Much*, she sang the song "Que Sera, Sera (Whatever Will Be, Will Be)." The song won an Academy Award and served as her signature song throughout her career.

Impact A popular actress throughout the 1950's, Day played wholesome, girl-next-door characters who exemplified the ideal American woman of her time. She continued her film career for another decade; during the 1960's, she starred in light comedies such as *Please Don't Eat the Daisies* (1960), *Touch of Mink* (1962), and *With Six You Get Eggroll* (1968), her last Hollywood film. From 1968 to 1973, she starred on a television comedy series, *The Doris Day Show*. A frequent costar with, and a close friend of, actor Rock Hudson, Day was one of the few to whom he revealed his illness as a result of HIV/AIDS during the 1980's.

Further Reading

Freedland, Michael. *Doris Day: The Illustrated Biography*. London: Andre Deutsch, 2000. Chronicles the life and career of the actor.

Rosen, Marjorie. "Sunny Side Up, Sunny Side Down: The Turbulent Life of Doris Day." *Biography* 7, no. 4 (2003): 76-81. A concise biography.

Bernadette Zbicki Heiney

See also Film in the United States; Hitchcock films; Hudson, Rock.

■ *The Day the Earth Stood Still*

Identification Science-fiction film
Director Robert Wise (1914-   )
Date Released in 1951

This film provided a social and political critique of the Cold War mentality during the early 1950's.

In the film, a ten-foot-tall robot, Gort, and an alien man, Klaatu (played by Michael Rennie), land their flying saucer on the Mall in Washington, D.C. Gort is a member of a police force with absolute and irrevocable power created by an interplanetary alliance of aliens. A messianic figure, Klaatu bears a message of warning because humanity has produced atomic bombs. After politicians explain that world suspicions make it impossible to meet Klaatu's demand to deliver his message to representatives of all countries simultaneously, he obtains the cooperation of Dr. Jacob Barnhardt (Sam Jaffe), a physicist. Right before the meeting with the world's scientists, a soldier kills Klaatu, but Gort restores him temporarily to life, thus enabling him to warn Earth's people that if they export their violence, their planet will be destroyed by the robots.

Impact *The Day the Earth Stood Still* represented multiple fears of the Cold War: the Soviet Union, nuclear proliferation after the Soviet's first atomic bomb test in 1949, the 1947 sightings of UFOs, and machines controlling humans. Because the alien, who at first is feared, proves to be beneficient and at times morally superior to humans, it also implicitly criticized McCarthyist paranoia and the U.S. government policy of using maximum force when others threaten. Finally, Doctor Barnhardt, with his Einstein-like haircut, portrayed the power and goodness of scientists, many of whom, including Einstein, had become suspect under McCarthyism.

Further Reading

Hendershot, Cyndy. "The Atomic Scientist, Science Fiction Films, and Paranoia: *The Day the Earth Stood Still, This Island Earth*, and *Killers from Space*."

Journal of American Culture 20 (Spring, 1997): 31-41. An examination of popular views of scientists in science-fiction films.

Henriksen, Margot A. *Dr. Strangelove's America: Society and Culture in the Atomic Age.* Berkeley: University of California Press, 1997. Discusses *The Day the Earth Stood Still* in the context of Cold War paranoia.

Kristen L. Zacharias

See also Cold War; *Destination Moon*; Disarmament movement; Einstein, Albert; Flying saucers; *Forbidden Planet*; House Committee on Un-American Activities; Hydrogen bomb; *Invasion of the Body Snatchers*; McCarthy, Joseph; *Thing from Another World, The.*

■ Dean, James

Identification American film actor
Born February 8, 1931; Marion, Indiana
Died September 30, 1955; Cholame, California

Because of his movie roles and the way he lived, and died, James Dean became a universal symbol of adolescent angst.

James Byron Dean lived the American Dream; he was born and raised in a small, rural Indiana town, and by the age of twenty-four was considered one of Hollywood's greatest stars. Dean grew up on a farm near Fairmount, Indiana, where he played on the local high school basketball team. Despite his rural upbringing, he studied violin, tap dancing, and art. Following graduation from high school, he moved to California, where he attended Santa Monica Junior College and the University of California at Los Angeles (UCLA). He also attended an acting workshop conducted by James Whitmore. He landed a few television commercials, including one for Pepsi. In the winter of 1951, he moved to New York to pursue a stage acting career. Following moderate stage success and a few television appearances, he was tapped in late 1954 to appear in the movie *East of Eden* (1955).

Before *East of Eden* even premiered, Dean got the starring role in the movie that was to define his legend, *Rebel Without a Cause* (1955). Prior to filming it, he moved to Hollywood. He celebrated the success of *East of Eden* by buying a Porsche and began entering road races—an activity typical of his fast-paced lifestyle. *Rebel Without a Cause* was filmed from March through May of 1955. He then traveled to Texas for the filming of his third movie, *Giant*

(1956), starring Rock Hudson and Elizabeth Taylor. When filming was completed, he returned to Hollywood. On September 30, 1955, on his way to a race in Salinas, California, Dean was killed in a highway accident while driving at a high rate of speed. Ironically, he had filmed a public service television commercial on highway safety only two weeks before his death.

By the time of his death, Dean had made only three films, two of which had not premiered by the time of his death, and had done so in less than a year, but they were enough to make him a widely admired star and ultimately a legend that spoke to the restless American youth of the 1950's. He had a charismatic screen presence and natural acting ability. He was posthumously nominated for Academy Awards for both *East of Eden* and *Giant*, but did not win.

James Dean as Jett Rink in his last film, Giant. *(Arkent Archive)*

Impact In the years since Dean's death, there have been hundreds of books and articles written about him; at least forty-three songs have been recorded in tribute to him. Artists portray him as the subject of their paintings. Perhaps because he never got old, he remains the symbol of adolescent angst that he portrayed in his three films. Fans make annual pilgrimages to his grave in Fairmount, Indiana, to honor his memory.

Further Reading

Dalton, David. *James Dean, the Mutant King: A Biography.* San Francisco: Straight Arrow Books, 1974. Shows how deliberately and carefully Dean crafted his own image and performances. An excellent bibliography is included.

Holley, Val. *James Dean: The Biography.* New York: St. Martin's Press, 1995. Concentrates on his Manhattan years. Bibliography, index.

Spoto, Donald. *Rebel: The Life and Legend of James Dean.* New York: HarperCollins, 1996. Excellent biography with extensive bibliography and index. The author takes a dispassionate look at the legend of Dean and argues that his untimely death was probably his greatest career move.

Dale L. Flesher

See also Actors Studio; Brando, Marlon; Clift, Montgomery; Conformity, culture of; Film in the United States; *Giant*; Hudson, Rock; *Rebel Without a Cause*; Steinbeck, John; Taylor, Elizabeth; Youth culture and the generation gap.

■ De Kooning, Willem

Identification Dutch American abstract expressionist painter
Born April 24, 1904; Rotterdam, the Netherlands
Died March 19, 1997; East Hampton, New York

During the 1950's, the work of Willem de Kooning helped abstract expressionism reach international scope and influence, becoming the first American movement to have such worldwide impact.

Willem de Kooning developed an interest in art early and apprenticed with a commercial art firm while taking night classes in fine art. In 1926, he entered the United States illegally (he became a U.S. citizen in 1962) and took up residence in Manhattan, where he made the acquaintance of artists Arshile Gorky, John Graham, and Jackson Pollock.

De Kooning had his first solo art show in 1948. In 1950, his painting *Excavation* was exhibited at the prestigious Venice Biennial and was subsequently purchased by the Art Institute of Chicago. Through the 1950's his fame increased, bolstered by retrospective exhibits in Boston and at the Venice Biennial.

De Kooning's work was highly gestural and appeared spontaneous, but in fact de Kooning worked over his paintings many times. While painters such as Pollock, Franz Kline, and Mark Rothko painted completely abstract paintings, de Kooning never entirely abandoned the human figure. During the 1950's, de Kooning's most celebrated works were of women. Brightly colored and painted in an aggressive style, these paintings were alternately viewed as misogynist and as representing the power of women. Other de Kooning works related to landscape or to the frenetic world of Manhattan.

Impact De Kooning was in many respects the quintessential American painter. His work linked both the

Willem de Kooning in 1959. (Hulton Archive | by Getty Images)

cubist tradition of Pablo Picasso and the pure abstraction of other abstract expressionists. His wild paintings of women look forward to the pop art of the 1960's.

Further Reading

Butler, Cornelia H., et al. *Willem de Kooning: Tracing the Figure.* Los Angeles: Museum of Contemporary Art, 2002. An insightful look at de Kooning's drawings.

Prather, Marla. *Willem de Kooning: Paintings.* Washington, D.C.: National Gallery of Art, 1994. This book combines a critical biography with numerous color reproductions.

Amy K. Weiss

See also Abstract expressionism; Art movements; Guggenheim Museum; Kline, Franz; Motherwell, Robert; Pollock, Jackson; Rauschenberg, Robert.

■ Demographics of Canada

The 1950's was a period of widespread demographic change worldwide, and in Canada, the population grew dramatically because of the postwar baby boom and immigration from war-torn countries in Europe. The country also experienced a face pace of urbanization, which affected immigration trends.

During the 1950's, Canada's total population grew 27 percent, one of the highest growth rates in the world. In contrast to the United States, the Canadian government conducts its census in years that end with the number "1," and it counted a population of 14,009,429 in 1951. By 1961, the count was 18,238,247; the Canadian statistical office had estimated that the figure in 1960 would be 17,814,000, and the actual count in 1961 tends to validate that estimate.

Two Native Canadian peoples, Indians and Eskimos, contributed very modestly to the total population count. At the end of the 1950's, the federal statistical service estimated that there were about 180,000 indigenous Indians living in Canada. The Indian population when the Europeans first arrived is thought to have been slightly more—around 200,000—but the numbers dropped to about 90,000 at the beginning of the twentieth century, and some people predicted the extinction of the aboriginal peoples. Instead, the population doubled during the first sixty years of the twentieth century. A distinctly different group, the Eskimos, was much

smaller—11,500 people, a figure that reflected the marginal resources at the northernmost part of Canada, where they live on lands bordering the Arctic Ocean. They survive from ocean harvests, principally seals.

Population Growth The startling increase in Canada's population in the 1950's was due, in large measure, to an increase in the number of Canadians of Canadian birth. The birthrate, which had fallen quite low in the Depression years of the 1930's, soared to 27.5 per thousand, one of the highest in the world. The result was a large number of births over deaths, and this fact accounted for 80 percent of the population increase. The numbers of individuals in the zero-to-fourteen age bracket stood at 29.7 percent of the population in 1950; it had increased to 33.7 percent in 1960, reflecting a significant increase in family size during Canada's baby boom. In 1959, there were 480,000 births in Canada, the largest number of births up to that time in a single year, and one-third of these births were children born to parents who already had three children.

Population growth was very unevenly distributed geographically. The province of British Columbia, on the Pacific Coast, experienced the largest increase of all the provinces—37.8 percent—though a significant part of this increase derived from "immigration," that is, people moving to British Columbia from elsewhere in Canada. Prince Edward Island, in the St. Lawrence River estuary, had the smallest increase at 4.6 percent. Alberta, where the oil industry was beginning to develop; Ontario, the country's manufacturing hub; and Quebec were the other provinces with substantial growth, much of it related to economic opportunity.

Immigration While 80 percent of Canada's population growth in the 1950's came from Canadians having larger families, 20 percent was the result of immigration. The peak of immigration occurred during the late 1950's, at about the same time the growth of the long-resident population tapered off. Canada's government adopted a policy in the immediate post-World War II years of encouraging immigration, on the grounds that the country was too sparsely settled for its own security. More than 100,000 immigrants reached Canada annually in the 1950's, peaking at more than 282,000 in 1957.

Until 1950, Canada's immigration policy had emphasized "family reunification," resulting initially in very large numbers of immigrants who came from the British Isles—some 600,000 of them arrived between 1945 and 1960. The first to arrive were the war brides, spouses of Canadian servicemen who had been stationed in Europe. The Canadian government also favored immigrants from Scandinavia and the Netherlands. By 1950, however, Canada had adopted a policy encouraging many of Europe's displaced persons to emigrate to Canada. Large number of these immigrants were ethnic Germans, pushed westward by the invading Soviet army in 1945 and subsequently housed in large refugee camps in West Germany. The International Rescue Organization as well as many church groups encouraged these people, who could not return to their homes in eastern Europe, to emigrate to Canada. After initial hesitation, Canadians welcomed these people, many of whom brought important skills with them: Some 40 percent of European emigrants to Canada brought with them managerial, professional, or industrial skills.

Urbanization Besides the sheer growth in numbers, the other startling change in the demographics of Canada was the concentration of the population in urban centers. In the pre-World War II period, Canada was largely an agricultural country, based on large-scale commercial farms in the plains provinces and small, often self-sufficient farms in the Atlantic provinces and in Quebec. Ontario, the most southerly province of Canada, had some market-based agriculture, but it was chiefly home to the manufacturing industry of Canada.

However, the economic growth of the postwar era was self-reinforcing: As the incomes of Canadians grew, so too did their ability to spend more on discretionary goods such as appliances, cars, and furnishings, which propelled the growth of manufacturing, especially in Canada's largest cities. Montreal increased in size in the 1950's by 43 percent, and Toronto grew by a staggering 53 percent. Thanks to the burgeoning oil sector, Edmonton grew 77 percent in the 1950's. By the end of the 1950's, 45 percent of Canada's population lived in urban areas.

Impact During the 1950's, Canada changed from being a colonial—albeit self-governing—settlement of Great Britain to an industrialized country and joined the developed world. Even though much of its economy was, by the 1950's, dominated by its much larger neighbor to the south, the United States, Canada acquired a much more distinctive and internationalized identity of its own. Its welcome to many of the Europeans displaced by World War II changed it into a multicultural nation, even though its elite continued to reflect the dominant influence of Britain during its formative years.

Further Reading

Broadfoot, Barry. *The Immigrant Years: From Europe to Canada, 1945-1967.* Vancouver: Douglas & McIntyre, 1986. Gives a broad survey of postwar trends in immigration.

Information Services Division, Dominion Bureau of Statistics. *Canada 1961.* Ottawa: Queen's Printer, 1961. A contemporary government document that gives statistics on immigration during the era.

Kerr, Don, and Bali Ram. *Population Dynamics in Canada.* Scarborough, Ont.: Statistics Canada and Prentice-Hall, Canada, 1994. Covers the demographic developments in Canada after World War II.

Lithwick, N. H. *Urban Canada: Problems and Prospects: Report to the Minister for Housing, Government of Canada.* Ottawa: Central Mortgage and Housing Corporation, 1970. Covers the trends in urbanization in Canada during the postwar years and how changes in the urban landscape fostered and reflected developments in immigration.

Nancy M. Gordon

See also Birth control; Business and the economy in Canada; Canada and Great Britain; Canadian regionalism; Demographics of the United States; Education in Canada; Health care systems in Canada; Immigration to Canada; Income and wages in Canada; Medicine; Minorities in Canada; Urbanization in Canada; War brides.

■ Demographics of the United States

During the 1950's, family and household demographics reflected the prosperous economy and conservative values of the decade. The baby boom created a bulge in the population's age distribution, while suburbanization facilitated home ownership and fueled consumerism in the United States.

The 1950's was a decade of both conformity and change. The decade is often viewed as a rather slow-paced, idyllic one, yet calm was overshadowed by the threat of nuclear war and social unrest. Many social and demographic trends of the 1950's resulted from a relative return to normalcy after World War II and resulting economic affluence and optimism for the future.

Population Size and Geographic Distribution In 1950, the population of the United States numbered 150.7 million for the forty-eight states in existence; more than half of the U.S. population (56.1 percent) lived in metropolitan areas. The metropolitan population exceeded the nonmetropolitan one by 18.3 million. Alaska and Hawaii were admitted to the United States in 1959, and by 1960, the total U.S. population was 179.3 million. Population density in the United States declined from 1950 (without Alaska and Hawaii) from 50.9 people per square mile of land area to 50.7 (with Alaska and Hawaii) in 1960. In 1950, the South had the largest proportion of the United States' total population (31.3 percent), followed by the Midwest (29.5 percent) and the Northeast (26.2 percent). The West contained only 13 percent of the U.S. population, although the region would prove to have the highest population growth of the decade, increasing its share of the population to 15.6 percent by 1960. By 1960, the Midwest and the Northeast experienced small declines in their share of the population as migration to the Sun Belt began.

Baby Boom Perhaps the most important demographic event of the 1950's was the baby boom: an unprecedented, unanticipated fertility explosion following World War II. The baby-boom generation included the approximately 76 million people born between 1946 and 1964. The baby boom reversed a century-long trend toward lower fertility but did not reflect a return to the large families of the nineteenth century. In fact, average household size declined from 3.68 in 1940 to 3.38 in 1950 and to 3.29 in 1960. The total fertility rate, which reflects the average number of births per woman, grew from 2.2 children in 1940 to 3.2 in 1950 to a high of 3.7 in 1957. However, fertility rates do not indicate best the magnitude of the baby boom. Prior to 1947, the number of births in the United States remained stable at about 2.5 million births per year. In 1947, the annual number of births was more than 1 million more than in 1945; and for the next seventeen years, approximately 4 million babies were born every year in the United States. The annual number of births

peaked in 1957 at 4.3 million; the same year the highest fertility rates were also recorded.

Many suggest the baby boom resulted from soldiers returning home from the war. Marriage rates increased and high fertility existed immediately after the war, but the substantial increase in births began in 1951 and persisted into the next decade. The primary factors contributing to the baby boom were more people marrying and having children at younger ages. Older women who had deferred childbearing during the Great Depression and the war also had "makeup" births. Extra income in the affluent postwar economy encouraged the births of additional children. The 1950's represent the decade of second-highest population growth in the United States both in numerical (28.6 million) and percentage (19 percent) terms. By the early twenty-first century, the 1990's had had the highest population growth.

The impact of the baby boom on the population composition in the United States is often compared to the process of a pig being digested by a python: A bulk of population moves slowly along a continuum as the years pass. After the year 1950, the largest age groups, measured in five-year increments, have coincided with the range of ages included in the baby boom. In 1950, the largest age group was children under age five. In 2000, those aged thirty-five to thirty-nine and forty to forty-four constituted the largest age groups. The year 2011 will mark rapid growth of the elderly population as the first of the baby boomers reach the age of sixty-five.

The baby boom reduced the median age of the U.S. population from 30.2 years in 1950 to 29.5 years in 1960 and 28.1 years in 1970. In subsequent decades, the median age of the U.S. population increased as baby boomers aged. As this cohort continues to age, demographers predict higher mortality rates and less residential mobility in the United States.

Desegregation, Race, and Fertility All demographic subgroups in the United States experienced higher birthrates during the baby boom with one notable exception. Many studies have documented that fertility is sensitive to social change. During the 1950's, this fact was evident following the 1954 *Brown v. Board of Education* Supreme Court ruling declaring segregation of public schools unconstitutional, when several southern states showed declines in

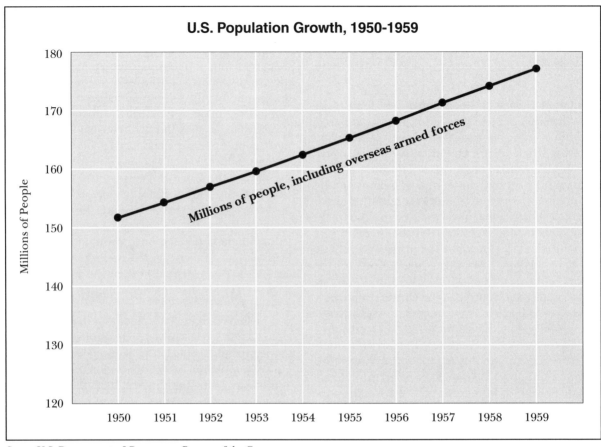

U.S. Population Growth, 1950-1959

Source: U.S. Department of Commerce, Bureau of the Census.

childbearing. Between 1953 and 1954, the white birthrate in the South increased 2 percent, faster than the overall U.S. birthrate of 0.8 percent. This trend suddenly reversed in 1954 and 1955. While the national birthrate increased 1.9 percent, the birthrate in nine of eleven former confederate states declined an average of 0.7 percent. Ending school segregation clearly affected southerners differently from the way it affected northerners. The decision threatened the status of white southerners and created a fear of violence that might accompany segregation. White southerners postponed childbearing as a result of social uncertainty.

Sex Distribution Before 1950, men outnumbered women in the United States, but beginning during the 1950's, the female population outnumbered the male population because of larger gains for women than men in life expectancy. In 1940, the sex ratio was 100.7 males per 100 females; by 1950, the bal-

ance had shifted to 98.6 males for every 100 females; and by 1960, the ratio was 97.1 males to every 100 females. In the United States, women outnumbered men by one million in 1950 and by 2.5 million in 1960. In 1950, men still outnumbered women in nonmetropolitan areas even though the sex ratio of men to women had fallen below 100 for the entire country.

Minority Populations According to the 1950 U.S. Census, African Americans made up 10 percent of the population and grew only 0.5 percent during the decade. In 1950, 68 percent of blacks resided in the South. By 1960, the effects of postwar black migration were evident, as the proportion of blacks living in the South had declined to 59.9 percent. The Midwest and Northeast experienced slight gains in their black populations, as African Americans from the South looked for job opportunities in the more industrialized regions.

Only 0.4 percent of the population reported a race other than "white" or "black" on the 1950 U.S. Census, and this figure increased to only 0.5 percent in 1960. Of those reporting race other than "white" or "black," Asian and Pacific Islanders were located primarily in western states (69.4 percent in 1950; 79.2 percent in 1960), and slightly more than half of those who reported "American Indian" and "Alaskan Native" (52.9 percent in 1950 and 51.8 percent in 1960) resided in a western state. The remainder of Native Americans lived predominantly in the Midwest and South.

Family and Household Demographics Families of the 1950's reversed previous demographic trends, and they differed qualitatively from families in the decades before and after. The 1950's family was not the last remnant of traditionalism but rather a focused effort to create a family-centered culture.

High marriage rates reflected the profamily values of the decade. While the marriage rate peaked in 1940 at 12.1 marriages per 1,000 members of the population, in 1950 the marriage rate was still relatively high at 11.3 marriages per 1,000; by 1960, the marriage rate had dropped to 8.5 per 1,000. The average age of marriage also fell after World War II. By 1950, the median age for marriage was 20.3 years for women and 22.8 years for men. This age remained steady throughout the decade. Divorce was uncommon, and divorce rates actually declined slightly over the ten-year period, from 2.6 divorces per 1,000 in 1950 to 2.2 per 1,000 in 1960. About 78 percent of households in 1950 were married-couple households. Only 9.3 percent of the population lived in single-person households in 1950. While in 1960 the proportion of married-couple households was about the same (74.8 percent), the proportion of single-person households had increased to 16.3 percent.

In spite of the almost mythical nature of the 1950's family, family life was not ideal. Only about 60 percent of children lived in the stereotypical two-parent, male-breadwinner, female-homemaker household. Furthermore, African American families experienced high rates of poverty and earned approximately half the income white families earned. Women often left college to occupy housewife roles, then found themselves bored at home in the suburbs as a result of an overall lack of professional or creative outlets. Half of all women marrying were

teenagers, and the teenage pregnancy rate stood at 96.3 per 1,000 in 1957, almost double the rate of the 1990's, although by the latter decade, most of the pregnant teenagers were unmarried.

Economic Change Economic prosperity typified the 1950's. War spending had ended the Great Depression, and military investment spurred the economy. By the mid-1950's, more than forty thousand defense contractors worked for the federal government. During a recession in 1957, President Dwight D. Eisenhower boosted the waning economy again by increasing defense spending. Many economists were concerned that the United States was establishing a permanent wartime economy.

However, during the 1950's, the U.S. economy changed from an industrial economy to a service economy. Workers left farms and factories for service positions in banking, advertising, health care, and sales. Technology also changed the face of the American workplace. In 1950, 11.8 percent of U.S. workers were in agriculture, 41.4 percent in industry, and 47.1 percent in services. By 1960, only 6.3 percent of workers remained in agriculture, industry was reduced to 39.7 percent of economic activity, and the service sector had expanded to 54.0 percent of the labor force. By 1956, white-collar jobs outnumbered blue-collar jobs.

The gross national product (GNP) increased tremendously during the 1950's, swelling from $294.3 billion in 1950 to $527.4 billion in 1960. Family income grew steadily as average salaries rose from an average of $2,992 in 1950 to $4,743 by 1960, and per capita income increased from $1,501 to $2,219.

The 1950's also witnessed middle-class expansion, low unemployment, and good wages. Government assistance to families and investment in technology and infrastructure projects contributed to economic prosperity. Additionally, the minimum wage was set at a sufficient level for a single earner to receive a living wage to support a family. Consumer spending increased rapidly during the 1950's. Expenditures for personal consumption increased from $192 billion in 1950 to $332 billion by 1960. Major appliances, processed foods, automobiles, televisions, and children's toys represented the wide range of consumer choices during the 1950's. Throughout the decade, Americans made up only 6 percent of the world's population but produced and consumed one-third of the world's goods and services.

Women and Employment Many women entered the paid workforce during the 1940's during the war effort. After the war, government propaganda and social commentary encouraged women to return to the home so that men returning from the war could have jobs. Public opinion polls showed that women who were employed during the war wanted to keep paid jobs. Consequently, many women moved into traditionally female occupations such as teaching and social services. Strong gender segregation existed in the workplace.

Men greatly outnumbered women in the labor force. In 1940, 55.2 percent of men and only 17.9 percent of women over the age of sixteen were employed in the labor force. In 1950, 55.9 percent of men and 34.5 percent of women participated in the labor force. By 1960, the percentage employed in the labor force was 60.2 for men and 37.5 for women. In 1950, 27.8 percent of the labor force were women, a figure that increased to 32.1 percent by 1960. Even though about one-third of all women were in the paid labor force, and women made up about one-third of the labor force, only 16 percent of married women with children worked outside the home in 1950. Society expected women to occupy domestic roles and care for their husbands and children rather than work outside the home for pay.

Suburbanization and Home Ownership Suburbs rapidly expanded during the 1950's. The number of suburban residents more than doubled, surging from 35 million to 84 million during the decade.

Many factors account for the high rate of suburban growth during the 1950's. The increased marriage rate and baby boom created a demand for housing because most young families desired a single-family home on a private lot. Suburbs had more land and lower-priced homes than inner cities. The federally financed highway system made a daily commute to cities possible, and liberalization of lending policies by government agencies made suburban home-ownership a realistic goal. Furthermore, mass-market home building contributed to suburbanization. Perhaps the most famous suburban development during the 1950's was Levittown, New York, where seventeen thousand families purchased a 750-square-foot home for $7,900 and received housing identical to everyone else in the neighborhood.

Suburban life was marketed as a move out of the city and up the socioeconomic ladder. Suburbs often were portrayed as demographically homogeneous, but they were actually more diverse than inner cities. Many religious, ethnic, and socioeconomic groups settled in the suburbs during the 1950's, although neighborhood race barriers were perpetuated. Affluent whites created formal and informal barriers that banned African Americans from many suburban developments. Cities lost white families during the 1950's, and real estate industry practices, bank lending policies, and legal segregation in the South kept most suburbs white.

African Americans experienced limited suburbanization during the 1950's. By 1960, black residents who did suburbanize migrated into established black, working-class suburban neighborhoods or became suburbanized because predominantly black city ghettos expanded into aging inner-ring suburbs. During the 1950's, a dual housing market kept black citizens restricted to traditionally black residential areas, especially in the suburbs. In 1960, the suburbs were only 4.6 percent African American.

Home ownership rose by 50 percent from 1940 to 1950 and another 50 percent from 1950 to 1960. By 1960, 25 percent of all housing units in the United States had been built in the previous decade. Thirteen million new homes were built during the 1950's, eleven million in the suburbs.

By 1950, many Americans owned their homes; home ownership stood at 55 percent and increased to 61.9 percent in 1960. Vacancy rates were low during the 1940's (6.6 percent), but demand for housing soared when veterans returned from World War II. Demand declined further as marriage and fertility rates sustained the demand for housing during the 1950's but increased by 1960 as the housing market declined.

Impact The decade of the 1950's is often considered a stagnant period in U.S. history. While conformity and homogeneity appeared to dominate the decade, remarkable changes actually occurred. More babies than ever before were born. The population shifted from farms and cities into suburbs. The isolated nuclear family characterized suburban living with stay-at-home mothers and breadwinning fathers and became the idealized family form. Consumerism replaced thriftiness as the economy shifted from lean war years to relative affluence.

The demographic trends of the 1950's set the stage for explosive changes of the 1960's. The rigid social expectations and conformity of the 1950's gave way to the youth rebellion of the 1960's. The Civil Rights movement and feminism arose from the baby boomers' concern for justice and their desire to right perceived societal wrongs. Suburbs became mainstream America, and suburbanization led to traffic, zoning issues, and the ugly realities of urban sprawl.

Because the baby-boom cohort is larger than those that went before and came after it, baby boomers have influenced culture and social structure at every stage of their lives. At first, increased fertility led to overcrowded maternity wards. The mid-1950's saw overcrowding in elementary and secondary schools resulting in mass construction of new schools, temporary classrooms, and teacher shortages. By the 1960's and 1970's, colleges enrolled record numbers of students, and during the 1970's and 1980's, the job market was flooded, and unemployment rose as young, college-educated job seekers entered the labor market. The divorce rate also increased during the 1980's as baby boomers entered their thirties and forties—ages at which divorce most typically occurs. At the turn of the twenty-first century, domestic policy makers anticipated that health care demands would increase and that Social Security would experience economic strains.

Further Reading

Bouvier, Leon F. *America's Baby Boom Generation: The Fateful Bulge.* Washington, D.C.: Population Reference Bureau, 1980. This publication offers an in-depth look at the causes and consequences of the baby boom.

Coontz, Stephanie. *The Way We Never Were: American Families and the Nostalgia Trap.* New York: Basic Books, 2000. Coontz examines the history of family life in the United States and shatters the myth of the 1950's family as the idealized two-parent homemaker-breadwinner family form.

Halberstam, David. *The Fifties.* New York: Ballantine Books, 1994. A wide-ranging book that offers a broad overview of cultural, political, and world developments during the 1950's. The author stresses how the 1950's were the impetus for change during the second half of the twentieth century.

Hobbs, Frank, and Nicole Stoops. *Demographic Trends in the Twentieth Century.* Washington, D.C.: U.S. Government Printing Office, 2002. This is a special Census Bureau report summarizing broad population trends over the course of the twentieth century.

Kallen, Stuart A., ed. *The 1950's.* San Diego, Calif.: Greenhaven Press, 2000. This informative book covers significant political and cultural events of the 1950's, including lifestyle and population trends.

Palen, J. John. *The Suburbs.* New York: McGraw-Hill, 1995. Palen offers a history of American suburbs, including information on the growth of cities during the 1950's.

Barbara E. Johnson

See also Affluence and the new consumerism; African Americans; Asian Americans; Baby boomers; Birth control; Demographics of Canada; Housing in the United States; Immigration to the United States; Latinos; Native Americans; Urbanization in the United States; War brides.

■ *Dennis v. United States*

Identification U.S. Supreme Court decision on freedom of speech
Date Decided on June 4, 1951

As a decision handed down in the McCarthy era, Dennis v. United States *strengthened the power of Congress to restrict subversive speech by distinguishing advocacy of "organized violent action" from advocacy of "belief."*

The Smith Act of 1940 (Internal Security Act) made it a felony to advocate the violent overthrow of the U.S. government or to conspire to organize a group advocating such violence. The Cold War, which had begun after World War II in response to Soviet communism, deepened after the United States became involved in the Korean conflict, and by the early 1950's, McCarthyism achieved substantial national influence. Against this background of Cold War hysteria, the Supreme Court reviewed and affirmed the convictions of twelve leaders of the Communist Party of the U.S.A.

Party Secretary Eugene Dennis and his eleven co-defendants had been convicted after a highly publicized nine-month federal trial for violation of the Smith Act. The defendants' convictions stemmed from their activities in organizing and furthering the purposes of communism in the United States. The Second Circuit Court of Appeals upheld the convictions, and the Supreme Court affirmed under what became known as the "clear and present danger" test, which balanced the perceived danger or gravity of evil, discounted by its improbability, against the invasion of free speech necessary to avoid the danger.

Impact In the aftermath of *Dennis*, as public opinion and the composition of the Court changed, there was a gradual movement away from its restrictive First Amendment interpretation. There was greater protection for the advocacy of ideas, and the "membership clause" of the Smith Act was confined to "active" rather than simply "nominal" membership in an organization advocating forcible overthrow of the government.

Further Reading

Domino, John C. *Civil Rights and Liberties: Toward the Twenty-first Century.* New York: HarperCollins, 1994. Analysis of Supreme Court rulings on civil rights and liberties in a historical context.

Lewis, Thomas T., and Richard L. Wilson, eds. *Encyclopedia of the U.S. Supreme Court.* Pasadena, Calif.: Salem Press, 2001. A comprehensive examination of landmark cases, including *Dennis.*

Stephens, Otis H., Jr., and John M. Scheb II. *American Civil Liberties.* Belmont, Calif.: West/Wadsworth, 1999. Casebook with useful introductory materials.

Marcia J. Weiss

See also Communist Party of the U.S.A.; Internal Security Act of 1950; McCarthy, Joseph; Red Monday; Supreme Court decisions, U.S.; *Yates v. United States.*

■ *Destination Moon*

Identification Science-fiction film depicting the first moon landing
Director Irving Pichel (1891-1954)
Date Released in 1950

Destination Moon is remembered for its reflection of early Cold War anxieties and for being the first serious cinematic treatment of spaceflight.

In George Pal's production of *Destination Moon*, an engineer and a military officer appeal to the patriot-

ism of American industrialists to finance a secret moon flight. Their effort encounters prelaunch conspiracies and postlaunch crises that include one crew member's drifting into outer space and another's nearly being left behind before the craft returns to Earth.

Novelist Robert A. Heinlein, the coauthor of the screenplay, borrowed from his *Rocket Ship Galileo* (1947), a young-adult novel about a backyard missile used by teenagers to defeat Nazis on the moon. The ninety-one-minute film retains the characteristic Heinlein theme of strong-willed, pioneer-spirited, and patriotically minded individuals who prevail despite obstructionist government policies.

Impact *Destination Moon* anticipated how, after the Soviets in 1957 launched the first artificial satellite, *Sputnik*, the early Cold War missile race would include the space race. Domination through weaponry was a key point of the film, a point made clear in the *Life* magazine article (April 24, 1950) on the movie, which specifically refers to four daring Americans who land on the moon to protect world peace. As the film's military officer notes, those who land on the moon first will control Earth.

Winning an Academy Award for special effects, benefiting from Chesley Bonestell's impressive matte paintings of the moon's surface, and appealing to audience concern with national security and the arms race, this movie was a financial success despite stock characterization, stiff acting, wooden dialogue, and its documentary manner. Now considered an influential classic of golden-age science fiction, *Destination Moon* was far more scientifically accurate and thematically optimistic than was customary in 1950's science-fiction cinema.

Further Reading

Hendershort, Cynthia. *Paranoia, the Bomb, and 1950's Science Fiction Films.* Bowling Green, Ohio: Popular Press, 1999. Examines how America's cultural paranoia during the 1950's was heightened by the arms race and the depiction of that race in Hollywood films.

Warren, Bill. *Keep Watching the Skies: American Science Fiction Movies of the Fifties.* Jefferson, N.C.: McFarland, 1997. Provides an alphabetical list of films, each of which includes synopses, quotes, cast and director information, and special effects listings.

William J. Scheick

The film Destination Moon *was praised for its realism; however, its depiction of the Moon's surface was far from realistic. For example, the lunar surface on which the spaceship stands in this scene bears the erosion marks of a former lake bed—an impossibility on the Moon.* (Hulton Archive | by Getty Images)

See also Cold War; Comic books; Film in the United States; Flying saucers; *Forbidden Planet*; Space race; *Sputnik I*; *Thing from Another World, The*; *War of the Worlds, The*.

■ DEW Line

Identification Ground-based radar installations designed to detect the approach of enemy bombers and intercontinental ballistic missiles (ICBMs) aimed at the United States from launch sites in the Soviet Union
Date Initiated in 1954; completed in 1957

The establishment of the Distant Early Warning (DEW) Line symbolized the realization that, in the nuclear Cold War age, America could ill afford a surprise attack of the type launched against Pearl Harbor in 1941.

In a report submitted to President Dwight D. Eisenhower in 1955, a panel of experts under the direction of presidential science adviser James R. Killian concluded that two hundred nuclear bombs, delivered in a surprise attack, would render the United States defeated, unable to mount a counterattack. To safeguard against such an event, Eisenhower approved the construction of long-range radar installations, sited at overlapping intervals within Canada, to create a virtual electronic "fence" from Alaska to Greenland. Data from this system were relayed to Strategic Air Command (SAC) headquarters in Omaha, Nebraska, providing an estimated thirty-minute warning of any attack.

Impact During the Cold War years, the DEW Line was thought to offer a defensive advantage by providing sufficient time for U.S. military forces to mount a

The Dew Line

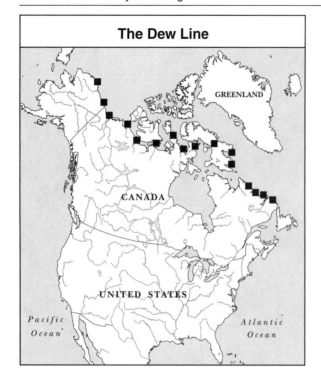

GREENLAND

CANADA

UNITED STATES

Pacific Ocean

Atlantic Ocean

counteroffensive against enemy attack. Even with these coordinated defenses in place, however, analysts estimated that as much as 50 percent of the enemy's nuclear attack force could most likely reach their targets. In the twenty-first century, even with the advent of more powerful hydrogen bombs, ballistic missile submarines, and sophisticated surveillance satellites, elements of the ground-based DEW Line concept still remain in use.

Further Reading

Keeny, L. Douglas. *The Doomsday Scenario.* St. Paul, Minn.: MBI Publishing Company, 2002. A declassified government document outlining the events and outcomes of a nuclear war.

Newhouse, John. *War and Peace in the Nuclear Age.* New York: Alfred A. Knopf, 1988. A comprehensive history of the nuclear age from the Manhattan Project to the Strategic Defense Initiative.

Larry Smolucha

See also Atomic bomb; B-52 bomber; Canada as a middle power; Civil defense programs; Cold War; Continentalism; Eisenhower, Dwight D.; Elections in Canada; Hydrogen bomb; North American Aerospace Defense Command; Polaris missiles; U-2 spy planes.

■ Diamond synthesizing

The Event First artificial transformation of graphite into diamond
Date First achieved in 1953

The ability to transform graphite into diamond revolutionized the diamond industry by providing durable material that allowed for the faster production of goods.

In 1796, Smithson Tennant discovered that although diamond was a form of carbon chemically, it was not physically identical to graphite, or pencil lead. Over the next century and a half, many scientists attempted to synthesize graphite or other soft forms of carbon into diamond. Research by Harvard University physicist Percy Bridgman developed the high-pressure techniques that would lead to his receiving the Nobel Prize in Physics in 1946 and would allow other researchers to synthesize diamond in the next decade.

In 1953, Swedish scientists at the Allmanna Svenska Elektriska Aktiebolaget (ASEA) Laboratory first produced diamond from graphite, but they did not publicize their invention. A team of American scientists working at General Electric Company (GE) also developed a process for producing synthetic diamonds and announced their invention in 1955. General Electric was awarded a world patent.

In 1957, the synthesization process was sufficiently developed by GE to produce commercial quantities of industrial diamonds, which became the basis for a group of hard industrial materials termed "superabrasives." These industrial diamonds were used to produce industrial cutting tools made from tungsten carbide, a very hard substance. In turn, the tools made from tungsten carbide were used to create machine metal parts for automobiles and other consumer products much faster than previous steel tools could.

Impact By the early twenty-first century, approximately 80 percent of all diamonds were synthetically produced, and more than 90 percent of all diamonds were being used for industrial applications.

Further Reading

Bruton, Eric. *Diamonds.* 2d ed. Radnor, Pa.: Chilton Book Company, 1978. A general book on diamonds.

Kalpakjian, Serope. *Manufacturing Engineering and Technology.* Reading, Mass.: Addison-Wesley, 1989. Explains common industrial uses of diamonds.

Robert E. Haag

See also Automobiles and auto manufacturing; Inventions; Science and technology.

■ Diddley, Bo

Identification African American rock-and-roll musician

Born December 30, 1928; McComb, Mississippi

As an early African American contributor to rock and roll, Bo Diddley helped steer the development of the genre.

Born Otha Ellas Bates, Bo Diddley moved with his family to Chicago in 1934. When he was eight, he

Bo Diddley with his trademark rectangular guitar. (Hulton Archive | by Getty Images)

asked for a violin, and the Ebenezer Missionary Baptist Church took up a collection for the instrument and lessons. He played classical violin until he broke a finger when he was fifteen. He received a guitar as a Christmas present in 1940 and taught himself to play, experimenting with duplicating the sounds of the violin and drums and developing his distinctive backbeat sound.

In 1955, Chicago's Chess Records recorded the double-sided "Bo Diddley" and "I'm a Man." This first record had the driving rhythm and sexual innuendoes typical of early rock-and-roll music, but his suggestive lyrics kept Diddley from receiving as much radio exposure as contemporaries such as Chuck Berry and Little Richard. Hits such as "Who Do You Love," "Road Runner," "You Can't Judge a Book by the Cover," "Pretty Thing," and "Mona" soon followed. Diddley's style merged blues and rhythm and blues to form a unique kind of guitar-based music, and his guitar work proved to be the contribution for which he was most noted.

Impact Diddley is widely acknowledged as one of the most influential pioneers of rock and roll. Echoes of his style can be heard in the music of Elvis Presley, Buddy Holly, the Rolling Stones, and Bruce Springsteen, and dozens of other performers have recorded his songs. He was elected to the Rock and Roll Hall of Fame in 1987 and received a Lifetime Achievement Award at the 1998 Grammys.

Further Reading

Weinraub, Bernard. "Pioneer of a Beat Is Still Riffing for His Due." *The New York Times* 152 (February 16, 2003): 1. Overview of Diddley's career and his struggles for recognition and recovery of unpaid royalties.

White, George R. *Bo Diddley: Living Legend.* New York: Music Sales, 1998. Biography based on interviews with Diddley.

Michael Adams

See also Berry, Chuck; Dance, popular; Domino, Fats; Haley, Bill; Holly, Buddy; Little Richard; Music; Presley, Elvis; Rock and roll.

■ Diefenbaker, John G.

Identification Prime minister of Canada from 1957 to 1963
Born September 18, 1895; Neustadt, Ontario, Canada
Died August 16, 1979; Ottawa, Ontario, Canada

John Diefenbaker was prime minister of Canada at a time when important issues related to Canada's relationship with the United States were developing, specifically in the areas of the economy and defense.

John Diefenbaker was born in 1895 in the province of Ontario, but eight years later, his family moved to western Canada—a region with which Diefenbaker would later be politically associated. After serving overseas in the Canadian military in World War I, he chose law as his career. Practicing law, however, lacked the appeal of politics for Diefenbaker. After losing five consecutive elections at three different political levels, he finally won a seat in the federal parliament in Ottawa in 1940 as a member of the Conservative Party. The fledgling politician soon sought the leadership of his party and failed in elections twice more before finally achieving his goal in 1956, at the age of sixty-one.

A Nationalistic Vision Diefenbaker had one more political goal, however. In 1957, members of the Liberal Party under Prime Minister Louis St. Laurent confidently sought reelection. Instead, they found themselves defeated by a reinvigorated Progressive Conservative Party under the leadership of Diefenbaker. The new prime minister quickly found himself having to make important Cold War decisions, including those that had ramifications for Canada's global diplomatic position. Diefenbaker, a firm supporter of Canada's close historical relationship with Great Britain, sought to strengthen that position by shifting trade away from the United States and toward Great Britain, a move that proved an impractical failure.

John Diefenbaker (center) shaking hands with former British prime minister Winston S. Churchill at the latter's London home in 1960. (AP/Wide World Photos)

In other arenas, Diefenbaker's nationalistic efforts had equally mixed results. The national government took a less rigid stance than the United States toward Fidel Castro's new government in Cuba, yet when it came to national defense, Diefenbaker avoided making a commitment to allowing the stationing of American nuclear weapons on Canadian soil, despite his predecessor's government having given permission for just such an undertaking. This vacillation prompted ridicule and pressure from Washington, D.C., and the entire matter would become an election issue during the 1960's.

Diefenbaker's policy decisions arguably made Canada more dependent on the United States. For example, in a controversial move, Diefenbaker cancelled the further development and manufacture of the Avro Arrow, an advanced jet fighter that was initiated in Canada. The administration feared the escalating costs associated with the production of the plane. Instead, the government opted to rely on Bomarc, the American surface-to-air missiles defense system, which became obsolete soon after its installation in Canada. Even more significantly, with little debate, Diefenbaker allowed Canada to join with the United States in a defense alliance, the North American Air Defense Command (NORAD), which Canada's American partner would come to dominate.

Impact Diefenbaker's policies ultimately proved divisive, and Canada found itself increasingly under American domination. Defense issues, particularly the continuing controversy over nuclear weapons on Canadian soil and Canada's relationship with the United States, bedevilled Diefenbaker's government and played a significant role in its defeat in the 1963 election. Although he introduced the Canadian Bill of Rights in 1960, his administration became unpopular as the government went into debt and domestic- and foreign-policy miscalculations embarrassed the nation.

The former prime minister continued to play an active political role in both his party and the federal parliament until his death in 1979.

Further Reading

Grant, George. *Lament for a Nation: The Defeat of Canadian Nationalism.* Montreal: McGill-Queens University Press, 2003. Study of Diefenbaker government's failed efforts to distance Canada from the United States.

Smith, Denis. *Rogue Tory: The Life and Legend of John G. Diefenbaker.* Toronto: Macfarlane Walter & Ross, 1997. Definitive biography of Diefenbaker.

Steve Hewitt

See also Avro Arrow; Canada and Great Britain; Canada and U.S. investments; Canada as a middle power; Canadian Labour Congress; Canadian regionalism; Continentalism; Elections in Canada; Foreign policy of Canada; International trade of Canada; North American Aerospace Defense Command; Pearson, Lester B.; St. Laurent, Louis.

■ Diggs, Charles C., Jr.

Identification African American congressman
Born December 2, 1922; Detroit, Michigan
Died August 24, 1998; Washington, D.C.

As the first African American elected to Congress from Michigan, Diggs fought for civil rights and improved relations with Africa.

The son of a wealthy undertaker in Detroit, Charles Diggs enjoyed opportunities in business and politics that were uncommon for African Americans during the 1940's. He served in World War II and graduated from Wayne State University with a degree in mortuary science. In 1946, he began working in the family business, and in 1951, he took over his father's seat in the Michigan state senate.

When Diggs was elected to the U.S. House of Representatives in 1954, he became one of only three African Americans in Congress. Appointed to the Veterans Affairs Committee, he focused on civil rights issues. He headed an investigation of segregation on army bases in Alabama and attended the trial for the murder of Emmett Till in Mississippi. In general, he was a powerful advocate for racial equality.

Diggs attended Ghana's independence celebration in 1957 and returned the following year for the All-Africa People's Conference. In 1959, he joined the House Foreign Affairs Committee and chaired its subcommittee on Africa. Until his resignation from Congress in 1980, he remained a central figure in U.S. relations with Africa, most notably as a cofounder of both the Congressional Black Caucus and TransAfrica.

Impact Diggs helped break new ground for African Americans in national politics during the 1950's and was one of a handful of U.S. policy makers who paid attention to Africa. He assisted the civil rights struggle and laid the foundation for other Americans interested in African issues.

Further Reading

Christopher, Maurine. *Black Americans in Congress.* New York: Thomas Crowell, 1976. Includes a chapter on Diggs.

DuBose, Carolyn. *The Untold Story of Charles Diggs.* Arlington, Va.: Barton, 1998. A good biography of Diggs.

Andy DeRoche

See also African Americans; Civil Rights movement; Congress, U.S.; Till lynching.

■ DiMaggio, Joe

Identification American baseball player

Born November 25, 1914; Martinez, California

Died March 8, 1999; Hollywood, Florida

An icon of 1950's masculinity, Joe DiMaggio was the one of the most successful and adored baseball players of his generation.

Joseph Paul DiMaggio was the son of Italian immigrant parents. Raised in San Francisco, DiMaggio played three seasons (1933-1935) for the San Francisco Seals of the Pacific Coast League. During DiMaggio's major league career (1936-1942, 1946-1951), punctuated by military service (1942-1945), the center fielder played exclusively for the New York Yankees.

Beset by age and injury, DiMaggio encountered disappointment during his final baseball seasons. In 1950, DiMaggio, playing inconsistently, was briefly benched by Yankee manager Casey Stengel. Nonetheless, DiMaggio finished the 1950 campaign with a .301 batting average, leading the Yankees to a World Series sweep. In 1951, the Yankee dynasty again won the Series, but DiMaggio's perfor-

mance suffered; he batted only .263, and Stengel increasingly relied on Yogi Berra and anointed young Mickey Mantle as the team's next superstar. Not wanting fans to remember him struggling, DiMaggio announced his retirement on December 11, 1951.

DiMaggio was central to the iconography of 1950's baseball and masculinity. His impressive record of nine World Series championships a .325 lifetime batting average, and a fifty-six-game hitting streak helped earn him a place in the National Baseball Hall of Fame in 1955. Pundits increasingly depicted DiMaggio as the greatest all-around player in baseball history. DiMaggio's dignity, grace, stoic

Joe DiMaggio (right) with New York Yankees general manager George Weiss, after signing his contract for the new season in 1950. Until free agency entered Major League Baseball during the 1970's, it was rare for players to sign for more than a single season at a time. (AP/Wide World Photos)

courage, and brief marriage to Hollywood sex symbol Marilyn Monroe rendered him emblematic of American masculinity. However, novelist Ernest Hemingway's evocation of DiMaggio in *The Old Man and the Sea* (1952), and the brief, tragic marriage in 1954 between DiMaggio and actor Marilyn Monroe helped tarnish DiMaggio's heroic status.

Sports fans saw little of DiMaggio after the 1950's, although he acted in television commercials for Mr. Coffee products during the 1970's. However, DiMaggio's mystique continued to grow, indicative in songwriter Paul Simon's "Mrs. Robinson" (1968), "Where have you gone, Joe DiMaggio?," a song which resonated in an America that longed again for such a hero.

Further Reading

Cramer, Richard Ben. *Joe DiMaggio: The Hero's Life.* New York: Simon & Schuster, 2000. A revisionist biography.

Gilliam, Richard, ed. *Joltin' Joe DiMaggio.* New York: Carroll & Graf, 1999. An excellent collection of essays.

William M. Simons

See also Banks, Ernie; Baseball; Berra, Yogi; *Damn Yankees*; Hemingway, Ernest; Mantle, Mickey; Monroe, Marilyn; New York Yankees; Stengel, Casey.

■ Disarmament movement

Definition Cold War-era attempts by the superpowers to bring about the reduction or abolition of troops and weaponry

The expanding stockpiles of nuclear weapons during the 1950's increased the urgency for disarmament negotiations to control an escalating and dangerous arms race.

With the devastation caused by both conventional and atomic weapons during World War II, hopes were high that the newly created United Nations (U.N.) would foster international peace and security by promoting disarmament. In a 1950 address to the U.N. General Assembly, President Harry S. Truman initiated a new American policy on arms control that coupled conventional and nuclear weaponry, but the outbreak of the Korean War brought negotiations to an impasse. Early in 1952, the United Nations set up a disarmament commission, and in April, the United States proposed that, before any arms reductions, an international inspection system

be established. However, the Soviet Union insisted on a cut in conventional arms and an atomic weapons ban before the creation of an inspection system. In the climate of the Cold War, the Soviets interpreted inspections as a subterfuge for intelligence gathering.

When, during the early months of 1953, Dwight D. Eisenhower became president and Soviet leader Joseph Stalin died, expectations were raised that these events would lead to progress in disarmament. At the end of 1953, President Eisenhower, in his famous "Atoms for Peace" speech, noted that he hoped that his plan to use nuclear materials for peaceful rather than military purposes would be a step toward nuclear disarmament. His plan did result in the International Atomic Energy Agency, a U.N. organization headquartered in Vienna, Austria, but it failed to realize the U.N. goal of total disarmament.

Multilateral Negotiations From 1954 to 1957, the most important agency for disarmament discussions was a five-nation subcommittee consisting of the United States, Soviet Union, Great Britain, France, and Canada. The Western powers emphasized onsite inspections, with the United States particularly concerned about surprise nuclear attacks. When President Eisenhower met the Soviet leaders at the Geneva Summit Conference in the summer of 1955, he introduced an "Open Skies" proposal that advocated mutual aerial inspections of the nuclear nations, but the Soviets were skeptical of Western intentions. The Western countries, concerned about possible clandestine nuclear weapons, withdrew their disarmament proposals until an effective scientific inspection system could be devised. Political events in 1956, such as the Suez Crisis and the Hungarian revolt, further complicated disarmament talks, from which the Soviet Union withdrew in 1957.

During the mid- to late 1950's an increasingly successful movement of scientists, who were troubled by the harm done by fallout to humans and the environment, urged banning tests of nuclear weapons. President Eisenhower appointed an advisory committee of scientists who concluded that a test ban was feasible, as did a conference of experts meeting in Geneva in the summer of 1958. Other negotiations, conducted apart from the U.N. disarmament agencies, involved several interested countries, all of which successfully concluded the Antarctic Treaty of 1959. This first postwar disarmament agreement, signed by twelve countries that participated in the International Geophysical Year (1957-1958), made Antarctica into a nuclear-weapons-free zone.

Toward the end of 1959, the U.N. General Assembly unanimously passed a resolution championing total disarmament, though recognizing that partial measures might be necessary to achieve this goal. The new committee to implement these recommendations was made up of five democratic and five communist countries. It began meeting in 1960, but when the Soviet Union shot down a United States U-2 spy plane over its territory, disarmament talks collapsed.

Impact The addition of nuclear weapons to the world's arsenal created a compelling need to control if not abolish them. Some initiatives developed during the 1950's continued into the 1960's, and these efforts resulted in the Limited Nuclear Test Ban Treaty of 1963, which prohibited the testing of nuclear weapons in the atmosphere, under water, and in outer space. The deep fears and suspicions of the Cold War prevented any agreement on general disarmament during the 1960's, but during the 1970's, arms limitation talks between the United States and the Soviet Union led to a series of accords that put limits on offensive nuclear weapons.

Further Reading

Divine, Robert A. *Blowing on the Wind: The Nuclear Test Ban Debate, 1954-1960.* New York: Oxford University Press, 1978. Divine, a historian, tells the story of the dilemmas that nuclear weapons and their testing posed for politicians, scientists, and the public.

Hewlett, Richard G., and Jack M. Hall. *Atoms for Peace and War, 1953-1961: Eisenhower and the Atomic Energy Commission.* Berkeley: University of California Press, 1989. A well-researched account of the arms control policies of the Eisenhower administration.

Robert J. Paradowski

See also Antarctic Treaty of 1959; Atomic bomb; Bomb shelters; Cold War; Foreign policy of the United States; Geneva Summit Conference; Hydrogen bomb; Oppenheimer, J. Robert; Pauling, Linus; Seaborg, Glenn; Tripartite Security Treaty; Truman, Harry S.

■ Disneyland

Identification Theme-oriented amusement park
Date Opened on July 17, 1955
Place Anaheim, California

Walt Disney redefined carnivals, gardens, and leisure time with Disneyland, the first "themed" entertainment park, which quickly became a California landmark and a leading U.S. tourist attraction.

Walt Disney was the world-renowned creator of Mickey Mouse and his cartoon friends, Academy Award-winning animated and live-action films, and World War II-era educational films and military insignias. Disney films espoused the virtues of American individualism, patriotism, sentimentalism, optimism, capitalism, and environmentalism.

From Vision to Reality Disney's theme park idea was sparked during the 1930's, when he took his two young daughters to the merry-go-round near his Los Angeles home. His vision was later refined after visits to the Chicago Railroad Fair (1948), Henry Ford's Greenfield Village in Michigan (1948), and Tivoli Gardens in Copenhagen (1950). Disney wished for a safe, clean, and comfortable place where children and parents could have fun together as well as learn about their heritage.

In 1952, Disney took a color rendering of a sixteen-acre Disney park to the Southern California city of Burbank and proposed it be built along Riverside Drive, across the street from his Disney Studio. Although Burbank officials rejected the idea, he was not discouraged. He established Walter Elias Disney (WED) Enterprises. WED, later renamed Walt Disney Imagineering, was a select group of Disney Studio employees—architects turned art directors, illustrators, machinists, model makers, landscape designers, and filmmakers—charged with the design and construction of Disneyland. In 1953, Stanford Research Institute found Disneyland a suitable location in Anaheim, thirty-eight miles southeast of Los Angeles, adjacent to the nearly completed Santa Ana Freeway, on 160 acres of orange grove land.

The remaining obstacle to building Disneyland was Disney's need for financial backing. Already wooed by the three major television networks for a weekly Disney show, Disney's brother and finance director, Roy Oliver Disney, presented a revised Disneyland painting at network negotiations in New

York. Roy stipulated that in addition to airing the Disney television program, the network would agree to help finance the building of Disneyland. ABC took the bait. Later, about sixty-five corporate sponsors backed many of Disneyland's stores and attractions.

Excavation began during the summer of 1954. After a year of feverish construction, at a cost of $17 million, Disneyland opened on Sunday, July 17, 1955. Twenty-five thousand invited guests attended the dedication ceremony, which was televised live on ABC's *Dateline Disneyland* and was hosted by television personalities Art Linkletter, Ronald Reagan, and Bob Cummings. Disney dedicated his theme park to "the ideals, the dreams, and the hard facts that have created America. . . . "

Design Arguably Disney's favorite project, Disneyland took his films to three dimensions. WED designers used principles of filmmaking and applied them to invent the world's first "theme park." Each of the themed "lands"—Adventureland, Frontierland, Fantasyland, and Tomorrowland—translated to ongoing Disney projects. Adventureland modeled the true-life adventure documentaries the Disney Studio had begun producing in 1948. Its Jungle Cruise attraction was inspired by director John Huston's *The African Queen* (1951). Frontierland, with its wilderness fort, Mark Twain steamboat, and Golden Horseshoe Revue, simulated the Old West, including the popular *Davy Crockett* television series. In Fantasyland, guests became lead characters inside the "dark rides" depicting some of Disney's most popular animated films such as *Snow White and the Seven Dwarfs* (1937) and *Peter Pan* (1953). Beautifully crafted miniature houses with bonsai trees in manicured minigardens were featured in the Storybook Land boat and Casey, Jr., train rides. Tomorrowland reflected Disney's interest in promised future technological change as well as corporate research; among its attractions were a rocket ship and a *Twenty Thousand Leagues Under the Sea* (1954) exhibit. Main Street U.S.A., through which all visitors passed while entering Disneyland, was an idealized, early twentieth century look at America and reflected Disney's fond memories of his small-hometown roots. The feelings of security, family cohesion, and optimism expressed in Disney films were also reflected in the park's design.

Disney had a hand in every detail of Disneyland, from the antique gas lampposts, comforting color scheme, and building heights on Main Street to the design of the trash receptacles. The whole park was designed to make visitors feel themselves to be part of the action, not merely observers. Disneyland was in a constant state of improvement and clean as a whistle. Disney used a term from silent-film comedies, "wienies," to describe Disneyland's tall landmarks that drew the pedestrian forward. Disney's fascination with trains and the virtues of public transportation provided the first "wienie" even before entering the park: The five-eighths scale "E. P. Ripley" freight train of the Santa

Walt Disney, with a grandson, in front of the entrance to Fantasyland, shortly after Disneyland opened in 1955. (Hulton Archive | by Getty Images)

Fe and Disneyland Railroad was elevated above Disneyland's entrance. Next, the majestic seventy-five-foot-high Sleeping Beauty castle at the end of Main Street beckoned pedestrians. Just in front of the castle was a circular space or "hub," a place from which the guest could walk into each of the four lands. Connecting all the lands together like the rim of a wheel was the railroad. Main Street at street level was also built to five-eighths scale. Disney said it cost him more but made Main Street a toy that one's imagination could play with more freely.

Impact Disneyland welcomed its one-millionth guest only seven weeks after opening day, and by 1956, five million people had walked through its gates. Every year new attractions were added, such as Junior Autopia, Tom Sawyer Island, Monsanto House of the Future (a four-winged house built of plastic), and an Alice in Wonderland ride. The country's first daily operating monorail and "E ticket" thrill rides were introduced in 1959. The one-hundredth scale Matterhorn bobsled ride took over as the park's newest "wienie" (it became an Anaheim landmark in its own right, visible from the freeway far outside Disneyland's berm). At the Matterhorn's base was the Submarine Voyage "through liquid space." Disney's net profits jumped from $1.3 million in 1955 to $3.4 million by the end of the decade.

At the dedication ceremony, California governor Goodwin J. Knight noted, "Disneyland is a monument to humanity's desire for happiness and enjoyment of life's blessings." By 1960, Disneyland annually attracted five million visitors. Disney and his Imagineers had provided in Disneyland a harmoniously designed environment that evoked stability and reassurance in spite of the Cold War. "I don't want the public to see the world they live in while they're in the park," said Disney, "I want them to feel they're in another world."

Further Reading

The Imagineers. *Walt Disney Imagineering: A Behind the Dreams Look at Making the Magic Real.* New York: Hyperion, 1996. Well-illustrated book that explores the role both of the artist and of the creative process at Disney Studios.

Marling, Karal Ann, et al., eds. *Designing Disney's Theme Parks: The Architecture of Reassurance.* Paris: Flammarion, 1997. Chronicles the development of Disneyland and assesses its importance on Americans' architectural imagination.

Tieman, Robert. *The Disney Treasures.* New York: Disney Editions, 2003. Handbook for memorabilia collectors.

Watts, Steven. *The Magic Kingdom: Walt Disney and the American Way of Life.* New York: Houghton Mifflin Company, 1997. A biography of Walt Disney that includes discussion of the creation of Disneyland.

Sheri P. Woodburn

See also Affluence and the new consumerism; Architecture; *Davy Crockett*; Khrushchev's visit to the United States; *Mickey Mouse Club*; Television for children.

■ DNA (deoxyribonucleic acid)

The Event Discovery by Francis Crick and James D. Watson of the structure of DNA (deoxyribonucleic acid) and the recognition that DNA is a critical genetic component of genes that determines the eventual expression of particular traits in living organisms

Date Announced in 1953

After genes were recognized early in the twentieth century as the determinants of heredity, their chemistry was in question. Once the chemistry was tied to DNA, the next major hurdle was to learn the nature of the molecule, a scientific discovery that subsequently occurred during the 1950's, paving the way for far-reaching advancements in science.

During the early decades of the twentieth century, there was great confusion over the basic nature of DNA and the role it played within cells. P. Aaron Levene, working at Columbia University, proposed the tetranucleotide theory, which indicated equal amounts of the four bases—adenine, guanine, thymine, and cytosine—which are always found in DNA. From this research, the conclusion was drawn that DNA is far too simple a molecule to function as the genetic material. However, using methods available after World War II, U.S. scientist Erwin Chargaff showed that the four DNA bases are not necessarily present in equal amounts. This led to the recognition for the first time that DNA was a complex polymer of great interest and most likely the principal component of genes. Therefore, by 1950, scientists had learned that genes were what determined heredity and that DNA, which contained the genes, was the key to this process. However, the molecular structure of DNA was still a scientific puzzle.

Stages in DNA Replication

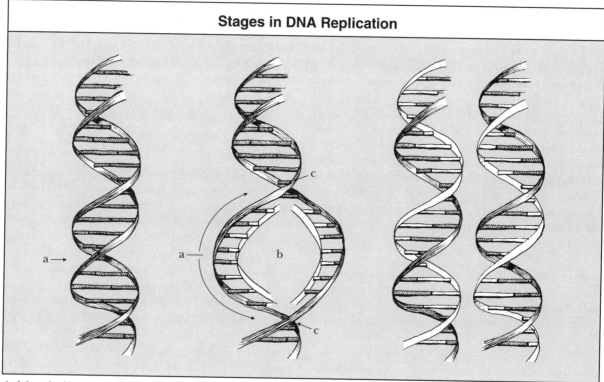

At left, a double-stranded DNA molecule, with the sides made of sugar-phosphate molecules and the "rungs" of base pairs. Replication begins at a point (a), with the separation of a base pair, as a result of the action of special initiator proteins (b). The molecule splits, or "unzips," in opposite directions (c) as each parental strand is used as a template for the formation of a new daughter strand (new bases pair with their appropriate "mate" bases to form new ladder "rungs"). Finally (right), one parental strand and its newly synthesized daughter strand form a new double helix, while the other parental strand and its daughter strand form a second double helix. (Kimberly L. Dawson Kurnizki)

The Watson-Crick Model During the early 1950's, U.S. researcher James D. Watson and his British colleague, Francis Crick, were able to explain the chemical nature of DNA. They did little or no experimental work but rather drew on the work of others. They visualized a DNA molecule consisting of two helices, or spirals, each wrapped around the other and consisting of alternating phosphate and sugar (deoxyribose) units. Next, Watson and Crick had to account for Chargaff's finding that the amounts of the bases adenine (A) and thymine (T) are always the same for a given source and that the same is true for the bases guanine (G) and cytosine (C). This formation is explained as an A and T pair and a G and C pair; in turn, both pairs form connections between sugar units opposite one another along the two helices. The basic unit of DNA is the nucleotide; there are four kinds of nucleotides, each containing a phosphate, a sugar, and one of the four bases.

The Watson-Crick model explained that all genes are diverse despite all being composed of DNA. The arrangement of nucleotides along the length of the long DNA molecule allows for information to be built into molecules. The model, announced in the journal *Nature* in 1953, explained the diversity of the millions of genes in all living organisms, how genes replicate, and how genes express themselves as visible traits, called phenotypes. In elucidating how genes replicate themselves, Watson and Crick explained that during interphase, when a cell is not dividing, the DNA molecule becomes "unzipped" and unwound as nucleotides of one half of the molecule pull apart from those of the other half. This process is followed by the attraction of "spare-part" nucleotides, resulting in two DNA molecules, each a copy of the original molecule. Each molecule will go into one of the two cells that will result from the subsequent cell division.

Watson and Crick's research enabled an understanding that genetic information flows in a path that begins with DNA, moves to ribonucleic acid (RNA), and ends with protein. This path came to be known as the Central Dogma of molecular biology: RNA, a nucleic acid similar to DNA and also composed of nucleotides, is synthesized, using DNA as a template (pattern), thus passing information to the RNA. The resulting RNA leaves the nucleus and becomes attached to a ribosome in the cytoplasm. There, proteins are assembled of amino acids, the sequence determined by the nature of the RNA. In this way, the nature of the DNA in the nucleus determines the kind of protein molecules that are formed in the cytoplasm.

Impact The elucidation of DNA's molecular structure through Watson and Crick's research made it possible to understand for the first time the nature of genes and how they control heredity. Watson and Crick's discovery paved the way for a new branch in science, molecular biology. Moreover, advancements in both medicine and crime investigation were enabled by Watson and Crick's work. In 1962, nine years after the publication of their landmark article on DNA, the two biologists were honored with the Nobel Prize for Physiology or Medicine, along with their colleague, Maurice Wilkins.

Further Reading

Edelson, Edward. *Francis Crick and James Watson and the Building Blocks of Life*. New York: Oxford University Press, 2000. Edelson concentrates on the development of molecular genetics, particularly the story of the discovery of the structure of DNA, which serves as a contextual biography for Watson and Crick.

Inglis, John R., Joseph Sambrook, and Jan Witkowski, eds. *Inspiring Science: Jim Watson and the Age of DNA*. Cold Spring Harbor, N.Y.: Cold Spring Harbor Laboratory Press, 2003. Colleagues and friends of Watson contribute anecdotes about their experiences of working with him.

Raven, Peter, and George B. Johnson. *Biology*. 7th ed. Boston: McGraw-Hill, 2004. A college textbook with a major section devoted to heredity and molecular biology.

Thomas E. Hemmerly

See also Genetics; Ribonucleic acid (RNA); Science and technology; Watson, James D.

■ Dodgers and Giants relocation

The Event Transfer of the Brooklyn Dodgers and New York Giants to Los Angeles and San Francisco

Date Announced in 1957; took place in 1958

By moving to California, the Dodgers and Giants initiated the geographical expansion of Major League Baseball beyond its original eastern and midwestern regions.

The Brooklyn Dodgers and New York Giants enjoyed great popularity and at times considerable success throughout their histories. Both were among the top major league teams of the 1950's. From the late 1940's through 1956, the Dodgers, known lovingly as "Dem Bums," won six pennants in ten years. Before leaving the team in 1950, Branch Rickey, the Dodgers' president and general manager, had assembled a great collection of star players, including Duke Snider, Roy Campanella, Pee Wee Reese, Don Newcombe, Gil Hodges, and Jackie Robinson. Robinson, an African American player, integrated the majors in 1947. Under Rickey's successor, Walter O'Malley, the Dodgers continued to excel, finally winning their first World Series in 1955 against the New York Yankees.

Meanwhile, the New York Giants were heated rivals of the Dodgers. In 1951, the Giants won a three-game playoff series with the Dodgers for the National League crown, when Bobby Thomson hit a dramatic ninth-inning home run in the final game. The Giants lost the World Series to the Yankees but again captured the pennant in 1954, this time upsetting the Cleveland Indians in the World Series. By 1954, Willie Mays was the Giants' greatest star and one of the most popular players in baseball history.

During the summer of 1957, fans were shocked and angered to learn that their teams were leaving for California after the season. Fans blamed O'Malley and Giants owner Horace Stoneham for forsaking the people who had supported the teams for decades in order to capture a more lucrative market in California. Others argued that O'Malley wanted to stay in Brooklyn but was unable to gain support from the city for a new stadium to replace an antiquated Ebbets Field. Once O'Malley decided to move, he persuaded Stoneham to follow suit and continue the rivalry out West.

The move to California was financially rewarding

for both teams, whose attendance increased dramatically in 1958 in their new locations. On-field success also came quickly, with the Los Angeles Dodgers winning the World Series in 1959 and the San Francisco Giants capturing the pennant in 1962. However, the beloved Bums and the "Say-Hey Kid" Willie Mays now belonged to the surfers and Hollywood stars of California.

Impact For more than fifty years, Major League Baseball remained more or less unchanged in the number of teams (sixteen, eight in each league) and in the cities in which they played. Although some switching of cities had started to occur as early as the 1953 season (the Braves' move from Boston to Milwaukee), these changes had remained within Major League Baseball's original geographical boundaries. Now, with improved air travel making cross-country competition feasible, the migration of the Dodgers

and Giants opened the gates for both geographical expansion and an increase in the number of major league teams.

Subsequent Events Within the next decade, Major League Baseball expanded beyond sixteen teams and also spread to the South. With the creation of the Arizona Diamondbacks and the Tampa Bay Devil Rays in 1998, Major League Baseball reached a total of thirty teams, including five in California.

Further Reading

Goldblatt, Andrew. *The Giants and the Dodgers: Four Cities, Two Teams, One Rivalry.* Jefferson, N.C.: McFarland, 2003. Examines the rivalry between the Dodgers and Giants before and after their move to California.

Schott, Tom, and Nick Peters. *The Giants Encyclopedia.* Champaign, Ill.: Sports, 2000. A lengthy and

Officials and employees of the Brooklyn Dodgers baseball team prepare to take off for Los Angeles, where the team relocated, on October 23, 1957. Team owner Walter O'Malley is at the top of the stairs, to the right. The only player in the picture is infielder Jim "Junior" Gilliam, second from the left in the front row, who was rookie of the year in 1955. (AP/Wide World Photos)

detailed history of the Giants in New York and San Francisco.

Sullivan, Neil J. *The Dodgers Move West.* New York: Oxford University Press, 1987. A detailed discussion of the decision by the Dodgers to move to Los Angeles.

Edward J. Rielly

See also Baseball; Baseball's exemption from antitrust laws; Campanella, Roy; Mays, Willie; New York Yankees; Snider, Duke; Sports; Stengel, Casey; Thomson, Bobby.

■ Domino, Fats

Identification American rhythm-and-blues pianist and singer

Born February 26, 1928; New Orleans, Louisiana

A major influence on several types of American music during the 1950's, Domino sold more records than any other recording artist of that decade except Elvis Presley.

Antoine "Fats" Domino's music-loving family taught him to play the piano, and he decided early in his life to make music his career. He dropped out of school and worked the day shift in a factory so he could perform at night. With a large and growing following, Domino signed a contract with Imperial Records in 1949.

Domino's records sold well from the start. His first release was "The Fat Man," a sanitized version of a drug song, which sold more than one million copies. He had several other huge selling singles on the rhythm and blues (R&B) charts before crossing over to a wider, largely white market in 1955 with "Ain't That a Shame." Domino's tremendous success was even more astounding considering certain circumstances, which might have ended his career. For an entertainer, Domino was surprisingly reticent and never enjoyed self-promotion; therefore, he rarely appeared on television. Moreover, other recording companies would release cleaned up versions of his songs by artists such as Pat Boone, thus subtracting from Domino's sales potential. Domino ill advisedly changed recording companies in 1963, and he gradually disappeared from the charts.

Impact Domino's record sales alone would make him noteworthy. He sold 65 million records and appeared on the Top 40 charts thirty-seven times and the R&B charts fifty-nine times. He was a recipient of the Grammy's Lifetime Achievement Award and was inducted into the Rock and Roll Hall of Fame in 1986.

Further Reading

Altschuler, Glenn C. *All Shook Up: How Rock 'n' Roll Changed America.* New York: Oxford University Press, 2003. Details the rise of rock-and-roll music during the 1950's, with vivid biographies of countless musicians, including Domino.

George-Warren, Holly, and Patricia Romanowski, eds. *The Rolling Stone Encyclopedia of Rock and Roll.* New York: Fireside, 2001. Contains a good article on Domino.

Koster, Rick. *Louisiana Music.* Cambridge, Mass.: Da Capo Press, 2002. Covers the many genres of music that have emanated from Louisiana, including R&B and gospel. Domino is part of the discussion.

Thomas W. Buchanan

See also Boone, Pat; Cole, Nat King; Dance, popular; Diddley, Bo; Freed, Alan; Holly, Buddy; Lewis, Jerry Lee; Little Richard; Music; Rock and roll; Top 40 radio.

Fats Domino in 1955. (Hulton Archive | by Getty Images)

■ *Dragnet*

Identification Television police drama
Date First aired in January, 1952

This long-running series by Jack Webb provided Americans with a realistic if dramatized view of crime and police work.

As producer, director, and star of the show, Jack Webb gave NBC television audiences thirty minutes of weekly excitement during the 1950's with *Dragnet*. Webb's button-down, clean-cop image as Sergeant Joe Friday was in contrast to the lawbreakers he and his partner apprehended. The program's classic opening—four musical notes with a view of sprawling Los Angeles—was followed by Friday's deadpan voice: "This is the city. Los Angeles, California." Viewers were told, "The story you are about to see is true. Names have been changed to protect the innocent."

Dragnet provided audiences with depictions of unglamorous, typical police work: interviewing witnesses, following dead-end leads, and filling out paperwork. Gunplay was rarely seen. Part of the show's realism was attributed to the voice-over that gave local weather conditions and the time of day, and spoke in typical police jargon. Friday often delivered a terse lecture to the subdued suspect, and each show ended with the police mug shots of the nervous criminal and the reading of the judge's sentence.

Impact *Dragnet* consistently conveyed the message that crime does not pay. Its realistic action format was a departure from the predominance of comedy and vaudeville shows, and it became an important prototype for similar programs in future years. *Dragnet*'s hero became one of the most popular police characters in television history. Phrases from the show even entered the decade's mainstream culture, including "Just the facts, ma'am," and "My name's Friday—I'm a cop."

Further Reading

Marling, Karal Ann. *As Seen on TV: The Visual Culture of Everyday Life in the 1950's.* Cambridge, Mass.: Harvard University Press, 1996. This book provides a social commentary on the early days of television and its influence on the decade's popular culture.

Moyer, Daniel, and Eugene Alvarez. *Just the Facts, Ma'am: The Authorized Biography of Jack Webb.* Carson, Calif.: Seven Locks Press, 2001. An account of Webb's rise from poverty to television producer and the contributions *Dragnet* has made to television's gritty realism.

Randy Hines

See also Freberg, Stan; Nielsen ratings; *Perry Mason*; Radio; Television in the United States.

■ Drive-in theaters

Definition Outdoor movie theaters at which audiences watched films from inside their own vehicles

Drive-in theaters entertained an affluent and car-loving postwar population and merged Americans' love of automobiles with community entertainment.

During the 1950's, the typical drive-in theater consisted of a large, painted outdoor screen at the front of a large parking lot. Visitors pulled their cars into parking rows sculpted into the pavement, their front tires elevated by mounded rises in the ground so that their cars' front ends were raised for viewing without interfering with the views of cars behind them. For good sound reception, poles with individual speakers for each car lined the parking spots, and visitors mounted the speakers on their side windows. Viewing the film from one's automobile provided privacy combined with the ability to stretch one's legs or consume snacks without affecting other theatergoers.

History The first drive-in theater was created during the early 1930's by Richard Hollingshead. He nailed a screen to his backyard trees and placed a radio behind the screen for sound. Hollingshead determined the best car parking distance and angle by arranging parked cars at different distances from one another and then placing them on angled blocks for good viewing. In 1933, he received the first patent for a drive-in theater. The popularity of the drive-in grew quickly: In 1948, there were fewer than one thousand drive-in theaters in the United States, and by 1958, there were almost five thousand in the United States and about three hundred in Canada. By the end of the 1950's, as television became more popular, drive-in theaters had reached their peak and began losing ground as people accessed entertainment in their homes.

Teenagers enjoyed the privacy afforded by drive-in theaters, which also served young families by pro-

Cars entering a Los Angeles drive-in theater in 1951. Drive-ins usually charged by the individual patron but occasionally had bargain nights with flat admission fees for entire carloads of patrons. (Hulton Archive | by Getty Images)

viding an opportunity to go to the movies affordably and not require children to be quiet and still, as in conventional theaters. Drive-in theater complexes began to offer amenities to attract children and families—outdoor playgrounds, snack bars, and even carhop food delivery. Theater owners discovered that large profits were enjoyed from the sale of food and candy, and many created movie shorts, concession advertising, and long intermissions in order to encourage the sale of these food items.

To keep children and families coming back, drive-in theaters began to include other children's activities such as miniature golf, trains, or pony rides. Many drive-in theaters opened as much as three hours before the shows began so that people could enjoy the festive and entertaining activities.

Impact Drive-ins reflected Americans' growing affluence. Families could afford automobiles and public entertainment. In addition, families of the 1950's

had a great fondness for their automobiles. Merging the public's interests in leisure activities and automobiles, drive-in theaters provided a place for youth and growing families to enjoy public entertainment with others in their community, in a safe, family-oriented environment.

Further Reading

Miller, Douglas T., and Marion Nowak. *The Fifties: The Way We Really Were.* Garden City, N.Y.: Doubleday, 1977. Overview of important cultural influences of the 1950's, including popular media.

Sanders, Don, and Susan Sanders. *American Drive-In Movie Theatre.* Osceola, Wis.: Motorbooks International, 1997. Offers informative details and photographs of drive-ins in their heyday.

Seagrave, Kerri. *Drive-in Theaters: A History from Their Inception in 1933.* New York: McFarland, 1992. Traces the rise of the drive-in theater, examining patent battles, concerns with morality, technological advances, and other factors that affected these theaters.

Megali Stuart

See also Affluence and the new consumerism; Automobiles and auto manufacturing; Baby boomers; Fads; Film in Canada; Film in the United States; Pay television; Surfing and beach culture; Wide-screen movies; Youth culture and the generation gap.

■ Dulles, John Foster

Identification U.S. secretary of state from 1953 to 1959
Born February 25, 1888; Washington, D.C.
Died May 24, 1959; Washington, D.C.

As secretary of state under President Dwight D. Eisenhower during the contentious Cold War era, John Foster Dulles exercised considerable control over U.S. foreign policy, which he used to take a hard stance in opposition to the spread of international communism.

When President Dwight D. Eisenhower selected John Foster Dulles as his first choice to be secretary of state in 1953, the decision elicited little surprise. Dulles had an impressive résumé of foreign service. He had participated in the Versailles Peace Conference following World War I, and between the world wars he had worked as a Wall Street attorney specializing in international law. After World War II, he was one of the few Republicans who worked closely with the Truman administration. In 1949, he served as a U.S. senator who supported the North Atlantic Treaty Organization (NATO), and in January, 1951, President Harry S. Truman named Dulles as head negotiator of the Japanese peace mission. In order to ensure that the Japanese Peace Treaty was not too harsh or vindictive, Dulles also played a major role in creating the Tripartite Security Treaty that resulted in the creation of ANZUS, the Australian-New Zealand-U.S. Tripartite Security Treaty, on September 1, 1951.

After signing the Japanese Peace Treaty on Sep-

John Foster Dulles (right) with President Dwight D. Eisenhower (left) and former British prime minister Winston S. Churchill in May, 1959, a few days before Dulles died. (Hulton Archive | by Getty Images)

tember 8, 1951, Dulles began distancing himself from the Truman administration. He became a vociferous critic of Truman's foreign policy, and he turned into the Republican Party's leading expert on foreign policy in the 1952 presidential campaign. His influence was so great that he wrote the Republican foreign policy platform during the campaign. Additionally, Dulles's views of foreign policy closely mirrored those of Eisenhower. Both men believed that the isolationist wing of the Republican Party was wrong and that the United States needed to be active in the international arena. Thus, when Eisenhower became president, Dulles was the natural choice for his secretary of state.

Impact As secretary of state, Dulles worked closely with Eisenhower to develop U.S. foreign policy throughout most of the 1950's. As in other Cold War administrations, the Eisenhower-Dulles policy emphasized a strong stance against communism. A devout Presbyterian, Dulles even went so far as to suggest that communism was an atheistic force of evil in the world while the United States, with Christianity as its dominant religion, was the leading force of goodness. Publicly, Dulles carried the dual worldview to the extreme. In his speeches, Dulles portrayed himself as an inflexible "Cold Warrior" intent on battling the communists and liberating the rest of the world despite the costs. Behind the scenes, Dulles had more complex beliefs. He truly believed in the evils of communism, but he was much more pragmatic and understood the benefits of negotiation.

In foreign policy matters, President Eisenhower often said little to the public, and there was a public perception that Dulles dictated policy. In effect, Dulles's bellicose speeches served as a lightning rod to insulate the president from the public fear that the Cold War might one day escalate. Dulles often came across as a warmonger, but President Eisenhower was always there to offer a smile and a measure of comfort. Dulles served as secretary of state and shaped American foreign policy until shortly before his death from cancer in 1959.

Further Reading

Immerman, Richard H. *John Foster Dulles: Piety, Pragmatism, and Power in U.S. Foreign Policy.* Wilmington, Del.: Scholarly Resources, 1999. A brief biography of Dulles emphasizing the secretary's close working relationship with President Eisenhower.

Marks, Frederick W. *Power and Peace: The Diplomacy of John Foster Dulles.* Westport, Conn.: Praeger, 1995. A study of Dulles's foreign policy that contrasts his true pragmatic, flexible diplomacy with his public image as a bombastic ideologue.

John K. Franklin

See also Brinkmanship; Central Intelligence Agency; Cold War; Eisenhower, Dwight D.; Eisenhower Doctrine; Foreign policy of the United States; Geneva Summit Conference; Guatemala invasion; Isolationism; Kennan, George F.; North Atlantic Treaty Organization; Southeast Asia Treaty Organization; Suez Crisis; Tripartite Security Treaty.

■ DuMont network

Identification Fourth U.S. television network
Date Broadcast nationally from 1950 to 1955

Although short-lived, the DuMont television network excelled in creating innovative programming concepts during the early years of commercial television.

DuMont was a late entrant into network television and, with limited resources, competed against the CBS, NBC, and ABC networks. To be successful DuMont had to try different program ideas, create imaginative schedules, and find primary affiliates that would approve shows to attract an audience.

The DuMont network was established by an electrical engineer, Allen B. DuMont. DuMont's previous work at Westinghouse Lamp Company and DeForest Radio Company led him to form his company, DuMont Labs, in 1933. His company produced cathode ray tubes used for oscillographs and eventually for home television receivers.

Television research and experimentation within the DuMont Labs broadcast division led to the manufacture of television cameras, transmitters, and other origination equipment. To finance his move into television, DuMont sold half of his interest in DuMont Labs to Paramount Pictures. DuMont received experimental television licenses in 1939 for two stations, W2XCD in Passaic, New Jersey, and W2XWV in New York City. The New York station was licensed commercially in 1944 as WABD-TV, which became the flagship station of a soon-to-be two-station regional DuMont network that linked WABD-TV and WTTG-TV in Washington, D.C., by 1945.

In 1947, DuMont submitted applications for additional stations in Pittsburgh, Cleveland, and Cincinnati and announced his intention to build a nationwide network. DuMont's business partner, Paramount Pictures, applied for two stations about the same time, and the Federal Communications Commission (FCC) ruled that only five VHF (very high frequency) stations could be licensed to both entities. The FCC decision obstructed network expansion into large cities.

Programming DuMont's programming featured new and creative talent that was frequently hired away by the larger networks. Since DuMont did not have a radio network and access to established talent, its programs featured less recognized performers such as Jack Carter, Jackie Gleason, Mike Wallace, Dennis James, and Ernie Kovacs. Many of these performers moved on to bigger career opportunities at other networks.

Dupont offered a wide variety of programming. Among the popular live prime-time DuMont shows were Ted Mack's *The Original Amateur Hour, Captain Video and His Video Rangers, Cavalcade of Stars,* and Bishop Fulton J. Sheen's *Life Is Worth Living.* The network regularly programmed shows with formats that highlighted drama, news, or music—the latter with an emphasis on big band and jazz groups such as those of Benny Goodman, Duke Ellington, Count Basie, Stan Kenton, James Brubeck, and the Dorsey Brothers. Interview and talk programs during the 1950's included several hosted by Mike Wallace. The network also provided extensive coverage of the Senate Army-McCarthy hearings. Two popular children's programs were *Quiz Kids* and *Small Fry Club.* Sports programming dominated the DuMont sched-

ule. Dumont telecast the first pro-football and pro-basketball games; boxing was carried four nights a week; wrestling was featured each Friday evening; and New York Yankee baseball filled Tuesday and Thursday afternoons. In 1950, Notre Dame football was introduced.

Impact DuMont never had the financial resources to produce shows like those of the CBS or NBC networks. Although DuMont programs attracted small audiences and did not achieve high ratings, the network outperformed ABC during the early 1950's. Because of a lack of large city primary affiliates, falling advertising revenues, and poor management decisions, network offerings decreased by the summer of 1955, and the network soon ceased operations. The DuMont-owned stations were acquired by John Kluge in 1959 and eventually became known as Metromedia, Incorporated.

Further Reading

Bergmann, Ted. *Whatever Happened to the DuMont Television Network?* Landham, Md.: Rowman & Littlefield, 2002. Details the rise, fall, and impact of the DuMont network.

Weinstein, David. *Forgotten Network: DuMont and the Birth of American Television.* Philadelphia: Temple University Press, 2004. Chronicles DuMont's role in early television.

Dennis A. Harp

See also *Captain Video;* Communications in the United States; *Goldbergs, The; Honeymooners, The;* Nielsen ratings; Sheen, Fulton J.; Television in the United States.

E

■ Economic Stabilization Agency

Identification U.S. government agency created to apply wage, price, and other economic controls to restrain inflation
Date Operated from 1950 to 1953

Inflation during the 1950's was fueled by fear of a return to the shortages and inflationary conditions of World War II; the government enacted controls to bolster consumer confidence.

President Harry S. Truman, under authority of the Defense Production Act of September, 1950, created the Economic Stabilization Agency (ESA) in response to the outbreak of the Korean War. Alan Valentine was its first director, Michael V. DiSalle headed ESA's price-control program, and Cyrus Ching was in charge of wage controls. In January, 1951, ESA ordered a freeze on most wages at their existing levels and most prices at recent levels.

In the spring of 1951, formula pricing standards were introduced to allow for adjustments in individual prices and to maintain seller profitability and adequacy of supplies. The law required that wage controls be imposed on any industry subject to price controls. Public opinion strongly favored such controls in October, 1950, but this support rapidly eroded. Congress weakened controls over agricultural products, and the American public was angered by price increases and supply shortages for meats. The excess-demand pressures driving inflation slackened in response to restrictive monetary and fiscal policies. Soon after his inauguration, President Dwight D. Eisenhower terminated the controls.

Impact Wage-price controls between 1951 and 1953 were relatively effective: Consumer prices rose only 2.1 percent per year under these controls. The next imposition of controls came under President Richard M. Nixon in 1971 in response to the Vietnam War.

Further Reading

Goodwin, Craufurd D., ed. *Exhortation and Controls: The Search for a Wage-Price Policy, 1945-1971.* Washington, D.C.: Brookings Institution, 1975. Chapter 1 examines the Truman administration's economic policies in detail.

Rockoff, Hugh. *Drastic Measures: A History of Wage and Price Controls in the United States.* New York: Cambridge University Press, 1984. Chapter 7 places the 1950's experience in broader historical context.

Paul B. Trescott

See also Bowles, Chester; Business and the economy in the United States; Income and wages in the United States; Inflation in the United States; Korean War; Recession of 1957-1958.

■ Edsel

Identification Automobile produced by the Ford Motor Company during the late 1950's
Date Sold during 1958-1960 model years

One of the most famous marketing flops in automotive history, the Ford Edsel has become synonymous with failure.

Produced by the Ford Motor Company and sometimes called the Ford Edsel, the Edsel became synonymous with a marketing and branding failure. The Edsel was introduced in 1957 to huge amounts of fanfare, bolstered by a "teaser" advertising campaign that showed the car blurred or hidden under wrap, but by 1959, the decision was made to cease production of the car. The car boasted several new innovations, including its "rolling dome" speedometer and its "teletouch" transmission shifting system on the center of the steering wheel.

The original Edsels were distinctive, with their large, circular "horse-collar" grill, which was most noticeable on the 1958 model but less pronounced on the 1959 model. By 1960, the last year of production, the Edsel collar had disappeared, and in the front center of the grill was a concave shape. Edsels were produced in a variety of types and styles, including two- and four-door models, convertibles, sedans, and station wagons, with varying amounts of chrome.

The car was named for Edsel Bryant Ford, the only son of Henry Ford, Ford Motor Company's founder. During his tenure with the company, Edsel Ford helped to design the Model A Ford, created the Lincoln, and founded and named the Mercury division. He served as president of Ford Motor from the early 1920's onward, although Henry Ford maintained direct power throughout Edsel Ford's tenure.

Edsel the Failure The Edsel motorcar was a failure for a number of reasons. First, production and management problems impeded its success. Ford tried to make Edsel a wholly separate division early in its production, a plan which was to include separate dealerships unconnected with Ford. Ford also wanted separate production plants, although this was never accomplished, and Edsels were built on Ford lines.

Workers subsequently found themselves building Ford automobiles one moment and Edsels the next, a task that proved difficult. Second, the quality of Edsels was problematic. In general, 1950's cars were poorly built, and the Edsel was one of the worst. For example, Edsels experienced the unique problem of having their trunk lids pop open when drivers put them into reverse. The car's push-button transmission controls in the center of the steering column also proved problematic.

Perhaps the greatest difficulty with the Edsel was related directly to its name and the way it was marketed to the public. The teaser campaign, combined with the fact that the Edsel name did not resonate with the public, confused potential buyers. Poor market timing was also a factor: The Edsel line was aimed at families who were ready to move "up" from their starter cars to larger and more expensive cars. However, the United States was just entering a recession, which limited the market of potential buyers that Ford counted on. People also began to buy

Before the Ford Motor Company unveiled the Edsel in 1957, it promised that the car would have a revolutionary new look. However, the car's only truly distinctive feature was its much-ridiculed "horse-collar" grill, which the last model of the Edsel eliminated. (Hulton Archive | by Getty Images)

things other than large cars to signal their growing affluence.

The Edsel quickly moved from being "the next big thing" at Ford to being discontinued. In 1957, Ford announced that it wanted to sell between 100,000 and 200,000 Edsels in 1958, but during the model's three-year production history, only about 100,000 cars were sold in total.

Impact The Edsel failure signaled a growing consumer savvy in the United States by the late 1950's: American marketers and car manufacturers learned that consumers were not going to buy everything that Detroit attempted to sell them, and other industries took this lesson to heart as well. In subsequent years, marketing failures have earned the colloquial distinction of being "an Edsel."

Further Reading

Bak, Richard. *Henry and Edsel: The Creation of the Ford Empire.* New York: Wiley and Sons, 2003. Provides one of the first thorough biographies of both Henry and Edsel Ford, detailing their teamwork in building the Ford Motor Company.

Banham, Russ, and Paul Newman. *Ford Century: Ford Motor Company and the Innovations That Shaped the World.* New York: Artisan, 2002. A lavish pictorial that features full-color layouts of twenty-five of Ford's most legendary cars, including the Edsel.

Scott A. Merriman

See also Automobiles and auto manufacturing; Chevrolet Corvette; Chrysler autoworkers strike; Ford Thunderbird; General Motors; Interstate highway system; Volkswagen.

■ Education in Canada

During the 1950's, Canada converted a hodgepodge of local and sectarian schools into a nationwide system in a national movement to consolidate schools into modern institutions and meld disparate educational philosophies.

Canada's school system at the end of World War II reflected the thinly settled nature of the country. In a nation where only a little more than half the population lived in major urban centers, the need for education on the part of many citizens involved attendance at rural, one-room schools. By the mid-1950's, Canada's population was still classified as one-half rural, even though significant urbanization was occurring.

The vast majority of the population was of European descent, though many were recent immigrants. The native population, comprising both Indians and Eskimos, was not served by the regular school system but by special schools administered by the Department of Indian Affairs and Northern Development. These two groups aside, by the end of the decade, essentially all members of the citizenry received formal education.

Each provincial government had a minister of education, who was a member of the provincial parliament. Each also had a deputy minister, who was usually the senior civil servant of the Department of Education. The department was responsible for oversight, curriculum, textbooks and school libraries, testing, teacher training, financing, and even adult education, which attracted growing attention in educational circles during the 1950's. Expenditures on public education increased sharply during the 1950's, with the per-student outlay rising from C$204 in 1952 to C$348 in 1960. The per-capita outlay doubled, from C$32 to C$68. Of these sums, some 25 percent was spent on new facilities during the 1950's, with another 25 percent going to administration and 50 percent to higher salaries for teachers.

Consolidation A major drive during the 1950's was for school consolidation, replacing the one-room schools that had served the rural populace for decades with modern, consolidated schools that depended on the widespread use of school buses. Consolidation proceeded most rapidly in those provinces with growing provincial economic resources, notably Alberta (with its oil revenues) and British Columbia.

Every province was divided into school districts, which were directly administered by a local school board of 5-20 local citizens. The boards governed such issues as attendance requirements, length of the school year, holidays, and staffing. This local element justified the fact that 40 percent of the school funding came from local tax receipts, 42 percent from the provinces, 8 percent from the federal government, and 10 percent from other sources. Every school had a principal, and districts of any size also had a superintendent of schools, directly responsible to the school board.

Educational Philosophy Canadian educators during the 1950's were deeply divided between those who advocated traditional educational methods and those who espoused "progressivism," that is, a more child-centered philosophy. This split was reflected in the deliberations of the royal commissions organized in each province to consider the needs of the schools, a development pioneered in Ontario with its Hope Commission. The commission, which issued its report in 1950, generally advocated more progressive approaches in the schools. The other side of the argument was articulated by Hilda Neatby, whose book, *So Little for the Mind*, appeared in 1953 and took issue with the progressive approach to education.

In part reflecting these different educational philosophies, many Canadian schools adopted a policy called "streaming," in which students were grouped according to their ability and their achievement. As in the United States, the policy in time produced significant criticism that it marginalized those of lesser abilities. However, because the policies recommended by the Hope Commission also recommended less rigid curricula and more freedom for teachers, they won a lot of support among educators. Many of these changes were highlighted at the First Canadian Conference on Education, which met in Ottawa in 1958.

Secondary Education and Sectarian Schools Further development of secondary education in Canada was a vital need during the 1950's, since in 1951, 55 percent of Canadians had less than nine years of schooling. Secondary schools, many of them one-room rural schools, were often taught by only one teacher. This circumstance was gradually made less common, as school consolidation proceeded apace during the decade. However, school completion rates continued to remain behind those in the United States.

One of the major defects of the Canadian educational system that came to light during the 1950's was the lack of vocational education. Almost no school system offered it, yet as Canadians moved off the farms and into the cities, there was a major need for such training. Technical training institutes, of which there were only twenty-seven during the early 1950's, provided vocational training for some 3,000 students; by the late 1950's, the number enrolled had increased to 8,300. In December of 1960, the federal parliament passed the Vocational Training Assistance Act, which provided subsidies that led

subsequently to a considerable expansion of the technical training institutes during the 1960's.

Alongside the regular public schools in every province, there were sectarian schools. In some provinces, as in Newfoundland, these types were the only schools and typically were affiliated with one or another of the major religious denominations of Canada: the Roman Catholic Church, the United Church of Canada, or the Church of England. Even Mennonites and Jews had their own schools. These schools were required to follow an official curriculum and could add their own religious instruction.

The most prominent place where sectarian schools continued to exist was in Quebec. There were seven primary grades in Quebec; after completion, those students aspiring to a university education would enroll in a "classical" curriculum. There were additional programs for those intending to work in business or industry and those aiming for a career in agriculture. There were also special schools for girls, which could feed into a normal school education (for work as a teacher) or a four-year commercial course. A two-year "domestic arts" course existed as well. The programs tended to reflect the fact that most residents of Quebec were most likely to return to the family farm after school. The instruction was in French.

Postsecondary Education At the end of World War II, Canada had only twenty-eight institutions of higher learning, and only twenty-one of those were universities. Twenty-five years later it had almost twice as many. There was a widespread realization that Canada's university world was too limited, both in space and in offerings, for the urbanized, mechanized world Canadians inhabited during the postwar era. However, there was much uncertainty about how to bring higher education up to date, given the limited financial resources available.

A model somewhat similar to that of the business world developed. Small colleges either amalgamated with other small colleges or became part of a university system. Sometimes the process worked in reverse: Elements hitherto part of a university became independent and gradually expanded to university status. In the years immediately following World War II, when Canadian veterans enjoyed a benefit equivalent to that offered to U.S. veterans by the American G.I. Bill, enrollment in Canadian

Schoolteacher Fred Sloman beside his School on Wheels mobile classroom, which moved on railroad lines through northern Ontario, whose remote communities had too few children to justify building regular schoolrooms during the 1950's. (Hulton Archive | by Getty Images)

universities more than doubled, from 40,000 in 1944-1945 to 83,000 in 1947-1948. Temporary facilities were employed to accommodate the crowds, but a long-term solution was essential, as enrollments after the bulge fell back to only 63,000 in 1952-1953.

A national conference of Canadian universities met in 1945 and pinpointed the major needs of the universities. On the list were plans for postgraduate studies, annuities for professors, the provision of funds for the expensive scientific disciplines, and the expansion of the administrative structures needed to support these additional activities. A special need in Canada was to develop a system of cooperation between the French-speaking institutions, largely in Quebec, and the majority English-speaking institutions spread over the rest of the country.

At the heart of the problem was maintaining some measure of independence from the United States. A substantial number of the professors teaching at Canadian universities had obtained part or all of their postgraduate training in either Great Britain or the United States, chiefly the latter. Canada needed to develop postgraduate programs that would lead to its independence from the United States in staffing its universities. This problem required a long-range solution, and much of it did not occur until after the 1950's. In the back of the minds of university leaders was a problem later exposed by John Porter in his book *The Vertical Mosaic: An Analy-*

sis of *Social Class and Power in Canada*, published in 1965, in which he charged that access to the top levels of society in Canada was severely limited.

As in the United States, Canada had long had postsecondary educational institutions that were not liberal arts colleges or universities, notably the normal schools, which provided teacher training before World War II. Normal schools were converted, as in the United States, into teachers' colleges, and helped to produce the large numbers of schoolteachers that the expansion of primary and especially secondary education required.

Like the teaching profession, nursing before World War II had its own educational system, mostly affiliated with hospitals. In time, many of these nursing schools became university affiliates, but that process took place more slowly than the upgrading of the teachers' colleges; most of the change occurred after the 1950's.

In Canada, and notably in Quebec, there developed institutions equivalent to the junior colleges in the United States. These often incorporated some of the formerly independent technical training institutes and art institutes that had long existed, but the program was expanded to include a two-year general studies program that could be used as a vehicle to gain entrance to a university. Although Quebec's CEGEPs (colleges of general and vocational education) were uniquely adapted to the existing educational system in that province, they offered a general model to the other provinces.

Canada had long provided adult education courses, mostly in the form of extension courses offered by universities or in the form of summer session courses. However, as the country's leaders came to understand the great need for further training for those running its economy, considerable attention was devoted to expanding adult education. The Canadian Broadcasting Corporation, tapped to help with this effort, ran broadcasts heavily promoting the updating of existing training programs.

Impact The 1950's were the years when Canadians came to understand that a modern, developed society needs a commensurate educational system. The first task addressed during the 1950's was to improve elementary and, especially, secondary education. In particular, a nationwide system of public education had to be available to supplement or replace the scattered religious schools that had hitherto served

as secondary schools. School districts had to be consolidated so that secondary education no longer took place in one-room schools. The rapidly urbanizing populace had to be served by modern facilities, many of which were constructed during the 1950's. Plans, at least, had to be made to expand university education to provide the technical schools essential in a developed country.

Many of the educational plans laid during the 1950's came to fruition during the 1960's and 1970's. Although Canada's link to the United States continued to be very strong, the country developed most of the capabilities needed to supply the educational requirements of its own population.

Further Reading

Guppy, Neil, and Scott Davies. *Education in Canada: Recent Trends and Future Challenges.* Ottawa: Ministry of Industry, 1998. Although focused on contemporary issues, contains a number of tables and other data going back to the 1950's.

Jones, Giles, ed. *Higher Education in Canada: Different Systems, Different Perspectives.* New York: Garland, 1997. Various authors describe the higher education in each of the provinces; the last chapter provides a synthesis.

Manzer, Ronald. *Public Schools and Political Ideas: Canadian Educational Policy in Historical Perspective.* Toronto: Toronto University Press, 1994. Uses a thematic approach, but the individual chapters are related to historical stages in Canadian educational development.

Porter, John. *The Measure of Canadian Society: Education, Equality, and Opportunity.* Ottawa: Carleton University Press, 1987. A new edition of an earlier work, still stressing the theme of his famous book, in which he accuses Canada's schools of perpetuating an elitist society.

Wilson, J. D., R. M. Stamp, and Louis-Philippe Audet, eds. *Canadian Education: A History.* Scarborough, Ont.: Prentice-Hall, 1970. Each chapter, by a different author, traces one of the stages in the evolution of Canada's schools.

Nancy M. Gordon

See also Canadian Broadcasting Corporation; Canadian regionalism; Communications in Canada; Demographics of Canada; Education in the United States; Minorities in Canada; Newspapers in Canada; Religion in Canada; Television in Canada; Urbanization in Canada; *Why Johnny Can't Read.*

■ Education in the United States

Developments in education during the 1950's, which pitted educational liberals against educational conservatives, resulted in a reconsideration of the methods and purposes of education in a free society and moved toward redefining the interrelationship of education, technology, and society.

The United States at mid-twentieth century had survived the Great Depression and then had come through World War II, among the most devastating wars in the history of the world. When the war ended in 1945, hundreds of thousands of people in the military (G.I.s), who had been uprooted by the war and whose personal lives had been put on hold, returned home, where they attempted to resume their normal lives. By 1950, a baby boom, unprecedented in the nation's past history, was under way. The decade of the 1950's was one in which elementary schools (and, by the end of the decade, secondary schools) were bursting at the seams with the baby boomers flocking into them.

The Postwar Baby Boom On January 1, 1950, the United States had eight million more children than demographers had predicted. Even without a baby boom, the country's schools would have been severely strained because few new schools had been built during the Great Depression of the 1930's, and, after 1939, 40 percent of the nation's teachers were lost to military service or to jobs in defense industries. With baby boomers entering schools in record numbers, schools were forced to resort to desperate measures. More than 100,000 emergency teaching certificates were issued to those who did not qualify fully as teachers. Many school districts handled the onslaught by operating schools on double shifts, which was disruptive to the lives of many families.

During the 1949-1950 school year, approximately 25.1 million students were enrolled in the public schools of the United States: 19.4 million in kindergarten through eighth grade, and 5,725,000 in grades nine through twelve. Institutions of higher learning enrolled another 2.7 million students in 1950. By the end of the decade—the fall of 1959—America's public schools served a total of 40.9 million pupils, with 29.9 million in kindergarten through eighth grade and 8.3 million in grades nine through twelve. College and university enrollments had increased to 3.2 million.

The large increase in the birthrate after 1945 and the crush of returning G.I.s combined to create a high demand for housing. Children born during these peak years entered kindergarten or elementary school during the early 1950's. Their siblings, arriving in substantial numbers during the late 1940's and early 1950's, added more than fifteen million students to school populations in the period between 1950 and 1959.

Many communities, in efforts to accommodate the increased numbers, were forced to build new schools in record time and had to find qualified people to teach in them. Attempts were made to draw people into the teaching profession by increasing remuneration. The average entry-level teacher in 1950 earned less than three thousand dollars a year. This figure increased to almost five thousand dollars by 1960.

In some instances, whole new communities were created to accommodate the returning G.I.s. Twenty miles outside New York City, William J. Levitt, using mass production techniques modeled on similar techniques that Henry Ford pioneered in the automotive industry fifty years before, built seventeen thousand homes in the potato fields of a small Long Island town, Island Trees (later renamed Levittown in honor of the man who had created it). In only five years, Levittown grew into a thriving community of 82,000 people.

Levitt's crews alone were building thirty-six new houses every day, 180 houses a week. Similar communities grew throughout suburban America. Levitt's bedroom community for New York City required five new elementary schools immediately. These schools were built at public expense, much to the displeasure of people living in the area before Levitt developed it. Although residents felt they were being coerced into paying for educational facilities they did not require but that the new arrivals sorely needed, they had no way to avoid the tax increases that such necessary construction demanded.

The G.I. Bill After 1945, postsecondary institutions began to be filled beyond their normal capacities as returning veterans enrolled in school to take advantage of the G.I. Bill, a government bill which provided them with educational expenses based on their military service.

Under the G.I. Bill, passed in 1944 as part of the Servicemen's Readjustment Act, returning service people became eligible to receive $500 annually toward tuition fees at approved institutions, as well as $50 a month for subsistence if they were unmarried and $75 if they were married. These stipends seem paltry by later standards, but it must be remembered that when the bill came into being, its tuition grant fell only $25 short of paying Harvard University's annual tuition fee of $525.

Returning G.I.s flocked into vocational schools, colleges, and universities, necessitating immediate expansion of such institutions. Housing these students became a major problem in schools with dormitories originally designed to accommodate only a fraction of the students who now needed housing. In many instances, three or four students were forced to occupy rooms designed to house only one or two. In other instances, students occupied Quonset huts, which were hastily erected on campuses or adjacent

to them. Such structures were used by many colleges and universities to house married students.

The returning G.I.s brought about substantive changes in the ways institutions of higher learning dealt with students. More mature than typical college students in earlier decades, the G.I.s were, as a group, serious and well motivated. They were attracted to schools able to provide them with curricula that would, when they completed their programs, quickly validate them as members of the workforce. Likewise, because many of these students were married and had children, educational institutions sometimes established care facilities and nursery schools to look after their children and, in some instances, tied these facilities into their teacher training programs in early childhood and elementary education.

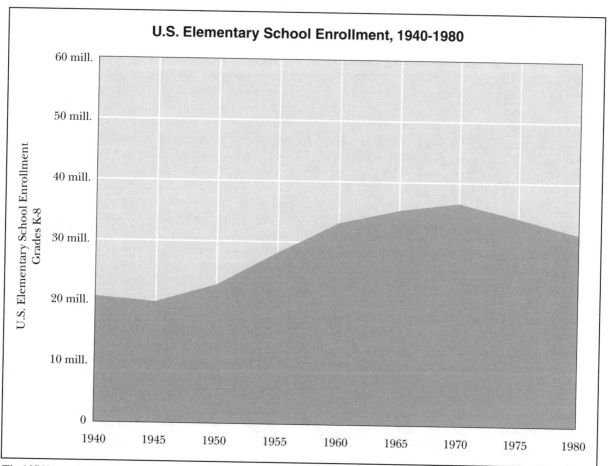

U.S. Elementary School Enrollment, 1940-1980

The 1950's saw the beginning of the spike in school enrollment as baby boomers (b. 1946-1964) entered elementary school nationwide.
Source: U.S. National Center for Educational Statistics.

The Communist Threat During the early 1950's, an ambitious junior senator from Wisconsin, Joseph McCarthy, embarked on a witch-hunt that focused on alleged communists in public life. He warned that the Department of State was riddled with communists, who had also penetrated the United States armed forces and other branches of government, including public schools and public universities. Although McCarthy's accusations were not buttressed by convincing evidence, they had a profound, if temporary, effect upon American society as a whole. McCarthy's power was weakened substantially in December, 1954, when the United States Senate, by a vote of 67 to 22, officially censured the senator for his badgering conduct in the notorious Army-McCarthy hearings.

During the four years in which McCarthy held sway over the country, his policies, all in the name of patriotism, had a significant effect upon public education. In 1951, largely at his instigation, the Supreme Court supported the imposition of loyalty oaths upon public employees, including teachers at all levels of public educational institutions. McCarthy boasted that he had caused more than six hundred college and university professors to be terminated because of their refusal to sign loyalty oaths or because they were suspected of being communists. The numbers of elementary and secondary school teachers who were similarly affected during the McCarthy era far exceeded the number of instructors terminated by institutions of higher learning.

Brown v. Board of Education **and Its Aftermath** Perhaps the most crucial single event affecting American education during the 1950's was a unanimous Supreme Court decision, issued on May 17, 1954, in *Brown v. Board of Education of Topeka, Kansas*, which declared unconstitutional the "separate but equal" doctrine established half a century earlier in *Plessy v. Ferguson* (1896). *Plessy*, although it addressed segregation in interstate travel rather than segregation in education, was used by many school districts as the legal basis for justifying the practice of racial segregation in their schools.

The Supreme Court had already handed down several decisions that strengthened the case for permitting African American citizens to participate fully in American society and for assuring that they received the constitutional rights that supposedly pertain to all Americans, not merely white citizens. In 1950, the Court ruled in favor of a black student wishing to enter the law school of the University of Texas at Austin rather than attend the law school Texas had established in Houston specifically for black students. This decision led to the integration of graduate and professional schools throughout the South. It also demolished Jim Crow laws that mandated school segregation and affected educational institutions in seventeen states and the District of Columbia. Similar laws in Arizona, Kansas, New Mexico, and Wyoming, where segregation was optional, were also dismantled.

Thurgood Marshall, who later was a Supreme Court justice from 1968 to 1991, worked with the National Association for the Advancement of Colored People (NAACP) to bring a case before the Court that would successfully abolish the "separate but equal" doctrine that school districts in many states used as a justification for operating dual school systems. The landmark *Brown* decision proclaimed that an inherent inequality existed in the public support of separate facilities for people of different races, even if such facilities were considered equal, because a vital part of one's education involves freedom to mix with one's colleagues regardless of race. Many opponents of integration took the Court's ruling calmly because they genuinely believed that it could never be implemented. A year following the decision, when little progress had been made toward integration, the Court mandated that the federal district courts enforce compliance with, in the Court's words, "all deliberate speed." However, no deadline was stipulated for enforcement, so recalcitrant school districts felt little pressure to rush toward integrating.

Integration occurred in the public schools of Washington, D.C., and in some of the border states, but the South as a whole resisted desegregating its schools. In 1956, Senator Harry Byrd of Virginia issued his doctrine of massive resistance. His state, Virginia, immediately enacted legislation mandating that any integrated school within the state be closed. The Southern Manifesto was drawn up, calling the *Brown* decision a clear abuse of judicial power and demanding that the decision be reversed. This manifesto was signed by most southern members of the House of Representatives and by every southern senator except Lyndon B. Johnson, Estes Kefauver, and Albert Gore, Sr.

White students jeer after being tear-gassed by police while demonstrating against the integration of the University of Alabama in February, 1956. (AP/Wide World Photos)

Implementing Integration The racial integration of schools did not proceed easily or well. In 1956, the University of Alabama at Tuscaloosa admitted its first black student, Autherine J. Lucy, amid considerable opposition that included threats upon her life and required that she be given around-the-clock police protection. When the 1957 school year began in early September, Little Rock's all-white Central High School had already filed a desegregation plan, but it would take eight years to implement. The NAACP was unwilling to wait that long. It lent its support to nine black students who attempted to enroll in the school.

Arkansas had never viewed itself as part of the Deep South, so it was not anticipated that the state's governor, Orval Faubus, who long had been considered politically moderate, would take a strong stand against integration. Nevertheless, on September 4, 1957, Faubus sent a contingent of 270 members

of the Arkansas National Guard to Central High School to prevent the black students from registering. This action provoked a confrontation, one of many that would follow throughout the southern states. Alex Wilson, a black journalist and a war veteran, was brutally beaten during this confrontation. The event received prominent national press coverage and was a precipitating event in the Civil Rights movement.

President Dwight D. Eisenhower, learning of Alex Wilson's beating and seeing pictures of the badly injured reporter, realized that the time had come for him to assume his responsibility as president and to take decisive action to implement the Court's call for "all deliberate speed." He acted despite being displeased by the Court's decision in *Brown v. Board of Education.*

On September 24, Eisenhower, seeking to end the educational firestorm that had been ignited in

Little Rock, deployed twelve hundred paratroopers from the area's 101st Airborne Division. By federalizing the Arkansas National Guard, Eisenhower made it virtually impossible for any racists in the Guard to oppose openly the orders of their commander-in-chief because to do so would violate the established chain of command.

The venomous objections by hordes protesting integration were trumped by the actions of the National Guard, who accompanied nine black students into Central High School and enabled them to register. Once classes began, the National Guard continued to provide protection for the black students who had taken this initial and decisive step toward forcing school integration that the Supreme Court had mandated three years earlier.

The integration of Central High School marked a turning point in school integration in the South, al-though in most of the country, de facto segregation remained a fact of life in the large cities, where blacks tended to cluster in their own neighborhoods and to attend neighborhood schools, which, al-though not segregated by law, were segregated by circumstance.

To overcome this problem, many school districts resorted to busing students to schools outside their neighborhoods in order to reflect a racial mix that achieved the spirit of school integration. The problem of neighborhood segregation was compounded by realtors who continued to practice discrimination, often refusing to show black clients available property in parts of town traditionally occupied by white residents.

Before the events in Little Rock, the Eisenhower administration sent Congress the first civil rights bill of the twentieth century. During the late 1940's, un-

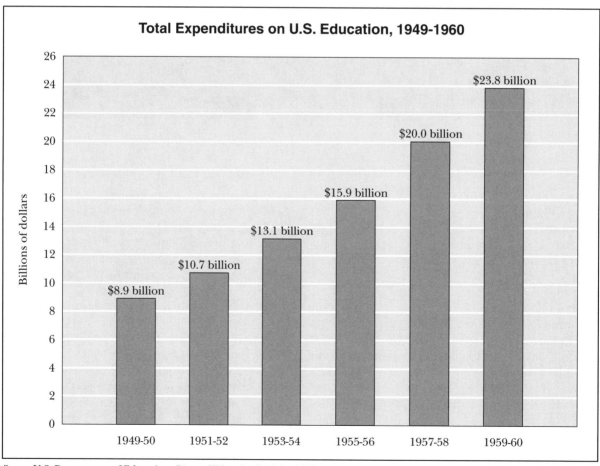

Source: U.S. Department of Education. *Digest of Education Statistics,* 1992. Data are given for alternate school years for all levels of education, public and private.

der the administration of Harry S. Truman, the armed forces had been integrated. The next logical step toward assuring that African Americans be treated on an equal basis with white Americans appeared to be the desegregation of other American institutions, notably schools. The Civil Rights Act of 1957 heralded a step toward acknowledging that black citizens deserved equal protection under the U.S. Constitution. Some months later, this act provided President Eisenhower with an acceptable and wholly legal rationale for the intervention of the federal government in the integration of Little Rock's Central High School.

The Critics of Public Education Although school integration was the salient educational issue of the 1950's, many other matters concerned educators and the general public. A constant flow of books commenting, often negatively, on American education angered taxpayers who, sometimes on very questionable evidence, accepted as fact that the nation's schools were dangerously substandard.

During the 1930's and 1940's, the educational philosophy of John Dewey was a pervasive influence in public education. Central to this philosophy was the concept that children learn by what they do. Educators who accepted Dewey's philosophy, labeled progressivism, created child-centered rather than subject-centered learning environments. In fairness, one must realize that doing so did not preclude the teaching of subject matter. Rather it shaped the subject matter so that it fit into activities in which schoolchildren were involved. Rote learning was deemphasized as children were encouraged to gain an understanding of what they were doing. The John Dewey concept was badly misunderstood by a public that had been schooled in more authoritarian ways. However, some teachers who attempted to adapt progressivism to their own classrooms and some school administrators who, in many cases, sought to impose it upon the schools in their jurisdiction, did not have a deep understanding of Dewey's tenets as set forth in his landmark books, *The School and Society* (1899) and *Experience and Education* (1938).

One of the more balanced, if arguably elitist critiques of education during the 1950's was Robert Maynard Hutchins's *The Conflict in Education in a Democratic Society* (1953). Less objective and temperate, as the title indicates, was Albert B. Lynd's *Quackery in the Public Schools* (1953), which attacked the

progressivism of past decades and called for a return to the study of what he considered the basic elements of education. During the same year, Arthur Bestor published *Educational Wastelands: The Retreat from Learning in Our Public Schools*, which decried emphasis on the learner rather than on the subject matter to be learned. He equated progressive education with regressive education and attacked progressive educationists as charlatans leading society to an educational abyss.

The climate was quite right for the publication in 1955 of Rudolf Flesch's *Why Johnny Can't Read—And What You Can Do About It*, a book that gained an enormous following and contributed to a growing public outcry against the schools and against public education. However, many of the most dedicated followers of Bestor and Flesch neither had spent much time in public schools since their own educational tenure nor fully understood what progressivism really was. Flesch supported a return to the teaching of phonics, at the time a disputed method of reading instruction but one familiar to those who had attended school two or three decades earlier.

The Conant Report Partly as a response to many educational critics, James Bryant Conant, a former president of Harvard University, undertook an extensive survey of American high schools, visiting and assessing 103 high schools in twenty-six states over a period of two years. Conant's study, *The American High School Today: A First Report to Interested Citizens* (1959), was well balanced and was conducted following established research criteria designed to produce objective and unbiased outcomes.

Conant concluded that the diversity of the United States, from large city to suburbia to small town and rural areas, made it impossible to determine what constituted a "typical" American school. In order to offer the most diverse educational opportunities to school populations in such a complex country, he supported the idea of comprehensive high schools. These schools would serve large areas and would offer diverse curricula that would approach meeting the needs of their heterogeneous populations in the most effective ways possible.

Among its twenty-one specific recommendations, the Conant Report called for an increased emphasis on teaching English composition, science and mathematics, and foreign languages, suggesting the school boards approve teaching the third and fourth years of foreign languages even if the enrollments were small. He urged schools to develop well-defined counseling programs and to emphasize individualizing instruction to meet the needs of students most effectively.

Conant recommended ability grouping, remedial classes for those who fell behind, and classes in developmental reading. He stipulated that minimal requirements for high school graduation, which should apply to all students, include four years of English (half of those years devoted to teaching composition); three or four years of social studies, including a senior course in American government; and one year each of mathematics and science in the ninth grade. He urged that the school day contain minimally six periods of academic classes, over and above such nonacademic subjects such as physical education and driver education.

Conant's study of the American high school led to the publication four years later of *The Education of American Teachers* (1963), in which he examined closely teacher training programs at seventy-seven institutions in twenty-two states. This study had a profound effect on how future teachers would be trained.

Vice Admiral Hyman Rickover's Admonitions As the arms race between the United States and the Soviet Union intensified, Americans became increasingly aware of the need to train large numbers of scientists. The launching of the Soviet satellite *Sputnik* in 1957 was a wake-up call for many Americans, as was the Soviet Union's successful mission to photograph the dark side of the moon two years later. These events clearly indicated that the Soviet Union, already a nuclear power, was surging ahead of the United States both in technology and in the exploration of outer space.

Spurred by this revelation and by the fear that the Soviet Union was perfecting long-range delivery systems for atomic weapons, Admiral Hyman Rickover, who established the nuclear navy by developing the first nuclear-powered submarine, the USS *Nautilus*, and by spearheading the development of a fleet of nuclear submarines, published *Education and Freedom* (1959). In this book, he called both for an increased emphasis on mathematics and science in the secondary schools of the United States and for a rigor in public education that he felt was lacking.

When Rickover turned his attention to public education in 1956, he found many supportive listeners. His speeches accused the schools of promoting dangerous educational practices that were a severe threat to America's national security. Along with many contemporary critics, he attacked the life adjustment curricula that had permeated school systems during the 1930's and 1940's.

Rickover declared that the fundamental purpose of education in modern America was to produce people capable of creating the science and technology upon which modern nations depend for winning wars. There was little room in Rickover's educational scheme for the arts or the humanities. His focus was on science. There was also little room in his proposals for any students save those who could gain proficiency in mathematics and science. The time was ripe for the kind of critiques that Rickover articulated since they seemed to echo the claims of Senator Joseph McCarthy that the armed forces and the United States government were infiltrated by communists.

The National Defense Education Act of 1958 Admiral Rickover's arguments were influential in the passage of the National Defense Education Act (NDEA) of 1958, which was aimed at producing more teachers for America's understaffed schools. This act was heavily weighted in favor of helping students to pursue studies in science, mathematics, foreign languages, and technology. Many public school teachers and prospective teachers received the financial support through NDEA that enabled them to continue their educations. Each NDEA grant provided five thousand dollars per year, one-half as an outright grant and one-half as a loan to be remitted upon the completion of a stipulated term of teaching in public schools, usually five years. Applicants planning to teach in the targeted subject areas received special consideration. The NDEA was so successful that by the mid-1960's, President Lyndon B. Johnson disbanded the program because an oversupply of teachers had been created.

Although the NDEA offered some assistance to those seeking vocational training, the Vocational Education Act placed greater emphasis on offering training in skilled, semiskilled, or technical vocations. This act provided incentives for potential school dropouts to continue in school and to complete their programs.

Despite giving fleeting attention to students with learning disabilities or to students who had not achieved basic literacy, Robert Hutchins, James B. Conant, and Hyman Rickover were concerned largely with secondary education as a prelude to higher education. They gave only passing attention to students for whom secondary school would be terminal or to the overwhelming problems of controlling school dropouts. They ignored to some extent the fact that public high schools were huge melting pots in which a broad variety of students representing all socioeconomic and ability levels were intermixed and in which a college preparatory curriculum was irrelevant to the goals of a large number of high school students.

Despite their limitations and occasional unfair attacks upon educators, the writings of the educational critics of the 1950's were of the utmost importance in helping to shape the schools and reform teacher training programs in future decades. The numerous critiques of public education, while demoralizing to many teachers and school administrators, served to bring serious discussions of education and of learning styles to public attention, which, in the long term, was beneficial.

Impact The 1950's was pivotal in determining the course of American education during the remainder of the twentieth century. Two major factors were instrumental in turning the tide: the integration of American schools that followed *Brown v. Board of Education* and the emphasis on science and technology stimulated both by the Soviet's launching of *Sputnik* and by that country's undisputed position as a nuclear power.

In 1955, when Rosa Parks's refusal to yield her seat on a bus in Montgomery, Alabama, led to her arrest and prompted a year-long boycott by African Americans of Montgomery's white-owned enterprises, U.S. society as a whole began to realize the concerted power that African Americans could wield in the United States if they were organized. Educational institutions were directly affected by the waves of social protest and political activism that ensued.

With the help of the NAACP and leaders such as Martin Luther King, Jr., the power of the people was unleashed and black citizens began to move decisively toward enjoying the full benefits of citizenship in a country that had largely scorned them for the nine decades following the end of the Civil War in 1865. The key to their achieving the benefits that were the right of all citizens lay in their being free to receive educational opportunities equal to those of their white counterparts.

Further Reading

Bestor, Arthur E. *Educational Wastelands: The Retreat from Learning in Our Public Schools.* Urbana: University of Illinois Press, 1953. One of the most condemnatory critiques of America's schools by an educational conservative, this book aroused considerable public passion in opposition to progressivism in education. In many venues, it led to a renewed emphasis on the basics.

Campbell, Will, et al. *A Life Is More than a Moment: The Desegregation of Little Rock's Central High.* Bloomington: Indiana University Press, 1999. Illustrated with haunting photographs of those involved in the controversial integration of Little Rock's Central High School. Both the text and the photographs bring to life the events of these turbulent days.

Conant, James Bryant. *The American High School Today: A First Report to Interested Citizens.* New York: McGraw-Hill Book Company, 1959. Spurred by the arms race, Conant made an exhaustive investigation of America's high schools and recommended significant reforms in how they were run.

_____. *The Education of American Teachers.* New York: McGraw-Hill Book Company, 1963. Following his comprehensive investigative visits to American schools, Conant presents a blueprint for drastic revisions in how to train teachers.

Cremin, Lawrence A. *American Education: The Metropolitan Experience, 1876-1980.* New York: Harper and Row, 1988. Although Cremin focuses more attention on other decades than the 1950's, his book remains valuable for the statistics it presents.

Elmore, Richard F. *Restructuring in the Classroom: Teaching, Learning, and School Organization.* San Francisco: Jossey-Bass, 1996. Elmore provides an excellent insight into the open-school concept initiated during the 1950's, which continued through the following two decades, as well as into some of the curricular reforms that were called for and partially implemented during the 1950's.

Flesch, Rudolf Franz. *Why Johnny Can't Read—And What You Can Do About It.* New York: Harper, 1955.

A conservative attack on progressivism that aroused those who favored a return to the basics.

Pulliam, John D. *History of Education in America.* 4th ed. Columbus, Ohio: Merrill, 1987. Pulliam regards the 1950's as a period of prosperity and relative calm until the launching of *Sputnik* in 1957, which aroused public criticism of American schools.

Ravitch, Diane. *The Troubled Crusade: American Education 1945-1980.* New York: Basic Books, 1983. A thorough and unbiased account of the major post-World War II debates about education.

Sadker, Myra Pollack, and David Miller Sadker. *Teaching, Schools and Society.* New York: McGraw-Hill, 1997. Chapter 9, "The History of American Education," and Chapter 14, "The Struggle for Equal Educational Opportunity," are especially relevant. Chapter 14 considers public school integration in detail.

R. Baird Shuman

See also *Bolling v. Sharpe; Brown v. Board of Education;* Civil Rights movement; Education in Canada; G.I. Bill; *God and Man at Yale;* Great Books movement; Health, Education, and Welfare, Department of; National Defense Education Act of 1958; School desegregation; Science and technology; Sex and sex education; *Sweatt v. Painter; Why Johnny Can't Read.*

■ Einstein, Albert

Identification German American theoretical physicist

Born March 14, 1879; Ulm, Württemberg, Germany

Died April 18, 1955; Princeton, New Jersey

Albert Einstein revolutionized physics with his special and general theories of relativity, his postulate of light quanta to explain the photoelectric effect, and his efforts to find a unified field theory.

Albert Einstein is revered as one of the greatest physicists ever to live. For his explanation of the photoelectric effect, he was awarded a Nobel Prize in Physics in 1921. Using his theory of special relativity, he discovered the relationship between matter and energy, the idea that led to the development of the atomic bomb.

During the 1950's, Einstein stirred controversy with his leftist political convictions, his support for socialism and civil rights, and his advocacy of nu-

Albert Einstein at his Princeton, New Jersey, home around 1950. (Hulton Archive | by Getty Images)

clear disarmament. His allegedly subversive political activities led to investigations from the House Committee on Un-American Activities and encouraged the Federal Bureau of Investigation to amass a fifteen-hundred-page file on him. Einstein persisted in publicly criticizing McCarthyism as a dangerous threat to democracy and to freedom of expression.

In 1953, Einstein completed the mathematical formulation of his unified field theory—an attempt to explain the four fundamental forces of nature, gravity, electromagnetism, and the two nuclear forces—as one basic force law. In 1955, one week prior to his death, he supported a manifesto urging all nations to give up nuclear weapons. Until his death, he continued to search for the fundamental laws that govern the universe.

Impact Although not agreeing with some of the end results and uses of his scientific research, Einstein fathered quantum physics and the atomic bomb. His ideas affected nearly every branch of science. He got closer to nature's truths than anyone had done previously. Physicists continue to explore his theories, with many seeking a unified field theory, a venture that has led to the unification of electromagnetism and the weak nuclear force into the electroweak force.

Further Reading

Mehra, Jagdish. *Einstein: Physics and Reality.* River Edge, N.J.: World Scientific, 1997. Provides insights into Einstein's life and theories.

Mih, Walter C. *The Fascinating Life and Theory of Albert Einstein.* Huntington, N.Y.: Kroshka Books, 2000. A good biography of Einstein.

Alvin K. Benson

See also Atomic bomb; Atomic Energy Act of 1954; Cyclotron; Oppenheimer, J. Robert; Pauling, Linus; Photovoltaic cell; Science and technology; Teller, Edward.

■ Eisenhower, Dwight D.

Identification President of the United States, 1953-1961

Born October 14, 1890; Denison, Texas

Died March 28, 1969; Washington, D.C.

Dwight D. Eisenhower became president during the early and most crucial years of the Cold War. He established the foreign-policy path that the United States would pursue regarding the Soviet Union until that country's collapse in 1991.

Eisenhower entered West Point in 1911. He was commissioned a second lieutenant in the U.S. Army in 1915. He advanced rapidly in the Army during World War I, reaching a temporary rank of lieutenant colonel. From 1929 to 1939, he served as an aide to General Douglas MacArthur, with whom he shared leadership of U.S. forces during World War II. After serving as supreme allied commander of the European theater and overseeing the Normandy Invasion, which turned the tide of war in favor of the Allies, Eisenhower was promoted to the rank of five-star General of the Army, one of only five men ever to achieve that honor. In 1946, while serving as Army chief of staff, he declared, "I hate war as only a soldier who has lived it can, only as one who has seen its brutality, its stupidity."

Political Career Both major political parties wanted to nominate Eisenhower for president in 1948. He declined, however, declaring that a professional soldier should stay out of politics. He served two years as president of Columbia University in New York City. In 1950, Eisenhower was named commander of the North Atlantic Treaty Organization (NATO) forces in Europe and sought to build an army that could stop any communist invasion of Western Europe. He retired from active military service on May 31, 1952.

On June 4, 1952, Eisenhower changed his view on soldiers in politics and announced his candidacy for the Republican nomination for president. A possible cause of the 1952 election's outcome was the role of the United States in NATO. The Democratic Party would likely have renominated President Harry S. Truman, who supported NATO but was considered too liberal in domestic affairs. The leading Republican candidate was Ohio senator Robert A. Taft, who opposed NATO and, as president, would likely have ended the U.S. role in it. After a hard-fought battle at the Republican national convention in Chicago, and with the backing of California senator Richard M. Nixon, Eisenhower won the nomination and named Nixon as his choice for vice president.

President Truman then decided not to seek reelection, and the Democrats nominated Illinois governor Adlai Stevenson. During the campaign, Eisenhower promised to take action concerning the Korean War, then two years old. The slogan "I Like Ike" helped lead Eisenhower to victory in November, carrying thirty-nine of the forty-eight states.

First Presidential Term, 1953-1957 After his election, President-elect Eisenhower visited Korea. He made it clear to the North Koreans and Communist Chinese that if an armistice could not be signed quickly, he would use any weapons necessary to end the war as president. This was a veiled threat of atomic power, and the armistice was signed in July, 1953.

Aided by his secretary of state, John Foster Dulles, Eisenhower developed a foreign policy that has been called brinkmanship, which included the capability of massive retaliation. Brinkmanship alerted the world that if the United States suffered a surprise attack, it could still deliver a devastating blow to the attacker. It was hoped that the knowledge of this capability would deter any nation from attacking the United States. The Suez Crisis of 1956 led to the issuance in January, 1957, of the Eisenhower Doctrine, which promised military and economic aid to anti-

President Dwight D. Eisenhower. (Library of Congress)

communist governments and primarily targeted the Middle East.

Part of the domestic agenda of Eisenhower's first term was to expand Social Security to include farmers. He also signed legislation to begin building the St. Lawrence Seaway in 1954 and to begin the development of the interstate highway system in 1956, a system now named for him.

Second Presidential Term, 1957-1961 In spite of a serious heart attack in September, 1955, Eisenhower again overwhelmingly defeated Adlai Stevenson in 1956. Richard M. Nixon was retained as vice president, after serving as acting president during Eisenhower's heart attack recovery.

Eisenhower's second term was again marked by foreign policy. His relationship with the new Soviet leader, Nikita Khrushchev, went from a high point, when Khrushchev toured the United States in 1959, to a low point in May, 1960, when in the U-2 incident, a U.S. spy plane was shot down over the Soviet Union.

Outer space became a real issue when the Soviets launched the first human-made satellite, *Sputnik I*, in October, 1957. The United States responded with a satellite launch of its own in January, 1958, followed by the creation of the National Aeronautics and Space Administration (NASA) in July of that year.

Eisenhower had mixed feelings about the 1954 Supreme Court *Brown v. Board of Education* decision banning the segregation of public schools. He supported integration but felt that the public schools were too sensitive a place for the process to begin. However, he felt duty-bound to support the decision and, in 1957, he sent U.S. troops to enforce desegregation in a Little Rock, Arkansas, high school. He also signed the 1957 Civil Rights Act.

A new phase in Eisenhower's foreign policy came in February, 1960, when he outlined a proposal for a nuclear test ban with the Soviet Union. Earlier he had declared, "The only way to win World War III is to prevent it." However, a Paris summit in May with Khrushchev to discuss the proposal was ruined by the U-2 incident.

On January 17, 1961, three days before leaving office, Eisenhower delivered his farewell address to the nation. Among other things, he warned of the danger of a military-industrial complex having undue influence on national policy. On January 20, he retired to his farm in Gettysburg, Pennsylvania.

Impact As president, Eisenhower symbolized the stability that Americans strongly desired after almost twenty-five years of depression, war, and other world conflicts. His quiet but firm leadership in world affairs convinced potential enemies that the United States would lead the quest both for peace and justice in the world and for the security of American freedoms and interests at home.

Further Reading

Ambrose, Stephen E. *Eisenhower: Soldier and President.* New York: Simon and Schuster, 1990. One of the best full-length biographies, which emphasizes Eisenhower's years as president.

Bowie, Robert, and Richard Immerman. *Waging Peace: How Eisenhower Shaped an Enduring Cold War Strategy.* New York: Oxford University Press, 1998. Details Eisenhower's impact on the world as president.

Damms, Richard. *The Eisenhower Presidency, 1953-1961.* Harlow: Longman, 2002. Brief coverage of the major events of Eisenhower's presidency.

Pruden, Caroline. *Conditional Partners: Eisenhower, the United Nations, and the Search for a Permanent Peace.* Baton Rouge: Louisiana State University Press, 1998. Emphasizes the foreign policy of Eisenhower.

Glenn L. Swygart

See also Conservatism in U.S. politics; Cuban Revolution; Dulles, John Foster; Eisenhower Doctrine; Eisenhower's heart attack; Elections in the United States, 1952; Elections in the United States, 1956; Marshall, George C.; Military-industrial complex; Nixon, Richard M.; Presidential press conferences; Stevenson, Adlai; Truman, Harry S.

■ Eisenhower Doctrine

Identification Document delineating U.S. foreign policy relating to the Middle East

Date Articulated on January 5, 1957; enacted by Congress on March 9, 1957

Stating that the United States would intervene with military force to defend the Middle East from Soviet incursion and communist encroachment, the Eisenhower Doctrine was an essential element in American Cold War foreign policy.

After World War II relations between the United States and the Soviet Union became strained as they viewed each other as rivals. The late 1940's and early 1950's witnessed a continuing collapse of that relationship: The Berlin Wall crisis of 1961, the victory of the Chinese communists, the Korean War, and the nuclear arms race all exacerbated U.S.-Soviet tensions.

During the mid-1950's, President Dwight D. Eisenhower and Secretary of State John Foster Dulles had mounting concern over the growth of nationalism among the Arab states, the subsequent unpredictability of Arab foreign policy, and the continuing decline of British power. From the American perspective, the situation appeared tenuous and ripe for Soviet exploitation through direct intervention or the establishment of satellite states.

In 1956, the Suez Crisis resulted in a British-French-Israeli attack on Egypt, which the United States denounced. During the months that followed the Suez Crisis, it appeared that the Egyptian president Gamal Abdel Nasser was moving toward accommodating the Soviet Union. American support for the new Israeli state compounded tensions; Arab nations refused to recognize Israel and demanded a return of the land to native Palestinians. On January 5, 1957, Eisenhower requested congressional authority to provide financial and military aid to any Middle Eastern nation that was threatened by communism. On March 9, 1957, Congress approved this request, which became formally known as the Eisenhower Doctrine. While Lebanon and Jordan applauded the policy, it was denounced by Syria, Egypt, Iraq, and Saudi Arabia as being an interventionist measure.

Impact In 1958, Eisenhower sent troops to Beirut, Lebanon, although he did not justify his actions via the doctrine. Through the administrations of subsequent American presidents, the Eisenhower Doctrine was used as an expression of American interest throughout the Middle East and as the threat to use force to sustain that interest. In 1980, during the Iranian hostage crisis, President Jimmy Carter used the Eisenhower Doctrine to threaten military action; during the 1980's, President Reagan deployed American military forces in Lebanon and justified that action by referring to the Eisenhower Doctrine. With the collapse of the Soviet Union and communism during the early 1990's, the United States continued its interest in the Middle East but not under the rationale of the Eisenhower Doctrine.

Further Reading

Brands, H. W. *Cold Warriors: Eisenhower's Generation and American Foreign Policy.* New York: Columbia University Press, 1988. A well-written and organized study of Eisenhower's foreign policy and its impact on subsequent decades of American policy toward the Soviet Union.

Takeyh, Ray. *The Origins of the Eisenhower Doctrine: The United States, Britain, and Nasser's Egypt, 1953-1957.* New York: St. Martin's Press, 2000. An excellent study of the Eisenhower Doctrine; it considers the origins of the policy from various perspectives and provides a comprehensive bibliography.

William T. Walker

See also B-52 bomber; Bowles, Chester; Disarmament movement; Dulles, John Foster; Eisenhower, Dwight D.; Foreign policy of the United States; Guatemala invasion; Hungarian revolt; Isolationism; Latin America; Lebanon occupation; Nixon's Latin America tour; United Nations.

■ Eisenhower's heart attack

The Event President Dwight D. Eisenhower had a
heart attack that made his health a national
issue

Date September 24, 1955

Eisenhower's heart attack led to concern about the president's ability to serve in office and run for a second term in 1956. Although the White House was secretive about some aspects of the president's illness, in comparison with previous presidential medical conditions it was rather straightforward. Not only did the incident increase public awareness of heart disease; it also made the subject of presidential health an acceptable topic for press discussion.

Before becoming president of the United States,
Dwight D. Eisenhower had suffered from intestinal
problems for decades. This long-term illness became more severe during his role as supreme allied
commander during World War II and as he became
older. Physicians were never able to diagnose his illness satisfactorily. In addition, Eisenhower's intensity made him prone to outbursts of temper, and he
suffered from high blood pressure. His medical difficulties were one reason why he decided to retire
from the military and become president of Columbia University in October of 1948. However, his status as wartime hero and five-star general meant that
he continued to be involved in military matters despite the toll it took on his health. He worked closely
with the Truman administration on a military reorganization plan.

When Eisenhower was elected president in 1952,
he looked the picture of health. The public's perception of him revolved around his charismatic smile.
Indeed, during the first few years of his administration, Eisenhower showed signs of being more relaxed than ever. Relieved of the pressures of military
command, he seemed to enjoy a more relaxed pace
of work as president. His chief of staff, Sherman Adams, was a dedicated member of the Eisenhower
team, and he made it his job to lessen the burdens
of the president. Eisenhower spent a considerable
amount of time playing golf, and this activity led
some press members to suggest that the president
did not have a good work ethic. Although Eisenhower seemed to be happy in his new role, the old
medical challenges continued to plague him and to
worry his doctors. Eisenhower's physicians were especially concerned about the possibility of stroke.

On September 24, 1955, Eisenhower's personal
physician was summoned to the president's side
while he was vacationing in Colorado. After adminis-
tering morphine, the doctor waited until the following afternoon to transfer the president to a nearby
hospital. At this time, treatments for heart disease
were not advanced and the president was in danger
of death or long-term damage to his heart. As a long-
term smoker, Eisenhower's medical condition had
undoubtedly been harmed by his use of cigarettes.
The president was incapacitated for only a week, but
this would be the first of three serious illnesses during his administration.

Impact Eisenhower won a second term in office in
1956. Plagued by significant health issues for the remainder of his second term, the White House had to
deal as openly as possible with the public about the
nature of the president's health. During the second
half of 1957 he suffered first from an ileitis attack,
which necessitated intestinal surgery (June), and
then a slight stroke (November). The White House
once again had to respond to press questions about
how these episodes had affected the president.

Moreover, Eisenhower's heart attack affected the
vice presidency when Richard M. Nixon had to act
as president while Eisenhower was incapacitated.
Since Eisenhower's poor health was a constant
threat, he worked with Nixon to create the office of
acting president in the event he again became incapacitated from illness. The formal agreement authorized the vice president to govern when the president could not discharge the powers and duties of
his office.

In the long term, Eisenhower's heart attack caused
a gradual opening of private medical records of
presidential candidates for public scrutiny. Prior to
this event, the press viewed presidential health as
a private matter not to be discussed in public settings.

Further Reading

Ambrose, Stephen E. *Eisenhower.* New York: Simon &
Schuster, 1984. Comprehensive biography.

Lasby, Clarence G. *Eisenhower's Heart Attack: How Ike
Beat Heart Disease and Held on to the Presidency.* Lawrence: University Press of Kansas, 1997. Detailed
examination of the crisis precipitated by Eisenhower's heart attack.

Pach, Chester J., and Elmo Richardson. *The Presidency of Dwight D. Eisenhower.* Lawrence: Univer-

sity Press of Kansas, 1991. Objective account of the Eisenhower administration that includes an account of Eisenhower's heart attack.

Michael E. Meagher

See also Adams, Sherman; Eisenhower, Dwight D.; Elections in the United States, 1956; Nixon, Richard M.

■ Elections in Canada

The Events Canadian federal elections
Dates August 10, 1953; June 10, 1957; March 31, 1958

During the 1950's, elections in Canada proved to be centered on such issues as nationalism, continentalism, debate over foreign dependence on the United States, and issues of unity between the country's French and English populations. Twenty-two years of Liberal dominance gave way in 1957 to a temporary Conservative resurgence.

Canadian federal elections during the 1950's were a contest between the Liberal Party (Grits) and the Progressive Conservatives (Tories). Minor parties that won some parliamentary seats and governed a few western provinces included the left-of-center Cooperative Commonwealth Federation (CCF) and the right-of-center Social Credit (Socreds). Another noteworthy political force, the Union Nationale of Quebec, did not participate in federal elections but controlled the country's second largest province from 1945-1960. The decade's most important political figures were Liberal Party leaders Louis St. Laurent and Lester Pearson, Progressive Conservative John Diefenbaker, and Quebec's premier Maurice Duplessis.

Elections of 1948 When Louis St. Laurent, a veteran French-Canadian politician from Quebec, succeeded party leader William L. Mackenzie King in late 1948, the Liberals had held power since 1935. St. Laurent's grandfatherly image, mastery of a highly qualified cabinet, self-assurance, and seemingly effortless leadership style were political assets. Moreover, a postwar economic boom with impressive growth rates, high employment, and rising prosperity continued unchecked. In their 1953 federal election triumph, the Liberals won 171 parliamentary seats to 51 for the Tories. The CCF gained 23, Social Credit 15, and other parties 5.

To sustain growth and bolster the infrastructure,

Liberal domestic policy encouraged foreign investment and undertook megaprojects such as the St. Lawrence Seaway, Trans-Canada Highway, and a Trans-Canada Pipeline providing industrialized eastern Canada with western natural gas. In the foreign policy sphere, Canada actively participated in NATO and the Korean conflict, developed closer military ties with the United States in joint hemispheric defense measures, and served as a mediator in international disputes. External Affairs minister Lester Pearson won the Nobel Peace Prize for his role in resolving the Suez Crisis in 1956.

Elections of 1957 A key factor in the Liberal Party's defeat in 1957 was a miscalculation over the Trans-Canada Pipeline bill. During this debate, the opposition objected to the presence of American capital in the pipeline construction and advocated giving the task to a purely Canadian firm. When a filibuster delayed the legislation, the government party resorted to a parliamentary procedure, which shut off debate. Opponents convinced many that an arrogant ruling party had bypassed the democratic process to suppress legitimate nationalist concerns. Election results on June 10, 1957, stunned the overconfident Liberals, ending twenty-two years of uninterrupted rule. The Tories formed a minority government with 112 seats to 105 for the Liberals. The CCF, Social Credit, and others won 25, 15 and 4 respectively.

Diefenbaker's Tenure John Diefenbaker, a small-town lawyer from Saskatchewan, became prime minister. Diefenbaker, who assumed his party's leadership in 1956, was a rousing orator with a theatrical and entertaining delivery, a staunch Canadian nationalist, and a western populist with sympathy for the working classes and the oppressed. Diefenbaker appeared dynamic and decisive in his first parliamentary session of 1957-1958. Then, opposition leader Lester Pearson, St. Laurent's successor as party head in 1958, asked Diefenbaker and his cabinet to resign without giving sufficient reasons, a move which further underscored the public's impression of Liberal arrogance. Diefenbaker quickly called an election. In a landslide victory, the Tories won 208 seats, the highest total for any party in Canadian history to date. The Liberals plummeted to 49 seats, while minor parties garnered merely 8 seats. This immense triumph was aided by the unprecedented defection of Quebec from the federal Liberal Party with Premier Duplessis's help.

Diefenbaker's achievements included aid for farmers, improving social legislation, and promoting human rights in Canada and abroad. However, the Tory leader's talents lay in parliamentary debate and campaigning rather than effectively directing his government in a definite plan. Diefenbaker's policies were sometimes radical and contrary to traditional Tory values. Quebec soon became disaffected with their temporary Tory alliance when Diefenbaker was unable to give the province any significant representation in his government. Moreover, the prime minister's nationalism and desire of escaping American domination in foreign policy was contradicted by his zealous "Cold Warrior" mentality. He defied American wishes on policy issues relating to China and Cuba, while he simultaneously integrated Canada further into the American military defense scheme designed for North America. Diefenbaker's efforts to seek closer political and economic ties with the British Commonwealth to alleviate increasing American economic domination proved futile.

Some of Diefenbaker's problems were not of his own making. The economic boom was giving way to recession near the time he took office. This situation required unpopular policies such as devaluation of the dollar. Moreover, the decision in 1959 to cancel the much-heralded but expensive Avro Arrow project, Canada's contribution to military technology and defense in the form of a formidable supersonic jet interceptor, cost the Tories popularity and contributed to the government's ultimate defeat during the early 1960's.

Impact Although the 1950's witnessed a dramatic interruption of a long one-party trend at the national level, the failure of Diefenbaker and the Tories to capitalize on their great electoral victory in 1958 had serious long-term consequences. The Tories were reduced to a minority government in the 1962 election, and narrowly defeated in 1963. Over the next twenty-one years, the Progressive Conservatives would again hold power for a mere nine-month span.

Further Reading

Bothwell, Robert, Ian Drummond, and John English. *Canada Since 1945: Power, Politics, and Provincialism.* Rev. ed. Toronto: University of Toronto Press, 1989. Informative treatment of Canadian political, economic, and cultural developments during the postwar decades.

English, J. Lester. *Pearson: The Worldly Years, 1949-1972.* Toronto: Alfred A. Knopf, 1992. Good biographical study of an important Liberal statesman and political leader in this era.

Smith, Denis. *Rogue Tory: The Life and Legend of John G. Diefenbaker.* Toronto: McFarlane, Walter & Ross, 1997. Most comprehensive study to date of this Canadian prime minister and his interesting career.

Whitaker, Roy. *The Government Party.* Toronto: University of Toronto Press, 1977. An excellent study of Canada's Liberal Party based on party documents and papers.

David A. Crain

See also Business and the economy in Canada; Canada and Great Britain; Canada as a middle power; Canadian regionalism; Diefenbaker, John G.; North American Aerospace Defense Command; Pearson, Lester B.; St. Laurent, Louis; Unemployment in Canada.

■ Elections in the United States, midterm

The Events National elections occurring between presidential elections

Dates November 7, 1950; November 2, 1954; and November 4, 1958

In keeping with a historical tendency in U.S. politics, the presidential parties lost congressional seats in each of the midterm (or off-year) elections of the 1950's.

Throughout the U.S. history of electoral politics, in the years of presidential elections, the political party of the winning president usually gains seats in both the Senate and House of Representatives. In midterm elections, by contrast, the presidential party tends to lose seats. Many voters blame the incumbent president for problems and undesirable situations, and they express their discontent at the ballot box during off-year elections. Historically, voters have punished the presidential party most severely in the sixth year of a two-term presidency—sometimes called the "six-year itch." However, midterm elections are not determined only by the approval rating of the president. Voters are also motivated by local issues and the personalities of the individual candidates.

Elections of 1950 In 1950, many Americans thought that Democratic president Harry S. Truman's policies were responsible for both the communist victory in China and the outbreak of the Korean War. In this context, Democrats had reason to be nervous about Republican senator Joseph McCarthy's assertion of communist infiltration in the government. With growing inflation and higher taxes, moreover, a significant percentage of the public was ready to believe that the New Deal-Fair Deal programs were too "socialistic." Conservative-leaning voters were particularly suspicious of Truman's proposal of compulsory health insurance for all citizens.

Preoccupied with the Korean conflict, Truman did not make any political speeches until three days before the election. He argued that Democratic policies of the previous seventeen years had ended the Depression and helped the average citizen, and he denounced the Republicans as the party of "special interests" and "isolationism." Replying for the Republicans, Harold Stassen of Minnesota asserted that the "blundering" policies of Truman's "spy-riddled" administration were responsible for casualties in Korea.

On November 7, Republican candidates won a number of unexpected victories in both the Senate and the House. Although the Republicans failed to gain control of either chamber, the Democratic majority in the Senate declined from twelve seats to only two, and in the House, it was reduced from seventeen to twelve. Republicans, moreover, prevailed in several high-profile Senate races. In California, Republican Richard M. Nixon defeated Helen Gahagan Douglas; in Illinois, Republican Everett Dirksen defeated Democratic Majority Leader Scott Lucas; and in Ohio, Senator Robert Taft, leader of the conservative Republicans, won by a huge margin.

The election further strengthened the coalition between the Republican Party and conservative southern Democrats. If the southern Democrats were not counted in the election returns, the Democrats prevailed in only 126 House contests, compared to 196 for the Republicans. During the following two years, Truman clearly found it impossible to get Congress to enact any major liberal Fair Deal legislation.

Elections of 1954 Until late in the campaigns of 1954, it appeared that the Republicans had a good chance of keeping the narrow congressional majority they had won two years earlier. In addition to President Dwight D. Eisenhower's great popularity, the economy was growing, unemployment was down, and the country was at peace. By accepting Social Security and other New Deal reforms, the Republicans had not alienated centrist voters. One of Eisenhower's special problems was deciding whether to support the movement in the Senate to censure McCarthy for his irresponsible allegations. Eisenhower avoided any direct involvement in the controversy, which allowed him to distance himself from the senator without completely alienating the senator's loyal followers.

In October, after the polls indicated a Democratic trend, Eisenhower decided to become more actively involved in the campaign. Over television, he warned that a Democratic Congress would mean "a cold war of partisan politics." On October 29, he made an unprecedented one-day flying trip of 1,521 miles, addressing large crowds in major cities. In his speeches, he was generally positive and emphasized the growing prosperity of the nation. Vice President Richard M. Nixon, in contrast, was quite partisan in his attacks, charging that the Democrats had been ineffective in dealing with the internal communist threat.

The election results of November 2 were unusually close, with the Democrats narrowly regaining control of Congress. The new balance in the Senate was forty-eight Democrats versus forty-seven Republicans. The new lineup in the House was 232 Democrats versus 203 Republicans. The Democratic Party, of course, was badly divided, especially on the issue of civil rights. Winning candidates included antisegregation Democrats such as senators Hubert H. Humphrey and Paul Douglas, but they also included prosegregation southerners such as Strom Thurmond. One notable result of the election was that the Eighty-fourth Congress would include seventeen women, a record for the legislative institution.

President Eisenhower promised at his press conference that he would work with the congressional leaders of both parties, and he conceded that he had exaggerated in speaking about a possible cold war between the executive and legislative branches. He strongly denied that the election returns implied a repudiation of his policies. Faced with a Democratic Congress for the next six years, Eisenhower would find it necessary to make numerous compromises. He would find it relatively easy, nevertheless, to cooperate with Speaker of the House Sam Rayburn and Senate Majority Leader Lyndon B. Johnson.

Elections of 1958 During the elections of 1958, Eisenhower traveled widely and gave many speeches in favor of Republican candidates. His speeches were more partisan in tone than in previous years. Claiming to have a record of the "finest six years of progress" in the nation's history, he accused the Democrats of favoring "harebrained spending schemes" that would saddle future generations with debt and inflation. Nixon's rhetoric was even more strident. Responding in kind, Illinois governor Adlai Stevenson charged that the "old Nixon" had been joined by the "new Ike" in a desperate and intolerable "demagoguery."

Republicans were at a disadvantage in 1958 because of the economic recession that had begun in late 1957. Although the recession ended by the middle of 1958, it nevertheless reinforced the tendency of voters to associate the Republican Party with hard times. In many states, Republican efforts to pass right-to-work laws inspired labor unions to organize their members to vote. The scandal involving White House aide Sherman Adams also damaged the Republican cause. Candidates said much about the launch of Soviet satellite *Sputnik* and the "missile gap," but neither party was able to gain much from the issue. Although most white Democrats of the South were angry about the official Democratic position on school desegregation, the Republican parties of the South were still too weak to benefit from this growing discontent.

On November 4, the Republicans suffered their worst defeat since the early years of the Depression. In the next Congress, the Democrats would outnumber Republicans by almost two to one in both chambers. The Senate would have 64 Democrats and 34 Republicans, while the House would have 282 Democrats and 154 Republicans. Democrats, moreover, would have thirty-five governors, compared to fourteen for the Republicans. At a press conference, Eisenhower expressed his disappointment that so many "spenders" had won, but he indicated that he would continue to work with moderate and conservative Democrats to keep spending under control.

Impact In each of the midterm elections of the 1950's, the party of the incumbent president suffered because of voter discontent. As a result, both presidents Truman and Eisenhower would be unable to pursue some of their preferred policies, and both would find it necessary to make many compromises.

Although the two-year periods following these elections were not times of great legislative accomplishment, the elections did not result in government paralysis or stalemate. The ideological divisions within both parties, especially in the area of civil rights, encouraged accommodation and shifting alliances.

Further Reading

Ambrose, Stephen. *Eisenhower: The President.* New York: Simon & Schuster, 1984. A standard work that includes good discussions of the elections from 1952 to 1960.

Donovan, Robert J. *Tumultuous Years: The Presidency of Harry S. Truman, 1949-1953.* Columbia: University of Missouri Press, 1996. Written by a reporter of the period, this standard work gives a very good account of the issues and personalities of the election of 1950.

Moore, John, ed. *Guide to U.S. Elections.* Washington, D.C.: Congressional Quarterly, 1994. Includes excellent summaries of both presidential and midterm elections, with abundant statistical information and tables.

O'Connor, Karen, and Larry Sabato. *American Government: Continuity and Change.* New York: Pearson Education, 2004. Chapters 12 and 13 are helpful for the reader desiring clear and informed discussions about the various kinds of elections.

Thomas Tandy Lewis

See also Conservatism in U.S. politics; Elections in the United States, 1952; Elections in the United States, 1956; Espionage and Sabotage Act of 1954; McCarthy, Joseph; Nixon, Richard M.; *Profiles in Courage*; Reagan, Ronald; Truman assassination attempt; Unemployment in the United States.

■ Elections in the United States, 1952

The Event Elections for the presidency and other federal offices
Date November 4, 1952

Voters elected Dwight D. Eisenhower to the first of two terms as president, ending twenty years of Democratic control of the White House, and gave the Republican Party temporary control of Congress.

The Twenty-second Amendment, ratified February 26, 1951, limited presidents to two terms. Because it did not apply to Democratic President Harry S. Truman, many Americans assumed that Truman would run for reelection in 1952. Truman announced his decision not to seek reelection in the spring of 1952. Skeptics and critics of Truman suspected that his decision was prompted by his defeat in the New Hampshire Democratic presidential primary in March, 1952. Senator Estes Kefauver of Tennessee, a prominent critic and investigator of organized crime and corruption in the Truman administration, defeated Truman 19,800 to 15,927 votes.

The Democratic Party Before the Democratic national convention opened in Chicago in July, the Democrats experienced a brief yet spirited contest for the presidential nomination. Although Kefauver won most Democratic presidential primaries, he competed against Alben William Barkley and Senators Richard Russell of Georgia and Robert Kerr of Oklahoma. Russell, an anti-civil rights conservative, decisively defeated Kefauver in the Florida presidential primary.

Since most delegates to the Democratic national convention were not chosen through binding primaries, it was unlikely that Estes Kefauver would be nominated for president. Southern conservative Democrats disliked Kefauver's moderate position on civil rights, and northern Democrats resented his widely publicized Senate investigation of corruption, organized crime, and apparent collusion between gangsters and Democratic machine politicians. Although Illinois governor Adlai Stevenson repeatedly stated that he would not run for president, a draft-Stevenson movement gathered momentum and attracted delegate support before the convention. After Stevenson's inspiring welcoming address stimulated a rousing response at the convention, the Illinois governor accepted the Democratic presidential nomination. In an effort to unite the Democratic Party for the election, Stevenson chose Senator John Sparkman of Alabama, an anti-civil rights economic liberal, as his running mate.

President-elect Dwight D. Eisenhower (right), vice-president-elect Richard M. Nixon (center), and Republican National Committee chairman Arthur Summerfield conferring shortly after the November election. (Hulton Archive | by Getty Images)

The Republican Party While the Democrats were plagued by Truman's low public approval ratings, inflation, a frustrating stalemate in the Korean War, and Republican charges of corruption and softness toward domestic and international communism, they at least retained their status as the majority party in voter identification. In preparing Stevenson's campaign, Democratic strategists emphasized twenty years of progress in economic reforms, domestic policy, and foreign policy during the Roosevelt and Truman administrations and portrayed a Republican victory in the elections of 1952 as a threat to popular Democratic-created policies that benefited farmers, union members, consumers, and the elderly. The Democrats hoped that the Republicans would nominate Senator Robert A. Taft of Ohio for president. Nicknamed "Mr. Republican," Taft was a conservative known for his controversial, acerbic criticism of New Deal programs.

Many leading Republicans, however, realized that in order to win control of the presidency and Congress, they needed to nominate a presidential candidate who could unite the Republican Party and attract the votes of most independents and a substantial minority of Democrats. Taft was too conservative, partisan, and divisive for this purpose. Although some Republicans persisted in promoting Taft's presidential candidacy at the Republican national convention in Chicago, former general Dwight D. Eisenhower won the Republican presidential nomination on the second ballot. From the perspective of moderate and liberal Republicans

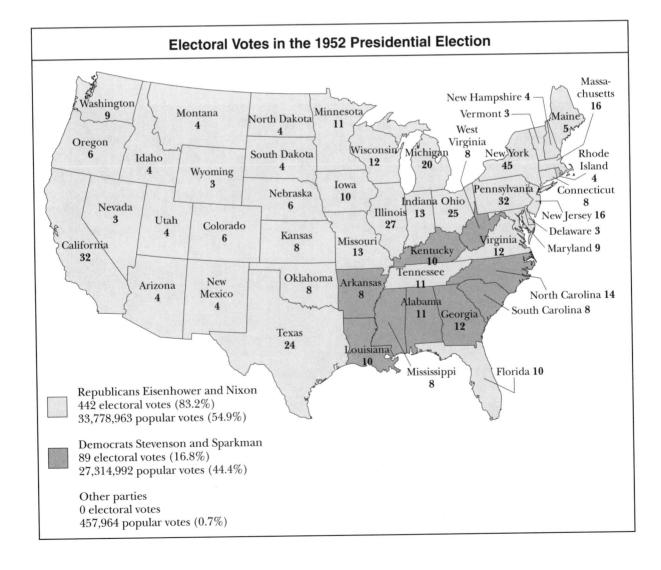

Electoral Votes in the 1952 Presidential Election

Republicans Eisenhower and Nixon
442 electoral votes (83.2%)
33,778,963 popular votes (54.9%)

Democrats Stevenson and Sparkman
89 electoral votes (16.8%)
27,314,992 popular votes (44.4%)

Other parties
0 electoral votes
457,964 popular votes (0.7%)

who led the draft-Eisenhower movement long before the convention began, Eisenhower was the ideal candidate. Eisenhower was an immensely popular hero of World War II who accepted major New Deal policies and an internationalist, bipartisan foreign policy.

The General Election Campaign In addition to choosing Senator Richard M. Nixon of California as his running mate, Eisenhower asserted that the three major issues of his presidential campaign were Korea, communism, and corruption. Regardless of their partisan and policy differences, many Americans were frustrated by Truman's failure to end the Korean War victoriously and perceived Eisenhower as better able to successfully end it than Truman or Stevenson. Eisenhower's charges of Democratic failure to combat domestic and international communism seemed to be substantiated by the popular appeal of Senator Joseph McCarthy's dramatic accusations of communist influence in American foreign policy, Truman's limited war strategy in Korea and his unpopular removal of General Douglas MacArthur from command there, the fall of China to communism in 1949, and the Soviet detonation of an atomic bomb linked to earlier communist infiltration of American atomic bomb research.

The credibility of Eisenhower's third campaign theme, corruption, was undermined by news that Richard M. Nixon, his running mate, had received an ethically questionable slush fund from California businessmen. After Nixon's televised "Checkers" speech, in which he explained the gifts, proved to be popular, Eisenhower retained him as his running mate. Although Stevenson had a reputation as a cerebral, articulate, "good government" reformer, he was often forced to defend the most unpopular, controversial aspects of Truman's presidency and the Democratic Party. Stevenson's campaign was also burdened by inadequate funds, disorganization, and Truman's harsh criticism of the Republicans.

Election Results Benefiting from a high voter turnout, the Republicans easily won the 1952 presidential election and narrowly gained control of Congress. This was the first time since 1928 that the Republicans won control of the presidency and Congress. Eisenhower carried thirty-nine of the forty-eight states in the electoral college and 55 percent of the popular votes. Stevenson carried a few border and southern states and lost his home state of Illi-

nois. The Republicans achieved a five-seat majority in the U.S. House of Representatives and a one-seat majority in the Senate.

Impact The results of the 1952 federal elections influenced American politics and public policy for the remainder of the 1950's. However, despite Eisenhower's popularity and his subsequent landslide re-election against Stevenson in 1956, the Republican Party failed to become the new majority party among voters. The Democrats regained control of Congress in 1954, and Eisenhower was faced with a Democratic Congress during most of his presidency. Eisenhower emphasized bipartisan moderation in developing most of his major foreign and domestic policies, such as the Civil Rights Act of 1957 and the National Defense Education Act of 1958. The most conservative Republicans and the most liberal Democrats in Congress were often dissatisfied with the moderate, bipartisan tone and content of the politics and policies of the 1950's.

Further Reading

Ambrose, Stephen E. *Eisenhower: Soldier and President.* New York: Simon & Schuster, 1990. A comprehensive biography of Eisenhower.

Pickett, William B. *Eisenhower Decides to Run: Presidential Politics and Cold War Strategy.* Chicago: Ivan R. Dee, 2000. Focuses primarily on the 1952 election year, detailing Eisenhower's strategy in his political win.

Savage, Sean J. *Truman and the Democratic Party.* Lexington: University Press of Kentucky, 1997. A study of Truman's party leadership with details on the 1952 elections.

Sean J. Savage

See also Army-McCarthy hearings; Barkley, Alben W.; Conservatism in U.S. politics; Eisenhower, Dwight D.; Elections in the United States, 1956; Gallup polls; Kefauver, Estes; Korean War; McCarthy, Joseph; Nixon, Richard M.; Steel mill closure; Stevenson, Adlai; Tidelands oil controversy; Truman, Harry S.; Twenty-second Amendment.

■ Elections in the United States, 1956

The Event Elections for the presidency and other federal offices

Date November 6, 1956

In a landslide, voters returned Republican president Dwight D. Eisenhower and Vice President Richard M. Nixon for a second term and gave the Democratic Party continued control of Congress.

The Eisenhower victory in 1952 had given the Republican Party control of Congress for the first time since before the Great Depression. However, the midterm elections of 1954 saw that fragile control disappear. The loss of one Senate seat gave the Democrats control of the Senate, as did the loss of eighteen seats in the House of Representatives. The loss by the Republicans was due in part to the public's continued perception of the Republican Party as the party of big business and of the Democrats as the party of the people. President Dwight D. Eisenhower hoped to change that perception, win reelection in 1956, and carry the Republican Party back into control of Congress.

Presidential Election Near the end of Eisenhower's first presidential term, the president suffered a heart attack that many feared would end his political career. Vice President Richard M. Nixon served as acting president for several weeks. However, when his doctors pronounced him fully recovered in early 1956, Eisenhower resumed plans for reelection to a second term. At the Republican national convention in the San Francisco Cow Palace that summer, the popular president was quickly renominated. There was a question about keeping Nixon on the ticket, but Eisenhower eventually decided to keep him.

The previous week, the Democratic Party met in Chicago and renominated Adlai Stevenson, the former governor of Illinois. Although being soundly defeated by Eisenhower in 1952, Stevenson again actively pursued the Democratic nomination. He ran in the state primaries and secured the nomination on the first ballot. For his vice president, in an effort

Republication campaign headquarters in New York City in September, 1956. (AP/Wide World Photos)

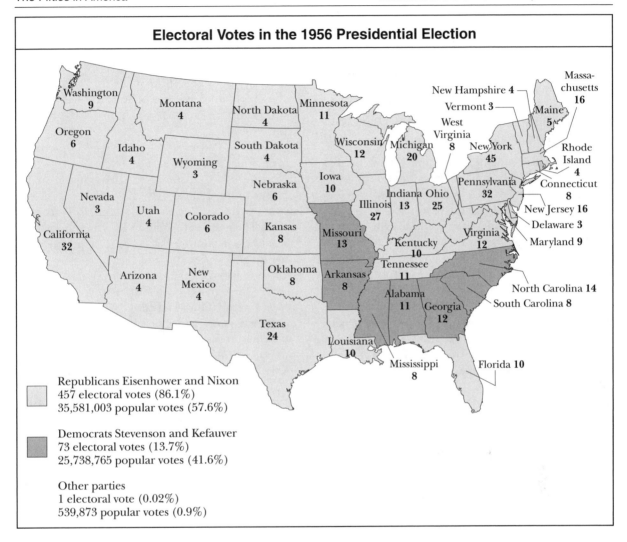

Electoral Votes in the 1956 Presidential Election

Washington 9
Montana 4
North Dakota 4
Minnesota 11
New Hampshire 4
Vermont 3
Massachusetts 16
Maine 5
Oregon 6
Idaho 4
South Dakota 4
Wisconsin 12
Michigan 20
West Virginia 8
New York 45
Rhode Island 4
Wyoming 3
Iowa 10
Pennsylvania 32
Connecticut 8
Nevada 3
Utah 4
Colorado 6
Nebraska 6
Illinois 27
Indiana 13
Ohio 25
New Jersey 16
California 32
Kansas 8
Missouri 13
Kentucky 10
Virginia 12
Delaware 3
Maryland 9
Arizona 4
New Mexico 4
Oklahoma 8
Arkansas 8
Tennessee 11
North Carolina 14
South Carolina 8
Alabama 11
Georgia 12
Texas 24
Louisiana 10
Mississippi 8
Florida 10

Republicans Eisenhower and Nixon
457 electoral votes (86.1%)
35,581,003 popular votes (57.6%)

Democrats Stevenson and Kefauver
73 electoral votes (13.7%)
25,738,765 popular votes (41.6%)

Other parties
1 electoral vote (0.02%)
539,873 popular votes (0.9%)

to hold the Democratic control of the South, he chose Senator Estes Kefauver of Tennessee. Kefauver had gained national attention as chairman of the Senate Crime Investigation Committee and with his 1951 book based on that work, *Crime in America.*

During the campaign, Stevenson did not heed advice to stress domestic issues. He disappointed liberal Democrats by not taking a strong stand on civil rights and was perceived as not caring about the needs of African Americans. Any concern he did have was overshadowed by his need for southern electoral votes.

Stevenson focused his campaign on foreign policy. He declared that U.S. security was at risk because of the failure of Eisenhower's policies during the most crucial years of the Cold War. Stevenson's sug-

gestion to halt hydrogen bomb testing was interpreted as a weakening of U.S. defenses at a time when most felt that they needed strengthening. Stevenson's opinion was based on the comment by Albert Einstein that a World War III involving nuclear weapons would be followed by a World War IV fought only with sticks and stones. However, when the Soviet Union began a new round of nuclear testing in 1956, President Eisenhower said the United States had to follow suit or lose its advantage in nuclear weapons.

Eisenhower and Nixon concentrated on domestic conditions, including what many have called the "affluent society." Americans were enjoying a prosperity never imagined one generation earlier, and the new medium of television was carrying that message into millions of American homes. However, the major factor in the campaign was the popularity of the president. The outcome of the election was never in doubt. Eisenhower won 57.6 percent of the popular vote and 457 electoral votes; Stevenson won only 73 electoral votes and only 7 southern states. Stevenson failed to win his home state of Illinois or Kefauver's home state of Tennessee.

Congressional Elections Unfortunately for the Republican Party, the coattails of President Eisenhower were not long enough to carry his party back into control of Congress. The losses the party suffered in 1954 were only a taste of what they would lose in 1956.

The Republican Party was still trying to carve for itself a reliable voting block in the post-Depression years. Eisenhower's personal popularity was not enough to perform that task. To help Eisenhower's efforts, Arthur Larson, Eisenhower's undersecretary of labor, wrote *A Republican Looks at His Party* in 1956. His theme was "New Republicanism," which included a major appeal to workers. He also emphasized Eisenhower's support for an increase in the minimum wage and other social welfare legislation.

Both parties moved toward the political center in 1956, trying to gain the votes of the moderate and independent voters. The mainstream of each party agreed on most domestic issues, such as the need to continue strengthening Social Security and to reduce budget deficits.

The outcome of the congressional elections was a sharp contrast to the presidential race. Three out of four voters for Eisenhower did not vote for Republican congressional candidates. The Democratic Party increased their majority in the House of Representatives by thirty-three. The trend continued in the off-year elections of 1958, when the Democrats secured a wide margin in both houses: In the House it was 282-154, and in the Senate it was 64-34. The Democrats held more than two-thirds of each branch of Congress. In the House, only 59 percent of incumbents were reelected.

Impact The 1956 elections produced the necessity of cooperation between a very popular president of one party and a congress heavily controlled by the opposition. On one hand, it enabled President Eisenhower to continue his leadership in the Cold War, which including inviting Soviet leader Nikita Khrushchev to visit the United States in 1959. On the other hand, the congressional elections gave the Democratic Party hope that they could win the White House in 1960.

Further Reading

Campbell, Angus, et al. *Elections and the Political Order.* New York: John Wiley and Sons, 1966. Discusses voting patterns and demographics of elections of the 1950's.

Diggins, John Patrick. *The Proud Decades: America in War and Peace, 1941-1960.* New York: W. W. Norton, 1988. Historical analysis of the major events of the 1950's.

Larson, Arthur. *A Republican Looks at His Party.* New York: Harper, 1956. Written by a member of the Eisenhower administration as a campaign manual in 1956.

Madaras, Larry. *Taking Sides: Clashing Views on Controversial Issues in American History Since 1945.* 2d ed. New York: McGraw-Hill, 2003. Gives opposing arguments on major political issues in the twentieth century, discussing Eisenhower's presidential tenure in the process.

Pickett, William B. *Eisenhower Decides to Run: Presidential Politics and Cold War Strategy.* Chicago: Ivan R. Dee, 2000. While focusing primarily on the 1952 election year, the book nonetheless details Eisenhower's strategy in his political wins.

Polsby, Nelson W., and Aaron Wildavsky. *Presidential Elections: Strategies and Structures of American Politics.* 10th ed. New York: Chatham House, 2000. Explores how a president becomes elected, highlighting the complexity of the selection process.

Glenn L. Swygart

See also Conservatism in U.S. politics; Eisenhower, Dwight D.; Eisenhower's heart attack; Elections in the United States, midterm; Elections in the United States, 1952; Gallup polls; Kefauver, Estes; Nixon, Richard M.; Rayburn, Sam; Reagan, Ronald; Stevenson, Adlai; Unemployment in the United States; Veterans organizations.

■ Eliot, T. S.

Identification American poet, essayist, and playwright
Born September 26, 1888; St. Louis, Missouri
Died January 4, 1965; London, England

T. S. Eliot earned celebrity status during the 1950's for literary and dramatic work that resonated thematically with the American public of the Cold War era.

Thomas Stearns Eliot grew up in an aristocratic Victorian family. He discovered poetry as an outlet to express his thoughts and observations and continued to write it as a Harvard student, grammar school teacher, bank clerk, and editor. In 1927, he became a British subject and converted to the Church of England.

Eliot gained a reputation as a poet who exposed the modern urban landscape as sordid and decaying, its inhabitants in need of human connection and spiritual enlightenment, as in one of his best-known poems, "The Love Song of J. Alfred Prufrock" (1915). He made frequent trips to the United States to visit family and give lectures on literature at various universities and organizations. The 1922 publication of Eliot's long poem, *The Waste Land*, earned for him international acclaim and established his role as a groundbreaking modern poet who influenced his contemporaries and all other poets after him.

Celebrity Status When he was awarded the Nobel Prize in Literature in 1948, Eliot was primarily writing plays, including *The Cocktail Party* (pr. 1949). Set at a social gathering hosted by a man whose wife has suddenly and mysteriously left him, it portrays the difficulty and sense of hopelessness in human relationships, a theme which also is found in Eliot's poetry and in his play *The Family Reunion* (pr. 1939). Both of these plays eventually reached a wider audience through the new medium of television, which helped catapult Eliot to celebrity status. After readings in the United States, photographers and autograph seekers pursued him. In 1950, when Eliot lectured at Harvard, loudspeakers were set up for those who could not gain access to the overcrowded auditorium. This period was also marked by a new play, *The Confidential Clerk* (pr. 1953).

In 1957, he married Valerie Fletcher, his secretary of eight years. His first marriage to Vivienne Haigh-Wood, from 1915 to 1933, had been a constant source of anxiety, because of Vivienne's mental instability, and with his second wife, he finally found a loving, fulfilling relationship, the lack of which so much of his work had been based upon. Despite the happiness of this relationship and a less demanding schedule—with only one play, *The Elder Statesman*, written during this time—in 1965, Eliot finally succumbed to the health problems that had been plaguing him throughout this decade, including emphysema, due to heavy smoking, and heart problems.

Impact Along with Ezra Pound, Eliot is considered one of the founders of literary modernism. In his poems, he showed the desolation of the postwar landscape and the difficulty of humans to reconnect not only to a fragmented consciousness but also to one another. In the plays of the 1950's, Eliot depicted the lack of progression in relationships between the repressed Victorian period, in which he had come of age, and the postwar years. The resonance this message had for audiences who were experiencing the conservative repression of the 1950's earned him a reputation as the voice of modern consciousness and paved the way for the experimentation of contemporary writers.

Further Reading

Ackroyd, Peter. *T. S. Eliot: A Life*. New York: Simon & Schuster, 1984. A biography of Eliot that discusses not only his work in different periods of his life, but also his life in the context of that work.

Moody, A. David, ed. *The Cambridge Companion to T. S. Eliot*. Cambridge, England: Cambridge University Press, 1994. A helpful introduction to the work of T. S. Eliot for students and scholars, providing essays on his poems and plays as well as examining his work in its historical context.

Holly L. Norton

See also Literature in the United States; Nobel Prizes; Poetry; Pound, Ezra.

■ Elizabeth II's coronation

The Event Formal crowning of Elizabeth II as queen of Great Britain and Northern Ireland
Date June 2, 1953
Place Westminster Abbey, London, England

The coronation festivities signaled Great Britain's emergence from the dark days of World War II and acknowledged the survival of the British crown of a thousand years. The magnificent and glittering ceremony with its ancient rituals gave the entire world reasons to celebrate.

Princess Elizabeth succeeded to the throne at the death of her father, King George VI, on February 6, 1952. Preparations for her formal coronation ceremony immediately began. Complicated and difficult decisions were made about the invitation list, precedence of visiting dignitaries and other protocol is-

Queen Elizabeth after receiving the crown, scepter, and rod from the archbishop of Canterbury during her coronation. (AP/Wide World Photos)

abbey, a relict of ancient practice of election of monarchs. She then took the oath to govern her peoples according to their laws and to preserve the state religion. Next, as part of the communion service, the queen was anointed with the holy oil that represented divine confirmation of the people's choice and was invested with the emblems of sovereignty. The archbishop of Canterbury then placed the St. Edward's crown on the queen. Finally, she was enthroned and received the homage of her subjects. Carrying the scepter with the cross and the orb, the queen, wearing the lighter imperial state crown and the purple velvet imperial robe of state for the first time, led the distinguished assembly from the abbey.

The return procession to Buckingham Palace included more than ten thousand soldiers and the Royal Canadian Mounties, who received a special cheer from the crowd that had been standing in the intermittent rain for hours. The queen and her family repeatedly appeared during the evening on the balcony of Buckingham Palace to great roars of approval from the gathered crowd.

sues, participants, music, and other minutiae of the ceremony. At London's Westminster Abbey, an annex was built, more than two thousand square yards of carpet were laid, and seating for seven thousand people was constructed. Stands for an additional 100,000 people were built along the royal route. London was refurbished from its gloomy wartime state and decorated with new paint, flags, flowers, banners, arches, and other street decorations.

Elizabeth herself, attired in a white satin gown embroidered with symbols of the Commonwealth nations and encrusted with precious and semiprecious stones, traveled to the abbey in a gilded coach. The roots of the coronation service went back to the coronation of King Edgar in the year 973 but had been altered and modified by successive generations. The ceremony had four major phases. First, the queen was accepted by the people in the

Impact While past coronations had been essentially private observations, witnessed by the relatively small groups of people who could fit inside Westminster Abbey, Elizabeth's coronation was very much a public event. Initially, media coverage of the ceremony was to be limited to print, radio, and cinema; however, the queen reversed the decision and permitted the ceremony to be broadcast on television as well. Still photos of the event were transmitted in two-minute intervals over new transatlantic cables to appear on television screens in North America within seven minutes. Audiences in Great Britain, France, Holland, and Germany viewed the events live while the Royal Air Force flew tapes of the ceremony to Canada and the United States that later were viewed on television by eighty-five million North Americans.

Television broadcasts in Canada and the United States showed the ceremony in color, and the scope of the audiences in both countries indicated the widespread fascination both with the pageantry itself and with the immediacy of television. Many North American schools were closed so that students could observe and report on the historic event. In all, the intense media coverage of the royal family and the events preceding the coronation as well as the ceremony itself generated a deep fascination with the British crown among North Americans that continued to grow in the following decades.

Further Reading

Barker, Brian. *When the Queen Was Crowned*. New York: David McKay, 1976. A participant's in-depth description of the planning for the coronation ceremony and the surrounding events.

McLeish, Kenneth, and Valerie McLeish. *Long to Reign Over Us: Memories of Coronation Day and of Life in the 1950's*. Leicester, England: G. B: Charnwood, 1993. Collection of individuals' memories of the events and of the decade.

Susan Coleman

See also Canada and Great Britain; Elizabeth II's visit to North America; Foreign policy of Canada; Television in Canada; Television in the United States.

■ Elizabeth II's visit to North America

The Event Goodwill visit to Canada and to the United States by the queen of Great Britain
Date October 12-21, 1957

Elizabeth II's visit helped the young queen reconnect with her Canadian subjects, after last visiting in 1951, and it helped heal the breach in British-United States relations caused by the Suez Crisis of 1956.

When Queen Elizabeth II and her husband and consort, Prince Philip, arrived in the Canadian capital of Ottawa, Ontario, she was greeted by thirty thousand Canadian subjects, a twenty-one-gun salute, and coronation trumpeters. At an evening press reception that day, the queen, in less than one hour, shook

Queen Elizabeth, President Dwight D. Eisenhower, First Lady Mamie Eisenhower, and Prince Philip, the duke of Edinburgh, at a White House banquet in October, 1957. (Hulton Archive | by Getty Images)

hands with about five hundred people. The next morning, the queen and Prince Philip attended church at Christ Church Cathedral, and that afternoon, she nervously prepared for her first television broadcast. Near airtime her look of "congealed terror," as the Canadian producer described it, was relieved by a humorous note from Prince Philip. She gave a successful speech, broadcast throughout Canada and the United States that evening.

During her four days in Canada, Elizabeth II opened the Canadian parliament and visited other sites in Ottawa and the nearby city of Hull, Quebec. On Wednesday, October 16, the queen and prince left for the United States.

United States Visit The first stop of Elizabeth's visit to the United States held great symbolism. Elizabeth and Philip landed at Patrick Henry Airport in Virginia, named for the American leader whose "Give me liberty or give me death" speech helped inspire the American Revolution. The airport was chosen to commemorate the 350th anniversary of the establishment of the Virginia Colony, named for England's Virgin Queen, Elizabeth I. The monarch also visited Jamestown, where Rappahannock Native Americans, whose ancestors met the first Englishmen, welcomed the British party. The visitors spent the night in Colonial Williamsburg and returned to the airport on Thursday for a flight to Washington, D.C.

President Dwight D. Eisenhower, whom Elizabeth had met during World War II, and Mrs. Eisenhower greeted the royal couple at the Washington Air Transport Service Air Base. Following a military parade, the monarch performed an official duty as British Head of State, by giving her approval to the forthcoming visit to the United States by British prime minister Harold Macmillan. The stay in Washington included nights at the White House, laying a wreath at the Tomb of the Unknown Soldier, and other visits. A train ride to New York was interrupted in Baltimore by the Maryland-versus-North Carolina football game, at which the queen asked many questions about this American Saturday afternoon pastime. Arriving in New York City, Elizabeth and Philip stayed at the Waldorf Hotel and saw many of the usual sites in that city. They departed for London from Idlewild Airport on October 21.

Impact Despite being called a "royal soap opera" by British writer Malcolm Muggeridge, the trip was a great success. It signaled a renewed friendship between Great Britain and its former colonies in the wake of the Soviet Union's launch of *Sputnik I*, the first artificial satellite, which occurred only a few days before the visit. The Cold War allies could now face together the threat of the Soviet lead in the space race.

Further Reading

Cathcart, Helen. *Her Majesty the Queen*. New York: Dodd, Mead, 1966. A biography of Elizabeth II that discusses the events surrounding the visit.

"Elizabeth II—America's Salute." *Newsweek* 50, no. 17 (October 21, 1957): 40-45. An analysis and itinerary of the visit.

Pimlott, Ben. *The Queen*. New York: John Wiley & Sons, 1996. A biography of Elizabeth II that puts the 1957 visit in the context of the domestic criticism of the British monarchy as a whole.

Glenn L. Swygart

See also Canada and Great Britain; Eisenhower, Dwight D.; Elizabeth II's coronation; Foreign policy of the United States; Khrushchev's visit to the United States; Space race; *Sputnik I*; Suez Crisis.

■ Emmy Awards

Identification Annual awards granted for outstanding achievement in the television industry

Date First awarded in 1949

The Emmy Awards signaled the growing influence of the new medium of television and became a significant public and television industry event after the ceremony's first national telecast on March 7, 1955.

The Academy of Television Arts and Sciences was founded in Los Angeles in 1946 by Syd Cassyd, an entertainment industry reporter. Like the Academy of Motion Picture Arts and Sciences upon which it was modeled, the fledgling trade association sought to encourage artistic and technological excellence through an annual awards ceremony. In 1948, Charles Brown, the president of the young organization, sought suggestions for a name and symbol for the organization's awards. "Emmy," a derivative of "Immy," a nickname for the then state-of-the-art image orthicon camera tube, was selected; the name was suggested by Harry Lubcke, who served as president of the academy between 1949 and 1950. For its symbol, the academy chose designer Louis Mc-Manus's winged "golden girl," whose outstretched hands hold the model of an atom.

When the debut Emmy ceremony was broadcast locally from the Hollywood Athletic Club on January 25, 1949, only several thousand television sets were tuned in. The first Emmy went to Shirley Dinsdale, a twenty-year-old Los Angeles ventriloquist, for most outstanding television personality. At its onset, the Emmy Awards ceremony was a distinctly local event centered on the nascent television industry then emerging in Los Angeles.

Coastal Rivalries Television, however, was growing up in New York as well as in Los Angeles. Indeed, during the 1950's, New York was the industry's business and production center. Not surprisingly, as the medium rapidly evolved into the nation's most important mass medium, professional jealousies developed between the industry's East and West Coast elites. Seeking to reduce these rivalries, and to recognize the contributions of industry professionals on both coasts, the Los Angeles-based academy produced its first national Emmy telecast on March 7, 1955, "simulcasting" from both New York City and Hollywood.

New York television professionals still were concerned about the ability of a Los Angeles-controlled organization to represent the industry at large. Led by television personality Ed Sullivan, a "Committee of One Hundred" was formed in 1955 to create a National Television Academy; here, "national" was used to signify a New York-dominated television industry. With the backing of influential industry leaders such as Walter Cronkite, Edward R. Murrow, Neil Simon, Mark Goodson, and Carl Reiner, Sullivan established the National Academy of Television Arts and Sciences (NATAS). Sullivan served as the New York City-based NATAS's first president.

Because New York was the industry's financial and production center throughout the 1950's, the National Academy was able to effect a merger with the Hollywood-based academy in 1957. In addition to reaffirming the academy's goal of excellence, the National Academy adopted the Emmy Awards.

Impact The national broadcasts of the Emmy Awards during the 1950's, like the national broadcasts of the film industry's Academy Awards, became glamorous and star-studded television events. While boosting the visibility of the television industry itself, the Emmy Awards were soon recognized for their success-begets-success impact on individual programs and stars. The Emmys were first broadcast in color in 1957, adding even greater luster to the event's already considerable status.

Further Reading
Barnouw, Erik. *The Image Empire: A History of Broadcasting in the United States.* New York: Oxford University Press, 1970.

O'Neil, Thomas, and Peter Bart. *The Emmys: The Ultimate, Unofficial Guide to the Battle of TV's Best Shows and Greatest Stars.* 3d ed. New York: Perigee, 2000. Provides a history of the awards, anecdotes from the shows, and trivia.

Chuck Berg

See also Academy Awards; *Father Knows Best; Lassie;* Linkletter, Art; *Perry Mason;* Serling, Rod; Silvers, Phil; Television in the United States; Thomas, Danny; Young, Loretta.

■ ENIAC computer

Identification First electronic digital computer
Date Introduced in 1946 and retired in 1955

Originally designed as a large multistep calculator to determine projectile paths, the Electronic Numerical Integrator and Computer (ENIAC) was actually the first stored program computer and influenced the design of computers throughout the 1950's.

In 1943, John Mauchly and Presper Eckert submitted the design for the ENIAC to the Ballistic Research Laboratory (BRL) in Aberdeen, Maryland. The design was accepted by the BRL, and assembly of the ENIAC was completed in 1945. While the ENIAC was originally designed to calculate ballistic trajectories, its first major use was in support of the development of the atomic bomb. During its ten years of service, the ENIAC was used to solve many scientific and military problems.

The ENIAC was based on an earlier computing device built by John Atanasoff in 1939. It had thirty separate units, 19,000 vacuum tubes, 1,500 relays, a processing unit, memory, and an internal clock. Each functioning unit was equipped with a local control program and some storage. The ENIAC was one thousand times faster than any of the earlier computing devices.

An ENIAC II mainframe computer. (Hulton Archive l by Getty Images)

Impact The 1950's saw an explosion of computing technology, much of which was a result of the hardware and software of the ENIAC. The designers of the ENIAC took the existing technology and created the first stored program computer. Admiral Grace Hopper helped develop its programming environment by stressing the use of subprogram.

Further Reading

Fritz, W. Barkley. "ENIAC: A Problem Solver." *IEEE Annals of the History of Computing* 16, no. 1 (1994): 25, 45. Contains detailed information about the ENIAC.

Stern, Nancy. *From ENIAC to UNIVAC: An Appraisal of the Mauchly-Eckert Computers.* Bedford, Mass.: Digital Press, 1981. Documents the influence of the ENIAC on computing during the 1950's.

George M. Whitson III

See also Computers; FORTRAN; International Business Machines Corporation; Science and technology; UNIVAC computer.

■ Espionage and Sabotage Act of 1954

Identification U.S. federal domestic security legislation

Date Became law on September 3, 1954

The Espionage and Sabotage Act was a hallmark of the Cold War and was passed in response to the perception that American citizens were providing critical information on American defense to the Soviet Union and its agents.

American politics were transformed during 1954. As the year began, Senator Joseph McCarthy—the decade's most notorious anticommunist figure—was still influential and the United States was uncertain about the direction and intent of the post-Stalinist Soviet Union. In March, 1954, Edward R. Murrow of CBS News denounced McCarthy, and support for the Wisconsin senator soon fell dramatically. During these same months, the French faced defeat in Indochina at Dien Bien Phu (it fell to the Vietnamese on May 7, 1954), and the communists appeared to be making headway in Guatemala and Iran. In the United States, there was fear that some Americans welcomed and supported the advance of communism and that some were involved in treason. The Eisenhower administration responded by addressing the situations in Latin America and the Near East, supporting the division of Indochina, and drafting new legislation that was directed at the internal threat.

Impact The Espionage and Sabotage Act was directed at curtailing the gathering or delivering of information for any foreign government that would impair the defense of the United States. It was focused on espionage and sabotage acts by American citizens who were sympathetic to or employed by the Soviet Union, communist China, and their satellite states. The act specified that the death penalty was authorized in the event of the killing of an American agent or if the information that was transferred concerned nuclear weapons, military spacecraft or satellites, war plans, early warning systems, codes, or any other major component associated with the defense of the United States. If a person were convicted under this law, the United States government had the right to seize the person's property that was used in the process of committing treason and all property that might have been acquired using the profits realized by the crime.

This law served as the basis for subsequent legislation, including the Foreign Intelligence Surveillance Act of 1978.

Further Reading

Damms, Richard V. *The Eisenhower Presidency, 1953-1961.* London: Longman, 2002. An excellent general review of Eisenhower's tenure as president, including relevant sections on the Cold War and McCarthyism and the domestic political environment of the 1950's.

Perret, Geoffrey. *Eisenhower.* New York: Random House, 1999. Using a wide range of primary sources, Perret's study is the best one-volume work to date on Eisenhower and the politics of the 1950's.

Taubman, Philip. *Secret Empire: Eisenhower, the CIA, and the Hidden Story of America's Space Espionage.* New York: Simon and Schuster, 2003. A worthwhile study of the American approach to Soviet espionage and how the United States countered it.

William T. Walker

See also Brinkmanship; Central Intelligence Agency; Cold War; Eisenhower, Dwight D.; Elections in the United States, midterm; Federal Bureau of Investigation; Hoover, J. Edgar; Internal Security Act of 1950; Loyalty oaths; McCarthy, Joseph; Rosenberg, Julius and Ethel.

■ *Explorer I*

Identification First American Earth-orbiting satellite

Date Launched on January 31, 1958

Explorer I, *the first American satellite to reach orbit, was launched only four months after the Soviet Union's* Sputnik I *and increased the stakes in the Cold War space race.*

The success of *Explorer I* came soon after the humiliating explosion of America's *Vanguard I* only seconds after its launch from Cape Canaveral in late 1957. With *Explorer I*, the embarrassment of *Vanguard* quickly diminished. The origin of the Cold War competition to orbit an artificial satellite can be traced to earlier attempts to develop rockets as military weapons. As World War II drew to a close, members of the scientific and engineering team that developed German V-1 and V-2 rockets sought the protection of either Allied or Soviet forces. Among those emigrating to the West was Wernher von

Braun. Von Braun and his colleagues began developing and testing missile systems for the U.S. Army. Captured V-2's test-fired in the New Mexico desert ultimately led to development of advanced rockets.

Amid Cold War tensions, the superpowers and their aligned countries agreed to mount a scientific program to better understand the earth. During the 1957-1958 International Geophysical Year (IGY), both superpowers declared intentions to launch an artificial satellite. The American effort was not well organized and did not enjoy strong White House support. President Dwight D. Eisenhower insisted that rather than using von Braun's Redstone rocket, the American satellite effort must use the new civilian Vanguard booster.

The Soviet program enjoyed tremendous support from the Soviet government, and even though Soviet intentions had been declared openly, when *Sputnik I* entered orbit on October 4, 1957, the West reacted with astonishment and fear. *Vanguard I* rushed to match that achievement but blew up on the pad before the eyes of the world. Restrictions on von Braun's team were lifted, and they quickly produced a Jupiter C booster and a primitive satellite. *Explorer I* launched in the evening of January 31, 1958; it performed flawlessly, and the satellite separated from it.

Two hours after liftoff, success was confirmed. The spacecraft's science package transmitted data, and ground stations could pick up that telemetry. Not long thereafter, President Eisenhower spoke to the nation on radio, stressing American participation in the peaceful exploration of space. "The United States has successfully placed a scientific satellite in orbit around the earth. This is part of our participation in the International Geophysical Year."

Impact *Explorer I* marked the successful American entry into the Space Race. Following *Vanguard, Explorer I* restored confidence that American technology could compete with Soviet efforts in orbit. Whereas *Sputnik I* merely housed a radio transmitter, *Explorer I* contained scientific instruments: two micrometeoroid detectors and a Geiger counter. *Explorer I* data quickly led to discovery of Earth's radiation belts. This first American satellite circled the globe 58,000 times before reentering the atmosphere over the Pacific in 1970. American space efforts became centralized within the National Aeronautics and Space Administration (NASA). President Eisen-

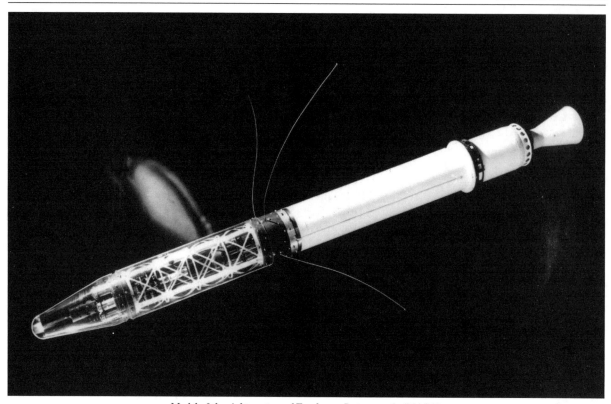

Model of the eighteen-pound Explorer I *spacecraft.* (NASA)

hower reacted slowly to the coming challenge of space, but, after *Sputnik* and *Explorer I,* he committed NASA to the manned orbital Mercury program. Meanwhile, NASA surpassed the success of *Explorer I* with subsequent unmanned efforts that led to extended Earth studies, development of communications and weather satellites, and space-based observatories.

Further Reading

Burrows, William E. *The Infinite Journey: Eyewitness Accounts of NASA and the Age of Space.* New York: Discovery Books, 2000. A coffee-table book detailing space program history.

Divine, Robert A. *The Sputnik Challenge: Eisenhower's Response to the Soviet Satellite.* Oxford: Oxford University Press, 1993. An academic treatise on the politics of the competition to launch early satellites.

Von Braun, Wernher, and Frederick I. Ordway III. *History of Rocketry and Space Travel.* Rev. ed. New York: Thomas Y. Crowell Company, 1969. Details the life of von Braun and of space flight history.

David G. Fisher

See also Astronomy; Mercury space program; National Aeronautics and Space Administration; Science and technology; Space race; *Sputnik I;* Television in the United States; Van Allen radiation belts.

F

■ Fads

Definition Fashions, entertainments, and products that experienced exceptional but brief popularity

The new affluence of the 1950's, coupled with the impact of advertising on television, created a culture ripe for fads.

The 1950's followed the Great Depression and World War II. North Americans were interested in restoring family life and, with the hard times behind them, they were ready for lighthearted amusement. The 1950's was also a time of economic affluence and consumer spending. Home ownership was widespread, unemployment was low, and new technologies and production methods spawned a consumer products revolution. Americans were able to spend both time and money on the latest fashions and entertainment, spurred by the growing impact of television advertising. The decade thus provided an atmosphere conducive to the development of fads. People were willing to spend their disposable income to obtain the latest styles, toys, or trends.

Fashion Fashionable teenage girls wore poodle skirts, which were full skirts with appliqués of poodles—fads in their own right as collectible figurines and adorning countless household items—flowers, or other images. This look was completed by blouses with Peter Pan collars, saddle shoes, bobby sox, ponytails with scarves tied around them, and letter sweaters, worn by girls to call attention to their boyfriends' athleticism. Many girls would also wear a boy's pin or his ring on a chain around her neck to show that they were dating exclusively, or "going steady." These fashion fads died out as the teenage styles matured into more sophisticated looks.

Many young men sported the rebel image popularized by such 1950's stars as singer Elvis Presley and actor James Dean. This look was characterized by leather jackets, jeans, plain white T-shirts—often with cigarette packs rolled into the sleeves—and shoes with taps fastened to the bottom. Sideburns

and a D.A. (duck's ass), or ducktail, hairstyle completed the look. Boys achieved the D.A. look by combing the hair back on the sides of the head and holding it in place with a styling product such as Brylcream, giving its wearers the name "greasers." This look was unpopular among adults, who often associated it with juvenile delinquency.

Adults of the decade were not immune to fashion fads either. The color pink—present in homes, accessories, cosmetics, and cars—was an important fad, even in menswear. The use of bright color on ties and shirts helped offset the drab, neutral colors most popular in the decade's menswear, such as the ubiquitous gray flannel suit. Bermuda shorts became a popular fad during the mid-1950's both at home and at work. Originally worn by British military officers, the style was imported by tourists from Bermuda to the United States. Other popular clothing styles included pedal-pusher (or capri) pants, bowling shirts, and cat's-eye glasses. Popular women's hairstyles of the 1950's included the poodle haircut—a cropped, curly style—with Lucille Ball as its most famous model.

Toys and Collectibles The Wham-O Company, founded by Richard Knerr and Arthur Melin, produced many of the best-selling toys of the decade. Boomerangs, originally wooden hunting tools used by Australian Aborigines, were first sold at the 1956 Summer Olympic Games in Melbourne, Australia. Wham-O hired American atomic weapons researcher Lorin Hawkes to design boomerangs for it during the late 1950's, and the contraptions quickly became a popular toy. The rumored crash of a flying saucer in Roswell, New Mexico, during the late 1940's and the subsequent UFO craze of the 1950's helped market another popular Wham-O toy, the Frisbee. The Frisbee quickly became known as a "flying saucer." Bamboo hoops that Australian children twirled around their waists during gym classes were the inspiration for the hula hoop. The company reproduced these hoops in a new, lightweight, durable plastic and named them after the Hawaiian dance that the twirling motion imitated. The company quickly sold millions of hula hoops, making them one of the most successful fads of all time.

Other researchers and companies profited from fad toys during the decade. Silly Putty, a derivative of silicone that bounced when rolled up and thrown, was originally developed by scientists but rejected as not useful. Advertising copywriter Peter Hodgson saw its potential as a novelty item, obtained legal rights to the name, and began selling it packaged in plastic eggs. A magazine article spread the craze, and its popularity increased further when it was discovered that the putty would duplicate newspaper copy when pressed against it. Richard James created a fad when he coiled an eighty-seven-foot piece of wire and marketed it as the Slinky. The popular toy performed numerous tricks, such as "walking" down stairs by turning end over end, and sold millions of units.

One of the decade's biggest fads was also a popular cultural milestone, serving as one of the first successful instances of advertising merchandise on a television show. Children first saw coonskin caps on a series of Davy Crockett features shown on the *Disneyland* television show during the mid-1950's. Actor Fess Parker achieved fame in the starring role of Davy Crockett and children around the country wanted coonskin caps like the one he wore in the show. Disney sold close to one hundred million dollars' worth of the caps in a single year. The Davy Crockett merchandising craze also included cap guns, watches, books, moccasins, lunch boxes, board games, and many other products. Although the appeal of the Crockett items dropped off almost as quickly as it had sprung up, it gave rise to themed merchandise, based on popular movie, television, or book characters.

Southeast Missouri State College students participating in one of the odder fads of the era: stuffing bodies into a telephone booth. This effort in 1959 set a record of thirty-five people. (AP/Wide World Photos)

Leisure Activities Paint-by-numbers kits attracted numerous followers and sold millions during the 1950's and early 1960's. Customers would purchase a drawing in which numbers corresponded to the colors of paint that came with the drawing. The painter simply would paint the appropriate colors into the areas with the corresponding numbers in order to complete the work. Some people saw these kits as a symbol of the era's emphasis on conformity, while others felt that the kits served as guides that allowed people to develop their own artistic talents.

Both 3-D films and drive-in movie theaters enjoyed popularity as 1950's fad entertainments. The technology that made 3-D films possible had existed since the 1920's; however, it did not become popular until the 1950's, when the motion picture industry recognized its potential as a hook to keep people interested in films as the television medium challenged the status of the film industry. The decade's first 3-D movie, *Bwana Devil*, premiered in 1952. A new Polaroid system called Natural Vision created a better 3-D picture, and moviegoers received special 3-D glasses. There were still problems with blurry pictures, and some viewers complained of headaches. As regular versions of popular films outsold their 3-D versions, the technique became reserved for low-budget films.

The rising number of automobiles and the creation of the interstate highway system meant that automobiles had an important influence on the decade's fad entertainments. Drive-in movies often featured fan-shaped, tiered parking lots, large movie screens, and individual speakers for each car. Some drive-ins also offered car washes, shuffleboard games, miniature golf, and other activities. Another popular automobile-based entertainment of the decade was eating at drive-in restaurants, which featured roller-skating carhops who took orders and delivered meals on trays to people through their car windows. The decade's large, luxurious cars even sported fad styles of their own, such as wrap-around windshields, tail fins, and the use of chrome trim.

Popular fad activities on 1950's college campuses included telephone booth stuffing and panty raids. Telephone booth stuffing, also called telephone box squash, spread from South Africa to England to California and the rest of the United States. Young people competed to see who could stuff the most people inside a telephone booth; the booth had to contain a phone and remain upright, the door could remain open, and at least half of a person had to be inside the booth to count. The popular Volkswagen Beetle was another site of such competitions. During panty raids, male students raided women's dormitories, stole lingerie, and paraded the stolen items in front of the dormitory. Sometimes women would raid male dormitories in revenge.

Dances that reached a height of popularity during the 1950's include the jitterbug, the stroll, the lindy, the jive, the limbo, and the mashed potato. The hit ABC television show *American Bandstand* popularized many of these dances. The limbo was a sacred West Indies funeral ritual that tourists brought to the United States during the mid-1950's,

where it spread from teenage gatherings to adult dinner parties. One of the limbo's most famous artists was Trinidad-born dancer Boscoe Holder. The limbo reached its height of popularity when it was featured in the 1960 movie *Where the Boys Are.*

Cold War Influence A number of 1950's fads were directly linked to the United States' involvement in the Cold War and its accompanying threat of nuclear war. Many people added either hand-built or catalog-ordered bombproof fallout shelters to their homes. Most shelters were small, with room for basic necessities such as a two-week supply of food and water. Other shelters were larger and more luxuriously equipped. This fad provided a source of comfort to many people, and its brief popularity is demonstrated by the fact that many real estate advertisements from this decade list such shelters as a selling point. Cold War plots of communist espionage frequently appeared in films, television shows, and pulp fiction novels, such as Mickey Spillane's popular Mike Hammer private detective series. While Cold War plots would remain a popular cultural staple for the next several decades, the construction of fallout shelters proved to be temporary.

Impact The 1950's produced a wide number and variety of fads because of the stable nature of society after the disruptions of the Great Depression and World War II. People were looking for amusements and had the disposable income to follow their pursuit, giving rise to the decade's consumer culture. At the same time, automobiles and highways provided mobile forms of entertainment, while the rise of television and advertising provided markets for fad styles and products. Even the era's Cold War tensions gave rise to fads. Fads themselves had a lasting impact on the link between entertainment and advertising and have influenced future generations' views of the 1950's and the decade's portrayal in popular culture. Some 1950's fashions, toys, and collectibles remained on the market long after their brief popularity, while others resurfaced decades later to become fads once again or even valuable antiques prized by collectors.

Further Reading

Drake, Albert. *Fifties Flashback: A Nostalgia Trip.* St. Paul, Minn.: Motorbooks International, 2003. Examines a wide variety of the decade's popular culture and fads, including television shows, automobiles, and comic books. It also includes numerous photographs.

Epstein, Dan. *The Fifties (Twentieth Century Popular Culture)*. New York: Chelsea House, 2000. This book for young adults provides an overview of the films, songs, celebrities, and fads popular in this decade.

Kallen, Stuart A., ed. *The 1950's*. San Diego, Calif.: Greenhaven Press, 2000. This book provides an excellent overview of the 1950's culture.

Long, Mark A. *Bad Fads*. Toronto: ECW Press, 2002. Examines the short-lived popular trends of the twentieth century in the categories of games, gags, dances, and styles.

Marling, Karal Ann. *As Seen on TV: The Visual Culture of Everyday Life in the 1950's*. Cambridge, Mass.: Harvard University Press, 1996. Provides a social commentary on the early days of television and its influence on the decade's popular culture.

Marcella Bush Trevino

See also Affluence and the new consumerism; Bomb shelters; *Davy Crockett*; Drive-in theaters; Fashions and clothing; Flying saucers; Hairstyles; Hula hoops; Paint-by-numbers movement; Scrabble; Silly Putty; 3-D movies.

■ *Fahrenheit 451*

Identification Dystopian novel envisioning a world in which firemen burn books, rather than save them from fires

Author Ray Bradbury (1920-   )

Date Published in 1953

In Fahrenheit 451, *Ray Bradbury used the increasingly popular futuristic science-fiction format to capture post-World War II concerns about the threats to individuality, freedom, and humanism posed by totalitarian government, censorship, technology, and humankind's failures of imagination and will.*

Scene from the 1966 film adaptation of Fahrenheit 451, *showing firemen gathering books to burn.* (Museum of Modern Art, Film Stills Archive)

Much of *Fahrenheit 451* is grim, but it is also a novel of awakening and possible recovery. The central character, Guy Montag, is a fireman whose job is to burn books, which have been outlawed because they are believed to cause confusion and unhappiness, to offend some groups, and to be fundamentally out of tune with an image-based society. However, Montag has an irrepressible curiosity for what he is called on to destroy and a growing despair of the casualties of the modern lifestyle, represented by his wife, Mildred.

Montag has some key allies. Montag's passion, memory, and inquisitiveness are rekindled by Clarisse, his neighbor who is eventually run over by reckless teenagers. Faber, an otherwise reclusive and ineffectual former college professor, revives Montag when he is on the run and offers him tangible as well as strategic assistance. Most important, the group that Montag joins at the end of the novel symbolizes Bradbury's central idea that books are people (each person, including Montag, has memorized a key text) but also, more subtly, people are books, at least insofar as humans are significantly shaped by their experience with books. Even as the city is blown up at the end of the novel, a remnant of culture and humanity lives on in the book-people, ready to be reborn, phoenix-like, from the ashes.

Impact Photographs and reports of book burnings in Nazi Germany and the Soviet Union haunted Bradbury as he wrote *Fahrenheit 451*. However, he was equally concerned with worrisome developments within contemporary America, especially the repressive activities of Senator Joseph McCarthy and others like him who used censorship, blacklisting, and intimidation as blunt instruments in their campaign against what they felt was creeping communism, subversive nonconformity, and anti-Americanism.

Further Reading

De Koster, Kate, ed. *Readings on "Fahrenheit 451."* San Diego, Calif.: Greenhaven Press, 2000. Wide-ranging collection of critical articles on Bradbury's style, *Fahrenheit 451* as a dystopian work, and its connection to contemporary social and political realities.

Mogen, David. *Ray Bradbury.* Boston: G. K. Hall, 1986. Reliable and informative overview of Bradbury's life, works, and critical reception, with a solid chapter on *Fahrenheit 451*, which emphasizes its critique of mass culture.

Reid, Robin Anne. *Ray Bradbury: A Critical Companion.* Westport, Conn.: Greenwood Press, 2000. Accessible survey of Bradbury's works, featuring summaries and applications of various critical approaches.

Sidney Gottlieb

See also Censorship; Conformity, culture of; Film in the United States; Literature in the United States; McCarthy, Joseph; Pulp magazines; Television in the United States.

■ Famous Artists School

Identification Correspondence school offering courses in fine and commercial art
Date Founded in 1948
Place Westport, Connecticut

The Famous Artists School, guided by a faculty of outstanding American artists, became one of the world's largest correspondence schools and began successfully training thousands of artists during this era.

Founded by twelve well-known artists, the Famous Artists School was approved for college credit. The entrance exam was simple: duplicate a sketch in the magazine advertisement and submit it for evaluation. Acceptance depended not on education, age, gender, race, or social status but on basic aptitude.

A self-taught artist and illustrator for *Life* magazine, Albert Dorne co-founded and directed the program, which provided students individual attention from artist-mentors in the form of written discussions along with specific critiques of student artwork. Another founder was Norman Rockwell, the prominent illustrator for *Saturday Evening Post*.

After a childhood of poverty and illness, Dorne quit school in seventh grade to follow the dream of being an artist, which he had held since the age of five. As director of the school, he was proof to students of their own potential for success. Never formally trained in the arts, he developed his innate talent into a successful career as the most sought-after illustrator for several national magazines. Truly a self-made man, Dorne received the Horatio Alger Award from the American Schools and Colleges Association in 1963.

Impact At a time when college education was becoming important for employment, the Famous Artists School offered affordable, entry-level training in one's own home. Furthermore, the school stressed that success depended on motivation and self-discipline supported by guidance from dedicated instructors.

Further Reading

Bogart, Michele. *Artists, Advertising, and the Borders of Art*. Chicago: University of Chicago Press, 1995. Examines the history of commercial art, with some discussion of the Famous Artists School.

Heiman, John. *All-American Ads: The Fifties*. Los Angeles: Taschen America, 2001. Showcases a collection of print advertisements from the decade, which provide good context for the rise of the commercial art form that the Famous Artists School encouraged.

Gale M. Thompson

See also Art movements; Disneyland; *Life*; *Look*; McLuhan, Marshall; Paint-by-numbers movement; *Saturday Evening Post*.

■ Farm subsidies

Definition Government-sponsored price supports for agricultural commodities and direct financial assistance to stabilize farm income

During the 1950's, U.S. government subsidies reduced the price volatility of farm products, shielded farmers from low commodity prices, protected farmers from crop loss disasters, encouraged the production of specific commodities, and produced agricultural surplus for export.

Large-scale federal intervention in agricultural markets began as temporary New Deal programs during the 1930's in response to the national economic Depression and drought in America's western states. Federal programs were gradually expanded to include risk reduction guarantees and direct payments to farmers for market transition costs, market losses, disaster relief, export assistance, loan deficiencies, conservation activities, water quality and environmental cost sharing, crop insurance, and more.

The main program provided deficiency payments to farmers based on the difference between legislated target prices for commodities and the national average market prices. However, price supports eventually created overproduction in more than one hundred supported commodities, primarily in corn, wheat, cotton, rice, sorghum, oats, and barley. The government paid farmers for their base

acreage in each particular crop so farmers were encouraged to continue raising the same crop and to expand the acres in production, even when market prices were declining. Continued planting and improvements in crop yields further reduced market prices and increased price support payments to farmers and costs to the taxpayers. Finally, to stem overproduction, the government enacted a flexible price support program in 1954 and began paying farmers to set aside land in acreage reduction programs, including the Soil Bank Act, begun in 1956.

Use of Surplus Commodities Surplus commodities were exported initially to support European and Asian postwar reconstruction, but global recovery rapidly reduced exports during the 1950's. Price support levels were reduced to discourage production. Economies of scale, hybrid seeds, improved farming methods, and consolidation of agricultural land into fewer but larger farms kept production and surpluses high. Through programs such as the 1954 Food for Peace Act, surplus commodities were provided free or at subsidized prices to nations that supported the United States in the Cold War or experienced famine or civil strife, and to nations the United States sought to lure from alliances with the Soviet Union, a country which had little surplus of its own to export. These surplus exports sometimes created chaos in the agricultural markets of the importing nations and hindered the development of the agricultural sector in many developing countries. Direct donations to needy American groups and expansion of the Food Stamp and Child Nutrition programs sought to reduce government stocks and to encourage market demand for agricultural products.

The federal government also provided farmers with short-term financing to pay farm expenses from the time crops were planted until they were sold. These were nonrecourse loans so farmers could default in times of economic hardship. When market prices were high, farmers sold the crop and repaid the loan. When market prices were low, farmers forfeited or sold the crop to government stockpiles at the support prices and then often defaulted on the loan.

Impact Subsidies helped many farmers remain in agriculture during the 1950's, provided food surpluses for Americans, and provided commodities for export. Ironically, the reduced financial risks of farming led to higher land values during the 1950's, gradually driving many small farmers and younger farmers out of agriculture.

Further Reading

Luttrell, Clifton B. *The High Costs of Farm Welfare.* Washington, D.C.: Cato Institute, 1989. Critique of the history of farm subsidies.

Orden, David, Robert Paarlberg, and Terry Roe. *Policy Reform in American Agriculture: Analysis and Prognosis.* Chicago: University of Chicago Press, 1999. Discussion of the origins and future direction of agricultural policy.

Gordon Neal Diem

See also Agriculture in Canada; Agriculture in the United States; Bracero program; Food for Peace; Soil Bank Act of 1956.

■ Fashions and clothing

Clothing from the 1950's showed a return to femininity for women and a sophisticated conservatism for men, and served as a mode of self-expression for teenagers.

Clothes during the 1950's were simpler and more convenient as a result of slimmer lines and synthetic fabrics. Christian Dior's "New Look," established in 1947, signaled a return to femininity in women's dress, a trend that carried over to the 1950's. Dresses of this style used many yards of fabric in the skirt and showcased tight waistlines. Women's clothing in general became more feminine by emphasizing the bust, waist, and hips in suits and sportswear.

Elegance also described women's dress during this period. Women used traditional corsets made of bone and pads, as well as multilayer petticoats, long-line bras, panty girdles, and other waist-cinching devices to sculpt their figures into the decade's desired hourglass shape. The days of war and manual toil were behind women; they could return to their feminine roles as housewives and mothers.

Fabrics during this time tended to be stiff rather than soft and draping. Buttons were fabric covered or made from natural materials such as bone or mother-of-pearl. Popular colors were often neutral-toned (white, beige, or gray), navy-blue, bold toned, or jewel toned (ruby, sapphire, and emerald). Color combinations not normally seen—such as red, pink, and orange—were also used by designers and manufacturers. Plaids became a popular fabric choice of the decade.

Influential Factors After working in factories, restaurants, and hospitals during World War II, women returned to homemaking and child rearing in the postwar years. Families grew and moved from urban areas to the suburbs. Activities that the family could do together, such as traveling and outdoor recreation, increased, and a more casual style of clothing was emphasized.

Television and films were important influences on fashion. By 1950, many American families had a television set in their own home. Television showed what celebrities were wearing and helped to disseminate fashion information more quickly than newspapers and magazines and to wider audiences. Film stars such as Marilyn Monroe, Jayne Mansfield, and Brigitte Bardot popularized the hyper-feminine "sex goddess" appearance; Audrey Hepburn sported a gamine look that promoted a simple elegance; and Grace Kelly became the epitome of sophisticated glamour. These stars and countless others were celebrated by haute couture and emulated by everyday Americans.

Teenagers and youth culture played an important role in setting fashion trends during the 1950's. The teen market was quickly growing, and designers began to cater to the young people. Designer Mary Quant opened her shop in London and designed innovative yet inexpensive garments for young men and women. In the United States, teenagers had become wage-earners during the war and continued to work for wages during the 1950's. Their rising incomes helped them become a mass market for designers and manufacturers of fashions and fads. Blue jeans, once the uniform of miners and farmers that had become popular during the late 1940's with high school and college students, increased in popularity during the 1950's, largely due to their presence in films—Elvis Presley and James Dean were two influential film stars who wore blue jeans—and television shows.

Many new fibers and fabrics were introduced to the market during the 1950's. Prior to this decade, most clothing was made from the four major natural fibers—cotton, silk, wool, and flax—and from the regenerated cellulosic fibers, rayon and acetate. However, nylon, which had been limited during World War II, was again available for clothing items. Other major fibers that appeared during the time included acrylic, polyester, and spandex. These new synthetic fibers introduced consumers to easy-care clothing that could be categorized as "wash and wear" and "drip dry."

Clothing manufacturing systems and processes also affected the fashion industry. New and improved technology, which included new machinery, automation, computers, and advanced techniques in pattern making, sped the process of making clothes and brought new designs to the market faster. Manufacturing plants could use automatic needle positioning and thread trimming, laser beams were being used to cut cloth, and computers were being used for pattern making and grading.

Dresses and Skirts Dresses and skirts that emphasized a silhouette look were popular during the era. The use of a long, very tight skirt fitted with the ideal figure of the time, tall and slim but with womanly curves.

Dresses of the decade generally had sleeves that were straight and narrow to go along with the silhouette look; puffed sleeves and a more glamorous approach were reserved for evening wear. Sleeveless dresses were seen in the summer. However, Dior's New Look also influenced the appearance of bell-shaped, fuller skirts.

The first major silhouette dress of the 1950's was created by Cristobal Balenciaga in 1953. It was a chemise dress, reminiscent of the adolescent "boy look" of the 1920's, later to be known as the sack dress. It was a simple, straight dress with a slightly bloused bodice over a dropped waistline. It had straight sleeves and a shorter skirt than the dresses from the first years of the decade. The chemise dress became ubiquitous during the decade. Balenciaga is perhaps best remembered for his flamenco evening dress, which was cut short in front and long in the back. Balenciaga's designs often featured jackets and dresses that were fitted in front and bloused away from the body in the back.

Dior introduced the A-line silhouette in 1955. Upon Dior's untimely death in 1957, his assistant, Yves St. Laurent, continued the A-line for the House of Dior and introduced the revolutionary trapeze dress in 1958. The trapeze was a tentlike dress with narrow shoulders, no waist, and a triangular shape, and it broke away from the conformity of postwar fashion. Other popular designers of the period were Molly Parnis, who popularized the shirtwaist dress, which buttoned down the front like a man's tailored shirt; and Larry Aldrich, who created formal gowns with slit skirts and an often asymmetrical projection. Aldrich's dresses emphasized the bust and hips and were usually decorated with large buttons.

During the first years of the 1950's, suits were very popular and consisted of a peplum jacket worn with a full gored skirt. Toward the middle of the decade, women began wearing a slimmer suit. Jackets with three-quarter length sleeves were shorter and worn with slim skirts. Famed 1920's and 1930's designer Coco Chanel returned to the fashion scene with her tailored suits. These suits had a jacket with no collar and no lapels and were often trimmed with decorative braids. Both the jacket and the skirt were lined, but the jacket usually had a lining made of printed silk fabric.

During the 1950's, formal gowns were very complex designs made of heavy, draped fabrics, often with asymmetrical details. The ballerina-length (above-the-ankle) dresses with nipped waists and various sleeve styles and details became popular. Both ballerina-length and full-length gowns were worn throughout the decade, and during the late 1950's, women began to wear high-waisted designs for evening. Formal gowns were often trimmed with large bows, large collars, or side streamers that fell to a floor-length hem. The "little black dress," first seen in the 1920's, experienced a resurgence and became a classic for evening wear and formal occasions.

Swimsuits and Casual Wear Swimwear for women was generally made of cotton and resembled short-skirted dresses. Bikinis were also popular and consisted of two-piece suits with a modest top and short trunks worn low on the hips. The name "bikini" came from a small island in the Pacific where the atom bomb was tested; the name was adopted for the skimpier version of the two-piece swimsuit because it was said to be "smaller than an atom." Women in the United States were slower than their European counterparts to adopt the bikini and often continued to wear the more modest swimsuits.

Beauty pageants were prominent in the 1950's and helped make swimwear part of the fashion industry. In 1952, Catalina Swimwear withdrew its support of the Miss America pageant when the year's winner refused to wear a bathing suit at a Milwaukee department store during the middle of winter. Catalina Swimwear then began both the Miss USA and Miss Universe pageants in order to rival the Miss

America contest. By 1959, all states in the country were represented in these types of beauty pageants.

Despite the formality and glamour of the decade, casual wear found its place among fashion-conscious consumers. "Pedal pushers" were tight, calf-length pants and were common among women of all ages during the 1950's. Culottes, which gave the appearance of a flared skirt but were actually short, full trousers, were equally popular and generally worn with a pullover blouse and jacket. Italian designer Emilio Pucci introduced Capri pants, which were longer and fuller than pedal pushers. The "dress-up sweater" was a novelty item created by the designer Mainbocher. It was a jacketlike sweater with a chiffon lining and heavily ornamented with sparkling beads and ribbons.

Casual sweaters were worn either tucked in, over skirts, or belted. Women often wore blouses with either small or large collars or those with a Mandarin-style, stand-up collar. Halter tops were also popular and were worn with a short, open-front bolero jacket. Bermuda shorts, thigh-length shorts that were tight in the legs, appeared during the middle of the decade and replaced the "short shorts" of the earlier years. In addition, dirndle skirts, simple slim skirts, tapered pants, and twin sweater sets were all popular casual garments for women during the 1950's.

Outerwear Coats for formal occasions were typically velvet or silk. Coats and suits for women were very tailored and most of the time had fabric-bound button holes. The predominant outer coat was a tent-shaped coat that flared from the shoulders. Other popular coats were the belted reefer and the princess coat. Reversible coats, with a wool side and a chemically treated (water repellant) gabardine side, made for versatile outerwear. Other wraps ranged from mink shoulder capes to coats with various collars.

The coats' hems rose with the dress hems of the decade. Clutch capes, which had no closures, were also popular. While mink commonly had been used for coats for many years, sable, fox, and leopard also gained popularity during this era. The use of fake furs was on the rise, however. Cloth coats often sported dyed mink collars, and, targeting college girls, designers and manufacturers produced short jackets, as well as full-length coats in moleskin and beaver.

Accessories, Hairstyles, and Cosmetics Hats for daytime during the early 1950's often were made of ve-

Model wearing a cape made of Canadian pearl platinum mink at a fashion industry fair in London in 1954. (Hulton Archive | by Getty Images)

lour and trimmed with feathers, flowers, or veils. Brims might be asymmetric, tilted, or pleated. Hats were generally small to coincide with the prominence of short hairstyles as the decade progressed. Also seen during this time were berets and tiny pillbox hats. Hairpieces began to appear during the late 1950's.

The fashionable woman wore gloves for day and evening wear, and wide elastic belts were worn with full skirts. Button-type earrings as well as hoops and drop earrings were worn throughout the 1950's. Choker necklaces were worn close to the neck, and bracelets were also popular. Chanel's return to the fashion world showcased costume jewelry made mainly of fake pearls and colored stones.

Handbags were tailored during this period and the less expensive cost of plastic and metal made them popular choices for handbag materials. Envelope and other styles of clutch purses, called "pouchettes," were commonly carried. One "rule" of being fashionably dressed was to use a matching handbag-shoes combination in both color and texture. Leather was still a leading choice for handbags and was available in antelope, ostrich, gazelle, and pigskin. Reptile-skin handbags were considered valuable investments; crocodile handbags were generally the most expensive. Most fine handbags were lined. Handles of bags also were becoming interesting. Bamboo, plastic, tortoiseshell, metal, and suede were all common materials for decorative handles. During the late 1950's, women began wanting fur handbags, so designers created flat bags and oval-shaped purses in cheetah, moleskin, and opossum. Moreover, toward the end of the decade, straw or woven basket bags decorated with fruit or flowers were being seen.

Scarves were another common accessory during the 1950's. Scarves could be found in squares or longer rectangles and were worn around the neck or head. Women complemented their outfits with scarves in solids and patterns.

Shoes with high, narrow heels and pointed toes were common at the beginning of the decade, as were "strappy" sandals. During the mid-1950's, penny loafers, ballet slippers, and thong sandals appeared. By the end of the decade, boots were being worn. Hosiery was made of very sheer nylon and was most often flesh colored, but black stockings were worn often during the early years of the decade.

The most common hairstyle during the early 1950's was the bouffant, which was a slightly wavy short cut that appeared voluminous. Mamie Eisenhower was considered a trendsetter when she became the First Lady of the United States. She was especially remembered for her signature hairstyle, which was a short cut with narrow bangs covering her forehead. Mrs. Eisenhower also wore charm bracelets and popularized her favorite color, pink.

Women cared a great deal about cosmetics and skincare. Most women used lipstick, which was usually bright red, but other cosmetics were also popular. Colored eye shadows and mascara were worn, and nail polish in shades of red or pink was common. The weekly visit to the beauty salon was also a tradition of the decade.

Menswear The 1950's was referred to as "the gray and black period" for menswear. Suits were conservative, and gray flannel was the most popular color and fabrication. Jackets were single-breasted with natural shoulders, had narrow lapels, and were worn with narrow cuffed trousers, often with zippers in the inner-leg seams so a man's foot could get through the trouser leg at the cuff. Suit jackets had a slight indentation at the waistline, and pants did not have pleats. This look was known as the "Ivy League suit" and was popular at the beginning of the decade.

Toward the middle of the 1950's, the "continental look," which was reminiscent of the Edwardian look, popularized a two-button coat that was a little shorter than the Ivy League look and had a more rounded cut-away front. The continental-look suit jackets were shorter and more fitted with peaked lapels. Breast pockets and lapel buttonholes returned with this style as did the matching vest.

Sport jackets and slacks started to replace the matching suit. Men's sportcoats might have two, three, or four buttons, and were made in fabrics ranging from solid gabardines, corduroy flannels, and cashmere to tweeds, checks, and plaids.

New fabrics for men included glen plaids, herringbone tweeds, and seersucker, and new colors included blues, golds, olives, and plums. Synthetic fibers were also making their way into the clothing market, usually blended with cotton, wool, linen, and silk.

Formal Wear Early in the decade, formal wear became less traditional, a trend reflected in President Dwight D. Eisenhower's refusal to wear a formal tuxedo coat and top hat for his 1953 inauguration, when he opted instead for a short suit jacket and striped trousers. For evening wear, men's jackets might be single- or double-breasted and might have a shawl collar or peaked lapels. Black or midnight-blue were the predominant colors for dinner jackets. Colors were also changing from the traditional black to reds, plaids, and pastels; white dinner jackets with black trousers were often seen during the summer. Sometimes men wore fancy shirts with ruffles, pleats, and tucks for formal occasions.

Shirts, Sportswear, and Outerwear White dress shirts with smaller rounded or pointed collars were made from a variety of fabrics and styled with button-down collars, short or long sleeves, and plain or French cuffs. Sport shirts, very similar to later decades' polo shirts or golf shirts, were made of knit material and worn for less formal occasions. Pink dress shirts began to join white ones in the latter part of the decade.

Bermuda shorts were also popular for men. Casual slacks, including khaki pants, were worn with button-down shirts or crew neck sweaters. Sweater vests became popular, and in the latter part of the decade, men's trousers had self-belts or were worn without belts. Furthermore, during this time, men—especially those in high school and college—began wearing solid white T-shirts without another shirt over them. These T-shirts were commonly worn with blue jeans or shorts.

The basic overcoat for men during the 1950's had raglan sleeves, a button-front, and slash pockets, and it was constructed from hound's-tooth fabric. Full-length Chesterfield coats, with their characteristic velvet collars, remained popular. Overcoats sometimes had linings that zipped out. Black leather jackets were popular for young men in high school and college, and the Eisenhower jacket (also called the "bomber" or "battle" jacket) was worn. This jacket was a waist-length jacket with several pockets and epaulets on the shoulders. During the late 1950's, wraparound coats that were belted were being worn.

Accessories Neckties were slender and had smaller knots during the 1950's. Some men wore tie pins, but these pins, as well as cuff links and wristwatches, were about the only jewelry worn by men during this time. Hats during the decade included small-brimmed straw hats, felt fedoras, and various caps such as the Russian-style fur cap, the leather-billed cap, and the ear-flap billed cap.

Most men's footwear had pointed toes and ranged from loafers to calf-high boots. Loafers commonly had tassels and could be made from calf leather, suede, or reptile skin. College students preferred white buck oxfords with red rubber soles.

Most men during the 1950's wore their hair short in crew cuts, but an alternative was longer hair greased back into a ducktail to emulate rock-and-roll star Elvis Presley. Facial hair was rare.

Impact Fashion and clothing of the 1950's introduced the world to new designers, couture fashion, new fibers and fabrics, and items of dress that later became fashion classics, including blue jeans, khaki pants, and navy-blue sport coats and blazers. The era's fashion signaled that the hardships of war were behind America and ushered in a formal, almost decadent era of glamour and beauty.

Further Reading

Arnold, R. *Fashion, Desire, and Anxiety: Image and Morality in the Twentieth Century.* New Brunswick, N.J.: Rutgers University Press, 2001. Explores the influences and contradictions of the fashion world.

Baker, Patricia, et al. *Fashions of a Decade: The 1950's.* Detroit: Facts on File, 1991. Examines postwar fashion and the rise of couture.

Marling, Karal Ann. *As Seen on TV: The Visual Culture of Everyday Life in the 1950's.* Cambridge, Mass.: Harvard University Press, 1994. Among other topics, examines how television influenced America's fashion trends in the 1950's.

Leigh Southward

See also Barbie dolls; Fads; Hairstyles; Kelly, Grace; Miss America pageants; Monroe, Marilyn; Parker, Suzy; Surfing and beach culture; Youth culture and the generation gap.

■ Fast-food restaurants

Definition Restaurants that serve rapidly prepared and low-cost food

Suburbanization, increased reliance upon automobiles, and an increase in the number of two-income families during the 1950's created a demand for inexpensive, efficient food service, resulting in the creation of standardized restaurant chains.

Prior to World War II, restaurant dining was an infrequent activity for most middle- and working-class North American families. Urban restaurants were generally expensive and intimidating to many consumers, and many roadside diners and taverns catered to an unsavory clientele. The quality of food and service often varied greatly, as did the time necessary for food to be prepared and served. A potential market for more efficient and inexpensive retail food service thus existed during the early twentieth century but was untapped until the advent of "fast food" during the 1950's.

The fast-food industry can be traced back to the short-order diners and food stands that dotted the North American landscape during the first half of the twentieth century. These restaurants offered low-priced, easy-to-prepare sandwiches and hand-held foods popularized by urban street vendors such as hot dogs and hamburgers. Food stands located near recreational facilities and on busy thoroughfares proved especially successful. Some hamburger stands became sufficiently popular to develop into chains—most notably White Castle, which opened its first restaurant in Wichita, Kansas, in 1921. Other notable examples of early diner chains were Stuckeys—the first of which opened in Georgia in 1936—and Dairy Queen, which began in Joliet, Illinois, in 1940.

The McDonald Brothers Dick and Maurice McDonald, who moved to California from New Hampshire in 1930 and opened a drive-in restaurant in San Bernardino in 1940, are often cited as the inventors of the fast-food restaurant. Following the end of World War II, the McDonald brothers noticed that a large number of their restaurant's customers were young working families looking for fast, inexpensive meals, and they began to explore ways of reducing the twenty-minute average wait time to process their orders. The brothers began by simplifying their menu to focus on their most popular items, such as hamburgers and milk shakes, which allowed them to mechanize their food-preparation process.

The McDonald's hamburger, which originally sold for fifteen cents, was smaller, pre-prepared, and standardized, eliminating the choices that created delays in traditional restaurants. Meals were served in paper bags, paper wrappers, and plastic cups and utensils, instead of cumbersome and expensive plates and silverware. This assembly-line method of food service dramatically cut the operating costs of the restaurant, allowing the brothers to keep their food prices low.

Franchising The McDonald's system was wildly successful, and the restaurant's business boomed; by 1951, their gross annual receipts exceeded a quarter of a million dollars. The low prices of McDonald's meals allowed working-class families to afford restaurant meals in a comfortable, family-friendly environment, and the speed with which orders were processed permitted harried commuters to conserve time and energy that would otherwise be spent preparing meals at home. However, despite their success, the McDonald brothers showed little interest in expanding their business. They rejected proposals from investors to build a nationwide chain of McDonald's restaurants and did not award their first franchise until 1952.

In 1954, the restaurant caught the attention of Ray Kroc, a kitchen appliance salesman and aspiring entrepreneur who was looking to enter the restaurant business. Kroc visited the restaurant one day during lunchtime and was impressed as much by the long lines as by the quality and efficiency of the service. Kroc offered to act as franchising agent for the McDonald brothers—an offer they readily accepted. Kroc ran the franchise operation with an iron fist and a cutthroat competitive mentality, insisting on total conformity on the part of each McDonald's restaurant and often visiting the restaurants himself to enforce cleanliness, dress codes, and adherence to uniform price and service standards. By the end of the decade, Kroc had awarded franchises to more than two hundred McDonald's restaurants.

Imitators Follow The success of McDonald's inspired numerous other restaurant chains to compete for a share of the fast-food market during the 1950's and 1960's. The first Jack-in-the-Box restaurant opened in San Diego, California, in 1951, and the first restaurant in what would become the Taco Bell chain began operating in San Bernardino, California, the following year. Although some time would pass before they would award their first franchises, these two restaurants were successful and innovative in their own right and contributed to the development of the fast-food industry. In 1952, Colonel Harlan Sanders sold the first franchise of his Kentucky Fried Chicken restaurant, which utilized a special method of rapidly preparing fried chicken. The first Burger King opened in Miami, Florida, in 1954, and the restaurant began awarding franchises by the end of the decade. Wendy's, Long John Silvers, and numerous other chains followed during the 1960's. Some of the old diner chains, such as White Castle and Dairy Queen, streamlined their operations to compete with the fast-food chains.

Impact The emergence of the fast food industry during the 1950's reflected the changing needs of a more mobile and leisure-conscious society. In subsequent decades, the increasing availability and popularity of fast food would dramatically alter the tastes and habits of American consumers, contributing to the development of a homogenized, commercially driven mass culture. The fast-food industry boomed during the waning decades of the twentieth century, generating gross annual revenues in excess of 100 billion dollars worldwide in 1999.

Further Reading

Halberstam, David. *The Fifties*. New York: Villard Books, 1993. Discusses the social and economic factors that led to the creation of the fast food industry, including an entire chapter on the establishment of the McDonald's chain.

Jakle, John A., and Keith A. Sculle. *Fast Food: Roadside Restaurants in the Automobile Age.* Baltimore: Johns Hopkins University Press, 1999. A comprehensive study of the origins and growth of fast-food chains in the twentieth century.

Kroc, Ray. *Grinding It Out: The Making of McDonald's.* New York: St. Martin's Press, 1992. Kroc's autobiographical account of the founding of McDonald's.

Schlosser, Eric. *Fast Food Nation: The Dark Side of the All-American Meal.* New York: HarperCollins, 2002. Critical analysis of the fast-food industry that includes detailed information on the establishment of several popular fast-food chains.

Michael H. Burchett

See also Affluence and the new consumerism; Automobiles and auto manufacturing; Kroc, Ray; McDonald's restaurants; TV dinners.

■ *Father Knows Best*

Identification Television situation comedy
Date Aired from 1954 to 1963

Father Knows Best *represented the ideal vision of American family life during the 1950's, which included an understanding and wise father; a beautiful, loving mother; and three attractive, lively children.*

Father Knows Best began as a radio show in 1949, starring Robert Young as Jim Anderson. The show, with Young, made the move to television in 1954, where it appeared at various times on each of the three national networks until 1963. The television version also starred Jane Wyatt as Margaret Anderson, Billy Gray as Bud, Elinor Donahue as Betty, and Lauren Chapin as Kathy. The show was set in a typical midwestern community called Springfield, where Jim works as the manager of an insurance company and Margaret is a housewife. At the program's inception, Betty was seventeen years old, Bud was fourteen, and Kathy was nine.

The show was based on real-life domestic experiences of its creators, Young and Eugene Rodney, expertly embedding moral lessons in comedic situations. Despite the title, father did not know best at all times, and the gentle comedy often depicted Margaret or one of the children teaching Jim a lesson. Like most situation comedies of the 1950's, *Father Knows Best* did not deal with difficult social issues or the grittier realities of family life, although, ironically, Rob-ert Young was an alcoholic, and Lauren Chapin later became a heroin addict.

Impact The phrase "Father Knows Best" became synonymous with the bland, simplistic, idealized situation comedies of the 1950's and early 1960's. Critics argued it portrayed an unrealistic version of family life that, although clearly unattainable, many Americans during the 1950's strove to achieve.

Further Reading

Jones, Gerard. *Honey, I'm Home! Sitcoms: Selling the American Dream.* New York: St. Martin's Press, 1993. An excellent analysis of the impact of television sitcoms from their beginnings in radio through the 1990's. Includes a discussion of *Father Knows Best.*

Leibman, Nina. *Living Room Lectures: The Fifties Family in Film and Television.* Austin: University of Texas Press, 1995. A strong analysis of family life during the 1950's, using film and television.

Robert Young and Jane Wyatt with the Emmy Awards they won for their lead-acting performances on Father Knows Best *during the 1957-1958 television season.* (Hulton Archive | by Getty Images)

Taylor, Ella. *Prime Time Families.* Berkeley: University of California Press, 1989. Analyzes family life as portrayed in the situation comedy.

Mary Virginia Davis

See also *Adventures of Ozzie and Harriet, The*; American Dream; Conformity, culture of; Emmy Awards; *Leave It to Beaver*; Nielsen ratings; Television in the United States.

■ Faubus, Orval

Identification Prosegregationist governor of Arkansas
Born January 7, 1910; near Combs, Arkansas
Died December 14, 1994; Conway, Arkansas

Orval Faubus gained national attention in 1957, when, as governor of Arkansas, he oversaw one of the most tense civil rights confrontations of the decade, the Little Rock Central High School integration crisis.

Born in the mountains of northwest Arkansas, Faubus won local elections until he volunteered for service in World War II. In 1954, Faubus challenged the incumbent for the governor's office. Despite being labeled a communist sympathizer, he unseated the first-term governor. His record during his early tenure was one of moderate reform regarding race relations, and in 1956, he ran for reelection while defending a moderate racial stance.

Under a plan mandated by the U.S. Supreme Court, desegregation was supposed to commence in Little Rock in September of 1957. Segregationists and the White Citizens' Councils pressured Faubus to stop the plan. After a plot to delay integration failed, a federal judge ordered desegregation to continue. African American students were scheduled to enter Little Rock's Central High School on September 2, 1957, but instead, Faubus called out the Arkansas National Guard to prevent them from entering. The troops stayed for three weeks and the crisis made national and international headlines. On September 14, he met with President Dwight D. Eisenhower in an effort to work out a solution, but the effort failed. The governor removed the troops on September 20 in response to a federal order. On September 24, President Eisenhower ordered U.S. troops to Little Rock to protect the nine students.

Impact Historians have debated whether Faubus deliberately instigated the crisis at Central High or took advantage of it for political opportunity. He became a famous symbol for southern resistance during the 1950's and was elected six times as governor and served for twelve years. He continued to support segregationist policies, but his efforts were mostly futile as the political climate in the South changed and African Americans finally were allowed to exercise their right to vote in 1965.

Further Reading

Bates, Daisy. *The Long Shadow of Little Rock.* Fayetteville: University of Arkansas Press, 1987. Bates was the head of the National Association for the Advancement of Colored People (NAACP) in Little Rock at the time and a major figure in the confrontation.

Jacoway, Elizabeth, and C. Fred Williams. *Understanding the Little Rock Crisis: An Exercise in Remembrance and Reconciliation.* Fayetteville: University of Arkansas Press, 1999. A collection of essays about the Central High crisis.

Reed, Roy. *Faubus: The Life and Times of an American Prodigal.* Fayetteville: University of Arkansas Press, 1997. An excellent biography of Faubus.

Charles C. Howard

See also *Brown v. Board of Education*; Civil Rights Act of 1957; Civil Rights movement; Education in the United States; Little Rock school desegregation crisis; National Association for the Advancement of Colored People; School desegregation; White Citizens' Councils.

■ Faulk, John Henry

Identification American folklorist, satirist, writer, and strong defender of the First Amendment
Born August 21, 1913; Austin, Texas
Died April 9, 1990; Austin, Texas

John Henry Faulk became known during the 1950's for his broadcasting career as well as for being blacklisted by Aware, Incorporated for alleged procommunist activity.

John Henry Faulk was an outstanding storyteller who blended humor, impersonations, and charm into his presentations, which frequently related societal customs, popular sayings, and incidents involving family members and friends. On radio broadcasts, he assumed the roles of several distinctive characters to portray humorous behavior and human situations.

Humorist John Henry Faulk during an appearance on a television program on folk music. (Hulton Archive | by Getty Images)

Politically, Faulk supported a liberal agenda and was involved in some leftist activities. He was actively involved in political affairs, participated in environmental protection campaigns, and opposed nuclear weapons proliferation and the Korean War. Faulk unsuccessfully sought a U.S. congressional seat to represent Texas.

Following his army discharge after World War II, Faulk moved to New York, where he hosted a weekly folk-humorist radio program for CBS Radio. In 1951, WCBS Radio introduced the daily *John Henry Faulk Show,* which was broadcast until the popular personality was blacklisted by Aware, Inc., in 1957 for his political beliefs.

Members of various broadcast unions had formed Aware in 1953, as a company which identified and blacklisted alleged communist influences in the broadcasting industry. As vice president of the actors' union, AFTRA, Faulk confronted the issue and sued Aware for libel. After a lengthy legal battle, Faulk was awarded $3.5 million, of which he only received $75,000 from the then-bankrupt Aware corporation.

Impact Blacklisting destroyed Faulk's career along with those of numerous other entertainers who became unemployable amid fears of industry subversion. Unable to regain prominence in the media, he became a popular lecturer and later appeared on the *Hee Haw* television program for five years. He re-

gained a measure of prominence in 1975 when his book titled *Fear on Trial* was made into a television film chronicling his blacklisting legal battles.

Further Reading

Burton, Michael C. *John Henry Faulk: The Making of a Liberated Mind.* Austin: Eakin Press, 1993. Biography reflecting Faulk's life and politics.

Faulk, John Henry. *Fear on Trial.* New York: Simon & Schuster, 1964. Chronicles the six-year successful lawsuit by John Henry Faulk against Aware, Inc.

Dennis A. Harp

See also Army-McCarthy hearings; Communist Party of the U.S.A.; House Committee on Un-American Activities; *I Led Three Lives*; Liberalism in U.S. politics; McCarthy, Joseph.

■ Federal Aviation Administration

Identification U.S. federal agency charged with the regulation of commercial aviation and airports, as well as air safety

Date Created in 1958

The Federal Aviation Administration (FAA) established the responsibility of the federal government for the regulation and oversight of the nation's airlines, airways, airports, and civil aviation industry.

In 1926, the U.S. Congress passed the Air Commerce Act, which charged the secretary of commerce with oversight of the civil aviation industry and established the Aeronautics Branch to do so. Twelve years later, Congress revisited the issue with the creation of the Civil Aeronautics Authority. Within two years, President Franklin D. Roosevelt authorized the division of the agency into a new Civil Aeronautics Authority (CAA) and the Civil Aeronautics Board (CAB). Roosevelt charged the CAA with air traffic control, safety enforcement, and airport oversight. To the CAB fell regulation of the civil aviation industry and accident investigation.

The rapid growth of the aviation industry during the 1950's, the emergence of jet airliners and widespread commercial air travel, and increasingly high accident rates prompted the federal government to reevaluate its oversight of civil aviation. In 1957, President Dwight D. Eisenhower appointed retired U.S. Air Force general Elwood R. "Pete" Quesada his special assistant for aviation matters and the next year asked Congress to create a new federal aviation agency. Congress, in turn, passed the Federal Aviation Act of 1958, which established the Federal Aviation Agency. The new agency took over from the CAA and CAB. Under the leadership of Quesada, it began the regulation of the nation's airlines, airways, and airports.

Impact The FAA was granted broader authority to combat aviation hazards and gained the sole responsibility for developing and maintaining a common civil-military system of air navigation and air traffic control, a responsibility the CAA had shared with others. The agency was renamed the Federal Aviation Administration in 1967, when it became part of the Department of Transportation.

Further Reading

Burkhardt, Robert. *The Federal Aviation Administration.* Florence, Ky.: International Thompson, 1967. Details the history of the organization.

Donald, David, ed. *The Complete Encyclopedia of World Aircraft.* New York: Barnes and Noble Books, 1997. Donald's comprehensive volume provides a detailed analysis of the commercial and military aircraft of the twentieth century.

Paul D. Gelpi, Jr.

See also Aircraft design and development; Boeing 707; Grand Canyon airliner collision; United States Air Force Academy.

■ Federal Bureau of Investigation

Identification Investigative arm of the U.S. Department of Justice

Date Founded in 1908 as the Bureau of Investigation; renamed the Federal Bureau of Investigation (FBI) in 1935

The FBI has the primary responsibility for enforcing federal law in the United States. During the 1950's, it played a leading role in investigating, and building dossiers on, persons and organizations suspected of being subversive at the height of the Cold War.

In 1950, J. Edgar Hoover was in his twenty-sixth year as director of the Federal Bureau of Investigation.

He was an autocratic leader whose parochial views were reflected in the agency he headed. Although he reorganized the FBI, increasing its efficiency and expanding its influence, he was not above using the organization to intimidate people on whom he had accumulated extensive secret files, including presidents and legislators. The bureau under Hoover had an undeniable anti-intellectual, politically reactionary climate.

The Anticommunist Crusade After World War II, the United States engaged in an arms race against the Soviet Union. The United States had nuclear weapons while the Soviets did not, although they were eager to produce such weapons and develop an arsenal of them. During the late 1940's, the FBI, through an intercept from the Soviet State Security Committee (known as the KGB for its Russian acronyms), identified Klaus Fuchs—a German-turned-British atomic scientist who worked at the Los Alamos, New Mexico, weapons laboratory during the 1940's—and his communist connections and informed the British that they likely had a Soviet spy in their midst.

Under questioning, Fuchs admitted his involvement in espionage and identified Harry Gold as his American informant. The day before Fuchs's confession, Gold made a confession to the FBI about his subversive activities. Before long, David Greenglass, brother of Ethel Rosenberg, was drawn into the investigation and, upon being accused of espionage, traded testimony against Ethel and her husband for promises of lenient treatment. The Rosenbergs were tried on charges of selling atomic secrets to the Soviets. On March 29, 1951, on meager evidence, both were found guilty of these charges and sentenced to death. The presiding judge congratulated the FBI for its assiduous cooperation in the prosecution of this case.

The case against Ethel Rosenberg was weak. Hoover hoped to use her as a means of getting her husband to reveal the names of others who were involved in leaking atomic secrets to the Soviets. Hoover made it clear that Ethel could save her life if she persuaded her husband to give the FBI the information it sought, although probably he did not possess such information. Because the Rosenbergs had sons aged three and seven at the time of their trial, Hoover felt certain that Ethel would cooperate rather than die and allow her sons to grow up parentless.

Ethel Rosenberg, however, refused to do Hoover's bidding, and on June 19, 1953, she and her husband were electrocuted in New York State's Sing Sing Prison. Subsequent investigations revealed that there was no hard evidence to link Ethel Rosenberg to the treasonous activities of which she was convicted. The FBI, indifferent to ensuring that justice be served in this celebrated case, used her to achieve its own ends.

The year before the Rosenbergs were tried, a maverick Republican senator from Wisconsin, Joseph R. McCarthy, seeking to draw attention to himself and to advance his incipient political career, made a historic speech in which he claimed that many government employees, including large numbers in the Department of State, were communists. McCarthy and Hoover were friends, and McCarthy used that friendship to champion his anticommunist agenda.

Finally, in 1953, McCarthy, capitalizing on the anticommunist hysteria that was gripping the country, accused former president Harry S. Truman and President Dwight D. Eisenhower of being soft on communism. McCarthy's attack on Eisenhower embarrassed Hoover, who avoided being seen in public with the senator, although he continued to see him socially. Hoover frequently invited McCarthy to dine with him in his home or met him for meals in the apartment of Jean Kerr, McCarthy's secretary whom the senator married on September 29, 1953, largely to quash rumors of his own homosexuality.

McCarthy, who on April 22, 1954, began hearings on communism in the U.S. Army, was censured by the Senate on December 22, 1954, for his behavior during those hearings. On May 2, 1957, having destroyed many lives and instigated the dismissal of more than six hundred college professors who refused to sign loyalty oaths, McCarthy died of acute hepatitis. Hoover's secret files contained considerable sensitive information about McCarthy that remained sealed.

FBI Files on Homosexuals in Government Hoover's FBI relied on large numbers of informants to infiltrate government agencies, gather information on government employees, and report to the bureau on their activities. FBI agents had dossiers on thousands of government employees. If a dossier revealed that an employee in a sensitive and strategic government position was homosexual, the bureau forced that employee to work clandestinely for the FBI under the threat of having the bureau reveal its damaging personal information, which would have led to immediate dismissal and utter humiliation. Many of these career government employees were married and had children. Any suggestion of their covert homosexual involvements would have destroyed them professionally and seriously affected their families. Hoover agreed to suppress such information as long as these employees provided the bureau with the intelligence it needed.

Hoover used these informants to report to the bureau about their colleagues' activities. At that time, government employment was officially denied to homosexuals because they were thought to be vulnerable to blackmail. It is ironic that under Hoover's direction, the FBI subjected homosexual government employees to the very blackmail that it claimed as its rationale for not employing homosexuals.

Desegregation of Public Education In a landmark decision handed down on May 17, 1954, the Supreme Court, in the case of *Brown v. Board of Education*, ruled that the concept of "separate but equal" that had been used to justify school segregation was unconstitutional. Arguing that a significant part of one's education involves the ability of people to mingle freely and acknowledging that in reality schools serving black students generally lacked many of the amenities found in schools serving white students, the court declared the separate-but-equal doctrine unconstitutional. On March 31, 1955, the Court ordered that America's public schools be integrated with "all deliberate speed."

Southern states used every tactic they could to thwart integration, but on April 20, 1957, Congress passed the Civil Rights Act of 1957, establishing a legal basis for equal rights for all Americans. With the passage of this act, Hoover declared that the FBI would do all in its power to assure that no Americans were deprived of their civil rights. Despite this public pronouncement, the bureau intensified its investigations of civil rights activists, focusing particularly upon leaders such as Martin Luther King, Jr., and Malcolm X. The bureau pried into the private lives of activists and leaked damaging information about them in its attempt to discredit them in the eyes of both their colleagues and the public.

On September 4, 1957, National Guardsmen from Arkansas refused to permit nine black students to enter Little Rock's Central High School, where they wanted to enroll. When President Eisenhower sent federal troops to Little Rock on September 24 to assure that the nine students who had been turned away be permitted to enter and enroll in the school, the desegregation struggle reached fever pitch. Hoover was displeased by Eisenhower's action and directed much of the FBI's attention to controlling civil rights groups that Hoover considered dissident.

COINTELPRO COINTELPRO was the acronym for the *Co*unter *Intel*ligence *Pro*gram that the FBI, at Hoover's bidding, launched in 1956. Aimed primarily at dissident groups and organizations thought to be communist-front groups, COINTELPRO was launched in considerable secrecy. It took two years for Hoover to provide the House appropriations subcommittee with a vague description of the program, contending only that it was directed toward disorganizing and disrupting the Communist Party.

Actually, the purpose of COINTELPRO was to infiltrate groups that Hoover considered a threat to the nation and to use whatever tactics it could to spread suspicion and encourage discord within these groups. The FBI planted newspaper stories, many of them untrue, about party officials. They wrote anonymous letters and made anonymous telephone calls spreading rumors about the sexual deviancy or alleged past indiscretions of those the bureau sought to discredit. FBI agents invaded people's places of employment to question them, thereby arousing suspicion in the minds of their coworkers. The antics of COINTELPRO often resembled fraternity house pranks, but they had lasting consequences and were generally manufactured and largely untrue.

Following the publication of Max Lowenthal's *The Federal Bureau of Investigation* (1950), a book that greatly embarrassed Hoover, Hoover had FBI informants infiltrate the publishing industry and the offices of major magazines so that the bureau could be informed of forthcoming articles or books that might embarrass the FBI and could block their publication. FBI publicist Louis Nichols had to approve anything that was to be published about the bureau.

The Jencks Decision On June 3, 1957, the U.S. Supreme Court decided to reverse a lower court's conviction of Clinton Jencks, a labor leader from New Mexico found guilty of perjury for signing a noncommunist affidavit. Jencks's lawyers asked to see the statements of his accusers, held in sealed FBI files. The one dissenting justice in this case, former

attorney general Tom Clark, warned that the Court's decision could result in a rush to open confidential files in other court cases. Indeed, the FBI vigorously guarded access to such files and supported Clark's stance.

Appalled by the Jencks decision, the bureau circulated rumors that if this decision stood, it might need to discontinue the investigation of some pending espionage cases. Hoover persuaded President Eisenhower to decry the damage that could be done to national security if FBI files were made available to defense attorneys. The American Bar Association issued a resolution that denounced the Court's decision. This resolution was secretly written by FBI publicist Louis Nichols, who is purported to have aspired eventually to replace Hoover as director. Hoover prevailed upon Congress to pass a bill to annul the Jencks decision and protect the sanctity of FBI files. It took the Supreme Court two years to rule on the constitutionality of this bill, and when it did, it was clear that Hoover, who had taken on the nation's highest court, had, for better or worse, triumphed over it.

Impact It is clear that the FBI generally concurred with and encouraged the anticommunist hysteria of the 1950's, often trampling on the rights of United States citizens under the banner of national security. Hoover's bureau, in exposing alleged political dissidents, homosexuals, and civil rights activists promoted a climate of fear and suspicion throughout the decade. By the end of the 1950's, Hoover still ruled the FBI with an iron hand. He remained in office until his death on May 2, 1972. His most secret files were destroyed immediately by his secretary and other staff members. Hoover had served under eight presidents of the United States and nineteen attorney generals.

Further Reading

Gentry, Curt. *J. Edgar Hoover: The Man and the Secrets.* New York: W. W. Norton, 2001. This thorough, well-documented study of the man who directed the FBI for forty-six years is exceptionally revealing. Well written and researched.

Kessler, Ronald. *The Bureau: The Secret History of the FBI.* New York: St. Martin's Press, 2002. This extensive overview of the FBI by a former investigative reporter for *The Washington Post* contains sharp insights developed from reviewing thousands of documents relating to the Bureau.

Theoharis, Athan G., ed. *The FBI: A Comprehensive Reference Guide.* Detroit: Facts on File, 2000. A thorough guide to countless FBI-related topics, including important cases, legislative and policy decisions, personalities, media portrayal, and FBI relationships with the president, members of Congress, and law enforcement agencies.

R. Baird Shuman

See also Army-McCarthy hearings; Brink's robbery; Central Intelligence Agency; Civil Rights movement; Cold War; Eisenhower, Dwight D.; Hoover, J. Edgar; House Committee on Un-American Activities; Internal Security Act of 1950; Loyalty oaths; McCarthy, Joseph; Rosenberg, Julius and Ethel.

■ Ferlinghetti, Lawrence

Identification Poet, publisher, and bookstore owner
Born March 24, 1919; Yonkers, New York

Lawrence Ferlinghetti became known as one of the best Beat poets of the 1950's and as a social activist who staunchly defended free speech and the controversial work of other writers during this era.

Shortly after Ferlinghetti was born in 1919, his mother was committed to an insane asylum. As a result, he was raised by relatives. As a boy, he was both an Eagle Scout and a gang member arrested for petty theft. He earned a bachelor's degree at the University of North Carolina, Chapel Hill, and a doctorate at the Sorbonne in Paris. He was in the U.S. Navy during World War II and visited Nagasaki six days after the second atomic bomb was exploded there; he later marked that event as the catalyst in his political thinking.

In 1951, Ferlinghetti moved to San Francisco and taught French and wrote art criticism. Within two years, he and Peter Martin started a magazine called *City Lights* and opened a bookstore of the same name. The bookstore grew in popularity, becoming a center for alternative culture in San Francisco and a meeting place for the large number of Beat poets who had congregated in the city.

In 1955, Ferlinghetti and Martin began the Pocket Poets Series and became publishers of the burgeoning Beat writers. One of the publishing house's most famous titles was *Howl, and Other Poems* by Allen Ginsberg, which led to Ferlinghetti's arrest in 1956 for obscenity. The ensuing trial brought na-

Poet Lawrence Ferlinghetti in 1960. (AP/Wide World Photos)

tional attention to the San Francisco Renaissance, the Beat generation, City Lights Publishing, and civil protections under the First Amendment. Ferlinghetti prevailed and the case became a precedent-setting judgment, favoring controversial works with so-called redeeming social value.

Ferlinghetti's dissertation at the Sorbonne was titled "The City as Symbol in Modern Poetry: In Search of a Metropolitan Tradition," a title that foreshadowed the very tradition his own poetry would embody. Ferlinghetti became an anomaly—a serious, skilled versifier who also possessed a wild sense of humor and keen ear for colloquial language. His first volume of poetry was *Pictures of the Gone World*, published by City Lights in 1955, but it was *A Coney Island of the Mind* (1958) that brought him national attention. The poetic voice here is that of a latter-day Walt Whitman, a figure who finds wonder in the smallest, most seemingly ordinary phenomena. Underneath the meditations on the works of painters and other writers and the personal revelations, there was the social critic who saw behind the bland exterior of affluent times and political conformity. In one of the most memorable of the collection's poems, titled simply "11," Ferlinghetti combined hilarity with mordant disgust:

> Oh the world is beautiful place
> to be born into
> if you don't mind
> a few dead minds
> in the higher places
> or a bomb or two
> now and then
> in your upturned faces

During the 1960's and 1970's, *A Coney Island of the Mind* gained increased popularity and became a best-selling collection of poetry in the United States.

Impact Ferlinghetti's was a voice of resistance, a writer with a conscience who refused to conform or pretend that prosperity was a sign of moral superiority. He did as much as anyone to foster the Beat generation and bring it to national attention.

Further Reading

Myrsiades, Kostas. *Beat Generation: Critical Essays.* New York: Peter Lang, 2002. Fourteen essays analyze the Beat generation's place in literature.

Silesky, Barry. *Ferlinghetti: The Artist in His Time.* New York: Warner Books, 1980. The first comprehensive biography, prepared with the author's cooperation.

Skau, Michael. *Constantly Risking Absurdity: The Writings of Lawrence Ferlinghetti.* Troy, N.Y.: Whitston, 1989. A brief monograph assessing the writer's works and career.

Smith, Larry R. *Lawrence Ferlinghetti, Poet At Large.* Carbondale: Southern Illinois University Press, 1983. the first serious critical study of Ferlinghetti's work.

David W. Madden

See also Beat generation; Book publishing; Burroughs, William; Censorship; Conformity, culture of; Ginsberg, Allen; Kerouac, Jack; Poetry; Rexroth, Kenneth; San Francisco Renaissance.

■ Film in Canada

The 1950's impetus toward documentary and animation filmmaking paved the way for Canada's national prominence as a maker of short films.

At the end of World War II, Canada had one of the world's largest film studios and a cadre of innovative documentarists and animators. The National Film Board of Canada (NFB), founded in 1939 by John Grierson, leader of the British School of Documentary, combined Grierson's expertise (and his hostility to fictional features) with Canada's own resources to produce distinguished short films. David Bairstow's *Royal Journey* (1951) won the British Film Academy award for best documentary and set new box-office records in Canada. In 1952, at the Cannes Film Festival, Colin Low won best animated short for *The Romance of Transportation in Canada.*

In 1941, Grierson brought a young Scot, Norman McLaren, into the NFB to make wartime promotional films. Through his constant experimentation with color transformation, cameraless animation, and frame-by-frame photography, McLaren became arguably the finest animator in the world, making almost fifty films for the NFB and winning more than one hundred international awards.

The postwar trend, begun in war-ravaged Europe, toward an intense realism (neorealism) achieved by filming on location and not in studios, flourished in Canada. Grierson's belief that documentaries should become government tools for public education succeeded in dramatized case histories with problem-solving outlines and in dramatized training films. The integration of documentary and fiction, which dominated documentary practice, was used by Julian Biggs in *The Son* (1951), which focuses on the difficulties of farm life, and in Gudrun Parker's *Opera Singer* (1951), an account of the rise of a fictional opera singer from training to public performance.

The advent of Canadian television in 1953 compelled the NFB to adapt to the demands of television programming, achieved by scheduling a weekly series of film. Two movements became visible about the same time—one among English-speaking Canadians and the other among the Francophones of Quebec.

English-Language Films Bernard Devlin, a prominent filmmaker at this time, originated a weekly reportage series, *On the Spot* (1953-1955), which was researched, shot, and edited in a week—all on a minuscule budget. Devlin's experimentation with a new sixteen-millimeter camera that recorded sound directly on the film led to *Survival in the Bush* (1954), which depicted a real-life film crew's experience and was accompanied by expert commentary.

The formation of a tightly knit group of intellectuals calling themselves "Unit B" rejected the prevalent tendency toward docudramas and the authority of the Griersonian style. Instead, their films became more lyrical and contained no didactic message or social injustice in need of correction. *Corral* (1954) demonstrates, without comment, the crucial stages of breaking a range horse over a score for two guitars. The idea that instances of human life require no commentary was pushed further with the "Candid-Eye" productions of 1958-1959. The camera observed impressive aspects of Canadian life, as in three films by Terence McCartney-Filgate: Montreal's pre-Christmas rush in *The Days Before Christmas* (1958); an inside view of the Salvation Army's work in *Blood and Fire* (1958); and a look at an Ontario onion farm in *The Back-Breaking Leaf* (1959).

In 1957, *City of Gold*—a meditation on the Klondike Gold Rush of 1897—was filmed. It used slides, personal reflection, and images combined with still photographs and live shots of contemporary Dawson, Yukon Territory, to produce a kind of dream-journey without closure, leaving the viewer with a sense of unresolved mystery. This type of meditative film continued into the 1960's.

Despite the success of short films in Canada during the 1950's, feature filmmaking was left almost exclusively to the U.S. film industry until the 1960's, and by then many Canadian directors and actors had migrated to the American industry.

French-Language Films The arrival of French-language television in 1953 stimulated NFB productions in French. The debate over entertainment programming for television was won by Devlin, who advocated noncritical magazine journalism. He initiated a twenty-six-part series, *Sur le Vif* in 1953 (similar to his English-language *On the Spot* series), that treated institutions such as the church, the police, and the army.

In 1956, the NFB relocated to Montreal, and one year later, it acquired its first French-Canadian commissioner. Soon the NFB attracted many talented French-Canadian filmmakers who, despite Canada's lack of a national policy of bilingualism and biculturalism, embarked on the so-called Quiet Revolution.

Educated film enthusiasts favored the idea of an uncontrolled documentary and deemed it necessary for the evolution of a personal vision. Turning their cameras toward Quebec, the new group of filmmakers attempted to establish in their films a sense of solidarity with the society they filmed. The candid-eye style of observing people from a distance gave way to a wide-angle method suggesting a sense of participation in their subjects' lives.

The milestone accomplishment was *Les Raquetters* (the snowshoers), a 1958 film that showed, with limited commentary, incidents in a small town during a snowshoe festival. Shunning the customary distancing shot, the film plunges into the midst of street revelers and, through the utilization of hand-held thirty-five-millimeter cameras, attempts to establish a connection between the viewers and the revelers. This style of documentary, with its emphasis on urban rituals, was to dominate French-language films for several years and was responsible for ushering in the golden age of Québécois documentary films.

Impact The 1950's marked a turning point for Canadian attitudes toward film. Intellectual filmmakers and enthusiasts encouraged creative freedom as the means of moving beyond the NFB provincial attitudes into the exploration of the camera's potential. French involvement in the NFB led to unexpected growth that ultimately brought Canada's film production from a cottage industry to a national cinema.

Further Reading

Baldassare, Angela, ed. *Reel Canadians: Interviews from the Canadian Film World.* Toronto: Guernica Editions, 2002. Interviews with Canadians in the film industry, including David Cronenberg, Dan Aykroyd, James Cameron, and Keanu Reaves.

Walz, Gene P. *Canada's Best Features: Critical Essays on Fifteen Canadian Films.* Rodopi BV Editions, 2002. Essays and in-depth analyses of fifteen films from various perspectives.

Wise, Wyndham, ed. *Take One's Essential Guide to Canadian Film.* Toronto: University of Toronto Press, 2001. Alphabetical listings and discussions of significant Canadians and Canadian films.

Mary Hurd

See also Canadian regionalism; Drive-in theaters; Film in the United States; Literature in Canada; Pay television; Theater in Canada.

■ Film in the United States

During the 1950's, the U.S. motion-picture industry tried to compete with the new medium of television by offering audiences features not available in their living rooms, such as wide-screen cinematography and more adult themes.

After the end of World War II, American moviegoers flocked to theaters in record numbers, enjoying the new freedom of not worrying about war and its accompanying deprivations and the benefits of the booming postwar economy. By 1950, however, this burst of prosperity for Hollywood began to slow down as television was introduced to households and slowly established itself as a major competitor for Americans' entertainment spending.

The average weekly film attendance in the United States declined from over seventy-eight million people in 1946 to fifty-eight million by 1950, with annual ticket sales dropping from $1,692,000,000 (the highest total ever) in 1946 to $1,379,000,000 in 1950. In contrast, the number of American households with television sets rose rapidly from nearly four million in 1950 to twenty-six million by 1954. The 1948 U.S. Supreme Court decision, based on an interpretation of antitrust laws, required the studios to divest themselves of their theater chains, which ended their virtual monopoly over the exhibition of their products and furthered the industry's financial hardship. Therefore, during the 1950's, film companies sought to survive by making their products "bigger and better than ever."

Big-Screen Technology Because audiences at home were watching only black-and-white images on small screens—and often with bad reception during this pre-cable era—the Hollywood studios decided to combat the upstart medium by making its images bigger. A wide-screen process developed in France during the 1920's was optioned by Twentieth Century-Fox and named CinemaScope. Cinemascope images were 2.35 times as wide as they were high, compared to the 1.33-aspect ratio of standard screen images. The first CinemaScope film, Fox's biblical epic *The Robe*, premiered at the Roxy Theater in New York in 1953 and opened slowly around the country as theaters installed wider screens. By 1957, 85 percent of theaters in the United States and Canada were equipped for wide-screen films.

The success of CinemaScope led other studios to develop their own wide-screen processes, including Paramount's VistaVision. Soon these processes allowed aspect ratios up to 2.55, as with Todd-AO, used for 70-millimeter films, and the more popular Panavision, first used for Metro Goldwyn Mayer's (MGM) *Ben-Hur* (1959).

A less successful technique, because of both production and exhibition expenses, was Cinerama. This wide-screen process required three cameras and three projectors in separate projection booths to capture and project a single image, thus creating an illusion of vastness. Showing Cinerama films required an even larger screen that was curved at an angle of 165 degrees. The process was unveiled in 1952 with *This Is Cinerama*, a travelogue featuring a roller-coaster ride and an airplane flight over the Grand Canyon. Most of the other Cinerama productions were also travel documentaries, such as *Cinerama Holiday* (1955) and *Seven Wonders of the World* (1956). A traditional narrative film in Cinerama did not appear until *How the West Was Won* (1962). Cinerama did not prove more popular because the cost of the special screen prohibited nonurban, smaller theaters from affording it, and during this era, the American population was becoming more suburban and leaving city areas.

The much cheaper process of three-dimensional or stereoscopic films was popular only for about a year and a half. The first Hollywood 3-D film was *Bwana Devil* in 1952, in which a lion seemed to leap from the screen into the audience. The technology proved to be only a novelty, with many viewers annoyed by the cheap cardboard-and-plastic glasses they needed to wear to see the 3-D effect.

In order to gain a competitive edge over television, the film industry needed to provide more color. In 1945, only 8 percent of Hollywood films were shot in color, but the percentage rose by 1955 to more than 50 percent. Audiences wanted wide-screen films but not black-and-white ones. While most color films before the 1950's had been in Technicolor, Twentieth Century-Fox discovered that Technicolor cameras could not accommodate CinemaScope lenses, so Eastmancolor was used instead.

Spectacles Prior to the 1950's, audiences went to the movies out of habit or to see favorite stars. Because people during the 1950's attended films much less routinely thanks to the relative ease and comfort of watching television at home, the movie industry understood that going to theaters had to become more of an event. Bigger and more colorful films created the sense of a film being something special, but not every film could achieve this must-see quality. As a result, more and more films during the 1950's became spectacles. If the screens were big, the actions appearing on them had to be large scale as well.

The Robe was only the first of several wide-screen biblical epics. One of the most popular films of the decade was director Cecil B. DeMille's large-scale remake of one of his silent films, *The Ten Commandments* (1955), shot in VistaVision. Such films were not filled only with stars and lavish costumes and sets, but each also had to have a special set piece to dazzle audiences and encourage word-of-mouth praise. Therefore, in *The Ten Commandments*, Charlton Heston, portraying Moses, parts the Red Sea, while the title character in William Wyler's *Ben-Hur,* competes with Messala (Stephen Boyd) in a spectacular chariot race.

The most typical of the nonbiblical epics was the all-star adaptation of Jules Verne's *Around the World in Eighty Days* produced by Michael Todd (owner of the Todd-AO process). Shot on locations throughout the world, with dozens of big names such as Frank Sinatra in cameo roles, it won the Academy Award for Best Picture, a win critics claim was less for its quality and more for Todd's cinematographic audacity. In addition to being grand in scale, such films, in an era when few films ran more than two hours, were also often long: *Around the World in Eighty Days* stood at two hours and fifty-eight minutes, *The Ten Commandments* at three hours and thirty-nine minutes, and King Vidor's version of author Leo Tolstoy's *War and Peace* (1956) at three hours and twenty-eight minutes. Even adaptations of Broadway musicals had to be bigger than ever. Fred Zinnemann's two-hour-and-twenty-three-minute film *Oklahoma!* (1955) was shot in Todd-AO, as was Joshua Logan's *South Pacific* (1958), which ran two hours and fifty minutes.

On Location Hollywood also tried to lure audiences away from home with authenticity. After the center of American film production shifted from New York to Los Angeles during the silent-film era, almost all films were made on sets within the boundaries of the studios. When a film called for more extensive outdoor shooting than could be found at the studio—a typical scenario with Westerns—the exterior scenes were shot at studio-owned locations within easy commuting distance from Hollywood.

To meet audiences' demands for realism after World War II, however, more and more films began shooting on location. The long-abandoned New York was rediscovered for the exterior scenes of films such as *Kiss of Death* (1947) and *The Naked City* (1948). This trend escalated during the 1950's with most big-studio films set in New York filming at least some scenes there. Elia Kazan's *On the Waterfront* (1954), one of the decade's most acclaimed films, was filmed extensively in New York and New Jersey. Stanley Kubrick's low-budget *Killer's Kiss* (1955) included startling images of Pennsylvania Station a decade before it was torn down.

Director John Ford began breaking away from Hollywood during the 1940's to make his Westerns in Utah. Throughout the 1950's, more and more Westerns were made in such locations as Arizona, Mexico, and Canada. The result was more lush colors and startling vistas than had been seen before. The size and scope of the images dwarfed what viewers at home could see on such popular televised Westerns as *Gunsmoke.*

The most significant development in location shooting, however, involved sites far away from North America. To show off the splendors of CinemaScope, Fox made *Three Coins in the Fountain* (1954), a lightweight romance, in Rome. While other postwar American films were made in Italy, most notably *Roman Holiday* (1953), they did not feature the widescreen locations in color seen in *Three Coins in the Fountain.* Most of the decade's big-studio films set abroad were filmed at least in part in the real locations: Ford's *The Quiet Man* (1952) in Ireland, Alfred Hitchcock's *To Catch a Thief* (1955) on the French Riviera and his *The Man Who Knew Too Much* (1956) in London and Marrakech, and Zinnemann's *The Nun's Story* (1959) in Belgium and the Belgian Congo. The era saw many films set in peacetime Japan, including *The Teahouse of the August Moon* (1956) and *Sayonara* (1957).

Because of the increasing international scope of Hollywood films and the attendant costs, more films became international coproductions. The Italians Dino de Laurentiis and Carlo Ponti coproduced *War and Peace* and other Hollywood films. Because there were political restrictions on cinematic realism, *War and Peace* was made in Italy rather than in Russia, where its story was set. Though the World War II prisoner-of-war drama *The Bridge on the River Kwai* (1957), made in Ceylon, had a British director, David Lean, and a mostly British and Japanese cast, economics demanded that such a large-scale war film become an American co-production, so Columbia Pictures financed it and required a big-name American star, William Holden, in the cast.

As more American films were made in Europe, more European stars came to Hollywood, including Rossano Brazzi, Gina Lollobrigida, Sophia Loren, and Anna Magnani from Italy, Leslie Caron from France, and Anita Ekberg from Sweden. The use of such performers in films set in both Europe and the United States deepened the international cross-pollination of Hollywood films.

Adult Themes Films of the 1930's and 1940's dealt only occasionally and usually superficially with social issues and sexuality because of restrictions placed on filmmakers by the Motion Picture Production Code Administration (PCA). For example, two people, even if married, could not be shown in the same bed, and miscegenation or drug trafficking were similarly off limits. However, just as the audiences of the 1950's expected more authentic settings in films, they also wanted more realistic representations of their lives, and the studios wanted to give them a view of life unavailable in television programs. As a result, the decade saw films dealing with drug addiction, as with *The Man with the Golden Arm* (1955) and *A Hatful of Rain* (1957), racial issues in *The Defiant Ones* (1958) and *Imitation of Life* (1959), and the very real threat of nuclear annihilation in *On the Beach* (1959).

Films of the 1950's dealt more openly and more often with such topics as alcoholism, juvenile delinquency, and rape. While the treatment of such subjects was more graphic than in the films of earlier decades, these films were still rather mild compared to those of the 1960's and 1970's for several reasons. The Production Code would remain in effect until 1966. Many states and communities had local censorship boards that would ban or drastically edit films. Studios did not want to risk alienating audiences, especially in the South, with racial themes. More important, Hollywood knew that films presenting African Americans as the equals of white characters would not be widely accepted. Even though the Civil Rights movement was making daily head-

lines during the decade, it barely existed on the big screen.

The hearings of the House Committee on Un-American Activities that began during the 1940's extended into the 1950's, resulting in the jailing of a handful of screenwriters and directors for contempt of Congress in failing to disclose their political affiliations. Dozens of others employed in the film industry were blacklisted for their political beliefs. Dealing with social issues, therefore, created the risk of being labeled sympathetic to communism. In the first half of the decade, there were many overly anti-communist films such as *My Son John* (1952). The studios had to maintain a balance between offering audiences who had endured the Depression and World War II more realism with their fear of offending other components of the potential film audience, politicians, and censors.

While the films of the era seem tame to later decades' audiences, many were much more sexually suggestive than those in prior decades. Such films as *A Streetcar Named Desire* (1951), *From Here to Eternity* (1953), *Picnic* (1955), and *Peyton Place* (1957) presented sexual undertones previously not seen in Hollywood films, though *Peyton Place* had to be toned down considerably from the Grace Metalious novel on which it was based. Films such as *Picnic* and *Peyton Place* suggested that, in contrast to the white-washed image of American life seen in the Andy Hardy films of the previous decades, small-town America portrayed during the 1950's was full of secrets, lust, and sins.

Comedies such as *The Seven Year Itch* (1955), *The Girl Can't Help It* (1956), and *Pillow Talk* (1959) offered what seems in retrospect a silly, leering approach to the relations between the sexes. Some sexual topics, however, were still forbidden. Films adapted from plays or novels with homosexual characters would find the movie versions transformed into heterosexuals or confused sexless characters. This transformation is most notable in *Tea and Sympathy* (1956) and *Cat on a Hot Tin Roof* (1958), both adaptations of successful, critically acclaimed Broadway plays. What was acceptable in Manhattan, however, would not necessarily play in Middle America.

Censorship Throughout the decade, films tackling adult themes had problems with the PCA, organizations such as the Legion of Decency, and local censorship boards, all groups having the power to define and enforce social mores. Ida Lupino, the only American woman director of the period, attempted to present the first realistic treatment of rape in *Outrage* (1950), but the PCA demanded that the rapist be an acquaintance rather than a stranger, that the victim could not be shown fighting off her assailant, and that the word "rape" could not be used.

A Streetcar Named Desire, Elia Kazan's film based on Tennessee Williams's play, was edited by Warner Bros. without the director's approval to respond to PCA and Legion of Decency complaints. The uncensored version was not seen until 1993. Otto Preminger's fluffy comedy *The Moon Is Blue* (1953), also based on a Broadway hit, was released without PCA approval and despite Legion of Decency opposition to its treatment of sex, which included the daring use of the word "virgin." Because the subject of narcotics was banned by the PCA, Preminger's heroin drama, *The Man with the Golden Arm*, was also released without a seal of approval, an action that led to a modification of the Production Code.

Kazan's *Baby Doll* (1956), also based on a Williams play, was condemned by the Legion of Decency and the Roman Catholic Church because of its depiction of sexual lust. Preminger's *Anatomy of a Murder* (1959) created controversy because of the language used in a court scene discussing rape. The film was banned in Chicago, but this ruling was overturned by a district court.

Anatomy of a Murder was one of several films experiencing local censorship problems. *Native Son* (1951), adapted from the Richard Wright novel of the same title, was banned in Ohio as contributing to immorality and crime. Several theaters canceled screenings of Charlie Chaplin's *Limelight* (1952) after Chaplin was denied a reentry permit to the United States because of alleged communist sympathies. In one of the most unusual cases, Walt Disney's *The Vanishing Prairie* (1954), a nature documentary that would win an Academy Award, was banned in New York because it showed a buffalo giving birth. An American Civil Liberties Union complaint led to a reversal of the ban.

Rock and Roll and Youth Culture One of the decade's most controversial subjects was, however, eagerly embraced by the film industry: juvenile delinquency. *Blackboard Jungle* (1955), noteworthy as one of the first of several films to acknowledge the restlessness and, in some cases, violence of teenagers,

featured "Rock Around the Clock" by Bill Haley and the Comets during its opening credits, marking the first use of rock-and-roll music in a film.

While television, with the notable exception of *American Bandstand*, approached the new musical form cautiously and allowed few African American acts on the popular variety programs of the time, films were a different matter. *The Girl Can't Help It* featured performances by Fats Domino, Little Richard, the Platters, and Gene Vincent, capturing the beginnings of rock and roll in "glorious" CinemaScope and Eastmancolor. Several films were built around such popular rock-and-roll acts. *Rock Around the Clock* (1956) featured Bill Haley and the Comets, Little Richard, and the Platters; *Rock Rock Rock* (1956) offered La Vern Baker, Chuck Berry, and Frankie Lymon and the Teenagers, not to mention the debut of fourteen-year-old actress Tuesday Weld, whose songs were dubbed by Connie Francis. Several of these films, such as *Don't Knock the Rock* (1956), helped explain or defend rock music to the older generation.

Many of the white rock singers of the period, including Frankie Avalon, Fabian, and Ricky Nelson, were given acting roles in films, but only one rock performer became a major star. Such films as *Loving You* (1957), *Jailhouse Rock* (1957), and *King Creole* (1958) capture the rebellious essence that made Elvis Presley the first rock superstar and a major box-office attraction as well.

Rock music became emblematic of adults not understanding young people and having little patience with them. While teenagers during the 1930's and 1940's appeared as characters in comedies and family dramas, they did not become "problems" until the 1950's: refusing to listen to their parents and teachers, joining youth gangs, getting into all kinds of trouble, looking for kicks, driving fast cars, and riding motorcycles. Low-budget films such as *Dragstrip Girl* (1957) were among the first to recognize the burgeoning youth market. Many films such as *Blue Denim* (1959), about teenage pregnancy, came with sociological trappings. The decade's major statement about the inability of cross-generation communication came with James Dean, Natalie Wood, and Sal Mineo in Nicholas Ray's *Rebel Without a Cause* (1955).

Science-Fiction Films While horror films were common during the previous decades, science-fiction films did not appear in great numbers until the

1950's. Some such films reflected increased interest in the possibility of space travel. Americans also wanted to reach outer space before the Soviet Union, the impetus behind *Destination Moon* (1950). Other films grew out of Americans' fear of the unknown and the tensions related to the Cold War. In *The Day the Earth Stood Still* (1951), an apparently benign visitor from outer space is treated with suspicion before warning the earth what will happen if its wars continue. Less friendly visitors bring destruction to the earth in *The War of the Worlds* (1953), adapted from H. G. Wells's novel. Alien creatures assume human form in the 3-D film *It Came from Outer Space* (1953).

Fears of the consequences of the atomic age appear in several films. Radiation from atomic-bomb testing creates predatory giant ants in *Them!* (1954), and a plutonium explosion causes an army colonel to grow ten feet a day in *The Amazing Colossal Man* (1957). After being caught in a radioactive mist, the hero of *The Incredible Shrinking Man* (1957) goes to the other extreme.

In general, these science-fiction films indicated a society comfortable with its mundane routines and fearful of uncontrollable forces that might disrupt and possibly destroy the American way of life. These forces might come in the form of communism or the technology that was advancing too quickly. Strong distrust of scientists—blamed for creating the atomic bomb—was prevalent in these films.

Other Genre Films In addition to the adaptations of Broadway musicals and rock-and-roll films, the 1950's was the last decade to see a large number of original musicals. MGM, as it had during the 1940's, continued to turn out musicals, including several such as *Jupiter's Darling* (1954), starring Esther Williams. These films featured elaborate sets and costumes and became even bigger than before with the advent of wide screens. The most enduring musicals included Fred Astaire in the sophisticated *The Band Wagon* (1953), directed by Vincente Minnelli, and the charming *Funny Face* (1957), directed by Stanley Donen and starring Astaire and Audrey Hepburn.

Donen also co-directed, with Gene Kelly, *Singin' in the Rain* (1952). This musical comedy treatment of how Hollywood coped with the invention of talking pictures, featuring the famous scene of Kelly splashing happily about while singing the title song, often appears on critics' polls of the greatest films ever made.

Gene Kelly's storm-drenched dancing scene in Singin' in the Rain *is one of the most famous moments in film history.* (Arkent Archive)

The era also saw the rise of the so-called adult Western. Instead of the simple good-guy-versus-bad-guy plots of the previous decades, many Westerns during the 1950's developed more complex characters. In Zinnemann's *High Noon* (1952), a marshal receives no help from the townspeople he must protect from vengeful bad men. *High Noon* was another depiction of the decade's desire for conformity. Nicholas Ray's highly unusual *Johnny Guitar* (1954) was a Freudian view of the role of the individual in society.

Native Americans were treated with more respect than in earlier years in films such as *Broken Arrow* (1950) and *Apache* (1954). These films made subtle commentaries about racial attitudes in contemporary America. John Ford's *The Searchers* (1956), with John Wayne tracking down the Native Americans who have murdered his brother and sister-in-law and kidnapped his niece, comments on racism and offers one of the decade's most psychologically complex and indelible characters.

Film noir, the dark, pessimistic, moody crime films that developed and flourished during the 1940's, continued with some of the best films of the genre: *The Asphalt Jungle* (1950), *D.O.A.* (1950), *In a Lonely Place* (1950), *Sunset Boulevard* (1950), *The Big Heat* (1953), and *Pickup on South Street* (1953). *Film noir* slowly dissipated during the decade because its cynical, existential fatalism clashed with the essential optimism of the time. Before taking a respite until the 1970's, however, two of the greatest films in this genre appeared: Robert Aldrich's *Kiss Me Deadly* (1955) and Orson Welles's *Touch of Evil* (1958). Racism toward Hispanics appears in *Touch of Evil*, and *Kiss Me Deadly* ends with what seems to be an atomic explosion, the suitcase its characters are pursuing becoming a symbol of the decade's potential for self-destruction.

Roles for Women For the most part, women played subservient roles in the films of the 1950's, typically portraying wives, mothers, secretaries, and waitresses. If a woman was a business executive, she would give up her career when she found the right man. The primary goals of American women in the films of the 1950's were exemplified by titles such as *How to Marry a Millionaire* (1953).

Women actors often found their most substantial roles in the era's soap operas. Universal International specialized in lushly produced tear-jerkers.

The best of this type of film was directed by Douglas Sirk: *Magnificent Obsession* (1954), depicting Rock Hudson as a doctor helping Jane Wyman regain her sight; *All That Heaven Allows* (1956), with Wyman daring to date a young gardener (Rock Hudson) against her children's wishes; and *Written on the Wind* (1957), in which Lauren Bacall marries into a wealthy dysfunctional family. Sirk gave these films more visual style and panache than seemed warranted by the melodramatic material. In such films, women survived and prospered through the strength of their characters, as with the previously wild Dorothy Malone at the end of *Written on the Wind*.

Stars and Directors As always, a major reason for audiences to attend films during the 1950's was to see stars. Many established stars continued to appear in major films. Marilyn Monroe was the major female film star of the decade, creating an overt sexuality not seen before. In melodramas such as *Niagara* (1953), musical comedies such as *Gentlemen Prefer Blondes* (1953), Westerns such as *River of No Return* (1954), and sex comedies such as *The Seven Year Itch* and *Some Like It Hot* (1959), Monroe displayed her distinctive breathy style. The studios desperately tried to create Monroe clones with Jayne Mansfield, Sheree North, Kim Novak, and Mamie van Doren. However, of these women, only Novak, with a much cooler, more aloof approach, had a substantial film career.

At the other extreme from the voluptuous Monroe was the thin Audrey Hepburn. Hepburn's gamine charm and distinctive mid-Atlantic accent helped, but the camera loved looking at her more than perhaps anyone before or since. In *Roman Holiday, Sabrina* (1954), *Funny Face*, and *Love in the Afternoon* (1957), she was always graceful and beautiful. Although the 1950's are often considered a decade of rigid extremes, it was flexible enough for two such different personalities as Monroe and Hepburn to become icons.

The major male star of the 1950's was Marlon Brando. Along with Montgomery Clift, James Dean, and Paul Newman, he personified the naturalistic Method approach to acting, popularized by the famed Actors Studio. With his patented mumble, relaxed posture, and often slovenly appearance, Brando was unlike anyone before or since, and he had perhaps the greatest impact ever on film acting styles. His performances in *A Streetcar Named Desire*,

Director Billy Wilder (left) issues instructions to actors Audrey Hepburn and Humphrey Bogart on the set of Sabrina *in 1954.* (Hulton Archive | by Getty Images)

Viva Zapata! (1952), *The Wild One* (1953), and *On the Waterfront* are seen by many as among the decade's best films. While the Method acting of Brando and Clift clashed strongly at the beginning of the decade with the traditionally polished Hollywood approach to acting, the two styles showed some signs of merging as the 1950's progressed, with established stars such as Robert Mitchum, in *The Night of the Hunter* (1955), and James Stewart, in the Westerns he made with director Anthony Mann, sometimes incorporating Method techniques.

Another major new star of the 1950's was Sidney Poitier, the first African American leading man. Poitier's roles, from *No Way Out* (1950) and *Blackboard Jungle* to *Edge of the City* (1957) and *The Defiant Ones*, grew increasingly substantial, though he would

have to wait until the more liberal 1960's for his best roles.

The end of the decade also saw the first stars to emerge from television, with James Garner and Steve McQueen receiving their first leading film roles. The impact of television was also seen with the emergence of directors such as John Frankenheimer, Sidney Lumet, Arthur Penn, and Martin Ritt, who had refined their skills directing live television dramas.

Future film director François Truffaut and other critics writing for the noted French film magazine *Cahiers du cinéma* (cinema notebooks) during the 1950's posited what came to be known as the auteur theory. Auteurists claimed that films are works of art reflecting the personalities of their creators and that the films of the best directors display their distinctive styles. This theory, which began having an impact on American film criticism during the 1960's, fittingly developed during an era when many of the directors beloved by the auteurists were doing their best work.

John Ford made *The Quiet Man* and *The Searchers.* Howard Hawks made *Gentlemen Prefer Blondes* and *Rio Bravo* (1959). Fritz Lang made *The Big Heat* and *While the City Sleeps* (1956). Orson Welles, who spent much of the decade acting to finance his film projects, nevertheless made *Touch of Evil.* Alfred Hitchcock was the most productive of all, making *Strangers on a Train* (1951), *Rear Window* (1954), *To Catch a Thief, Vertigo* (1958), and *North by Northwest* (1959). By appearing as the host of his television series *Alfred Hitchcock Presents,* he also became the nation's most recognizable filmmaker.

Impact The American films of the 1950's both reflected and molded the values of the time. Films became increasingly less timid about such matters as sex and race. They acknowledged the previously ignored youth market and quickly recognized the significance of rock and roll. Because Hollywood was being pulled in different directions by conservative and liberal forces and influences, often the decade's films arguably had an almost schizophrenic quality.

However, the impact of 1950's film went beyond technological innovation and socioeconomic issues; the stars, filmmakers, and the entertainment and artistic values of the films themselves were significant draws during this era. Brando, Clift, and Dean changed the way audiences perceived film stars. Here were stars with the same weaknesses and neuroses as the viewers. While many of the award-winning and most popular films of the time seem dated to later audiences, critics argue that the best films by the best directors of the era have endured in their impact and often seem more profound decades later. The filmmakers who emerged during the 1960's and 1970's, such as Francis Ford Coppola, Martin Scorsese, and Steven Spielberg, grew up with these films and were heavily influenced by them. Films such as *Rio Bravo*, *The Searchers*, *Touch of Evil*, and *Vertigo*, whose distinctiveness went unrecognized at the time, are now considered among the greatest ever made.

Further Reading

Biskind, Peter. *Seeing Is Believing: How Hollywood Taught Us to Stop Worrying and Love the Fifties.* Rev. ed. New York: Pantheon Books, 2000. Examination of how films dealt with the social, political, and family tensions of the decade and includes detailed looks at such films as *All That Heaven Allows* and *I Was a Teenage Werewolf* (1957).

Cohan, Steven. *Masked Men: Masculinity and the Movies in the Fifties.* Bloomington: Indiana University Press, 1997. Looks at how male characters evolved from generally aggressive to more domesticated as the decade progressed and discusses the homoerotic subtext in films such as *Pillow Talk*.

Dowdy, Andrew. *The Films of the Fifties: The American State of Mind.* New York: William Morrow, 1973. General overview of the trends of the decade and how Hollywood sold its product.

Harvey, James. *Movie Love in the Fifties.* New York: Alfred A. Knopf, 2001. Argues that films such as *Johnny Guitar*, *Vertigo*, and *Written on the Wind* subverted audience's values and redefined the aesthetics of genres.

Kashner, Sam, and Jennifer MacNair. *The Bad and the Beautiful: Hollywood in the Fifties.* New York: W. W. Norton, 2002. Gossipy look at several controversial films, such as *The Night of the Hunter* and *The Sweet Smell of Success* (1957), and the impact of tabloid journalism.

Leibman, Nina C. *Living Room Lectures: The Fifties Family in Film and Television.* Austin: University of Texas Press, 1995. Includes examinations of how American family life is represented in such films as *Rebel Without a Cause* and *A Summer Place* (1959).

Sterritt, David. *Mad to Be Saved: The Beats, the 1950's, and Film.* Carbondale: Southern Illinois University Press, 1998. *Christian Science Monitor* film critic discusses how Beats and intellectuals were mocked by Hollywood in films such as *Funny Face* and how directors such as Vincente Minnelli and Douglas Sirk were able to bridge the experimental and the mainstream.

Warren, Bill. *Keep Watching the Skies: American Science Fiction Movies of the Fifties.* Jefferson, N.C.: McFarland, 1997. Detailed analyses of science-fiction films from 1950 to 1957.

Michael Adams

See also Academy Awards; Broadway musicals; Censorship; Drive-in theaters; Film in Canada; Hitchcock films; Pay television; Rock and roll; Television in the United States; 3-D movies; War films; Widescreen movies.

■ Fitzgerald, Ella

Identification African American jazz vocalist
Born April 25, 1917; Newport News, Virginia
Died June 15, 1996; Beverly Hills, California

During the 1950's, Ella Fitzgerald, who established herself as a well-known vocalist during the preceding swing era, enjoyed a new surge of popularity, achieving a level of virtuosity and creativity that rivaled the most recognized jazz instrumentalists.

At the beginning of the decade, Ella Fitzgerald's career was in transition. *Gershwin Songs* (1950), her first recording to be released in the new long-playing (LP) format, and her duets with Louis Armstrong were recorded for Decca records, her label from the previous decade. She had just started singing in promoter Norman Granz's "Jazz at the Philharmonic" concerts the year before but remained under obligation to continue recording for Decca. Granz was comparatively well regarded by his artists as someone who treated African American musicians with respect. In 1953, Ella accepted him as her manager. By 1954, which marked her nineteenth year as a professional musician, she had sold twenty-two million records for Decca. Later that year, she performed at the first Newport Jazz Festival and was warmly received.

In 1956, after her contract with Decca expired, Fitzgerald recorded her first LP for Granz's new Verve label, *The Cole Porter Songbook*, which was a great success and was followed quickly by other "songbook" albums, each focusing on a specific songwriter.

Impact Through her prolific recordings, her television appearances, and almost constant touring, Fitzgerald solidified her place at the heart of American musical culture in this decade. She continued to delight audiences all over the world until succumbing to illness in 1996.

Further Reading

Fidelman, Geoffrey Mark. *First Lady of Song: Ella Fitzgerald for the Record.* New York: Birch Lane Press, 1994. Organized by record label, with emphasis on recordings but includes other information and anecdotes.

Nicholson, Stuart. *Ella Fitzgerald: A Biography of the First Lady of Jazz.* New York: Charles Scribner's Sons, 1994. General, comprehensive biography.

John Myers

See also Cole, Nat King; Jazz; Long-playing records; Music; Newport Jazz Festival; Peterson, Oscar; Sullivan, Ed.

■ Flying saucers

Definition Unexplained aerial phenomena

During the 1950's, fascination with flying saucers reflected not only the curiosity of Americans at the dawn of the space age but also their fears of invasion and conquest during the Cold War.

Reports of anomalous objects in the skies of the United States date back at least as far as the nineteenth century. Such objects were first dubbed "flying saucers" in the summer of 1947, when amateur pilot Kenneth Arnold reported seeing metallic objects flying in formation over Mount Rainier in Washington State. A reporter coined the term "flying saucers" when he mistook Arnold's description of how the objects moved through the air—as flat objects skim across water—for a description of their shapes. The misnomer was maintained in media and public usage, however, and Americans routinely used it in discussing the frequent sightings of airborne oddities throughout the decade, regardless of the shape of the purported objects.

A popular debate raged across North America about the validity of witnesses' claims, with skeptics attributing the accounts to hoaxes, lies, hallucinations, and misidentification of conventional aircraft and meteorological phenomena. "Believers" tended to see the saucers as craft, probably extraterrestrial spaceships piloted by visitors from other planets.

Tales and Texts Flying-saucer reports during the 1950's offer some of the most colorful stories in the history of what has come to be called "ufology" (the study of UFOs, or Unidentified Flying Objects, which became a less sensational phrase later adopted by both skeptics and believers alike). For example, one night in September of 1952, a saucer supposedly set down on a hilltop in Flatwoods, West Virginia, discharging a strange mist, a fetid odor, and a tall, monstrous humanoid alien with fiery orange eyes that chased a woman and some children who had come to investigate. In August of 1955, members of a family were allegedly besieged in their house in a remote region near Hopkinsville, Kentucky, by a band of hideous, goblinlike aliens with clawed hands.

Such stories inspired much derision during the decade; however, it is also true that the 1950's witnessed some of the more credible UFO incidents to date as well as the publication of some of the most credible and serious-minded investigations into the mystery. For example, photos of metallic-looking disks speeding through foggy skies near McMinnville, Oregon, in May of 1950, resisted debunking as a hoax or depiction of conventional objects. In the summer of 1952, a widely publicized spate of sightings in Washington, D.C., provided dozens of credible witnesses, and the objects sighted actually registered on local radar screens.

Both the American and Canadian governments set up official entities to investigate saucer sightings—Project Grudge in the United States, Project Second Storey in Canada—and a retired Marine Corps officer, Major Donald Keyhoe, wrote a number of best-selling books on the subject, including

The Flying Saucers Are Real (1950) and *Flying Saucers from Outer Space* (1953). In 1959, Swiss psychologist Carl Jung, who remains the most respected figure ever to undertake an investigation of the subject, wrote *Flying Saucers: A Modern Myth of Things Seen in the Skies.* In it, Jung considered sightings from the standpoint of mythic and psychological archetypes but without wholly ruling out the possibility that some saucers may represent a physical reality.

Hopes of Contact, Fears of Conquest As reports of sightings appeared in newspapers and magazines around America, flying saucers also became a major presence in films of the decade that reflected the era's worries about communist infiltration and Soviet invasion. Film after film—including *Invaders from Mars* (1953), *Earth vs. the Flying Saucers* (1956), and *Invasion of the Saucer Men* (1957)—dealt explicitly both with imminent threats of violent attacks on America by outsiders and with subtler, insidious invasions by "fifth-columnists" of otherworldly origin.

One of the best of the era's saucer films—*The Day the Earth Stood Still* (1951)—demonstrated an opposite reaction to the phenomenon, one of a near-religious hope for planetary redemption. In this film, a messianic alien lands his flying saucer in Washington, D.C., to preach a gospel of brotherhood and pacifism. This movie captured the spirit of a reaction that contrasted quite sharply with fears that many Americans held of invasion and conquest by "others": The hope that saucer aliens would prove to be "Space Brothers," highly advanced humanoids that could save Earth from war, pollution, greed, and nuclear annihilation. This interstellar gospel of good will was spread by colorful prophets and pundits such as George Adamski, Truman Bethurum, and Orfeo Angelucci, who claimed contact with the saucer beings and presented themselves as the aliens' messengers, sent forth to proclaim doctrines of nonviolence and the essential confraternity of all sentient beings. Dubbed "contactees," these people traveled America throughout the decade giving lectures on the dangers of war and nuclear weapons and regaling their audiences both with accounts of tours of the solar system that they had taken with their alien friends and with reports of the tranquillity of the utopian societies on the saucer beings' home worlds.

Impact As humanity began to venture out into space during the late 1950's, it was only natural that curiosity about what was "out there" would consume Americans. In many ways, the flying-saucer mythos of the decade constituted a popular, folkloric manifestation of that curiosity, but, more important, it mirrored the fears of conquest by outsiders and destruction by nuclear warfare that haunted people during this era. Moreover, in the tales of the contactees, flying-saucer lore addressed Americans' hopes and dreams that perhaps their current problems might have a peaceful outcome.

Further Reading

Evans, Hilary, and Dennis Stacy. *UFOs 1947-1997: Fifty Years of Flying Saucers.* London: John Brown, 1997. A concise history by two UFO historians and investigators, containing a very thorough chapter on the phenomenon during the 1950's.

Peebles, Curtis. *Watch the Skies! A Chronicle of the Flying Saucer Myth.* Washington, D.C.: Smithsonian Institution Press, 1994. A thorough history of the topic from a skeptical viewpoint.

Rux, Bruce. *Hollywood vs. the Aliens: The Motion Picture Industry's Participation in UFO Dis-information.* Berkeley: Frog, 1997. A worthwhile analysis of saucers and aliens in films, which includes interesting information on 1950's saucer films.

Thompson, Keith. *Angels and Aliens: UFOs and the Mythic Imagination.* New York: Addison-Wesley, 1991. An overview from a folklorist's standpoint.

Thomas Du Bose

See also Army-McCarthy hearings; Atomic bomb; Cold War; Comic books; *Day the Earth Stood Still, The; Destination Moon;* Fads; *Forbidden Planet; Invasion of the Body Snatchers;* Pulp magazines; Space race; *Sputnik I; Thing from Another World, The.*

■ Food for Peace

Identification Agricultural surplus program created under Public Law 480
Date Signed into law on July 10, 1954

Food for Peace created markets for large postwar farm surpluses, while providing food to nations in need.

During World War II, U.S. agricultural policies were designed to achieve maximum food production for Americans, their soldiers, and many of the war-torn countries around the world. When the war ended, farming was resumed throughout the world, and, as a result, the U.S. produced huge quantities of agricultural commodities for which the demand was woefully inadequate.

The specter of drastically deflated farm prices generated policy responses during the late 1940's and early 1950's that sought to restore the supply-and-demand balance through government supply controls and price supports. However, Section 416 of the Agricultural Act of 1949 provided that food could be purchased by the U.S. government and given to foreign countries through humanitarian organizations. This demand-side approach to agricultural surpluses was included and expanded in Public Law 480, the Agricultural Trade Developmental and Assistance Act of 1954, which came to be called "Food for Peace."

The main objectives of the Food for Peace program were to establish markets for U.S. agricultural surpluses to foster economic development and to alleviate hunger in foreign countries. Another important objective was to further U.S. interests in the Cold War by mitigating the appeal of communism in recipient nations. These objectives were to be met through the provisions of the program's three main sections. Title I of Public Law 480 provided that surplus agricultural products could be bought by foreign governments with low-interest, long-term loans that were to be repaid with local currency. The uses of this currency had to include creating new markets for U.S. agricultural commodities, promoting economic development, and paying U.S. government expenses in the purchasing country. Titles II and III provided both for famine relief by government agencies and private organizations and for barter arrangements involving surplus food.

Impact Food for Peace was viewed by many Americans during the 1950's as an effective mechanism for addressing some important economic and humanitarian concerns. U.S. exports to foreign markets created by Public Law 480 increased continuously during the 1950's, amounting to tens of millions of tons and representing one-third of the value of all U.S. agricultural exports during that decade. There was also clear evidence that world hunger and malnutrition had been reduced and the progress of development enhanced in developing nations.

However, this program was not without its critics. Some economists claimed that low-cost imports depressed farm prices in importing countries, creating disincentives for increasing domestic production while simultaneously increasing prices for U.S. consumers because of the increase in demand created by the program. Additionally, U.S. allies, including Canada, the world's second largest grain producer, complained that low-cost Food for Peace exports made it impossible for them to compete effectively with their own exports.

Subsequent Events Since the 1950's, there have been numerous amendments to Public Law 480, such as the 1966 requirement that payments must be made in U.S. dollars rather than local currency. In 1996, Public Law 480 was amended, reauthorizing it for seven years with its original objectives essentially intact. Under a new agricultural law passed in 2001, Food for Peace was reauthorized through 2011. Since 1954, the program has provided billions of tons of agricultural commodities to more than one hundred countries.

Further Reading

Hopkins, Raymond F. "Reform in the International Food Aid Regime: The Role of Consensual Knowledge." *International Organization* 46, no. 1 (1992): 225-264. A comprehensive discussion of the provisions and objectives of the Public Law 480 food aid program of the 1950's, and how those original objectives were subsequently questioned and modified because of economic analyses and political dynamics.

Singer, Hans W. *The Challenge and the Opportunity.* Oxford, England: Clarendon Press, 1987. Summarizes and reviews early food aid programs, including those during the 1950's, and emphasizes the objectives of using food assistance to foster economic development and avoiding possible negative effects in developing nations.

Jack Carter

See also Agriculture in Canada; Agriculture in the United States; Bowles, Chester; Cold War; Farm subsidies; Foreign policy of Canada; Foreign policy of the United States; International trade of Canada; International trade of the United States.

■ Football

With the televising of professional games and the growth of teams across the country, football expanded its fan base throughout the decade.

The American game of football evolved from the older game of rugby shortly after the Civil War. Football was initially a collegiate sport, with matches between the Ivy League schools. It was considered dangerous, and in the wake of a series of exposés detailing the rash of injuries caused by the sport, President Theodore Roosevelt convened a meeting at the White House in October, 1905, during which he urged colleges to institute changes to make the sport safer. Following the death of a player later that year, and in response to the negative publicity about the violence, the universities created the Intercollegiate Athletic Association to help monitor the sport. In 1910, the organization became the National Collegiate Athletic Association (NCAA), which had authority to adopt rules changes. Football became increasingly popular across college campuses, and by 1920, as the National Football League (NFL) began operations, there were a number of semiprofessional clubs.

The Professional Game Over the next two decades, football continued to grow. Although it did not match baseball as a spectator sport, football nonetheless had a wide fan base. The sport, particularly the professional game, took off during the 1950's. More than anything else, the marriage of football and television explains the American public's new awareness of the game. The Chicago Bears were the first team to have their home games televised, during the 1947 season, and three years later, the Los Angeles Rams had their entire season telecast. NFL games were nationally televised on the DuMont network during the 1951 season, but it was not until 1955 that the National Broadcasting Company (NBC) began showing NFL games. League owners were wary at first about the effect television might have on attendance; however, those fears proved groundless. Average NFL game attendance in 1950 stood at 25,000; ten years later the figured was more than 40,000.

The NFL was divided into eastern and western divisions during the 1950's, with six to seven teams in each division. The Detroit Lions dominated the league during the early part of the decade, winning the league championship in 1950, 1952, and 1953. Led by Doak Walker, a Heisman Trophy winner from Southern Methodist University who led the NFL in scoring twice in his six-year career, Detroit dominated its competition. The New York Giants and Cleveland Browns were two of the other top franchises, with the teams winning two championships each during the decade.

Integration The NFL racially integrated a year before Jackie Robinson played his first Major League Baseball game. In 1946, the Los Angeles Rams signed running back Kenny Washington, a former star at the University of California at Los Angeles (UCLA). The signing of Washington reversed a twelve-year period during which the NFL had no black players on its rosters. At its inception in 1933, the NFL had included black players, but after the 1933 season, the owners adopted an informal policy of not signing black athletes. The Rams added Washington and future film actor Woody Strode to their roster, and the Cleveland Browns also had two African American players in 1946. Many of the other franchises soon ended their white-players-only policy, with the glaring exception of the Washington Redskins, whose owner, George Preston Marshall, was believed by many to be responsible for instituting the segregation policy. Marshall stubbornly refused to sign any black players until 1962, when the Kennedy presidential administration refused to allow his team to play in the new District of Columbia stadium; Marshall finally relented.

For the most part, integration progressed smoothly in the NFL, but during the 1956 season, there were still only thirty-four African Americans on NFL rosters. In 1957, the Cleveland Browns drafted African American running back Jim Brown of Syracuse. A powerful runner with sprinter's speed, Brown quickly became the NFL's best player. During his rookie season, Brown won rookie-of-the-year honors and was named an all-pro. He rushed for more yards than any other player and would eventually lead the league in rushing in eight of his nine seasons. When Brown retired in 1965, he held numerous records, including most rushing yards, most touchdowns scored, and most yards per carry.

The NFL Comes of Age The biggest event for the NFL during the decade was the December, 1958, championship game between the New York Giants and the Baltimore Colts. Going into the game, the Giants had come off a tough victory over the powerhouse Cleveland Browns. The Colts, who had joined the NFL in 1953, were the underdogs, though the team had an array of talent, with a roster that included quarterback Johnny Unitas, wide receiver

Raymond Berry, and defensive linemen "Big Daddy" Lipscomb, Art Donovan, and Gino Marchetti. Played at Yankee Stadium, where the Giants had moved two years earlier, the game attracted 64,185 fans. Some thirty million Americans tuned in on television, but most of the people in the New York metropolitan area could not watch the contest in their own homes because of the NFL's strict blackout policy. In a close match, the Colts battled back in the last few minutes of regulation to tie the score and send the game into overtime. Halfback Alan Ameche scored the winning touchdown on a one-yard run, giving the Colts a 23-17 victory and their first-ever championship. The game instantly became a classic and marked the emergence of football as a sport that rivaled baseball in popularity.

As professional football gained in popularity and grew increasingly profitable for the owners, cities across the country vied for the chance to get a new franchise. Texas multimillionaire Lamar Hunt applied for a franchise during the late 1950's, but his request was rebuffed. In response, Hunt started his own league, the American Football League (AFL).

The College Game The collegiate game did not experience the same growth during the 1950's, and the period was a time of trouble for college football. Because of rising costs, several schools simply disbanded their programs, including Georgetown, Catholic University, and the City College of New York. The Ivy League universities did not go that far, but they decided to deemphasize football: The schools dropped football scholarships and prohibited players from attending postseason bowl games.

A number of scandals called into question the integrity of the college game. Two major incidents raised particular concern. The College of William and Mary admitted that it had altered high school transcripts and assigned grades to football players who had not actually taken the classes. At West Point, thirty-seven cadets, including the coach's own son, were thrown out of the school after they admitted violating the university's honor code. Several of the players had cheated on their exams, while the others had failed to report their knowledge of the cheating. The sordid exposures forced the NCAA to make major changes. After World War II, the NCAA created the "Sanity Code" to regulate recruiting practices and the doling out of athletic scholarships. However, the numerous scandals demonstrated how ineffective those rules were. After scrapping the Sanity Code, the NCAA created a membership committee, which could investigate allegations of misconduct and penalize schools found to be in violation of NCAA rules. One of the major changes the NCAA instituted was the decision to allow schools to grant scholarships without having to justify need for the student.

On the field, the programs from the major conferences retained their customary places atop the polls. Big Ten powerhouse Michigan State captured consecutive national titles in 1951 and 1952. The Oklahoma Sooners, coached by Bud Wilkinson, won three national championships and at one point had a winning streak of forty-seven games. The streak came to an end in November of 1957, when visiting Notre Dame, an eighteen-point underdog, upset Oklahoma 7 to 0. Notre Dame, perhaps the nation's most storied program, struggled throughout most of the decade, although it claimed a national championship in 1953.

Cleveland Browns quarterback Otto Graham (14) scores a touchdown against the Los Angeles Rams in the 1955 NFL championship game, which Cleveland won, 38 to 14. (AP/Wide World Photos)

The number of postseason bowl games expanded during the decade. The Liberty Bowl and the Blue Bonnet Bowl were two of the games that were added to the postseason schedule. The bowl games generated huge revenues for the colleges. Television played an instrumental role in the increase of the bowls. Just as pro-football owners did, the NCAA expressed concern about the effect television might have on attendance figures. In 1951, the Big Ten Conference issued a mandate prohibiting the televising of any Big Ten games; earlier the same year, the NCAA recommended a ban on televising games live. A battle ensued, with the NCAA eventually allowing the broadcasting of a few games, although there were several blackouts on Saturdays during the season. Eventually the NCAA relented and allowed regional and national broadcasts.

College coaches continued to emphasize the running attack. At Oklahoma, Bud Wilkinson used the T formation and many teams adopted the wing formation. Programs placed less emphasis on the passing game, as evidenced by the combined 195 passing yards per team on average for the college game in 1958. By comparison, teams averaged 333 yards rushing per contest. Not until the early 1980's would teams average more yards through the air than on the ground.

The stars during the decade were running backs. The Heisman Trophy, the annual award given by the New York Downtown Athletic Club, was won by a running back during every year of the decade except 1954, when fullback Alan Ameche captured the award. The scoring system underwent significant changes in the last part of the decade. For the first time in nearly fifty years, the NCAA made alterations in the scoring policies. In a controversial 1958 decision, the rules committee established a change that allowed teams to attempt two-point conversions after touchdowns—a rule change that would later be copied by the AFL and NFL. After 1959, field goals became a far more significant aspect of the collegiate game. The rules committee widened the field goal posts by five feet to twenty-three feet, four inches, a move that led to more field goals being attempted and the development of the placekicker as a significant player on the roster.

Impact As the 1950's ended, football was on a solid footing and stood poised for even more growth. In 1960, a rival league, the American Football League,

began operations. Attendance figures rose steadily throughout the 1950's, at both the professional and collegiate levels. The college game had weathered turmoil but retained its loyal following.

Subsequent Events The AFL began its first season in 1960. The league had a television contract with ABC, and the Houston Oilers signed Heisman Trophy-winner Billy Cannon from Louisiana State University. Originally ignored by the NFL, the AFL would soon sign some of the best collegiate graduates and also begin bidding for NFL players. The two leagues did not compete against each other on the field until January, 1967, when the NFL's Green Bay Packers defeated the AFL's Kansas City Chiefs. The two leagues merged in 1970, by which time their annual championship game was known as the Super Bowl. By the middle of the 1970's, football had overtaken baseball as America's most popular spectator sport.

Further Reading

Peterson, Robert W. *Pigskin: The Early Years of Pro Football.* New York: Oxford University Press, 1997. A short but lively study of the National Football League, with a strong analysis of how television transformed the game in American culture.

Ross, Charles K. *Outside the Lines: African Americans and the Integration of the National Football League.* New York: New York University Press, 1999. Ross details the integration of the NFL and the struggles African Americans had after 1946.

Watterson, John Sayle. *College Football: History, Spectacle, Controversy.* Baltimore: Johns Hopkins University Press, 2000. An excellent summary of college football from its origins.

Justin P. Coffey

See also Baseball; Basketball; Brown, Jim; Oklahoma football team; Soccer; Sports; Television in the United States; Unitas, Johnny; West Point honor code scandal.

■ *Forbidden Planet*

Identification Science-fiction film adapted from a William Shakespeare play and set on a remote planet
Director Fred McLeod Wilcox (1905-1964)
Date Released in 1956

Combining a venerable plot with sophisticated production values, this comparatively high-budget film thrilled audi-

ences of the mid-1950's with its special effects and challenged them with its ideas.

Forbidden Planet recasts English playwright William Shakespeare's play about a marooned magician and his daughter, *The Tempest* (1611), on the imaginary planet Altair-IV in the twenty-third century. A United Planets spaceship, in the form of a flying saucer, arrives to determine the fate of an earlier mission. However, the crew find only two survivors, Dr. Morbius (played by Walter Pidgeon) and his daughter Altaira (Anne Francis), who are being waited upon by an ingenious robot.

Morbius explains to the cruiser's commander, John J. Adams (Leslie Nielsen, who would later win fame in comic roles), that the rest of the mission's crew died at the hands of a savage, invisible monster. Later he reluctantly reveals an underground network built by a vanished race known as the Krell and boasts that he has used one of their machines to "boost" his own intelligence. Adams realizes that the doctor's own energized id is the "monster" that killed his colleagues and that has now begun attacking Adams's crew.

Impact Aside from Walter Pidgeon, the cast of *Forbidden Planet* was unremarkable. However, its psychological theme, spectacular imagery, and otherworldly soundtrack set it apart from most science-fiction films of the decade. It influenced films and television series for decades to come and is considered one of the primary inspirations for the 1960's television series *Star Trek*.

Further Reading

Harris, Steven B. "A.I. and the Return of the Krell Machine: Nanotechnology, the Singularity, and the Empty Planet Syndrome." *Skeptic* 9, no. 3 (2002): 68-79. Harris argues that *Forbidden Planet* is important for the questions it raises about advanced technologies.

Kennedy, Harlan. "Prospero's Flicks." *Film Comment* 28 (1992): 45-59. Kennedy discusses several filmed adaptations of *The Tempest*, including *Forbidden Planet*.

Grove Koger

See also *Captain Video; Day the Earth Stood Still, The; Destination Moon;* Film in the United States; Flying saucers; *Invasion of the Body Snatchers; Sputnik I; Thing from Another World, The; War of the Worlds, The.*

■ Ford Thunderbird

Identification Luxury-oriented automobile model

Date Entered the consumer market on October 22, 1954

Ford, with its introduction of the Thunderbird, became the first car manufacturer to create the market segment for personal luxury cars. The car became the trendsetting automobile of the 1950's and defined personal status during the decade of consumer excess.

The concept for the Thunderbird—named after a mythical bird of great power and beauty in Indian lore—reflected the American public's passion for automobiles during the early 1950's, an era during which there existed a significant interest in V-8 engines and performance, European sports cars, and California's leisure lifestyle. As a result, the first Thunderbird mixed a touch of European influence, a hood scoop, "frenched headlights," and fender louvers. Despite occasional marketing references to it as a sports car, Ford created a unique niche by calling it a "personal luxury car" in the hope that it could distinguish the Thunderbird from its primary American rival, the Chevrolet Corvette from General Motors (GM).

In the fall of 1952, Ford's chief designer, Frank Hershey, learned of the GM Corvette project, and with assistance from William Boyer, he began work on a car that would have a distinctive American and Ford appearance. Initially the car was named after Henry Ford's estate, Fairlane, but after an employee contest, the name "Thunderbird" was assigned to the car. Compared to the Corvette's six-cylinder engine and automatic transmission, the Thunderbird had a V-8 engine, both manual and automatic transmission options, and a level of comfort that included power steering, brakes, seats, and windows. The spartan Corvette, fitted with side curtains instead of roll-up windows, simply could not match the Thunderbird for luxury and comfort. After its unveiling, interest in the two-seat Thunderbird, with its clean styling, luxurious comforts, and V-8 refinements, was immediate.

Impact Given the era's affluence and desire for status-oriented consumer goods, it was no surprise that the introduction of the 1955 Thunderbird was a huge success, easily filling a market niche. Actor

The first model of the Ford Thunderbird featured a wrap-around windshield, fender skirts, and modest tail fins. (AP/Wide World Photos)

Clark Gable was photographed in his 1955 Thunderbird cruising Hollywood; Marilyn Monroe owned a 1956 model painted in Sunset Coral. The car's preeminence with noted Hollywood celebrities was only one indication of its success during the decade. Initially a two-seat car, the roadster eventually was changed to four seats after the public indicated it wanted a car with more passenger and cargo room. The revamped 1958 Thunderbird was an instant success, and it was named *Motor Trend Magazine*'s Car of the Year in 1958.

Further Reading

Boyer, William P. *Thunderbird: An Odyssey in Automotive Design.* Dallas, Tex.: Taylor, 1986. An important history written by one of the early designers of the Thunderbird.

Gunnell, John, ed. *T-Bird: Forty Years of Thunder.* Iola, Wis.: Krause, 1995. A history of the car containing detailed information.

John A. Heitmann

See also Automobiles and auto manufacturing; Chevrolet Corvette; Edsel; General Motors; Interstate highway system; Volkswagen.

■ Foreign policy of Canada

Canadian foreign policy during the 1950's vacillated between Canada's strong alliance with the United States and its opposition to the Soviet Union and international communism and Canada's efforts to be an independent nation with its own policies distinct from those of the United States.

Canada emerged from World War II in a relatively strong defense position, holding the world's fourth largest military. However, in terms of its foreign policy, Canada was in an awkward position. Traditionally, as a member of the British Empire, its closest ally always had been Great Britain. In fact, the war demonstrated that Canada could no longer depend solely on Britain to defend its security. The obvious successor in that role was the United States, and as early as 1940, Canada pursued a closer defense relationship with it. This shift, however, meant a movement toward continentalism, an approach prior Canadian governments had resisted historically because of the potential for Canada's domination by the much larger and more powerful United States.

A Multilateral Approach Considered by the international community as a "middle power," Canada lacked the strength to impose its will by acting unilaterally. Instead, it had to balance its close and dependent relationship with the United States through a policy of multilateralism, which encouraged collective security by active participation in a wide range of international organizations. For a Canada long ruled by a series of administrations controlled by the Liberal Party, strength came in numbers and—beginning in 1945 with Louis St. Laurent's tenures first as minister of external affairs and, in 1948, as prime minister—an increasingly activist foreign policy.

Aspects of the multilateral approach, carried out by St. Laurent and his successor as minister of external affairs, Lester Pearson—individuals who would dominate Canadian foreign policy during the 1950's—were evident by the end of the war. For instance, Canada played an active role in the development of the United Nations. It was also an enthusiastic supporter of the Commonwealth, made up of those nations that once were part of the British Empire. The Canadian government provided twenty-five million dollars and additional support toward the 1950 Colombo Plan, which was designed to foster democracy among the Commonwealth's Asian nation members. Finally, during the late 1940's, with heightened Cold War tensions, the Canadian government enthusiastically participated in the development of the North Atlantic Treaty Organization (NATO). The national government's enthusiasm for the new alliance went beyond expected military benefits as the government pushed for, ultimately unsuccessfully, an economic component to the new alliance.

Canada's desire for multilateralism and collective security, combined with a belief in Cold War anti-

Brigadier General Jean Allard, the commanding officer of the Canadian Brigade in Korea, and Colonel K. L. Campbell, read about the truce in the Korean War in the American servicemen's newspaper, Stars and Stripes, *in August, 1953.* (Hulton Archive | by Getty Images)

communism, made Canadian participation in the United Nations effort in Korea in 1950 almost inevitable. The national government initially hesitated, however, out of concern that Korea was a cover for a communist military strike elsewhere in the world. Anticommunism was significant in determining governmental policy during this era, as it meant that even the politically important province of Quebec, who historically opposed overseas Canadian military intervention in three previous wars, supported Canadian involvement in the conflict on the Korean peninsula. Cutbacks to the Canadian military that had occurred after World War II were reversed by the government of St. Laurent, and eventually 26,791 soldiers fought in Korea with more than one thousand suffering wounds and 518 dying. Behind the scenes, the Canadian government, to the occasional chagrin of U.S. leaders, attempted to assert influence over American policy toward the Korean War, arguing against both the use of nuclear weapons and the singling out of China as an aggressor.

The 1956 Suez Crisis served as an additional test of the St. Laurent government's multilateral principles since it—much to the unhappiness of many Canadians, the media, and the main opposition party—pitted Canada against its oldest friend and ally, the United Kingdom. Canada cooperated with Israel in its confrontation with Egypt over that country's nationalization of the canal, a stance that was in opposition to Britain and France's military involvement in the matter.

The United States, a nation with increasing influence over Canadian policy, also stood in opposition to Egypt, Britain, and France. Articulating Canada's position to the international community was Minister of External Affairs Lester Pearson. During the crisis, Pearson flew to New York and participated in the debate in the U.N. General Assembly. It was during this period that Pearson proposed the creation of a permanent United Nations' peacekeeping force composed of military units of member countries to handle similar disputes in the future. In early November, 1956, all fifty-seven members of the United Nations supported Pearson's plan. Canadian soldiers would be among the first peacekeepers, and for his efforts, Pearson received the 1957 Nobel Peace Prize.

Canada faced one other foreign policy crisis in 1956: the Soviet invasion of Hungary, which crushed a reformist movement that had proved popular across the country. Although a military response was out of the question, Canada did accept approximately 37,000 Hungarian refugees who fled as a result of Soviet intervention.

A Shift to Continentalism Although multilateralism was important to Canadian foreign policy during the 1950's, Canada's relationship to the United States remained critical. Even the policy of multilateralism was, in practical terms, a response to Canada's position vis-à-vis the United States. Canada's economy had become increasingly tied into its southern neighbor, although efforts at creating a free trade zone between the two nations during the late 1940's failed when the Canadian government backed away from negotiations as a result of fears of a loss of sovereignty. Nonetheless, Canada's economic dependence on the United States as a market for its products only grew during the 1950's. By the first part of the decade, 59 percent of Canadian exports went to the United States, which, in turn, was responsible for 70 percent of Canadian imports. Particularly significant during the Cold War were exports of Canadian natural resources, such as uranium, aluminum, and zinc, destined for use by the American military.

A key to Canadian foreign policy during this era was the country's military relationship with the United States. U.S. leaders, fearing the potential of a nuclear strike borne by Soviet bombers, focused on Canada as the chief Soviet attack route in the event of war. One result of this preoccupation was three separate radar systems built in Canada at the behest of the United States and with continual controversy surrounding their financing and which country would oversee their control. The Canadian government held that any defense establishments on its soil had to be under domestic control and that any American military presence should be minimized or be solicited by Canada. Such a stance proved impractical given the state of the world, and by the middle of the decade as many as fifteen thousand U.S. soldiers were in Canada. Furthermore, in places such as the American base in Newfoundland, U.S. governmental institutions such as the post office and the Internal Revenue Service operated and subjected Canadian civilian employees to the American legal system.

The first radar system to be built, the Pinetree Network, was in service to the north beyond major

Canadian cities by 1954; it stretched from Vancouver Island to Newfoundland. When the United States requested another line farther north, the Canadian government developed the Mid-Canada Line in 1957. American military planners still sought additional security and requested a radar system in the Arctic. That project, the most famous of the three, became known as the Distant Early Warning (DEW) line and was operational by 1959. Built along the seventieth parallel, it featured forty-two radar stations across the Canadian north.

The subject of nuclear weapons remained a contentious one between the governments of the two countries. Canada had not pursued diligently a nuclear weapons program for itself, but American defense strategists envisioned Canada as the ideal storage area for American nuclear weapons. As a means of encouraging further military integration, the U.S. government encouraged Canada to engage in talks to formalize the defense relationship between the two nations. Eventually, an agreement was formed, initially by the St. Laurent government and then formally ratified by the government of Prime Minister John Diefenbaker.

Nationalism and the Diefenbaker Era The growing alliance between Canada and the United States worried many Canadian nationalists, who feared their country's loss of independence in a wide number of arenas. In 1957, a special commission perpetuated these fears when it warned of the growing American control over Canada's economy. A figure who portrayed himself as resisting this trend was John Diefenbaker, leader of the Progressive Conservative Party and elected as prime minister in 1957.

Although generally friendly with the administration of American president Dwight D. Eisenhower, Diefenbaker, a committed Anglophile, criticized the St. Laurent government's position during the Suez Crisis and expressed concern about his country's growing dependence on its southern neighbor. In turn, he announced that his government intended as one of its foreign policy objectives to shift 15 percent of Canada's trade away from the United States and toward Britain. Diefenbaker's promise had been a mere rhetorical flourish since in practice, such a fundamental economic shift was nearly impossible.

Equally contradictory to the United States was the Diefenbaker administration's defense policy. Ignoring the rest of the federal cabinet, Diefenbaker

and his defense minister made the decision to ratify the North American Air Defense Command (NORAD) agreement, inaccurately portraying it, perhaps deliberately, as being nothing more than an extension of the generally popular NATO. Moreover, the Diefenbaker administration was faced with having to decide whether to proceed with the production of a Canadian-designed advanced fighter aircraft, the Avro Arrow. In the end, the government canceled the program for practical economic reasons: the aircraft would be too expensive to produce. The choice, however, meant using American-built Bomarc surface-to-air missiles, designed to carry nuclear warheads, a path that ultimately tied Canada more closely to the United States.

Impact Despite being a middle power, Canada's foreign policy, primarily because of the nation's geographic proximity to the United States, was of international significance during the 1950's. The country not only played a leading multilateral role in conjunction with its allies but also with a wider group of countries through the United Nations. Canada's foreign policy from that decade contributed to international peacekeeping plans, which remains a lasting legacy in international affairs. However, in terms of Canada's relationship to its closest ally, the United States, its foreign policy during the 1950's would see, despite occasional efforts to the contrary, a growing integration into the military and economy of the superpower next door.

Further Reading

Hilliker, John, and Donald Barry. *Coming of Age.* Vol. 2 in *Canada's Department of External Affairs, 1946-1968.* Montreal: McGill-Queen's University Press, 1995. An institutional look at both the governmental department responsible for generating Canadian foreign policy and some of the policy it has generated.

Hillmer, Norman, and J. L. Granatstein. *Empire to Umpire.* Toronto: Irwin, 1994. A history of Canada's foreign policy.

_____. *For Better or for Worse: Canada and the United States to the 1990's.* Toronto: Copp Clark Pitman, 1991. A specialized look at Canada's historical relationship with the United States.

Whitaker, Reg, and Steve Hewitt. *Canada and the Cold War.* Toronto: James Lorimer, 2003. A popular examination of some of the key Cold War events, including several that occurred during the 1950's.

Whitaker, Reg, and Gary Marcuse. *Cold War Canada: The Making of a National Insecurity State, 1945-1957.* Toronto: University of Toronto Press, 1994. A detailed examination of Canada, in particular its foreign policy, during the early years of the Cold War.

Steve Hewitt

See also Avro Arrow; Canada and Great Britain; Canada as a middle power; Diefenbaker, John G.; Food for Peace; Israel; Korean War; North American Aerospace Defense Command; North Atlantic Treaty Organization; Pearson, Lester B.; St. Laurent, Louis; Suez Crisis; United Nations.

■ Foreign policy of the United States

During the Cold War of the 1950's, the American goal of preventing the expansion of communism required large military budgets and resulted in participation in the Korean War as well as growing involvement in numerous places throughout the world.

The presidential administrations of Harry S. Truman and Dwight D. Eisenhower pursued foreign policies that were designed to protect national security and promote national interests. Although emphasizing the containment policy, which meant the attempt to prevent the expansion of communism, both administrations were committed to avoiding any direct military confrontation with the Soviet Union or China. They also attempted to encourage the expansion of democracy and human rights, but such idealistic concerns were secondary to concerns of American military and economic power. In order to oppose communism, U.S. officials did not hesitate to cooperate with authoritarian and dictatorial regimes that disregarded human rights.

By the end of the 1940's, the United States had abandoned many of its traditional tenets in foreign policy, most notably its isolationism and neutrality toward foreign conflicts. Although there were always a few dissenting voices, most political leaders of the 1950's agreed on the basic assumptions of the Cold War. Before the Republican victory of 1952, Republican politicians commonly criticized President Truman's policies as being too conciliatory toward communist countries. When Eisenhower became president, however, his administration made only modest changes in the policies pursued by the previous administration. In the presidential elections of 1956 and 1960, Democratic candidates did not challenge the assumptions of Eisenhower's foreign policies. Likewise, most influential journalists and intellectuals accepted the Cold War approach to foreign policy.

The Soviet Threat and Nuclear Deterrence After the firm establishment of the containment policy in 1947, U.S. foreign policy centered on the perceived threat of the Soviet Union. President Truman greatly distrusted Soviet intentions, and following the Potsdam Conference of 1946, he never expressed any interest in having another meeting with the Soviet dictator Joseph Stalin. In the election of 1952, Republican candidate Eisenhower occasionally spoke of "rolling back" the Iron Curtain. After he took office, his anticommunist secretary of state, John Foster Dulles, even asserted the need of going to the "brink" of war, if necessary. When Soviet troops invaded Hungary in 1956, however, the Eisenhower administration never considered giving support to the Hungarian freedom fighters because officials recognized the awful consequences of a nuclear war between the two superpowers.

The Eisenhower administration formulated a "New Look" in defense strategy, which emphasized nuclear weapons and delivery systems. Eisenhower and his advisers believed that deterrence based on the threat of "massive retaliation" was less costly than reliance on large armies and conventional weapons. Defense Secretary Charles Wilson argued that nuclear power provided more "bang for the buck." The Soviet Union responded by building up its own nuclear arsenal. In 1957, when the Soviets launched *Sputnik I,* a rocket-launched satellite, Congress quickly approved a huge increase in space research. Eisenhower, nevertheless, correctly insisted that the United States possessed overall nuclear superiority.

Despite his anti-Soviet statements, Eisenhower wanted to reduce tensions between the two superpowers. After Stalin died in 1953, the emergence of a more moderate Soviet leader, Nikita Khrushchev, allowed for a lessening of tensions. At the Geneva Conference of 1955, the conciliatory tone led to optimistic references to "peaceful coexistence" and "the Spirit of Geneva." When the Paris Conference began in May, 1960, the prospects for a ban on nuclear testing appeared promising. However, the shooting down of a U-2 spy plane over Soviet territory resulted in a failed conference and promoted an expanded arms race. By the time Eisenhower left office in early 1961, the United States had installed seventy-two intercontinental ballistic missiles and launched a Polaris submarine carrying nuclear weapons.

Anticommunist Policies in Asia Americans were shocked when Chinese communists, led by Mao Zedong, established the People's Republic of China (PRC) in October, 1949. Even though President Truman refused to recognize the PRC, many Republicans, including Wisconsin senator Joseph McCarthy, charged that Truman and procommunist officials in the State Department had lost China. The Democrats reacted to these charges by resolving not to follow policies that could be characterized as soft on communism. When it appeared that China would be a close ally of the Soviet Union, the Truman administration emphasized the importance of military and economic cooperation with Japan. In September, 1951, the United States and Japanese governments signed a peace treaty and a mutual security pact.

In June, 1950, the Cold War suddenly became a fighting war, when the Democratic Republic of Korea, a communist country, attacked noncommunist South Korea. The Truman administration immediately assumed that either the Soviet Union or China had instigated the invasion. Without asking for a declaration of war, Truman committed ground troops to support South Korea and obtained a United Nations endorsement for a U.S.-led coalition. In October, the intervention of Chinese troops marked an expansion of the war. General Douglas MacArthur wanted to bomb China and to seek a military victory regardless of the cost. Truman feared that such policies might result in a third world war, and he fired MacArthur for failure to support official policies. The brutal fighting continued until President Eisenhower negotiated an armistice in July, 1953.

Another major communist-inspired conflict took place in Southeast Asia, where Vietnamese nationalists called the Viet Minh, led by Ho Chi Minh, fought to win their independence from France. Because Ho Chi Minh was a communist, President Truman quietly began providing aid to the French. After 1953, President Eisenhower expanded the commitment, warning that the fall of Vietnam would result in the triumph of communism throughout the region (called the "domino theory"). In 1954, when French troops were surrounded by the Viet Minh in the remote village of Dien Bien Phu, members of the administration failed to persuade Eisenhower to intervene militarily.

After the French defeat, the United States joined an anticommunist alliance for the region, the Southeast Asia Treaty Organization (SEATO). The next year, the United States participated in the Geneva Conference, which divided Vietnam along the seventeenth parallel into a communist country in the north and a noncommunist country in the south. Between 1955 and 1961, U.S. assistance to South Vietnam totaled $1 billion. The Eisenhower administration also supported South Vietnam's refusal to hold elections for unifying the country, as promised in the Geneva agreements.

The Middle East and Latin America American officials were determined to protect access to Middle Eastern oil. In 1951, Iran's prime minister, Mohammad Mosadegh, nationalized the country's oil fields and refineries, and he also eliminated the power of Iran's pro-American monarch, Shah Mohammad Reza Pahlavi. American officials viewed Mosadegh's actions as a threat to economic interests in the region. President Eisenhower authorized the Central Intelligence Agency (CIA), headed by Allen Dulles, to finance pro-shah demonstrations and to encourage Iranian army officers to overthrow the Mosadegh regime.

In contrast to President Truman's outspoken support for Israel, the Eisenhower administration attempted to encourage better relations with Arab countries. However, when Arab nationalist Gamal Abdel Nasser came to power in Egypt in 1954, the administration was hostile toward his anti-Israeli and left-leaning policies. In 1956, American refusal to support the construction of the Aswan Dam provoked Nasser to take control over the Suez Canal. When Great Britain, France, and Israel attacked Egypt without consulting American officials, Eisenhower, fearing Soviet intervention, condemned the invasion and stopped oil shipments to England and France. The Suez Crisis came to an end, but the underlying conflict continued.

Although Eisenhower refused to use force against Nasser, he clearly indicated his intentions to actively combat communism in the Middle East. In 1957, Eisenhower persuaded Congress to pass a joint resolution promising assistance to any nation in the region threatened by "any country controlled by international Communism." The resolution, called the Eisenhower Doctrine, seemed to equate communism with left-leaning Arab nationalism. In 1958, Eisenhower ordered five thousand marines to the unstable country of Lebanon, based on reports of a threat from Nasser's supporters. Secretary Dulles claimed that the action prevented a communist victory, but most observers disagreed with his analysis.

Because of geographical proximity, the Eisenhower administration was even more concerned about a possible communist threat in Latin America. In 1954, the CIA supported a coup in Guatemala to remove the leftist government of Jacobo Arbenz, which was replaced with a military dictatorship. In 1959, when leftist Fidel Castro overthrew dictator Fulgencio Batista y Zaldívar in Cuba, Eisenhower was suspicious of the direction of the Cuban Revolution. Following negative responses to his requests for loans from the United States, the Cuban leader began to look to the Soviet Union for assistance. Eisenhower was especially upset by Castro's nationalization of American-owned property: One of his last official acts was to break off diplomatic relations with Cuba, and he also authorized CIA agents to train Cuban exiles to invade the island.

Impact Among historians, there is much disagreement about the wisdom of the foreign policies of the Truman and Eisenhower administrations. Those endorsing the so-called orthodox perspective interpret the policies as a defensive reaction to the Soviet attempts to expand communist hegemony. In contrast, those holding to the "revisionist" viewpoint argue that Soviet policies were defensive in nature, and radical revisionists hold that the engine behind American foreign policy was economic greed. A small minority of historians support an additional perspective, arguing that General MacArthur was correct in calling for more aggressive policies in pursuit of victory in Korea and elsewhere.

The Eisenhower administration introduced the use of covert operations by the CIA. Although the interventionist policies in Guatemala and Iran worked in the short term, they resulted in bitter feelings that would have serious repercussions for years thereafter. The two operations encouraged the CIA to expect that an invasion of Cuba could also be successful, but wishful thinking and poor planning would

result in a major foreign policy fiasco: the Bay of Pigs invasion of 1961.

During the 1950's, the Soviet model of communism had international appeal because it seemed to present a practical way for poor countries to achieve greater prosperity. Given the economic interests and dominant ideology of the United States, it was probably inevitable that the government opposed the further expansion of communism. Nevertheless, in dealing with the Soviet Union, the Truman and Eisenhower administrations alternated between reliance on military threat and attempts to reduce tensions—a process that would continue until the fall of the Soviet Union in 1991. In the case of Vietnam, officials in charge of foreign policy unduly minimized the role of Vietnamese nationalism. By the time that Eisenhower left office in 1961, the foundations for later American participation in the Vietnam War were firmly in place.

Further Reading

Alteras, Isaac. *Eisenhower and Israel: U.S.-Israeli Relations, 1953-1960.* Gainsville: University Press of Florida, 1994. A detailed account of the Suez crisis and its impact on U.S. relations with Israel.

Arnold, James. *First Domino: Eisenhower, the Military, and America's Intervention in Vietnam.* New York: William Morrow, 1991. A detailed study showing how the policy decisions of Truman and Eisenhower began the process of involvement in the Vietnam quagmire.

Bowie, Robert, and Richard Immerman. *Waging Peace: How Eisenhower Shaped an Enduring Cold War Strategy.* New York: Oxford University Press, 1998. Argues that the Eisenhower administration succeeded in formulating coherent and sustainable policies for preventing Soviet expansion and mitigating Soviet hostility.

Brown, Seyom. *The Faces of Power: United States Foreign Policy from Truman to Clinton.* New York: Columbia University Press, 1994. An interesting book that discusses policy decisions from the perspective of how officials have viewed their adversaries and options.

Divine, Robert. *Eisenhower and the Cold War.* New York: Oxford University Press, 1995. A clearly written and interesting synthesis that generally endorses Eisenhower's containment policies, which are viewed as a combination of idealism and pragmatism.

Melanson, Richard, and David Mayer, eds. *Reevaluating Eisenhower: American Foreign Policy in the Fifties.* Urbana: University of Illinois Press, 1990. Includes a variety of interpretive essays about the diplomatic and military policies of Eisenhower and John Foster Dulles.

Offner, Arnold. *Another Such Victory: President Truman and the Cold War, 1945-1953.* Stanford, Calif.: Stanford University Press, 2002. Highly critical of Truman's anticommunism, Offner views Mao Zedong as a "populist" despot and considers Stalin obsessed by legitimate concerns of national security.

Paterson, Thomas, and J. Garry Clifford. *America Ascendant: U.S. Foreign Relations Since 1939.* Lexington, Mass.: Heath, 1995. A clear and concise summary from a revisionist perspective, criticizing U.S. policy makers for their anticommunism and support for right-wing dictators.

Rabe, Stephen. *Eisenhower and Latin America: The Foreign Policy of Anticommunism.* Chapel Hill: University of North Carolina Press, 1988. A study of how the Cold War affected U.S. policy toward Latin America, with an emphasis on revisionist interpretations.

Schlesinger, Arthur, Jr., and Richard Rovere. *General MacArthur and President Truman: The Struggle for Control of American Foreign Policy.* New York: Farrar, Straus, & Giroux, 1965. A dramatic and classic account of the controversy about whether to expand the war by attacking China and using troops from Taiwan.

Thomas Tandy Lewis

See also Acheson, Dean; Central Intelligence Agency; Cold War; Cuban Revolution; Dulles, John Foster; Eisenhower Doctrine; Guatemala invasion; Isolationism; Israel; Korean War; Latin America; Lebanon occupation; North Atlantic Treaty Organization; Organization of American States; Southeast Asia Treaty Organization; Truman Doctrine.

■ Formosa Resolution

Identification Federal legislation regarding U.S. foreign and military policy in Asia

Date Signed on January 29, 1955

As a means to prevent communist expansion in East Asia, the Formosa Resolution became part of Cold War foreign policy and set a precedent by allowing congressional advance authorization for a president to deploy U.S. forces in overseas conflicts.

The U.S. Congress adopted the Formosa Resolution during the first Taiwan Strait Crisis, which began in September, 1954, when the People's Republic of China (PRC) commenced the artillery bombardment of the islands of Jinmen and Mazu. The bill authorized President Dwight D. Eisenhower to utilize U.S. armed forces to defend Taiwan and nearby islands against armed attack. Eisenhower also received power to protect "such related positions and territories of that area now in friendly hands" as he determined was necessary or appropriate to secure their defense. Moreover, to secure U.S. interests in the region, the resolution identified the need for friendly governments to possess the Western Pacific island chain that included Taiwan.

In January, 1955, Eisenhower asked Congress to pass the Formosa Resolution after PRC forces threatened to seize several islands 200 miles north of Taiwan, which were under control of the Nationalist government ruled by Chiang Kai-shek. Drafters of the legislation purposely included elastic language in order to authorize U.S. action to defend Nationalist-held offshore islands without specifically naming them. Following a strategy of deterrence, Eisenhower wanted to signal to both the PRC and the Soviet Union that the United States would protect its vital security interests and defend the Republic of China on Taiwan, especially because the Senate had yet to ratify the U.S.-China Mutual Defense Treaty signed the prior December. Some Democrats in Congress doubted the wisdom of a U.S. commitment to defend the offshore islands, but the vote for passage was 410 to 3 in the House and 85 to 3 in the Senate.

Impact The Formosa Resolution strengthened the United States' political and military connection with the Republic of China on Taiwan. The Eisenhower administration later relied on it to justify protecting Jinmen and Mazu during the Taiwan Strait Crisis of 1958.

Further Reading

Accinelli, Robert D. *Crisis and Commitment: United States Policy Toward Taiwan, 1950-1955.* Chapel Hill: University of North Carolina Press, 1996. A balanced and judicious study that demonstrates how the Formosa Resolution provided a way for the Eisenhower administration to assume a firm stand against communist expansion in East Asia but at the price of formalizing the previously avoided U.S. commitment to defend Taiwan.

Chang, Gordon. *Friends and Enemies: The United States, China, and the Soviet Union, 1948-1972.* Stanford, Calif.: Stanford University Press, 1990. This thorough account of the early Cold War shows that the United States began to pursue a partnership with the Soviet Union against China long before the Nixon administration adopted the policy of détente.

James I. Matray

See also Chiang Kai-shek; China; Cold War; Congress, U.S.; Dulles, John Foster; Eisenhower, Dwight D.; Foreign policy of the United States; Korean War; Southeast Asia Treaty Organization; *Ugly American, The*; United Nations.

■ FORTRAN

Identification First popular high-level computer programming language
Date Designed in 1954

Before the development of the FORTRAN (Formula Translating System) compiler, most programming was done in machine or assembly language to generate small efficient code modules since computers were slow and had little memory. The first FORTRAN compiler produced code that was almost as efficient as that written in machine language and demonstrated that programming in a high-level language was feasible.

In 1953, John W. Backus and a team of programmers from International Business Machines Corporation (IBM) started a project to develop a high-level language for its 700 series of computers. By 1954, the name FORTRAN was adopted as an abbreviation for IBM's FORmula TRANslating System. The FORTRAN I compiler was developed in 1957 for the IBM 704 computer. It had most of the features of later FORTRAN compilers, including variables, arrays, and functions. FORTRAN was primarily developed to support scientific programming with applications coming from areas such as matrix algebra, linear programming, and differential equations.

FORTRAN II added the ability to compile program and subprogram modules separately, which was a major addition to the FORTRAN language. FORTRAN III added few new features and was never

released to the public. FORTRAN IV was developed from 1958 to 1961 and was the standard version of FORTRAN for the next ten years.

Impact FORTRAN demonstrated that it was possible to have a user-friendly, high-level language that generated efficient machine code. The other compilers of the 1950's, such as ALGOL and COBOL, leaned heavily on the concepts of Backus's FORTRAN compiler.

Further Reading

Backus, John. "ENIAC: The History of FORTRAN I, II, and III." *IEEE Annals of the History of Computing* 20, no. 4 (1998): 68-78. Complete description of the development of FORTRAN.

Sammet, Jean. *Programming Languages: History and Fundamentals.* Englewood Cliffs, N.J.: Prentice Hall, 1969. Excellent overview of FORTRAN with historical comments.

George M. Whitson III

See also Computers; ENIAC computer; International Business Machines Corporation; Science and technology; UNIVAC computer.

■ Freberg, Stan

Identification American satirist, comedian, and advertising executive
Born August 7, 1926; Los Angeles, California

In his recorded albums and television appearances, Stan Freberg brought a satirical approach to comedy and helped bridge the mediums of radio and television.

Stan Freberg got his start in show business as a voice for cartoon characters for Warner Bros. and other Hollywood studios during the 1940's, when he was recently out of high school. After World War II, he played guitar and wrote comedy sketches for comedian Redd Foxx, whose band allowed him to utilize his talents. Freberg's record "John and Marsha," a parody of contemporary soap operas, consisted of two characters endlessly repeating each other's names in varying tones. He next moved to television, where he was voice, puppeteer, and writer for *Time for Beany*, a precursor of *Sesame Street*. He went on to lampoon the popular *Dragnet* series with "St. George and the Dragonet," an album that he recorded for Capitol Records.

Freberg then turned to writing parodies of popular songs. Among his targets were Johnnie Ray's

"Cry," Eartha Kitt's "C'est Si Bon," and the hits of Lawrence Welk. In his version of the Platters' "The Great Pretender," Freberg added hiccups and a pianist unwilling to play "kling-kling-kling jazz"; Harry Belafonte's "Banana Boat Song" was also subjected to ridicule. His most outrageous parody was his "Green Chritma," an attack on materialism and consumerism which Capitol was unwilling to release. Verve Records released it and it became a big hit. Freberg also had trouble getting Capitol to release his parodies of the television shows of Arthur Godfrey and Ed Sullivan, and he had to water down his parody of Senator Joseph McCarthy.

Impact Freberg, who often "crossed the line" with his criticism of popular culture, went on to advertising during the 1960's but remained one of the 1950's most gifted parodists. His album *Stan Freberg Presents the United States of America* (1961) was a hit, and in 1988 "A Child's Garden of Freberg," a compilation work, was released. Many comedians and actors, including the likes of Sir Anthony Hopkins and Tom Hanks, have memorized some of his work and praised his comedic talent.

Further Reading

Freberg, Stan. *It Only Hurts When I Laugh*. New York: Crown, 1988. Freberg's career in his own words.

Nachman, Gerald. *Seriously Funny: The Rebel Comedians of the 1950's and 1960's*. New York: Pantheon Books, 2003. Explores the ways in which comedians of the era redefined the approach to comedy and performance by employing cynicism, satire, and a new awareness of socially relevant topics.

Thomas L. Erskine

See also Belafonte, Harry; Caesar, Sid; Kovacs, Ernie; Lehrer, Tom; Radio; Sahl, Mort; Television in the United States.

■ Freed, Alan

Identification Radio disc jockey
Born December 15, 1921; Windber, Pennsylvania
Died January 20, 1965; Palm Springs, California

Alan Freed introduced a generation of young white people to African American rhythm-and-blues music, which he called "rock and roll," and became a pivotal figure in pop-music history.

Alan Freed is sometimes credited with inventing the term "rock and roll," which he used in reference to

Alan Freed at his new WABC disc jockey job in New York City in June, 1958. (AP/Wide World Photos)

rhythm-and-blues music. Freed was a journeyman disc jockey when a Cleveland record store owner suggested he play "black music" to white teenagers. "Moondog's Rock and Roll Party" debuted on radio station WJW in July, 1951. Freed's musical taste and hyperactive on-air personality won him many fans. In 1952, he organized the "Moondog Coronation Ball," considered to be the first rock concert.

In September, 1954, Freed moved to WINS in New York. His nightly "Rock and Roll Party" soon became the city's most popular program. During the 1950's, white artists recording for major labels often "covered" songs by black singers on independent labels. Freed insisted on playing the original versions, enabling black musicians such as Chuck Berry and Fats Domino to become major stars. A tireless promoter of rock-and-roll music and himself, Freed hosted stage shows and two television programs and appeared in five musical films. He was attacked by conservatives for corrupting young people.

Freed's legal troubles began in 1958, when he was charged with "incitement to riot" after violence erupted outside his Boston stage show. Although the charges were eventually dropped, his contract was not renewed by WINS. However, he bounced back on WABC, a larger station. Freed added to his problems by drinking excessively and associating with organized crime figures. In November, 1959, he was accused of accepting money to play records ("payola"), payments which he claimed were "consulting fees." Fired by WABC for the scandal, his career was destroyed. In 1962, he pleaded guilty to commercial bribery and was fined three hundred dollars. After two unsuccessful comeback attempts, he died of cirrhosis of the liver at age forty-three.

Impact Alan Freed was the best known of the white disc jockeys who first played black music on mainstream radio stations. A tragically flawed man, he forever changed popular music and indirectly affected race relations in the United States. In 1986, he was part of the first class inducted into the Rock and Roll Hall of Fame.

Further Reading

Altschuler, Glenn C. *All Shook Up: How Rock 'n' Roll Changed America.* New York: Oxford University Press, 2003. Places rock-and-roll music in the context of the cultural conservatism of 1950's America and emphasizes the effects of race and class on the genre.

Fong-Torres, Ben. *The Hits Just Keep on Coming: The History of Top 40 Radio.* San Francisco: Backbeat Books, 2001. Provides behind-the-scenes stories of the decade's most popular disc jockeys, including Freed.

Jackson, John A. *Big Beat Heat: Alan Freed and the Early Years of Rock and Roll.* New York: Schirmer, 1991. The definitive biography of Alan Freed.

Lloyd K. Stires

See also Berry, Chuck; Domino, Fats; Little Richard; Music; Radio; Rock and roll; *Rock Around the Clock*; Top 40 radio; Youth culture and the generation gap.

■ *From Here to Eternity*

Identification Novel set during World War II
Author James Jones (1921-1977)
Date Published in 1951

A best-selling novel about the lives of enlisted men, along with the people with whom they interact, in the U.S. Army on the eve of World War II. Critics and audiences alike lauded it for its unglamorous portrayal of war as well as the beauty and power of its narrative.

James Jones served in the United States Army from 1939 to 1944 and rose to the rank of sergeant. He was at Pearl Harbor when the Japanese attacked. He was injured in combat on Guadalcanal in the South Pacific. A decorated soldier, Jones was awarded the Bronze Star and Purple Heart.

From Here to Eternity probes the effects of World War II on the individual soldier. Private Robert E. Lee Prewitt and Sergeant Milton Anthony Warden are the principal protagonists whose lives are defined by power, sexuality, and violence. The army in which they serve is a mirror of American society during the Great Depression: a class-oriented institution populated by automatons and sadists, as well as individuals and philosophers. The rebellious Prewitt and conservative Warden represent the two futures of the working class: the revolutionary and the conformist. In the end, Jones suggests there is no future for the revolutionary in the United States, an apparent parable for an America under the threat of McCarthyism during the 1950's.

Impact *From Here to Eternity* topped the national best-seller lists in 1951, became a Book-of-the-Month Club selection, and won a National Book Award in 1952. Its 1953 film adaptation garnered an Academy Award for Best Picture. For many Americans, *From Here to Eternity* came to symbolize the contradictions, fears, and hopes of their wartime experiences.

Further Reading

Beidler, Philip D. *The Good War's Greatest Hits: World War II and American Remembering.* Athens: University of Georgia Press, 1998. Provides a thoughtful analysis of the cultural influences on the nation's collective memory of the war. Included is a study of the transformation of *From Here to Eternity* from best-selling novel to top-grossing film.

Fussell, Paul. *Wartime: Understanding and Behavior in the Second World War.* Oxford: Oxford University Press, 1989. An insightful study of the World War II experience, which echoes many of the themes in Jones's novel.

Paul D. Gelpi, Jr.

See also Academy Awards; Clift, Montgomery; Film in the United States; Literature in the United States; Sinatra, Frank; Uris, Leon; War films.

G

■ Gaines, William M.

Identification American comic book and magazine publisher
Born March 1, 1922; New York City
Died June 3, 1992; New York City

William M. Gaines revolutionized the comic book field during the 1950's with his comics that emphasized crime and horror and with MAD *magazine.*

In 1950, William M. Gaines, publisher of the unsuccessful Entertaining Comics (EC) line, instituted a series of well-written and well-drawn horror, war, crime, and science-fiction comic books. These titles made EC one of the best-regarded and influential lines of comics during the 1950's. Most famous and controversial were the horror comics such as *Tales from the Crypt,* with their gruesome and shocking covers. In 1952, Gaines began publishing *MAD,* a parody and satire comic that ridiculed various forms of popular culture. However, disagreements with the Comics Code Authority (CCA) caused Gaines to discontinue his comic book line in 1954, while *MAD* continued as a magazine.

Impact Gaines's early career was affected by the decade's controversies regarding popular culture and its alleged impact on American youth: Psychologists and others argued that crime and horror comic books, like those Gaines published, caused juvenile delinquency. Gaines testified before the Senate Committee on Juvenile Delinquency on comic books' role in this issue. The comic book industry instituted the CCA in 1954 to regulate comics, causing a downturn in the comics field and eventually driving Gaines out of comics. However, his production of satirical bombast made a lasting impact on other irreverent popular media throughout later decades.

Further Reading

Jacobs, Frank. *The Mad World of William Gaines.* Secaucus, N.J.: L. Stuart, 1972. The only full-length work on Gaines.

Wright, Bradford W. *Comic Book Nation: The Transformation of Youth Culture in America.* Baltimore: Johns Hopkins University Press, 2001. A well-regarded history of comics, which discusses EC Comics and its place in 1950's American culture.

Anthony J. Bernardo, Jr.

See also Capp, Al; Censorship; Comic books; *MAD*; Youth culture and the generation gap.

■ Gallup polls

Definition Means of surveying a particular group of people using standardized questions and conducted by the organization founded by George Gallup, Sr.

George Gallup, Sr., achieved unprecedented success during the 1950's by applying scientific methods to the polling process. The success of polls during this decade offered policy makers accurate readings of current attitudes and a historical perspective of major social trends. It assured pollsters a continuing role in the political process.

After 1900, polls had been used sporadically to assess public sentiments. Early polling consisted of unsystematic questioning of unspecified people who happened to be available. In 1935, George S. Gallup, Sr., began to employ the new approach of "scientific polling," in which the sample of people questioned did not have to be large, but it had to be chosen to reflect the members of an entire group, including important subgroups. Gallup polls first won acclaim in 1936 by predicting President Franklin D. Roosevelt's election victory. In 1948, Gallup suffered a humiliating setback by incorrectly predicting the defeat of presidential candidate Harry S. Truman.

Political Uses As a result of this error, Gallup modified his procedures during the 1950's. He polled preferences in presidential contests continuously until the eve of the election. Gallup no longer selected his samples by choosing a quota of cases from each subgroup but instead selected samples by a random process from the entire population.

During the 1950's, Gallup's predictions in presidential elections were notably successful. Dwight D. Eisenhower's approval ratings in polls—usually in the 60- to 70-percent range—predicted his two electoral victories. Polls during 1958-1959 anticipated the close 1960 presidential race by documenting a fluctuating 50-50 percentage split between John F. Kennedy and Richard M. Nixon. In contrast, President Harry S. Truman's 1950-1952 approval ratings stayed in a dismal 20- to 30-percent range; the president judged by historians as "near great" had the poorest poll ratings of all.

During the 1950's, political leaders began, more than before, to take poll results seriously. Eisenhower's 1952 selection as the Republican candidate over established Republican politicians was influenced greatly by his dramatic 70-percent approval ratings. The "man of peace" theme in Eisenhower's 1952 campaign was introduced after poll results showed that by a majority of 52 to 25 percent, Americans called the Korean War a "mistake." Senator Joseph McCarthy's wild accusations of communist infiltration lost any power to intimidate after polls in August of 1954 showed that most Americans rated him "unfavorably."

Reflecting Social Change The Gallup polls also reflected some of the broader social trends of the 1950's. A majority of Americans supported equal pay for women when they did the same work as men but continued to prefer such occupations as "physician and engineer" for sons and "nurse and secretary" for daughters. A modest majority supported racially desegregating schools yet stated they would not vote for an African American presidential candidate. Polls reflected a traditional country, but one that contained the seeds of change.

Impact The decade's successful use of polls assured them a continuing place in business and political life, and Gallup acquired an international reputation. Increasingly, political leaders commissioned private polls. Critics of the day charged that too many politicians were tempted to rely on favorable poll ratings as the sole criterion of their success. Gallup himself was well aware that the ultimate success of policies depended upon future consequences, not measures of current popularity. The contemporary political climate required that leaders not only reflected popular opinion but also sought to change it.

Further Reading

Bradburn, Norman M., and Seymour Sudman. *Polls and Surveys: Understanding What They Tell Us*. San Francisco: Jossey-Bass, 1988. A thorough but readable discussion of the techniques of polling. It views Gallup polls in the context of other survey techniques.

Eisinger, Robert M. *Evolution of Presidential Polling*. Cambridge, England: Cambridge University Press, 2002. Chronicles how presidents from Franklin D. Roosevelt onward have used public polls to further their policies and campaigns.

Gallup, George H. *The Gallup Poll: 1935-1971*. New York: Random House, 1972. This series of volumes describes the results of actual Gallup polls organized chronologically by date. Volume 2 describes poll results during the 1950's.

Thomas E. DeWolfe

See also Eisenhower, Dwight D.; Elections in the United States, 1952; Elections in the United States, 1956; Kennedy, John F.; Korean War; McCarthy, Joseph; Nielsen ratings; Nixon, Richard M.; School desegregation; Truman, Harry S.

■ General Motors

Identification Largest automobile manufacturing company in the world during the 1950's

During the economic boom of post-World War II in the United States, General Motors (GM) capitalized on the great demand for cars fostered by the new interstate highway system and the increasing popularity of suburbs. GM owned not only automobile companies but also the companies that made the components of automobiles. General Motors believed that what was good for General Motors was good for America.

In the 1950's, automobile use mushroomed, with the number of vehicles in use increasing by more than seven million from 1951 to 1959. Planned obsolescence ensured that cars were replaced regularly, and greater national prosperity meant that families often bought a second car—the decade saw an 8 percent increase in the number of families owning two cars.

General Motors capitalized on the 1950's car culture; it was a conglomerate consisting of five sepa-

Workers assembling Chevrolet station wagons at the General Motors plant in Euclid, Ohio, in August, 1950. The wood-sided models being assembled are examples of the cars later known as "woodies." (AP/Wide World Photos)

rate automobile companies as well as many of the companies that provided supplies needed to make the cars, such as spark plugs and ball bearings. The company became the first corporation in history to gross one billion dollars in a single year, and in some years, General Motors sold more cars than all its competitors combined. At the end of the decade, when GM's influence was waning, imports accounted for 8 percent of total American automobile sales, but GM continued to hold 42 percent of the U.S. market, leaving 50 percent to be divided among the other manufacturers—Ford, Chrysler, and American Motors.

During the 1950's, carmakers strove to create unique identities for their automobiles, and GM was no exception. Its Oldsmobile, Buick, Pontiac, Cadillac, and Chevrolet models each had an individual identity, with the different models easily distinguishable from one another. Design elements, often unnecessary, flourished on these cars during the decade. Huge tail fins decorated some models, as did bullet bumpers and round air vents, with lots of

chrome and white-wall tires adding status to cars. Air conditioning and automatic transmission were available on all cars. The V-8 engine, while relatively lightweight, was big and powerful. All 1950's-era cars were heavy gas guzzlers, but gasoline was plentiful, and gas consumption was not an issue at the time. Many of the cars were modeled after the sleek style of an airplane, and the word "aerodynamic" soon became synonymous with "modern styling."

Chevrolet was both the cheapest and the most popular of the General Motors cars; it, by itself, was the largest corporation in the United States. By 1960, there were forty-six Chevrolet models, thirty-two engine types, twenty transmissions, twenty-one colors, and more than four hundred accessories.

Decline of General Motors By the end of the 1950's, several trends adversely affected the fortunes of General Motors. Compact cars were becoming popular. Although GM introduced its Chevrolet Corvair model in 1959 for the 1960 model year, that car was riddled with problems. It handled badly, largely because of all the compromises made to keep costs down. Lawsuits that resulted from problems with the car plagued GM well into the 1960's. Moreover, the German Volkswagen company, at which American automobile executives initially had sneered, was making a dent in the American market. The cars' style stayed the same each year, which meant that replacing parts was easy. Volkswagens were inexpensive to buy, and service was good. While the Volkswagen was slow to become popular in the United States, it soon had a dedicated following of people who in turn were not buying GM cars. Finally, the top management at GM changed fundamentally; instead of executives who knew and loved cars, GM's new executives came from business divisions and not the creative or technical divisions.

Impact In its 1950's heyday, GM was the standard by which corporations in the United States measured themselves and against which all automobile companies tried to compete. Because of its size and dominance in the automobile market, GM came to symbolize to the world American industrial might. However, the philosophies that drove the company— planned obsolescence and "bigger is better"— became outmoded, which contributed to its demise.

Further Reading

Farber, David. *Sloan Rules: Alfred P. Sloan and the Triumph of General Motors.* Chicago: University of Chicago Press, 2002. This history of General Motors focuses on the corporation in its prime, which includes the 1950's.

Halberstam, David. *The Fifties.* New York: Fawcett-Columbine, 1993. Gives the reader a fascinating look inside the design studios and boardrooms of General Motors, as well as detailing the American psyche in relation to cars.

Keller, MaryAnn. *Rude Awakening: The Rise, Fall, and Struggle for Recovery of General Motors.* New York: Morrow, 1989. Keller details the history of General Motors, focusing on what made General Motors great, what brought it down, and how it attempted to recover in subsequent decades.

Tracy E. Miller

See also Advertising; Affluence and the new consumerism; AFL-CIO merger; Automobiles and auto manufacturing; Business and the economy in the United States; Chevrolet Corvette; Chrysler autoworkers' strike; Edsel; Ford Thunderbird; Volkswagen.

■ Genetics

Definition Science that explains the control of heredity by means of genes, or discrete sequences of DNA, and the proteins that these genes instruct our cells to make

The science of genetics made giant strides in North America and elsewhere during the 1950's. At the start of the decade, there was a lack of universal agreement even as to the chemical nature of genes. At the conclusion of the decade, it was known that genes are composed of deoxyribonucleic acid (DNA). Furthermore, the mechanism by which genes express themselves as observable traits had also been established.

During the early twentieth century, genetics became established as an important branch at the heart of biology. By 1920, it was recognized that genes are distinct particles arranged on chromosomes, thread-like bodies in the nuclei of cells. The American biologist Thomas H. Morgan helped to establish the important concept of the gene-chromosome theory. During the 1940's, Americans George Beadle and Edward Tatum proposed the one-gene/one-enzyme hypothesis, which stated that genes express themselves by producing enzymes (proteins) that control the eventual expression of particular traits.

Despite these and other advances of the early twentieth century, one major puzzle remained unsolved by 1950: What is the chemical nature of the gene? Conventional wisdom seemed to point toward proteins as the likely compound. Nevertheless, continued research pointed increasingly to DNA as the substance in which information is encoded.

The DNA Molecule During the early 1950's, scientists hurried to elucidate the nature of the DNA molecule. It was two young and relatively unknown scientists who would soon become famous for their work on DNA: American James D. Watson and British scientist Francis Crick. Drawing on the experimental work of others, in 1953 they proposed the double-helix model of DNA. The Watson-Crick model is useful because it explains the nature of genes and how they function. Specifically, the Watson-Crick model explains the diversity of the millions of genes of all living organisms, how genes replicate or duplicate, and how genes express themselves as visible traits, or phenotypes.

From Watson and Crick's model, it became understood that each molecule of DNA consists of two helices (spirals), each wound around the other. Each helix is composed of alternating phosphate and sugar (deoxyribose) units. Connecting these helices are bases arranged in pairs, which connect a sugar on one side with one on the other, like the rungs on a twisting ladder. As a result of the size and shapes of the bases and the constant distances between the sugars, the base adenine pairs only with the base thymine, and the base guanine only with the base cytosine. However, each pair can be reversed, left to right, making a total of four kinds of "stair-steps" arranged in a linear fashion along the long DNA molecule. The pairs thus act as an alphabet in which the sequence of base pairs stores information much as the sequence of letters in an English-language sentence contains meaning depending on the way in which letters are arranged.

This information then passes from the DNA molecule to a molecule of ribonucleic acid (RNA), "copying" the genes of the DNA molecule in a process called translation. In this process, the RNA leaves the nucleus and moves to the cytoplasm, where it becomes attached to a ribosome. There, the RNA directs the assembly of a chain of amino acids, eventually becoming a long protein molecule. Subsequently, the protein enzymes produced in this way control a series of biochemical reactions, which result in a particular end product, or a compound. For example, a compound can be the pigment that accumulates and results in a trait such as brown eyes in a human or red eyes in a fruit fly.

All organisms, from bacteria to plants to humans, use this same basic mechanism for passing information from the genes in the nucleus to a ribosome of the cytoplasm to the synthesis of proteins. This basic concept, which became crystallized during the 1950's, came to be called the Central Dogma of molecular biology.

Impact The basic research of the 1950's set the stage for increasingly sophisticated and useful scientific advances that were to follow in the field of genetics. The Human Genome Project, which had mapped the entire human genome by 2003, held great promise for medical applications. Because of the monumental advances of the 1950's, crops later were able to be genetically engineered and animals cloned, and scientists continued to work toward the prevention or treatment of diseases via the manipulation of genes.

The widespread testing of atomic bombs following World War II, especially by the United States and the Soviet Union, was of great concern to many geneticists and other scientists. In 1954, leading genetics researcher A. H. Sturtevant expressed a legitimate concern about the effects of low doses of high energy radiation resulting from testing of bombs on human heredity. He emphasized that such effects, though subtle, may have long-lasting effects on humans for centuries. These types of warnings from 1950's-era scientists helped the scientific and medical communities understand that excessive and unnecessary exposure to harmful radiation should be averted.

Further Reading

Edelson, Edward. *Francis Crick and James Watson and The Building Blocks of Life.* New York: Oxford University Press, 2000. A fascinating account of the biologists' work to uncover the mysteries of DNA.

Inglis, John R., Joseph Sambrook, and Jan Witkowski, eds. *Inspiring Science: Jim Watson and the Age of DNA.* Cold Spring Harbor, N.Y.: Cold Spring Harbor Laboratory Press, 2003. Colleagues and friends of Watson contribute anecdotes about their experiences of working with him, giving a good context to the era of DNA discovery.

Magner, Lois. *A History of the Life Sciences.* New York: Marcel Dekker, 2002. Places the advances in genetics in historical perspective.

Peters, James A., ed. *Classic Papers in Genetics.* Englewood Cliffs, N.J.: Prentice-Hall, 1959. Presents eight contemporary publications in genetics.

Thomas E. Hemmerly

See also DNA (deoxyribonucleic acid); Nobel Prizes; Ribonucleic acid (RNA); Science and technology; Watson, James D.

■ Geneva Summit Conference

The Event Meeting of major world leaders to discuss world issues and to ameliorate Cold War tensions

Date July, 1955

Place Geneva, Switzerland

High-level negotiations between leaders of France, Great Britain, the Soviet Union, and the United States offered the possibility to reduce Cold War tensions. However, the summit did not resolve existing issues and disputes.

The Cold War confrontation between the Soviet Union and Western democratic countries began soon after the end of World War II. Disputes over territory, a continuing and expanded arms race, deployment of opposing military forces, and rival ideological systems threatened world peace.

Americans during the 1950's had to adjust to living with the potential dangers of nuclear war. However, the decade occasionally provided hopeful signs that suggested that the great powers might succeed in reducing postwar tensions—a new American president was elected in 1952, while in 1953, Soviet leader Josef Stalin's death brought new officials to power in that country, and the Korean War ended. Moreover, several agreements in 1954 and 1955 dealt with trouble spots in Europe and Asia. Combined, these events suggested greater world political stability and positive changes in the Cold War climate.

The chief delegates to the Geneva Summit Conference, from left to right: Soviet premier Nikolai Bulganin, U.S. president Dwight D. Eisenhower, French premier Edgar Faure, and British prime minister Anthony Eden. (National Archives)

A meeting in Geneva, Switzerland, of prominent government officials in July of 1955 exemplified this trend. U.S. president Dwight D. Eisenhower, French premier Edgar Faure, and British prime minister Anthony Eden represented the western democracies. Premier Nikolai Bulganin and Communist Party head Nikita Khrushchev led the Soviet delegation. The summit was the first face-to-face meeting of the top leaders of these nations since 1945, an event that added to the optimism among the public. The discussions, often described as cordial, lasted nearly a week. Photographs showed the leaders in friendly poses, leading many to speak hopefully of the "spirit of Geneva" and the possibility of finding solutions to disputes.

Topics and Negotiations The summit talks considered many important topics, especially the troublesome subject of a divided Germany. Negotiations for possible reunification of the two German regions through democratic elections initially looked hopeful, but further negotiations following the Geneva meeting failed to achieve either elections or unification.

Another major topic dealt with reducing weapons systems. Public opinion in the United States optimistically hoped for a successful reduction or elimination of growing stockpiles of destructive nuclear weapons, a task that would require meaningful and comprehensive inspections of military sites in nations possessing nuclear weapons. President Eisenhower proposed an "open skies" plan at Geneva to achieve this objective. The Soviet Union rejected the details to implement the proposal, and the plan failed. The Soviet government also called for the end of the western defense alliance, the North Atlantic Treaty Organization (NATO), a demand the Western states rejected.

Impact The Geneva Summit promised more than it could produce. While helpful in bringing important leaders together, the "spirit of Geneva" could not break the Cold War impasse. Major issues could not be resolved easily or quickly. In 1956, the situation deteriorated with the continued nuclear arms race, including the development of long-range missiles, and the Soviet military intervention in Hungary. By the end of the decade, tensions between the West and the Soviet Union had intensified.

In the aftermath of Geneva, the American public understood that the Cold War would continue.

Their optimism gradually faded, recognizing that future crises could lead to a conflict that might escalate into nuclear conflagration.

Further Reading

Bischof, Gunter, and Saki Dockrill, eds. *Cold War Respite: The Geneva Summit of 1955.* Baton Rouge: Louisiana State University Press, 2000. Provides details and interpretations of the Geneva meeting.

Eisenhower, Dwight D. *Mandate For Change, 1953-1956.* Garden City, N.J.: Doubleday, 1963. The American president describes the Geneva meeting and its significance.

LaFeber, Walter. *America, Russia, and the Cold War, 1945-2000.* Boston: McGraw-Hill, 2002. This comprehensive and readable survey of Cold War issues and crises includes discussion of the Geneva summit.

Taylor Stults

See also Cold War; Disarmament movement; Dulles, John Foster; Eisenhower, Dwight D.; Foreign policy of the United States; Kennan, George F.; North Atlantic Treaty Organization; Warsaw Pact.

■ *Gentlemen Prefer Blondes*

Identification Film about a woman who wants to marry for diamonds
Director Howard Hawks (1896-1977)
Date Released in 1953

Gentlemen Prefer Blondes *featured the first scene ever filmed in CinemaScope as well as an outstanding performance by Marilyn Monroe as Lorelei Lee, which made her famous.*

Gentlemen Prefer Blondes, a female buddy film, was one of the most popular, funny, and sexy musicals of the 1950's and featured outstanding performances by Marilyn Monroe and Jane Russell as showgirls looking for husbands. It was a box-office hit largely because of Monroe and Russell's sexy, wicked comic timing and for its over-the-top song-and-dance numbers. Monroe made history as she danced sensuously in a dazzling, vivid pink strapless dress while singing "Diamonds Are a Girl's Best Friend."

Gold digger Lorelei Lee and her companion Dorothy Shaw (played by Russell), set off for a luxury cruise to Paris, France. Dorothy flirts with the men on the ship, singing and dancing with the male Olympic team, yet remains protective of the naïve

Marilyn Monroe (left) and Jane Russell posing for a dance number in Gentlemen Prefer Blondes. *(AP/Wide World Photos)*

Lorelei, who is planning to marry for love and for diamonds. Hawks, who was one of the most outstanding directors of the 1950's, gave this film snappy dialogue with the perfect balance of sex and humor, although he made certain that the women never lost respect as they romped their way toward marriage.

Impact This film was a turning point in the career of Marilyn Monroe, who won *Photoplay*'s best-actress-of-the-year award for both *Gentlemen Prefer Blondes* (1953) and *How to Marry a Millionaire* (1953).

Further Reading

Beauchamp, Cari, and Mary Anita Loos, eds. *Anita Loos Rediscovered: Film Treatments and Fiction by Anita Loos, Creator of "Gentlemen Prefer Blondes."* Berkeley: University of California Press, 2003. Chronicles the career of screenwriter, novelist, and playwright Anita Loos and explores the 1953 film version of *Gentlemen Prefer Blondes*.

Loos, Anita. *Gentlemen Prefer Blondes: The Illuminating Diary of a Professional Lady.* New York: W. W. Norton, 1998. The original book from the 1920's that inspired the movie.

Garlena A. Bauer

See also Film in the United States; Monroe, Marilyn.

■ Geodesic dome

Identification Architectural structures built from interlocking triangles
Date Patented in 1954

Buckminister Fuller's invention made possible the construction of one of the most cost-efficient structures ever designed.

During the 1950's, Buckminster Fuller, who had dedicated his life to the betterment of humanity, was recognized internationally after a large cardboard prototype of his geodesic dome, an original architectural design built from triangles, won the highest award at the 1954 Triennale in Milan. Concurrently, the U.S. military considered the use of his domes for rapid construction under harsh conditions. Based on his principle of tensegrity, the domes were minimalist spherical structures created from triangles, and they became stronger as they got larger. Fuller designed these domes as his solution to global homelessness and the wasting of resources.

Impact The geodesic dome is considered the most cost-effective, strongest, most energy-efficient, and lightest structure ever created. At the Montreal Expo of 1967, Fuller's twenty-story dome housed the U.S. Pavilion. Other famous domes are at Florida's Walt Disney World's EPCOT Center. Today, more than 200,000 geodesic domes are found throughout the world. Scientists have also discovered a class of carbon molecules of geodesic sphere shape, possibly the oldest molecules in the universe, and named them "fullerenes."

Further Reading

Baldwin, J. *Bucky Works: Buckminster Fuller's Ideas for Today.* New York: Wiley, 1996. Written by an inventor who worked with Fuller for thirty-three years, this interesting introduction to Fuller's ideas and inventions contains discussions of domes. Includes more than two hundred archival photos and drawings.

Buckminster Fuller standing in front of one of the geodesic domes he designed. (Hulton Archive | by Getty Images)

Zung, Thomas. *Buckminster Fuller: Anthology for the New Millennium.* New York: St. Martin's Press, 2001. Includes a history of geodesic domes, a chronology, and bibliography.

Alice Myers

See also Architecture; Housing in the United States; Inventions.

■ Germany's postwar occupation

The Event American control of a region of defeated Germany after World War II
Date 1945-1955

The United States administered part of Germany in the post-World War II years, but in 1955, it restored full political authority to the new German government and supported its admission into the North Atlantic Treaty Organization (NATO).

Germany's defeat in World War II led to the partition of the nation in 1945 into four occupation zones under the control of the four primary victorious allies: France, Great Britain, the Soviet Union, and the United States. Berlin, which lay with the Soviet sector, was divided in turn into four occupation sectors. The policies of the occupying powers in postwar Germany were outlined in extensive detail in several major agreements.

The United States took responsibility for central and southern Germany, an arrangement that required the presence of U.S. military forces. Other Americans served in oversight capacities to deal with issues such as political governance in the occupied region, promotion of economic reconstruction and recovery, coping with significant health needs, and reviving the educational system. The occupation sought to remove the remnants of the Nazi dictatorship and move the region toward a democratic future, a goal that included the trial and punishment of leading Nazi and German leaders at Nuremberg during 1945 and 1946.

The three occupying Western states worked reasonably effectively together in their occupation efforts, while the Soviet Union followed different policies in the eastern part of the nation it controlled. By 1948, the disagreements and confrontations between the allied victors could no longer be denied, and the Cold War in Europe existed as a reality, exemplified by the dangerous Soviet blockade of Berlin in 1948 and 1949.

A Return to Democracy Seeking to return Germany to a self-governing democratic system, in July, 1948, the three Western states adopted a revised "occupation statute" to permit German authorities to exercise legislative, executive, and judicial control over some functions previously controlled by the occupation powers. It took effect in April of 1949. The same year, the three western zones established a new state, the Federal Republic of Germany (West Germany). In response, the Soviet Union created the German Democratic Republic (East Germany) from its occupation zone. The Berlin sector plan remained intact.

In October of 1951, President Harry S. Truman signed a proclamation formally ending the state of war between Germany and the United States. This further illustrated the Western effort to permit the German people to ultimately govern themselves. Although the American occupation continued into the early 1950's, and its military forces remained in the U.S. zone, the effort clearly sought to return the West German state to the community of democratic nations. This contrasted with the communist regime in East Germany.

To implement the 1948 "occupation statute," the United States created the office of high commissioner as the highest governing official in the American zone. Two prominent Americans served in this capacity until the position was abolished in 1955: John J. McCloy, between 1949 and 1952, and James B. Conant, between 1952 and 1955. Negotiations with the West German government of Chancellor Konrad Adenauer replaced portions of the "occupation statute" in 1952 by contractual agreements between the Federal Republic and the three Western powers. These continued until the British, French, and Americans terminated the existing arrangement in October of 1954. Consequently, West Germany regained its full political sovereignty in May, 1955, and joined the Western military alliance NATO the same month. U.S. military forces remained in West Germany after the occupation ended during the 1950's but only as part of NATO's common defense against possible Soviet attack in Central Europe.

Impact American public opinion favored the occupation of Germany after its surrender in 1945. The devastating effects of the war and the evidence of Nazi tyranny, including the Holocaust, convinced Americans that the United States should take an active role in dominating the defeated enemy. Trials of Nazi war criminals matched the public mood seeking justice and punishment. With the emergence of the Cold War between the United States and the Soviet Union during the late 1940's and into the following decade, Americans supported continued U.S. involvement in Europe against further communist expansion. The public viewed the Cold War as a striking contrast between the values and institutions of the Western democracies as compared to the one-party dictatorships of communist regimes in the Soviet Union, Eastern Europe, and East Germany. During this period, the majority of Americans interpreted the United States occupation in its designated region of Germany as justified and necessary. The Marshall Plan also assisted the German postwar economic recovery, which proved to be an impressive success by the mid-1950's. As a result, Americans believed it was time to let the West Germans regain their political rights as a sovereign nation and provide military support for NATO in facing the communist bloc in Europe.

Subsequent Events The continuation of the Cold War between NATO and the Soviet Union and its East European partners under the Warsaw Pact made the German region a tense area of confrontation in succeeding decades. The Berlin crisis of 1961, which included the communist erection of the Berlin Wall, exemplified the tensions. However, in 1989, the communist regime in East Germany fell, the Berlin Wall and other frontier fortifications were removed, and the two Germanys united in 1990. The partition of the city of Berlin ended in 1994, as the four allied occupying powers formally terminated their rights based on prior agreements. Clearly, events in postwar Germany affected Europe for decades.

Further Reading

Davidson, Eugene. *The Death and Life of Germany: An Account of the American Occupation.* Columbia: University of Missouri Press, 1999. Good description of the American occupation period.

Schwartz, Thomas A. *America's Germany: John J. McCloy and the Federal Republic of Germany.* Cambridge, Mass.: Harvard University Press, 1991. Covers McCloy's career as U.S. high commissioner in Germany.

Williamson, D. G. *Germany from Defeat to Partition, 1945-1963.* Harlow: Longman, 2000. Describes the challenges and issues facing Germany after its defeat.

Wolfe, Robert, ed. *Americans as Proconsuls: United States Military Government in Germany and Japan, 1944-1952.* Carbondale: Southern Illinois University Press, 1984. Describes the planning for the occupation, the policies and programs of the American government in both countries, and the results.

Zink, Harold. *The United States in Germany, 1944-1955.* Princeton, N.J.: Van Nostrand, 1974. Excellent coverage of the tasks facing the Americans during the occupation era.

Taylor Stults

See also Acheson, Dean; Cold War; Dulles, John Foster; Eisenhower, Dwight D.; Foreign policy of the United States; Kennan, George F.; North Atlantic Treaty Organization; Truman, Harry S.; Truman Doctrine; Volkswagen; Warsaw Pact.

■ Getty, J. Paul

Identification American oil business billionaire and art collector
Born December 15, 1892; Minneapolis, Minnesota
Died June 6, 1976; Sutton Place, Surrey, England

During the 1950's, J. Paul Getty became the world's richest private person and founded the J. Paul Getty Museum to display some of his art collection.

After graduating from college in 1914, Jean Paul Getty began in the oil business in Oklahoma with the backing of his millionaire father. Within two years, he had made his first million dollars. For the remainder of his life, he would continue in the oil business, and when he died at age eighty-three, he was still president of the Getty Oil Company. His most profitable oil deal began in 1949, when he purchased a sixty-year-oil concession from King Saud of Saudi Arabia. In 1953, enormous oil deposits were discovered in the Arabian oil field, which made Getty a billionaire.

During the 1930's, Getty began collecting art. He purchased a ranch in Malibu, California, in 1943, and later added a gallery wing to house some of his collection. In 1954, he opened it to the public as the J. Paul Getty Museum.

Impact An article in *Fortune* magazine in 1957 propelled the relatively reclusive Getty into the public spotlight when it named him the world's richest private person. He became a symbol of the success of American capitalism. His development of oil fields in the Persian Gulf region also had an important effect on the role of oil in international trade and relations.

Further Reading

Economides, Michael, and Ronald Oligney. *The Color of Oil: The History, the Money, and the Politics of the World's Biggest Business.* Houston, Tex.: Gulf, 2000. While this book does not discuss Getty, it offers insight into the business that made him rich.

Getty, J. Paul. *As I See It: The Autobiography of J. Paul Getty.* Englewood Cliffs, N.J.: Prentice Hall, 1976. Getty's autobiography.

Robert E. Haag

See also Affluence and the new consumerism; Guggenheim Museum; International trade of the United States.

■ G.I. Bill

Identification Educational benefits provided for military veterans

Date Approved on July 16, 1952

The G.I. Bill dramatically increased the number and type of college students, which resulted in major changes in higher education and society as a whole.

Prior to World War II, only about 10 percent of adult Americans attended college. The middle class was very small and mostly made up of white male Protestants. Women, minorities, and the poor had few opportunities for higher education.

Originally enacted as the Servicemen's Readjustment Act of 1944, the G.I. Bill was designed to provide educational benefits as well as to help ease transition back into civilian life for World War II veterans. The G.I. Bill provided for education and training; loan guarantees for homes, farms, or businesses; unemployment pay of twenty dollars per week for up to fifty-two weeks; job-finding assistance; building materials for Veterans Affairs (VA) hospitals; and military review of dishonorable discharges. The VA paid a maximum of five hundred dollars per year for tuition, books, fees, and other costs, with payments going directly to the educational institution and monthly allowances to the veterans.

The number of veterans enrolling in colleges during the middle and late 1940's was immense, with almost eight million of the fifteen million eligible veterans using the G.I. Bill to obtain an education. With veterans totaling between 40 and 50 percent of the total college enrollment, new facilities and programs had to be developed. The 1944 bill program ended July 25, 1956, and cost approximately $14.5 billion.

The Veterans Readjustment Assistance Act of 1952, approved on July 16, 1952, by President Harry S. Truman, was not as economically favorable to the veterans of the Korean War. These veterans received only three-fourths the benefits of World War II veterans. Korean War veterans had to pay their own tuition and expenses, but they received a higher monthly allowance. The 1952 G.I. Bill did not include an unemployment allowance but did provide education and training benefits, and funds for home, farm, and business loans. A movement by the Association of American Colleges in 1954 to equalize benefits for all veterans was unsuccessful in

Congress. The Korean War G.I. Bill program ended January 31, 1965. More than two million eligible veterans received training at a total cost of $4.5 billion.

American Society Transformed The G.I. Bill literally transformed the United States. Because of assistance with housing costs and the educational benefits of the bill, the middle-class lifestyle was available to more Americans. Home ownership, white-collar work, and suburban life became more obtainable, and millions of veterans and their families joined the middle class. In turn, this middle class contributed to the financial stability of the nation, leading to an unprecedented period of economic growth. According to the U.S. Department of Veterans Affairs, the veterans who were educated under the G.I. Bill typically gave back two to eight times as much in income taxes as was spent on their educational benefits.

The effects of the G.I. Bill went far beyond merely increasing income and economic opportunities for the veterans. Families and children also benefited, and college enrollment increased dramatically from 1950 to 1970. The increase resulted in expansion of physical facilities and the creation of new colleges. Community colleges grew tremendously to accommodate the veterans, the adult educational system was developed, and the concept of continuing education was introduced. Many of the new institutions were in underserved areas, which brought the opportunity for higher education to more Americans.

The number of research universities grew from 25 to 125. Educational restrictions against Jews and Roman Catholics were dropped, and African Americans began to attend previously all-white colleges. Americans came to expect that everyone, not merely the wealthy, should have the opportunity to pursue a higher education and middle-class lifestyles. The change in educational philosophy, with an emphasis on advanced education and training for everyone, contributed to the shift to a knowledge-based economy and society.

An unexpected consequence of the G.I. Bill was to help African American men, which led to the development of the black middle class and the education of the people who became leaders in the Civil Rights movement. African American enrollment at traditional black land-grant colleges increased by 50 percent by 1950, and enrollment in predominantly white colleges increased tremendously, especially in the North, Midwest, and West. Although segregation continued to hinder the employment opportunities of African Americans, often they were able to make the same wages as whites in the South, and their educational opportunities resulted in an increased number of African Americans in education and civil service, greatly expanding the black middle class.

Impact Beginning during the 1940's and 1950's, higher education became important to most Americans and necessary to supply the quality of labor force needed in modern society. Millions of people were able to attend college because of the G.I. Bill, and the educational benefits available to veterans and military personnel and their families continued into the twenty-first century to be an important recruiting element for the volunteer military. Additionally, the original G.I. Bill served as a model for future federal student loan and grant plans, such as Pell grants and Stafford and Perkins loan programs.

Subsequent Events President Lyndon B. Johnson signed the Veterans Readjustment Benefits Act of 1966 on March 3, 1966, for post-Korean War and Vietnam-era veterans. Other bills enacted to extend educational benefits to veterans included the Montgomery G.I. Bill, as well as various bills to assist members of the military reserves and survivors and dependents of veterans.

Further Reading

Bennett, Michael J. *When Dreams Came True: The G.I. Bill and the Making of Modern America.* McLean, Va.: Brassey's, 1996. A highly readable, fascinating, and detailed account of the history of the G.I. Bill and its far-reaching impact on society.

Greenberg, Milton. *The G.I. Bill: The Law That Changed America.* West Palm Beach, Fla.: Lickle, 1997. A short book that includes the basic information about the G.I Bill, as well as numerous photographs and personal narratives of its effects.

Roach, Ronald. "From Combat to Campus: G.I. Bill Gave a Generation of African Americans an Opportunity to Pursue the American Dream." *Black Issues in Higher Education* 14, no. 13 (August 21, 1997): 26. An interesting report on the unintentional benefits of the G.I. Bill for black veterans and their families.

Wilson, Reginald. "The G.I. Bill and the Transformation of America." *National Forum* 75, no. 4 (Fall, 1995): 20. Discusses the social and economic im-pact of the G.I. Bill, especially on segregation and the poor.

Virginia Hodges

See also African Americans; Baby boomers; Business and the economy in the United States; Civil Rights movement; Education in the United States; Housing in the United States; Income and wages in the United States; Korean War; National Defense Education Act of 1958; Truman, Harry S.; Unemployment in the United States; Urbanization in the United States; Veterans organizations.

■ *Giant*

Identification Film about rich versus poor on a Texas ranch
Director George Stevens (1904-1975)
Date Released in 1956

The film Giant, *based on Edna Ferber's best-selling novel, is chiefly remembered as being the last film in which actor James Dean appeared. The movie was giant in scope in all respects: It was more than three hours long, was filmed on a huge Texas ranch, and included many of Hollywood's greatest stars.*

Rock Hudson and Elizabeth Taylor were considered the main stars of *Giant* initially, but it was the performance of James Dean that is best remembered. Other notable actors in the cast included Mercedes McCambridge, Chill Wills, Carroll Baker, Dennis Hopper, Earl Holliman, and Sal Mineo. The saga begins when Texas rancher Bick Benedict (played by Rock Hudson) visits Maryland to buy a prize horse. While there, he falls in love with the owner's daughter, Leslie (Elizabeth Taylor); they are married immediately and return to his ranch. The story of their family and its rivalry with Jett Rink, a cowboy and later oil tycoon portrayed by Dean, unfolds across two generations. Rink is looked down upon by Bick and his family, but they cannot ignore his success.

Impact Many critics agree that *Giant* is one of the greatest films of all time, an epic in the grand tradition of *Gone with the Wind* (1939). The film garnered ten Academy Award nominations in 1956, winning the award for best directing for George Stevens. Hudson, Taylor, and Dean gave outstanding performances, but Dean's untimely death in 1955 and the ensuing mythology surrounding his life ultimately overshadowed the film and its performances.

James Dean costarred in Giant *as Jett Rink, a cowboy who strikes oil on his little plot of land and becomes a tycoon.* (Arkent Archive)

Further Reading

Dalton, David. *James Dean, the Mutant King: A Biography.* San Francisco: Straight Arrow Books, 1974. Shows how carefully Dean crafted his own image and performances. A bibliography is included.

Hendler, Jane. *Best Sellers and Their Film Adaptations in Postwar America: "From Here to Eternity," "Sayonara," "Giant," "Auntie Mame," "Peyton Place."* New York: Peter Lang, 2001. Examines film adaptations of novels during the 1950's, focusing primarily on the portrayal of gender identity and conflict.

Spoto, Donald. *Rebel: The Life and Legend of James Dean.* New York: HarperCollins, 1996. Excellent biography with extensive bibliography and index. The author takes a dispassionate look at the legend of Dean and argues that his untimely death was probably his greatest career move.

Dale L. Flesher

See also Dean, James; Film in the United States; Hudson, Rock; *Rebel Without a Cause;* Taylor, Elizabeth.

■ Gibson, Althea

Identification African American tennis player
Born August 25, 1927; Silver, South Carolina
Died September 28, 2003; East Orange, New Jersey

One of the first African American tennis stars, Althea Gibson won five singles and six doubles "grand slam" titles during the 1950's.

Althea Gibson moved from her native South Carolina to New York City as a youngster. Her ability in paddle ball, played in urban neighborhoods, led to her interest in tennis. A natural athlete, Gibson won a New York state junior tennis championship when she was fifteen. She then attended Florida A&M University on a tennis and basketball scholarship.

In 1950, Gibson became the first African American to play in the U.S. National Tennis Championships (now the U.S. Open); the next year, she broke the racial barrier at Wimbledon in England. In 1956, she won the French national title, the first of her "grand slam" (major) tennis titles. In 1957 and 1958, she won both Wimbledon and U.S. championships in singles. She earned women's doubles titles at Wimbledon (1956, 1957, 1958), France (1956), and Australia (1957); she was half of a "mixed doubles" team to win a U.S. title (1957).

However, Gibson's grand slam victories occurred when only amateurs could play in the tournaments and winners received no money (later, these events became open to professionals and awarded cash prizes). Consequently, Gibson abandoned her tennis career in 1958 to earn a living. In 1959, she toured with the Harlem Globetrotters, an exhibition basketball team. She later recorded an album and acted in a film (*The Horse Soldiers*, 1959) with John Wayne.

In 1964, Gibson became the first black woman to compete on the Ladies Professional Golf Association tour. She played until 1978 but never won a tournament. Moreover, her paychecks were small—typical of professional sports of that era. In her later years, she was plagued by financial problems.

Impact Gibson was a great athlete and a true pioneer in race relations in sports. Later African American female tennis stars—including Zina Garrison, Venus Williams, and Serena Williams—all cited Gibson as a heroine who had paved the way for their athletic and financial successes.

Althea Gibson. (International Tennis Hall of Fame)

Further Reading

Biracree, Tom. *Althea Gibson, Tennis Champion.* New York: Chelsea House, 1990. A title aimed at young adults that covers Gibson's life until 1975.

Davidson, Sue. *Changing the Game: The Stories of Tennis Champions Alice Marble and Althea Gibson.* Seattle: Seal Press, 1997. A good biography of Gibson.

Gibson, Althea. *I Always Wanted to Be Somebody.* New York: HarperCollins, 1958. Gibson's autobiography.

Roger D. Hardaway

See also African Americans; Connolly, Maureen; Gonzáles, Pancho; Racial discrimination; Sports; Tennis.

■ Ginsberg, Allen

Identification Iconoclastic American poet and political activist of the Beat generation
Born June 3, 1926; Newark, New Jersey
Died April 5, 1997; Manhattan, New York

A 1957 obscenity trial marked the beginning of Allen Ginsberg's long public career. Like other members of the Beat generation, Ginsberg used his writings and readings to promote controversial themes of political activism, altered states of consciousness, and explicit sexuality.

Allen Ginsberg grew up in Paterson, New Jersey. He was the second son of Naomi and Louis Ginsberg, a poet and schoolteacher. They surrounded their children with storytelling and recitations of poetry. Naomi Ginsberg's struggle with mental illness affected her family, and she died when Allen was thirty.

Ginsberg attended Columbia University in New York City. While there, he met Jack Kerouac, Lucien Carr, William Burroughs, and Neal Cassady—who all later became celebrated members of the Beats. However, their extreme lifestyles resulted in legal difficulties. Ginsberg interrupted his college studies with time in a mental institution to avoid charges for his misdemeanor crimes. After graduation from Columbia, Ginsberg worked in an advertising agency. He also acquired disdain for the conformity of corporate life. After five years, he left for San Francisco.

In California, Ginsberg met Gary Snyder, Kenneth Rexroth, and Philip Whalen, a group of writers influenced by Zen Buddhism. Another acquaintance was Peter Orlovsky, who became his companion for three decades. Other San Francisco writers and artists were Robert Duncan, Diane DiPrima, Michael McClure, Lew Welch, and Jack Spicer. In October, 1955, Ginsberg first read his most famous poem, "Howl," at Six Gallery. Soon after, Lawrence Ferlinghetti of City Lights Bookstore published a small staple-bound edition of poems, one of which was "Howl." American and San Francisco officials declared the book obscene. The ensuing trial resulted in a landmark ruling against censorship. It also gained the poet fame, as the book eventually sold one million copies.

Ginsberg spent the remainder of the 1950's traveling, writing, and performing his poetry to enthusiastic audiences. Another major publication was the book *Kaddish, and Other Poems, 1958-1960* (1961), which included a long poem about the death of his mother. In these books, Ginsberg used a conversational, jazz-influenced style that resembled Walt Whitman's verse. Like rap music, Ginsberg's poetry celebrates a wide range of sacred and profane human experience. His work challenged the elitist role of 1950's academic literature.

Impact Ginsberg and the Beats expanded the role of American literature during the post-World War II era. A positive outcome of the obscenity trial, in which Ginsberg was acquitted, was that street slang began to be tolerated in broadcast and print media. At the same time, Ginsberg championed a spiritual ethic, based on expansion of consciousness. Ferlinghetti credits Ginsberg with creating a coherent literary movement: "Without Allen, it would've been separate great writers in the landscape, it wouldn't have been known as the Beat generation." The Beats continued to be influential during the counterculture movement of the 1960's and 1970's. Public free expression and poetry slams are echoes of Beat influence.

Poet Allen Ginsberg (right) with author Norman Mailer on a television talk show around 1957. (Hulton Archive | by Getty Images)

Subsequent Events During the 1960's and 1970's, Ginsberg became a hero of the counterculture movement. He protested the Vietnam War and campaigned for gay rights. Gradually, his writing gained national acceptance. He won the National Book Award in 1973, and in 1990, he won an American Book Award. During the 1970's, he began teaching at Naropa Institute in Boulder, Colorado, a Buddhist-influenced college, and he also taught at Brooklyn College. He resided in the East Village of New York City until his death. In all, he published forty books of poetry and prose.

Further Reading

Caveney, Graham. *Screaming with Joy: The Life of Allen Ginsberg.* New York: Random House, 1999. A good biography that contains 150 photos and illustrations.

Raskin, Jonah. *American Scream: Allen Ginsberg's "Howl" and the Making of the Beat Generation.* Berkeley: University of California Press, 2004. Primarily an analyses of "Howl," this book also offers insight into Ginsberg's role in the Beat generation, his association with other Beats, the nexus of politics and literature during the 1950's.

Denise Low

See also Beat generation; Burroughs, William; Corso, Gregory; Ferlinghetti, Lawrence; Homosexuality and gay rights; Jazz; Kerouac, Jack; *Naked Lunch*; *On the Road*; Poetry; Rexroth, Kenneth; San Francisco Renaissance.

■ Gobel, George

Identification Movie and television comedian
Born May 20, 1919; Chicago, Illinois
Died February 24, 1991; Los Angeles, California

The George Gobel Show, a variety show that revolved around Gobel's family problems, was a successful program during the first decade of television. Gobel portrayed the stereotypical henpecked husband.

George Gobel began in show business as a singer, eventually developing a comedy routine. His first entertainment job was with radio's WLS Barn Dance in Chicago, where he sang, played guitar, and cracked jokes. Often called Lonesome George, he culivated a meek persona that belied a significant talent. Gobel's comedy routines generally centered on family life and humorous stories. His "Well, I'll be a dirty bird" line became standard within many of his stories. He frequently utilized deprecatory humor in describing himself: "I'm the type of guy who will

have nothing all my life, but then they'll discover oil when they're digging my grave."

From 1954 to 1960, Gobel starred in *The George Gobel Show,* a variety program that always included a sketch dealing with family problems. His real-life wife, Phyllis Avery (known as "spooky old Alice"), was his co-star and played the family antagonist for two of the show's years. The show was a significant hit until *Gunsmoke* began to appear on another network during the same time slot. In later years, Gobel appeared on numerous celebrity quiz shows and late-night talk shows.

Impact Gobel was one of many comedians who made a successful transition to television during the 1950's. His variety show was typical of the era's depiction of domesticity and family life.

Further Reading

Brooks, Tim, and Earle Marsh. *The Complete Directory to Prime Time Network TV Shows: 1946-Present.* 8th ed. New York: Random House, 2003. Provides plot summaries, cast, and air dates, among other information.

Jones, Gerard. *Honey, I'm Home! Sitcoms: Selling the American Dream.* New York: St. Martin's Press, 1993. An excellent analysis of the impact of television sitcoms from their beginnings in radio through the 1990's.

Richard Adler

See also Berle, Milton; Caesar, Sid; *I Love Lucy*; Television in the United States; *Tonight Show.*

■ *God and Man at Yale*

Identification Book that critiqued postwar American higher education
Author William F. Buckley, Jr. (1925-   )
Date Published in 1951

As a book that questioned the level of secularization in schools and critiqued America's educational system both for its move away from individualism and for its erroneous claim to academic freedom and impartiality, God and Man at Yale: The Superstitions of "Academic Freedom" *sparked considerable debate during the early 1950's.*

William F. Buckley, Jr.'s book was both an autobiography and a critique of his years at Yale University from 1946 to 1950. It consisted of five chapters: "Religion at Yale," "Individualism at Yale," "Yale and Her Alumni," "The Superstitions of 'Academic Freedom,'" and "The Problem of the Alumnus." Arguing that he was compelled to write this book because of his love of God, country, and Yale, Buckley contended that American values were under attack or, at the very least, were ignored by the Yale faculty and derided or absent from the Yale curriculum. He argued for the restoration of traditional Christian values and for individualism.

Impact The immediate impact of *God and Man at Yale* resulted in a major discussion of academic freedom in higher education and the widespread denunciation of Buckley as an individual who had no sympathy for academia. More important, *God and Man at Yale* established Buckley as a force in American conservatism; he served as the most visible spokesperson for American conservatism throughout the twentieth century.

Further Reading

Dunn, Charles W., and J. David Woodard. *American Conservatism from Burke to Bush: An Introduction.* Lanham, Md.: Madison Books, 1991. A solid study of American conservatism, which discussed the impact of *God and Man at Yale* and its author.

Kirk, Russell. *Academic Freedom: An Essay in Definition.* Chicago: Henry Regnery, 1955. A scholarly argument by the intellectual leader of American conservatism during the 1950's; it followed in the wake of the discussion and criticism of *God and Man at Yale.*

William T. Walker

See also Conservatism in U.S. politics; Education in the United States.

■ God's Country and Mine

Identification Book exploring American culture that pays particular attention to domestic and foreign expressions of anti-Americanism

Author Jacques Barzun (1907-   )

Date Published in 1954

Written during an era of intense preoccupation with defining a national "self," God's Country and Mine commented on American national character and furthered the formal study of cultural history.

French American writer and philosopher Jacques Barzun became one of the founders of the discipline of cultural history with the publication of several books during his long tenure as a professor and ad-

ministrator at Columbia University. In 1954, he published *God's Country and Mine: A Declaration of Love Spiced with a Few Harsh Words*, a book that addressed many aspects of American culture, including science, entertainment, advertising, medical facilities, marriage, and child rearing. The book celebrated the fact that the United States was "peopled by underdogs, refugees, nobodies, and . . . it keeps on being run by them." Barzun considered the United States a testing ground for the possibility of diverse people living together and contrasted this U.S. situation with that of Europe and the endemic warfare that historically has ravaged the European continent.

Barzun also wrote that the U.S. economy was more or less aligned to promote equality and fair treatment. He praised competition, supermarkets, and installment credit for consumers and argued that "the world's work is going to be done by organized self-interest." He denied that Americans were greedier and more materialistic than the rest of the world—one of many criticisms emanating from Europe that the author attempted to debunk. Rather, he noted, the U.S. society displays a moral core with wide acceptance of the "social gospel," a stance reflected in private philanthropy and government welfare-state programs. Furthermore, while deploring racial injustice, Barzun rejected the view that Americans should "give every group its orbit and be very tender of peculiarities and touchiness."

Impact A preoccupation with national character and social psyche, as well as a struggle to define the national self, were paramount during the intense postwar years, and *God's Country and Mine* fit well into this climate. Barzun's views overall served as an antidote to the attacks on American culture that emerged from many intellectuals during the later years of this decade. Books such as William H. Whyte's *The Organization Man* (1956), John Kenneth Galbraith's *The Affluent Society* (1958), and Rudolf Flesh's *Why Johnny Can't Read* (1955) critiqued American conformity and the inadequacies of American economic policies and education. While Barzun acknowledges the materialism of American culture, he also celebrates Americans' simultaneous individualism and teamwork, social mobility and friendliness; he claims the good of the United States predominates. Ultimately, with his accessible writing, Barzun helped extend discussions about national character and culture from the realm of academia into the homes of average Americans.

Further Reading

Barzun, Jacques. *God's Country and Mine.* Westport, Conn.: Greenwood, 1973. Barzun's exploration of mid-century national character.

Murray, Michael, ed. *A Jacques Reader: Selections from His Works.* New York: HarperCollins, 2002. Provides essays from several of Barzun's important works, including *God's Country and Mine.*

Weiner, Dora B., and William R. Keylor. *From Parnassus: Essays in Honor of Jacques Barzun.* New York: Harper and Row, 1976. Includes biographical and bibliographic information on Barzun.

Paul B. Trescott

See also Affluence and the new consumerism; *Affluent Society, The;* American Dream; *Lonely Crowd, The; Organization Man, The;* Packard, Vance.

■ *The Goldbergs*

Identification Pioneering radio and television family drama

Date Aired on television from 1949 to 1955

The Goldbergs was a forerunner of both ethnic and family situation comedies, and it anticipated Desilu and MTM as entertainment companies dominated by a multifaceted woman.

Ward Cleaver, the archetypal father figure of *Leave It to Beaver,* and many another sitcom characters owe a great deal to Gertrude Berg, a woman who pioneered both the sitcom format and the warm, parental approach to dealing with the challenges of modern America. Berg was the creator, producer, writer, and star of a program known by several names but mainly as *The Goldbergs.*

Broadcast live on radio from 1929 until 1947 and on television from 1949 to 1955, *The Goldbergs* was one of a handful of shows that made a successful transition from radio to television. Beginning with *The Rise of the Goldbergs* in 1929, Berg drew upon both the ironies and situations of the Yiddish theater and the broader themes characteristic of every immigrant group trying to assimilate, or at least survive, in the United States. Appropriately, the show was set in the leading center of immigrants, New York City.

Although the cast, except for Berg, varied over the life of the show and the show's family moved from the Bronx to the suburbs, the situation, the characters—Molly, Jake, Rosalie, Sammee, and Uncle David—and the approach remained the same. Life's daily challenges were dealt with through the practical Yiddish American wisdom of the quintessential Jewish mother, Molly Goldberg.

The greatest challenge to both show and creator occurred when Philip Loeb, the first television Jake, was branded a communist sympathizer. After Loeb refused to name communist sympathizers when he was questioned by the House Committee on Un-American Activities in 1951, General Foods canceled its sponsorship of *The Goldbergs,* and CBS dropped the show. According to one version of the affair, Loeb resigned to save the jobs of the remaining cast and crew, despite Berg's refusal to fire him. Another version holds that Berg forced him out to save those jobs, mainly hers. In any case, eight months later *The Goldbergs* returned to the air on NBC. The next season it was on the DuMont network, and in the final season it was offered for first-run syndication under the title *Molly.*

Impact *The Goldbergs* was one of the few network television shows to depict Jewish American life, and it made an indelible mark on the many family sitcoms that followed it.

Further Reading

Berg, Gertrude. *Molly and Me.* New York: McGraw-Hill, 1961. Berg's autobiography covers more of her life and career than her years on *The Goldbergs.* It is a lively, opinionated, and somewhat self-aggrandizing memoir by a woman whose achievements were remarkable.

Brooks, Tim, and Earle Marsh. *The Complete Directory to Prime Time Network TV Shows: 1946-Present.* 8th ed. New York: Random House, 2003. Contains a brief but useful sketch of *The Goldbergs* on television, including a discussion of Philip Loeb's resignation.

Dunning, John. *Tune in Yesterday: The Ultimate Encyclopedia of Old-Time Radio, 1925-1976.* Englewood Cliffs, N.J.: Prentice Hall, 1976. Provides useful background information on *The Goldbergs* before it went to television.

Daniel J. Fuller

See also DuMont network; Radio; Television in the United States.

■ Golden, Harry

Identification American humorist
Born May 6, 1902; New York, New York
Died October 2, 1981; Charlotte, North Carolina

During the 1950's, Harry Golden introduced to Americans the life, culture, and folklore of the Jews of New York's lower East Side.

Had his collection of essays *Only in America* (1958) not become a national best-seller, Harry Golden might have remained merely a regional writer, unknown beyond the boundaries of North Carolina and the limited subscription list of his oddly named newspaper, *The Carolina Israelite*. Instead, he became a national voice for the downtrodden, one of the best-known Jewish writers in the United States, and a man identified by Martin Luther King, Jr., as one of the four white journalists who did the most for the Civil Rights movement in the South.

Harry Golden was born Herschele Lewis Goldhurst in New York City. His father, an educated man who had been highly respected in his Jewish village in the Austro-Hungarian Empire, had the simple goal of offering his children more choices in life than had been available to Jews in late nineteenth century Europe. Golden grew up on the lower East Side of New York during the early years of the twentieth century—an experience he later recounted in *For Two Cents Plain* (1959) and several other books. He attended the City College of New York for three years, worked at his sister's brokerage firm for a brief period, and then left it to found one of his own. However, after a speculative deal failed to materialize, he was arrested for mail fraud in 1926, convicted in 1929, and served several years in prison. That was an experience he did not recount in his popular memoirs but finally made public in 1958. (In one of history's little ironies, he was granted a full pardon by President Richard M. Nixon in 1973.) After his release, he managed a hotel for five years and followed that with a stint writing and selling ads for the *New York Mirror.*

After nearly thirty years of being known as Goldhurst, he changed his surname to Golden and moved to Norfolk, Virginia, where he worked as an advertising salesman. Finally, he settled in Charlotte, North Carolina, where he worked for both the *Labor Journal* and the *Observer.* In 1941, he founded a small newspaper, *The Carolina Israelite,*

which he was to publish until 1968. Whatever his original intentions—his newspaper contained Jewish news and reminiscences about his childhood—he realized that he was essentially a northerner living in the South, a Jew in "the most Gentile community on the continent," and an integrationist surrounded by white supremacists. Like many other American Jews, he saw in the Jim Crow laws of segregation a parallel to the world from which his family had escaped in Europe and began editorializing about the plight of African Americans and calling for reform. The warmth and humor of Golden's social criticism may have made it more palatable to his southern readers. For example, he wrote many essays about the "Vertical Negro," a concept based on his observation that a black man was welcome everywhere in the South—so long as he did not try to sit down.

Golden collected some of his essays in *Only in America*, which became a best-seller in 1958. He followed that with two more best-sellers, *For Two Cents Plain* in 1959, and *Enjoy, Enjoy* in 1960. Altogether he wrote more than twenty books, including a biography of Carl Sandburg, the well-received *Mr. Kennedy and the Negroes* (1964), and a number of books on the American Jewish experience.

Impact By the time Golden died in 1981, he had traded the identity of an ex-convict for that of a respected author, a chronicler of Jewish life, and a hero of the Civil Rights movement. As he himself might have observed, his life could have happened "only in America."

Further Reading

Golden, Harry. *The Best of Harry Golden.* New York: World Publishing, 1967. There is no substitute for reading Golden himself, and this is an excellent starting place.

Solotoff, Theodore. "Harry Golden and the American Audience." *Commentary* 31, no. 1 (January, 1961). Convincing contemporary analysis of the Golden phenomenon and its wide appeal.

Thomas, Clarence W. *The Serious Side of Harry Golden.* Landham, Md.: Rowman & Littlefield, 1996. Study of Golden's writings on the Civil Rights movement.

Daniel J. Fuller

See also Armour, Richard; *Goldbergs, The*; Jewish Americans; Lehrer, Tom; Shulman, Max.

■ Golf

American golf grew dramatically in popularity as both a participation sport and a spectator sport, as professional golfers such as Ben Hogan, Sam Snead, and Babe Didrikson Zaharias ushered in the era of televised golf.

During the early 1950's, with the end of the Korean War and the country at peace, attention was refocused on pursuits at home, which included a renewed interest in the sport of golf. President Dwight D. Eisenhower brought much attention to the game. He played several times a week when he was in Washington, D.C., and practiced around the White House, hitting iron shots on the lawn or putting on the green constructed outside the Oval Office. Eisenhower's enthusiasm for the sport stimulated great interest in the game, particularly among the middle class. In 1950, there were more than three million golfers and nearly five thousand courses; by the end of the decade, there were more than four million participants and nearly six thousand golf courses. Interest among women soared as women's play increased from 10 percent to 30 percent.

Golf Technology Improved golf technology played an important role in promoting the sport during the period. The steel shaft was replaced during the 1950's with lighter fiberglass shafts. Golfcraft Incorporated of Escondido, California, introduced its Glasshaft clubs, made of fibers laminated to a thin steel core. These clubs were ideal for increasing swing speed and significantly improving how far golf balls would travel.

The postwar years saw major improvements in the golf courses as well. The first major development came in weed control. Course superintendents also used grasses that were tested by scientists. By the early 1950's, 116 strains of Bermuda grass were being tested for use on putting greens and fairways. Penncross, the most widely used of the grasses for golf courses, was first developed at Pennsylvania State University in 1954 by H. B. Musser. Better drainage, aeration, and frequent fertilizing also improved the conditions of both public and private courses. Electronic golf carts entered the scene during the 1950's. The use of these carts created disputes on whether they should be used since initially, members bought their own carts and drove them to the course. Soon, golf carts were made available at the courses for a nominal fee and their presence became standard on courses across the country.

Professional Golf The Men's Professional Golf Association (PGA) expanded during this period. Not only did tournament tour prize money increase but so also did the attendance at these events. The average purse in an official PGA event was $12,183 in 1945 in contrast to $23,108 in 1954. By 1958, the PGA tour passed the million-dollar annual mark in prizes. Ben Hogan, who ranks as one of the best golfers of all time, won numerous major tournaments during the decade. In addition to winning four U.S. Opens, two PGAs, two Masters, and a British Open, Hogan remarkably came back to win six of his nine major titles after a car accident in 1949 that nearly took his life. Other high-profile golfers such as Arnold Palmer and Jack Nicklaus came into competitive golf at a time when television was ready to create instant star performers. Nicklaus, who would go on to be one of the greatest golfers in the game, launched his career when he won the U.S. Amateur Championship in 1959.

International golf also took hold during this period, evidenced by the feats of several foreign-born players, such as Bobby Locke and Gary Player of South Africa and Peter Thomson of Great Britain, the latter of whom won four out of five British Opens between 1954 and 1958. The World Cup Match, introduced in 1953 by John Jay Hopkins to stimulate interest in international golf competition, continued its tenure into the twenty-first century.

Women's professional golf also came into its own during the 1950's. The Ladies Professional Golf Association (LPGA) was officially chartered in 1950 with eleven members. The growth of the LPGA was largely a result of the efforts of Fred Corcoran, its executive director. In 1950, the season had nine tournaments with the total prize money estimated at 45,000 dollars. The LPGA provided a regular stage on which women could display their golfing talents, and the number of tournaments and prize money available to them grew. The most visible tournament was the Women's Open Championship.

The LPGA also had its share of stars. One of the most successful performers was Louise Suggs, who won the U.S. Open twice and the LPGA championship once. Her best year was in 1953, when she won eight tournaments and collected nearly twenty thousand dollars—an unusually large sum on the

Golfers Ben Hogan, Sam Snead, Cary Middlecoff, and Byron Nelson at the 1955 U.S. Open Golf Tournament in San Francisco. (AP/ Wide World Photos)

women's tour. The LPGA tour expanded and prize money grew over the years, thanks to the successes of the LPGA's two most popular stars, Mildred (Babe) Didrikson Zaharias and Patty Berg. The two women were competitive rivals until the untimely death of Zaharias in 1956. These two, together with Suggs and Betty Jameson, constituted the Big Four in women's golf during the decade.

Impact The 1950's set the stage for the golf boom that followed in subsequent decades. With the help of a president who freely promoted the game and the successes of both the men's and women's professional tours, interest in the game was at an all-time high. The recognition of golf as a business and the increased attractiveness of the game to the middle and lower classes stimulated a great demand for public and private golf facilities. Poised at the threshold of the modern era, golf course architects examined ways to present new challenges to players. Golf course designers such as Robert Trent Jones called for longer and more challenging courses that would push the limits of the better players and produced many of the great courses that are still in use decades later.

Further Reading

Labbance, Bob, and Gordon Wittenveen. *Keepers of the Green: A History of Golf Course Management.* Ann Arbor, Mich.: Ann Arbor Press, 2002. Details course design, innovations, and management.

McGrath, Charles, and David McCormick, eds. *The Ultimate Golf Book: A History and a Celebration of the World's Greatest Game.* New York: Houghton Mifflin, 2002. A collection of essays and photographs celebrating the sport.

Nickerson, Elinor. *Golf: A Women's History.* Jefferson, N.C.: McFarland, 1987. Concise but interesting accounting of the history of women's golf.

Mary McElroy

See also Eisenhower, Dwight D.; Hogan, Ben; Snead, Sam; Sports.